Microsoft Office Home and Student 2013

Step by Step

Beth Melton

Mark Dodge

Echo Swinford

Ben M. Shorr

Published with the authorization of Microsoft Corporation by:
O'Reilly Media, Inc.
1005 Gravenstein Highway North
Sebastopol, California 95472

ISBN: 978-0-7356-6940-6

1 2 3 4 5 6 7 8 9 QG 8 7 6 5 4 3

Printed and bound in the United States of America.

Microsoft Press books are available through booksellers and distributors worldwide. If you need support related to this book, email Microsoft Press Book Support at mspinput@microsoft.com. Please tell us what you think of this book at *http://www.microsoft.com/learning/booksurvey*.

Microsoft and the trademarks listed at *http://www.microsoft.com/about/legal/en/us/IntellectualProperty/ Trademarks/EN-US.aspx* are trademarks of the Microsoft group of companies. All other marks are property of their respective owners.

The example companies, organizations, products, domain names, email addresses, logos, people, places, and events depicted herein are fictitious. No association with any real company, organization, product, domain name, email address, logo, person, place, or event is intended or should be inferred.

This book expresses the author's views and opinions. The information contained in this book is provided without any express, statutory, or implied warranties. Neither the authors, O'Reilly Media, Inc., Microsoft Corporation, nor its resellers, or distributors will be held liable for any damages caused or alleged to be caused either directly or indirectly by this book.

Acquisitions and Developmental Editor: Kenyon Brown

Production Editor: Kara Ebrahim

Editorial Production: Online Training Solutions, Inc. (OTSI)

Technical Reviewer: Kristen Merritt

Indexer: Bob Pfahler

Cover Design: Girvin

Cover Composition: Karen Montgomery

Illustrator: Online Training Solutions, Inc. (OTSI)

[2013-05-09]

Contents

Introduction xv

    Who this book is for. xv

    How this book is organized xv

    Download the practice files xvi

    Your companion ebook. xix

    Getting support and giving feedback. xix

        Errata xix

        We want to hear from you xx

        Stay in touch xx

PART 1

Office Home and Student 2013 fundamentals

1   Getting comfortable in Office Home and Student 2013   3

Exploring the Office environment. 4

Working with Office files 16

Recovering unsaved files and versions. 23

Customizing the user interface 25

    Customizing the Office environment 27

    Customizing the Quick Access toolbar. 28

    Customizing the status bar. 30

Customizing the ribbon. 32

Choosing the right application for the task at hand 35

Key points 38

2   Using shared Office features   41

Identifying new shared features in Office Home and Student 2013 .42
Applying Office themes 47
Inserting graphics, videos, charts, and diagrams 50
           Inserting charts. 54
Searching for online templates 58
Presenting Office documents online. 62
           Inserting online video 65
Key points 69

3   Sharing and collaborating   71

Defining the term *cloud service* 72
Signing in and managing your Office account 74
Connecting cloud services to your Office account. 78
           Saving files on SharePoint Online and SkyDrive. 85
           Sharing files with others from SharePoint Online or SkyDrive. 88
           Opening files from the cloud. 90
Syncing files with SkyDrive for offline use 92
           Syncing with SkyDrive Pro 93
           Syncing with SkyDrive for a Microsoft Account 94
Getting started with co-authoring 97
Key points 99

4   Using touch in Office   101

Getting comfortable with Office on a tablet. 101
           Looking at unsupported features 102
Using touch mode 103
Selecting content with touch 106
Working with ink in Office 108
Key points 112

PART 2

Word 2013

5   Getting comfortable in Word 2013   115

Exploring the Word 2013 user interface. 115
Modifying your document view 119
Changing other view options. 122
Discovering what's new in Word 2013 123
Key points 130

6   Navigating and reading documents   133

Navigating a document by scrolling and using keyboard shortcuts 134
Searching and navigating a document by using the Navigation pane. 135
Collapsing and expanding document content 141
Working with documents in the new Read Mode 144
Exploring research tools in Read Mode 148
Key points 153

7   Editing and composing documents   155

Moving the cursor by using keyboard shortcuts 155
Selecting text by using the keyboard and mouse 156
       Selecting text by using the keyboard. 157
       Selecting text by using the mouse 159
       Using other selection methods 160
Using formatting marks during document composition. 161
Inserting symbols, international characters, and other special characters 165
       Inserting special characters 169
Using AutoCorrect. 172
Composing documents faster by using building blocks 176
Key points 181

8 Formatting documents 183

Formatting documents more efficiently. 183
Setting default document formatting for your documents 188
Setting section formatting 190
Using styles for paragraph and character formats 192
Exploring other paragraph formats. 196
Exploring other character formats 200
       Changing case 202
Managing pagination through formatting 203
Key points 207

9 Presenting information 209

Formatting simple lists by using bullets and numbering 210
Creating tabbed lists 213
Inserting tables. 217
Enhancing tables 223
Key points 227

10 Finalizing documents 229

Correcting proofing errors 230
Inspecting documents before publishing. 233
Marking documents as final. 238
Creating PDF files in Word 239
Printing documents 245
Key points 250

PART 3

PowerPoint 2013

11   Getting comfortable in PowerPoint 2013   253

Getting started working with PowerPoint 2013 253
Exploring the PowerPoint 2013 tools 256
Discovering the new features in PowerPoint 2013 259
Key points 265

12   Designing and creating presentations   267

Creating a new presentation based on a theme or template 268
Applying a theme to an existing presentation 269
Customizing your file with colors, fonts, and effects 271
    Theme fonts 272
    Theme colors 273
Applying theme effects to your presentation 277
    Applying background styles to your presentation 281
    Formatting placeholders on the slide master 283
Adding graphics to the slide master and layouts 288
Creating a custom slide layout 291
Changing your presentation from a 16:9 format to a 4:3 format 297
Key points 301

13   Creating on-slide content   303

Choosing a slide layout and adding text in placeholders 304
Adding manual text boxes 308
Adding and formatting a table 313

Inserting and formatting charts. 316
Creating and formatting SmartArt diagrams 320
Reusing slides and keeping their source formatting 326
Key points 333

14   Creating Office graphics   335

Adding and formatting shapes 336
Applying enhanced fills and effects 342
Creating your own shapes 349
Inserting, cropping, and formatting pictures 354
Key points 363

15   Adding animation and multimedia   365

Adding animation to text and shapes. 366
Editing video and applying transitions. 371
Inserting and playing online video 374
Saving your presentation as a video. 375
Key points 377

16   Finalizing and presenting   379

Adding and renaming sections 380
Inserting comments. 384
Printing slides and notes. 386
Finalizing your presentation. 391
Delivering a presentation 394
Practicing with Presenter view 401
Key points 406

PART 4

Excel 2013

17 Getting comfortable in Excel 2013   409

Starting Excel 2013. 409
Identifying what's new in Excel 2013 413
Key points 419

18 Creating and editing worksheets   421

Entering and organizing data. 422
Changing column widths 423
Using formatting to alter the appearance of data 426
Extending a series with AutoFill. 429
      Introducing Flash Fill 431
Selecting and naming cell ranges 434
Using column headers to define names. 437
Moving around in the worksheet 439
Moving and adjusting cells. 442
Moving and copying rows and columns 445
Copying one or more cells to many 447
Key points 449

19 Manipulating numbers and text   451

Creating, editing, and copying formulas 452
Using functions. 456

Using the AutoSum button and built-in function 457
Inserting functions. 464
Using relative, fixed, and mixed cell references 467
Using names in formulas and validating cell entries 470
Looking at useful functions 473
Working with text in Excel 479
Combining text from multiple cells into one string 479
Removing extra spaces 482
Copying cells containing formulas and pasting only their resulting values 484
Changing the case of text. 485
Restricting cell entries 487
Key points 492

20   Analyzing data   495

Exploring a built-in template 495
Performing what-if analyses. 498
Managing multiple what-if models. 499
Using the Quick Analysis tools. 502
Formatting conditionally 504
Analyzing data from another source 508
Filtering data with tables. 512
Filter menu commands 518
Adding data to tables 519
Sorting data. 521
Creating a custom sort list 523
Creating a PivotTable. 526
Key points 535

21   Formatting worksheets   537

Applying number formatting. 538
Formatting with styles. 542
Creating custom themes. 546

Formatting in cells 550
Working with custom number formats 551
Working with percentage formats 558
Working with fraction formats. 560
Working with date formats. 564
Protecting worksheets. 570
Setting view options 574
Storing formats in templates 579
Key points 581

22   Manipulating workbooks and worksheets   583

Inserting rows and columns 583
Inserting and deleting cells. 587
Working with panes and page layout options 591
Printing row and column labels on every page 599
Adjusting page breaks. 602
Creating a multisheet workbook. 606
Manipulating sheets. 610
Summarizing a multisheet workbook. 613
Working with sheet references 617
Managing multiple workbooks 618
Key points 621

23   Creating charts and graphics   623

Creating and modifying a chart. 623
Adding a slicer to a PivotChart 629
Manipulating chart elements. 632
Adding a timeline to a chart. 637
Manipulating objects. 640
Creating and sharing graphics. 642
Using graphics elsewhere. 648
Key points 654

PART 5

OneNote 2013

24   Getting comfortable in OneNote 2013   657

Getting started with OneNote 2013 657
Exploring the OneNote interface 659
Identifying new and improved features in OneNote 2013 665
Key points 667

25   Working with notebooks, sections, and pages   669

Creating a notebook 670
Creating and organizing sections 671
         Section groups 673
Creating and organizing pages 674
         Creating subpages 675
         Adding and organizing notes 675
         Inserting images 676
Working with ink and shapes 677
         Custom pens 679
         Shapes 679
         Erasing ink or shapes 681
         Inserting space 682
         Arranging shapes 683
Recovering deleted sections or pages 684
Key points 685

26   Using organizational tools   687

Using tags 688
Creating and customizing tags 690
Using styles to format your notes 692

Connecting OneNote to Outlook 693

    Sending email messages to OneNote 693

    Connecting appointments to OneNote 695

    Annotating contacts 697

Connecting OneNote tasks to Outlook 698

Using hyperlinks to tie your notes together 700

Creating custom hyperlinks to other pages 702

Creating and organizing tables 704

Using the Insert Table feature 705

Searching your notes to find information quickly 707

Changing your search scope 709

Key points 711

27   Sharing notes with others   713

Creating a new notebook on SkyDrive 713

Moving a notebook to SkyDrive 716

    Stopping sharing in SkyDrive 718

Using a file server to share notes 718

    Stopping sharing on a file server 721

Sharing notes via SharePoint 723

Sharing notes with others during a meeting 727

Sending notes via email 728

Exporting to other formats 730

Key points 733

28   Using OneNote everywhere   735

Syncing your notes by using SkyDrive 735

Accessing your notes in a web browser 738

Using OneNote on your phone or tablet 740

Using OneNote on an iPhone or iPad 741

Using OneNote Mobile for Android 743

Using OneNote Mobile on a Windows Phone 746

Using OneNote with a Windows 8 tablet 747

Key points 749

29   Saving time with OneNote   751

Finding tags. 751

Recording audio 755

Using Quick Notes 756

Using screen clipping. 758

Using linked notes 759

Searching your images 761

Inserting a spreadsheet. 763

Using the Napkin Math feature 765

Formatting with templates 765

Key points 768

Index 769

About the authors. 805

Introduction

The Microsoft Office Home and Student 2013 suite of programs provide the tools you need for easy and efficient word processing, presentation planning, spreadsheet creation, and note taking. *Microsoft Office Home and Student 2013 Step by Step* offers a comprehensive look at the features of Office that most people will use most frequently, particularly those new to Office Home and Student 2013.

Who this book is for

Microsoft Office Home and Student 2013 Step by Step and other books in the Step by Step series are designed for beginning to intermediate level computer users. Whether you are already comfortable working in Office and want to learn about new features in Office Home and Student 2013 or are new to Office, this book provides invaluable hands-on experience so that you can work with Microsoft Word, PowerPoint, Excel, and OneNote.

How this book is organized

This book is divided into 29 chapters. Chapters 1–4 provide information on Office fundamentals, including how to work in the Office environment, how to avail yourself of shared Office features across applications, and how to share and collaborate with Office 365 services. Chapters 5–10 show you how to create, read, and navigate, format, organize, and share Word documents. Chapters 11–16 cover how to design and create impactful presentations in PowerPoint, including working with themes, masters, and layout, along with multimedia, creating customized graphics, and finalizing and making your presentation. Chapters 17–23 take you through the steps of creating, editing, and formatting database worksheets and workbooks, manipulating and analyzing data in spreadsheets, and creating charts and graphics. Chapters 24–29 cover all the features of OneNote, and show how to work with notebooks, sections, and pages, and how to organize and share your notes.

The first chapter of each of the five parts of the book contains introductory information that will primarily be of interest to readers who are new to a particular Office application or are upgrading from an earlier version. If you have worked with a more recent version of Office, you might want to skip past that material.

This book has been designed to lead you step by step through all the tasks you're most likely to want to perform with Office Home and Student 2013. If you start at the beginning and work your way through all the exercises, you will gain enough proficiency to be able to work with all the Office Home and Student applications. However, each topic is self-contained, so you can jump in anywhere to acquire exactly the skills you need.

Download the practice files

Before you can complete the exercises in this book, you need to download the book's practice files to your computer. These practice files can be downloaded from the following page:

http://aka.ms/OfficeHomeStudent2013SbS/files

IMPORTANT Microsoft Office Home and Student 2013 is not available from this website. You should purchase and install that program before using this book.

The following table lists the practice files for this book.

Chapter	File
Chapter 2: Using shared Office features	Fabrikam Management Team.pptx
	Sample Picture.jpg
	Simple to-do list.xlsx
Chapter 6: Reading and navigating documents	Fabrikam Rebrand Campaign.docx
	Newsletter_A.docx
	Newsletter_B.docx
Chapter 7: Creating and editing documents	List Example.docx
	Newsletter_C.docx
	Sample Logo and Address.docx
Chapter 8: Formatting documents	Fabrikam Rebrand Campaign_A.docx
	Fabrikam Rebrand Campaign_B.docx
	Fabrikam Rebrand Campaign_C.docx
	Fabrikam Rebrand Campaign_D.docx
	Fabrikam Rebrand Campaign_final.docx
Chapter 9: Organizing documents	Example Newsletter.docx
	List Example.docx
	List Example_B.docx
	List Example_C.docx

Chapter	File
Chapter 10: Finalizing documents	Fabrikam Newsletter.pdf
	Newsletter_B.docx
Chapter 12: Working with themes, masters, and layouts	SampleContentA_Start.pptx
	SampleContentB_Start.pptx
	SamplePictureB.JPG
Chapter 13: Creating on-slide content	SampleContentA_start.pptx
	SampleContentA_end.pptx
	SampleContentB_start.pptx
	SampleContentB_end.pptx
	SampleContentC_start.pptx
	SampleContentC_end.pptx
	SampleContentD_start.pptx
	SampleContentD_end.pptx
	SampleContentE_start.pptx
	SampleContentE_end.pptx
	SampleContentF_start.pptx
	SampleContentF_end.pptx
	SampleContentG_start.pptx
Chapter 14: Creating Office graphics	SampleContentA_Start.pptx
	SampleContentB_Start.pptx
	SamplePictureB.JPG
Chapter 15: Working with multimedia	Fabrikam Employee Excursion.wmv
	SampleContentA_start.pptx
	SampleContentA_end.pptx
	SampleContentB_start.pptx
	SampleContentC_start.pptx
	SampleContentD_start.pptx
Chapter 16: Finalizing and presenting	SampleContentA_Start.pptx
	SampleContentB_Start.pptx
	SampleContentC_Start.pptx
	SampleContentD_Start.pptx
Chapter 18: Creating and editing worksheets	Fabrikam-Employees_start.xlsx
	Fabrikam-Management_start.xlsx

Chapter	File
Chapter 19: Manipulating numbers and text	Fabrikam-Management2_start.xlsx
	Fabrikam-Seven-Year-Summary_start.xlsx
	Fabrikam-Seven-Year-Summary2_start.xlsx
	Loan_start.xlsx
	Real-Estate-Transition_start.xlsx
Chapter 20: Analyzing data	2015Projections_start.xlsx
	Fabrikam-Jan-2013-Sales_start.xlsx
	FabrikamJanSales2013.txt
	FabrikamQ1SalesDetail_start.xlsx
	JanSales2_start.xlsx
	RealEstateTransition_start.xlsx
Chapter 21: Formatting worksheets	Custom Formats 2_start.xlsx
	Custom Formats 3_start.xlsx
	Custom Formats_start.xlsx
	FabrikamSummary_start.xlsx
	FabrikamSummary2_start.xlsx
	FabrikamSummaryTheme_start.xlsx
	FabrikamSummaryTheme.xlsx
	Real-Estate-Transition_start.xlsx
Chapter 22: Manipulating workbooks and worksheets	FabrikamQ1_start.xlsx
	FabrikamQ1-B_start.xlsx
	Q1-Summary_start.xlsx
	Q1-Transactions_start.xlsx
	Q1-Transactions2_start.xlsx
	UnitSales_start.xlsx
	UnitSales2_start.xlsx
Chapter 23: Creating charts and graphics	FabrikamLogo_start.xlsx
	FabrikamSalesTable_start.xlsx
	FabrikamSalesTable2_start.xlsx
	FabrikamSalesTable3_start.xlsx
	FabrikamSalesTable4_start.xlsx
	FabrikamSalesTable5_start.xlsx
	Logo_start.xlsx
	Report_start.xlsx

| Chapter 29: Saving time with OneNote | 29 Practice Image 1.jpg |
| | 29 Practice Spreadsheet 1.xlsx |

Your companion ebook

With the ebook edition of this book, you can do the following:

- Search the full text
- Print
- Copy and paste

To download your ebook, please see the instruction page at the back of the book.

Getting support and giving feedback

The following sections provide information about getting help with Office Home and Student 2013 or the contents of this book and contacting us to provide feedback or report errors.

Errata

We've made every effort to ensure the accuracy of this book and its companion content. Any errors that have been reported since this book was published are listed on our Microsoft Press site at oreilly.com:

http://aka.ms/OfficeHomeStudent2013SbS/errata

If you find an error that is not already listed, you can report it to us through the same page.

If you need additional support, email Microsoft Press Book Support at *mspinput@microsoft. com.*

Please note that product support for Microsoft software is not offered through the addresses above.

We want to hear from you

At Microsoft Press, your satisfaction is our top priority, and your feedback our most valuable asset. Please tell us what you think of this book at:

http://www.microsoft.com/learning/booksurvey

The survey is short, and we read every one of your comments and ideas. Thanks in advance for your input!

Stay in touch

Let's keep the conversation going! We're on Twitter at: *http://twitter.com/MicrosoftPress/.*

Part 1
Office Home and Student 2013 fundamentals

1 Getting comfortable in Office
Home and Student 2013   3

2 Using shared Office features   41

3 Sharing and collaborating   71

4 Using touch in Office   101

Chapter at a glance

Explore

Explore the Office environment,
page 4

Work

Work with Office files,
page 16

Recover

Recover unsaved files and versions,
page 23

Versions

- Today, 6:13 PM (autosave)
- Today, 6:03 PM (autosave)
- Today, 5:27 PM (autosave)

Manage Versions ▾

Customize

Customize the ribbon,
page 32

Getting comfortable in Office Home and Student 2013

IN THIS CHAPTER, YOU WILL LEARN HOW TO

- Explore the Office environment.

- Work with Office files.

- Recover unsaved files and versions.

- Customize the user interface.

- Customize the ribbon.

- Choose the right application for the task at hand.

One of the biggest advantages of using Microsoft Office Home and Student 2013 is the similarities across the applications. The most obvious is the user interface, which is the overall look and feel of the application and how you interact with it. If you've used previous versions of Office, you may notice that many commands and features are nearly identical to those in past releases of Office, if not exactly the same, such as the commands for copying and pasting information, formatting text, creating charts, or inserting pictures. All of these similarities greatly reduce the learning curve, which allows you to apply the functionality in one application across the entire Office suite.

As you apply that knowledge and learn more about each application, you'll likely discover similar functionality that may not be initially obvious. For example, you can create a company newsletter by using Microsoft Word or PowerPoint. You can document company meeting notes in Microsoft OneNote or Word. And you can store lists of data in both Word and Microsoft Excel.

In this chapter, you'll learn about the Office environment, which includes the user interface, application options, and Office settings, plus you'll learn about Office terminology, Help options, and other functionality available in Office. This chapter also covers basic instructions for starting an Office application and working with Office files. At the end of this chapter, you'll get an overview of each application and tips for choosing the right application for various tasks.

Exploring the Office environment

The first step in getting comfortable with Office Home and Student 2013 is to become familiar with your Office surroundings. In this section, you'll explore the user interface along with application options and settings that are shared across the Office applications.

TIP Even if you're already comfortable with this information from working with a previous version of Office, please read this section for tips that you may have not previously discovered.

You typically start an Office application from the Windows Start screen in Windows 8 or the Start menu in Windows 7. You can also start an application and open a file at the same time by opening a file sent to you as an email attachment or by double-clicking a file from somewhere in your computer environment, such as your Windows desktop.

With the exception of OneNote, when you start an application without opening a file, the new application Start screen appears.

TIP OneNote doesn't have an application Start screen. When you start the application, the main window is displayed.

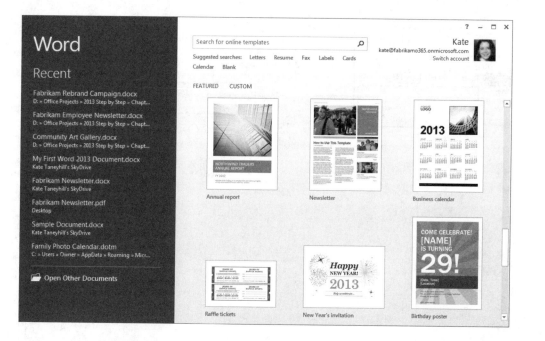

From the application Start screen, you can open a recently used file, open an existing file, or create a new file from a template. After you create a new file or open an existing one, the main window will be displayed.

The figure illustrates the Microsoft Word application window with labeled components: File tab, Quick Access Toolbar, Ribbon tab, Dialog box launcher, Ribbon, Gallery, More button, Window controls, Group, Status bar, and Collapse ribbon.

The application window has the following elements:

- **Ribbon** The main component of the Office user interface and where you'll find the primary commands for working with the content of your Office files. The ribbon includes tabs that have commands associated with a specific task. For example, objects that you insert in an Office document; like a picture, chart, or shape; are located on the Insert tab. This task-oriented organization also extends to the commands themselves, which are placed in related groups. For example, frequently used commands for formatting text are all located in a group named Font in most applications.

  TIP Some commands on the ribbon have what's known as a split control, which is a combination of a button and an arrow. An example is the Bullets command, found in Word on the Home tab in the Paragraph group. If you click the button, the default option, or the last option you selected during your editing session, will automatically be applied. When you click the arrow next to the button, a list of options will display, such as a list of available bullets.

Note that for larger split controls, like the Paste button, the arrow will appear below the button instead of to the right. An easy way to determine if you're using a split control is to point to the button. If only the button or the arrow is highlighted rather than the entire button, then it's a split control.

- **Title bar** Appears at the top of the application window and displays the name of the active file and application name. In most standard Windows applications, including the Office applications, the title bar also has the program icon on the far left.

- **Window controls** Located on the far right of the title bar. Along with the standard Minimize, Restore Down/Maximize, and Close buttons, there are two additional buttons:

  - **Help** Clicking this button displays help for the application.

  - **Ribbon Display Options** Clicking this button gives you a list of choices for viewing the ribbon.

The Auto-Hide Ribbon option gives you nearly a full-screen view because it also hides the status bar along with the ribbon. Show Tabs and Show Tabs And Commands toggle the ribbon between a collapsed or expanded state, displaying only the ribbon tabs or displaying both the ribbon tabs and commands.

SEE ALSO For more information about how to hide, collapse, and expand the ribbon, see the "Customizing the user interface" section later in this chapter.

- **Quick Access Toolbar** Appears on the left end of the title bar by default. Each application has its own set of frequently used commands that are specific to the application. The most common commands are Save, Undo, and Redo.

- **Status bar** Located at the bottom of the application window; displays information about the application or current file. In most applications, view controls and the zoom slider are located on the right end of the status bar.

- **Dialog box launcher** Appears in the lower-right corner of a group when additional options for the related set of commands are available. Clicking the dialog box launcher opens a dialog box or task pane.

- **Tool tabs** Appear in the ribbon when additional commands are available for a selected object, such as a table, picture, chart, or drawing object.

TIP You can quickly activate a tool tab for most objects by double-clicking the object.

- **Gallery** A visual list of choices, such as a collection of formats that offer multiple options. A gallery also refers to a set of related tools.

TIP Many galleries have additional options that may not appear in the ribbon. To view gallery options, right-click a gallery item. For example, to lock a shape for multiple uses, right-click a shape in the Shapes gallery and then click Lock Drawing Mode. To dismiss this mode, press the Esc key.

- **Live Preview** Enables you to view changes like pasted text or picture formatting prior to making a modification.

TIP Live Preview is available in all applications except OneNote.

- **Mini toolbar** Appears on the screen in most applications when you have text or an object selected; provides quick access to the most-used formatting commands.

☐ Leave house and car keys, and your complete itinerary, with a trusted friend.

☐ Lock windows, garages, and

| Calibri (Headin ▾ | 12 ▾ | A˄ A˅ ✎ | A ▾ |
| B I U aby ▾ A ▾ ☷ ▾ ☷ ▾ | | | Styles |

3. PACKING FOR THE TRIP

☐ Make a list of the specific items of clothing you'll need to pack for your trip to you'll attend.

TIP The Mini Toolbar may also appear when you right-click selected text or objects.

- **ScreenTips** ScreenTips provide descriptions of commands and are displayed when you point to a ribbon command. If the command has an associated keyboard shortcut, that shortcut will appear in parentheses next to the name of the command. Several ScreenTips also include detailed help or a feature preview. For instance, in Excel, the ScreenTip for the Conditional Formatting command on the Home tab in the Styles group includes a detailed explanation for how to use conditional formatting. It also includes a preview of how data bars and an icon set are displayed for a range of values.

| Conditional Formatting ▾ | Format as Table ▾ | Cell Styles ▾ | Insert ▾ | Delete ▾ | Format ▾ |
| | | Styles | | Cells | |

Conditional Formatting

		Easily spot trends and patterns in your data using bars, colors, and icons to visually highlight important values.
	6	
⊗	4	
⊘	9	
	7	
⊗	3	

❔ Tell me more

TIP If a command has an associated Help topic, Tell Me More is displayed at the bottom of the ScreenTip. Clicking the link displays the Help topic.

- **KeyTips** Enable you to navigate the ribbon by using the keyboard. To display KeyTips, press and release the Alt key. The KeyTips are the letters, numbers, or combinations of letters and numbers that appear on the ribbon. When you press only the Alt key, Key-Tips for the ribbon tabs and Quick Access Toolbar are displayed. To view KeyTips for a specific ribbon tab, after you press the Alt key, press the corresponding KeyTip on the keyboard. For example, to navigate to the Home tab and view the KeyTips for that tab, press Alt+H. Or to view the KeyTips for the Backstage view, press Alt+F.

TIP Commands on the Quick Access Toolbar have sequential KeyTips associated with the position of the command. For example, your first command is automatically assigned Alt+1.

The Office environment also extends to an area called the Backstage view, which is displayed by clicking the File tab on the ribbon.

Whereas the ribbon and Quick Access Toolbar are used for working with the content inside a file, the Backstage view is used for working with the entire file and for changing application settings.

The commands in the Backstage view are separated into two groups. The first set is for file-related commands, such as Info, Open, Save As, and Print. These commands are covered in the next section of this chapter.

The last set, specifically the Account and Options commands, are related to the application and are considered part of the Office environment.

- **Account** This is where you manage a new feature in Office Home and Student 2013 called an Office cloud account and get information about your Office installation.

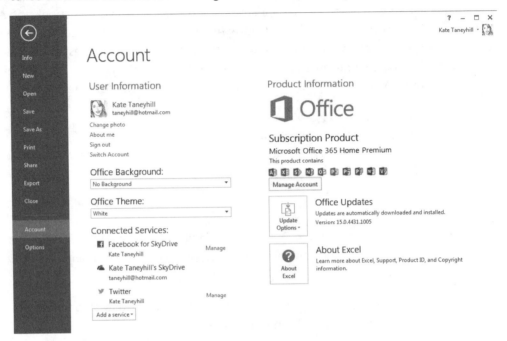

NOTE The previous image is from Microsoft Office 365 Home Premium, which is a subscription based edition of Office. The Microsoft Office Home and Student 2013 edition only includes Word, Excel, PowerPoint, and OneNote.

The User Information area has information about your Office cloud account, like your user name and your photo if you've elected to add one. This location is also where you can set a preferred Office background, with designs such as clouds or circles that appear in title bar of your Office applications, or where you can change the Office Theme.

SEE ALSO For more information about Office cloud accounts and connected services, see Chapter 3, "Sharing and collaborating."

The Product Information area is where you find information about your Office installation such as the Office suite you have installed and the applications that are included. This is also where you can choose how your Office installation is updated and view your update history.

- **Options** This is where you can change a variety of application preferences and customize certain behaviors that are specific to the application. In some applications, such as Excel and Access, there are also options specific to the active file.

To close the Backstage view and return to the application window, click the arrow in the upper-left corner or press the Esc key.

Adjusting your ribbon display

The ribbon is dynamic and adjusts to the size of the application window, your screen resolution, and your screen magnification. If you're using a low resolution, one that makes everything appear larger, a small application window, or a screen magnification of more than 100 percent, the appearance of groups and buttons may be affected. For example, a gallery or an entire group of commands may collapse to a single group button, or button images may appear without labels, or buttons may appear stacked vertically instead of horizontally. And when you are resizing an application window, if there isn't enough room to display the ribbon, it could disappear completely. You may want to take a few minutes to resize an application window to become more familiar with the dynamic ribbon changes.

To modify your screen resolution in both Windows 8 and Windows 7, right-click an empty area of your desktop and then click Screen Resolution. In the Screen Resolution dialog box, click Resolution and drag the slider to adjust your resolution.

TIP Screen resolution is expressed as pixels wide × pixels high, such as 1024×768. The greater the screen resolution, or the higher the numbers, the greater the amount of information that will fit on your screen. The greater the number of pixels wide (the first number), the greater the number of buttons that can be shown on the ribbon. Note that screen resolution options are dependent on your monitor, but they typically range from 800×600 to 2048×1152.

As previously noted, the ribbon also adjusts to your screen magnification. To modify your screen magnification in both Windows 8 and Windows 7, right-click an empty area of your desktop and then click Personalize. In the lower-left corner, click Display and then select your preferred screen magnification.

Working with Office files

In the previous section you learned about the Backstage view and how this area of the application is used for file-oriented tasks. In this section, you'll explore the primary file options that are available across the Office applications.

IMPORTANT The images and content provided in this section are from Excel. The other Office applications have similar options, and major differences between the applications are described in tips.

The pages in the Backstage view that contain commands for working with files are described in the following list:

- **Info** In most applications, the Info page displays information about the active file, such as the name and location of the file, the author, and the date the file was last modified. In all of the applications, you'll find specialized file management tools that are specific to the file and application. The following list provides an overview of some of the management tools and features you'll learn about in other chapters and sections of this book.

  - In Excel, PowerPoint, and Word, you'll find tools for opening previous versions of your current document and recovering files you forgot to save.

  - In OneNote you use the Info page to manage your open notebooks, by using tools such as syncing and sharing options.

SEE ALSO For more information about versions and recovering unsaved documents, see the "Recovering unsaved files and versions" section later in this chapter.

- **New** The New page is available in most applications and provides access to templates that enable you to create new files in the application. You can choose to start from scratch and select a blank template, or you can select one that already has content to help you get started on a specific type of task. For example, across the applications you'll find templates that range from newsletters, budgets, and sales reports, to contact information and asset tracking.

NOTE The templates shown in this book may not be the same as those that appear on your screen. New templates are added regularly, which may alter the results.

To create a new file in the applications that offer templates, simply double-click the template you want. Depending on the application and template, you may need to provide additional information before a new file is displayed in the application window. For example, in OneNote, you need to provide a location and file name and then save the file before it's created. This is because OneNote automatically saves certain changes.

TIP In OneNote, there are page templates available in the application, and you can find entire notebook templates in the Templates gallery on Office.com. PowerPoint templates include designs and layout templates along with task-oriented templates.

■ **Open** The Open page lists the recent files you previously opened and displays a list of available places from which you can open files.

Pinning the files you use the most

To pin the files you use the most to the recent file list, point to the file and then click the pushpin to the right of the file name. Pinned files are placed at the top of the list.

Recent Workbooks

> Fabrikam Info.xlsx
> https://fabrikamo365.sharepoint.com » sites » authors » Shared Documents

To unpin the file, click the pushpin a second time. You can pin and unpin frequently used folders to the Recent Folders list on the Open and Save As pages as well. You can also right-click a recently used file for additional options such as the ability to remove a file from the list and clear all pinned files.

TIP Your recent files list can also be accessed from the main list of tabs in the Backstage view. To make this change, click Options, and then click Advanced. Locate the Display options and then click Quickly Access This Number Of Recent Workbooks. Note that in other applications the option text reflects the type of Office document you use for that application. Also in the Display area are options to change the number of recent files and unpinned folders that appear on the Open and Save As pages.

SEE ALSO For more information about opening files from Microsoft SkyDrive, Microsoft SharePoint Online, or other web locations, see Chapter 3.

To view your recent files, click the Recent option near the top of the view, such as Recent Workbooks in Excel.

To open a file, if it's in the recent file list, you can click the file to open it in the application. If the file you need isn't in the list, first click the location where the file is stored, such as Computer, and then to the right of the location, click a recent folder. Or, if the folder you need isn't in the recent list, click the Browse button at the bottom. Either action displays the Open dialog box. After you select a file to open, click the Open button to open the file in the application.

TIP You can also double-click a location, like Computer, to quickly display the Open dialog box.

- **Save** When you save a file for the first time and click Save, the Save As page is displayed. After a file has been saved, clicking Save in the Backstage view will update the file and return you to the application window.

- **Save As** The options on the Save As page are similar to those on the Open page. The main difference is that there isn't a recent file list.

To save a file, select the location you want, and if the folder you want isn't in the recent folders list, click the Browse button. Either action displays the Save As dialog box. After you provide a file name, and if necessary, a different location in the Save As dialog box, click the Save button to save the file.

TIP As with the Open page, you can double-click a location to quickly display the Save As dialog box.

- **Print** In all Office applications except OneNote, the Print page provides printing and page layout options along with a preview of your file. In the Printer area, you can choose a different printer and set printer options. In the Settings section, you can specify various print and page settings prior to printing your file.

To print your file, click the Print button at the top of the view.

TIP OneNote has similar print and preview options, but they aren't combined in the same view.

There are also additional file options available on the Share and Export pages. The Share page gives you ways to share your file with others, such as sending your file as an email attachment or sharing it with others online in a web location or through a web browser.

On the Export page, you'll find the ability to save your file in a Portable Document Format (PDF) or XML Paper Specification (XPS) format. And in PowerPoint, you have options for converting your presentation to a video.

Because the majority of these options vary across Office applications or depend on additional components, you'll learn more about them and get step-by-step instructions in other chapters.

Recovering unsaved files and versions

There's a very good chance you will accidentally close a file without saving it, if you haven't already made such a mistake. The good news is that in Excel, PowerPoint, and Word, you may be able to recover your unsaved changes. And if you've spent some time working on an Office document and discover you'd like to return to a previous version of it, you may be able to do that too. File management tools for both of these situations are located in the Backstage view, on the Info page.

In the Versions area, a list of autosave files of your current document might be displayed.

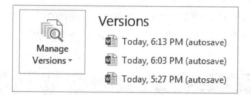

These versions are automatically created while you're working and are deleted when you save and close your Office document. There are a couple of requirements that need to be met before an autosave version is created.

- You must choose to save AutoRecover information, which is turned on on the Save page of the Options dialog box by default.

- An AutoRecover save must be made. This save is based on the time interval next to the AutoRecover information option and depends on whether you've made changes that need to be saved.

When these conditions are met, you can recover up to your last five autosave versions of your current file.

To open a previous version, click the file you want to open in the list and the autosave version will open in a separate window. You can then choose to restore your file, save the version as a new file, or close it without saving changes.

TIP If you only need to recover a portion of an autosave version, you don't need to restore your file to the earlier version. Simply copy the information you need and paste it in your main document.

The Versions area is also where you can recover a file you closed without saving. There are two types of unsaved files: those you never saved and unsaved autosave versions. The latter applies to files that were previously saved. It's the last autosave version of a file you closed without saving current changes.

IMPORTANT Files you never previously saved are automatically deleted after four days. Unsaved autosave versions are automatically deleted the next time you edit the file and save changes.

As with the autosave version requirements, in order to recover an unsaved file, you must elect to save AutoRecover information. And to recover an unsaved autosave version, you must also elect to keep the last autosaved version when you close without saving. The latter option is also found in the Options dialog box near the top of the Save options.

To recover unsaved files, click Manage Versions and then do one of the following.

- In Excel, click Recover Unsaved Workbooks.
- In PowerPoint, click Recover Unsaved Presentations.
- In Word, click Recover Unsaved Documents.

1

The Open dialog box appears and lists the files you can recover for the application you are using. Select the file you want and then click Open to open it in the application. And if you to want to keep that file, make sure you save your changes.

Customizing the user interface

In the first section of this chapter, you explored the user interface and became familiar with terminology and product-specific functionality. The next step is to personalize your Office surroundings to help you settle in and begin making yourself at home.

Here are some of the ways you can customize your user interface:

- To free up space on your screen, you can set the ribbon to auto-hide or you can toggle the ribbon between a collapsed and expanded state. A ribbon set to auto-hide is hidden from view. A collapsed state shows only the tabs, and the expanded state shows both the tabs and the commands.

- Set the Quick Access Toolbar to appear above or below the ribbon.

- Add additional commands to the Quick Access Toolbar or remove commands you don't need.

- Choose the information you prefer to display in the status bar, if applicable to the application.

Adapting exercise steps

The screen shots shown in this book were captured at a screen resolution of 1024×768, at 100 percent magnification. If your settings are different, the ribbon on your screen might not look the same as the one shown in this book. As a result, exercise instructions that involve the ribbon might require a little adaptation. Our instructions use this format:

- On the **Insert** tab, in the **Illustrations** group, click the **Chart** button.

If the command is in a list, our instructions use this format:

- On the **Home** tab, in the **Editing** group, click the **Find** arrow and then, in the **Find** list, click **Go To**.

If differences between your display settings and ours cause a button to appear differently on your screen than it does in this book, you can easily adapt the steps to locate the command. First click the specified tab, and then locate the specified group. If a group has been collapsed into a group list or under a group button, click the list or button to display the group's commands. If you can't immediately identify the button you want, point to likely candidates to display their names in ScreenTips.

In this book, we provide instructions based on traditional keyboard and mouse input methods. If you're using Office on a touch-enabled device, you might be giving commands by tapping with your finger or with a stylus. If so, substitute a tapping action any time we instruct you to click a user interface element. Also note that when we tell you to enter information in Office, you can do so by typing on a keyboard, tapping in the entry field under discussion to display and use the On-Screen Keyboard, or even speaking aloud, depending on your computer setup and your personal preferences.

Customizing the Office environment

In this exercise, you'll customize your Office environment by collapsing and expanding the ribbon, setting it to an auto-hide state, and moving the Quick Access Toolbar below the ribbon.

 SET UP **You don't need any practice files to complete this exercise. Start Word and follow the steps.**

> **IMPORTANT** Unless otherwise noted, the customizations in this section are not application specific.

1   On the Word Start screen, click **Blank document**.

2   Double-click the active ribbon tab to collapse it.

KEYBOARD SHORTCUT Press Ctrl+F1 to toggle the ribbon between a collapsed and expanded state.

3   Click the **Home** tab to expand the ribbon, and in the **Font** group, click the **Bold** button.

4   Click in the document to return the ribbon to a collapsed state.

5   In the window controls at the right end of the title bar, click the **Ribbon Display Options** button and then from the list, click **Auto-hide Ribbon**.

6   Click the top of the application window to display the ribbon.

7   On the **Home** tab, in the **Font** group, click the **Bold** button.

8   Click in the document to return the ribbon to an auto-hide state.

9   Click the arrow at the end of the **Quick Access Toolbar** and then near the bottom of the list, click **Show Below the Ribbon**.

CLEAN UP Set the ribbon to your preferred auto-hide, expanded, or collapsed state. Set the position of the Quick Access Toolbar to your preference, either shown above or below the ribbon. If you're continuing to the next exercise, leave Word and your document open. Otherwise, exit Word without saving changes to the document you created.

Customizing the Quick Access toolbar

As noted in the introduction of this section, you can also customize the Quick Access Toolbar by adding frequently used commands, such as New or Open, or by adding commands directly from the ribbon. Here are two ways you can add additional commands:

- Click the arrow at the end of the **Quick Access Toolbar** and then select a command from the **Customize Quick Access Toolbar** list.

- Right-click a command on the ribbon and then click **Add to Quick Access Toolbar**.

To remove a command from the Quick Access Toolbar, right-click the command and then click Remove From Quick Access Toolbar.

In this exercise, you'll customize the Quick Access Toolbar by adding and removing commands.

SET UP **You don't need any practice files to complete this exercise. If Word and your blank document are still open from the previous exercise, follow the steps. Otherwise, start Word, create a new document, and follow the steps.**

1 Click the arrow at the end of the **Quick Access Toolbar** and then in the list, click **Open**.

2 On the **Home** tab, in the **Font** group, right-click the **Bold** button, and then click **Add to Quick Access Toolbar**.

TIP You can also add dialog boxes or a group on the ribbon, such as the Font group, to your Quick Access Toolbar for faster access. To do so, right-click a dialog box launcher or right-click a group name and then click Add To Quick Access Toolbar.

3 On the **Quick Access Toolbar**, right-click the **Open** button and then click **Remove from Quick Access Toolbar**.

4 Remove the **Bold** button from the **Quick Access Toolbar**.

CLEAN UP **If you're continuing to the next exercise, leave Word and your document open. Otherwise, exit Word without saving changes to the document you created.**

TIP For more information about how to rearrange the commands on your Quick Access Toolbar or to add commands that don't appear on the ribbon, see "Customizing the ribbon" later in this chapter.

Customizing the status bar

You can also customize the status bar by choosing what you prefer to display. Similar to how you customize the Quick Access Toolbar, you can right-click the status bar to customize it. The Customize Status Bar list shows the available status bar items, and a check mark will appear next to those that are currently displayed. You then select or deselect items in the list to add or remove them. Note that some items only appear in the status bar when a feature is turned on, to help reduce status bar clutter. For example, if you choose to show Caps Lock, it will only display in the status bar if you've turned caps lock on and are typing in all caps.

Customize Status Bar	
Formatted Page Number	1
Section	1
✓ Page Number	Page 1 of 1
Vertical Page Position	1"
Line Number	1
Column	1
✓ Word Count	0 words
✓ Number of Authors Editing	
✓ Spelling and Grammar Check	
✓ Language	English (United States)
✓ Signatures	Off
Information Management Policy	Off
Permissions	Off
Track Changes	Off
✓ Caps Lock	Off
Overtype	Insert
Selection Mode	

In this exercise, you'll customize the status bar in Word.

SET UP You don't need any practice files to complete this exercise. If Word and your blank document are still open from the previous exercise, follow the steps. Otherwise, start Word, create a new document, and follow the steps.

1   At the bottom of the Word window, note **Page 1 of 1** on the left end of the status bar.

2   Right-click the status bar and then in the **Customize Status Bar** list, click **Page Number** to turn it off.

3   In the **Customize Status Bar** list, click **Page Number** again to turn it back on.

4   Click in the application window to close the **Customize Status Bar** options.

CLEAN UP Exit Word without saving changes in the document you created.

TIP You can also customize the behavior of the mini toolbar, Live Preview, or ScreenTips. To access these settings, display the Backstage view and then click Options. These user interface options are located at the top of the General section. Note that the user interface options vary across the applications. For example, OneNote does not support Live Preview.

Customizing the ribbon

As noted at the beginning of this chapter, one of the biggest advantages of Office is the similarities across the applications. In this section, you'll start applying what you learn about one feature to other components that are similar, like the Quick Access Toolbar and ribbon.

In comparison, both the Quick Access Toolbar and ribbon contain the primary commands for an application and can be customized. The main difference between them, other than appearance, is that the Quick Access Toolbar holds your most frequently used commands, whereas the ribbon provides a more standardized set of commands. However, there may be times when you want to make modifications to the ribbon. For instance, there are more advanced commands that aren't in the ribbon by default that you may find beneficial. Or you might find you can work more efficiently by moving a command or group to another location or tab.

To customize the ribbon, you display the Backstage view, click Options, and then click Customize Ribbon.

The left side of the ribbon customization settings area lists commands that can be added to the ribbon, and the right side lists the ribbon tabs. You can add commands from the list of available commands to any existing group on the ribbon, or you can create a new group and add commands to it.

You can also create a new ribbon tab and add new groups and commands or modify the tool tabs that appear when a specific object is selected, like a picture. To access all available ribbon tabs, in the Customize The Ribbon area, click the arrow next to Main Tabs and then click All Tabs.

Additionally, you can reorder built-in tabs, groups, and commands using the Move Up and Move Down arrows on the right side of the dialog box.

In this exercise, you'll customize the ribbon by adding a new tab, group, and command to the ribbon in PowerPoint. You'll then delete your customizations. At the end of this exercise, you'll apply what you learned about ribbon customization to the Quick Access Toolbar.

➡️ SET UP **You don't need any practice files to complete this exercise. Start PowerPoint, create a blank presentation, and follow the steps.**

1 In the **Backstage** view, click **Options**, and then click **Customize Ribbon**. Below the ribbon tab list, click **New Tab**.

2 Click **New Tab (Custom)** to select it, and then click the **Rename** button near the bottom.

3 Enter **MY CUSTOM TAB** and then click **OK**.

4 Click **New Group (Custom)** and rename it to **My custom group**.

5   From the **Popular Commands** list, select any command. For instance, select **Email**. Click **My custom group** and then click the **Add** button near the middle of the **Options** dialog box.

> **IMPORTANT** Commands can only be added to groups on the ribbon. If you don't select a group prior to adding a command, you will encounter an error message.

6   To review your customizations, click **OK** at the bottom of the **Options** dialog box.

7   On the ribbon, click **MY CUSTOM TAB** and note your custom group and newly added command.

8   Reopen the **Options** dialog box and display the ribbon customization options.

9   If necessary, select **MY CUSTOM TAB**.

10   Near the middle of the **Options** dialog box, click the **Remove** button to delete your custom tab and custom group.

11   Experiment with other ribbon customizations. For example, to reorder tabs, groups, or individual commands, make a selection, and then on the right side of the dialog box, click the **Move Up** and **Move Down** buttons.

12   After you're comfortable customizing the ribbon, in the **Options** dialog box, click **Customize Quick Access Toolbar** and apply what you learned in the previous steps. For example, reorder the commands or add new ones.

13   To reset all of your ribbon and **Quick Access Toolbar** customizations, click the **Reset** button near the bottom of the **Options** dialog box, and then click **Reset all customizations**.

14   Click **Yes** to confirm the deletion of your customizations.

> **TIP** To back up your ribbon and Quick Access Toolbar customizations or to share them with others, use the Import/Export options at the bottom of the dialog box.

❌ CLEAN UP **Close the Options dialog box and exit PowerPoint without saving the presentation.**

Choosing the right application for the task at hand

As noted at the beginning of this chapter, many of the applications have similar functionality. In the next chapter, you'll learn about shared features that are available to most of the Office applications. With so many overlapping capabilities, you may be wondering how to determine the application you need to use for your various projects.

In this section, you'll get an overview of various tasks you can perform in each application that's available in the Office Home and Student 2013 suite. For the applications that have similar functionalities, you'll receive more information at the end of this section on how to choose an application to perform a specific task.

Application	Tasks
Excel	■ Calculate and analyze numeric information such as budgets, income, expenses, loans, and scientific or statistical data. ■ Organize and track information, such as inventory, task lists, projects, financial data, and address lists. ■ Summarize numeric and other data and display results in charts and PivotTables. ■ Create forms that include controls, such as check boxes, drop-down lists, and option groups, to be filled in by other users.
OneNote	■ Organize and keep track of your notes and other information in searchable notebooks. ■ Collect information from other Office applications or Windows Internet Explorer. ■ Capture your notes in text, ink, drawings, images, audio, and video. ■ Insert pictures, tables, files, spreadsheets, or diagrams. ■ Collaborate in real time with other people.
PowerPoint	■ Create presentations for a speech, class, or demonstration. ■ Create photo albums to share with friends and family or for personal use. ■ Add multimedia such as graphics, video, and audio along with animations. ■ Present your presentation to a live audience or in an online meeting, or transform it into a video.
Word	■ Create general documents such as letters, memos, term papers, essays, or reports. ■ Create documents that contain graphics, such as newsletters, cards, flyers, invitations, and photo calendars. ■ Create advanced documents, such as mass mailings that can be printed and mailed or sent by email. ■ Create a book or report with a table of contents, indexes, and cross references. ■ Create forms that include controls such as check boxes, drop-down lists, and date pickers, to be filled in by other users. ■ Generate other documents, such as envelopes, labels, blog posts, and webpages.

As previously discussed, several of the Office applications provide similar functionality. For instance, you can use Word or PowerPoint to create Office documents that include graphics, such as flyers or photo albums. You can create forms in Excel and Word. And you can use both Word and Excel for lists of information.

More often than not, you'll likely choose the application you're most comfortable with and forgo learning something new. Before you do, keep in mind that each application specializes in specific capabilities and can produce better results when selected for certain tasks. Think of it as going to a restaurant—if you go to one that specializes in seafood, you might find steak on the menu, but it may not be as good as a steak you get from a steak house.

Also keep in mind that what you learn in one application can be applied to another, so the learning curve may be easier than you think. Here are a few tips to help you determine the right application for specific tasks.

- For files that include graphics, consider the type of content you want to include, the amount of text, and the complexity of the layout. If it's a small amount of text and you don't need to use cross-references, fields, or other advanced text features, then use PowerPoint. In PowerPoint, it's easier to move your content and visually align objects. Plus, you can add vertical and horizontal guides for precision placement.

- For photo albums, think about the end result you want. If you want to display the album electronically on a computer or projection screen, use PowerPoint. It also enables you to add transitions and animations for a professional-looking result. Plus, you can convert your presentation to a video that can be published on websites like YouTube.

- For simple lists of data, such as an inventory or making a task, address, grocery, or birthday list, consider using Excel. It has tools for sorting, filtering, and managing your lists.

- For forms, determine whether the form contains calculations. Although Word supports calculations, creating formulas in Excel is easier and more reliable. However, if your form needs to contain advanced text features or needs the page flexibility of a word processor, then create your form in Word.

This list is certainly not an exhaustive list of all of the different types of files you can create or tasks you'll perform in your projects. This is a vast topic that could easily warrant its own book. But the information provided here should be enough to give you a good start in choosing the right application.

Key points

- The ribbon and Quick Access Toolbar have commands for working with the content of a file.

- The Backstage view has commands for working with the entire file or the application.

- You can create new documents, workbooks, presentations, publications, notebooks, and databases on the New page in the Backstage view.

- You can open, save, print, share, and export documents in the Backstage view.

- You can customize the Office user interface and modify application settings to fit your workflow.

- Choosing the right application for specific tasks can help you be more productive and get better results.

Chapter at a glance

Identify

Identify new shared features in Office Home and Student 2013, page 42

Apply

Apply Office themes,
page 47

Insert

Insert graphics, videos, charts, and diagrams,
page 50

Search

Search for online templates,
page 58

Using shared Office features

2

IN THIS CHAPTER, YOU WILL LEARN HOW TO

- Identify new shared features in Office Home and Student 2013.
- Apply Office themes.
- Insert graphics, videos, charts, and diagrams.
- Search for online templates.
- Present Office documents online.

As noted in Chapter 1, "Getting comfortable in Office Home and Student 2013," the biggest advantage of Office Home and Student 2013 is the similarities across the applications, which help greatly reduce the learning curve. Along with a common user interface, there are also features that work nearly the same regardless of the application you're using. For example, after you learn how to insert and work with SmartArt graphics, you can apply that knowledge to all of the applications that support SmartArt.

In this chapter, you'll get a look at the new shared Office features and learn how to get started with the primary features that are shared across the applications. You'll learn how to apply Office themes; insert graphics, videos, charts, and diagrams; search for online templates; and present Office documents online.

PRACTICE FILES To complete the exercises in this chapter, you need the practice files contained in the Chapter02 practice file folder. For more information, see "Download the practice files" in this book's Introduction.

Identifying new shared features in Office Home and Student 2013

Each Office release brings new features to help you make short work of otherwise cumbersome tasks, and Office Home and Student 2013 is no different from the rest. Along with new and improved productivity tools, this version of Office also gives you more Internet integration so you can use and access content stored in online locations, referred to as *cloud services*. Plus, with the addition of Touch Mode, you can work with your files on almost any device that supports touch.

In this section, you'll learn about new and improved features that are shared across the Office applications.

TIP The first chapter of each part of this book contains a list of key features that are specific to that Office application. Some of the new features discussed in this section may have previously been included in the Office applications but have been improved or are significantly different.

- **Microsoft SharePoint Online and Microsoft SkyDrive integration** Now you can open and save files stored in online locations from your Office applications. When your files are stored in the cloud, you can access them from other computers and devices, share them with people outside your school or home network, or work with others on the same file at the same time.

  TIP Cloud locations such as SharePoint Online and SkyDrive require a Microsoft Office 365 account or a Microsoft Account. Other online locations, such as a hosted SharePoint site, can also be accessed from the Office applications.

  SEE ALSO For more information on an Office 365 or Microsoft Account, see Chapter 3, "Sharing and collaborating."

- **Online templates** New templates offer a wide variety of content for business, school, and home. They range from letters, flyers, brochures, calendars, and newsletters, to industry-specific presentations, sales reports, inventory tracking, and project management, to coordinating sets of templates across the applications and more. There are thousands of templates available to help you get started.

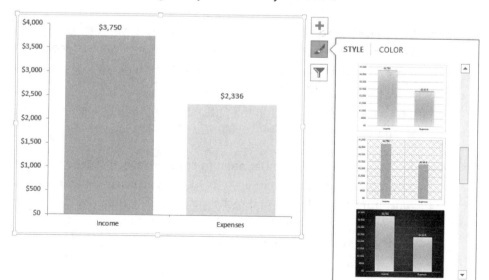

TIP New online templates are applicable to Microsoft Excel, PowerPoint, and Word.

- **Chart formatting controls** Modify your chart formatting, such as color and style, and add chart elements like titles, legends, and data labels by using new controls that are displayed when a chart is selected. The new chart filter enables you to select which data series or categories you want on your chart.

TIP New chart formatting tools are applicable to Excel, PowerPoint, and Word.

- **Rich data labels** You can now format and size chart labels like shapes and you can clone your modifications and apply them to other data labels. Information from other cells can also be included in your labels, and leader lines can be added for almost all chart types.

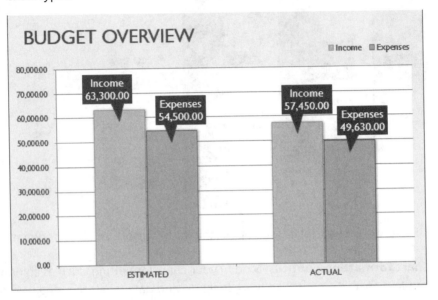

TIP New chart formatting tools are applicable to Excel, Outlook, PowerPoint, and Word.

- **Online presentation** Share your Office documents with others through the new free Office Presentation Service from your Office application. Meeting participants can view your online presentation on their computers, tablets, or most smartphones through a web browser.

TIP Presenting online through the Office Presentation Service is applicable to PowerPoint and Word.

- **Online pictures** You no longer need to copy or save an online picture to your local or network drive in order to insert it in your Office documents. You can now embed pictures from online locations directly into an Office document. And when you're signed in to Office with a Microsoft Account, you can access other places such as social networks like Facebook and Flickr.

TIP The online pictures feature is applicable to Excel, PowerPoint, and Word.

- **Online video**   Add a link to a video from an online location, like your SkyDrive or YouTube, in an Office document and play it without leaving the application.

TIP Online video is available in PowerPoint and Word. An Internet connection is required for video playback.

- **Posting to social networks** You can share your Office documents with your social networks, like Facebook and Twitter, directly from the application. When you set your edit or view permissions, a sharing link will be created and posted on the social networks you select. When others click the link, your shared file will open in the associated Office Web App.

TIP The Get A Sharing Link option is similar to the Post To Social Networks option. You can generate a link—for viewing only or for editing—that you can share with others through email, a website, or whichever method you choose. Posting to social networks and getting a sharing link is available in Excel, PowerPoint, and Word. You must be signed in to Office with a Microsoft Account and have previously connected your social networks to your Office account, and your Office document must be saved in a shared location, such as SkyDrive, in order for the additional sharing options to be available.

SEE ALSO For more information on Microsoft Accounts and connecting services, see Chapter 3.

- **Apps for Office** Insert apps in your Office documents to extend application functionality. Apps range from online dictionaries and application add-ins, such as templates for mailing labels, to interactive apps like Bing Maps, which enables you to map and visualize your geographic data.

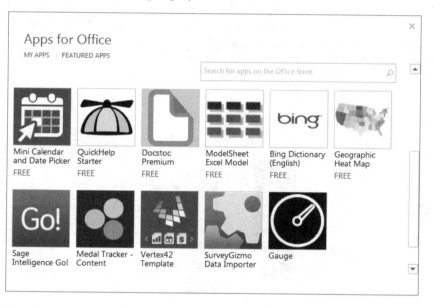

- **Touch Mode** All of the Office applications now support touch. When touch is enabled, the Office user interface is optimized for touch commands. The user interface increases in size, and more space is added between the buttons on the ribbon and Quick Access Toolbar.

Applying Office themes

Files you create in Access, Excel, PowerPoint, and Word all include a base set of formats called a *theme*. The theme is what controls the theme colors in the color palettes and the choices in numerous formatting galleries. It also controls the headings and body theme fonts at the top of the font list in most applications. Some applications also support theme effects, which apply to formatting for illustrations, such as pictures, shapes, SmartArt, and charts. Examples of these formats are border style and shadow. And in PowerPoint, formatting for slide masters and slide layouts are also part of the theme.

Files can be formatted by using theme elements, such as theme colors and theme fonts. Then if you choose a different theme from the themes gallery, the formatting will automatically update to match the formatting stored in your selected theme.

You can also start with a theme and then select different theme elements to create a custom theme. For example, you might like the colors of a theme but prefer different theme fonts or theme effects. Along with the themes gallery, which modifies all theme elements, you can modify individual theme elements by using the colors, fonts, and effects galleries.

In PowerPoint and Word, theme commands are located on the Design tab. In Excel, they're found on the Page Layout tab.

In this exercise, you'll explore themes and individual theme elements.

➜ SET UP **You need the Simple To-Do List workbook located in the Chapter02 practice file folder to complete this exercise. Start Excel, open the Simple To-Do List workbook, and follow the steps.**

1 Examine the **Simple To-Do List** workbook and take note of the colors and font appearance.

TIP The Simple To-Do List workbook is based on one of the new online Excel templates that are available on the New page in the Backstage view.

2 On the **Page Layout** tab, in the **Themes** group, click the **Themes** button.

3 In the **Themes** gallery, click **Integral**.

The fonts and colors automatically update to the Integral theme colors and theme fonts.

Task	Priority	Status	Start Date	Due Date	% Complete	Done/Overdue?	Notes
Task 1	Normal	Not Started	9/12/2012	9/21/2012	0%		
Task 2	High	Complete	9/2/2012	9/27/2012	100%		
Task 3	Low	In Progress	8/23/2012	10/7/2012	50%		
Task 4	Normal	Not Started	10/12/2012	11/16/2012	0%		

TIP The formatting of the title shape also changed from a gradient fill to a textured fill. This may appear to be a theme effect, but it's actually a theme fill. You can access theme fills for shapes at the bottom of the Shape Style gallery on the Drawing Tools Format tool tab.

4   Experiment with other themes by applying them to the workbook.

5   After you're comfortable with themes, experiment with changing only the theme colors or theme fonts, which are also available in the **Themes** group. For example, you may like the colors of a theme but prefer to use a different set of fonts.

❌ CLEAN UP **Close the Simple To-Do List workbook without saving your changes.**

SEE ALSO For more on themes and to learn how to create a custom theme, see Chapter 12, "Designing and creating presentations."

Inserting graphics, videos, charts, and diagrams

Documents have evolved from simple text-based files to those that contain rich images that help convey and illustrate information. For instance, graphics, like pictures or shapes, can be added for visual organization and to help break up large blocks of text. And for a combination of text and graphics, you can use SmartArt to help convey a concept. You can also use it for diagrams, lists of information, or for a collection of captioned pictures.

You don't need to hire a professional to add these visual elements. After an illustration is inserted, a variety of tools are available to help you create polished graphics and diagrams. And using those tools is much easier than you might think.

In this exercise, you'll insert a picture, shape, and SmartArt graphic by using features shared across Excel, PowerPoint, and Word. You will also explore basic formatting options that are available to these features.

SET UP **You need the Sample Picture image located in the Chapter02 practice file folder to complete this exercise. Start Word, create a blank document, and follow the steps.**

1   To insert an illustration, click the **Insert** tab and then locate the **Illustrations** group.

2   You are going to insert a picture, so click the **Pictures** button.

TIP In PowerPoint, the Pictures button is located in the Images group. You can use the Online Pictures button to insert pictures stored on the Internet, including in places like your SkyDrive or social networks like Facebook and Flicker. Or, if the picture you want to insert is on your screen rather than a stored in a file, use Insert Screenshot to add a picture of an entire window or a screen clipping.

3   Navigate to the **Chapter02** practice file folder and select **Sample Picture**.

4   Near the bottom of the **Insert Picture** dialog box, click the **Insert** button.

5   Note the **Picture Tools Format** tool tab that appears in the ribbon when the picture is selected.

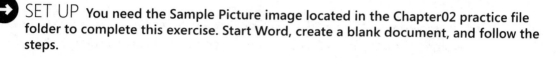

6   Click in the document away from the picture to deselect the picture and to remove the display of the picture tools.

7   Click the picture to redisplay the picture tools. Explore the commands on the **Picture Tools Format** tool tab.

For example, in the Picture Styles gallery, click a picture style or use Live Preview to explore them. Or, in the Adjust group, click Color and apply a color wash to the picture.

TIP You can swap a picture with another one and retain the size and formatting options. To do so, right-click the picture and then click Change Picture.

8   When you're finished checking out the various formatting options, select the picture and press the **Delete** key to remove the picture from the document.

9   Next you're going to insert a shape. On the **Insert** tab, in the **Illustrations** group, click the **Shapes** button, and then click the rectangle shape.

10   Point to an area in the document, and then click and drag to draw a rectangle.

11   Explore the **Drawing Tools Format** tool tab.

For example, in the Shape Styles group, use the Shape Styles gallery to apply different styles, or click Shape Effects and explore preset shadows, reflections, glows, or 3-D effects.

12   When you're finished exploring, delete the rectangle.

13   To insert a SmartArt graphic, on the **Insert** tab, click the **SmartArt** button.

14 In the **Choose a SmartArt Graphic** dialog box, select the different SmartArt categories and review the types of graphics that are available for the selected category.

15 To get more information on a specific graphic, click once on the preview and view the additional details on the right side of the dialog box.

16 Select the **List** category and then select **Basic Block List**.

17 Click **OK** to insert your SmartArt graphic in the document.

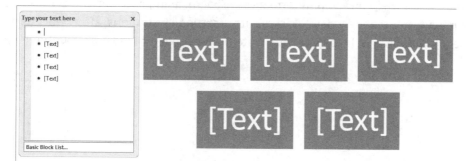

18   In the text pane, click to the right of the first bullet and enter **Word**.

19   Click in the next bullet placeholder and enter **PowerPoint**.

TIP Did you notice that the text font size decreased after you entered the word *PowerPoint*? SmartArt will reduce the size of the font to help maintain uniform formatting.

20   In the text pane, enter additional text or delete the remaining bullet placeholders to remove the empty shapes.

TIP To add additional shapes, click at the end of the last text entry and then press Enter.

21   On the **SmartArt Tools Design** tool tab, explore the design options.

For example, use the Layouts gallery to switch to a different SmartArt layout, or in the SmartArt Styles gallery, select a different style to change the format of the graphic.

22   When you're comfortable with the basic SmartArt formatting options, click the edge of the graphic in your document to select it, and then press **Delete**.

❌ CLEAN UP **Close the document without saving changes, and Exit Word.**

Inserting charts

A chart is often included alongside a list of values to convey how those values relate to each other. Charts help give your information visual meaning and context, and can be comprehended faster than raw data. And as with inserting illustrations, after your chart is inserted, the Chart Tools tool tabs help you create professional-looking charts without a lot of effort.

When you insert a chart, you start with a default chart, such as a column, line, bar, or pie chart, and then customize the style, layout, and formatting to fit your needs. In PowerPoint and Word, after you insert a chart, a small Excel window, called a *chart sheet*, is displayed. You use the chart sheet to replace the placeholder data with your own by entering your data in place of the sample information provided. The chart will update automatically.

In Excel, you first add your chart sheet information to a workbook. Then you select that information and insert your chart. Although the steps to insert a chart may vary between the applications, the tools for working with a chart, such as those for applying formatting and layout features, are shared across the applications.

SEE ALSO For more information on inserting charts in Excel, see Chapter 23, "Creating charts and graphics."

In this exercise, you'll insert a default column chart in Word and explore basic formatting options.

TIP The steps for inserting a chart in this exercise are applicable to PowerPoint and Word.

SET UP You don't need any practice files to complete this exercise. Start Word, create a blank document, and follow the steps.

1   To insert a chart, on the **Insert** tab, in the **Illustrations** group, click the **Chart** button to display the **Insert Chart** dialog box.

2   In the **Insert Chart** dialog box, click the various chart categories and explore the available chart types.

TIP If you're not sure which type of chart best represents your data, try the new Recommended Charts feature in Excel. It analyzes your information by looking for patterns in your data arrangement and suggests the most relevant chart types.

SEE ALSO For more information on the Recommended Charts feature, see Chapter 23.

3   From the **Column** category, select **Clustered Column**, and then click **OK**.

4   In the chart sheet, click a cell that contains a value, enter another number, and then press **Enter** to update the chart.

> **TIP** To add an additional series or category, enter your information to the right of the last series name or below the last category name. You can delete a series or category by right-clicking the row or column heading and then clicking Delete.

5   On the chart sheet, click the **Close** button to remove the chart sheet from the screen.

> **TIP** To redisplay the chart sheet, on the Chart Tools Design tool tab, in the Data group, click the Edit Data button. Note that this is a split control, so make sure you click the button and not the arrow.

6   On the **Chart Tools Design** tool tab, experiment with the various design options.

For example, in the Chart Layouts group, click Quick Layout and select a different layout to add or remove multiple chart elements, such as the legend, titles, or gridlines. Or, in the Chart Styles group, click the Chart Styles gallery and select a different style to modify multiple formats at the same time.

> **SEE ALSO** For more information on formatting charts, see Chapter 23.

✖ CLEAN UP Close the document without saving changes, and exit Word.

Searching for online templates

For some tasks, you may know exactly how to begin, including the types of features you need to convey your information. For the times when you're unsure, don't stare at a blank file hoping something will magically appear. Turn to the online templates for inspiration. The online templates that appear when you first start almost all Office Home and Student 2013 applications, as well as those available on the New page in the Backstage view, may provide a starting point or give you ideas for how to get started.

The templates that appear first on the application Start screen are featured templates. Typically these templates are new or are those you recently used. You can choose from these templates or search the online templates to find one that is more specific to your needs.

TIP All of the online templates created for Office Home and Student 2013 are theme enabled. As you learned in the "Applying Office themes" section earlier in this chapter, this means that the fonts and colors can be modified to match your preferred colors, such as those for a special event or your school colors.

SEE ALSO For more information on creating your own theme, see Chapter 12.

TIP To use online templates, you must be connected to the Internet. Online templates can be accessed from the New page in the Backstage view in Excel, PowerPoint, and Word. For OneNote, you can find a variety of notebook templates, such as planners, meeting notes, and appointment trackers, in the Templates gallery on Office.com.

In this exercise, you'll search for online templates by using Word.

➜ SET UP **You don't need any practice files to complete this exercise. Make sure you're connected to the Internet, start Word, and follow the steps.**

1   Let's start by searching for a specific type of template. Next to the list of suggested searches, click **Labels**.

TIP The number to the right of each category is the number of templates currently available for your specified search. Note that some templates may be assigned to more than one category.

IMPORTANT The online templates shown in the graphics in this exercise may not be the same as those that appear on your screen. New templates are added regularly, and this may alter your search results.

2   Point to a template thumbnail to view a ScreenTip, which displays additional details about a template, such as label vendor and product number.

3   Click once on any template to view more information and a larger preview of the template.

IMPORTANT For templates other than Blank Document, double-clicking a template thumbnail creates a new document based on the selected template. Be sure to click one time if you want to view details.

TIP You can use the arrows that appear to the left and right of the preview to browse the available templates. If the template has multiple views, More Images will display below the preview, along with navigation arrows. And in PowerPoint, if there are additional theme color variations included in the template, they are shown to the right of the template.

4   Click the **Close** button in the upper-right corner to close the preview.

5   In the Category pane on the right, click **Business** to narrow your search results.

6   To narrow your search results even further, click **Industry**.

Both categories will be highlighted at the top of the pane.

7   To remove the filtered category and return to a broader set of search results, point to the **Business** category and click the X that appears to the right.

8　To return to the featured templates, to the left of the **Search** text box, click **Home**.

TIP You can also use the Search For Online Templates text box to find specific templates. You can use single words or phrases, but single words will return the most results. After you enter your search string, press Enter to perform the search. For applications with similar functionality, when you search for a template, you may get results for other applications below the template thumbnails. For example, if you search for *Calendar*, you'll find results for almost every application.

Search results from your other Office applications

› ☒ Excel: 45

› ☒ PowerPoint: 27

To view the other templates, click the arrow to the left of the application name to expand the list. When you double-click a template, the application will start, and then a new file is created based on the template.

✖ CLEAN UP **Exit Word without saving changes to your document.**

The templates across the applications include examples of many of the features you'll learn about in this book. Though some of them may include more advanced capabilities, such as macros used to automate tasks, we'll introduce you to the tools you'll need to utilize them so they can be modified to fit your needs.

Presenting Office documents online

In Office Home and Student 2013 you can share your documents in real time with a live audience with the free Office Presentation Service. The best part is participants don't need the application to view your PowerPoint presentation or Word document. They can view it in a web browser on their computer, tablet, or most smartphones.

TIP If you have notes stored in a OneNote notebook, you can share that notebook with participants during your presentation. Even if you don't have specific notes, you can use a shared notebook for taking notes, capturing a brainstorming session, or as a whiteboard. For more information about sharing OneNote notebooks, see Chapter 27, "Sharing notes with others."

TIP Presenting online through the Office Presentation Service is applicable to PowerPoint and Word. It requires an Office account and that the presenter and participants have an Internet connection. Saving the presentation in a shared location isn't required for presenting online. For more information about Office accounts, see Chapter 3, "Sharing and collaborating."

When you use the free Office Presentation Service, you present your slide show in PowerPoint or your Word document in Word and the participants view it in the corresponding Office Web App. To include audio or video, you'll need a conference line or an online service, such as Skype.

In this exercise, you'll present a PowerPoint presentation through the Office Presentation Service.

 SET UP **You need the Fabrikam Management Team presentation located in the Chapter02 practice file folder to complete this exercise. Make sure you are signed in to Office, start PowerPoint, open the Fabrikam Management Team presentation, and follow the steps.**

1   Click the **File** tab to open the **Backstage** view, and then click **Share**.

2   On the **Share** page, in the **Present Online** options to the right, make sure **Office Presentation Service** is selected.

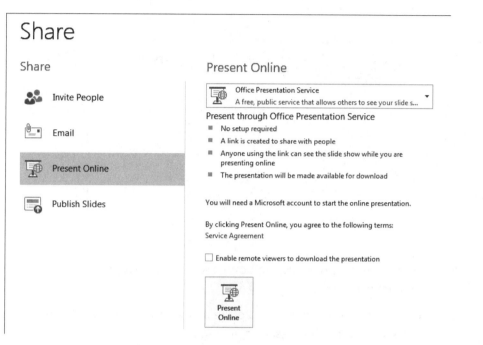

TIP In PowerPoint, the Present Online button is also available on the Slide Show tab, in the Start Slide Show group.

3   Above the **Present Online** button, note the **Enable remote viewers to download the presentation** check box. You can select this option if you want participants to be able to save a copy of your presentation.

4   Click the **Present Online** button to view additional sharing options.

5   In the **Present Online** dialog box, click either the **Copy Link** or **Send in Email** option to share your presentation.

TIP You can copy the link and paste it in your web browser to view what the participants view when the presentation begins.

6   Click **Start Presentation**.

TIP After you start your presentation, participants will view your presentation in PowerPoint Web App.

7   To advance to the next slide, press the **Enter** key.

8   To end the presentation, press **Esc** to suspend it, and then on the **Present Online** tab, click **End Online Presentation**.

9   In the message box that confirms ending your presentation, click **End Online Presentation**.

TIP After you end your presentation, participants will view a black screen in Power-Point Web App.

✖ CLEAN UP **Exit PowerPoint without saving changes to the practice file.**

When using the Office Presentation Service, you may want to explore the participant's view and options. As noted in a tip in this exercise, you can copy the presentation link and paste it in your web browser to view what the participants view while you're presenting. For instance, they can scroll through the presentation or document on their own, or they can use the Follow Presenter option so their screen changes as the presenter's screen changes.

Inserting online video

In both PowerPoint and Word, you can insert a linked video that's stored in an online location, like your SkyDrive, Facebook, YouTube, or another website. Note that because online videos are linked, in order to play an online video during a PowerPoint presentation or from a Word document, you must have an Internet connection, and your computer must have access to the website where the video is stored.

To insert an online video, use the Insert tab. In Word, you can then play the video from the document. In PowerPoint, you need to be in Slide Show view to play your video.

In this exercise, you'll add a link to a video into a Word document and play it after it's inserted.

➜ SET UP **You don't need any practice files to complete this exercise. Start Word, create a blank document, and follow the steps.**

1   On the **Insert** tab, in the **Media** group, click the **Online Video** button.

TIP In PowerPoint, on the Insert tab, in the Media group, click Video, and then from the list, click the Online Video button.

Insert Video

⊙	**Bing Video Search** Search the web	Search Bing 🔍
☁	**Kate Taneyhill's SkyDrive** someone@example.com	**Browse ›**
🌐	**From a Video Embed Code** Paste the embed code to insert a video from a web site	Paste embed code here ➡

Also insert from:

[f] [You Tube]

IMPORTANT In order to access social networking sites like Facebook or YouTube, you need to be signed in to Office with a Microsoft Account. For more information about Microsoft Accounts and signing in to Office, see Chapter 3.

2 In the **Insert Video** dialog box, click in the Search Bing text box, enter **Office 2013 microsoft.com** and then press the **Enter** key to view your search results.

> **IMPORTANT** Because you're browsing online videos, your search results may vary from those shown in this exercise.

3 Click once on any video to select it and display more information about the selected video at the bottom of the dialog box.

4 To preview the video, click the **View Larger** button in the lower-right corner of the video.

5 In the video preview, click the **Play** button in the center to play the video.

6 Click the **Close** button in the upper-right corner to close the preview.

7   Next let's insert a video in the document. Click a video to select it, and in the lower-right corner of the **Insert Video** dialog box, click **Insert**.

8   Click the **Play** button in the center of the video preview picture to play the inserted video from the Word document. If the video doesn't begin to automatically play, click the **Play** button at the bottom of the video.

TIP When the video is playing, controls to pause, adjust the volume, and show the video in a full screen are available.

TIP In PowerPoint, you need to be in Slide Show view to play a video.

9 Click anywhere in the Word document that is outside of the video screen to end the video.

TIP In PowerPoint, clicking a slide away from the video will advance to the next slide. In either application, you can also press the Esc key to end a video.

CLEAN UP **Exit Word without saving changes to your document.**

SEE ALSO For more information on working with video in PowerPoint, see Chapter 15, "Adding animation and multimedia."

Key points

- The Office applications have features that are shared across Office, which means they work almost the same regardless of the application you're using.

- You use the Insert tab to add illustrations, such as pictures, shapes, SmartArt graphics, and charts.

- To format illustrations and charts, click the object to select it, and then use the tools that automatically appear in the ribbon for the selected object.

- You can share your Office documents with others in real time through the free Office Presentation Service.

- When you insert an online video in an Office document, only a link to where the video is stored online and a preview picture are inserted. You need to be connected to the Internet to play the video.

Chapter at a glance

Explore

Explore the Office account,
page 74

page 74

Connect

Connect cloud services,
page 78

Open

Open files from the cloud,
page 90

Sync

Sync your files with the cloud,
page 94

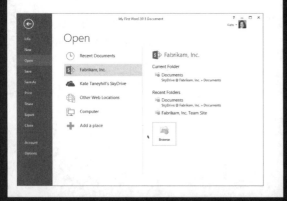

Sharing and collaborating

3

IN THIS CHAPTER, YOU'LL LEARN HOW TO

- Define the term *cloud service*.

- Sign in and manage your Office account.

- Connect cloud services to your Office account.

- Sync files with SkyDrive for offline use.

- Get started with co-authoring.

A cloud service typically refers to online file storage, resources, or applications that are accessed through the Internet. These can range from apps for your smartphone, Internet games, social networks, and web-based email to secure private networks.

These services are becoming part of our everyday lives. You may have documents and other files like pictures or videos stored on Microsoft SharePoint, Microsoft SkyDrive, Flickr, or YouTube. And you may have contact information stored on various social networks like Facebook, Twitter, or LinkedIn.

In this chapter, you'll learn about how Microsoft Office Home and Student 2013 connects you to your various cloud services through your Office account. You'll also learn how you can use cloud services to share and collaborate with others, such as working with a group on a school project or planning a family reunion.

PRACTICE FILES You don't need any practice files to complete the exercises in this chapter.

Defining the term *cloud service*

These days you may work across numerous computers and devices. You may use a desktop computer while at your desk and use a laptop, Microsoft Surface, or other tablet, or smartphone when you're on the go. And there may be times when you use a public computer, such as one in a hotel business center or Internet café. Or, if you're a student, you may use various computers at school.

Imagine switching to another computer or device and picking up exactly where you left off, right down to the last paragraph in a document you were editing in Microsoft Word or the last slide you were working on in Microsoft PowerPoint.

You could have almost achieved this capability in past versions of Office, but it may not have been as seamless as you'd have liked it to be. Prior to Office Home and Student 2013, personal settings, such as recently used document and folder lists, were associated with the account you used to log in to Windows. That account may be limited to a specific computer, such as your home computer, or if you're a student, you may have a roaming profile that lets you access your information when you're connected to your school network.

Office Home and Student 2013 takes the concept of the roaming profile a step further. Instead of a profile that can be accessed only by a specific computer or while you are connected to your school network, personal settings can now be stored online in your Office account. This lets you access your information from almost anywhere. And not just from another computer, but also from devices such as Surface or a Windows Phone.

Plus, you can connect other cloud services that store contact information, documents, photos, and videos and access them right from your Office applications.

TIP To access your Office account on another computer, it must be running Windows 7 or Windows 8 and be connected to the Internet. It also needs to either have Office Home and Student 2013 installed, or you need a Microsoft Office 365 subscription that includes Microsoft Office on Demand.

SEE ALSO For more on connecting cloud services, see "Connecting cloud services to your Office account" later in this chapter; for more on Office 365 or Office on Demand, see the sidebar "What is Office 365?" later in this chapter.

In order to store your information in the cloud, you need an Office account. This account is associated with an email address that you use for various Microsoft services, such as those in the following account types:

- **Microsoft Account** This account type, previously called Windows Live ID, is typically associated with a personal email address. For example, if you use Windows Live Messenger, Windows Live Hotmail, or Microsoft Xbox LIVE, you have a Microsoft Account.

  TIP Even though a Microsoft Account is typically associated with a personal email address, you can use almost any email address to create a Microsoft Account.

- **Organizational account** This account type is provided to you by an administrator for Microsoft SharePoint Online services. If your company or educational organization uses Office 365, then you have an organizational account.

> **IMPORTANT** If you have an organizational (Office 365) account, your personal settings aren't stored on SharePoint but are stored in your Office account.

If your email account lets you use Microsoft services, then you already have an Office account. All you need to do to start using it is sign in to Office, and you'll learn how to do that in the next section.

Need a Microsoft Account for Office?

Outlook.com, an upgrade to Hotmail, is a new email service from Microsoft. It has a better Office integration experience than its predecessor, along with features that are more like the desktop version, Microsoft Outlook. And as with Hotmail, SkyDrive is included for online file storage along with Microsoft Office Web Apps.

SEE ALSO For more information on SkyDrive, see the sidebar "What is SkyDrive?" later in this chapter.

To get your new email account, go to *www.outlook.com* and sign up. Or, if you already have a Hotmail account, you can upgrade it to an Outlook.com account in your Hotmail account options.

Signing in and managing your Office account

As previously mentioned, in order to take advantage of the cloud integration features, you need to sign in to your Office account with an email address that gives you access to various Microsoft services.

Although the option to sign in occurs during the Office Home and Student 2013 installation or appears the first time you start Office Home and Student 2013, you may have skipped that step, or Office may have already been started on your computer.

TIP If you're using Windows 8 and are logged in with an account that's connected to Microsoft services, the Office installation signs you in to your Office account.

In this exercise, you'll sign in to your Office account.

➡ SET UP **You don't need an email address that lets you use Microsoft services to complete this exercise. Start Word, create a blank document, and follow the steps.**

1 Click the **File** tab to display the **Backstage** view, and then click **Account**.

2 Below the **User Information** section, click **Sign in**.

×

Sign in

Type the email address of the account you would like to use with Office.

Type your email address

Sign In

When you sign in, your documents and settings are online
Learn more | Privacy statement

3 On the **Sign in** screen, enter your email address and then click the **Sign In** button.

4 Complete one of the following actions:

- If you already have email address that lets you use Microsoft services, enter your Microsoft Account password and then click **Sign In**.

- If you don't have an email address that lets you use Microsoft services, click **Sign Up Now**, and then complete the sign up form.

TIP If you're signing up for a Microsoft Account, you can use an email address you already have for the account name. For security purposes, you may want to create a password that's different from your email account password for your Microsoft Account.

❌ CLEAN UP **Close the document without saving changes.**

When you sign in to Office, you sign in across the Office applications. And in any application, your sign in name will appear in the upper-right corner above the ribbon.

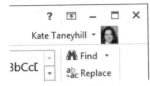

Additionally, you're not limited to a single Office account and can have more than one. Some people have accounts for school or business and personal use. This lets them keep their recently used files and other preferences separate and easier to manage.

If you have multiple Office accounts, you can easily switch between them from any Office application.

To switch accounts, use the Account page in the Backstage view and the Switch Account option, or click your name in the right corner above the ribbon and then click Switch account, and complete the sign in process.

Note that after you sign in to Office, you stay logged in even if you have switched to another Office account. This way, after you have added at least two Office accounts, you can switch between them without the need to repeat the sign in process.

In this exercise, you'll switch to another Office account.

➡ SET UP **You need a second Office account to complete this exercise. Start Word if necessary, create a blank document, and follow the steps.**

1   In the **Backstage** view, click **Account**.

2   Click **Switch Account**.

TIP You can also click your name in the upper-right corner above the ribbon and click Switch Account.

3   On the **Sign in** screen, enter your email address and then click the **Sign In** button.

4   Enter your account password, and then click **Sign In** to log in to your other Office account.

5   To view your available accounts, display the **Switch Account** screen again.

6 To switch between accounts, click an account name below **Other Accounts**.

✖ CLEAN UP **Close the document without saving changes.**

As noted, after you sign in to Office, you stay signed in on that computer. This isn't an issue if it's your work or personal computer, but if you're using a public computer, it's important that you sign out of Office.

When you sign out of your Office account, you're removing the account from the computer you are using. Part of the sign out process is to delete any personal data that an Office application may have created while you were using the computer. However, it won't remove documents or other information you may have created. So, if you don't want that information on the computer, you'll need to manually delete those items. For example, if you saved a file to the computer's local drive, then it will still be there after you sign out of your account. And even though you removed your account from the computer, you can sign back in at any time and all of your personal settings that are stored in your Office account will be redisplayed.

In this exercise, you'll sign out of your Office account.

➡ SET UP **You need to be signed in to Office to complete this exercise. Start Word if it's not already running, create a blank document, and follow the steps.**

1   In the **Backstage** view, click **Account**.

2   Below the **User Information** section, click **Sign out**.

> **Remove Account**   ✕
>
> ⚠ Removing this account will remove all customizations, and documents and notebooks may no longer sync to the server. For this change to fully take effect, please log off/log in to Windows at the next opportunity. Do you want to remove the account now?
>
> [Yes]   [No]

3   In the **Remove Account** confirmation message box, click **Yes** to remove the account.

4   Exit Word and restart Windows to complete the sign out process.

✖ CLEAN UP **If you exited Word and restarted Windows, there are no additional clean up steps.**

Connecting cloud services to your Office account

Cloud services help us stay connected to our information and other people. However, these services can result in information that's scattered in several different locations, depending on the number of cloud services you have. For example, you could have an organizational account, a Microsoft Account, as well as personal accounts on social networks. You might often need to sign in to various websites to locate a document or recall which social network you need to access to find contact information for someone.

As noted in the section titled "Defining the term *cloud service*" earlier in this chapter, you can connect these various online services to your Office account. Doing so gives you the ability to open and save files to your cloud locations and insert your online pictures or videos in an Office document.

SEE ALSO For more information on Office 365, see the sidebar "What is Office 365?" later in this section. For more information on SkyDrive, see the sidebar "What is SkyDrive?" also later in this section.

You can connect to cloud services on the Account page in the Backstage view. The available connected service options for your Office account depend on the type of account you're using for Microsoft services. For example, with either a Microsoft Account or an organizational account, both SharePoint Online and SkyDrive connections are available. But if you have a Microsoft Account type, you'll have sharing options for personal cloud services like Facebook, LinkedIn, Twitter, and Flickr. These may not be shown if you have an organizational account, because this account type is more school oriented or business oriented.

TIP If you have an Office 365 account, your file storage locations on SharePoint Online may be connected and available when you sign in.

In this exercise, you'll first connect a SharePoint Online or SkyDrive cloud storage service to your Office account. Then you'll have the option to connect a personal cloud service like LinkedIn.

➡ SET UP **You need to be signed in to Office and be connected to the Internet. To complete the optional steps for connecting a personal cloud service, you must be signed in with a Microsoft Account and have a Facebook, LinkedIn, or Twitter account. Start Word if necessary, create a blank document, and follow the steps.**

1   In the **Backstage** view, click **Account**.

2   In the account options, click **Add a service**, point to **Storage**, and then click either **Office 365 SharePoint** or **SkyDrive**.

> **IMPORTANT** If you have SharePoint Online, click Office 365 SharePoint.

3   On the **Sign in** screen, enter the email address for your cloud storage account and complete the sign in process.

Your connected service will be listed under the account settings in the **Backstage** view.

Account

User Information

Kate
kate@fabrikamO365.onmicrosoft.com

Sign out

Switch Account

Office Background:

No Background	▼

Office Theme:

White	▼

Connected Services:

Fabrikam, Inc.
Kate@FabrikamO365.onmicrosoft.com

Fabrikam, Inc. Team Site
Kate@FabrikamO365.onmicrosoft.com

Kate Taneyhill's SkyDrive
someone@example.com

SkyDrive @ Fabrikam, Inc.
Kate@FabrikamO365.onmicrosoft.com

Add a service ▼

If you have a Microsoft Account type and want to connect a personal cloud service like Facebook, LinkedIn, or Twitter, then follow these optional steps.

IMPORTANT You must be signed in to Office with a Microsoft Account in order to add a personal cloud service.

4   In the **Backstage** view, click **Account**.

5   Click **Add a service**, point to **Sharing**, and then click the cloud service you want to add to display the options for connecting your Office account.

For example, if you have a LinkedIn account, click **LinkedIn**.

in Share to LinkedIn

Update your LinkedIn status and share documents and photos with your LinkedIn contacts from Office. Just connect **LinkedIn** to **someone@example.com**.

> What else happens when I connect?

Connect   Cancel

Next, you'll go to linkedin.com to sign in.

6   Complete the sign-in steps as directed by the service you selected.

IMPORTANT The service may require that you authorize the connection. This process is typically accomplished through an email message that is sent to the email address you used to log in to the service. If authorization is required, it must be completed before you can access the service through Office.

✖ CLEAN UP **Close the document without saving changes.**

TIP Some personal cloud services have additional options that let you choose the type of information you share between the service and your Microsoft Account. In the Backstage view, on the Account page, if a Manage link appears next to the service, click the link to view the options. For example, if you click the Manage link for LinkedIn, you'll find options for viewing LinkedIn contacts, their status updates, and using LinkedIn email in Outlook. You'll also find an option for sharing status updates and files with your LinkedIn contacts through other social services like Microsoft Messenger, SkyDrive, or your Windows phone.

Your Microsoft Account options are also where you'll find the ability to remove the personal cloud service. Other services, such as SkyDrive, can be removed from the Backstage view.

What is Office 365?

Office 365 is a subscription-based cloud service for Microsoft Office as well as hosted Microsoft server products, such as Microsoft Exchange Server, SharePoint Online, and Microsoft Lync Server. The subscription can include a variety of services, such as Skype minutes, email and shared calendars, online file storage and sharing, or instant messaging and web conferencing. Office 365 can also include Office on Demand along with the desktop version of Office Home and Student 2013.

TIP Office on Demand is a service that lets you take Office Home and Student 2013 with you to other locations. You can temporarily use, or stream, an Office Home and Student 2013 application on computers in which Office Home and Student 2013 isn't installed, such as those in a hotel business center or Internet café. In order to stream Office Home and Student 2013 on another computer, it must be running Windows 7 or Windows 8 and be connected to the Internet.

What you get with your subscription depends on the plan you choose. You can select home and family plans, such as Microsoft Office 365 Home Premium, small business plans, or a large enterprise plan.

SEE ALSO For more information on Office 365, along with plans and pricing, visit *www.Office365.com*.

One of the biggest advantages of using Office 365 is you don't need to make a large investment in hardware or software. Nor do you need expert knowledge of server installation or even administration. And, with your subscription, you'll always get the most current Office technologies.

If you already have an Office 365 account, to access it from a web browser, go to *www.Office365.com* and sign in.

3

What is SkyDrive?

SkyDrive is a cloud storage service hosted by Microsoft for storing documents, photos, and other files and is included with your Microsoft Account. If your school uses SharePoint Online, you'll get a version of SkyDrive called SkyDrive Pro for your school-related files. To access your SkyDrive account from a web browser, go to *www.SkyDrive.com* and sign in. To access SkyDrive Pro, go to *www.Office365.com* and sign in.

> **IMPORTANT** Even though there are two SkyDrive types, the general term *SkyDrive* is used throughout this book to refer to both types unless it's important to distinguish between them.

With your SkyDrive, you can access your files on almost any device with an Internet connection. It gives you the ability to share files with others too. For example, if a file attachment is too large to be sent through email, you can save it on your SkyDrive. Then in the email message, you can send a link to the file.

SkyDrive also includes Office Web Apps, which are browser-based companions to your Office applications. As an added bonus for those with a Microsoft Account, you can access various SkyDrive applications from both Microsoft and third parties. For example, there are SkyDrive apps that let you manage your SkyDrive files on most smartphones.

Most importantly, SkyDrive now has more integration across Office applications, and you'll learn more about those features throughout this book.

Saving files on SharePoint Online and SkyDrive

In the previous sections, you learned how your Office cloud account lets you take your Office settings with you. You also learned how to sign in to your Office account and connect to cloud services. But, if you want to access your recently used files or other files across various computers and devices, those files need to be saved in a cloud service like SharePoint Online or SkyDrive. Now that Office has integrated cloud services for opening and saving documents, you'll find that using these locations is just as easy as using a local or network drive.

In this exercise, you'll create a new document in Word and save it to either SharePoint Online or SkyDrive.

SET UP **You need either a SharePoint Online location or SkyDrive added to your connected services to complete this exercise. Start Word if necessary, and follow the steps.**

TIP The steps for saving files to the cloud also apply to Excel and PowerPoint. For Microsoft OneNote, saving a notebook is part of the creation process, and the steps you use are slightly different than the following procedure.

SEE ALSO For information about creating and saving a new OneNote notebook to a cloud location, see Chapter 25, "Working with notebooks, sections, and pages."

1   From the Word **Start** screen, click **Blank Document**.

    KEYBOARD SHORTCUT Press Ctrl+N to create a new blank document.

    TIP If Word is already running and the Start screen doesn't appear, click the File tab and then click New to display the Start screen.

2   In the blank Word document, enter some sample text.

    TIP To quickly add sample text, you can enter *=rand* or *=lorem* followed by an open and close parenthesis, such as *=rand()*, and then press Enter.

3   Click the **File** tab, and then click **Save As**.

KEYBOARD SHORTCUT Press Ctrl+S to save the document.

TIP In the Backstage view, you can click Save instead of Save As. However, since the document hasn't been previously saved, the Save As option will be displayed.

4   In the Backstage view, click your SharePoint Online or SkyDrive location.

IMPORTANT If you're saving a file to a SharePoint Online location, you may want to select your SkyDrive for your practice files. Otherwise, locations such as a group site for your school may be shared with others.

5   To the right of your selected location, either click a recent folder or click **Browse** to
    select an alternate folder.

6   In the **Save As** dialog box, in the **File name** text box, enter **My First Word 2013
    Document** and then click **Save**.

7   To close the document, click the **File** tab, and then click **Close**.

❌ CLEAN UP **Close the document without saving changes.**

Sharing files with others from SharePoint Online or SkyDrive

After you save a document or notebook to SharePoint Online or to your SkyDrive location, you can share the file with others. For example, you might have a file that's too large to send in an email message. You could be collaborating with other people on a document and everyone needs to work on it at the same time, which is referred to as *co-authoring*. Or, you might have a notebook with notes that you want to share with others. Office Home and Student 2013 has made sharing easier than ever before by adding sharing options for Excel, OneNote, PowerPoint, and Word files right in the Backstage view.

SEE ALSO For more information on co-authoring, see "Getting started with co-authoring" later in this chapter.

When you share a file from your Office application, you can also set one of two permission types, Can Edit and Can View. As each option name implies, those with Can Edit permission can edit your file and update their changes on the cloud location. Those with Can View permission have read-only access to your file, which means any changes they may make cannot be saved to the cloud location.

You also have the option to require people to sign in with either their Microsoft Account or their organizational (Office 365) account in order to access the file. Although requiring others to sign in may seem like an extra step, it helps protect your file. When you share a file, you send a sharing link, which can potentially be sent to other people. If you require sign in, only those you've explicitly shared your file with will be able to access it.

In this exercise, you'll share the document that you created in the "Saving files on SharePoint Online and SkyDrive" section with others.

➡ SET UP **All of the steps in the previous exercise need to be completed. Start Word if it's not already running, and follow the steps.**

TIP The steps for sharing files also apply to Excel, OneNote, and PowerPoint.

1   Click the **File** tab to display the **Backstage** view, and then click **Open**.

2   From the **Recent Documents** list, click **My First Word 2013 Document** to open the document in Word.

3   In the **Backstage** view, on the **Share** page, click **Invite People**.

TIP After you send your sharing invitations, the people you shared your file with will be displayed in the Shared With section, along with the type of permission you assigned to them.

4   In the **Invite People** section, enter the names or email addresses of the people with whom you want to share the document.

TIP To gain a better understanding of how this works, you can enter your own email address for testing purposes.

5   Note the **Permissions** drop-down box on the far right of the names and email addresses text box. You can change the permissions from **Can Edit** to **Can View**, if you want.

6   Enter a message in the **Include a personal message** text box, if you want.

7   Select the **Require user to sign in before accessing the document** option, if you want.

8   Click **Share** to share the document and send the sharing invitation.

✖ CLEAN UP **Close My First Word 2013 Document without saving changes.**

After you send your sharing invitation, each person will also receive an email message that contains a link to your file. Clicking the link will open the file in the corresponding Office Web App. For example, if the file is a Word document, it will open in Word Web App.

Kate has a document to share with you on SkyDrive. To view it, click the link below.

My First Word 2013 Document.docx

Share your files with SkyDrive.

TIP You can change or remove sharing permissions for a user after the invitations have been sent. To do so, open your shared file and in the Backstage view, on the Share page, right-click the person to view the change and remove options.

Opening files from the cloud

After you have saved files on SharePoint Online or on SkyDrive, you essentially use the same steps for opening a file from the cloud as you would for saving files to the cloud.

In the previous exercise, you opened My First Word 2013 Document from your Recent Documents list. In this exercise, you'll open the document by using the Open dialog box.

 SET UP **All of the steps in the exercise from the "Saving files on SharePoint Online and SkyDrive" section earlier in this chapter need to be completed. Start Word if necessary, and follow the steps.**

TIP The steps for opening files from the cloud also apply to Excel, OneNote, and PowerPoint.

1   Click the **File** tab and then click **Open**.

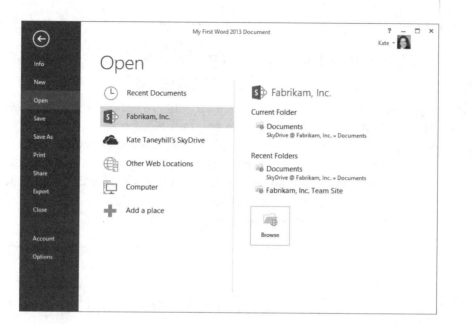

2   In the **Open** options, click the same location in which you saved **My First Word 2013 Document**, such as your SkyDrive.

3   On the right side, below **Recent Folders**, click the folder where you saved **My First Word 2013 Document** to display the **Open** dialog box.

4   Select **My First Word 2013 Document** and then click **Open** to view your document in Word.

5   On the **Quick Access Toolbar**, note the green arrows in the lower-right corner of the **Save** button, which indicate that your changes will be synced with your cloud location when you save the document.

✖ CLEAN UP   **Close My First Word 2013 Document without saving changes.**

Can I access my files through SharePoint locations hosted by my school or a company?

Although connected services for your Office account are designed to be used with Office 365 and SkyDrive, you can still open and save files stored on a hosted, on-premises SharePoint Server from Office applications. In the Backstage view, from either the Open or Save As option, click Other Web Locations and then enter the URL for the server. After you've used another web location, it will be added to your Recent Folders list for quick reference. These locations are also saved in your Office account so you'll be able to access them whenever you sign in to Office.

Syncing files with SkyDrive for offline use

In the previous exercises, you learned how to open and save files in the cloud. You may be wondering at this point about what happens if you don't have an Internet connection, or if you're limited to using a web browser to manage your files. The good news is SkyDrive has an answer for both. You can create a sync location for files stored in the cloud to a network or local drive so they can be used even when an Internet connection isn't available. The sync folder also provides the ability to access and manage your files directly from Windows 8 File Explorer or Windows Explorer on Windows 7. Best of all, after you create the location, your files will sync when you're connected to the Internet.

TIP In Windows 8, *File Explorer* has replaced *Windows Explorer*. Throughout this book, we refer to this browsing utility by its Windows 8 name. If your computer is running Windows 7, use Windows Explorer instead.

If you're wondering how this works exactly, when you create a sync location, you're essentially creating a shortcut to your cloud service that can be accessed from your computer. But unlike a shortcut that needs the location to be available in order to access it, in a sync location offline copies of your files are created in the folder. Then when an Internet connection is available, your online files are updated.

In this exercise, you'll create a sync location for SkyDrive Pro, and then you'll get the SkyDrive app for a Microsoft Account to sync your files. If you don't have both SkyDrive Pro and a Microsoft Account, choose the set of instructions in this exercise that fits the type of SkyDrive you're using.

SEE ALSO For more information on determining the type of SkyDrive you have, see the sidebar "What is SkyDrive?" earlier in this chapter.

Syncing with SkyDrive Pro

If you have an Office 365 account with SharePoint Online and want to sync your files with SkyDrive Pro, follow these steps.

➡ SET UP **You need an Office 365 account that includes SharePoint Online for this exercise. Open a web browser and follow the steps.**

1   In the address bar of your web browser, enter **www.Office365.com** and press the **Enter** key.

2   If necessary, sign in to Office 365 with your email address and password.

3   In the navigation options near the top of the page, click **SkyDrive**.

4   In the upper-right corner, below your sign-in name, click **SYNC**.

5   In the **Microsoft SkyDrive Pro** dialog box, click **Sync Now** to create a folder with a name similar to **SkyDrive @ Fabrikam, Inc.** in the location you specified.

> **TIP** If you want to use a location other than the default sync folder, click Change and select an alternate location or folder.

❌ CLEAN UP **Close your web browser.**

Syncing with SkyDrive for a Microsoft Account

If you have a Microsoft Account and want to sync your files with SkyDrive, follow these steps.

➡ SET UP **You need a Microsoft Account for this exercise. Open a web browser and follow the steps.**

1   In the address bar of your web browser, enter **www.SkyDrive.com** and press the **Enter** key.

2   If necessary, sign in to SkyDrive with your email address and password.

3   In the navigation options on the left, near the bottom of the screen, click **Get SkyDrive apps**.

4   Locate the SkyDrive app for Windows Desktop, then download and install the application.

TIP You may need to log in to your Microsoft Account during the installation.

5   When the **Introducing your SkyDrive Folder** message box displays, click **Next** and complete the installation.

TIP If you want to use a location other than the default sync folder, click Change and select an alternate location or folder.

Microsoft SkyDrive

Introducing your SkyDrive folder

Look for your SkyDrive folder in File Explorer. Files in here are on your other devices and SkyDrive.com.

▲ ☆ Favorites
　　　 Desktop
　　　 Downloads
　　　 SkyDrive

Your SkyDrive folder is here: C:\Users\taney_000\SkyDrive

Change

Next

❌ CLEAN UP **Close your web browser.**

After you follow either set of steps, a shortcut to your SkyDrive folder is created and added to your Favorites list in File Explorer. Additionally, because your Favorites list appears in most Windows dialog boxes for opening and saving files or inserting file attachments in an email message, you can access your SkyDrive from almost every application.

TIP You can use also use the SkyDrive Pro 2013 or Microsoft SkyDrive apps on your Windows 8 Start screen to quickly access your SkyDrive sync location.

Getting started with co-authoring

When you collaborate with others on Office documents, you may encounter a situation in which more than one person needs to work on a file at the same time. Consider the following scenarios:

- Multiple people need to contribute to a school newsletter, and the deadline is in a few hours.

- Several people are taking part in a last-minute presentation, and they all need to add speaker notes to their slides.

- Your team's project notes for an upcoming class project are stored in a OneNote notebook, and you need to collaborate on them during a meeting.

- Several people are responsible for adding budget and cost data to a workbook for an upcoming class or family reunion.

If you've ever encountered any of these scenarios, you've likely waited for the original file to be available. With the co-authoring feature, you don't need to wait. Multiple people can edit an Office document or a notebook at the same time.

TIP In OneNote, co-authoring is typically referred to as *sharing* rather than *co-authoring*.

Here's a list of the Office applications that support co-authoring:

- Excel Web App

- OneNote and OneNote Web App

- PowerPoint and PowerPoint Web App

- Word and Word Web App

To start a co-authoring session, the following requirements must be met:

- The file must be opened in a supported application.

- The Office document or notebook must be stored on SharePoint, SharePoint Online, or SkyDrive.

- The file needs to be shared with other co-authors.

Ideally, co-authoring is seamless, and it's not something you necessarily plan. If the requirements are met and more than one person edits a document or notebook at the same time, co-authoring is automatic. With the exception of Excel files, one person can even be using the desktop application and another can be using the associated Office Web App.

For Excel, if multiple people need to edit a workbook at the same time, all they need to do is open it in Excel Web App. For this scenario, some coordination with others may be necessary.

When more than one person opens the same shared file, a notification appears in the status bar and reflects the total author count. When you click the count in the status bar, you'll get a list of the people currently using the file.

Key points

- A cloud service is an online file storage service, resource, or application that is accessed through the Internet.

- To store your Office settings, such as recently used files and folders, in the Office cloud, you need an email account that gives you access to Microsoft services.

- Examples of Microsoft services are SharePoint Online, SkyDrive, Hotmail, and Windows Live Messenger.

- You can connect cloud services like SkyDrive, Facebook, Twitter, LinkedIn, and Flickr to your Office account to share information between the service and Office.

- To access your Office documents from almost any computer or device, the files need to be stored in a cloud service such as SharePoint Online or SkyDrive.

- Co-authoring is supported in Excel Web App, OneNote, OneNote Web App, PowerPoint, PowerPoint Web App, Word, and Word Web App.

- To start a co-authoring session, the Office document or notebook must be stored in a cloud service such as SharePoint Online or SkyDrive and shared with your co-authors.

3

Chapter at a glance

Get

Get comfortable with Office on a tablet,
page 101

Use

Use touch mode,
page 103

Select

Select content with touch,
page 106

Work

Work with ink in Office,
page 108

Using touch in Office

4

IN THIS CHAPTER, YOU WILL LEARN HOW TO

- Get comfortable with Office on a tablet.

- Use touch mode.

- Select content with touch.

- Work with ink in Office.

One of the biggest enhancements made to Microsoft Office Home and Student 2013 is the addition of touch mode. Though you can use previous versions of Office on a touch-enabled device, the previous Office applications didn't include features that optimized touch input and focused more on using inking features, such as annotating files in your own handwriting. The new touch mode and better gesture support makes using touch in Office as easy as using a mouse and a keyboard.

In this chapter, you'll get an overview of using Office Home and Student 2013 on a tablet, such as Microsoft Surface. You'll learn how to adapt the exercises in this book to touch gestures, and how to select text and multiple objects. At the end of this chapter, you'll use inking tools.

PRACTICE FILES You don't need any practice files to complete the exercise in this chapter.

Getting comfortable with Office on a tablet

For using Office on a tablet, two editions of Windows 8 are available. The tablet edition of Windows 8, called *Windows RT*, comes with Microsoft Office Home and Student 2013 RT, which includes Microsoft Word 2013 RT, PowerPoint 2013 RT, Excel 2013 RT, and OneNote 2013 RT. Tablets that support the full edition of Windows 8, such as Surface with Windows 8 Pro, also support the installation of a full edition of Office, such as Microsoft Office Home and Student 2013.

Regardless of the edition you're using, using Office on a tablet isn't too different from using Office on your desktop or laptop computer. In fact, the user interface and your Office files look almost identical when viewed on a tablet device.

Looking at unsupported features

If you're using a tablet that has the Office Home and Student 2013 RT edition preinstalled, it's important to note that it doesn't have all of the same features as the full editions of Office. This is primarily due to security and mobility requirements. The following is a list of the primary unsupported features, along with any available workarounds.

- **Macros and add-ins** Programs created in Microsoft Visual Basic for Applications (VBA) to automate various tasks or to add additional functionality to an application are not supported. Developers are creating apps for Office, available from the Microsoft Office Store, as an alternative.

    TIP You can find available apps for Office on the Insert tab, in the Apps group. Additionally, some of the templates created for Office Home and Student 2013 also include apps, such as the Bing Finance app, which is included in the Financial Portfolio online template for Microsoft Excel.

- **Email features** Emailing from inside an application isn't supported, because Microsoft Outlook and other desktop email applications aren't supported on Windows RT. These commands include the Email options on the Share page in the Backstage view and email-related commands on the ribbon. The commands are still present in the user interface, but they are either unavailable or result in an error message when you try to use them. An alternative is to create a new email message by using the Windows RT email app, or another email app from the Windows Store, and manually attach your documents or links.

- **Flash video and recording narrations in PowerPoint** Inserting or playing back Flash videos isn't supported, and you can't record audio narrations. However, presentations that already include audio narrations will still play correctly.

- **Audio and video recordings and inserting from a scanner in OneNote** Recording and scanning through OneNote isn't supported, but you can use other third-party software for these types of content and then insert the file into a OneNote page.

TIP Tablets that support the full version of Windows 8 and Office, such as Surface with Windows 8 Pro, will support the items in this list.

Using touch mode

The primary difference with using touch mode in Office is that the user interface is optimized for touch commands. When touch is enabled, the user interface increases in size, and more space is added between the buttons on the ribbon and Quick Access Toolbar.

TIP To enable or disable touch mode, tap the Touch Mode button on the Quick Access Toolbar. When you enable or disable touch mode, it takes effect across the Office applications. If the Touch Mode button isn't visible, tap the arrow at the end of the Quick Access Toolbar, and then in the Customize Quick Access Toolbar list, tap Touch Mode.

You can work through the majority of the exercises provided in this book by using touch input and gestures, if you opt to use them instead of keyboard and mouse input. The following list provides the primary methods you can use to adapt the exercises to touch, along with additional touch tips.

- Substitute tap or double-tap for click and double-click.

- To right-click, press and hold until the shortcut menu is displayed. One exception to this is for spelling errors that appear in most applications that check your spelling as you type. When you tap a word to correct a spelling error, the list of spelling suggestions is displayed at the same time.

◢ DOG WALKING FOR FITNESS & CHARITY

After discovering his local animal rescue in Chestnut Ridge was in need of dog walkers, Laurent Penisson contacted our corporate Fabrikam offices and pitched his plan for a new Employee Give Program that offers employees the opportunity to help a dog, get fit, and give to charity.

We've partnered with local animal shelters throughout the US and together we've created the Dog Walking for Fitness & Chrit~ Program. All program participants will be given a Fabrikam-sponsored ped~ miles of logged dog walking, Fabrikam will donate $ participant's choice.

| Charity |
| Christy |
| Christi |
| Christie |
| Chitty |
| Ignore All |
| Add to Dictionary |
| Hyperlink... |
| New Comment |

Orientation for this program will be held the first starting in November. Attendance does not obligate program. For more information about the Dog Walking for Fitness & Charity program volunteer wiki.

◢ FABRIKAM'S FIRST COMMUNITY KITCHEN

Greenville is set to launch our pilot Community Kitchen program starting in Novembe program is to offer low-cost healthy eating classes to the local community. The Eating fo to increase healthy food preparation skills and knowledge. Our goal is to involve the sustainable food practices and start developing farm-to-table relationships with area gro

PAGE 3 OF 4   1177 WORDS

TIP To correct grammar errors as you type, or in OneNote, to correct spelling errors, press and hold to right-click and then tap the arrow at the end of the mini toolbar to display a list of suggestions.

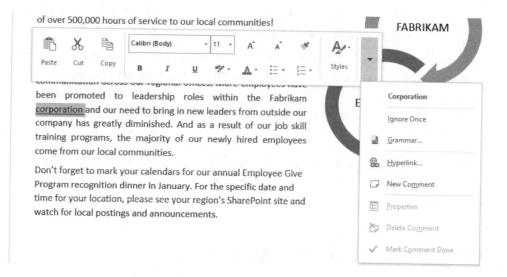

- To enter information, you can type on a keyboard or tap the On-Screen Keyboard. You can also use voice or handwriting recognition if your device supports these capabilities. Additionally, many of the applications, such as Word and PowerPoint, offer word completion when you enter text by using the On-Screen Keyboard. When the correct suggested word is displayed, tap the suggestion to insert it.

  TIP The word completion feature may not be supported, depending on the device you are using.

- To move the cursor or in Excel, the cell pointer, tap the desired location on the screen. Depending on your device, after you tap to move the cursor, the On-Screen Keyboard may appear. If you're not entering text, you can tap the X in the upper-right corner of the On-Screen Keyboard to dismiss it. If the On-Screen Keyboard doesn't appear, tap the keyboard icon located in the Windows taskbar.

- To scroll, swipe your finger up, down, left, or right, in the direction you want to navigate.

- To zoom in by using pinch gestures, use two fingers and stretch them apart. To zoom out, pinch your fingers together. You can use more than two fingers to pinch and stretch, but using only two fingers typically produces the best results.

- To move or resize an object, such as a shape, tap it once to select it and then drag it to another location, or drag a sizing handle to change its size.

Additionally, some features may work a little differently when you are using touch. For example, when you insert a shape, the shape you tap is inserted directly into your file in a predetermined size, rather than drawn with the mouse. The majority of the differences are minor and you may need to modify your steps slightly, but they shouldn't prevent you from completing a task by using touch.

If you're having difficulty adapting an exercise, you can use a mouse instead. For example, if you use your mouse to select a shape instead of tapping it, you can draw it the same way you would do it on a non-touch enabled device.

Selecting content with touch

Selecting content by using touch is similar to using the mouse. The main difference is that your finger or stylus is your mouse pointer, and you drag it on the screen. First, you tap to start your selection, and then you drag the selection handle below the cursor, called a *gripper*, through the area you want to select. In Excel, the active cell has grippers in the upper-left and lower-right corners, and you can drag either of them to select a range. When text or a cell range in Excel is selected, grippers are displayed at the beginning and end of the selection, and you can use them to adjust your selection at any time.

To remove a selection, tap in an area that's not part of your selection.

To select multiple objects by using touch, such as shapes or pictures, keep your finger on one object and then use another finger to tap each object you want to include in your selection. Note that not all applications support this selection method, and that you can also hold the Shift key on the keyboard and tap each object you want to select.

TIP In PowerPoint, you can select multiple slides in the Slides pane or in the Slide Sorter view by dragging them slightly to the right.

When you are working with dialog boxes, such as the Insert Picture dialog box, to select multiple files, tap the check boxes that appear in the upper-left corner for each file you want to select.

Working with ink in Office

When Office is installed on a device that supports ink, tools for inking are enabled. In Word, Excel, and PowerPoint, the Start Inking button is located at the end of the Review tab, in the Ink group.

TIP Using ink isn't the same as using handwriting recognition, which converts your handwriting to digital text characters as you write.

After you tap the Start Inking button, the Ink Tools Pens tool tab is displayed on the ribbon. Prior to inking, you can choose a different pen style, color, or pen thickness. Then, use your finger or stylus on the screen to add inked handwriting or drawings in your file.

TIP In OneNote, the inking tools are located on the Drawing tab, and you don't need to use a Start Inking command in order to use them. You start inking by selecting a pen style. Additionally, the ink tools in OneNote are also enabled on devices that don't support touch, because you can also use a mouse to add ink.

The following list provides a few ways you can incorporate ink in your Office files:

- Add drawings and handwritten annotations.

- If your touch device supports the full version of Office, you can send handwritten email messages in Outlook.

- Add handwritten comments in Word while reviewing a document.

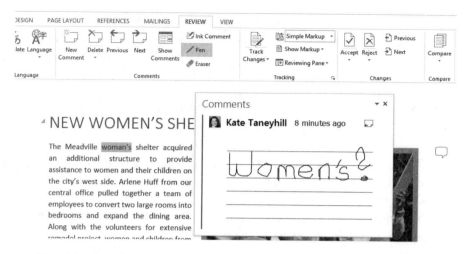

TIP To add a handwritten comment, on the Review tab, in the Comments group, tap the Ink Comment button.

- In PowerPoint, notate slides while creating your presentation or while presenting it on-screen.

- In OneNote, use handwriting to capture your notes during a meeting or sketch your ideas to capture them.

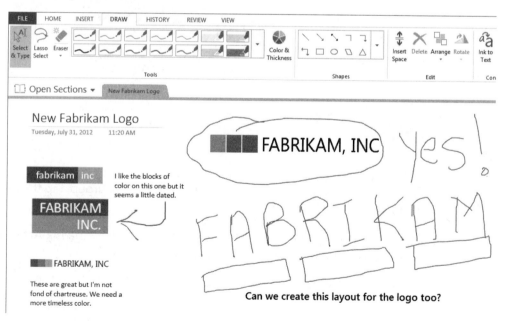

The available ink tools also include commands to select your inked handwriting or drawings as well as an eraser to remove them. Additional inking tools vary across the Office applications. For example, in PowerPoint, you can convert your drawings to shapes as you draw them in ink. In OneNote, you can convert your handwriting to text.

In this exercise, you'll convert an inked drawing to a shape in PowerPoint, move the converted shape, and resize it by using touch.

➡ SET UP You don't need any practice files to complete this exercise. Start PowerPoint, create a blank presentation, and then follow the steps.

1 To change the layout to a blank slide, on the **Home** tab, in the **Slides** group, tap **Layout**, and then tap **Blank** in the gallery.

2 To activate the ink tools, on the **Review** tab, in the **Ink** group, tap the **Start Inking** button.

3 Before drawing a shape, on the **Ink Tools Pen** tool tab, in the **Ink Art** group, tap the **Convert to Shapes** button.

4   Using your finger or stylus, draw a rectangle on the slide.

5   Lift your finger off the screen after the drawing is complete.

The inked rectangle is converted to a shape.

6   To move the converted shape, on the **Ink Tools Pens** tool tab, in the **Write** group, tap the **Select Objects** button.

7   Tap the border of the converted rectangle to select it.

8   Place your finger or stylus on the border of the rectangle between the sizing handles and drag to move it.

9   To change the size, place your finger or stylus on the sizing handle in the lower-right corner and drag to resize the rectangle.

TIP To format the shape, use the commands on the Drawing Tools Format tool tab, which is displayed when a shape is selected.

❌ CLEAN UP **Close the presentation without saving changes, and exit PowerPoint.**

Key points

- The tablet edition of Windows 8, called *Windows RT*, includes Microsoft Office Home and Student 2013 RT.

- The Office Home and Student 2013 RT edition doesn't support all features available in the full edition of Office.

- Tablets that support the full edition of Windows 8, such as Surface with Windows 8 Pro, also support the installation of a full edition of Office, such as Microsoft Office Professional 2013.

- To adapt the exercises in this book to touch gestures, substitute tap for click and double-tap for double-click. To right-click, press and hold, and to scroll, swipe the screen in the direction you wish to navigate.

- You can add handwritten comments in Word, convert handwriting to text in OneNote, and convert ink drawings to shapes in PowerPoint.

- Using ink in Office applications isn't the same as using handwriting recognition, which converts your handwriting to digital text characters as you write.

Part 2
Word 2013

5 Getting comfortable in Word 2013   115

6 Navigating and reading documents   133

7 Editing and composing documents   155

8 Formatting documents   183

9 Presenting information   209

10 Finalizing documents   229

Chapter at a glance

Modify

Modify your document view,
page 119

Change

Change other view options,
page 122

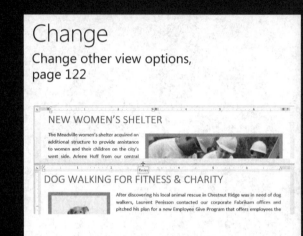

Discover

Discover what's new in Word 2013,
page 123

Getting comfortable in Word 2013

IN THIS CHAPTER, YOU WILL LEARN HOW TO

- Explore the Word 2013 user interface.

- Modify your document view.

- Change other view options.

- Discover what's new in Word 2013.

Microsoft Word 2013 is a word processing application that you can use for a wide range of tasks. You can create basic documents, such as letters, memos, reports, forms, newsletters, envelopes, labels, contracts, and more. And you can use Word for more complex documents, like a book or report that includes a table of contents, figures, indexes, footnotes, endnotes, and cross-references.

Whether your document is simple or complex, this part of the book provides you with the foundation for all of your document needs—from creating, formatting, layout, and pagination essentials to preparing your document for print, sharing, or exporting.

In this chapter, you'll get familiar with the Word 2013 user interface and learn how to modify your document view options so they're more suited to your specific work flow. And at the end of this chapter, you'll get an overview of the key new and improved features for Word 2013.

Exploring the Word 2013 user interface

You typically start Microsoft Word 2013 from the Start screen in Windows 8 or the Start menu in Windows 7. You can also start Word and open a file at the same time by opening a document from an email attachment or by double-clicking a document from a place like your desktop.

TIP If you have Windows set to view file extensions, the primary file extension for Word documents is .docx. Windows associates a file extension with an application, which enables you to open a document and start Word at the same time.

When you start Word without opening a file, the new Word Start screen appears.

From the Start screen, you can open a recent document, open an existing document, or create a new one from a template.

TIP If you haven't previously used Word 2013, the Recent documents list on the Start screen may appear empty.

After you create or open a document, the main window is displayed with a blank document along with the tools for working with the content of a document, such as the ribbon and Quick Access Toolbar.

The figure at the top of the page is a labeled screenshot of the Word 2013 user interface. Labels point to various parts of the interface:

- File tab
- Quick Access Toolbar
- Ribbon tab
- Dialog box launcher
- Ribbon
- Gallery
- More button
- Window controls
- Group
- Status bar
- Collapse ribbon

The screenshot shows the Word ribbon with tabs: FILE, HOME, INSERT, DESIGN, PAGE LAYOUT, REFERENCES, MAILINGS, REVIEW, VIEW. The Home tab is displayed showing Clipboard, Font, Paragraph, Styles, and Editing groups. The title bar reads "Document1 - Word" and the user name "Kate Taneyhill". The status bar shows "PAGE 1 OF 1", "0 WORDS", "ENGLISH (UNITED STATES)", and a zoom control at "100%".

■ **Ribbon** The ribbon is the main component of the Word interface and where you'll find the primary commands for working with the content of your documents. The ribbon is comprised of task-oriented tabs and each tab has groups of related commands. For example, on the Home tab, the Clipboard group contains commands for copying and pasting information in your Word documents. Groups that have additional commands that aren't shown on the ribbon have a dialog box launcher. Clicking the dialog box launcher will display a task pane or dialog box with options that are related to the group. For example, if you click the dialog box launcher for the Font group, the Font dialog box will be displayed, giving you more formatting choices such as Strikethrough, Superscript, and Subscript.

IMPORTANT In this book, the images of the ribbon were captured with a screen resolution of 1024x768, at the default 100 percent magnification. If your display settings are different than these, the images of the ribbon will appear differently on your screen due to its dynamic capabilities. For example, buttons may appear stacked vertically instead of horizontally. If you notice these differences, you can either adapt the exercise instructions to your screen or modify your display settings to match ours.

SEE ALSO For instructions on how to modify your display settings and adapt exercise instructions, see Chapter 1, "Getting comfortable in Office Home and Student 2013."

- **File tab** This is the first tab on the ribbon. Unlike other ribbon tabs, the File tab displays the Backstage view where commands for working with the entire document, such as Save As, Print, Share, and Export, are located. The Backstage view is also where application options are located and where you can find information about your user account and your version of Office.

- **Quick Access Toolbar** This toolbar holds your most frequently used commands. By default, Save, Undo, and Redo have already been added.

  TIP To add other commands to your Quick Access Toolbar, right-click the command you want and then click Add To Quick Access Toolbar. To remove a command from the Quick Access Toolbar, similar to adding a command, just right-click the command you wish to remove and then click Remove From Quick Access Toolbar.

- **Title bar** This bar is located at the top of the window, and it displays the name of the active document along with the application name. If you're working with a document that hasn't been saved, a name such as *Document1—Word* is displayed. After the document has been saved, the title bar will reflect the name of the saved document.

- **Window controls** These controls are displayed at the right end of the title bar. Along with the standard Minimize, Restore Down/Maximize, and Close buttons, there are two additional buttons—Help and Ribbon Display Options.

  TIP To minimize the ribbon, you can use the Ribbon Display Options, click the Collapse Ribbon button located on the far right end of the ribbon, or press Shift+F1.

- **Status bar** The status bar is located at the bottom of the window and displays information about the current document, such as the page and word count. On the far right end of the status bar are the viewing options for switching your document to a different view, along with a zoom slider to change the magnification of your active document.

SEE ALSO For a more comprehensive list of ribbon and user interface elements, along with detailed instructions on how to customize your user interface, including the ribbon and Quick Access Toolbar, see Chapter 1.

Modifying your document view

You can modify how Word displays a document on your screen by changing the document view and zoom level on the View tab.

Word 2013 has five main document views:

- **Read Mode** The new Read Mode is optimized for reading and hides the ribbon and other elements that aren't specific to reading a document. Unlike the Full Screen Reading view in earlier versions of Word, Read Mode allows you to zoom in on objects, like pictures and charts, and adjust the column layout. This view is also the default view when you open a document from an Internet source, such as an email attachment.

  SEE ALSO For more information on using Read Mode, see Chapter 6, "Navigating and reading documents."

- **Print Layout** This is the default view for Word 2013. In this view, your document looks almost identical to how it will look when it's printed. All page margins and other elements of your document are displayed, such as multiple columns, tables, graphics, headers, and footers.

TIP To toggle the view of the top and bottom page margins along with any headers and footers in Print Layout view, place your mouse pointer between two pages and double-click to suppress the white space. To redisplay the white space, double-click the line that divides the pages.

- **Web Layout** This view is used when creating a webpage or a blog post. Similar to viewing a webpage, text will wrap to the size of your window and zoom setting, rather than page margins. Objects like pictures and charts will align differently than in other views and will appear as they will be displayed when viewed in a web browser.

- **Outline view** The Outline view shows the document's organization according to paragraphs that have been formatted with a heading style, such as Heading 1, Heading 2, and Heading 3. In Outline view, you can choose to show only specific heading levels and quickly rearrange entire sections of your document by dragging a collapsed section to another location.

- **Draft view** Formerly known as Normal view in earlier versions of Word, Draft view is similar to the old Normal view, because it displays the page margins and headers; the footers are suppressed. However, Draft view also suppresses the view of objects, such as pictures and charts, and multi-column layouts are displayed as a single column.

In the Zoom group, the majority of the options are fairly self-explanatory, such as setting your zoom to 100% or choosing whether you want to view a single page or multiple pages. Of the zoom options, the Page Width command is one that may need a little more explanation. When you click Page Width, your document is scaled to fit the width of the available document space. The available space for your document is determined by the size of your application window and any task panes you have displayed. For example, if you're using a wide screen monitor and do not have any task panes open, your zoom level may increase to 154%. But if your application window is restored and the Clipboard task pane is open, your zoom level may decrease to 80%.

You can also switch to Read Mode, Print Layout, or Web Layout and set your zoom level in the lower-right corner of the status bar.

View toolbar   Zoom slider   Zoom level

To increase or decrease your zoom level, drag the slider or click the plus and minus icons. You can also click the Zoom Level button to display the Zoom dialog box, which lets you set several zoom options at the same time.

With the exception of the Draft and Outline views, your last view and zoom level will be saved with your document. If you save and close a document in Draft or Outline view, the document will reopen in Print Layout view. Additionally, new documents you create will inherit your last zoom setting.

TIP To enable documents to be opened in Draft view, click the File tab to display the Backstage view, and then click Options. On the Advanced page, scroll to the bottom of the options to the General section, and then select Allow Opening A Document In Draft View. Note that this is an application option, which means it isn't saved with the document. If you send your document to someone else, whether it opens in Draft view depends on their settings.

IMPORTANT A document change, such as a text edit, is required in order to save your zoom or desired view with your document. If you want to make sure these settings have been saved, after modifying your view settings and prior to saving your document, press the Spacebar key and then press the Backspace key to create a text edit. This will force Word to save any changes you've made to your view.

Changing other view options

You can modify your document's view by turning on the ruler display or splitting your screen into two panes that can be scrolled independently of each other. You can use the ruler to view or modify page margins or to set tabs and modify indents. And you can split a document window if you want to compare or refer to portions of your document that aren't located beside each other, or you can move content between two areas without scrolling back and forth.

Both of these options are also on the View tab.

To toggle the ruler view, on the View tab, in the Show group, select the check box for Ruler.

To split your document window, on the View tab, click Split. After you click Split, the name of the command changes to Remove Split. Your document window will be split into two equal panes. Initially, the split will appear on your current page. Scroll the contents in either pane to view different areas of your document. If you prefer a larger top or bottom pane, you can drag the splitter to resize them.

NEW WOMEN'S SHELTER

The Meadville women's shelter acquired an additional structure to provide assistance to women and their children on the city's west side. Arlene Huff from our central

DOG WALKING FOR FITNESS & CHARITY

After discovering his local animal rescue in Chestnut Ridge was in need of dog walkers, Laurent Penisson contacted our corporate Fabrikam offices and pitched his plan for a new Employee Give Program that offers employees the

To remove the split view, click Remove Split, drag the splitter to the top or bottom of your document window, or double-click the splitter.

TIP In earlier versions of Word, a toggle for showing and hiding the ruler and the ability to split the window are located above the horizontal scrollbar. These options are no longer available in Word 2013. If you frequently use these commands, you can add them to your Quick Access Toolbar. To do so, right-click the command in the ribbon and then click Add To Quick Access Toolbar.

SEE ALSO For more information on how to customize your Quick Access Toolbar, see Chapter 1.

Discovering what's new in Word 2013

This section introduces you to key new and improved features for Word 2013 along with screenshots where applicable. The majority of the features included are discussed in detail along with step-by-step instructions throughout this part of the book.

- **Read Mode** In Read Mode, commands that aren't essential for reading are hidden from view and text is reflowed in columns to fit the available screen. While in Read Mode, you can right-click or double-click objects, like tables, charts, and images, to zoom in and view the details.

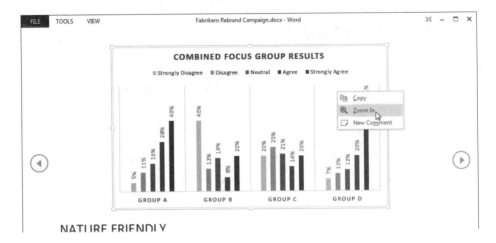

NATURE FRIENDLY

- **Resume reading** When you close a document, Word creates a bookmark of the last location where you were working inside the document. When you reopen a document, click the resume reading notification to pick up right where you left off.

Welcome back!
Pick up where you left off:

Employee Highlights
1 hour ago

- **PDF Reflow** Now you can open and convert PDF files in Word for editing. With PDF Reflow, tables, headers, footers, footnotes, and lists are all converted into editable content.

Recent Documents

 Fabrikam Newsletter.pdf
Desktop

- **One-click table row/column insertion** Insert new rows and columns without the need to visit the ribbon or use a shortcut menu. Point to the left of the table between two rows or above the table between two columns. Watch for the on-screen insertion indicator to appear, and then click the indicator to insert a new row or column.

- **Table Border tools** The new Border Styles gallery provides you with a variety of border formatting choices that are coordinated to match the current theme. After you make a selection from the gallery, you use the new Border Painter to apply, or "paint" the border formatting on your tables. With the new Border Sampler, you can transfer existing border formatting to the Border Painter for reuse.

- **Collapsible headings** While editing or reading a document, you can expand or collapse paragraphs that are formatted with a Heading style. When a heading is collapsed, all of the content that's associated with it is hidden from view. Large documents can be collapsed to a summary view for faster navigation.

- **Threaded comments** When multiple people review a document, they can reply to each other's comments and check them off as they're completed. With the new comment indicator, you can click to show or hide a specific set of comments.

- **Simple markup** When working with tracked changes, simple markup reduces the view of revisions in your documents. Clicking a revision mark will toggle the display of all changes, making it easier to switch between a clean and marked-up view.

Save time in Word with new butto
fits in your document, click it and a
you work on a table, click where yo

Click to show tracked changes.

Reading is easier, too, in the new F

- **Alignment guides and Live Layout** New alignment guides help you visually align objects, like pictures, shapes, and diagrams, to paragraphs and page margins. With **Live Layout**, now you can view the exact placement of a photo, video, or shape as you drag it into position in a document.

- **Layout Options** When you select an image, shape, or SmartArt graphic, the Layout Options button will appear. Clicking the button displays layout options, such as text-wrapping choices, along with a link to view more advanced layout options.

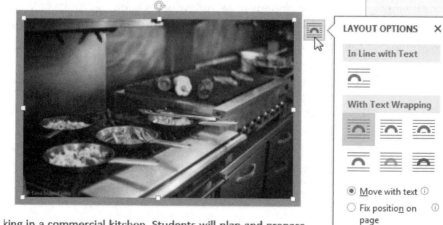

- **Design tab** The new Design tab contains commands for setting default formatting for your documents. Now you can change a document's theme, colors, fonts, paragraph spacing, and more from a single place. And the new Style Sets gallery enables you to quickly change the collection of styles that are displayed on the Home tab in the Styles gallery.

- **Building Blocks** New cover page, header, and footer building blocks have been added to help you create coordinating documents across the applications. For example, find new cover pages along with headers and footers that match the Ion slide design in Microsoft PowerPoint.

Ion (Dark)   Ion (Light)

- **File Format** The Word file format has been updated to accommodate page layout improvements. Along with improvements for graphics, text wrapping, and pagination, the most noticeable change is to table layout. In earlier versions of Word, the text in a table aligned to text outside of the table. In Word 2013, the table borders, rather than the text in the table, now align to the surrounding text.

Past versions of Word

Word 2013

SEE ALSO For more information on the layout changes in Word 2013, see *www.support. microsoft.com/kb/2740483*.

What happens to documents created in an earlier version of Word?

Documents created in an earlier version of Word will open in *compatibility mode* in Word 2013 and [Compatibility Mode] will be displayed to the right of the file name in the title bar. This mode will maintain the previous file format and layout. To convert the document to the new file format, click the File tab and then on the Info page, click the Convert button.

However, if you have a document that contains tables, graphics, multiple columns, or a more complex layout, it's recommended that you create a backup copy of your document prior to converting it, or choose to not convert the document and continue to use compatibility mode.

SEE ALSO For more information on sharing documents that you create in Word 2013 with an earlier version of Word, see Chapter 10, "Finalizing documents."

5

Key points

- You start Word 2013 from the Start screen in Windows 8 or the Start menu in Windows 7.

- The ribbon is made up of task-oriented tabs for working with your document's content.

- Use the View tab to change your document's view, modify your zoom settings, turn on the ruler display, or split your screen.

- With the exception of the Draft and Outline views, your last view and zoom level will be saved with your document.

- New documents will inherit your last zoom setting.

- You can also modify your zoom settings and switch to the Read Mode, Print Layout, and Web Layout views in the status bar on the View toolbar.

Chapter at a glance

Move

Move around in documents by using the keyboard and mouse, page 134

Search

Navigate documents by using the navigation pane, page 135

Collapse

Collapse and expand document content, page 141

Read

Read documents in Read Mode, page 144

Navigating and reading documents

IN THIS CHAPTER, YOU WILL LEARN HOW TO

- Navigate a document by scrolling and using keyboard shortcuts.

- Search and navigate a document by using the Navigation pane.

- Collapse and expand document content.

- Work with documents in the new Read Mode.

- Explore research tools in Read Mode.

In the previous chapter, you were introduced to various ways of viewing a document, such as switching to Read Mode, viewing options, and turning on the ruler display. In this chapter, you'll learn more methods for navigating documents that range from scrolling to using the Navigation pane. You'll also learn about new features that have been added, such as collapsing and expanding document content for quick navigation. In addition, you'll learn how to use the new Read Mode and research tools.

PRACTICE FILES To complete the exercises in this chapter, you need the practice files contained in the Chapter06 practice file folder. For more information, see "Download the practice files" in this book's Introduction.

Navigating a document by scrolling and using keyboard shortcuts

The most common method for document navigation is scrolling, which is achieved by using the scroll bars, the mouse wheel, or the scroll area on a touchpad. You can also use keyboard shortcuts to navigate, which also moves the cursor. When using the scroll bars to navigate in a document, you need to click the mouse to position your cursor at your desired location.

TIP In Microsoft Word 2013, the scroll bars will disappear from view after a few seconds of mouse inactivity or when you begin entering text. They will reappear after you move your mouse.

The size of a scroll box is related to the size of the document—the smaller the scroll box, the larger the document. Additionally, the position of the scroll box in the scroll bar indicates where you are in a document.

Use the following methods for scrolling by using the vertical scroll bar. Keyboard shortcuts that produce the same or a similar action follow each item in the list.

- Click above or below the scroll box to scroll one screen forward or backward.

    KEYBOARD SHORTCUT Press Page Up or Page Down.

- Click the arrows on the scroll bar to scroll one line at time.

    KEYBOARD SHORTCUT Press the Up Arrow or Down Arrow key.

- Drag the scroll box to scroll a greater distance forward or backward.

    KEYBOARD SHORTCUT Press Ctrl+Home to move to the beginning of the document and press Ctrl+End to move to the end of the document.

- Right-click the scroll bar to display a list of scrolling options. For example, if you want to scroll down one page, click the Page Down command.

NEW LOGO

Our research team determined the key to other successful rebrand campaigns was logo simplicity and familiarity. To test that research, our marketing team created five proposed logos that were presented to focus groups familiar with our current branding throughout our markets. Three of the proposed logos were comprised of a dramatic new look and the other two, a simplified version of our old one. Our focus group results confirmed our research analysis and key elements of our old logo have been maintained in order to preserve a sense of familiarity for our loyal customers.

Along with our traditional vertical logo, we've add a new horizontal logo. As we are still in the process of rolling out our new brand, please see our team site for guidelines on new logo usag

FABRIKAM
Vertical logo

FABRIKAM, INC
Horizontal logo

Scroll Here

Top
Bottom

Page Up
Page Down

Scroll Up
Scroll Down

PAGE 2 OF 5   895 WORDS   100%

TIP The Scroll Here command that appears when you right-click the scroll bar will scroll the document relative to the location at which you right-clicked. For example, if you right-click at the top of the scroll bar and then click Scroll Here, you'll scroll to the top of the document. Additionally, scrolling by using the horizontal scroll bar is similar to scrolling with the vertical scroll bar, but you move left and right instead of up and down.

When you are using a mouse wheel or scroll area on a touchpad, the number of lines you scroll, or whether you scroll a full screen of text, is dependent on the wheel settings for your mouse or touchpad as set in the Mouse Properties of the Control Panel.

Searching and navigating a document by using the Navigation pane

Another way to navigate a document is to use the Navigation pane. Unlike scrolling, using the Navigation pane navigates based on the content of your document, such as a search term, heading, graphic, or table, rather than by screens or lines.

The Navigation pane is accessed on the View tab, in the Show group. To view other navigation methods or search options, click the magnifying glass displayed on the right side of the Search box on the Navigation pane.

TIP You can also click the page number on the left end of the status bar to toggle the view of the Navigation pane.

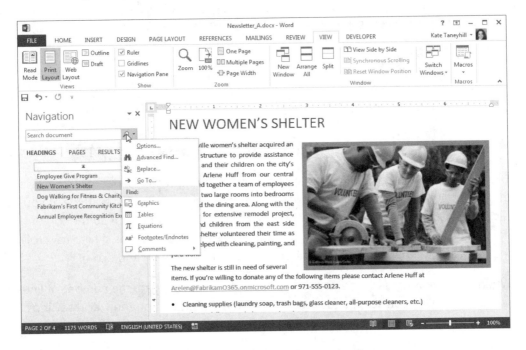

The following options are initially displayed in the Navigation pane:

- **Search document** Enter a search term in the Search box. Yellow highlighted results are shown in both the document and the Navigation pane as you enter the text. To jump between search results, click the Next and Previous buttons below the Search box.

TIP The Next and Previous buttons will cycle through the entire document. For example, if you're at the beginning of the document and click Previous, you'll jump to the last search result in the document.

- **Headings** The Headings section provides a clickable mini table of contents. The text that appears in the Navigation pane corresponds to paragraphs that are formatted with heading styles that are used to outline a document. To jump to a different heading in a document, click the corresponding heading.

  When you are searching a document, the headings in the Navigation pane will also be displayed with a yellow highlight, indicating that the search term can be found below the heading. You can click a highlighted heading to jump to that location in the document and then use the Next button to find your search term below the heading.

  TIP The heading for the current cursor location in a document will have a blue highlight. When you are searching a document, if your current location heading is included in the search results, it will be displayed with an outline and blue font color.

  SEE ALSO For more information about formatting a document by using heading styles, see Chapter 8, "Formatting documents."

- **Pages** The pages feature displays a thumbnail of each page in the document. Click a thumbnail to navigate to that page.

  When you are searching for a specific term or phrase in a document, the yellow highlighted search results will also be displayed on the page thumbnails.

- **Results** This option displays a summary of search results with the term formatted in bold. As with the other Navigation pane views, you can click a search summary to jump to that location in the document.

The other search options that are displayed when you click the magnifying glass to the right of the Search box, such as Advanced Find, Graphics, and Tables, work the same as searching for a term. You use the Next and Previous buttons below the Search box to jump between results or click a highlighted heading to jump to the general location. However, you won't find highlighted results or a summary of results when viewing Page or Results in the Navigation pane.

To clear the search results for both search terms and other search options, click the X that appears to the right of the Search box. The results will also be cleared when you close the Navigation pane.

In this exercise, you'll navigate a document by using the Navigation pane and then search for text and graphics.

 SET UP **You need the Newsletter_A document located in the Chapter06 practice file folder to complete this exercise. Open the Newsletter_A document and then follow the steps.**

1   On the **View** tab, in the **Show** group, select the **Navigation Pane** check box.

KEYBOARD SHORTCUT Press Ctrl+F.

2   On the **Navigation** pane, in the **Search** box, enter **employee**.

3   Note the total of 29 results that is displayed below the **Search** box and the first occurrence of the word **employee** in the document.

4   Below the **Search** box, click the **Next** button a few times to navigate to additional occurrences of the word **employee**.

KEYBOARD SHORTCUT Click in the document and then press Ctrl+Page Down.

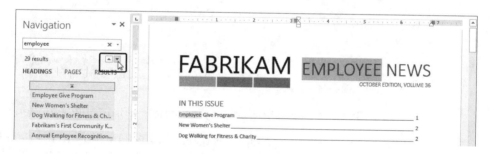

5   Click the **Previous** button to navigate to the previous occurrence of the word **employee**.

KEYBOARD SHORTCUT Click in the document and then press Ctrl+Page Up.

6   On the **Navigation** pane, in the **Headings** section, click **Dog Walking for Fitness & Charity** to view the occurrences of the search term **employee** below that heading. Also note how only the exact letters you entered in the **Search** box are highlighted in the word **employees** rather than the entire word.

DOG WALKING FOR FITNESS & CHARITY

After discovering his local animal rescue in Chestnut Ridge was in need of dog walkers, Laurent Penisson contacted our corporate Fabrikam offices and pitched his plan for a new Employee Give Program that offers employees the opportunity to help a dog, get fit, and give to charity.

We've partnered with local animal shelters throughout the US and together we've created the Dog Walking for Fitness & Charity Program. All program participants will be given a Fabrikam-sponsored pedometer and for every 50 miles of logged dog walking, Fabrikam will donate $25 to the charity of the participant's choice.

Orientation for this program will be held the first Saturday of the month starting in November. Attendance does not obligate you to participate in the program.

For more information about the Dog Walking for Fitness & Charity program for your area, visit the volunteer wiki.

7   To specify that you want only whole words highlighted, on the **Navigation** pane, click the arrow at the end of the **Search** text box and then click **Options**.

8   In the **Find Options** dialog box, select **Find whole words only** and then click **OK**.

TIP Your changes in the Find Options dialog box will be reset to the defaults after you exit Word. To make your modifications the default settings, click the Set As Default button.

9   When you change the search settings, the results are cleared. Search for **employee** again and note there are now 14 total results instead of 29.

10   Click the **X** on the right side of the **Search** box to clear the results.

11   Press **Ctrl+Home** to navigate to the beginning of the document.

12   To navigate by graphics, on the **Navigation** pane, click the magnifying glass and then click **Graphics**.

13   Click the **Next** button to jump to the next graphic.

14   Clear the search results and move the cursor back to the beginning of the document.

15   Close the **Navigation** pane.

❌ CLEAN UP **Exit Word without saving changes to the document.**

Collapsing and expanding document content

As noted in the previous section, the headings in the Navigation pane are paragraphs that are formatted with heading styles that create outline levels in a document. For example, a paragraph formatted with Heading 1 is a first level paragraph. Heading 2 is a second level paragraph, or subheading, and so forth. Along with providing a quick way to jump to different locations from the Navigation pane, heading styles are also used to create a table of contents, to create chapter-style numbering, and more. In Word 2013, headings play an even greater role. Now you can collapse all content below a heading or quickly collapse an entire document and display only the first level headings, making it even easier to navigate within a document.

Expand button

FABRIKAM EMPLOYEE NEWS

OCTOBER EDITION, VOLUME 36

▷ EMPLOYEE GIVE PROGRAM

▷ NEW WOMEN'S SHELTER

▷ DOG WALKING FOR FITNESS & CHARITY

▷ FABRIKAM'S FIRST COMMUNITY KITCHEN

▷ ANNUAL EMPLOYEE RECOGNITION EXCURSION

TIP The title of the newsletter isn't included in the collapsed view, because the paragraphs formatted with heading styles begin after the title.

To collapse a heading, point to the left of a paragraph that has been formatted with a heading style, and then click the triangular collapse button that is displayed. When a heading is collapsed, the expand button will always show. Clicking the button will expand the content that appears below the heading.

If a document contains subheadings, there will be collapse and expand buttons in the Navigation pane as well. Clicking these buttons only affects the headings in the Navigation pane and not the document's contents.

In this exercise, you'll use the new collapse and expand capabilities of headings in both the document and the Navigation pane.

 SET UP **You need the Newsletter_B document located in the Chapter06 practice file folder to complete this exercise. Open the Newsletter_B document and then follow the steps.**

1 In the document, point to the left of the heading **Employee Give Program** and click the collapse button.

FABRIKAM EMPLOYEE NEWS

OCTOBER EDITION, VOLUME 36

▷ EMPLOYEE GIVE PROGRAM

NEW WOMEN'S SHELTER

The Meadville women's shelter acquired an additional structure to provide assistance to women and their children on the city's west side. Arlene Huff from our central office pulled together a team of employees to convert two large rooms into bedrooms

2 To expand the heading, click the expand button.

3   To quickly collapse the entire document and display only the first level headings, right-click the first heading, point to **Expand/Collapse**, and then click **Collapse All Headings**.

TIP Collapsing all headings is a quick way to display an outline view of your document for printing.

4   Expand the **Annual Employee Recognition Excursion** heading.

5   At the end of **Annual Employee Recognition Excursion**, expand the, **Next Year's Destination Is...** subheading.

6   To expand all headings, right-click a heading, point to **Expand/Collapse**, and then click **Expand All Headings**.

7   View the **Navigation** pane and, below **Annual Employee Recognition Excursion**, note the subheading **Next Year's Destination Is....**

NEXT YEAR'S DESTINATION IS...

Next year's destination is Hawaii! Fabrikam employees of the month and the top Employee Give Program participants will take a magnificent private luxury cruise to exotic ports including Hilo, Kahului, Nawiliwili, and Kona. From tours of active volcanoes and deep lush canyons to relaxing on endless beaches, this trip is packed with exhilarating shore excursions.

Don't forget to nominate deserving employees for this prestigious award and yes, you can nominate yourself! Forms received by the 23rd of the month will be considered for the following month's recognition.

And don't forget -- the more volunteer hours you log for the Employee Give Program the better your chances of being one of the top 10% of participants who are eligible for our annual Employee Recognition Excursion program.

Note that eligibility rules for the recognition program have changed in order to give more employees an opportunity to share in our one-of-a-kind excursions. To view the full list of eligibility rules, see the Human Resources area on our company SharePoint site.

TIP Only the Annual Employee Recognition Excursion heading has the expand/collapse button in the Navigation pane, since it's the only heading that has a subheading.

8   In the **Navigation** pane, click the collapse button to the left of **Annual Employee Recognition Excursion** and note that the document content does not change.

9   Click the expand button to redisplay it.

10   Turn off the display of the **Navigation** pane.

❌ CLEAN UP **Exit Word without saving changes to the document.**

Working with documents in the new Read Mode

When you're viewing a document in Read Mode, the primary focus is placed on reading rather than how the document looks when printed. The size of text is increased and reflowed into columns that automatically adjust to fit the available space on your screen. The size of objects, such as charts, tables, and pictures, are decreased to fit the available column width. In addition, words are automatically hyphenated, the ribbon and Quick Access Toolbar are not displayed, and the available commands pertain to reading and commenting rather than editing.

and were given a brief overview of our new international products and services.

As expected, the vivid colors in Group A were well received in our East Asian focus groups. But unexpectedly, those in other regions preferred the familiar blue and green tones of our old brand colors in Group D. Considering the focus group participants were introduced only to a product overview and not our company, this was indeed an interesting discovery.

In order to appeal to all markets, our research team conducted a second focus group for our East Asian markets using color combinations from Groups A and D. Of the choices, fuchsia pink and turquoise were both well received. After careful consideration of all focus group results, we've elected to retain the majority of our old colors and introduce turquoise. We believe we've successfully achieved our branding goal of simplicity and familiarity while establishing a fresh new look.

COMBINED FOCUS GROUP RESULTS

▨ Strongly Disagree   ▨ Disagree   ▪ Neutral   ▪ Agree   ▪ Strongly Agree

Group	Strongly Disagree	Disagree	Neutral	Agree	Strongly Agree
Group A	5%	11%	16%	28%	40%
Group B	40%	13%	19%	8%	20%
Group C	20%	25%	21%	14%	20%
Group D	7%	10%	12%	20%	51%

NATURE FRIENDLY

While we've selected new company colors and created a new logo, our new look is only the first step in our international growth and new opportunities. We believe our continuous core aspect of striving for more nature friendly offices and stores is key to position Fabrikam as the leader in the industry.

6

Although the focus is placed more on reading text than viewing objects, you can double-click an object to magnify it and zoom in on the details.

The following list provides the view options that are located on the View menu for Read Mode:

- **Edit Document** Closes Read Mode and returns to Print Layout view.

- **Show Comments** Displays review comments in the markup area on the right side of the screen.

- **Navigation Pane** Toggles the view of the Navigation pane. If you previously turned on the Navigation pane, it will automatically be displayed in Read Mode.

- **Column Width** This option changes the number of columns that will display the document's contents. If you're viewing multiple columns of text, called *screens*, a dividing line is displayed between them. To navigate to the next or previous set of screens, click the arrows on the far right and left side of the window.

There are three options for Column Width: Narrow, Default, and Wide. The narrower the column, the smaller the line of text on each screen. For both the Narrow and Default options, the number of viewable screens depends on your display settings, such as resolution, magnification, document zoom level, and the size of your document window. For example, if you select Narrow and you're using a small restored document window, the text may only appear on a single screen. Typically, when you choose Narrow, the information is displayed in three screens; Default displays two screens, and Wide displays the content in one screen.

TIP When using Read Mode on devices that automatically rotate the screen, such as Microsoft Surface, select either Narrow or Default. This will allow the columns to adjust to an optimal reading width when you rotate the device.

- **Page Color** There are three page color options: None, Sepia, and Inverse. Sepia uses a brown color scale instead of a black-and-white scale. If your page is white, the content will be displayed as a light pinkish-brown color. Inverse is similar to a photo negative. Dark colors become light and light colors are dark. If you're reading black text in a document with a white background, it will appear as a document with a black background with white text.

TIP The inverse colors are dependent on your format settings, such as font color and paragraph or table shading rather than page color, which is located on the Design tab in the Page Background group.

- **Layout** This option toggles the document's content between Column Layout and Paper Layout. When using Paper Layout, the document view is similar to Print Layout, but the ribbon and Quick Access Toolbar are suppressed and editing is disabled. Additionally, column and page color modifications are not displayed.

In this exercise, you'll explore the available view options for Read Mode.

➡ SET UP **You need the Fabrikam Rebrand Campaign document located in the Chapter06 practice file folder to complete this exercise. Open the Fabrikam Rebrand Campaign document and then follow the steps.**

1 If the practice file isn't already displayed in Read Mode, on the **View** tab, in the **Views** group, click the **Read Mode** button.

2 To advance to the next set of screens, click the arrow at the right side of the window.

TIP The number of the current screens you're viewing and the total screen count are displayed on the left side of the status bar. Keep in mind that your status bar may not look the same as the ones in the screenshots due to your display settings.

3   To return to the previous screen, click the arrow on the left side of the window.

4   If the **Navigation** pane isn't displayed, click **View** and then click **Navigation Pane**.

5   In the **Navigation** pane, click **Brand Colors**.

6   In the document, click the collapse button to the left of **Brand Colors** to collapse the heading.

7   If the **Combined Focus Group Results** chart and table are not shown, below **Brand Colors**, use the horizontal scroll bar to scroll to the right.

8   To magnify the chart, double-click the chart.

     TIP Right-click the chart and then click Zoom In.

9   In the upper-right corner of the magnified chart, click the **magnifying glass** to increase the chart's magnification.

10   To close the magnified view, click away from the chart in the document window.

11   Double-click the table to increase its magnification and then close the magnified view.

12   To view a single screen of text, click the **View** menu, point to **Column Width**, and then click **Wide**.

13   To change the page color, click **View**, point to **Page Color**, and then click **Sepia**.

14   Repeat step 13 but change the page color to **Inverse**.

15   To view a layout that includes headers, footers, and page margins, click **View**, point to **Layout**, and then click **Paper Layout**.

16   Use the vertical scrollbar on the right side of the window to scroll through the document.

17   To return to a column layout, click **View**, point to **Layout**, and then click **Column Layout**.

18   Set the page color and column width to your preference.

19   Turn off the display of the **Navigation** pane.

20   To exit Read Mode, click **View** and then click **Edit Document**.

        KEYBOARD SHORTCUT Press the Esc key to exit Read Mode.

✖ CLEAN UP **Exit Word without saving changes to the document.**

      TIP When you open a document that originated from an Internet location, like an email attachment, it will be displayed in Read Mode by default. To bypass Read Mode for those documents, click the File tab to display the Backstage view, click Options, and then near the bottom of the General tab, clear the check box for Open Email Attachments And Other Uneditable Files In Reading View.

Exploring research tools in Read Mode

While reading a document, you may encounter words or phrases you're not familiar with or that you may want to find more information about on the Internet. Instead of reaching for a dictionary or opening a web browser, you can use the research tools available on the shortcut menu in Read Mode. To use these tools, right-click a word and then click Define, Translate, or Search With Bing.

FABRIKAM'S FIRST COMMUNITY KITCHEN

Greenville is set to launch our pilot Community Kitchen program starting in November. The first phase of the program is to offer low-cost healthy eating classes to the local community. The Eating for Health series is created to increase healthy food preparation skills and knowledge. Our goal is to involve the community in local and sustain... start developing farm-to-table relations...

When classes aren't i... the kitchen will be av... those in need of co... kitchen space certifie... Health Department f... food-related business such as

Phase two of our pilot community kitchen program is to develop a curriculum with volunteer chefs and offer culinary classes to help increase job skills within the community. The culinary program will also provide students with real-life experience working in a commercial kitchen. Students will plan and prepare meals that will be served in the community center and for organization fundraising events. Along with determining cost and nutrition analysis for each meal, students will also be responsible for cooking, expediting, and food service for each dinner. All dinner proceeds will benefit the culinary program.

IMPORTANT You need to have an Internet connection to use the online research tools.

Below is an overview of the research tools:

- **Define** This option searches for a word in an online dictionary and displays the results in a pop-up window. Along with a definition, most dictionaries include a list of synonyms and a verbal pronunciation of the word. To hear a verbal pronunciation of a search term in an online dictionary, click the speaker button displayed next to the word.

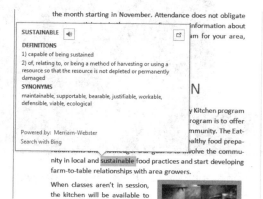

IMPORTANT You need to be signed in to Office with a Microsoft Account and have a dictionary installed in order to look up words from an online source. Definitions, synonyms, and other results may vary depending on the installed dictionary. If a dictionary isn't installed, a Dictionary pane will be displayed with available dictionaries from the Office Store, including those that are free. To install a dictionary, click the Download button for the dictionary you want to install.

SEE ALSO For more information on signing in to Office and using a Microsoft account, see Chapter 3, "Sharing and collaborating."

- **Translate** When you want to translate a word into another language, this feature opens the Research pane with a translation of the word or selected sentence. While the pane is displayed, when you click another word or select another sentence, the word or phrase will be translated.

KEYBOARD SHORTCUT Press the Alt key and then click the word or selected phrase to translate it.

TIP Subsequent automatic translation may not occur on all devices. For example, when using Microsoft Surface, you may need to tap or click the Translate command each time you want to translate a word or selected sentence.

IMPORTANT You may need to configure the From and To language pairs and install the bilingual dictionaries before you can use the translation service. To configure the language pairs, in the Research pane, below Translate A Word Or Sentence, use the drop-down lists to the right of From and To. If you need to install a bilingual dictionary, you'll be prompted with a message box the first time you use the translation service. Click OK to complete the installation.

You can also obtain dictionary definitions and synonyms in the Research pane. To change from the translation option to another option, near the top of the pane, click Translation to display a list of choices.

Research ▾ ✕

Search for:

sustainable →

Translation ▾

All Reference Books
  Encarta Dictionary: English (North America)
  Thesaurus: English (United States)
  Thesaurus: French (France)
  Thesaurus: Spanish (Spain)
  Translation
All Research Sites
  Bing
  Factiva iWorks™
  HighBeam (TM) Research
All Business and Financial Sites
  Thomson Gale Company Profiles

TIP A translation service provided by a computer only gives you a basic translation and does not change sentence structure or tone that might be required in order to convey meaningful information in another language. It's recommended that you use a human translation service for important or sensitive files.

- **Search with Bing** When you choose this option, a web browser opens and uses Bing as the web search engine to search and display results for the word or phrase you specified.

The research tools are also available when you right-click a word or phrase in the other document views, such as Print Layout. The Define and Translate commands are also located on the Review tab, along with Thesaurus. However, the results may be displayed differently in other views. For example, when you use the Define command, the results will be displayed in a Dictionary pane instead of a small window like you previously viewed in Read Mode.

Key points

- The most common document navigation method is scrolling.

- Heading styles are used to outline a document, to create a table of contents, and for viewing features, such as the Navigation pane.

- The Navigation pane can be used as a mini table of contents for documents that have paragraphs formatted with heading styles.

- With the Navigation pane, you can move through a document based on the content, such as a search term, heading, graphic, or table, rather than by screens or lines.

- You can click the arrow to the left of a heading paragraph to collapse and expand the content below the heading.

- The primary focus of Read Mode is to read a document rather than edit it or view how it will look when it is printed.

- Almost all editing commands are disabled when using Read Mode.

- Research tools, such as Define and Translate, are available when you right-click a word or selected phrase.

6

Select

Select text by using the keyboard and mouse, page 156

Use

Use formatting marks during document composition, page 161

Name		Amount¶
Kim·Abercrombie	→	$11¶
Tomasz	→	$502¶
Cornelius	→	$66¶
Michiyo	→	$67¶

Insert

Insert symbols, international characters, and other special characters, page 165

Compose

Compose documents faster by using building blocks, page 176

Editing and composing documents

IN THIS CHAPTER, YOU WILL LEARN HOW TO

- Move the cursor by using keyboard shortcuts.

- Select text by using the keyboard and mouse.

- Use formatting marks during document composition.

- Insert symbols, international characters, and other special characters.

- Use AutoCorrect.

- Compose documents faster by using building blocks.

In this chapter, you'll learn basic editing techniques, such as using the keyboard to quickly move between sentences or paragraphs, along with text selection methods. You'll also learn document composition essentials and how to insert symbols, international characters, and other special characters. At the end of this chapter, you'll learn how to compose documents by using building blocks to insert frequently used information and save valuable time.

PRACTICE FILES To complete the exercises in this chapter, you need the practice files contained in the Chapter07 practice file folder. For more information, see "Download the practice files" in this book's Introduction.

Moving the cursor by using keyboard shortcuts

The first step in editing a document is to move the cursor to the location where you want to make a change. If you're using the mouse, click the left (primary) mouse button to position the cursor.

If you're using the keyboard, use the keyboard shortcuts listed in the following table.

Navigation	Keyboard shortcut
Next or previous character	Right Arrow key or Left Arrow key
One line up or down	Up Arrow key or Down Arrow key
Word to the right	Ctrl+Right Arrow
Word to the left	Ctrl+Left Arrow
Beginning of the line	Home
End of the line	End
One paragraph up	Ctrl+Up Arrow
One paragraph down	Ctrl+Down Arrow
One screen up	Page Up
One screen down	Page Down
Top of the document	Ctrl+Home
End of the document	Ctrl+End

After you've moved the cursor, you can begin entering text or editing. To remove characters or words, use one of the keyboard shortcuts listed in the following table.

Delete	Keyboard shortcut
Character after the cursor	Delete
Character before the cursor	Backspace
Word after the cursor	Ctrl+Delete
Word before the cursor	Ctrl+Backspace

TIP To delete several characters or words, hold down the shortcut keys. If you delete too much, you can reverse your action by clicking the Undo button on the Quick Access Toolbar or by pressing Ctrl+Z.

Selecting text by using the keyboard and mouse

For larger edits, such as deleting a paragraph or making formatting changes, you highlight, or *select*, the text you want to change. When you make a selection, you're identifying *what* you want to work with. After it's selected, you then specify *how* you want to work with it by using your mouse or keyboard to issue a command.

Selected text

EMPLOYEE GIVE PROGRAM

Here at Fabrikam, we never cease to be amazed by the spirit of volunteerism in our employees. Last month marked the five year anniversary of our Employee Give Program and after tallying all hours logged by our employees, we've reached our first milestone of over 500,000 hours of service to our local communities!

The Employee Give Program is mutually beneficial to our company, the employees, and our local communities. Since starting this campaign we've seen an increase in job satisfaction, morale, and communication across our regional offices. More employees have been promoted to leadership roles within the Fabrikam corporation and our need to bring in new leaders from outside our company has greatly diminished. And as a result of our job skill training programs, the majority of our newly hired employees come from our local communities.

TIP Although this chapter talks about working with text, the selection methods can be applied to almost all of your document's content, such as pictures, SmartArt graphics, or charts.

You can use a variety of methods to select text. The most common is the click-and-drag method. That is, you move the mouse pointer to where you want to begin your selection, click and hold the left (primary) mouse button, and then drag through the text you want to select. Additional methods include using the keyboard and other mouse actions, which are discussed in the following sections.

IMPORTANT When using the mouse to select text, don't drag text that's already selected, because that action will move the selected text to a different location. If you accidently move text, you can reverse your action by clicking the Undo button on the Quick Access Toolbar or by pressing Ctrl+Z. If you want to make sure you don't accidentally move text by dragging, click the File tab to display the Backstage view, and then click Options. On the Advanced page, below the Editing options heading, clear the check box for Allow Text To Be Dragged And Dropped.

Selecting text by using the keyboard

You can use the keyboard to select text by pressing the Shift key in combination with a navigation keyboard shortcut. Your selection starts from the location of the cursor. For example, if your cursor is positioned at the beginning of a paragraph, you can press Shift+Ctrl+Down Arrow to select the entire paragraph. But if your cursor is positioned in the middle of the paragraph when you press Shift+Ctrl+Down Arrow, you'll select all the text from the location of the cursor to the end of the paragraph.

The following table provides the most frequently used methods for selecting text by using the keyboard. Keep in mind that these are the navigation shortcuts combined with the Shift key, and that you can also use the Shift key in combination with any of the navigation keyboard shortcuts provided in the previous section.

To make a selection from the cursor through the...	Keyboard shortcut
Next character	Shift+Right Arrow
Previous character	Shift+Left Arrow
Word to the right	Shift+Ctrl+Right Arrow
Word to the left	Shift+Ctrl+Left Arrow
End of the paragraph	Shift+Ctrl+Down Arrow
Beginning of the paragraph	Shift+Ctrl+Up Arrow
Beginning of the document	Shift+Ctrl+Home
End of the document	Shift+Ctrl+End

IMPORTANT If the cursor is in the middle of a word, the keyboard shortcut to select the word to the left or right will select a portion of the current word instead. Additionally, if the cursor is already at the beginning of a paragraph, by pressing Shift+Ctrl+Up Arrow, you'll select the previous paragraph.

Another method for selecting text by using the keyboard is to use selection mode, which is turned on by pressing the F8 key. When selection mode is activated, it's similar to holding the Shift key, and you can use any of the navigation shortcuts to select text without pressing and holding the Shift key. You can also press F8 consecutively to select specific amounts of text. For example, pressing F8 two times will select the current word; three times will select the current sentence; four times will select the current paragraph; and five times will select the entire document. To turn off selection mode, press the Esc key or perform an action on your selection, such as editing or formatting.

TIP To visually determine if selection mode is turned on, you can display an indicator in the status bar. Right-click the status bar and in the Customize Status Bar options, click Selection Mode. When section mode is turned on, the words *Extend Selection* will appear in the status bar.

Selecting text by using the mouse

When using the mouse to select text, you can place your mouse pointer in the document and use the text select arrow, also called an *I-beam pointer*. Or, you can point to the area to the left of the document margin. This area is called the *selection bar*. It isn't labeled, but you know you're in the selection bar when your mouse pointer changes from the text select arrow to an arrow that points up and to the right. Each time you click in the selection bar you select text.

EMPLOYEE GIVE PROGRAM

Here at Fabrikam, we never cease to be amazed by the spirit of volunteerism in our employees. Last month marked the five year anniversary of our Employee Give Program and after tallying all hours logged by our employees, we've reached our first milestone of over 500,000 hours of service to our local communities!

The Employee Give Program is mutually beneficial to our company, the employees, and our local communities. Since starting this campaign we've seen an increase in job satisfaction, morale, and communication across our regional offices. More employees have

FABRIKAM

The following table lists mouse actions for both the text select arrow and the selection bar.

Selection	Mouse action
One word	Double-click
One line	Click the selection bar next to the line
Multiple lines	Click next to the first line in the selection bar and then drag up or down
One sentence	Press the Ctrl key and click the sentence
One paragraph	Triple-click in the paragraph or double-click next to the paragraph in the selection bar
Entire document	Press Ctrl and click in the selection bar or triple-click in the selection bar

You can also use a combination of the mouse, keyboard, and Shift key to select text. For example, if you didn't select enough text, simply press the Shift key and then click where you want your selection to end, or use the keyboard to modify your selection.

Using other selection methods

Microsoft Word also has selection methods for selecting multiple words, phrases, sentences, and columns of text anywhere in a document.

To make text selections that are not next to each other, after you make your first text selection, press the Ctrl key and use a mouse action to select additional text.

EMPLOYEE GIVE PROGRAM

Here at Fabrikam, we never cease to be amazed by the spirit of volunteerism in our employees. Last month marked the five year anniversary of our Employee Give Program and after tallying all hours logged by our employees, we've reached our first milestone of over 500,000 hours of service to our local communities!

The Employee Give Program is mutually beneficial to our company, the employees, and our local communities. Since starting this campaign we've seen an increase in job satisfaction, morale, and communication across our regional offices. More employees have been promoted to leadership roles within the Fabrikam corporation and our need to bring in new leaders from outside our company has

To select a vertical column of text, press and hold the Alt key and use the mouse to drag through the text you want to select.

Name	Amount
Kim Abercrombie	$11
Tomasz	$502
Cornelius	$66
Michiyo	$67

IMPORTANT Holding down the Alt key and clicking a word or selected phrase will display the Research pane. When using the Alt key to select a column of text, make sure you click and drag. If the Research pane is displayed, close it, and then press the Alt key while selecting the column of text again.

TIP You can also use the Navigation pane to select a heading and its related content. On the Navigation pane, right-click the heading you want to select, and then click Select Heading And Content. For more information about using the Navigation pane, see Chapter 6, "Navigating and reading documents."

Using formatting marks during document composition

Each time you press the Tab, Spacebar, or Enter key, characters called *formatting marks* are inserted into the document. Normally these formatting marks are not shown on the screen, but you can toggle their display by clicking the Show/Hide ¶ button, located on the Home tab in the Paragraph group.

KEYBOARD SHORTCUT Press Ctrl+Shift+8.

When you press Enter, a paragraph mark (¶), also called a *pilcrow sign*, is inserted into your document. Each press of the Tab key adds a right-pointing arrow (→), and a dot in the middle of the line (·) indicates that the Spacebar was pressed.

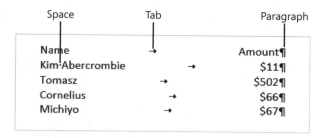

TIP To always view specific formatting marks on the screen without using the Show/Hide ¶ button, click the File tab to display the Backstage view, click Options, and then on the Display page, select the formatting marks you want to make visible.

If you use multiple spaces and tabs for horizontal alignment, or press the Enter key several times to change vertical alignment or to create blank lines, it can complicate the editing and formatting processes, because each character uses a specific amount of space.

The best practices for document composition include using formatting methods rather than pressing the Tab, Spacebar, and Enter key multiple times:

- To add space between information on the same line, add formatted spacing by setting a manual tab.

- To add space between paragraphs, add formatted spacing before or after paragraphs.

TIP The blank lines that are created by pressing the Enter key multiple times are called *empty paragraphs*.

SEE ALSO For information about setting manual tabs, see Chapter 9, "Presenting information." For information about adding paragraph spacing, see Chapter 8, "Formatting documents."

In this exercise, you'll examine how document composition can have an impact on editing. You'll edit two lists of information. One list uses tabs and spaces for alignment, and the other uses a manual tab to achieve the same result. You'll also use formatted space to change the position of a paragraph.

➡ SET UP **You need the List Example document located in the Chapter07 practice file folder to complete this exercise. Open the List Example document and then follow the steps.**

1   Below the **List with multiple tabs and spaces** heading, move the cursor to the right of **Kim**.

   KEYBOARD SHORTCUT Press the Down Arrow key twice and then press Ctrl+Right Arrow.

2   Press the **Spacebar** key, enter **Abercrombie**, and note how the **$11** amount for Kim moved to the right when you added her last name.

List with multiple tabs and spaces		
Name	Amount	
Kim Abercrombie		$11
Tomasz	$502	
Cornelius	$66	
Michiyo	$67	

3   To realign $11 to the other amounts, with the cursor still positioned after **Abercrombie**, press the **Delete** key two times.

4   To add a new item to the **List with multiple tabs and spaces** list, move the cursor to the end of the last line, after the **$67** amount.

   KEYBOARD SHORTCUT Press the Down Arrow key three times and then press the End key.

5   Press **Enter**.

6   On the newly added line, enter **Kate**, and then press the **Tab** key or **Spacebar** as needed to move the cursor to the **Amount** column.

7   Enter **$400**.

8   Add tabs or spaces if needed to align the amount you entered to the other amounts in the list.

List with multiple tabs and spaces	
Name	**Amount**
Kim Abercrombie	$11
Tomasz	$502
Cornelius	$66
Michiyo	$67
Kate	$400

9   Below the **List without multiple tabs and spaces** heading, move the cursor to the right of **Kim** and enter **Abercrombie**. The amount didn't move and additional edits aren't needed.

   TIP If you want more insight into the underlying differences between the lists, on the Home tab, in the Paragraph group, click the Show/Hide ¶ button to display the formatting marks.

List·with·multiple·tabs·and·spaces¶

Name→	→	→	→	·············Amount¶
Kim·Abercrombie	→	→	→	·······$11¶
Tomasz⁺	→	→	→	·····$502¶
Cornelius·	→	→	→	·······$66¶
Michiyo	→	→	→	·······$67¶

List·without·multiple·tabs·and·spaces¶

Name	→	Amount¶
Kim·Abercrombie	→	$11¶
Tomasz	→	$502¶
Cornelius	→	$66¶
Michiyo	→	$67¶

Examine the number of tabs and spaces in the first list. Because Kim's last name takes about as much space as two default tabs, you'll need to remove two tabs to correct the alignment. For the second list, a manual tab was used to add formatted space. This enables you to enter text up to the amount while maintaining the alignment.

10 Below the last list item, enter your name, press the **Tab** key, and then enter an amount, which will be aligned with the other amounts.

11 Make other edits to both lists. For example, change **$11** to **$110** and notice that additional edits aren't needed to align the amounts in the second list.

12 To demonstrate the advantage of using formatted space to modify the position of a paragraph, place the cursor in the **List without multiple tabs and spaces** paragraph.

TIP The cursor doesn't need to be at the beginning of the paragraph.

13 On the **Page Layout** tab, in the **Paragraph** group, next to **Spacing Before,** click the **Up Arrow** to increase the space from **6 pts** to **18 pts**.

PAGE LAYOUT	REFERENCES	MAILINGS	REVIEW

Indent	Spacing
₃ks ▾	
₂ Numbers ▾ ⊞ Left: 0"	↑⊟ Before: 6 pt
₁henation ▾ ⊞ Right: 0"	↓⊟ After: 0 pt
Paragraph

❌ CLEAN UP **Close the document without saving changes.**

Inserting symbols, international characters, and other special characters

To insert symbols, such as the ohm sign (Ω), or international characters, such as the letter "a" with an acute accent (á), you can use the Symbol dialog box or a keyboard shortcut.

To display the Symbol dialog box, on the Insert tab, in the Symbols group, click the Symbol button, and then click More Symbols.

From the list of symbols, double-click the symbol you want to insert, or click the symbol once to select it and then click the Insert button.

TIP You don't need to close the Symbol dialog box to insert multiple symbols. After your first insertion, click in your document to activate it, and then move the cursor to a new location. Then, click the Symbol dialog box to activate it and insert another symbol. If the dialog box is in your way, drag its title bar to move it to another location on your screen.

Here are a few tips for using the Symbol dialog box:

- When (normal text) is selected in the Font drop-down list, symbols will be inserted by using the current font. If you select a different font, the insertion will be the same as the font you selected from the Font list.

- After you insert a symbol, it will be added to the Recently used symbols list near the bottom of the Symbol dialog box and on the Symbol drop-down list in the ribbon.

- As you scroll through the available symbols, the Subset area to the right of the font will change. You can jump to a specific group of symbols by selecting an item from the Subset drop-down list, such as Mathematical Operators.

- To insert glyph characters, select Webdings or any of the three Wingdings fonts from the Font drop-down list.

    TIP Webdings, Wingdings, Wingdings 2, and Wingdings 3 are the main Windows fonts that contain glyphs. You may have other glyph fonts installed that you can use as well.

If a selected symbol has an associated keyboard shortcut, it will be listed near the bottom of the dialog box next to the Shortcut Key button. There are four basic keyboard shortcut methods that you can use to insert symbols.

The following table provides an example of each method and a description of how to enter the keyboard shortcut.

Symbol	Keyboard shortcut	How to enter it
¿	Alt+Ctrl+?	Press the Alt, Ctrl, and ? keys simultaneously. You may also need to hold the Shift key in order to enter a question mark.
¥	Alt+0165	Make sure Num Lock is turned on, hold the Alt key, and then press the numbers on the numeric keypad. The character will be inserted after you release the Alt key. The numbers on the main keyboard can't be used for this keyboard shortcut.
Ø	Ctrl+/, Shift+O	Press Ctrl and / simultaneously and release the keys. Then press Shift and O simultaneously.
≤	2264, Alt+X	Enter 2264 and then immediately press Alt and X simultaneously. The numbers will be replaced with the character after you press Alt+X.

TIP You can also use AutoCorrect to enter frequently used symbols. Select the symbol and then click the AutoCorrect button near the bottom of the dialog box. For information about how to create a custom AutoCorrect entry, see the "Using AutoCorrect" section later in this chapter.

If you use international characters that have accents, such as á or ÿ, you don't need to memorize each individual keyboard shortcut for them. You can use the built-in keyboard shortcuts for the accent character instead, which are listed in the following table.

To insert an accent, first press the keyboard shortcut, release the keys, and then enter the character.

Accent	Keyboard shortcut	Character	Example
acute	Ctrl+'	a, e, i, o, u, y, d	ý
cedilla	Ctrl+,	c	ç
circumflex	Ctrl+^	a, e, i, o, u	î
grave	Ctrl+`	a, e, i, o, u	ò
tilde	Ctrl+~	a, n, o	ñ
umlaut	Ctrl+:	a, e, i, o, u, y	ë

IMPORTANT On most standard keyboards, to enter the caret (^), tilde (~), or colon (:) you also need to hold down the Shift key. For example, a tilde is entered by pressing Shift and the single left quotation mark, which is typically the key to the left of the number 1. Another example is the caret, which is entered by pressing Shift+6. To help you remember the shortcuts, the keyboard shortcuts provided deliberately use keys for characters that are similar to the accent character.

Assigning a custom keyboard shortcut to a character or symbol

If you frequently use the same character or symbol that has a complex keyboard shortcut, you can define your own custom keyboard shortcut instead of memorizing the built-in one. In the Symbol dialog box, select a character or symbol, and then click Shortcut Key. In the Customize Keyboard dialog box that appears, in the Press New Shortcut Key text box, press the keys for your preferred keyboard shortcut. For example, press Ctrl+Shift+Y.

It's important to note that prior to assigning your new keyboard shortcut, you should first check whether the keyboard shortcut you want to use is assigned to another command. After you enter your keyboard shortcut, the existing keyboard shortcut assignment will be listed below the Current Keys list box.

If the shortcut is already assigned, and it's one you don't use, you can override the built-in assignment with your custom keyboard shortcut by clicking the Assign button. If you later decide you want to use the originally assigned keyboard shortcut, you can redisplay the Customize Keyboard dialog box for your symbol, select your custom keyboard shortcut from the list of current keys, and then click Remove. To reset all custom keyboard shortcuts, click Reset All.

Inserting special characters

The Special Characters page of the Symbol dialog box has a collection of special punctuation symbols, such as an em dash (—), and formatting characters, such as a nonbreaking space, that aren't available on most keyboards. You can insert them exactly like you insert symbols or international characters, by using the Symbol dialog box or the corresponding keyboard shortcut.

7

Symbol	? x

| Symbols | Special Characters |

Character: **Shortcut key:**

—	Em Dash	Alt+Ctrl+Num -
–	En Dash	Ctrl+Num -
-	Nonbreaking Hyphen	Ctrl+Shift+_
¬	Optional Hyphen	Ctrl+-
	Em Space	
	En Space	
	1/4 Em Space	
°	Nonbreaking Space	Ctrl+Shift+Space
©	Copyright	Alt+Ctrl+C
®	Registered	Alt+Ctrl+R
™	Trademark	Alt+Ctrl+T
§	Section	
¶	Paragraph	
...	Ellipsis	Alt+Ctrl+.
'	Single Opening Quote	Ctrl+`,`
'	Single Closing Quote	Ctrl+`,`
"	Double Opening Quote	Ctrl+`,`
"	Double Closing Quote	Ctrl+`,`

| AutoCorrect... | Shortcut Key... |

| Insert | Cancel |

Of the available special characters, there are a few that are especially useful for specifying how words or phrases should wrap between lines of text if they fall at the end of a line. The following table describes each of these and provides a description of the formatting mark that's displayed for each when you click the Show/Hide ¶ button on the Home tab.

Character	Description	Formatting mark
Optional Hyphen	An optional hyphen is displayed only when part of the text wraps to the next line. If the text remains on the same line, the hyphen doesn't appear.	hooked hyphen (¬)
Nonbreaking Hyphen	Keeps text before and after the nonbreaking hyphen together on the same line.	long hyphen(–)
Nonbreaking Space	Keeps text before and after the nonbreaking space together on the same line.	small raised circle (°)

TIP The formatting marks for an em space and en space are also displayed as a small raised circle, but extra space is added to the left of the symbol for an en space and extra space is added to the left and right for an em space. A 1/4-em space is shown as a vertical bar (|).

A manual line break, which isn't in the Symbol dialog box, is another special formatting character for controlling line wrapping. This type of break is used to force text to start on a new line without starting a new paragraph. For example, you may have several short lines that you want to treat as a single paragraph, such as an address. To enter a manual line break, press Shift+Enter. The formatting mark that represents a manual line break is a right-angle arrow pointing to the left.

In this exercise, you'll use the Symbol dialog box to insert a nonbreaking space to prevent a telephone number from wrapping across multiple lines.

SET UP **You need the Newsletter_C document located in the Chapter07 practice file folder to complete this exercise. Open the Newsletter_C document and then follow the steps.**

1   On the **View** tab, in the **Show** group, select the **Navigation Pane** check box.

2   In the **Navigation** pane, click **New Women's Shelter**. If necessary, scroll to view the text below the picture.

3   On the **Home** tab, in the **Paragraph** group, click the **Show/Hide ¶** button.

4   Select the space after **(971)**.

5   On the **Insert** tab, in the **Symbols** group, click **Symbol**, and then click **More Symbols**.

6   On the **Special Characters** page, double-click **Nonbreaking space**.

     KEYBOARD SHORTCUT Press Ctrl+Shift+Spacebar.

7   Close the **Symbol** dialog box and note that the entire phone number wrapped to the next line.

8   Edit the first part of the sentence with the phone number to read **To donate** instead of **If you wish to donate** and note that the phone number moves to the previous line.

     TIP Move the cursor to the beginning of the sentence and press Ctrl+Delete three times. Then press Delete to remove the lowercase t, and enter a capital T.

❌ CLEAN UP **Close the document without saving changes.**

Using AutoCorrect

As you enter text into a document, various typing mistakes and misspellings are corrected for you by a feature called *AutoCorrect*. If you're familiar with using AutoCorrect on a smartphone, the feature in Word is similar, but it does more than correct commonly misspelled words. Other corrections range from capitalizing the first letter of sentences and days of the week to toggling the case of characters if you accidently enter them with Caps Lock on. For example, if you enter the word "teh" as the first word of a sentence, AutoCorrect will both capitalize the first letter and change the word to "the" after you press the Spacebar.

You also have the ability to reverse the action if it isn't correct and remove words that you don't want corrected automatically. When a correction is made, point to the word to display the AutoCorrect Options button, and then click the button to display a menu of choices.

The quick brown fox jumped over the lazy dog.

↩ Undo Automatic Corrections

Stop Auto-capitalizing First Letter of Sentences

Stop Automatically Correcting "teh"

⚡ Control AutoCorrect Options...

To reverse the correction, click the first option, which will start with either *Change back* or *Undo*. For the example previously provided, when the word "teh" as been entered at the beginning of a sentence, the first option is Undo Automatic Corrections, because two corrections were made. Clicking the option will reverse both the spelling of the word "the" and the capitalization.

TIP You can also press Ctrl+Z to undo a correction immediately after it's made.

If you never want the correction to be made again, click a *Stop* option, such as Stop Automatically Correcting "teh". Keep in mind that this will delete the entry and will take effect for all documents. After an entry is deleted, you'll need to manually add the entry in the AutoCorrect dialog box in order for Word to start correcting it again.

To view all of the AutoCorrect options, click Control AutoCorrect Options at the bottom of the menu to display the AutoCorrect dialog box.

TIP To display the AutoCorrect dialog box, you can also click the File tab to display the Backstage view, and click Options. Then on the Proofing tab, click the AutoCorrect Options button. Alternatively, you can press Alt, T, A. That is, press and release the Alt key, press and release T, and then press A.

In the AutoCorrect dialog box, you can choose to turn the options on or off, delete words that are automatically corrected, or add your own entries to the AutoCorrect list.

To add custom entries, enter the characters you want to replace in the Replace text box. In the With text box, enter your replacement text, and then click the Add button.

Here are a few tips for using the AutoCorrect dialog box:

- Don't use a word for your Replace text. If you do, each time you enter that word in a document, it will be corrected. It's best to use abbreviations or a group of characters you wouldn't normally use as a word in your documents.

- Enter your text in the Replace text box in lowercase characters in order to make your entry case insensitive. That is, if you enter your Replace text in lowercase characters, you can use uppercase or lowercase characters in your document to trigger a correction. If you enter your Replace text in all uppercase or mixed case, you must enter it exactly as it's displayed in the AutoCorrect dialog box in order to have AutoCorrect correct your entry.

- Enter your text in the With text box exactly as you want it to be entered in your document, including punctuation and uppercase, lowercase, or mixed case characters.

- To quickly find an entry in the AutoCorrect list, enter it in the Replace text box. As you enter the text, the list will scroll to matching characters.

- Custom entries aren't only for words you frequently misspell. You can also use the AutoCorrect feature for frequently used phrases or your company name. For example, you can create an entry such as Replace: *finc* With: *Fabrikam, Inc.* Then to add your company name in a document, you would enter *finc*, and after you press the Spacebar, *Fabrikam, Inc.* will be inserted.

- You can add exceptions to prevent corrections from being made that change the case of words. To add exceptions, click the Exceptions button in the AutoCorrect dialog box.

Following are the types of exceptions you can add:

- **First Letter** A list of abbreviations that end with a period. If exceptions for these aren't specified, the first letter of the word after the abbreviation will automatically be capitalized.

- **Initial Caps** A list of words that have mixed uppercase and lowercase letters that should not be corrected.

> **IMPORTANT** Words on the Other Corrections page are those that are corrected by the spelling dictionary, and manual additions to the list are ignored. You can, however, use this page to delete entries that were added in error.

- You can also use AutoCorrect to insert formatted text, like a symbol. Select your formatted text in a document. When you display the AutoCorrect dialog box, your selection will be added in the With text box. Then, add your Replace characters and select the Formatted Text option before clicking the Add button.

> **TIP** Several frequently used symbols, such as ©, ™, and ®, are already included in AutoCorrect. To view them, scroll to the top of the AutoCorrect list.

Composing documents faster by using building blocks

Building blocks, formerly known as AutoText in previous versions of Word, are pieces of information that you can quickly insert into your documents. You can insert built-in building blocks, such as watermarks and cover pages, or your own custom entries.

TIP The built-in building blocks are theme enabled, which means that the fonts and colors will match your document's current theme. Also, if you change the theme, the thumbnails in the galleries will reflect the theme change. For more information about using themes, see Chapter 2, "Using shared Office features."

Following is a list of the primary building block galleries and their locations on the ribbon:

- **Cover Page** On the **Insert** tab, in the Pages group.

- **Quick Tables** On the Insert tab, in the Tables group. (Click Table and then point to Quick Tables.)

- **Headers**, **Footers**, **and Page Numbers** On the Insert tab, in the Header & Footer group.

- **Text Box and Quick Parts** On the Insert tab, in the Text group.

- **Watermark** On the Design tab, in the Page Background group.

- **Tables of Contents** On the References tab, in the Table of Contents group.

  TIP The Automatic Table 1 and Automatic Table 2 built-in building blocks in the Tables Of Contents gallery use heading styles in your document to generate a table of contents. For more information on using heading styles, see Chapter 8.

To insert a building block, simply click the building block you want to insert in your document. Some of the building block galleries, like the Cover Page gallery, have additional commands for inserting building blocks. To display these commands, right-click a building block in the gallery.

| Insert at Beginning of Document |
| Insert at Current Document Position |
| Insert at Beginning of Section |
| Insert at End of Section |
| Insert at End of Document |
| Edit Properties... |
| Organize and Delete... |
| Add Gallery to Quick Access Toolbar |

The Quick Parts gallery doesn't have built-in building blocks and can be used for your custom entries. Custom building blocks can range from frequently used text, such as a signature block or boilerplate text for a letter or other document, to pictures and other graphics. Additionally, unlike built-in building blocks, custom building blocks can be inserted by using the keyboard. Just enter the name of the building block and watch for the AutoComplete ScreenTip. When the ScreenTip is displayed, press Enter to insert the building block. Typically, you only need to enter the first few characters of the name and the AutoComplete ScreenTip will be displayed.

Company Logo and Address (Press ENTER to Insert)
comp

In this exercise, you'll create a custom building block for the Fabrikam company logo and address and then insert it by using the ribbon and keyboard.

SET UP You need the Sample Logo and Address document located in the Chapter07 practice file folder to complete this exercise. Open the Sample Logo And Address document and then follow the steps.

1   Point to the left of the logo and address in the selection bar and click once to select it.

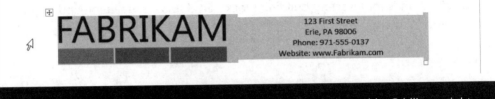

> **IMPORTANT** The logo and address are located in a borderless table. Gridlines might appear in the document, and your selection may look odd. If you used the selection bar to select the logo and address, your selection is correct.

2   On the **Insert** tab, in the **Text** group, click **Quick Parts**, and then click **Save Selection to Quick Part gallery**.

KEYBOARD SHORTCUT Press Alt+F3.

3   In the **Create New Building Block** dialog box, in the **Name** text box, enter **Company Logo and Address**.

4   In the **Save-in** list, click **Normal**.

TIP To add custom building blocks to other galleries, such as Cover Page or Header, select the gallery you want in the Gallery list. If you create a lot of building blocks, you can use the Category option to organize them in the gallery.

5 Click **OK**.

6 To test your newly created building block, create a blank document.

   KEYBOARD SHORTCUT Press Ctrl+N.

7 On the **Insert** tab, click **Quick Parts**, and then click **Company Logo and Address**.

8 To insert the logo by using the keyboard, add a new paragraph below the previously inserted logo and begin entering **Company**. When the **AutoComplete** ScreenTip is displayed, press **Enter** to insert the logo.

   KEYBOARD SHORTCUT Enter the first few characters of the building block name, and then press F3.

✖ CLEAN UP **Close the document without saving changes, and exit Word.**

Here are some important tips to remember when you are creating custom building blocks:

- To use the keyboard to insert your building block by using the AutoComplete Screen-Tip, you must save your entry in the Normal template or a custom template.

- When you are creating more than one custom building block, if the first few characters of the building block name aren't unique, you'll need to enter the first non-unique character before the AutoComplete ScreenTip will be displayed.

- The AutoComplete ScreenTip will not be displayed for building blocks containing pictures or other objects unless text is also included.

- To revise a building block, recreate the entry by using the same name and other properties, such as category, gallery, and save location. When you save the building block, you'll be prompted to redefine the entry.

- You can edit building block properties or delete a building block in the Building Blocks Organizer. To display it, on the Insert tab, in the Text group, click Quick Parts, and then click Building Blocks Organizer.

Key points

- To select text by using the keyboard, you can use navigation keyboard shortcuts combined with the Shift key.

- The selection bar is the area to the left of your document's left margin, rather than to the left of your text. If your pointer does not point up and to the right, try moving the pointer further to the left.

- To select pieces of text that are not next to each other, press the Ctrl key between selections and use a mouse action to add to your selection. If you use a keyboard action, your previous selection will be removed.

- When you are composing a document, avoid pressing the Spacebar, Tab, and Enter keys multiple times to move the cursor or add extra space.

- AutoCorrect actions are triggered when you press the Spacebar.

- You can press Ctrl+Z to undo an AutoCorrect action immediately after the correction has been made.

- To display the AutoComplete ScreenTip for a building block, you must save the entry in the Normal template, and the first few characters of the name must be unique.

7

Chapter at a glance

Set

Set default document formatting, page 188

Modify

Modify character and paragraph formats, like font color and indents, page 192

Use

Use styles for fast and flexible formatting, page 194

Manage

Manage how text flows between pages through formatting, page 203

Formatting documents 8

IN THIS CHAPTER, YOU WILL LEARN HOW TO

- Format documents more efficiently.

- Set default document formatting for your documents.

- Apply section, paragraph, and character formatting to text.

- Use styles to format documents faster and increase formatting flexibility.

- Manage document pagination through formatting.

Document formatting is one of the primary tasks in Microsoft Word and has the broadest set of features. Formatting ranges from changing a font or font size, to modifying line spacing or paragraph indents, to setting page margins and pagination options, such as specifying that all lines of a paragraph should stay together on the same page.

In this chapter, you'll learn about the four main categories of formatting and how you can format documents faster and more efficiently by using styles. At the end of this chapter, you'll learn how to manage document pagination through manual page breaks and formatting.

PRACTICE FILES To complete the exercises in this chapter, you need the practice files contained in the Chapter08 practice file folder. For more information, see "Download the practice files" in this book's Introduction.

Formatting documents more efficiently

Formatting can be one of the most time-consuming tasks if you're not familiar with the fundamentals. Similar to how document composition can affect editing, as covered in the previous chapter, the methods you use to format a document determine the amount of time you spend formatting, and many times, reformatting.

The primary document formatting fundamental to become familiar with first is the fact that, when you begin entering text into a document, the text you're entering is already formatted. For example, when you create a new blank document, default formats are already applied. The font is Calibri and the font size is 11 points. There are other default formats as well. The space between each line of a paragraph, which is called *line spacing*, is by default 1.08 points, and the space after each paragraph, which is referred to as *paragraph spacing*, is 8 points by default.

The next fundamental to understand is that all text is associated with a named set of formatting attributes called a *style*. Styles that are frequently used in a document are on the Home tab, in the Styles gallery.

TIP To expand the Styles gallery, click the More button in the lower-right corner.

You don't have to implement styles in your documents, but they give you flexibility and consistent formatting. Best of all, you can apply multiple formats with a single click, which enables you to instantly change text formatting associated with a style throughout a document simply by modifying the style's formatting attributes. You'll learn more about styles throughout this chapter.

The last formatting fundamental is to break formatting down into separate tasks to help make it more manageable. Here are the four main formatting categories:

- **Document** Initial formatting attributes that are applied to the entire document, referred to as *document defaults*. These formats include a set of fonts for your heading and body text and the initial colors displayed in the color palettes. They also include paragraph and line spacing formats. The primary location for setting these formats is on the **Design** tab.

TIP Examples of heading text are the section titles in this book, which are formatted with the Segoe Light font. Other text is considered body text, which is formatted as Segoe.

To modify document defaults, you don't need to select any text, because these formats are applied to the entire document.

SEE ALSO For more information on text selection, see Chapter 7, "Editing and composing documents."

The Design tab also has sets of pre-built styles called *style sets* in the Document Formatting group. The formatting that appears in the preview of each style set gives you a general idea of how your document will look when it's formatted with the available styles.

TIP If you select a different theme or change individual theme elements, the fonts and colors that are displayed in the style set preview will be updated to match your selection.

When you select a style set, you're changing both the document defaults and the collection of styles that are displayed on the Home tab in the Styles group. If you're working with a document that already has styles that are named the same as those in the style set applied, such as Title and Heading 1, the formatting will be updated to match your selected style set. Keep in mind that the set you choose only provides the initial formats. You can change a style's formatting attributes at any time.

- **Section** Formats that are applied to a division in a document such as a page or a group of pages. All pages within a section have the same section formats, such as page margins, orientation, and page size. These formats are located on the **Page Layout** tab.

To apply section formats, make sure your cursor is positioned in the section you want to modify.

SEE ALSO For more information on how to create additional sections in a document, see "Setting section formatting," later in this chapter.

- **Paragraph** Formats that are applied to a paragraph as a whole, such as alignment, indents, line spacing, and paragraph spacing. Other paragraph formats include page break options, such as specifying that all lines of a paragraph should stay together on the same page. The primary paragraph formats are located on the **Home** tab, in the **Paragraph** group.

To apply paragraph formatting for a single paragraph, text selection isn't necessary. You can place your cursor in the paragraph you want to format and then make your modifications. For multiple paragraphs, select all paragraphs you want to format.

- **Character** Formatting that can be applied to individual characters, such as font, font size, color, or bold. Primary character formatting is located on the **Home** tab, in the **Font** group.

TIP You can specify a font size as small as 1 point and as large as 1,638 points by entering it in the Size text box. You can also enter half-sizes, such as 10.5 points. When you enter a specific size, enter decimals for half-sizes and don't include a comma for large numbers.

To apply character formatting to a single word, click in the word you want to format and then make your changes. To format a single character or multiple words, select the text you want to format. Note that commands such as bold, italic, subscript, and superscript are toggle commands. This means you perform the same action when you want to apply and remove the formatting.

For setting other formats, such as the font type and font color, you can either apply a different format or remove it. For formats such as text effects, typography, and text highlight color, you remove applied formats by selecting the option that starts with the word *No*, such as No Color for Text Highlight Color.

TIP Text Highlight Color is an example of a split control, and it's one that works without the need to select text. You can click the Text Highlight Color button to apply the color that's shown on the button, or you can click the arrow next to the button and select your preferred highlight color. If your text is highlighted, the color will be applied. If you don't have text selected, your mouse pointer will change to a highlighter tool that you can drag through text to highlight it. If you use the latter method, to turn off the highlighter, click the button again or press the Esc key.

You don't necessarily need to format your document in the same order that the formatting categories have just been described. However, a best formatting practice is to start with your document and section formats, because these can affect your paragraph and character formatting. The remaining sections of this chapter cover each formatting category in more detail, along with step-by-step exercises.

8

Serif and sans serif fonts

Fonts are either serif or sans serif. The way to differentiate between them is that serif fonts have "hooks," called *serifs*, at the end of each stroke of the character. Sans serif fonts, however, do not have "hooks." In French, *sans* means *without*; therefore, sans serif fonts do not have hook characters. Examples of serif fonts are Cambria and Times New Roman. Examples of sans serif fonts are Calibri and Arial.

Cambria: The quick brown fox jumps over the lazy dog.

Times New Roman: The quick brown fox jumps over the lazy dog.

Calibri: The quick brown fox jumps over the lazy dog.

Arial: The quick brown fox jumps over the lazy dog.

It's fairly common for printed content to have a sans serif font for headings and serif fonts for body text, because this combination is the easiest to read on paper. But for online documents, the combination is often reversed for easier onscreen reading; a serif font is used for headings, and a sans serif font is used for body text. The main reason for this is that serifs may appear faint or jagged on a screen due to the display itself and various display settings. When choosing fonts, you may want to keep the main output of your document in mind. If it's to be read electronically, then choose a sans serif font for your body text to help make sure it's easy to read on all devices.

Setting default document formatting for your documents

The first set of formats you should change for a document are the document defaults, because they affect your entire document and set the base formats for your paragraph and character formatting.

In this exercise, you'll change document defaults by modifying theme elements and by changing line and paragraph spacing. You'll also select a style set for initial paragraph and character formats.

SET UP You need the Fabrikam Rebrand Campaign_A document located in the Chapter08 practice file folder to complete this exercise. Open the Fabrikam Rebrand Campaign_A document. Then follow the steps.

1   Scroll through the document and take note of the current fonts, font color, line and paragraph spacing, and how the colors don't match the Fabrikam logo colors on the first page.

2   To change the document theme, on the **Design** tab, in the **Themes** group, click **Themes** and then click **Retrospect**.

3   To change only the theme colors so they match the colors in the Fabrikam logo, on the **Design** tab, in the **Document Formatting** group, click **Colors** and then click **Blue II**.

4   To select an initial style set, on the **Design** tab, in the **Document Formatting** group, in the **Style** gallery, click **Basic (Elegant)**.

TIP The title, Rebrand Campaign, is now formatted as uppercase. It's no longer centered, but you'll correct this in another exercise.

5   To change the default paragraph and line spacing, on the **Design** tab, in the **Document Formatting** group, click **Paragraph Spacing**, and then click **Tight**.

SEE ALSO For more information about themes, see Chapter 2, "Using shared Office features."

CLEAN UP Save Fabrikam Rebrand Campaign_A as My Rebrand Campaign_B. If you're proceeding to the next exercise, leave the My Rebrand Campaign_B document open. Otherwise, close My Rebrand Campaign_B and exit Word.

TIP To view your current document defaults along with all of the document defaults that can be changed, on the Design tab, in the Document Formatting group, click Paragraph Spacing. Then click Custom Paragraph Spacing to view the Set Defaults page of the Manage Styles dialog box.

Setting section formatting

When you think of page margins and page orientation, you probably think of formats that belong to a page. Though they are essentially page formats, it would be time consuming to set page formatting for every single page in a document. Instead, you can format a document section so that all pages in the section will have the same formats applied.

Every new blank document starts with a single section. To add additional sections, you insert section breaks by using the Breaks command, located on the Page Layout tab, in the Page Setup group.

Here is a list of each type of section break, along with some examples for how they're used:

- **Next Page** If your document needs pages with both portrait and landscape orientation, different page margins, or different headers and footers, you can add a **Next Page** section break at the beginning of each change in section formats.

  TIP You don't need to use section breaks for a different first page header and footer or for different odd and even headers and footers.

- **Continuous** This is the only type of section break that doesn't result in a new page. Typically, a continuous break is used to add newspaper-style columns on the same page as text that spans the entire width of the page.

- **Even Page or Odd Page** This type of break forces a page to start on an even-numbered or odd-numbered page and is typically used in documents with multiple chapters that are printed on both sides of the paper. The most common usage is adding an odd page section break at the beginning of a chapter to make sure the first page of the chapter is an odd-numbered page.

TIP To view section information in your status bar, right-click the status bar, and in the Customize Status Bar options, click Section.

In this exercise, you'll insert a section break and set different page margins starting on page 2.

SET UP **If the My Rebrand Campaign_B document you saved in the previous exercise is still open, follow the steps. If you skipped the previous exercise, open the Fabrikam Rebrand Campaign_B document located in the Chapter08 practice file folder to complete this exercise, then follow the steps.**

1   To place the title and logo on its own page, place the cursor at the beginning of the first full paragraph that begins with **Our international office**.

2   On the **Page Layout** tab, in the **Page Setup** group, click **Breaks**, and then click **Next Page**.

3   To change the margins starting at the second page, on the **Page Layout** tab, in the **Page Setup** group, click **Margins**, and then click **Normal**.

CLEAN UP **Save the document as My Rebrand Campaign_C. If you're proceeding to the next exercise, leave the My Rebrand Campaign_C document open. Otherwise, close My Rebrand Campaign_C and exit Word.**

SEE ALSO For more information on section breaks and using headers and footers, see *Microsoft Word 2013 Step by Step* by Joan Lambert and Joyce Cox (Microsoft Press, 2013).

Using styles for paragraph and character formats

Many Word tutorials consider styles to be an advanced formatting technique. Though there are some advanced style topics, styles are such an integral part of Word that you need to know style essentials and how to use them, even if you're a beginning Word user. As noted in the "Formatting documents more efficiently" section earlier in this chapter, frequently used styles are located on the Home tab, in the Styles group.

Styles are document specific. This means that any changes you make to styles will be applied only to your current document. The two primary types of styles in Word are related to the paragraph and character formatting categories. A character style contains only character formats and is applied to individual words and even single characters. A paragraph style is applied to an entire paragraph and contains both character and paragraph formatting. Of the two, paragraph styles are used more frequently, because they enable you to apply more formats at the same time.

Another type of style to know about is a linked style, which is a combination of a paragraph style and a character style. A linked style has the same characteristics as a paragraph style, but if you apply it to a selected portion of a paragraph, only the character formats are applied. In contrast, if you're using a paragraph style, the entire paragraph is formatted, even if you have only a portion of it selected.

Of all the built-in styles, those that have other features connected to them are the heading styles, which are Heading 1 through Heading 9. For example, the headings that are displayed in the Navigation pane are paragraphs that have a heading style applied. And heading styles are also used for creating a table of contents.

SEE ALSO For more information on how to create a table of contents, see *Microsoft Word 2013 Step by Step* by Joan Lambert and Joyce Cox (Microsoft Press, 2013).

Each heading style has an outline level associated with it, which helps give your documents structure. Heading 1 is the highest outline level and Heading 9 is the lowest. This chapter is a good example of a structured document. Each main topic is formatted as Heading 1, and related content, or subtopics, are formatted as Heading 2.

TIP By default, only the Heading 1 and Heading 2 styles are displayed in the Styles gallery. After you apply Heading 2, the Heading 3 style will appear, and so on.

In this exercise, you'll modify paragraph and character formats, apply a style to a document, and modify style formatting.

➡️ SET UP **If the My Rebrand Campaign_C document that you saved in the previous exercise is still open, follow the steps. If you skipped the previous exercise, open the Fabrikam Rebrand Campaign_C document located in the Chapter08 practice file folder to complete this exercise, then follow the steps.**

1   To make the document easier to navigate, on the **View** tab, in the **Show** group, select the **Navigation Pane** check box.

2   In the **Navigation** pane, click **Nature Friendly Products**.

3   Place your cursor in the paragraph with the text **Sustainable products**.

4   On the **Home** tab, in the **Styles** gallery, click **Heading 2**.

5   Apply the **Heading 2** style to the following paragraphs: **Other materials**, **Fixtures and appliances**, and **Miscellaneous**.

KEYBOARD SHORTCUT After applying the first Heading 2 style, place your cursor in the next paragraph that needs the Heading 2 style applied and press F4 to repeat your last action of applying the Heading 2 style.

6   To change the font color and font size for all paragraphs with the **Heading 2** style applied, select **Sustainable products**.

TIP You can select any paragraph that has the Heading 2 style applied.

7   On the **Home** tab, in the **Font** group, click the arrow next to **Font Color**, and from the color palette, select the last color in the top row, **Teal, Accent 6**.

8   Change the font size from **16** points to **14** points.

9   To update all **Heading 2** paragraphs to the new font color and font size, with **Sustainable products** still selected, on the **Home** tab, in the **Styles** gallery, right-click **Heading 2**, and then click **Update Heading 2 to Match Selection**.

TIP Keep in mind that the changes you are making to the styles are limited to this document.

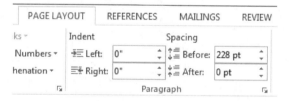

10   Move the cursor to the top of the document.

KEYBOARD SHORTCUT Press Ctrl+Home.

TIP Your cursor should be in the title paragraph, Rebrand Campaign. Because you're making a paragraph formatting change, the title doesn't need to be selected.

11   To center the title, on the **Home** tab, in the **Paragraph** group, click **Center**.

KEYBOARD SHORTCUT Press Ctrl+E.

12   To add formatted space before the first paragraph and to position it vertically on the page, on the **Page Layout** tab, in the **Paragraph** group, change the **Before** spacing to **228** points.

PAGE LAYOUT	REFERENCES	MAILINGS	REVIEW
Indent		Spacing	

ks ▾

Numbers ▾   ≡ Left: 0"   ↕≡ Before: 228 pt

henation ▾   ≡ Right: 0"   ↓≡ After: 0 pt

Paragraph

TIP You can click the up arrow to change the spacing or enter 228 in the text box, and then press the Enter key. You don't need to enter *pts*, because Word will add that for you.

13   In the **Styles** gallery, update the **Title** style to match your current selection.

TIP Repeat step 9 to update the Title style.

14   Scroll through the document and view the formatting changes.

✖ CLEAN UP Save the document as My Rebrand Campaign_D. If you're proceeding to the next exercise, leave the My Rebrand Campaign_D document open. Otherwise, close My Rebrand Campaign_D and exit Word.

You can also add additional formats to text that aren't already included in the style. However, if you have several places that use the same style and need the same format, it's best to modify the style or create a new style instead.

TIP To reset all character formats to only those formats that are included in the style, press Ctrl+Spacebar. To reset paragraph formats only to those included in the style, press Ctrl+Q. If you want to reset text to the document defaults, or the Normal style, on the Home tab, in the Font group, click Clear All Formatting.

Word has over 200 built-in styles that you can use and modify to fit your formatting needs. However, there may be times when you need to create a custom style. The easiest way to do this is to create a new style based on your existing formatting. To do so, add the formatting changes you want to include in your style to your text. Then, on the Home tab, in the Styles group, click the More button in the lower-right corner of the Styles gallery, and then click Create A Style. Then in the Create New Style From Formatting dialog box, name your style and then click OK. The style you created will appear in the Styles gallery for your current document.

SEE ALSO For more information about styles and style management options, see *Microsoft Word 2013 Step by Step* by Joan Lambert and Joyce Cox (Microsoft Press, 2013).

Exploring other paragraph formats

In addition to the basic formatting options on the Home tab in the Paragraph group, Word provides a number of other paragraph formats, which are available in the Paragraph dialog box. To display it, click the dialog box launcher in the Paragraph group.

Here's a list of the additional formats:

- **Outline level** This format is what triggers paragraphs to be displayed in the **Navigation** pane. The heading styles already have an outline level format, but you can use this format for any paragraph.

- **Indentation** You can use the **Increase Indent** and **Decrease Indent** commands in the **Paragraph** group on the **Home** tab for left indents only. If you want to set a right indent or a special indent, such as **First Line** or **Hanging**, you can use the **Paragraph** dialog box or ruler.

  Here are the indent types:

  - **Left Indent** Indents each line of a paragraph on the left.

  - **Right Indent** Indents each line of a paragraph on the right.

  - **First Line** Indents only the first line of a paragraph on the left.

- **Hanging** Indents every line of a paragraph on the left with the exception of the first line. This indent type is typically used for paragraphs with bullets or numbering.

- **Space Before and Space After** Adds formatted space before or after each paragraph. As a general rule, 12 points is around the same size as a line of text formatted with a 12-point font size for most fonts. The default setting for new blank documents is 8 points of space after each paragraph.

   The Don't Add Space Between Paragraphs Of The Same Style option will suppress formatted space both before and after paragraphs that are next to each other and have the same style applied. This option is typically used for lists of information, such as a bulleted or numbered list.

- **Line Spacing** Changes the space between the lines of a paragraph. The default setting for a new blank document is **Multiple**, **1.08** lines.

TIP You can also set left and right indents and change before and after paragraph spacing on the Page Layout tab in the Paragraph group.

Setting indents by using the ruler

To use the ruler to modify text indents, drag the indent markers on the ruler. The indent marker on the left, which looks like an hourglass, has three indents. The top triangle sets a first line indent, the bottom triangle sets a hanging indent, and the box at the bottom sets a left indent. The indent marker on the right changes the right indent only.

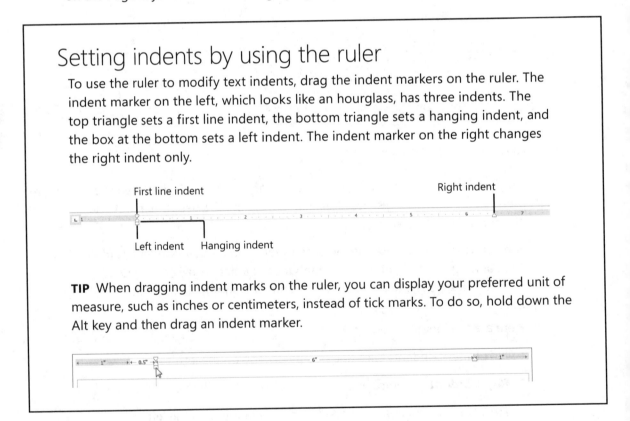

TIP When dragging indent marks on the ruler, you can display your preferred unit of measure, such as inches or centimeters, instead of tick marks. To do so, hold down the Alt key and then drag an indent marker.

TIP To change the unit of measure on the ruler to your preferred setting, click the File tab to display the Backstage view and then click Options. On the Advanced page, in the Display section, from the Show Measurement In Units Of list, select Inches, Centimeters, Millimeters, Points, or Picas.

When a paragraph is indented, the indent markers on the ruler will reflect the indent type and size of the indent for the current paragraph.

No Indent

Video provides a powerful way to help you prove your point. When you click Online Video, you can paste in the embed code for the video you want to add. You can also type a keyword to search online for the video that best fits your document.

Left Indent

To make your document look professionally produced, Word provides header, footer, cover page, and text box designs that complement each other. For example, you can add a matching cover page, header, and sidebar. Click Insert and then choose the elements you want from the different galleries.

Right Indent

Themes and styles also help keep your document coordinated. When you click Design and choose a new Theme, the pictures, charts, and SmartArt graphics change to match your new theme. When you apply styles, your headings change to match the new theme.

First Line Indent

Save time in Word with new buttons that show up where you need them. To change the way a picture fits in your document, click it and a button for layout options appears next to it. When you work on a table, click where you want to add a row or a column, and then click the plus sign.

Hanging Indent

- Reading is easier, too, in the new Reading view. You can collapse parts of the document and focus on the text you want. If you need to stop reading before you reach the end, Word remembers where you left off - even on another device.

Additional paragraph formats on the Line And Page Breaks page of the Paragraph dialog box are covered later in this chapter, in the section titled, "Managing pagination through formatting."

8

Exploring other character formats

Like paragraph formats, additional character formats can be accessed in the Font dialog box, which can be displayed by clicking the dialog box launcher in the Font group.

KEYBOARD SHORTCUT Press Ctrl+D.

Here is a list of those additional formats:

- **Double Strikethrough** Similar to **Strikethrough**, but an additional horizontal line is added in the middle of the text.

- **Small Caps** Displays lowercase characters as uppercase but maintains the lowercase character height.

  KEYBOARD SHORTCUT Press Ctrl+Shift+K.

- **All Caps** All characters appear in uppercase.

  KEYBOARD SHORTCUT Press Ctrl+Shift+A.

- **Hidden** Used to exclude text from printing or appearing on the screen. Additionally, several advanced features use hidden text formatting, such as table of contents and index fields. To display hidden text, click the **Show/Hide ¶** command on the **Home** tab in the **Paragraph** group. The formatting mark for hidden text is a dotted underline.

  KEYBOARD SHORTCUT Press Ctrl+Shift+H.

  This·is·text·with·the·Hidden·format·applied.¶

  TIP To print hidden text, click the File tab to display the Backstage view, and then click Options. On the Display tab, under the Printing options section, select Print Hidden Text.

8

Changing case

You might encounter a situation in which you want to change lowercase text to all caps, all caps to lowercase, mixed-case text to title case, and so on. Instead of making a lot of edits, you can change the case of text in Word as easily as changing the font, by using the Change Case command, located on the Home tab, in the Font group.

TIP Even though it's placed among other formatting commands, the Change Case feature isn't considered formatting, because it actually converts text characters. Keep in mind that formatting only changes the appearance of your text in a document, which may not be preserved if you make other changes, or if your text is pasted into a different application. The All Caps format in the Font dialog box, however, is a format. You may have noticed that the case of the title for the practice file used in this chapter changed to uppercase in the exercise for the section titled, "Setting default document formatting for your documents." This is because the All Caps format is included in the Title style, and the actual case of the text isn't changed.

You can change the case to one of the following options:

- **Sentence case** Capitalizes the first letter of each sentence

- **Lowercase** Converts all characters to lowercase

- **Uppercase** Converts all characters to uppercase

- **Capitalize each word** Capitalizes the first letter of each word, including words that aren't typically capitalized, such as *and*, *the*, and *or*

- **Toggle case** Converts each uppercase letter to lowercase and each lowercase letter to uppercase

KEYBOARD SHORTCUT You can also use Shift+F3 to change the case of text. Unlike with most keyboard shortcuts, each time you press Shift+F3, it will cycle through the Change Case options, which are determined by your text selection. If you select a paragraph or sentence, provided the period or full stop is selected, Shift+F3 will cycle through uppercase, lowercase, and sentence case. If your selection doesn't include a period or full stop, it will cycle through uppercase, lowercase, and capitalizing each word.

Managing pagination through formatting

Pagination is how your document is divided into pages and how your content flows from one page to the next. Word sets page breaks, called *automatic page breaks*, based on the amount of text and other elements, like pictures and charts, that can fit on a page. If you want to change where Word ends a page, you have two options:

- **Manual Page Break** Sets a point where the following content will begin on a new page, similar to a **Next Page** section break. The best practice for using manual page breaks is to add them where you want to always start a new page. For example, you might add a manual page break after a cover page to force content that doesn't belong on the cover page to start on a new page. If you use a manual page break to keep content together on the same page, then this can result in pages with large amounts of white space when your document is opened on another computer. The reason for this is that every printer has a different printable area. For example, some ink jet printers don't print below 0.7 inches on a page, compared to most laser jet printers, which can print to the edge of a page. Because Word takes the printer you're using into account when it paginates a document, where it places an automatic page break may not always be the same.

  To insert a manual page break, on the Insert tab, in the Pages group, click Page Break.

  KEYBOARD SHORTCUT Press Alt+Enter.

8

- **Paragraph pagination options** These pagination options give you the most control over how text flows from one page to the next and are located on the **Line and Page Breaks** page of the **Paragraph** dialog box.

- **Widow/Orphan Control** This option is set by default for all text. It keeps at least two lines of a paragraph on a page. It prevents the last line of a paragraph from being printed by itself at the top of a page or the first line of a paragraph from being displayed by itself at the bottom of a page.

- **Keep with next** Keeps text on the same page as the next paragraph. The built-in **Heading** styles include this option, because you typically don't want a heading to print at the bottom of a page without accompanying text. Another example is if you have text that refers to a picture and you want to keep the picture with the descriptive text.

  You can also use this option to keep table rows together. If you want to keep all rows of a table together on the same page, add this format to every row except the last one.

  SEE ALSO For more information on tables, see Chapter 9, "Presenting information."

- **Page break before** This format is similar to a manual page break. It's added as a paragraph option so it can be included in a style. For example, if each chapter of a book needs to start on a new page, you can add the page break before to the style you're using for the chapter title. This way, each time you use the style, you're also starting a new page.

- **Keep lines together** Keep all lines in a paragraph on the same page. Set this option if you don't want a paragraph to break across two pages.

The formatting mark for all paragraph pagination options is a tiny black square to the left of the first line of the paragraph; it looks similar to a square bullet character.

■ Along·with·our·traditional·vertical·logo,·we've·add·a·new·horizontal·logo.·As·we·are·still·in·the·process·of·rolling·out·our·

new·brand,·please·see·our·team·site·for·guidelines·on·new·logo·usage.·¶

FABRIKAM
¶

Vertical·logo¶

8

In this exercise, you'll add a pagination format to keep a paragraph on the same page as a picture.

 SET UP **If the My Rebrand Campaign_D document you saved in the previous exercise is still open, follow the steps. If you skipped the previous exercise, open the Fabrikam Rebrand Campaign_D document located in the Chapter08 practice file folder to complete this exercise, and then follow the steps.**

1   On page **3**, notice how the top of the page displays a picture and text, and the previous page has the heading, **Brand Colors** and a short introduction paragraph.

Brand Colors

Another set of focus groups were conducted to determine our new colors. These groups were not informed of our company and were given a brief overview of our new international products and services.

Group A   Group B

As expected, the vivid colors in Group A were well received in our East Asian focus groups. But unexpectedly, those in other regions preferred the

2   To move the **Brand Colors** introduction text to the next page, place your cursor in the paragraph below the **Brand Colors** heading.

3   On the **Home** tab, in the **Paragraph** group, click the dialog box launcher to display the **Paragraph** dialog box.

4   On the **Line and Page Breaks** page, select the check box for **Keep with next,** and then click **OK**.

5   Notice how both the **Brand Colors** heading and introduction paragraph were moved to the next page.

Brand Colors

Another set of focus groups were conducted to determine our new colors. These groups were not informed of our company and were given a brief overview of our new international products and services.

Group A

Group B

Group C

Group D

As expected, the vivid colors in Group A were well received in our East Asian focus groups. But unexpectedly, those in other regions preferred the familiar blue and green tones of our old brand colors in Group D. Considering the focus group participants were introduced only to a product

TIP Because the Brand Colors paragraph is formatted with the Heading 1 style, the Keep With Next format has already been applied, and it moves to the next page as well.

✖ CLEAN UP **Save the document as My Rebrand Campaign_final, close it, and exit Word.**

TIP The Chapter08 practice file folder also has a Fabrikam Rebrand Campaign_final document, if you want to compare yours to the completed result.

Key points

- The first set of formats you should change in a document is the document defaults, located on the Design tab.

- Use section breaks to change page formats such as page margins, page orientation, and paper size, in a portion of a document.

- Utilize styles in your documents to help save time when formatting a document, and to help maintain consistent formatting.

- The Change Case command, on the Home tab, in the Font group, converts your text characters.

- The All Caps format in the Font dialog box doesn't convert your text and only makes text characters appear uppercase.

- Use a manual page break only when you always want to start a new page.

- Use paragraph pagination options to control how text flows from one page to the next.

Chapter at a glance

Format

Format simple lists by using bullets or numbering, page 210

Create

Create tabbed lists by using manual tabs, page 213

Convert

Convert tabbed lists to tables and insert new tables, page 217

Convert from this...

First·Name	→	Last·Name·	→	Amount¶
Kim	→	Abercrombie	→	$150¶
Tomasz	→	Mieszkowski	→	$100¶
Cornelius	→	Ang	→	$100¶
Michiyo	→	Sato	→	$50¶

To this...

First Name	Last Name	Amount
Kim	Abercrombie	$150
Tomasz	Mieszkowski	$100
Cornelius	Ang	$100
Michiyo	Sato	$50

Enhance

Enhance tables by using built-in table styles, page 223

First Name	Last Name	Amount
Kim	Abercrombie	$150
Tomasz	Mieszkowski	$100
Cornelius	Ang	$100
Michiyo	Sato	$50

Presenting information

9

IN THIS CHAPTER, YOU WILL LEARN HOW TO

- Format simple lists by using bullets and numbering.
- Create tabbed lists.
- Insert and convert tables.
- Enhance tables.

Most of the time you can use paragraphs of text to convey your information. Other times you may need to present your information in a more structured format, such as in a list or in multiple columns. Or you may use structured elements to make your document easier to follow. For example, if you have a long list of information separated by commas, you can use bullets or numbering to break it down into smaller paragraphs. Or if you have several pieces of related information that you want to keep next to each other on the same line, you can use a tabbed list or a table.

The following provides a description of various ways to present information in a structured format in Microsoft Word.

- **Numbered list** This is a series of paragraphs that begin with a number and are usually formatted with a *hanging indent* so wrapped lines of the paragraph align to the text and not the number. This type of list is typically used for sequential steps when the order is important, such as a set of step-by-step instructions.

- **Bulleted list** This is similar to a numbered list, but each item begins with a symbol instead of a number. Like a numbered list, it's usually formatted with a hanging indent so wrapped lines of the paragraph align to the text and not the bullet. You use a bulleted list when the order of the paragraphs isn't important, such as a list of inventory items or a summary of information.

- **Tabbed list** This is simply columns that are separated by tabs, such as a list of names and addresses.

- **Table** A table is an arrangement of rows and columns typically used for more complex information. Unlike the other list types, tables have more formatting options, such as the ability to add shading to alternating rows or columns. You can also add table column headings that can be set to repeat at the top of a page for long lists of information.

In this chapter, you'll create a simple numbered and bulleted list, and a tabbed list that uses manual tabs. At the end of the chapter, you'll create tables and convert existing text into a table. You'll also enhance tables by using built-in table styles and new border formatting features.

PRACTICE FILES To complete the exercises in this chapter, you need the practice files contained in the Chapter09 practice file folder. For more information, see "Download the practice files" in this book's Introduction.

Formatting simple lists by using bullets and numbering

There are two methods you can use to create a simple list formatted with bullets or numbers:

- **Automatic** Word has an AutoFormat As You Type feature that converts characters you enter into a bulleted or numbered list. For a bulleted list, precede your paragraph text with an asterisk and then press the Spacebar. After the space is added, the asterisk is converted to a bullet character, and then a bulleted list is created. For a numbered list, precede your paragraph text with the number 1 followed by a period or closing parenthesis. As with a bulleted list, a numbered list is created when you press the Spacebar. You can also press Tab after the number and the numbered list will be created when you press Enter.

  TIP To turn off the automatic bullets and numbering feature, or to explore other AutoFormat As You Type options, click the File tab to display the Backstage view, and then click Options. On the Proofing page, click the AutoCorrect Options button and then click the AutoFormat As You Type tab. In the Apply As You Type section, clear the check boxes for Automatic Bulleted Lists and Automatic Numbered Lists.

- **Bullets and Numbering galleries** The Bullets and Numbering galleries are located on the Home tab, in the Paragraph group.

You can use these galleries to format existing selected paragraphs as a bulleted or numbered list, or you can select a bullet or numbering format before you begin creating the list.

When you use either method, Word also formats your text with the built-in List Paragraph style, which adds an indent and suppresses the space between the paragraphs.

SEE ALSO For more information on styles, see Chapter 8, "Formatting documents."

In this exercise, you'll create an automatic numbered list, modify the number format, and then change the numbered list to a bulleted list.

➡ SET UP **You don't need any practice files to complete this exercise. Start Word, create a blank document, and then follow the steps.**

1   On the first line of your document, enter **1)** and press the **Spacebar**.

   TIP If you click the AutoCorrect Options button that's displayed to the left of your numbered list, you can undo the automatic numbering, turn the feature off, or display the AutoFormat As You Type dialog box.

2   Enter **First list item** and then press **Enter** to create list item 2.

3   Next to the second list item, enter **Second list item** and press **Enter**.

4   Create a total of five list items.

   1) First list item
   2) Second list item
   3) Third list item
   4) Fourth list item
   5) Fifth list item

5   After you enter the fifth list item, press **Enter** two times to end the numbered list and
    return to normal text.

    TIP Pressing Enter twice is built-in functionality for ending a numbered or bulleted
    list, and you're not adding an empty paragraph. Within a list, if you place your cursor
    at the beginning of the paragraph, you can press Backspace to remove the number
    or bullet and keep the indent. Pressing Backspace twice will format the paragraph as
    normal text.

6   Select all of your list items, and on the **Home** tab, in the **Paragraph** group, click the
    arrow next to the **Numbering** button, and in the **Numbering Library**, select another
    numbering format, such as one that uses Roman numerals or alpha characters.

7   To change your numbered list to a bulleted list, on the **Home** tab, in the **Paragraph**
    group, click the arrow next to the **Bullets** button, and in the **Bullets Library**, select
    another bullet style, such as a square bullet.

    - First list item
    - Second list item
    - Third list item
    - Fourth list item
    - Fifth list item

❌ CLEAN UP **Close your document without saving changes.**

SEE ALSO For more advanced information on formatting bulleted and numbered lists and
using multilevel lists, see *Microsoft Word 2013 Step by Step* by Joan Lambert and Joyce Cox
(Microsoft Press, 2013).

9

Creating tabbed lists

A tabbed list can be used for a small amount of information that will stay together on the
same page and within a small number of columns. To easily control the position of each
column and align the data in the columns, you set your own tabs, called *manual tab stops*.
When you press the Tab key without first setting a manual tab stop, you move between
default tab stops that are left aligned and occur every 0.5 inches, or 1.27 centimeters.

As demonstrated in the exercise for composing documents in Chapter 7, "Editing and composing documents," you only want to press the Tab key once to align information horizontally. A manual tab stop overrides the default tab stop, enabling you to press the Tab key once to position your data. This functionality also enables you to reposition a column after your data is entered, by moving the tab stop.

There are three tabs for aligning text: left, center, and right. Similar to the text alignment commands, the tabs align text within the columns to the specified type. For example, a center tab will align each item in a column at the center of the tab stop. The manual tab used specifically for numbers is a decimal tab. This tab type aligns numbers to the decimal point position, and the numbers in a table will align to a decimal tab without being preceded by a tab character.

TIP Decimal tabs are preferred over right tabs when aligning numbers, because this setting aligns numbers according to the position of the decimal, or period, even if you're not using decimals. You can also use a decimal tab to align any type of data that contains a period or full stop.

To select a manual tab type, click the tab selector, located at the intersection of the vertical and horizontal ruler. Each time you click the tab selector, you cycle through the different types of tabs. Then, to set a tab, click the ruler at the location where you want the tab to be set. To remove a tab, drag it up or down off the ruler.

Tab selector

TIP The first line and hanging indent markers are also available when you cycle through the tab selector, and you can set those like you do manual tabs. Another tab type is the vertical bar. This tab doesn't position data. Instead, it inserts a vertical bar at the manual tab stop position. To determine the type of tab or indent that's displayed in the tab selector or on the ruler, point to the tab and view the ScreenTip.

In this exercise, you'll set a manual tab stop for existing data and change the position of the tab after it's been set. You'll also set a manual tab to create a memo heading.

 SET UP **You need the List Example document located in the Chapter09 practice file folder to complete this exercise. Open the List Example document, and then follow the steps.**

1   If your ruler isn't displayed, on the **View** tab, in the **Show** group, select the check box for **Ruler**.

2   On the **Home** tab, in the **Paragraph** group, click the **Show/Hide ¶** button to view the formatting marks.

3   Note the single tab between all of the list items and how the amounts don't align correctly. Place your cursor in one of the lines in the list and note the left manual tab stop in the ruler.

   TIP The list doesn't have additional formatted space between the list items. This is because the built-in No Spacing style has been applied to all paragraphs in the list.

4   To set a decimal tab and align the amounts, select the list headings and all employee information.

   TIP To select the list data, place your mouse to the left of the list items, point at the list headings, and then click and drag down through Michiyo Sato's data.

![Screenshot of a Word document showing the ruler and a document titled "EMPLOYEE GIVE PROGRAM UPDATE" with a paragraph of text and a tabbed list of First Name, Last Name, and Amount data including Kim Abercrombie $150, Tomasz Mieszkowski $100, Cornelius Ang $100, and Michiyo Sato $50.]

5   At the intersection of the vertical and horizontal ruler, click the tab selector until a **Decimal Tab** is displayed.

6   On the ruler, click the 5-inch or 13-centimeter mark to set the decimal tab and note how the amounts correctly align.

IMPORTANT Make sure you click on the ruler and not above or below it.

7   To reduce the amount of space between the last names and amounts, with the list selected, drag the decimal tab to the 3.5-inch or 9-centimeter mark.

TIP For precision, hold the Alt key while dragging to view measurements on the ruler instead of the tick marks.

8   To demonstrate how numbers align to the decimal point position, change the first amount in the list to **$150.50**.

9   Press **Ctrl+End** to move your cursor to the end of the document and remove the text selection.

10   To set a manual tab for the memo heading, move the cursor after the word **TO:** near the top of the document.

11   Click the tab selector until a left tab is displayed, and set a left tab at the 1-inch or 2.5-centimeter mark.

12   Press the **Tab** key, enter **All Employees**, and then press **Enter**.

13   Enter **FROM:**, press the **Tab** key, and then enter **Human Resources**.

MEMORANDUM¶

TO: →   All·Employees¶
FROM: →   Human·Resources¶

EMPLOYEE·GIVE·PROGRAM·UPDATE¶

We've·reached·our·six·month·milestone·for·our·newly·created·Dog·Walking·for·Fitness·&·Charity·Program·and·four·
Fabrikam·employees·have·already·logged·over·50·miles·of·dog·walking·and·earned·money·for·the·charity·of·their·
choice.·If·you·see·the·following·people·in·the·hallways·of·your·office·building·today,·be·sure·to·congratulate·them·
for·helping·a·dog,·getting·fit,·and·giving·to·charity!¶

First·Name   →   Last·Name·   →   Amount¶
Kim   →   Abercrombie   → $150.50¶
Tomasz   →   Mieszkowski   → $100¶
Cornelius   →   Ang   → $100¶
Michiyo   →   Sato   → $50¶

❌ CLEAN UP **Turn off the display of formatting marks, save the List Example document as My List Example, and then close the document.**

Inserting tables

A table is a grid-like structure with columns and rows. The intersection of each column and row forms a *cell*, and the data you enter is entered in the cell. You can put almost anything in a cell that you can put in normal document text, and you can format table text the same way you format a paragraph of text. There are several methods you can use to create a table, which are located on the Insert tab, in the Tables group.

- **Table gallery** Creates an empty table using the dimensions you select by clicking the table grid at the intersection of the number of columns and rows you want to use in your table. The inserted table spans the width of the text area with evenly distributed columns and rows.

9

- **Insert Table** For adding additional options to a table before it's created, the Insert Table dialog box enables you to select the number of rows and columns, similar to the Table gallery. But unlike the Table gallery, the Insert Table dialog box allows you to select an AutoFit behavior.

The following provides descriptions for each of the AutoFit options:

- **Fixed Column Width** You can set a default size for each column or use the Auto setting to insert a table that spans the width of the text area with evenly distributed columns and rows.

- **AutoFit to contents** Inserts a table with small columns that resize as you enter your information.

First Name	Last Name	Amount		

- **AutoFit to window** The inserted table initially spans the width of the text area with evenly distributed columns and rows. But unlike in the fixed column width option, column sizes and the table size are based on percentages rather than fixed measurements. If you change the paper size or page orientation, the table will be resized to fit the new text area.

- **Draw Table** For a less structured table that doesn't have uniform columns and rows, you can use the Draw Table command to draw your table in a document. This type of table is good for creating a fill-in-the-blank type of form or for a complex page layout.

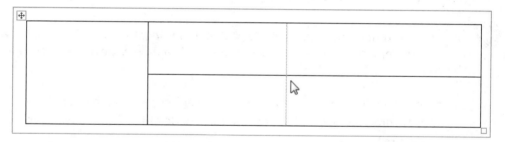

SEE ALSO For more information on using a table for a complex page layout, see the sidebar titled "Using tables to lay out information on a page" at the end of this section.

- **Convert Text to Table** Converts list data that is separated by a divider, such as a tab or comma, to a table. The Convert Text to Table dialog box has the same AutoFit behavior options as the Insert Table dialog box, and it also includes options to identify the character to replace with a table column.

9

Convert Text to Table dialog box

Table size
Number of columns: 4
Number of rows: 5

AutoFit behavior
○ Fixed column width: Auto
● AutoFit to contents
○ AutoFit to window

Separate text at
○ Paragraphs   ○ Commas
● Tabs   ○ Other: -

[OK]   [Cancel]

Convert from this...

First·Name	→	Last·Name·	→	Amount¶
Kim	→	Abercrombie	→	$150¶
Tomasz	→	Mieszkowski	→	$100¶
Cornelius	→	Ang	→	$100¶
Michiyo	→	Sato	→	$50¶

To this...

First Name	Last Name	Amount
Kim	Abercrombie	$150
Tomasz	Mieszkowski	$100
Cornelius	Ang	$100
Michiyo	Sato	$50

In this exercise, you'll convert the tabbed list you created in a previous exercise to a table that will always maintain the same width of the text area, and you'll change the page orientation to gain a better understanding of the AutoFit To Window option. You'll then insert a new table by using the Table gallery.

SET UP **You need the List Example_B document located in the Chapter09 practice file folder to complete this exercise. Open the List Example_B document, and then follow the steps.**

1   Select the list of names, including the headings, and on the ruler, at the 3.5-inch mark, drag the decimal tab off the ruler to delete it. (You'll add it back in another exercise.)

     TIP If you have difficulty deleting the decimal tab, point to the tab and watch for the ScreenTip. After it appears, click the tab and drag it up or down off of the ruler.

2   On the **Insert** tab, in the **Tables** group, click the **Table** button, and then click **Convert Text to Table**.

3   In the **Convert Text to Table** dialog box, note that the number of rows and columns match the tabbed selection, and near the bottom, under **Separate text at**, the **Tabs** option is selected.

4   Click **OK** to convert the tabbed list to a table.

5   To view how the table will be resized to fit your text area, on the **Page Layout** tab, in the **Page Setup** group, click the **Orientation** button, and then click **Landscape**.

FILE | HOME | INSERT | DESIGN | PAGE LAYOUT | REFERENCES | MAILINGS | REVIEW | VIEW

Margins | Orientation | Size | Columns | ⊢ Breaks ▾ | Indent | Spacing | Position | Wrap Text | Bring Forward | Send Backward | Selection Pane
Line Numbers ▾ | ⊞ Left: 0" | Before: 0 pt |
bc Hyphenation ▾ | ⊟ Right: 0" | After: 10 pt

Portrait

Landscape

...IVE PROGRAM UPDATE

We've reached our six month milestone for our newly created Dog Walking for Fitness & Charity Program and four Fabrikam employees have already logged over 50 miles of dog walking and earned money for the charity of their choice. If you see the following people in the hallways of your office building today, be sure to congratulate them for helping a dog, getting fit, and giving to charity!

First Name	Last Name	Amount
Kim	Abercrombie	$150
Tomasz	Mieszkowski	$100
Cornelius	Ang	$100
Michiyo	Sato	$50

6   Change the page orientation back to portrait.

7   To insert a table by using the **Table** gallery, press **Ctrl+End** to move the cursor to the end of the document and press **Enter** twice.

   TIP A paragraph must be added between two separate tables.

8   On the **Insert** tab, in the **Tables** group, click **Table** and then, in the grid, select a 3-column-by-5-row table.

   TIP In the Table gallery, above the grid, a 3 x 5 Table label will appear, and the table will be shown being created in the document as you make your grid selection.

✖ CLEAN UP **Save the document as My List Example. If you're proceeding to the next exercise, leave Word and My List Example open. Otherwise, close the document and exit Word.**

When you create a table, you're not limited to the number of rows and columns you initially selected, and you can resize both the columns and the rows. To add new rows or columns, point to the left of the table between two rows or above the table between two columns. Watch for the on-screen insertion indicator to appear, and then click the indicator to insert a new row or column. When you are inserting new columns, if the width of the table is the same size as the text area, the width of the table columns will be reduced to accommodate the newly added column.

9

TIP You can also use the Table Tools Layout tools tab and the Rows & Columns group to insert new rows and columns.

To change the width of a column or height of a row, point at the right border of the column you want to resize or point to the bottom border of the row you want to resize. Watch for the mouse pointer to change to a sizing pointer, and then drag.

To delete cells, rows, columns, or the entire table, place your cursor in the table element you want to delete. On the Table Tools Layout tool tab, in the Rows & Columns group, click Delete, and then click the command that corresponds with what you want to delete, such as Delete Rows.

TIP To delete multiple cells, rows, or columns, select what you want to delete before clicking your desired delete command.

SEE ALSO For more information on creating tables, such as drawing tables, see *Microsoft Word 2013 Step by Step,* by Joan Lambert and Joyce Cox (Microsoft Press, 2013).

Enhancing tables

When you insert a table, all of the columns and rows are formatted with a 1/2 point border by default. After your table is created, you can modify the border formatting or shade rows and columns. To format a table, place your cursor in the table, and then click the Table Tools Design tool tab.

The following list provides descriptions of the primary tools that are located on the Table Tools Design tool tab:

- **Table Styles gallery** The Table Styles gallery contains preformatted table styles that match your current document theme. To apply a table style, click a style in the gallery.

- **Table Style Options group** The options in the Table Style Options group enable you to turn on or off special formats that are included in most of the table styles. For example, if the first row of your table has text that identifies each column, you can use the Header Row option to format it differently than other rows. The Total Row, First Column, and Last Column options will also add different formatting to the corresponding table element. The Banded Rows and Banded Columns options will format odd and even rows or columns differently. The exact formats that are added by these options will vary depending on the table style you choose. You can select options in this group before you apply a table style, and the gallery will be updated to reflect the formats. You can also turn the table style options on or off after a table style has been applied to modify the table formatting.

  TIP The Total Row is the last row of a table. You typically use Total Row formatting for tables with values. However, if you're not working with values and need to format the last row of a table differently, you can still add Total Row formats.

9

- **Border Styles gallery** The Border Styles gallery provides a collection of border styles that match the current document theme.

When you select a style from the gallery, it turns on the Border Painter, located at the end of the Table Tools Design tool tab, in the Border group. Using the Border Painter is similar to drawing a table, because you *paint* borders by dragging through the borders you want to format.

TIP The Border Sampler command at the bottom of the Border Styles gallery can be used to pick up existing table border formats for the Border Painter, which makes it easy to ensure that you have consistent formatting.

After your table is formatted, you can add additional formats to the contents of a table just like you would do for text and paragraphs, using the Home tab and either the Font or Paragraph group.

In this exercise, you'll format names and amounts in a table that you created in the previous exercise, using the Table Styles gallery, the Table Style options, and the Border Painter.

➡ SET UP **If the My List Example document and Word are still open from the previous exercise, then follow the steps. Otherwise, you need the List Example_C document located in the Chapter09 practice file folder to complete this exercise. Open the List Example_C document, and then follow the steps.**

1   Place your cursor in the table of names and amounts.

2   On the **Table Tools Design** tool tab, in the **Table Styles** gallery, click the third table style, **Plain Table 1**.

3   To remove the bold formatting from the first column, in the **Table Style Options** group, clear the check box for **First Column**.

4   To gain a better understanding of alternating row formatting, in the **Table Style Options** group, clear the check box for **Banded Rows**.

5   Turn the banded row formatting back on.

6   To resize the **Last Name** column, place your mouse pointer on the right border of the column, watch for the sizing pointer, and then drag to the left until it's about 1.27 inches or 3.23 centimeters wide.

TIP Hold the Alt key while you're dragging to display measurements instead of tick marks on the ruler.

7   Resize the **Amount** column so it's about 0.8 inches or 2 centimeters wide.

8   To add the decimal tab back and align the values in the **Amount** column, point to the top edge of the **Amount** column, watch for the column select arrow, and then click to select the entire column.

TIP To select a row, place your mouse in the selection bar, point at the row you want to select, and then click to select the entire row. To select the entire table, click the icon with the multidirectional arrows in the upper-left corner of the table. You can also use the icon to drag a table to another location, so make sure you click, rather than click and drag, when using it to select a table.

9   On the ruler, click the tab selector until a **Decimal Tab** is displayed, and then set a decimal tab near the right end of the **Amount** column.

10   Click anywhere in the document to remove the column selection.

First Name	Last Name	Amount
Kim	Abercrombie	$150
Tomasz	Mieszkowski	$100
Cornelius	Ang	$100
Michiyo	Sato	$50

TIP You don't need to delete the decimal tab prior to converting your text to a table. This step is added to demonstrate how numbers in a table are aligned to a decimal tab without a preceding tab character. To enter a tab in a table, press Ctrl+Tab.

❌ CLEAN UP **Save the document as My List Example_B, and exit Word.**

Using tables to lay out information on a page

Though tables can be used for lists of data, they can also be used for complex layouts, to position information, or to flow paragraphs in parallel side-by-side columns. When tables are used in this manner, columns and rows don't appear in a printed document; all you get is the information. In the document, you can turn the table gridlines on or off while you're working by using the Gridlines button in the Tables group on the Table Tools Layout tool tab. This type of table is called a *borderless table*.

An example of a borderless table is located in the Example Newsletter document included in the Chapter09 practice file folder. The top of the newsletter has a two-column table. It is used to place the newsletter title along with the edition and volume to the right of the company logo. The second column is divided into two rows in order to create a taller cell for the newsletter title, *Employee News*, so more space can be added above and below the title.

To remove border formatting from a table, select the table and on the Table Tools Design tool tab, in the Borders group, click the arrow below Borders, and then in the Borders gallery, click No Border.

Key points

- You can present your information in a more structured format, such as in a list or in multiple columns.

- To create a bulleted list while entering text, enter an asterisk and then press the Spacebar.

- To create a numbered list while entering text, enter the number 1 followed by a period or closing parenthesis and then press the Spacebar.

- You can change a bulleted list to a numbered list by choosing a number format from the Numbering Library, and vice versa.

- A tabbed list is best for small amounts of information that will stay together on the same page and for a small number of columns.

- For lists that may not stay together on the same page or have several columns, use a table instead of a tabbed list.

- You can convert a tabbed list to table.

- The AutoFit To Window option in the Insert Table dialog box will create a table that automatically resizes to the text area if the page orientation or page margins change.

- When you are formatting tables by using built-in table styles, the Table Style Options group on the Table Tools Design tool tab enables you to turn special table formats, such as a header row, on or off.

Chapter at a glance

Correct

Correct proofing errors,
page 230

Inspect

Inspect documents before publishing,
page 233

Create

Create PDF files in Word,
page 239

Print

Print documents,
page 235

Finalizing documents 10

IN THIS CHAPTER, YOU WILL LEARN HOW TO

- Correct proofing errors.

- Inspect documents before publishing.

- Mark documents as final.

- Create PDF files in Word.

- Print documents.

There are two different ways to distribute a final Microsoft Word document: You can print a hard copy of your document or publish it electronically through email, your company network, or on a website. Prior to its delivery, there are a few things you should consider.

First, regardless of how your document will be distributed, you want to ensure there are no proofing errors you haven't already addressed. Second, if you'll deliver your document electronically, you may want to remove personal data and make sure there isn't other information in your document that you don't know about, such as hidden text. Then for an electronic file, you can mark it as a final copy to let others know additional edits shouldn't be made, or deliver it as a PDF file rather than as a Word document. Finally, it's also a good idea to review it in its final format to make sure there are no errors you may have previously missed. Keep in mind that the proofing tools won't catch everything, and you are the best proofreader.

In this chapter, you'll learn how to perform a final proofing check, use the Document Inspector to inspect a document, and remove personal information. You'll also learn how to mark your document as a final copy and create a PDF file that contains navigation bookmarks. At the end of this chapter, you'll learn how to print your entire document, along with how to print a portion of it if you find that certain pages need to be reprinted after your final review.

PRACTICE FILES To complete the exercises in this chapter, you need the practice file contained in the Chapter10 practice file folder. For more information, see "Download the practice files" in this book's Introduction.

Correcting proofing errors

By default, the following types of proofing errors are flagged as you enter text in Word 2013:

- **Spelling errors** A red wavy line is displayed below words that might be misspelled. The red wavy line doesn't necessarily mean that a word is misspelled; it means that the word isn't in a built-in or custom dictionary.

- **Grammar errors** A blue wavy line is displayed below a word, phrase, or sentence that breaks a grammar rule or a frequently confused word, such as *affect* or *effect*. The blue wavy line doesn't always mean that there's an error; as with misspelled words, it's up to you to determine if it's correct.

    TIP In previous versions of Word, grammatical errors are identified with a green wavy line. Additionally, grammar errors may not be identified until you correct spelling errors or complete a sentence by entering a period, or full stop, and pressing the Spacebar key. A blue wavy line under a frequently confused word might also appear as you're typing a sentence and then disappear as you provide more context. Because of this, it's best to correct grammar errors after you've entered the full sentence.

To correct a proofing error as you enter text, you can right-click the word or phrase that has a wavy line underneath it and select an option from the list of available corrections.

If you're like most users, you likely correct spelling and grammar errors as you're composing a document. Even if you may have made corrections while working, as noted at the beginning of this chapter, it's a good idea to perform a final proofing check prior to distribution. A quick way to determine if your document has proofing errors is to view your status bar.

If the Spelling And Grammar Check icon, which looks like a book, displays an X, there are errors in your document. If the icon shows a check mark, then there are no proofing errors.

— Proofing errors

PAGE 1 OF 4   2151 WORDS   — No proofing errors

If your document has proofing errors, you can perform a final proofing check by using one of the following methods:

- On the Review tab, in the Proofing group, click the Spelling & Grammar button.
- Click the Spelling and Grammar Check icon in the status bar.

Either method will display the new Proofing pane, which identifies the type of error and the error itself at the top of the pane. It also provides suggestions and more information to help you make the right correction.

Spelling ▾ ✕

grammer

[Ignore] [Ignore All] [Add]

grammar
grimmer
grammars
rammer
gramper

[Change] [Change All]

grammar ◄))
1. the study of the classes of words, their inflections, and their functions and relations in the sentence
2. the characteristic system of inflections and syntax of a language
3. a grammar textbook
See more...

Powered by: Merriam-Webster

Grammar ▾ ✕

Neither the men or

[Ignore]

Neither the men nor
Either the men or

[Change]

Conjunction Use
Some words work together in pairs, such as "both/and," "either/or," and "neither/nor." It is incorrect to interchange the parts of these different pairs.

• Instead of: You may have both candy or ice cream.
• Consider: You may have both candy and ice cream.
• Or consider: You may have either candy or ice cream.

TIP If the listed suggestions for a spelling error aren't correct or if you don't get any suggestions, edit the word in the document and try to get closer to the correct spelling.

If the error is a spelling error, you can click each suggested alternate word and obtain a definition to help you make the right selection. For grammar errors, suggestions are

10

provided along with details about the error. Most have additional examples for rewording the sentence or phrase to make it grammatically correct. As you correct or ignore the various errors, Word will find the next error and display it in the Proofing pane. You can also click a spelling or grammar error in a document and the Proofing pane results will reflect your current selection.

TIP If you choose to add a correctly spelled word to your dictionary, note that it's added to your custom dictionary only and may appear as a spelling error if the document is opened on someone else's computer.

Additionally, if you often enter words in all caps, a default setting in Word ignores words in uppercase. You may want to change this setting to ensure a more accurate spell check. Another default setting ignores words that contain numbers. If you don't work with a lot of numbers, you may want to change this setting as well. Otherwise, words that may have a number one instead of an *L*, or a zero instead of an *O*, could be missed. To view the available proofing options, click the File tab to display the Backstage view, click Options, and then click Proofing.

Inspecting documents before publishing

If you're publishing your document electronically outside your company—for example, sending it by email, or publishing it on a webpage or as a PDF file—it's a good idea to remove information that's stored with your document in the document properties. The properties of a document can contain personal information, such as the name of the author and other data that may have been added to the document, including document tags. It's also a good idea to make sure your document doesn't contain information that is not visible, such as hidden text or collapsed headings that may be suppressed from view, even if you don't intend to distribute it externally. To view both document properties and a list of items that you may not be aware of, click the File tab to display the Backstage view, and then click Info.

Document properties are listed on the right side of the Info page. A list of items to review before publishing is located under the Inspect Document heading.

TIP To view all document properties, on the right side of the Info page, click Properties and then click Advanced Properties.

Instead of manually scrutinizing your document and deleting information you may not want to share, you can use the Document Inspector to check your document and remove that information for you. To view the Document Inspector, on the Info page, click the Check For Issues button, and then click Inspect Document.

Document Inspector	?	X

To check the document for the selected content, click Inspect.

☑ **Comments, Revisions, Versions, and Annotations**
Inspects the document for comments, versions, revision marks, and ink annotations.

☑ **Document Properties and Personal Information**
Inspects for hidden metadata or personal information saved with the document.

☑ **Task Pane Apps**
Inspects for task pane apps saved in the document.

☑ **Collapsed Headings**
Inspects the document for text that has been collapsed under a heading.

☑ **Custom XML Data**
Inspects for custom XML data stored with this document.

☑ **Headers, Footers, and Watermarks**
Inspects the document for information in headers, footers, and watermarks.

☑ **Invisible Content**
Inspects the document for objects that are not visible because they have been formatted as invisible. This does not include objects that are covered by other objects.

Inspect   Close

When you inspect a document, the Document Inspector doesn't automatically remove document properties or other data. It checks whether the document contains the type of content listed and presents you with the inspection results for each type of check it preforms. You can then choose to remove the data, make corrections in your document, or not change the information after you've determined it's okay to keep.

In this exercise, you'll run the Document Inspector and correct the issues it discovers.

SET UP You need the Newsletter_B document located in the Chapter10 practice file folder to complete this exercise. Open the Newsletter_B document, and then follow the steps.

1   On page **1**, to the left of the **Employee Give Program** heading, click the **Collapse** button.

   TIP You can also right-click the Employee Give Program heading, point to Expand/Collapse, and then click Collapse Heading.

2   Scroll through the document and note the footer, **Fabrikam Employee News** along with the page number, at the bottom of each page.

3   Click the **File** tab to display the **Backstage** view. If the **Info** page is not displayed, click **Info**.

4   Review the document properties on the right side of the **Info** page, such as the title, tags, and author names. Review the list of items to be aware of prior to publishing, below the **Inspect Document** heading.

5   To the left of the **Inspect Document** heading, click the **Check for Issues** button and then click **Inspect Document**.

6   In the **Document Inspector** dialog box, click the **Inspect** button to run it and review
     the inspection results.

7   To the right of **Document Properties and Personal Information**, click the **Remove
     All** button.

8   To the right of **Collapsed Headings**, click the **Remove All** button.

9   Close the **Document Inspector** dialog box without removing additional data.

     TIP Because there is a visible footer at the bottom of each page, you don't want to
     remove it. Additionally, the table of contents in the newsletter creates both custom
     XML data and hidden table of contents fields. The custom XML data can't be re-
     moved, and even though hidden text is reported in the list of items on the Info page,
     because it's associated with the table of contents, it passed the test and the Docu-
     ment Inspector doesn't offer to remove it.

10   On the **Info** page, note that the title, tags, and author names were removed.

11   Click the **Back** arrow to close the **Backstage** view and return to the document.

         KEYBOARD SHORTCUT Press the Esc key to close the Backstage view.

12   View page **1** and note that the **Employee Give Program** heading is now expanded.

❌ CLEAN UP   **Save the document as My Newsletter_B. If you're proceeding to the next exercise, leave the document and Word open. Otherwise, close the document and exit Word.**

The Document Inspector will continue to remove document properties each time you save your document. Other elements, such as headers, footers, or comments, aren't automatically removed, and you'll need to run the Document Inspector again if you make additional editing changes.

To allow Word to start saving document properties after they're removed, on the Info page, below the list of items to be aware of, click the link titled Allow This Information To Be Saved In Your File.

Inspect Document

Check for Issues ▾

Before publishing this file, be aware that it contains:
- Footers
- Characters formatted as hidden text
- Custom XML data
- Content that people with disabilities are unable to read
- A setting that automatically removes properties and personal information when the file is saved

Allow this information to be saved in your file

TIP To review and correct content that people with disabilities are unable to read, such as missing alt text for graphics, you can run the Accessibility Checker. To run it, click the Check For Issues button and then click Check Accessibility.

10

Marking documents as final

If you're publishing a final version of your document and want to make sure additional edits aren't made, you can mark your document as final to let others know they're viewing the final version. To do so, on the Info page, click the Protect Document button, and then click Mark As Final.

Keep in mind that marking a document as final isn't a security option, and other users can still edit the document. After a document has been finalized, an Info bar is displayed at the top of the document. Although it discourages editing, it also includes an Edit Anyway button. If this button is clicked, the Mark As Final option is removed.

Creating PDF files in Word

If you're sharing a final document with others, your document may not look the same as it does on your computer. The recipient may be using a different printer, which can change document pagination, or he or she may be viewing it in Word Web App, or on another device, such as a Microsoft Surface or smartphone. If exact layout and pagination is a concern, you can save your document as a PDF file, which helps prevent layout changes and can be viewed using a number of PDF viewers, such as the new Windows 8 Reader.

IMPORTANT Creating a PDF file doesn't prevent it from being edited. And editing a PDF file is easier now that Word can convert a PDF file into editable content. If you have sensitive documents that need additional protection, you need to use a PDF application that has extra security options to restrict editing, such as Adobe Acrobat Pro, instead of using Word to create your PDF files.

To create a PDF file, click the File tab to display the Backstage view, click Export, and then click the Create PDF/XPS button.

When you publish a document as a PDF file, rather than using a PDF printer to create it, you also have the ability to include additional options. For example, you can use heading styles in the document to create navigation bookmarks when it's viewed in readers such as the Windows 8 Reader or Adobe Reader.

SEE ALSO For more information on heading styles, see Chapter 8, "Formatting documents."

In this exercise, you'll create a PDF document and add navigation bookmarks by using the heading styles.

SET UP **If Word and My Newsletter_B are still open from the previous exercise, then follow the steps. Otherwise, you need the Newsletter_B document located in the Chapter10 practice file folder to complete this exercise. Open the Newsletter_B document, and then follow the steps.**

1 Click the **File** tab to display the **Backstage** view, and then click **Export**.

2 Verify that the **Create PDF/XPS Document** page is selected, and then click the **Create PDF/XPS** button to display the **Publish as PDF or XPS** dialog box.

   TIP You can also double-click Create PDF/XPS Document below the Export heading to display the Publish As PDF Or XPS dialog box.

3 If you prefer to save the PDF in a location other than your Chapter10 practice files folder, navigate to that location. For example, choose your Microsoft SkyDrive, if desired.

4 In the **File Name** text box, enter **My Newsletter_PDF**.

5   Click the **Options** button.

6   In the **Options** dialog box, below **Include non-printing information**, select the check box for **Create bookmarks using** and verify that the **Headings** option is selected.

Options

Page range
- ● All
- ○ Current page
- ○ Selection
- ○ Page(s) From: `1` To: `1`

Publish what
- ● Document
- ○ Document showing markup

Include non-printing information
- ☑ Create bookmarks using:
  - ● Headings
  - ○ Word bookmarks
- ☑ Document properties
- ☑ Document structure tags for accessibility

PDF options
- ☐ ISO 19005-1 compliant (PDF/A)
- ☑ Bitmap text when fonts may not be embedded
- ☐ Encrypt the document with a password

    OK   Cancel

7   Click the **OK** button.

8   In the **Publish as PDF or XPS** dialog box, click the **Publish** button to save the newsletter as a PDF file.

TIP When you publish a document as a PDF file, your Word document remains open and is saved with the original file name. The saved PDF file is not opened in Word.

❌ CLEAN UP **Close My Newsletter_B and exit Word.**

TIP The Export page in the Backstage view also has a Change File Type option for saving your Word documents in other formats files, such as OpenDocument or HTML.

Export

Create PDF/XPS Document

Change File Type

Change File Type

Document File Types

Document (*.docx)
Uses the Word Document format

Word 97-2003 Document (*.doc)
Uses the Word 97-2003 Document format

OpenDocument Text (*.odt)
Uses the OpenDocument Text format

Template (*.dotx)
Starting point for new documents

Other File Types

Plain Text (*.txt)
Contains only the text in your document

Rich Text Format (*.rtf)
Preserves text formatting information

Single File Web Page (*.mht, *.mhtml)
Web page is stored as a single file

Save as Another File Type

Save As

Converting PDF files for editing

A new feature in Word 2013 is PDF Reflow, which converts tables, headers, footers, footnotes, and lists into editable content in Word. You open a PDF file just like you do other Word documents. However, Word doesn't open the original PDF file for editing. Instead, it converts the contents of the PDF file to a Word document. After you make your modifications, you'll need to create the PDF file again by using the steps provided in the "Creating PDF files in Word" section earlier in this chapter.

10

TIP If you want to try this feature, open the My Newsletter_PDF document you created in the previous exercise in Word. If the PDF files are not displayed in the Open dialog box, to the right of the file name near the bottom, click the File Type list and select All Word Documents or PDF files.

Printing documents

To print a document in Word, you click the File tab to display the Backstage view, and then click Print. The Print page displays a full-page print preview along with printing and page layout options.

TIP If you want to send your document directly to your default printer without previewing it first, you can use the Quick Print command. To add the command to your Quick Access Toolbar, click the arrow at the end of your Quick Access Toolbar and then click Quick Print.

10

SEE ALSO For more information on customizing your Quick Access Toolbar, see Chapter 1, "Getting comfortable in Office Home and Student 2013."

In the Printer section, if the printer shown isn't the printer you want to use, click the printer to display a list of additional printers. In the Settings section, there are several options that change your document settings and those that change only how the document will print. The options that will modify your document are page orientation, paper size, and page margins.

The options that will effect only how the document is printed are:

- **Print One-Sided** If your printer can automatically print on both sides of the paper, which is called *duplexing*, then you'll have an option to print on both sides. Otherwise, you'll have a manual option that requires you to reload the paper to print on the other side of the page when prompted.

- **Collated** If you are printing multiple copies of your document, the **Collated** option will print each copy of your document in sequential order. If you want to group each copy of a page together when it prints, select **Uncollated**.

- **1 Page per Sheet** You can change this option to print multiple pages of your document on a single sheet. For example, you may want to print two pages per sheet to proof a draft copy of your document to save paper.

  TIP The 1 Page Per Sheet list also has a Scaling option that will print your document on a different paper size. This option only affects how the document prints and doesn't change the page settings in your document.

Word also allows you to print only a portion of your document; for example, if you want to only print the current page. To choose what part of the document to print, click Print All Pages, directly below the Settings heading, and select another option, such as Print Selection, Print Current Page, or Custom Print.

Most of the options are self-explanatory, such as printing only your selected content in the document or the current page. When you select the Custom Print option, you enter a print range in the Pages text box. To print multiple pages that aren't next to each other, enter each page number separated by a comma, as in *3, 6, 8*. To enter a range of pages, separate the starting page number and ending page number with a hyphen, as in *2-5*.

TIP When you choose an option other than Print All Pages, the document preview to the right will not update to reflect your selection and will still show all pages in your document.

After you've made any needed adjustments, click the Print button at the top of the page to send your document to the printer.

Printing documents with sections

If your document has section breaks, and you want to print a portion of your document, you use the Custom Print option and enter the section and page information.
If you want to print an entire section, enter an *s* followed by the section number. For
example, if you want to print only section 1, you enter *s1*. To enter a specific page in
a section, you enter a *p* followed by the page number and then an *s* followed by the
section number. For example, to print page 4 in section 3, you enter *p4s3*. If you want
additional examples of how to enter pages and sections, point to the information icon
to the right of the Page text box to display the ScreenTip.

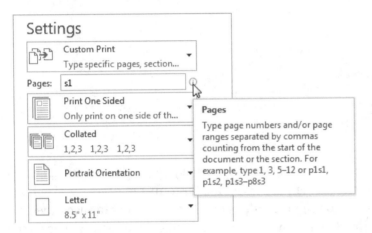

TIP To determine section numbers for your pages, click in the part of the document
you want to print and view the section information in the status bar. If this
information is not displayed, right-click the status bar and in the Customize Status Bar
options, click Section. The page number information should be displayed in the status
bar, by default. If it is not displayed, right-click the status bar and then click Page
Number.

SEE ALSO For more information on working with sections, see Chapter 8.

TIP If your document has heading styles, and you want to print a specific heading and its related content, you can use the Navigation pane to select that portion of your document and set the print options on the Print page in the Backstage view. To do so, in the Navigation Pane, right-click the heading you want to print and then click Print Heading and Content.

10

Key points

- Even if you correct spelling and grammar errors while you're composing your document, you should include a final proofing check prior to finalizing a document.

- To quickly check for proofing errors, view the Spelling And Grammar icon on your status bar. If the icon displays an X, there are still proofing errors in your document.

- You can use the Document Inspector to remove personal information, such as document properties, and check for items you may not be aware of, such as collapsed headings, hidden text, or other data that may not be visible in a document.

- You don't have to remove all items identified by the Document Inspector. Some information may need to be kept, such as headers and footers. Other information can't be removed, such as the custom XML data that is created by the table of contents feature.

- A document that's been marked as final can still be edited.

- If you're creating a PDF file and your document contains headings, you can add navigation bookmarks that can be used in the PDF viewer.

- Creating a PDF file doesn't prevent it from being edited.

- PDF files can be converted into editable content in Word 2013.

- You can print an entire document or print only a portion of it.

Part 3

PowerPoint 2013

11 Getting comfortable in PowerPoint 2013   275

12 Designing and creating presentations   289

13 Creating on-slide content   325

14 Creating Office graphics   357

15 Adding animation and multimedia   387

16 Finalizing and presenting   401

Chapter at a glance

Familiarize

Familiarize yourself with new features,
page 259

Resume

Resume where you left off,
page 261

Welcome back!

Pick up where you left off:

Slide 5
10/08/2012 - 1:36 PM

Add

Add guides to slide masters,
page 262

Getting comfortable in PowerPoint 2013

11

IN THIS CHAPTER, YOU WILL LEARN HOW TO

- Get started working with PowerPoint 2013.

- Explore the PowerPoint 2013 tools.

- Discover the new features in PowerPoint 2013.

Microsoft PowerPoint is arguably the world's most common presentation tool, and PowerPoint 2013 makes it even easier to create and deliver presentations than ever before. Better integration with the cloud and Internet means that accessing online content is more streamlined, and online storing, sharing, and collaboration tools are front-and-center features.

In this chapter, you'll explore the PowerPoint 2013 interface and work with new and improved features.

Getting started working with PowerPoint 2013

As with Microsoft Word and Excel, you typically start PowerPoint 2013 from the Start screen in Windows 8 (not the Start screen in PowerPoint) or the Start menu in Windows 7. You can also start PowerPoint 2013 and open a file at the same time by opening a presentation from an email attachment or by double-clicking one from a place like your Windows Desktop.

Regardless of how you open or start a presentation, before too long, you will more than likely create and edit slides in the PowerPoint workspace interface, which is also known as Normal view.

Collapse ribbon

Window controls

Title placeholder   Dialog box launcher

File tab   Quick Access Toolbar   Group   Ribbon   Gallery   More button

Slides pane   Status bar   Footer placeholders   Notes pane   View shortcuts
and slide   (date, footer text, and   Comments pane   Zoom slider
thumbnails   slide number)   Content placeholder   Fit slide to current window

- **Ribbon** The ribbon is the main component of the PowerPoint interface. It's where you'll find most of the tools for working with your presentations. The ribbon contains task-oriented tabs, and each tab has groups of related commands. For example, on the Home tab, the Clipboard group contains commands for copying and pasting information in your files. Groups that have additional commands that aren't shown on the ribbon have a Dialog Box Launcher. Clicking the Dialog Box Launcher will display a task pane or dialog box with options that are related to the group. For example, if you click the Dialog Box Launcher for the Font group, the Font dialog box will be displayed, giving you more formatting choices, such as Small Caps, Superscript, and Subscript.

- Also note the More button, which is found on most galleries. Clicking the More button expands a gallery and displays all of its options at once. (Alternatively, you can use the up and down arrows immediately above the More button to scroll through the gallery line by line.)

> **IMPORTANT** The screen shots of the ribbon and interface were captured with a screen resolution of 1280x800. If your display settings are different, the screen shots of the ribbon will appear differently on your screen due to its dynamic capabilities. For example, buttons may appear stacked vertically instead of horizontally. If you experience these differences, you can either adapt the exercise instructions to your screen or modify your display settings to match those in this book.

SEE ALSO For instructions on how to modify your display settings and adapt exercise instructions, see Chapter 1, "Getting comfortable in Office Home and Student 2013."

- **File tab** This is the first tab on the ribbon. Unlike other ribbon tabs, the File tab displays the Backstage view where commands for working with the entire contents of a document, such as Save As, Print, Share, and Export, are located. The Backstage view is also where application options are located and where you can find information about your user account and your version of Microsoft Office.

- **Quick Access Toolbar** This toolbar holds your most frequently used commands. By default, Save, Undo, Redo, and Start Slide Show have already been added.

  TIP To quickly add other commands to your Quick Access Toolbar, right-click a command on the ribbon, and then click Add To Quick Access Toolbar. To remove a command from the Quick Access Toolbar, right-click the command you wish to remove and then click Remove From Quick Access Toolbar. Opting to show the Quick Access Toolbar below the ribbon gives you more room for tools and puts them closer to your workspace.

- **Title bar** The title bar appears at the top of the window and displays the name of the active document, along with the application name. If you're working with a presentation that hasn't been saved, the title bar will display a name such as *Presentation3 - PowerPoint*. After the file has been saved, the title bar will reflect the name of the saved file.

11

- **Window Controls** These display at the right end of the title bar. Along with the name of the account you signed into Office with, there are standard Minimize, Restore Down/Maximize, and Close buttons, as well as the Help and Ribbon Display Options.

- **Collapse ribbon** To collapse the ribbon, click the button on the right end of the ribbon. Double-click any tab (except the File tab) to restore the ribbon.

- **Status bar** This appears at the bottom of the window and displays information about the current presentation, such as the number of slides. You can also open the Notes and Comments panes from here. The right end of the status bar has view options for switching your presentation to a different view, along with a zoom slider to change the magnification of your active document and a button that resizes your slide to fit the available workspace.

- **Slides pane** This pane appears at the left of the window and lets you access any slides in the presentation. Click a thumbnail to select a slide, and it will appear in the main workspace so you can edit it.

- **Notes pane** Click this button to open a pane where you can enter notes. These notes will be available to you in Presenter view, but will not be displayed for the audience to see.

- **Placeholders** Placeholders are preformatted content holders. PowerPoint has placeholders for slide titles, for subtitles, and for content such as text, pictures, tables, charts, SmartArt graphics, and video.

Exploring the PowerPoint 2013 tools

The Home tab in PowerPoint contains most of the tools you'd use to create a quick, basic presentation. You'll find the same Clipboard tools here that you'll find in Word, Excel, and Publisher, along with font and paragraph formatting tools.

In addition, the Home tab has drawing tools that include the Shapes gallery, Arrange tools (for alignment, ordering, and so on), and object formatting tools. Find, Replace, and Selection tools are at the end of this tab. When in doubt, head to the Home tab.

If a button is unavailable and appears to be grayed out, then try selecting an object that can use that command. For example, in order for the buttons in the Font group on the Home tab to be available, you need to select a text box or shape on a slide.

Don't forget about the ability to right-click. You might find tools you didn't even know existed. For example, on the Design tab, right-click one of the themes in the gallery, and you'll notice that an option will appear that allows you to set that theme as your default theme.

11

Access the formatting panes quickly and easily by right-clicking an object. For example, right-click a shape and choose Format Shape to open the Format Shape pane.

The best thing you can do to become quicker and more proficient with PowerPoint 2013 is to set up your Quick Access Toolbar. You can right-click any command on the ribbon and add it to the Quick Access Toolbar. You can also right-click the Quick Access Toolbar itself and choose Customize Quick Access Toolbar to add tools that are not available on the ribbon and to apply other customizations.

SEE ALSO For more step-by-step instructions on customizing your Quick Access Toolbar, see Chapter 1.

Discovering the new features in PowerPoint 2013

This section introduces you to key application features for PowerPoint 2013, offering screen shots where applicable. Many of the features included are discussed in detail along with step-by-step instructions throughout this part of the book.

- **16:9 slide size default** New presentations are automatically created with a 16:9 aspect ratio for widescreen monitors and displays. And the new scaling options help you convert a widescreen slide size (16:9) to a standard slide size (4:3).

- **Presenter view** The redesigned look of Presenter view makes it easier to determine exactly what the audience sees. And you can now rehearse your presentation in Presenter view without the need for two monitors.

- **Navigation grid** The new navigation grid in Slide Show view displays thumbnail views of your slides so you can jump to the slide you need faster.

- **Slide Show zoom** Now you can call attention to specific details during your presentation by zooming in on a portion of your slide.

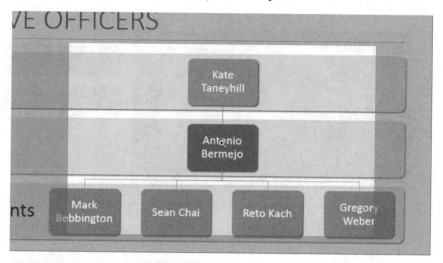

- **Slide Show pop-up toolbar** The new pop-up toolbar in Slide Show view gives you more tools for presenting.

- **New Transitions** New transitions include Page Curl and Peel Off.

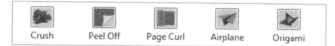

- **Resume Reading** When you close a presentation, PowerPoint automatically creates a bookmark for your last position. When you reopen the presentation, you can pick up right where you left off.

Welcome back!
Pick up where you left off:

Slide 5
10/08/2012 - 1:36 PM

11

- **Theme variants** New themes for PowerPoint now include variants to give you more color choices for a specified theme.

- **Master and slide layout guides** Now you can set guides on slide masters and layouts so you won't accidently move them when you're working on slides. For the guides you want to move, you can still add those to individual slides.

- **Eyedroppers** Select fill, outline, and glow colors for text and shapes and apply them to others. Use colors from within your presentation or from any color that appears on your screen. You can also use the Eyedropper to add a color wash to pictures.

- **Improved motion paths** When you add or edit a motion path, a subdued view of your object will appear at the endpoint so you can visually see where the object will begin and end.

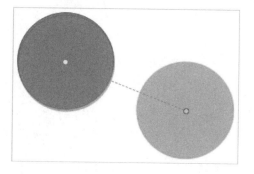

- **Fragment shapes** Use the new Fragment tool to break up overlapping shapes into new separate shapes.

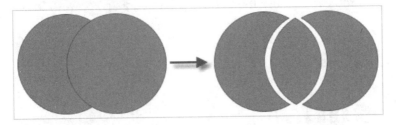

- **Smart Guides for equal distance** Smart Guides now appear when shapes are placed an equal distance from each other.

- **Threaded comments** When multiple people review a presentation, they can now reply to each other's comments. And the new Comments pane makes it easier to keep track of those conversations.

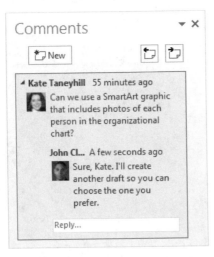

Key points

- Setting up your Quick Access Toolbar helps you work more quickly.

- The PowerPoint interface will change depending on your log-in status and your screen resolution.

- PowerPoint 2013 introduces a number of new tools for presenters: enhanced Presenter view, a navigation grid, a newly designed pop-up toolbar, and slide show zoom.

11

Chapter at a glance

Create

Create a new presentation,
page 268

Customize

Change theme colors,
page 271

Add

Add graphics to the slide master,
page 288

Create

Create a custom layout,
page 291

Designing and creating presentations

12

IN THIS CHAPTER, YOU WILL LEARN HOW TO

- Create a new presentation based on a theme or template.

- Apply a theme to an existing presentation.

- Customize your file with colors, fonts, and effects.

- Apply theme effects to your presentation.

- Add graphics to the slide master and layouts.

- Create a custom slide layout.

- Change your presentation from a 16:9 to a 4:3 format.

Microsoft PowerPoint is such a popular tool because it is practically synonymous with presentations. Used thoughtfully, it is a great program for producing clear, professional presentations to share ideas and concepts with an audience.

Creating an effective PowerPoint presentation is mostly a matter of form following function. You don't want the available features to overwhelm the content of your presentation. For that reason, when you are planning a presentation, it's best to work on the content before you bring PowerPoint and all its bells and whistles into the mix.

There are a number of recommendations for ways of doing this—jot ideas on sticky notes and rearrange them into blocks of content, create an outline in Microsoft Word, or even scribble thoughts on the back of a napkin. Regardless of how you do it, the goal is to concentrate on the content before you worry about how things look.

With that said, Microsoft Office themes and PowerPoint templates give you a lot of power and flexibility so you don't have to worry so much about how things look as you're creating your content. A good theme or template can help make that happen, because nearly everything in a presentation is affected by one or more theme elements.

In this chapter, you'll start creating a presentation based on a variant of an existing theme, and then you'll tweak the layout to better suit your needs. You'll learn how to change colors and font themes as well as create your own customized layout. You'll also learn how to add graphics to a slide master.

PRACTICE FILES To complete the exercises in this chapter, you need the practice files contained in the Chapter12 practice file folder. For more information, see "Download the practice files" in this book's Introduction.

Creating a new presentation based on a theme or template

Like all the other Office Home and Student 2013 applications, PowerPoint uses the new Start user interface, complete with a thumbnail gallery and dynamic previews of available themes. The themes that appear might vary a bit depending upon whether you're signed into Office. Either way, PowerPoint 2013 takes the theme preview concept a step further—each theme now has variations where the fonts or colors have been changed. These are called variants, and they're displayed in the preview windows. You can select a variant to quickly change the look and feel of a theme or template.

In this exercise, you'll start a new presentation based on a theme variant.

➡ SET UP **You don't need any practice files to complete this exercise. Just start PowerPoint and follow the steps.**

1   On the PowerPoint **Start** screen, click the **Retrospect** theme thumbnail to open the **Preview** window.

   TIP If you've already moved past PowerPoint's Start screen, you can click the File tab and then click New to return to the Start screen.

2   In the **Preview** window, click the blue variant.

3   Click the arrows next to **More Images** to view how the blue variant looks on some sample content.

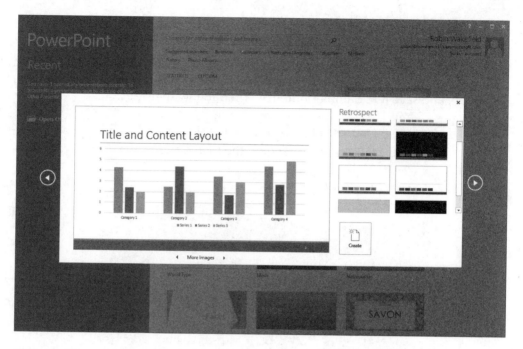

4   Click **Create** to create a new presentation based on the blue variant of the **Retrospect** theme.

❌ CLEAN UP **Save the presentation if you want, and then close it.**

SEE ALSO For more information about the Start screen, see Chapter 1, "Getting comfortable in Office Home and Student 2013." For more information about themes and templates, see Chapter 2, "Using shared Office features." For more information about signing into Office, see Chapter 3, "Sharing and collaborating: getting more from the cloud."

Applying a theme to an existing presentation

12

You won't always start from scratch when creating a presentation. In fact, you'll often begin with a presentation you've already done. That's not a problem, because you can apply a theme and its variants to your slides from the Design tab in PowerPoint. You can even right-click the thumbnails in the Themes and Variants galleries to apply them to specific slides in the presentation.

In this exercise, you'll apply a theme and a variant to an existing presentation.

➡️ SET UP **You need the SampleContentA_start presentation located in the Chapter12 practice file folder to complete this exercise. Open the SampleContentA_start presentation, and save it as SampleContentA. Then follow the steps.**

1   In the slide thumbnails pane on the left side of the PowerPoint workspace, click slide **2** so you can view how changing the theme affects the sample content.

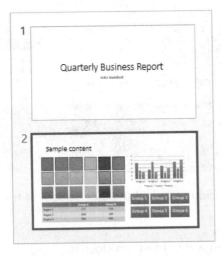

2   Click the **Design** tab, and then in the **Themes** gallery, click the **Retrospect** theme to apply it to the presentation.

Design tab

Blue variant

Retrospect theme

More button

TIP You can scroll through the Themes and Variants galleries by using the arrows on the right, or you can click the More button to expand the gallery.

TIP The theme name will appear in a ScreenTip when you point to a thumbnail in the gallery.

3   In the **Variants** gallery, click the blue variant to apply it to all slides in the presentation.

4   Select the title slide (slide **1**) in the slide thumbnails pane.

5   In the **Variants** gallery, right-click the gray variant and choose **Apply to Selected Slides** to apply this variant to the title slide only.

TIP If you want to apply a theme to multiple slides (but not to the entire presentation), select those slides in the thumbnails pane first.

6   Click the blue variant again to reapply the color change to the title slide.

KEYBOARD SHORTCUT Press Ctrl+Z to undo the previous action.

✖ CLEAN UP Save the SampleContentA presentation and then close it.

TIP If you don't find the theme or template you want to apply, click the More button to expand the Themes gallery and then choose Browse For Themes. Even though it specifies "themes" there, both themes and templates are displayed in the folders.

Customizing your file with colors, fonts, and effects

Every theme, even the blank Office theme, has a set of colors, fonts, and effects built in. And since every template is based on a theme, the colors, fonts, and effects are also built into every template. Of course, because every PowerPoint file is based on a template or a theme, the colors, fonts, and effects sets are built into every presentation as well.

As shown in the two previous exercises, applying a theme to a presentation can completely change its appearance. This is because the slide master and layouts are part of the theme, and they affect how the content is positioned on the slides. You'll learn more about this in upcoming exercises.

For now, it's most important for you to know that you don't have to apply an entire theme (the full set of colors, fonts, effects, and slide layouts) to a presentation. You can change the look and feel of a presentation at any time by simply applying different theme colors, fonts, or effects.

12

Theme fonts

You'll find the theme fonts that are used in a presentation listed on the Home tab in the Font gallery. Click into any text on a slide, and then on the Home tab, click the arrow to open the Fonts list. At the top of the Fonts list are the theme fonts that are used in the presentation.

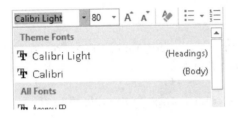

Heading fonts are generally applied to titles and subtitles, whereas the Body font is used for most other text.

You can choose a different theme font set from the Theme Font gallery by expanding the Variants gallery on the Design tab of the ribbon. If you don't find a font set you like, you can create your own there as well.

TIP You can also access theme colors, fonts, effects, and background styles from Slide Master view, but it's usually faster to access these galleries by expanding the theme Variants gallery on the Design tab. To access Slide Master view, click the View tab, and then the Slide Master button.

TIP Click the More button on the Variants gallery to expand it.

Theme colors

You'll find theme colors in almost every option that has anything to do with color. They show up in all formatting galleries—Shape Styles, Tables, Charts, SmartArt, and Pictures—as well as in the fill and outline colors for shapes, lines, and fonts.

Theme color sets consist of 12 colors: two light/dark combinations, six accent colors, and a hyperlink and a followed hyperlink, although the hyperlink and followed hyperlink colors don't actually show in any of the galleries. The full palette is derived from tints and shades of the theme colors.

12

The two light and dark combinations are generally used for text and slide background colors. They're designed to work together. If you change your slide background style from white to black, for example, any text that was black will turn white so it will be visible on the black background. SmartArt, tables, and charts all rely on dark/light combinations for their font colors as well.

Text color changes to
contrast with background

Text color changes to
contrast with background

The accent colors are used for everything else. You'll find these on every color gallery throughout the PowerPoint interface—Shape Styles, Table Styles, Chart Styles, SmartArt Styles, fill, line, and font colors, and more.

When you are applying a theme color to an object (or when PowerPoint applies it for you), that color is really just referencing a position in the theme color gallery. For example, if you fill a square shape with Accent 2 (which happens to be orange in the default Office theme), and you change themes, your orange shape will become whatever color the new theme uses for Accent 2. Think about how the colors changed in the SampleContentA file when you changed from Retrospect with its brown and yellow colors to the blue variant; that is a color theme in action.

You can choose a new theme color set from the Colors gallery that's accessed by expanding the Variants gallery. If you don't find a color set that you like, you can create your own set of theme colors.

Using absolute colors

Sometimes a red is just a red, and you don't have one in your theme colors. No problem! You can always use colors that aren't part of your theme. These colors are known as *absolute colors*, and they won't change when you change theme colors.

To access non-theme colors, choose one of the standard colors or click More Colors on any color gallery. For example, if you're using the Fill color gallery, click More Fill Colors. If you're using the Outline color gallery, choose More Outline Colors.

This opens the familiar honeycomb where you can choose from one of the standard colors, or you can insert your own RGB (red, green, blue) or HSL (hue, saturation, luminosity) values on the Custom tab.

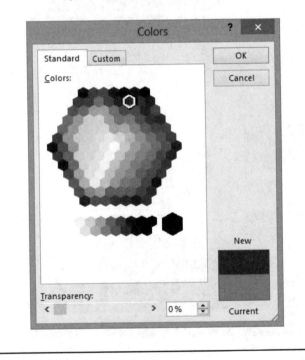

Applying theme effects to your presentation

Theme effects are things like default shadows and gradients or other fill styles that are built into a theme. You can view different theme effects in action by expanding the Variants gallery and pointing to the various sets of effects to view how they affect and change your slides. Some of the theme effects, like the default Office theme, will be fairly subtle. Others, like Grunge or Milk Glass, will have textured fills or extreme gradients and shadows.

SEE ALSO For an overview of how themes work, see Chapter 1.

In this exercise, you'll apply new theme fonts and effects to an existing presentation. You'll also customize and apply a new theme color set to the presentation.

➡ SET UP **You need the SampleContentB_start presentation located in the Chapter12 practice file folder to complete this exercise. Open the SampleContentB_start presentation, and save it as SampleContentB. Then follow the steps.**

1   With slide **2** selected (to demonstrate how changing theme effects, colors, and fonts affects the sample content), expand the **Variants** gallery on the **Design** tab and click **Fonts** to open the **Theme Fonts** gallery. Scroll through the theme font sets to display a live preview of their effect on the fonts in the presentation.

2   Click the **Franklin Gothic** theme font set. This applies the **Heading font, Franklin Gothic Medium**, to slide titles and subtitles, and the **Body font, Franklin Gothic**, to all other text.

   TIP To create your own theme font set, click Customize Fonts at the bottom of the Theme Fonts gallery.

3   Expand the **Variants** gallery again and click **Colors**. Scroll through the **Theme Colors** gallery to view how the different theme color sets would affect your presentation.

12

4   Click **Customize Colors** at the bottom of the **Theme Colors** gallery.

5   Click **Accent 6**, and then click the **More Colors** option.

6　On the **Custom** tab, enter **122** for **Red**, **188** for **Green**, and **50** for **Blue**, and then click **OK** to close the **Colors** dialog box.

7　Click the **Hyperlink** color swatch, and then click **Turquoise, Accent 3** in the **Theme Colors** palette.

TIP When you point to each color swatch in the Theme Colors palette, the name of the color will appear in a ScreenTip.

12

TIP The Hyperlink color is automatically applied to hyperlinked text. The Followed Hyperlink color will only be displayed in the Slide Show view after a hyperlink has been clicked. These colors will not be shown in the color galleries, so you won't be able to choose them for other objects.

8   Click the **Followed Hyperlink** color swatch and change it to a shade of gray by selecting a tint or shade of black or white in the **Theme Colors** palette.

9   Name your new **Theme Colors** set by entering **Fabrikam** in the **Name** box.

10 Click **Save** to save and apply the new theme colors.

TIP If you want to edit or delete a custom color theme, you can expand the Variants gallery and right-click the color set in the Theme Colors gallery.

11 Expand the **Variants** gallery and click **Effects**. Point to the different theme effects sets to see how they will affect your content.

12 Click **Office** to apply the **Office Home and Student 2013** theme effects to your file.

TIP Although you can customize theme fonts and colors, you cannot customize Theme Effects sets from within PowerPoint.

⊗ CLEAN UP Save the SampleContentB presentation, and then close it.

Applying background styles to your presentation

Every theme includes a set of background styles, which are also accessed by expanding the Variants gallery on the Design tab.

These background styles work with the text and background color combinations (the first four color swatches) in your color theme to ensure that text is always visible. That's why it's important to make sure those dark and light text and background colors have enough contrast when you're creating a custom color theme. It's also generally a good idea to choose your text colors from those background and text colors, because then the text color will be updated when you change the slide background style or paste the slide into a new presentation.

12

TIP In the Create New Theme Colors dialog box, the first four theme colors are called Text/Background Dark 1, Text/Background Light 1, Text/Background Dark 2 and Text/Background Light 2. In the ScreenTips that appear when you point to a color in the various color galleries in PowerPoint, they're called Background 1, Text 1, Background 2, and Text 2.

In this exercise, you'll apply new theme background styles to view how they affect font colors and visibility.

 SET UP **You need the SampleContentC_start presentation located in the Chapter12 practice file folder to complete this exercise. Open the SampleContentC_start presentation, and save it as SampleContentC. Then follow the steps.**

1 Expand the **Variants** gallery on the **Design** tab and click **Background Styles**. Notice that the slide uses the white background style.

2 Point to the lower-right thumbnail in the **Background Styles** gallery. (The ScreenTip will say **Style 12**). Click to apply this dark background to all slides. Black text that wouldn't be visible on the dark background changes to white.

3 Open the **Background Styles** gallery again and click **Style 5** (first column, second row) to apply a subtle light gradient to all slides.

4 With slide **1** selected, open the **Background Styles** gallery again, right-click **Style 12**, and choose **Apply to Selected Slides** to give the title slide a more dramatic look.

CLEAN UP **Save the SampleContentC presentation, and then close it.**

TROUBLESHOOTING If your text disappears when you copy a slide from a dark presentation to a light one or vice-versa, make sure the slide background style is selected, and make sure the text uses a contrasting text or background color.

Formatting placeholders on the slide master

Many people don't realize that the PowerPoint slide master and layout features give you a lot of control over the look of your slides. You can add graphics and images to the master, and you can format the placeholders on the master as well. These settings trickle down to the individual layouts, which provide combinations of placeholders to help you create content for your slides.

Placeholders are preformatted content containers. When you apply formatting to them on the slide masters and layouts, then any content that's created in a placeholder on a regular slide will inherit those settings.

Although PowerPoint provides you with a set of layouts built into each theme, template, and presentation, you can still create your own custom layout that has exactly the placeholders and graphics you need.

Most formatting that can be applied to shapes can be applied to placeholders as well, but the most common way to format a placeholder is to format the settings that are specific to the text; for example, the font color and size, paragraph settings, and bullet points.

TIP Text formatting can be applied to any text in your presentation, but it's best to apply these settings to the placeholders on the slide master and layouts to create consistency throughout your slides. You can always apply manual formatting to override the placeholder, if necessary.

Text formatting, such as bold, italics, and underlines, is probably obvious to most PowerPoint users, but you might not think of PowerPoint as having "paragraphs," and you'd be right! A PowerPoint paragraph is the text that's included in a bullet point. You can have up to nine levels of text in a presentation (although this is definitely not recommended), but PowerPoint shows only five by default in Slide Master view. You'll want to specify common paragraph settings, such as line spacing and the indentation size for each paragraph level of text.

SEE ALSO For more about formatting text, see Chapter 13, "Creating on-slide content."

12

In this exercise, you'll format placeholders on the slide master and layouts.

SET UP You need the SampleContentD_start presentation located in the Chapter12 practice file folder to complete this exercise. Open the SampleContentD_start presentation, and save it as SampleContentD. Then follow the steps.

1   Click the **View** tab, then **Slide Master** to open Slide Master view. Scroll to the top of the **Slides** pane and click the large **Slide Master** thumbnail.

2   Select the **Title** placeholder (the one that says, **Click to edit Master title style**) by clicking its edge.

TIP If you're having trouble selecting a placeholder, click inside the text area, and then press the Esc key on your keyboard.

Body placeholder   Title placeholder

Click to edit Master title style

Click to edit Master text styles
- Second level
  - Third level
    - Fourth level
      - Fifth level

12/27/2012   FOOTER

3   Click the **Home** tab and then click the **Font Size** drop-down list. Click the **Decrease Font Size** button twice to apply a smaller font size to the title placeholder.

KEYBOARD SHORTCUT Press Ctrl+Shift+< to decrease font size.

TIP You can apply a different font size by clicking the arrow next to the Font Size box on the Home tab and selecting from the list. Or you can enter a number directly into the Font Size box. To apply your new font size, press the Enter key after you enter the number.

4   Select the **Body** placeholder (the one with five levels of bulleted text). On the **Home** tab, click the **Increase Font Size** button once to increase the size for all levels of text in the placeholder.

KEYBOARD SHORTCUT Press Ctrl+Shift+> to increase font size.

12

5   Click in the top level of text in the **Body** placeholder. On the **Home** tab, expand the **Bullets** gallery by clicking the arrow next to the **Bullets** button. Choose **Filled Round Bullets** to add a bullet to the top level of text.

TIP If you need to change the color or size of the bullet symbol, expand the Bullets gallery, click Bullets And Numbering, and change the color and size there. You can also click Customize to choose a different symbol or even a picture.

6   To adjust the positioning of the bullet, first turn on the ruler by selecting the **Ruler** option on the **View** tab.

7   With your cursor still in the top line of text, on the ruler, click and drag the upward-pointing indent marker to adjust the space between the bullet point and the text.

TIP Press the Ctrl key for finer control over the indent markers on the ruler.

8   With your cursor still in the top level of text, click the **Paragraph** dialog box launcher on the **Home** tab to adjust the line spacing between first-level paragraphs of bulleted text.

Dialog box launcher

12

9   In the **Paragraph** dialog box, increase the **Before** spacing from **12 pt** to **18 pt**, and click **OK** to close the dialog box.

Paragraph

Indents and Spacing

General

Alignment: Left

Indentation

Before text: 0.25"   Special: Hanging   By: 0.25"

Spacing

Before: 18 pt   Line Spacing: Multiple   At 0.9

After: 2 pt

Tabs...   OK   Cancel

TIP Before and After spacing refers to the space before and after the paragraph levels of the bulleted text. Line spacing refers to the space within a level of text. Click the Line Spacing box and select Single for single-spaced text. Use Multiple at .9 for line spacing that is 90% as tall as single-spaced text. Going below about .7 will cut off the ascenders and descenders of letters on many fonts.

10   Click the **Title Slide** layout directly below the **Slide Master**. Select the **Title** placeholder and change the font size to **66 pt**.

11   Review the slide layouts to confirm that the bullet has been added to all top-level text and the spacing has been adjusted according to the changes you made on the master.

✖ CLEAN UP **Save the SampleContentD presentation, and then close it.**

Adding graphics to the slide master and layouts

In this exercise, you'll add graphics to the slide master and layouts.

SET UP You need the SampleContentE_start presentation and the Fabrikam_Logo_Large.png and Fabrikam_White_Small.png images located in the Chapter12 practice file folder to complete this exercise. Open the SampleContentE_start presentation, and save it as SampleContentE. Then follow the steps.

1   On the **View** tab, click **Slide Master** to open Slide Master view.

2   With the **Slide Master** selected, on the **Insert** tab, click **Pictures**. Navigate to the **Fabrikam_White_Small.png** file and click **Insert**.

3   Select the **Fabrikam** logo in the center of the **Slide Master** and then click the **Picture Tools Format** tab. In the **Size** group, enter **2** in the **Width** box and press **Enter**. The logo height will change proportionately.

   TIP You can drag a corner of a picture (or other object) to resize it. Press Shift while you drag to be sure the picture or object doesn't stretch out of proportion.

4   Drag the logo to the lower-right corner of the slide. Pay attention to the PowerPoint Smart Guides. They will help you align the logo vertically and horizontally to the footer placeholders that hold dates, page numbers, and footer text. Place the logo so its left edge is in the same position as the left edge of the slide number placeholder. It should also align vertically with the center of the slide number placeholder.

Smart guides

5   Select the slide number placeholder. Press **Shift** and drag the placeholder to the left so it's no longer behind the logo.

   TIP Use the tools on the status bar to zoom in while you're positioning the logo and moving the slide number placeholder. Click the Fit Slide To Current Window button to return to the normal zoom status.

12

6   Select the **Title Slide** layout (the first layout beneath the slide master). Right-click away from the slide and choose **Format Background**.

       TIP Point to a layout in the Layouts pane, and its name will appear in a ScreenTip.

7   In the **Format Background** pane, clear the **Hide Background Graphics** check box to unhide the graphics that the layout has inherited from the **Slide Master**. The thin gray line inherited from the **Slide Master** appears near the top of the **Title** placeholder.

Format Background ▾ ✕

◢ FILL
- ⦿ Solid fill
- ○ Gradient fill
- ○ Picture or texture fill
- ○ Pattern fill
- ☐ Hide background graphics

Color

Transparency ⊢——— 0%

8   Select the two blue rectangles at the bottom of the slide and move them so you can view the identical graphics and small **Fabrikam** logo from the **Slide Master** beneath.

       TIP Selecting Hide Background Graphics on a layout hides all the graphics inherited from the Slide Master. If you need some of the graphics, copy them from the Slide Master and paste them onto the slide layout.

9   Press **Ctrl+Z** twice to undo steps 6 and 7.

10   Click the **Insert** tab and then click **Pictures**. Navigate to **Fabrikam_Logo_Large.png** and click **Insert**.

11   Select the logo, and change its width to **3**″. Drag the logo to the upper-right corner of the slide.

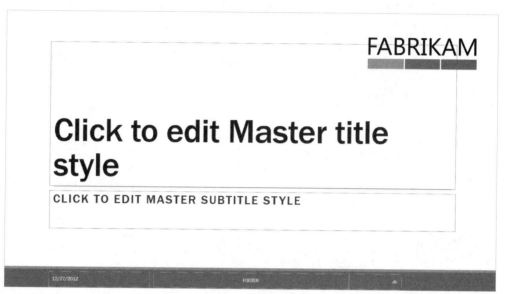

Creating a custom slide layout

In this exercise, you'll create a custom slide layout, rename it and the Slide Master, and save the file as a template.

➡️ SET UP **You need the SampleContentF_start presentation located in the Chapter12 practice file folder to complete this exercise. Open the SampleContentF_start presentation, and save it as SampleContentF. Then follow the steps.**

1   On the **View** tab, click **Slide Master** to open Slide Master view. Right-click the **Slide Master** and choose **Rename Master**.

12

2   In the **Rename Master** dialog box, enter **Fabrikam, Inc** and click **Rename**.

3   Point to the layouts beneath the **Slide Master** to find the one called **Title and Content Layout**. Select that layout.

4   On the **Slide Master** tab, click **Insert Layout** to add a new layout after the **Title and Content** layout.

The new layout will have title and footer placeholders.

TIP You can turn off the title and footer placeholders by clearing their check boxes on the Slide Master tab.

5   Right-click the new layout and choose **Rename Layout**. Name the layout **Speaker Bio**.

6   With the **Speaker Bio** layout selected, on the **Slide Master** tab, click **Insert Placeholder**, then **Picture**. Drag the slide to create a rectangular picture placeholder for the speaker's headshot. It should be about as wide as the date placeholder.

7   Click inside the picture placeholder and enter **Click icon to insert speaker photo**.

12

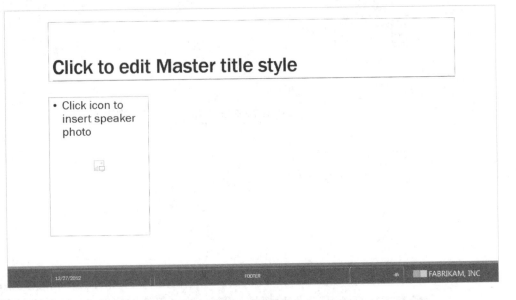

8   On the **Slide Master** tab, click **Insert Placeholder** again, and then click **Text**.

9   Click and drag on the slide to create a text placeholder. It should start near the upper-right corner of the picture and extend the width of the title placeholder.

10 Select the edge of the placeholder you just created, and change the font size to **16 pt** by selecting that size from the **Font Size** list on the **Home** tab. Click the bullet icon to remove the bullets from all levels of text.

11 Select the first level of text and enter **Type speaker affiliations here**.

Click to edit Master title style

- Click icon to insert speaker photo

Type speaker affiliations here
Second level
Third level
Fourth level
Fifth level

12/27/2012   FOOTER   FABRIKAM, INC

12   Copy the text placeholder (**Ctrl+C**) you added in step 9 and press **Ctrl+V** to paste it onto the layout. Drag the new placeholder into position directly beneath the original.

13   Select the edge of the placeholder and increase the font size to **20 pt**. Select the first level of text and enter **Type speaker biography here**.

12

14 Click **Close Master View** on the **Slide Master** tab to return to **Normal** view.

15 Click **File**, then **Save As**. Under **Save As**, select **Computer**, then click **Browse** to open the **Save As** dialog box.

16   In the **Save As** dialog box, click the **Save As Type** drop-down list and choose **PowerPoint Template (*.potx)** to save your file as a template. Enter **Fabrikam** in the **File name** field, and then click **Save**.

TIP When you save a PowerPoint template, PowerPoint will automatically take you to the folder where your custom templates should be saved. Templates saved here will appear in the File, New interface on the Custom tab.

TIP You can change the location of your custom PowerPoint templates by going to File, Options, then Save and typing a file path in the Default personal templates location field.

❌ CLEAN UP **Close the file after you save it as a template.**

Changing your presentation from a 16:9 format to a 4:3 format

You've probably noticed this already, but in case you haven't, the default slide size in PowerPoint 2013 is 16:9. Actually, that's the default proportion. The actual slide size is 13.33 inches wide by 7.5 inches tall. Previous versions of PowerPoint used a default slide size of 10 inches wide by 7.5 inches tall, which is a 4:3 proportion. The 4:3 format is the typical sort-of-square, old-school slide projector and screen size, whereas a 16:9 format is considered wide-screen, which is more in line with most of our computers, monitors, and television screens today.

You might be wondering why this is important. In previous versions of PowerPoint, when you would change an existing presentation from 16:9 to 4:3 (or vice versa), your content would be distorted. Squares would become narrow rectangles, people in pictures would look skinnier, and SmartArt diagrams would get rearranged.

12

Shapes and other content

Accent 1	Accent 2	Accent 3	Accent 4	Accent 5	Accent 6
Accent 1	Accent 2	Accent 3	Accent 4	Accent 5	Accent 5
Accent 1	Accent 2	Accent 3	Accent 4	Accent 5	Accent 5

Series 1   Series 2   Series 3

Category 1   Category 2   Category 3   Category 4

| Group 1 | Group 2 | Group 3 |
| Group 4 | Group 5 | Group 6 |

	Group A	Group B
Region 1	122	233
Region 2	406	189
Region 3	760	958

Shapes and other content

Acce nt 1	Acce nt 2	Acce nt 3	Acce nt 4	Acce nt 5	Acce nt 6
Acce nt 1	Acce nt 2	Acce nt 3	Acce nt 4	Acce nt 5	Acce nt 5
Acce nt 1	Acce nt 2	Acce nt 3	Acce nt 4	Acce nt 5	Acce nt 5

Series 1   Series 2   Series 3

Category 1 Category 2 Category 3 Category 4

Group 1	Group 2
Group 3	Group 4
Group 5	Group 6

	Group A	Group B
Region 1	122	233
Region 2	406	189
Region 3	760	958

PowerPoint 2013 works a lot better than previous versions, and it actually gives you a couple of options when you're changing the proportions of a presentation or template. You'll still want to choose your proportion before developing your content whenever you can, but at least now when you change the slide size, you'll have a choice of whether to make the content as large as it can be (taking into account that it might extend beyond the edge of the slide), or scale your content so it will fit on the new slide size. Either way, your content won't be distorted!

In this exercise, you'll change a 16:9-proportioned slide to a 4:3 format, and then you'll revert to the original size.

→ SET UP **You need the Fabrikam.POTX template located in the Chapter12 practice file folder to complete this exercise. Double-click the Fabrikam.POTX template to open a presentation based on the Fabrikam PowerPoint template. Save the file as SampleContentG. Then follow the steps.**

1   On the **Design** tab, click **Slide Size**, then click **Standard (4:3)**.

2   Choose **Maximize**, which doesn't scale your content.

PowerPoint maximizes the slide content, keeping everything the same size and letting it fall off the edges of the new 4:3 slide as necessary.

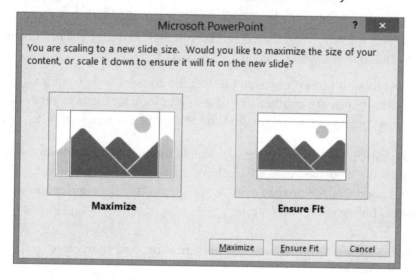

TIP You can click either the icons or the buttons in the Slide Size dialog box.

3   Press **Ctrl+Z** to undo the last step and return to the original slide size.

4   Click **Slide Size**, then **Standard (4:3)**, and choose **Ensure Fit**.

     PowerPoint scales the content so it fits on the slide without distortion.

5   On the slide, select the first blue shape labeled **Accent 1**, and look at its font size on the **Home** tab. You'll notice that PowerPoint changed it to **13.5** to help with the fit.

6   Click **Slide Size** again, and this time, click **Widescreen (16:9)**.

     PowerPoint will reposition the objects on the slide, but they will not become any larger. The font size will remain at 13.5 points.

     TIP Even though PowerPoint won't distort the content on your slides, graphics on the slide backgrounds are another story. Be sure to look for logos or other content that may have become distorted on the Slide Master or any of the layouts.

     TROUBLESHOOTING PowerPoint will reapply the original theme when it resizes a presentation. If you've made any customizations to your theme, template, or Slide Masters and layouts, you may need to resave the template and reapply it to your presentation before using this feature.

❌ CLEAN UP **Save the SampleContentG presentation, and then close it.**

Key points

- A theme is a set of colors, fonts and effects, along with Slide Masters and layouts for PowerPoint.

- A template is a theme plus content (usually sample slides). A PowerPoint presentation can be based on either a template or a theme.

- The theme elements are built into all template and presentation files.

- You aren't required to apply the whole theme. You can apply theme colors, fonts, and effects separately. Mix and match 'em! Have fun!

- Slide layouts inherit their settings from the Slide Master.

- Graphics added to the Slide Master appear on all slide layouts unless you choose to hide background graphics.

- Placeholders are preformatted content holders that can help you create consistency and cohesion throughout your presentation.

- Right-click a theme or variant to apply it only to selected slides as opposed to the entire presentation.

12

Chapter at a glance

Add

Add and format tables,
page 313

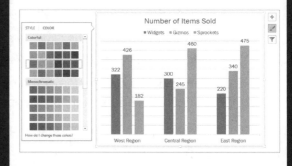

Insert

Insert and format charts,
page 316

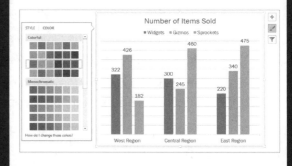

Create

Create SmartArt diagrams,
page 320

Reuse

Reuse existing slides,
page 326

Creating on-slide content

13

IN THIS CHAPTER, YOU WILL LEARN HOW TO

- Choose a slide layout and add text in placeholders.

- Add manual check boxes.

- Add and format tables.

- Insert and format charts using chart styles and layouts.

- Create and format SmartArt diagrams.

- Reuse slides and keep their source formatting.

You can add many different types of content to a presentation. Some of it, like text and SmartArt graphics, is created directly within Microsoft PowerPoint. Other types, such as pictures or video, are developed elsewhere and simply added to PowerPoint. Either way, there are multiple methods of adding or constructing content and then modifying it once it's on the slide.

In this chapter, you'll learn to leverage slide layouts to quickly create and position content. You'll also learn more about formatting text as well as creating SmartArt, charts, and tables.

PRACTICE FILES To complete the exercises in this chapter, you need the practice files contained in the Chapter13 practice file folder. For more information, see "Download the practice files" in this book's Introduction.

Choosing a slide layout and adding text in placeholders

When you begin a new presentation, PowerPoint provides you with a title slide to help you get started. The title slide has two text placeholders: one for the title of the presentation, and the other for a subtitle. If you insert another slide, you'll typically get a title and content layout. This layout also provides you with two placeholders: one for the slide title and another that can hold a variety of content, such as text, tables, charts, SmartArt diagrams, video, or pictures from either your computer or online sources.

These placeholders are preformatted containers just waiting for your content. They provide consistency throughout your presentation and eliminate repetitive formatting tasks. Remember how we formatted the graphic and placeholders on the slide master in the previous chapter? As you know, that formatting (including colors, fonts, effects, and graphics from the theme or template) trickles down to all the slide layouts. Taking it a step further, the actual slides inherit their formatting from the layout they're based on.

To experience this in action, click the bottom of the New Slide button on the Home tab. Choosing the layout that most closely matches your intended content can save you a lot of time.

TIP If you don't find a layout that works with your content, you may want to create your own custom layout, which might save you time in the long run.

SEE ALSO For more about placeholders and creating custom layouts, see Chapter 12, "Designing and creating presentations."

In this exercise, you'll insert a slide and add text in a placeholder. You'll also change text from first-level bulleted text to second-level and vice versa.

➡ SET UP **You need the SampleContentA_start presentation located in the Chapter13 practice file folder to complete this exercise. Open the SampleContentA_start presentation, and save it as SampleContentA. Then follow the steps.**

1   On the first slide, click in the title placeholder, which prompts you with **Click to add title**, and enter **Quarterly Report**.

![Quarterly Report title slide with FABRIKAM logo and "CLICK TO ADD SUBTITLE" placeholder]

2   Click in the subtitle placeholder, which reads **Click to add subtitle**, and enter **Robin Wakefield**.

3   On the **Home** tab, in the **Slides** group, click the top of the **New Slide** button to add a new slide based on the title and content layout.

TIP When you click the top of the New Slide button, PowerPoint inserts a new slide based on the layout of the selected slide. The exception is when you've selected a slide that uses the title slide layout. In such a case, PowerPoint always inserts a slide based on the title and content layout. If you want to choose a different type of layout, click the bottom of the New Slide button.

TIP Clicking the bottom of the New Slide button lets you choose the layout you want to use when you create a slide. If you want to change the layout of an existing slide, just click the Layout button and choose a different layout.

13

4   Click in the title placeholder of the slide you just created and enter **Fabrikam employee community contributions make a difference**.

(Don't enter the period. Punctuation at the end of bullet points can add a lot of clutter to a slide, so it's a common practice to omit it.)

5   Click in the content placeholder and enter **Women's shelter**. Press the **Enter** key and then press **Tab** to create a second-level bullet point, then enter **Raked leaves**. Press **Enter** to create another second-level bullet and enter **Repaired windows**. Press **Enter** and enter **Painted 2 rooms**.

6   Press **Enter** to create the next line, then press **Shift+Tab** to change the text to first-level bulleted text. Enter **Local animal shelter**.

KEYBOARD SHORTCUT Press Tab or Alt+Shift+Right Arrow to demote text. Press Shift+Tab or Alt+Shift+Left Arrow to promote text.

TIP You can also use the Decrease List Level and Increase List Level buttons to promote or demote the text to different levels.

TROUBLESHOOTING Many templates don't have a bullet point on the first level of text. This looks great, but it can cause problems if you're used to using the Tab key to create lower levels of bulleted text. If your first-level text doesn't have a bullet point and you press Tab to create second-level bulleted text, the bullet character won't appear as expected on the second level. Instead, enter the first-level text, then press Enter and use the Increase List Level button on the ribbon or the keyboard shortcut Alt+Shift+Right Arrow to create second-level text with a bullet character. Alternatively, click View, then Outline, and enter your text in the Outline pane, where Tab and Shift+Tab create levels of text as expected.

7   Press **Enter** and enter **Cleaned kennels**. Press **Enter** and enter **Walked dogs**. Press **Enter** and enter **Participated in food drive**. Press **Enter** and enter **Regional art museum**.

8   Click anywhere in the **Cleaned kennels** text. Press and hold the left mouse button and drag until you've selected at least part of the **Participated in food drive** text.

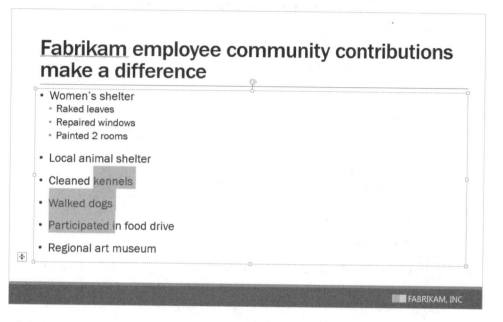

9   Click the **Increase List Level** button on the ribbon to change the three primary bullet points into second-level bulleted text.

10   Place the cursor at the end of the word **museum** and press **Enter**, then press **Shift+Alt+Right Arrow** on the keyboard to create second-level bulleted text. Enter **Decorated for new exhibition**. Press **Enter**, then enter **Taught art class for elderly**.

11   Click the **Autofit Options** button that appears near the bottom of the placeholder and select **Stop Fitting Text to This Placeholder** to prevent PowerPoint from shrinking the text and line spacing to force it to fit within the placeholder.

TIP Experiment with the various selections in the Autofit Options menu. For example, if you want to move some of the text to a new slide, choose Split Text Between Two Slides.

❌ CLEAN UP **Save the presentation if you want, and then close it.**

Adding manual text boxes

PowerPoint automatically formats and positions any text you add to placeholders. This saves a tremendous amount of time, but it's not always what you want. For example, sometimes you might need to label a diagram or graphic, or maybe you want to add a reference to the slide. For this, you'll use a manual text box.

In this exercise, you'll create and format text in manual text boxes.

TIP These ad hoc, manual text boxes are designed for small bits of text, so they're not very robust when it comes to things like multiple levels of bullets.

SET UP You need the SampleContentB_start presentation located in the Chapter13 practice file folder to complete this exercise. Open the SampleContentB_start presentation, and save it as SampleContentB. Then follow the steps.

1   On either the **Home** tab or the **Insert** tab, click the **Shapes gallery**.

   TROUBLESHOOTING Depending on the size of your screen and your PowerPoint window, the Shapes gallery may appear as a lot of shapes or it may appear as a big icon. (See Chapter 1, "Getting comfortable in Office Home and Student 2013," for more information about how screen resolution and window size affect your display.) In the gallery with a lot of shapes, click the arrows or the More button (see Chapter 11, "Getting comfortable in PowerPoint 2013") to display all the shapes. If your Shapes gallery is a large icon, just click it to display the entire set of shapes.

2   Click the **Text Box** shape. It will be in **Basic Shapes** if it's not already at the top in the **Recently Used Shapes** section.

Text box

3   Click anywhere on the slide and begin entering text to create a text box that expands as you enter the text. Enter the words **Conference Area**.

   TIP If you click and drag to create the text box on the slide, it will remain that width as you enter information, but its height will expand to accommodate your text.

4   Click the edge of the text box to select it.

13

TIP When your cursor is inside the text box, the text box edge will display a dotted line, which indicates that you're working with the text and not the entire text box. Press Esc or the F2 key on your keyboard or click the edge of the text box to select the text box itself. Then format all of the text in it at once. You'll know you've selected the text box when its edge is a solid line.

5   On the **Home** tab, in the **Font** group, click **Bold** to make the text bold.

   KEYBOARD SHORTCUT Ctrl+B applies bold formatting to selected text. Ctrl+I applies italics, and Ctrl+U applies underlining.

6   Click the **Decrease Font Size** button twice to change the font size to 14 points like the rest of the labels in the diagram.

7   Click the dialog box launcher in the **Font** group to open the **Font** dialog box.

8   Select the **All Caps** check box to change the text to uppercase, and then click **OK** to close the dialog box.

9   Select the text box by clicking its edge, and then drag it into place in the upper-left corner of the diagram. Smart Guides will appear to help you align the label with the others in the diagram.

SEE ALSO For more information about SmartGuides, see Chapter 14, "Creating Office graphics."

10 With the **Conference Area** text box selected, click the arrow next to the **Copy** button on the **Home** tab and select **Duplicate** to create a duplicate text box. Drag the duplicate away from the original text box so it's easier to work with.

KEYBOARD SHORTCUT Use Ctrl+C to copy the selected text or object. Use Ctrl+V to paste it. Ctrl+D will duplicate an object; it's like a combined copy-paste. Pressing Ctrl while you drag an object will also create a copy!

11 Click in front of the **C** and drag until you've selected all the text. Enter the words **Break Area**. The selected text will be replaced with the new text as you enter it.

TIP You don't have to worry about pressing the Caps Lock key, because you changed the formatting to All Caps.

TIP You can select a single word by double-clicking it. Triple-clicking selects all text in the paragraph. Try it for yourself!

12   Select the **Break Area** text box and click the rotation arrow at the top. When the pointer turns into a circular arrow, click and drag to the right to rotate the text box 90 degrees.

TIP Press Shift while you rotate to constrain the rotation to 15-degree increments.

TIP There are additional rotation tools available on the Home tab, in the Drawing group under Arrange tools, and on the Drawing Tools Format tab, in the Arrange group. These let you flip objects and rotate them 90 degrees with just one click.

13   Drag the **Break Area** label into place next to the icons for the sink, stove, and refrigerator at the right end of the **Conference Area** text.

14   Change the color of the **Break Area** text by selecting the text box (the edge will display a solid line) and, on the **Home** tab, in the **Font** group, clicking the arrow next to the font color icon. In the **Theme Colors** gallery, click the **Accent 2 (orange)** color swatch.

TIP All the formatting you're doing with manual text can be done to text in place-holders as well. If you need to apply a lot of manual formatting (for example, making all top-level text a different color or size), you should probably make that change on the slide master or on one of the slide layouts.

15 Create another duplicate of the **Conference Area** text box, replace the text with the word **Storage**, and place it in the small square at the upper-right of the diagram.

❌ CLEAN UP **Save the presentation if you want, and then close it.**

Adding and formatting a table

There are a number of ways to add a table to a slide. You can click the table icon in the content placeholder, or you can use the Table tool on the Insert tab, which gives you three additional options! If you use the icon in the placeholder, the inserted table will fill the width of the placeholder. If you use the table tool on the Insert tab, the table will be inserted into the center of the slide.

Regardless of how you add the table, after it's on the slide, you can easily format the table by using the Table tools.

In this exercise, you'll add and quickly format a table.

SET UP **You need the SampleContentC_start presentation located in the Chapter13 practice file folder to complete this exercise. Open the SampleContentC_start presentation, and save it as SampleContentC. Then follow the steps.**

1   Select slide 2. In the content placeholder on the left, click the **Table** icon to open the **Insert Table** dialog box. Enter **3** in the **Number of Columns** field and **4** for the number of rows. Then click **OK** to close the dialog box and insert the table.

2   Place your cursor in the first cell of the table, then press the **Tab** key to move to the second cell of the top row. Enter **Q1**. Press **Tab** again and enter **Q2** in the last cell of the top row.

3   In the first cell of the second row, enter **Widgets**. Press **Tab** to move to the next cell and enter **$129**. Press **Tab** to move to the third cell and enter **$254**. Press **Tab** again to move to the first cell in the third row.

4   Enter **Sprockets** in the first cell of the third row. Press **Tab** and enter **$653**. Press **Tab** again and enter **$997**. Press **Tab** again to move to the first cell in the fourth row.

5   Enter **Gizmos** and press **Tab** to move to the next cell. Enter **$278**, press **Tab** again, and enter **$690.**

6   Press **Tab** to create another row. Enter **Total** in the first cell. Press **Tab** and enter **$1060**. Press **Tab** again and enter **$1941.**

7   On the **Table Tools Design** tab, in the **Table Style Options** group, click **Total Row** to apply special formatting to the last row in the table.

	Q1	Q2
Widgets	129	254
Sprockets	653	997
Gizmos	278	690
Total	1060	1941

8   With the cursor in the table, on the **Table Tools Design** tab, in the **Table Styles** gallery, click the style labeled **Medium Style 3 - Accent 2.**

TIP As with all the other galleries, you can click the single arrows to scroll through the gallery line by line, or you can click the More button to expand the gallery completely.

IMPORTANT If tool tabs do not appear, make sure you have selected the object. For example, if you don't have the Table Tools Design or Layout tab, make sure your cursor is inside the table or click the edge of the table to select it.

13

9   Select the table and drag the bottom edge to increase the height of the table and give the text a bit of breathing room.

10   With the table still selected, click the **Table Tools Layout** tab, then in the **Alignment** group, click the **Center Vertically** button to center the text vertically within the cells. (This small task makes your table look 100 percent better!)

11   Move your mouse pointer above the middle column until the pointer changes to a downward-pointing arrow. Click and drag to the right to select the **Q1** and **Q2** columns.

	Q1	Q2
Widgets	129	254
Sprockets	653	997
Gizmos	278	690
Total	**1060**	**1941**

12   On the **Table Tools Layout** tab, in the **Alignment** group, click the **Center** alignment button to horizontally center the text in those two columns.

KEYBOARD SHORTCUT Ctrl+E centers text. Ctrl+L left-aligns text, and Ctrl+R right-aligns it.

✖ CLEAN UP **Save the presentation if you want, and then close it.**

Inserting and formatting charts

As with tables, there are multiple ways to add a chart to a slide. The most straightforward ways are to click the chart icon in a content placeholder or to use the Chart tool on the Insert tab. Either way, the Insert Chart dialog box will appear; in it you can choose the type of chart you want to add. You can format charts with just a few clicks.

In this exercise, you'll insert a chart, add your own data, and apply formatting with just a few clicks.

SEE ALSO For more about creating and formatting charts, see Chapter 23, "Creating charts and graphics."

➡️ SET UP **You need the SampleContentD_start presentation located in the Chapter13 practice file folder to complete this exercise. Open the SampleContentD_start presentation, and save it as SampleContentD. Then follow the steps.**

1 Click the chart icon in the empty placeholder on slide **3**.

2 Click **OK** to insert the default **Clustered Column** chart.

TIP Select the type of chart (such as column, line, or pie) from the list on the left of the Insert Chart dialog box. Select the subtype from the options across the top (such as clustered column or stacked column).

TIP Three-dimensional charts can make data very difficult to discern, and in fact, they can be quite misleading. It's really best to stick with two-dimensional charts.

3 In the chart sheet that appears above the chart on your slide, replace the sample data with your own. As you enter your own data over the sample data, the chart will update.

4 Click and drag the lower-right corner of the blue line that indicates the data range to eliminate any cells that shouldn't be included in the chart. Again, the chart's information will update.

	A	B	C	D	E
1		Widgets	Gizmos	Sprockets	
2	West Region	322	426	182	
3	Central Reg	300	245	460	
4	East Region	220	340	475	
5	Category 4		2.8	5	
6					
7					

5 When you've finished entering your data, click the **X** in the upper-right corner of the chart sheet to close it.

TROUBLESHOOTING You must close the chart sheet before inserting another chart. If you don't, you'll get this message: The Chart Data Grid Is Open ... To Insert A New Chart You Need To Close It First.

TIP Reopen the chart sheet by right-clicking the chart and selecting Edit Data.

6 Select the **Chart Title** text and change it by entering these words: **Number of Items Sold**.

7 Click the + icon next to the chart to open the **Chart Elements** list.

8 Click the arrow next to **Axes** and uncheck **Primary Vertical** to turn off the vertical axis.

9 Select the check box next to **Data Labels** to add those to the chart.

10 Click the arrow to the right of **Legend** and then click **Top** to reposition the legend.

TIP Click the More Options button on any element to access the Formatting pane, where you'll find many more options.

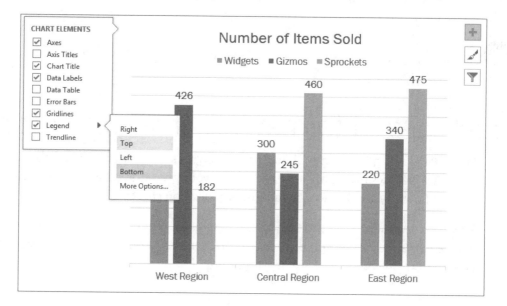

11 Click the paintbrush icon next to the chart and then click **Color**. Select the third color set so the data is easier to discern.

13

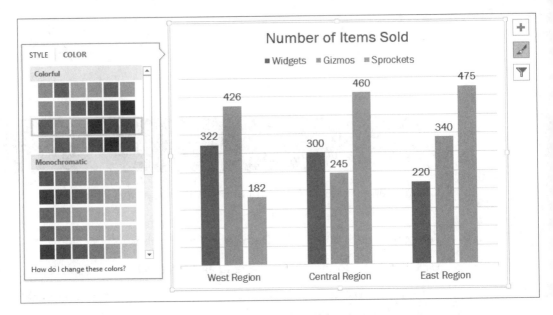

TIP Use the Chart Filters tool (the funnel icon) to highlight specific series or categories of data on the chart.

❌ CLEAN UP **Save the presentation if you want, and then close it.**

Creating and formatting SmartArt diagrams

SmartArt is a diagramming tool that helps you create visual representations of information. SmartArt graphics match the look and feel of your presentation and can be used to create process flows, cycle diagrams, pyramids, organization charts, and more.

There are several ways to add SmartArt diagrams to your presentation. As you might guess, you can always click the icon in a content placeholder to open a dialog box where you can choose from any number of SmartArt graphics.

You can, of course, use the SmartArt icon on the Insert tab as well, and it will open the same dialog box. But PowerPoint also lets you turn bulleted text into SmartArt graphics with just a few clicks! It's a quick and easy way to make a boring bulleted slide into a more visual presentation.

In this exercise, you'll change bulleted list text into a SmartArt graphic and format it.

➡ SET UP **You need the SampleContentE_start presentation located in the Chapter13 practice file folder to complete this exercise. Open the SampleContentE_start presentation, and save it as SampleContentE. Then follow the steps.**

1   Select slide **2** in the thumbnail pane on the left of the workspace. Right-click and choose **Duplicate Slide** to create a copy of the slide.

   TIP Always create a copy of your slide before drastically changing the formatting. In case you don't like the new slide, you can go back to the original!

2   With your cursor inside the body text on slide **2**, right-click and select **Convert to SmartArt**. Point to the **SmartArt graphic** options in the gallery to determine if any are appropriate for your text. Click the one labeled **Horizontal Bullet List** to apply it.

Horizontal Bullet List Smart Art

TIP If you don't like any of the diagrams in the gallery, click More SmartArt Graphics to open the Choose A SmartArt Graphic dialog box, where you can select from the entire set of diagrams.

3   Click at the end of the text in the Text pane, then press **Enter** and type **Regional Art Museum**, which adds the text both in the pane and in the diagram. Press **Enter** again and type **Decorated for new exhibition**. Press **Enter** again and type **Taught art class for elderly.**

TIP You can add or edit text in the Text pane or in the diagram itself, whichever is easier for you. If you add or delete bullet points in the pane, shapes will be added or removed from the diagram and vice versa.

TIP Click the **X** in the upper-right corner of the Text pane to close it. Use the small arrow on the left side of the diagram to reopen the pane. Or turn it on and off by toggling the Text Pane button on the SmartArt Tools Design tab, in the Create Graphic group.

4   Click the **Up Arrow** key on your keyboard until your cursor is in the line of text reading **Regional Art Museum**, and then press **Shift+Tab** to promote that text in the pane and create a new shape in the diagram at the same time.

5   Click the **Change Colors** button on the **SmartArt Tools Design** tab and select
     Colorful Range - Accent Colors 2 to 3 to change the colors of the diagram.

TIP You can use the SmartArt Styles gallery on the SmartArt Tools Design tab to apply various looks to your diagram. Use the tools in the Create Graphic group of the SmartArt Tools Design tab to rearrange and add shapes to your diagram.

6   Click the **More** button in the **SmartArt Layouts** gallery to expand the gallery. Click
     More Layouts to display the entire dialog box.

7   Click **List** on the left and choose **Stacked List**.

8   Click **OK** to change the diagram.

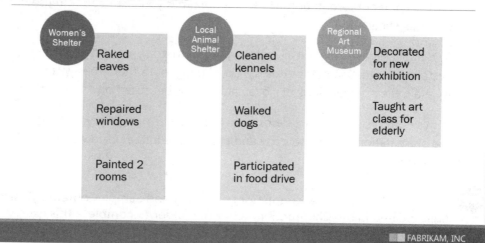

TROUBLESHOOTING Sometimes the text in a diagram doesn't size like you think it should. You can use any of the text tools on the Home tab to change the text size, but then your diagram won't resize the font if you later add or remove text.

TIP Because SmartArt diagrams are essentially Office graphics, you can apply manual formatting to any elements in tables, charts or SmartArt diagrams just like you can with any shape. See Chapter 14 for more information.

❌ CLEAN UP **Save the presentation if you want, and then close it.**

13

Reusing slides and keeping their source formatting

Creating content directly in your presentation is great, but often that content will already exist in another presentation. Those are the times you just need to reuse the slide, not reinvent the wheel!

By default, slides automatically take on the formatting attributes of any presentation you paste them into. Sometimes this is a good thing, but other times you might want the slides to retain their original look. It's okay either way, because PowerPoint lets you do both!

In this exercise, you'll insert slides from the Reuse Slides gallery and move them around in the presentation. You'll also copy and paste slides into a presentation and keep the original formatting.

➜ SET UP **You need the SampleContentF_start and SampleContentG_Start presentations located in the Chapter13 practice file folder to complete this exercise. Open the SampleContentF_start presentation, and save it as SampleContentF. You will open SampleContentG_Start as part of the exercise.**

1 Select slide **3**. On the **Home** tab, click the bottom of the **New Slide** button and select **Reuse Slides** to open the **Reuse Slides** pane.

2 In the **Reuse Slides** pane, click the **Browse** button and then **Browse File** to insert slides from a file on your hard drive. Alternatively, click the **Open a PowerPoint File** link just below the **Browse** button. The link will take you to the same **Browse** dialog box so you can find the file on your computer.

13

TIP If your company uses the Slide Library feature on Microsoft SharePoint, choose Browse Slide Library to access files from that location.

TIP When you've accessed a file from the Reuse Slides pane, you can select it from the drop-down list at the top of the pane, which provides handy access to files you frequently use to copy slides.

3　In the **Browse** dialog box, navigate to the **SampleContentG_Start** file and click **Open**.

4   In the **Reuse Slides** pane, click the sixth thumbnail, titled **International growth plan**, to add it to the presentation. Then click the last thumbnail to add it. Note that the formatting of the inserted slides is updated to match the template used in the SampleContentF file.

TIP If you want to insert all slides in the Reuse Slides pane, right-click one of the thumbnails and choose Insert All Slides.

5   Select the **Keep Source Formatting** check box at the bottom of the **Reuse Slides** pane, and then click the first thumbnail (**New Seattle office floor plan**) to insert it into the presentation.

IMPORTANT When you select Keep Source Formatting in the Reuse Slides pane (or when copying and pasting slides from one presentation to another), PowerPoint adds the original slide master each time. This can result in very large files with multiple duplicate slide masters.

13

6   Because **Keep Source Formatting** was selected, this slide doesn't pick up the formatting of the SampleContentF presentation when it's inserted. To change this slide to the blue Fabrikam template so it matches the rest of the presentation, select it and on the **Home** tab, click the **Layout** button. Select the **Title Only** layout from the **Fabrikam, Inc** set of layouts.

TIP When your slide has a title, but your content doesn't lend itself to including it in a placeholder, at least choose the Title Only slide layout. This ensures that your slide titles are all located in the same place and won't jump around as you move from slide to slide in your presentation. Jumping titles, logos, and other repeated graphics are telltale signs of an amateur-designed presentation.

7   Click the **X** in the upper-right corner of the **Reuse Slides** pane to close it.

8   Click the **File** tab, then **Open**, **Computer**, and then **Browse**. Navigate to the **SampleContentG_Start** file and click **Open** to open it.

9   Click the **View** tab, and in the **Window** group, click **Arrange All** to position the presentations side by side.

10   In the **SampleContentG_Start** file, click slide **2**, press and hold the **Shift** key, and click slide **5** to select slides **2**, **3**, **4**, and **5**.

   TIP Press and hold the Shift key, then click the first and last slides to select a set of contiguous slides. Press and hold the Ctrl key to select noncontiguous slides.

11   Right-click and choose **Copy**, or press **Ctrl+C** to copy the four slides.

12   In the **SampleContentF** file, right-click slide **6** and choose the **Use Destination Theme** paste option (the first paste icon).

   KEYBOARD SHORTCUT You can use Ctrl+C to copy and Ctrl+V to perform the default paste action, which is to use the destination theme.

   TIP Click the second paste icon to paste the slides and keep the source formatting.

13   Slides **7** through **10** should still be selected following the paste procedure. If they are not, then select them by pressing **Shift** and clicking slide **7** and then slide **10**. Drag them into position immediately following the first slide.

13

14   Click the **Slide Sorter** button on the status bar to switch to **Slide Sorter View**.

Slide Sorter button

15   Select slide **6**, the text version of the Fabrikam employee community contributions, and press **Delete** on your keyboard to delete it.

16   After you delete slide **6**, the **Employee Contributions** SmartArt graphic slide will become the new slide **6**. Select it and drag it to the end of the slides.

17   Click the **Normal** button on the status bar to return to **Normal** (editing) view.

❌ CLEAN UP   **Save the presentation if you want, and then close both presentations.**

TIP PowerPoint 2013 remembers the view you're in, the slide you're on, and the zoom percentage you're at when you save a presentation.

Key points

- Slide layouts can save you time and effort by providing consistency throughout your presentation.

- Placeholders can also save you time and effort by providing formatting for your text and positioning for your other content.

- Quickly format charts, tables, and SmartArt graphics by choosing styles and color combinations from the galleries on the Chart, Table, and SmartArt tool tabs.

- Chart, Table, and SmartArt styles are all based on the colors in the Color Theme.

- You can reuse slides by copying and pasting them into your presentation or by inserting them through the Reuse Slides pane.

- By default, old slides inserted into your new presentation will use the new formatting.

- If you want inserted slides to maintain their original formatting, select Keep Source Formatting in Paste Options or in the Reuse Slides pane.

13

Chapter at a glance

Add

Add and format shapes,
page 336

Apply

Apply enhanced fills and effects,
page 342

Create

Create your own shapes,
page 349

Insert

Insert, crop, and format pictures,
page 354

Creating Office graphics | 14

IN THIS CHAPTER, YOU WILL LEARN HOW TO

- Add and format shapes.

- Apply enhanced fills and effects.

- Create your own shapes.

- Insert, crop, and format pictures.

Many people don't realize it, but Microsoft PowerPoint is actually an extremely powerful drawing application. Not only can you format shapes as you'd expect by applying solid and gradient fills and outlines, but you can also add 3-D effects and other enhancements, such as shadows and reflections. PowerPoint even gives you some new tools to create your own shapes.

You can apply most of this formatting to pictures as well, all of which helps you create an attractive, cohesive presentation. Picture features in PowerPoint 2013 include a background removal tool, a picture cropping tool, recoloring options, and artistic filters to go along with the more common shadows, reflections, and 3-D settings.

After you've gotten your shapes and pictures looking beautiful, you need to position them on the slide. PowerPoint 2013 has a number of enhanced features to help with alignment and distribution, including enhanced Smart Guides and new colorable guides that can be locked to the slide master.

In this chapter, you'll learn all about creating and formatting shapes and pictures. You'll also learn about using the alignment tools and the new guides and Smart Guides to position objects after you've created them.

PRACTICE FILES To complete the exercises in this chapter, you need the practice files contained in the Chapter14 practice file folder. For more information, see "Download the practice files" in this book's Introduction.

Adding and formatting shapes

You may already be familiar with the Shapes gallery in PowerPoint. It gives you common shapes like lines, rectangles, arrows, and other frequently used shapes. What you may not realize is that there are a number of different ways to add and format these shapes.

In this exercise, you'll insert a shape. You'll also position shapes by using the Smart Guides, and format them by using the Shape Styles gallery, the Theme Color palette, and the new Eyedroppers.

➡️ SET UP **You don't need any practice files to complete this exercise. Open PowerPoint to a new, blank presentation, and then follow the steps.**

1   Select the first (and only) slide. On the **Home** tab, click the **Layout** button and choose the **Blank** layout so the content placeholders don't get in your way while you're drawing.

2   On either the **Home** or the **Insert** tab of the ribbon, click the **Shapes** button to expand the **Shapes** gallery.

   SEE ALSO For more information about how screen resolution and window size affect your display, see Chapter 1, "Getting comfortable in Office Home and Student 2013."

3   Click the **Rectangle** tool, (accessed from **Rectangles** or **Recently Used Shapes**), then click and drag on the slide to create a rectangle.

   TIP To create a perfect square, circle, or other shape, select the shape from the Shapes gallery and press the Shift key while you click and drag on the slide. Or just click once on the slide to create a 1" x 1" square, circle, triangle, or similar.

4   Select the **rectangle** and enter **Rectangle 1**.
   The text is added to the rectangle.

5   Select the rectangle and press **Ctrl+D** to duplicate it.

6   Drag the duplicated rectangle alongside the original rectangle.
   Smart Guides appear to help you align the two shapes.

7   Press **Ctrl+D** again. PowerPoint creates a duplicate rectangle perfectly aligned and distributed with the other two! Press **Ctrl+D** again to create a fourth aligned and distributed rectangle.

8   Select the number **1** in the second rectangle. Enter **2** so the text reads **Rectangle 2**. Change the text in the third and fourth shapes to **Rectangle 3** and **Rectangle 4**.

     TIP Shapes with text behave like manual text boxes. Look for a solid outline to indicate that the shape itself is selected. If your cursor is inside the text, the shape's outline will be dotted.

9   Right-click **Rectangle 1**. Click the **Style** button to expand the **Shape Styles** gallery.

     TIP You can also access the Shape Styles, fill color, and outline color galleries from the Drawing Tools Format tool tab, which appears when you select a shape.

14

TROUBLESHOOTING If a menu displaying options to Move Here, Copy Here, or Cancel appears when you right-click an object on a slide, you've moved your mouse (probably very slightly) when you right-clicked. Just click away from the object and try again.

10   Point to the different formatting chips in the gallery to view how each would affect the selected shape. (This is called Live Preview.) Scroll to the bottom of the gallery and click the green chip in the bottom row to apply it. (It's labeled **Intense Effect - Green - Accent 6**.)

11   Right-click **Rectangle 2**. Click the **Fill** button, then select the chip that represents **Orange, Accent 2** on the top row of the **Theme Colors** palette.

12   Click the **Outline** button and select the last chip in the **Accent 2 Orange** column to change the outline color of the rectangle to dark orange.

13   Click **Outline** again, then **Weight**, then **3 pt** to add a thicker border to the rectangle.

14   Right-click **Rectangle 3**. Click the **Fill** button to expand the **Fill Colors** gallery, and choose **Eyedropper** from the list.

15   Move the **Eyedropper** to **Rectangle 2** and click when the color swatch turns orange to apply the orange color to **Rectangle 3**.

16   Right-click **Rectangle 3** and click **Outline**, then **Eyedropper**. Move the **Eyedropper** over **Rectangle 4** until it turns blue, then click to apply a blue outline to **Rectangle 3**. Click **Outline** again, then **Weight**, then **3 pt** to apply a 3-point border to **Rectangle 3**.

14

TIP The Eyedropper Text Fill tool works on text, too. Select the text and click the Font button on the Home tab so you can access the Eyedropper. You can also access this tool from the Drawing Tools Format tool tab, in the WordArt Styles group, by clicking the Text Fill button.

❌ CLEAN UP **Save the presentation if you want, and then close it.**

Alignment tools

The enhanced Smart Guides in PowerPoint 2013 are extremely helpful. They assist not only with alignment, but also with spacing (also known as *distributing*) objects on the slides. But sometimes they can get in the way. If that happens, you can always turn them off by right-clicking the slide and choosing Grid And Guides. Clear the Smart Guides option to turn them off. Of course, select the Smart Guides option if you want to turn them on again.

In addition to the powerful Smart Guides, PowerPoint 2013 also has enhanced guides. Guides are dotted lines that show up on the sides. They're very useful for indicating text-safe zones and margins, for example. To turn them on, right-click the slide, choose Grid And Guides, and then either Add Horizontal Guide or Add Vertical Guide. Turn the guides on and off by selecting Guides in that same dialog box. To change the color of any guide, right-click it, and then select Color. Drag to position guides on your slide.

KEYBOARD SHORTCUT Use Alt+F9 (the function key) to toggle guides on and off. Press Ctrl and drag a guide to create more guides.

New in PowerPoint 2013 is the ability to add guides to the slide master and layouts! Users have asked for lockable guides for a long time, and this is the next best thing. Put guides that you don't want to grab and move by mistake onto the slide masters and layouts. You can still create guides directly on the slides when you need them quickly, and these guides will be selectable and moveable on the slides.

Finally, the conventional Alignment And Distribution tools are still available from the Arrange group on either the Home tab or tool tabs, but with the new guides and Smart Guides, you may never need to use them!

Theme colors vs. direct colors

It can be really confusing when you copy objects or slides from one presentation to another and all the colors change. It might seem like PowerPoint is doing something wrong, but it's actually just PowerPoint trying to be helpful.

The colors at the top of any of the Color galleries are called Theme Colors, and as you learned in Chapter 12, "Designing and creating presentations," all templates and presentations have a set of theme colors built in. If you think about the theme colors as being positional, that might help. For example, if you apply the Accent 2 color—whatever it might be—to a rectangle, when you apply a different template (which often happens if you copy a slide into a new presentation), then the rectangle updates its color to the new template's Accent 2 color.

Theme colors — Theme colors

Tints and shades of theme colors

Standard colors (direct formatting)

Recently used non-theme colors (direct formatting)

Color honeycomb (direct formatting)

Eyedropper (direct formatting)

14

Not all colors are theme colors, though. If you click More Colors, the familiar honey-comb will appear. You can select colors from it, or you can click the Custom tab and input your own RGB (red, green, and blue) values.

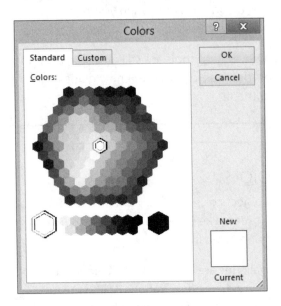

The colors you select in this dialog box show up in the Color Gallery as Recent Colors, and they are all considered direct or absolute formatting. This means that they are not theme colors, so they will not change when you apply a new template or color theme. Any colors you apply with the Eyedropper tools are also direct colors, not theme colors.

Finally, the Standard Colors are also direct colors. Hey, sometimes a red is just a red and you need it even though there's not a red in your template color theme. That's the purpose of the standard colors.

Applying enhanced fills and effects

Although the Shape Styles gallery often includes at least one gradient style, there are times when you need to create your own. In addition to enhanced fills, PowerPoint also offers a wide variety of effects; for example, soft shadows, reflections, and bevels.

In this exercise, you'll apply and edit a gradient fill. You'll also apply a shadow and 3-D effects to a shape.

➡ SET UP **You don't need any practice files to complete this exercise. Open PowerPoint to a new, blank presentation, and then follow the steps.**

1   Select the first (and only) slide. On the **Home** tab, click the **Layout** button and choose the **Blank** layout so the content placeholders don't get in your way while you're drawing.

2   Draw a rectangle on the slide.

3   Double-click the rectangle to activate the **Drawing Tools Format** tool tab, and then click the **Shape Fill** button to open the **Shape Fill** list.

4   Click **Gradient** and then select the **Linear Down** option from the gallery.

14

5   Right-click the rectangle and choose **Format Shape** to open the **Format Shape** pane.

TIP You can also access the Format Shape pane by selecting More Gradients at the bottom of the Gradient gallery.

6   On the **Shape Options Fill and Line** (paint bucket) pane, click **Fill** to expand the fill options part of the pane.

7   Look for the **Gradient stops** slider. Click the first gradient stop on the left, then click the **Color** button and select the black swatch in the **Theme Colors** gallery to change the first gradient stop to black.

8   Select the second gradient stop (in the middle),and then click the **Remove Gradient Stop** button to delete it.

9   In the **Format Shape** pane, with the **Fill and Line** pane still active, click **Line** to expand that section of the pane, and then click **No Line** to remove the border from the rectangle.

> **TIP** You can use the tools that appear on the Drawing Tools Format tool tab, on the Format Shape pane, or on the shortcut menu to format shapes.

10   In the **Format Shape** pane, click **Shape Options**, then click **Shadow** to access the shadow options. Click **Presets** and choose **Offset Diagonal Bottom Right** to apply a soft drop shadow.

14

11   In the **Distance** field, enter **10**. In the **Blur** field, enter **12** to soften the shadow.

12   With the rectangle still selected, click **Shadow** in the **Format Shape** pane to collapse those tools. Click **3-D Format** to expand those options.

13   In the **Format Shape** pane, in **3-D Format** tools, click **Top Bevel** and choose the **Circle** option. In the **Depth** field, enter **75**.

TIP All the fills, outlines, and effects that you can apply to shapes can also be applied to text, because PowerPoint 2013 considers text to be just another type of shape. Look for the text formatting tools on the Drawing Tools Format tool tab in the Word-Art Styles group. Or click Text Options in the Format Shape pane.

TIP If you're looking for a way to make circular text, don't despair! Select your text, then head to the Drawing Tools Format tool tab. In the WordArt Styles group, click the Text Effects button and choose Transform.

14   Collapse the **3-D Format** tools and expand the **3-D Rotation** options. Click the **Presets** button (which is also available on the **Drawing Tools Format** tool tab in the **Shape Effects** list) and choose **Perspective Left**.

15   Enter **40** in the **X Rotation** field, **5** in the **Y rotation** field, and **50** in the **Perspective** field.

16   Expand the **Shadow** tools in the **Format Shape** pane and change the **Angle** to **0**.

Format Shape

SHAPE OPTIONS | TEXT OPTIONS

▲ SHADOW

Presets

Color

Transparency ————|——— 60%

Size ————————|— 100%

Blur —|——————— 12 pt

Angle |——————— 0°

Distance —|—————— 10 pt

▷ REFLECTION

✖ CLEAN UP Save the presentation if you want, and then close it.

Creating your own shapes

In addition to allowing you to format shapes with a huge variety of options, PowerPoint gives you the ability to manipulate shapes as well as create your own. These are wonderful things to know about so you can create exactly the shape you need.

In this exercise, you will use the adjustment handles and edit points to modify shapes. You'll also use the new Merge Shapes tools to create your own.

➜ SET UP You need the SampleContentA_start presentation located in the Chapter14 practice file folder to complete this exercise. Open the SampleContentA_start presentation, and save it as SampleContentA. Then follow the steps.

1   Select the arrow on the first slide.

2   Click the yellow adjustment handle on the head of the arrow and drag it to the left. Release the mouse button to apply the change to the arrow.

14

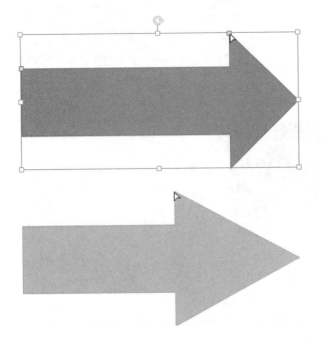

3 Click the yellow adjustment handle on the shaft of the arrow and use it to make the arrow slightly narrower.

4 Select the rounded rectangle. Drag the adjustment handle to the left to make the round corner less round.

5   On either the **Home** or **Insert** tab, in the **Shapes Gallery**, in the **Lines** area, choose
      Freeform.

6   Click the slide to begin your freeform. Click again a few inches away. Click again as
      though you were creating a rough rectangle. Click a fourth time near the first point
      to close the rectangle.

7   Right-click the shape and choose **Edit Points**, the PowerPoint equivalent of Bezier
      Curves.

8   Click one of the points and move it to change the shape of the freeform.

14

TIP You can also right-click the points in Edit Points mode to change them to Corner, Straight, or Smooth points. Grab the white square on the adjustment handles to modify the curve of the segments adjacent to these points. Right-clicking also lets you add and delete points and segments.

TIP You can use Edit Points on all shapes (except lines), not only on freeform shapes you've created yourself.

9   Click away to deselect the shape and exit **Edit Points**.

10   On **Slide 2**, select the red circle on the right and drag it toward the two circles above. Let go when the arrows appear on the **Smart Guides** to indicate that the distance between the circles is equal.

11   Duplicate one of the circles and drag it into place at the end of the row.

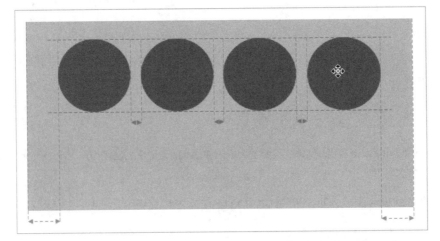

12   Press **Shift** and click each circle to select all four. Press **Ctrl+C** to copy them and **Ctrl+V** to paste.

13   With all four circles still selected, drag them into place below the top row. The **Smart Guides** will appear again to assist.

14 Press the **Esc** key to ensure you have nothing selected. Click the gray rectangle to select it. Press **Shift** and click each red circle in turn to select them all.

15 On the **Drawing Tools Format** tool tab, click **Merge Shapes**, then click **Combine** to cut out the circles from the rectangle.

IMPORTANT The order in which objects are selected is important when you're using the Merge Shapes tools. If things aren't turning out like you expect, try selecting the shapes in a different order.

14

16   Right-click the shape and choose **Format Shape** to open the **Format Shape** pane. Use the techniques you learned in the previous exercise to apply a bevel and shadow to the shape.

TIP You can format your new custom shape just as you would any other shape.

✖ CLEAN UP **Save the presentation if you want, and then close it.**

Inserting, cropping, and formatting pictures

As with most things in PowerPoint, there are a number of ways to insert pictures into your presentation. And, as with most other types of graphics in PowerPoint, pictures have a huge set of formatting tools to enhance their look and feel. Applying these effects to pictures throughout your presentation can also make a set of disparate images look like they go together.

In this exercise, you'll insert a screen shot as well as a picture from your computer. You'll use the crop tool and the picture formatting tools to enhance it.

 SET UP **You need the SampleContentB_start presentation and the SamplePictureB image file located in the Chapter14 practice file folder to complete this exercise. Open the SampleContentB_start presentation, and save it as SampleContentB. Then follow the steps.**

1 Select the last slide, and then on the **Insert** tab of the ribbon, click **Screenshot**.

2 Thumbnails of your open windows appear. This includes other PowerPoint files, but not the current file. (If only PowerPoint is open, there will be only one thumbnail.) Click a thumbnail to add it to your presentation.

3 Press **Ctrl+Z** to undo the action and remove the screen shot.

4 On the **Insert** tab, click **Pictures** to insert a picture from your computer or network drives. Navigate to the **SamplePictureB.png** file and click **Insert** to add it to the slide.

14

SEE ALSO For more information about inserting online pictures, see Chapter 2, "Using shared Office features."

5   Press and hold **Ctrl+Shift** and drag a corner of the picture toward the center. (**Shift** keeps the image aspect ratio intact, and **Ctrl** sizes it from the center.)

6   On the **Picture Tools Format** tool tab, click the top of the **Crop** button. Move your pointer toward the crop handle on the right edge of the picture until it turns into a black T-bar. Click the right edge of the picture and drag it left to crop. Click away from the picture to apply the crop.

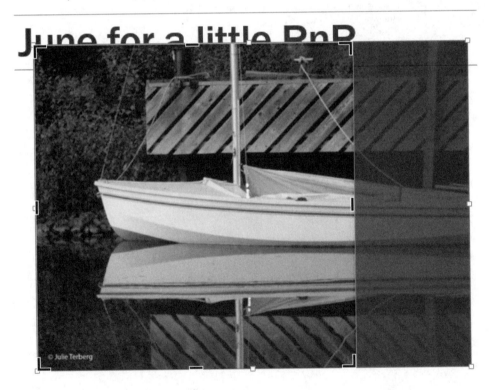

7   On the **Picture Tools Format** tool tab, click **Color** to open the **Recolor** gallery. Select **Turquoise, Accent color 1 Light** to apply a duotone look to the image.

Color Saturation

Color Tone

Recolor

More Variations

Set Transparent Color

Turquoise, Accent color 1 Light

8   To give the image a more abstract look, click the **Artistic Effects** button. Select **Pencil Grayscale**.

Corrections Color Artistic Effects

Compress Pictures
Change Picture
Reset Picture

Pencil Grayscale

Artistic Effects Options...

14

Picture tools are right at your fingertips

You can access the PowerPoint picture formatting tools in a couple of different places. Throughout this picture exercise, we've been using the tools on the Picture Tools Format tool tab that appears when you select a picture. You can also right-click a picture and choose Format Picture to access formatting options in a task pane. Artistic Effects settings are accessed from the Effects button, and settings for Picture Corrections (sharpen/soften, brightness/contrast), Picture Color, and Crop are accessed from the Picture button.

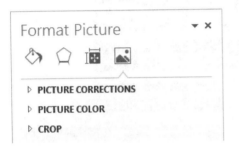

If your pictures are very large, you may want to use Compress Pictures to help keep your PowerPoint file size manageable. Select this tool from the Picture Tools Format tool tab that appears when you select a picture. It gives you options to permanently delete the cropped parts of pictures, and you can choose from four compression options.

9   To add a frame to the image and make it look like a snapshot, click the **Picture Tools Format** tool tab, then click the **More** button to expand the **Picture Styles** gallery. In the gallery, select **Rotated, White**.

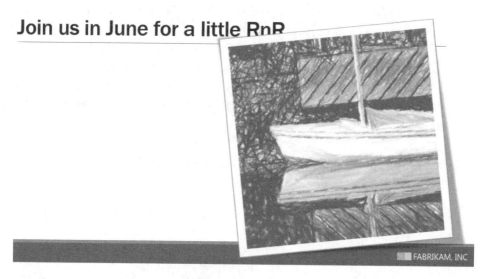

Join us in June for a little RnR

FABRIKAM, INC

TIP If you mess up your picture while you're playing with the picture formatting tools (after all, they're pretty darned fun!), click the Reset Picture button on the Picture Tools Format tool tab.

10   Move and size the picture so it overlaps the title a bit.

14

11   Click inside the **Title** placeholder. On the **Home** tab, click **Arrange** and then **Bring to Front** so the text is in front of the image.

TIP The Order Objects tools (Bring to Front, Send to Back, and so on) can be used on all images and objects, including shapes, SmartArt graphics, tables, charts, videos, placeholders, and text boxes. They are located on the Home tab in the Drawing Group, from the Arrange button. They can also be accessed from the formatting tabs. The Selection pane is an extension of these tools. It can be accessed from the Editing group on the Home tab. Click the arrow next to the Select button, and then choose Selection Pane from the list.

 CLEAN UP **Save the presentation if you want, and then close it.**

Removing the background from a picture

PowerPoint has a couple of tools you can use to remove backgrounds from pictures. These can be especially handy, for example, when you are working on a dark slide and your logo or other image has a white background.

To use the Remove Background tool, insert a picture, then click the Remove Background button on the Picture Tools Format tool tab.

PowerPoint will add a selection area to the part of the picture it thinks you want to keep.

Expand or contract the selected area by dragging the selection handles, and use the tools on the Background Removal tool tab to mark additional areas to keep or remove.

When you apply the changes, PowerPoint will remove parts of the image that are colored magenta. Click Keep Changes (or simply click away from the picture to deselect it) to apply the changes.

14

The other tool you can use to remove some backgrounds is the Transparent Wand tool. It's located on the Picture Tools Format tool tab, under the Color button, as the Set Transparent Color tool.

Click it, then click the color you want to remove on your image. The transparent wand tool removes pixels of color with the exact RGB values as the pixel you click.

Key points

- Using the styles galleries can save you time and provide consistency for your presentation.

- PowerPoint lets you apply and tweak settings for special effects such as shadows, reflections, glows, soft edges, and 3-D.

- Formatting tools can be found on the tabs that appear when you select an object.

- Most of the same formatting tools can be found by right-clicking an object and selecting Format Shape, Format Picture, or Format Text.

- You can create your own shapes by using the Merge Shapes tools.

Chapter at a glance

Animate

Animate by using the Animation Painter, page 366

Edit

Edit video and apply transitions, page 371

Save

Save your presentation as a video, page 375

Adding animation and multimedia

IN THIS CHAPTER, YOU WILL LEARN HOW TO

- Add animation to text and shapes.

- Edit video and apply transitions.

- Insert and play online video.

- Save your presentation as a video.

Microsoft PowerPoint 2013 makes it easy to include audio and video in presentations, along with more common animation and transition effects. In fact, you can even perform some basic multimedia editing tasks right inside PowerPoint. Have you ever needed to snip just a couple of seconds off the end of a video in your presentation? Well, now you can.

As we become increasingly more dependent on the cloud, PowerPoint follows suit, offering a number of options for inserting online media content. In addition, PowerPoint 2013 takes it a step farther and gives you the ability to save your own presentations as videos, in either MPEG-4 or Windows Media Video format.

In this chapter, you'll learn how to apply basic animations to text and shapes, how to add video to your slides, how to edit videos, how to insert an online video, and how to save your presentation as a video.

PRACTICE FILES To complete the exercises in this chapter, you need the practice files contained in the Chapter15 practice file folder. For more information, see "Download the practice files" in this book's Introduction.

Adding animation to text and shapes

Animation can add splash to your presentation, but it's important to use it effectively. Animation should have a purpose—to demonstrate a process, to emphasize a point, to control the flow of text, and so on. It should not be added "just because." Keeping it simple is a good rule of thumb when working with animation effects in PowerPoint.

In this exercise, you'll apply entrance and exit animation effects to placeholder text and shapes.

➜ SET UP **You need the SampleContentA_start presentation located in the Chapter15 practice file folder to complete this exercise. Open the SampleContentA_start presentation, and save it as SampleContentA. Then follow the steps. The SampleContentA_end. PPTX file has also been included in the practice file folder to help you monitor your success with this exercise.**

1   Click the edge of the text placeholder on slide **3** to select it.

   TROUBLESHOOTING If you're having trouble selecting a placeholder by clicking its edge, click the text inside, and then press the Esc key on your keyboard.

2   On the **Animations** tab, click **Fade** in the **Animation** gallery. The animation will be displayed on the slide.

Animation gallery

3   Notice the numbers next to the text on the slide. These will be displayed when the **Animations** tab is active on the ribbon. This shows you the sequential order of the animated objects.

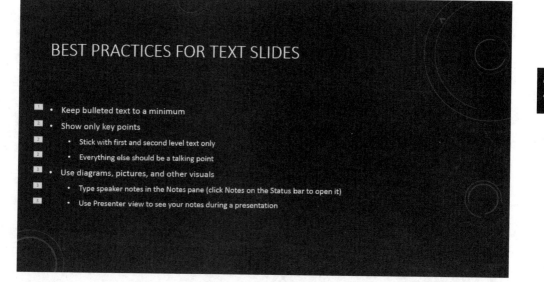

TIP When you select an object on the slide, its animation is highlighted in the Animation pane. Likewise, if you select an animation in the Animation pane, the sequence number will be highlighted next to it on the slide.

4 Press **Shift+F5** to start a presentation on this slide and review how the animation works in Slide Show view. Click once to reveal the first bullet point, and then click a second time to reveal the second point and its sub-bullets. Click again to reveal the third point and its sub-bullets. Keep clicking or press **Esc** to end the slide show.

5 Go to slide **2** and select the top rectangle. In the **Animation** gallery, click **Wipe**, which will bring the object onto the slide with a wiping motion from bottom to top.

6 With the top rectangle still selected, click **Effect Options** on the **Animations** tab, then click **From Top** to change the direction of the wipe animation you just added.

7   With the top rectangle still selected, click **Add Animation**. Scroll down to the **Exit** animations and click **Fade**. A **Fade** exit animation will be added to the top rectangle.

8   Click the **Animation** pane button on the ribbon to open the **Animation** pane.

TIP Entrance animations are indicated with a green icon, exit animations with red, and emphasis animations with yellow.

9   Select the second animation in the **Animation** pane. This is the exit animation you applied to the rectangle in step 7. On the ribbon, change **Start (On Click)** to **Start**

With Previous so that the rectangle disappears at the same time the previous animation occurs.

TIP If there is a number next to the animation in the Animation pane, then that animation starts when you click the mouse. If there is no number alongside the animation, then it is set to Start With Previous (which means it starts at the same time as the prior animation), or After Previous (which means the animation starts at the completion of the prior animation).

10 Select the top rectangle on the slide, and then double-click the **Animation Painter** to activate it.

TIP Click the Animation Painter once to paint animation settings from one object to another. Double-click the Animation Painter to make it "sticky" so you can apply animations to more than one object. Press Esc to deactivate it when you're finished.

11 Click each of the remaining rectangles on the slide to apply the same animation settings as you did with the top rectangle. Press **Esc** to exit the **Animation Painter**.

12 In the **Animation** pane, select the **Rectangle 6** exit animation. Drag it into position after the **Rectangle 9** entrance animation. This causes **Rectangle 6** to fade away at the same time **Rectangle 9** wipes in.

TIP PowerPoint 2013 lets you drag animations into the Animation pane. Or, you can use the up and down arrow buttons to reorder animations.

13 Select the **Rectangle 9** exit animation and drag it into place immediately following the **Rectangle 12** entrance animation. This causes **Rectangle 9** to fade away at the same time **Rectangle 12** wipes in. Rearrange the remaining exit animations so that one rectangle exits when the next rectangle enters.

14 Select the **Rectangle 18** exit animation in the **Animation** pane and press **Delete** to remove the animation. This guarantees that **Rectangle 18** won't disappear as it appears!

TIP If you have a long or complex animation sequence, select one of the animations in the Animation pane and then click Play From at the top of the pane. PowerPoint will begin playing the animation from that point, temporarily hiding the previous animations, so you don't have to watch them.

15 Press **F5** to begin the presentation from the first slide and click through it to review the animations. The **SampleContentA_end.PPTX** file has been included in your practice files to help you monitor your success with this exercise.

❌ CLEAN UP **Save the presentation if you want, and then close it.**

Editing video and applying transitions

Animation lets you add movement to an object on a slide. Transitions let you add movement between one slide and the next slide. And video adds another dimension of movement altogether. You can easily add all these to your presentations.

In this exercise, you'll add and edit a video and apply transitions to your presentation.

➡ SET UP **You need the SampleContentB_start presentation and the Fabrikam Employee Excursion.wmv video located in the Chapter15 practice file folder to complete this exercise. Open the SampleContentB_start presentation, and save it as SampleContentB. Then follow the steps.**

1 With slide **3** selected, click the bottom of the **New Slide** button on the **Home** tab, then click **Blank** to add a new slide based on the **Blank** layout.

2 With the new slide (slide **4**) selected, on the **Insert** tab, click **Video**, and then click **Video on My PC**.

3 Navigate to the **Fabrikam Employee Excursion.wmv** file, select it, and then click **Insert** to add the video to slide **4**. The video will be inserted in the middle of the slide.

TIP Audio and video files are embedded by default when you insert them into PowerPoint 2013. If you prefer to link a multimedia file, in the Insert dialog box, click the arrow next to the Insert button and choose Link To File.

4 With the video selected, click the **Video Tools Playback** tab and change the **Start On Click** setting to **Start Automatically** so the video begins playing as soon as you transition to slide **4**.

TROUBLESHOOTING When an animation is set to Start On Click, the animation begins when you click the mouse. You don't have to click anything special or have your mouse pointer in a specific location. With video, however, Start On Click indicates that the video will start when you click the multimedia controls, which appear when you move your mouse pointer near the video. This means you must move your pointer to the video in order to play it; a random mouse click won't do.

5 With the video still selected, click the **Trim Video** button to open the **Trim Video** dialog box.

6 Slide the green **Start Time** indicator to the right until it is at timepoint **00:10.669**. Use the arrows in the **Start Time** field, if necessary, or enter **10.669** directly into the **Start Time** field and press **Tab** to set the **Start** time.

7 Slide the red **End Time** indicator to the left until it is at timepoint **00:33.213**. As with the **Start Time** field, you can manually input time into the **End Time** field as necessary.

8 Click **OK** to apply the trims.

9 On the **Transitions** tab, scroll through the transitions until you can click **Peel Off**, which is located in the **Exciting** group of transitions. Click **Apply To All** to add a page turn transition to all of your slides.

TIP Use simple transitions for the bulk of your slides. Nobody wants to sit through a whole presentation of Vortex or Glitter transitions! When in doubt, a modest fade is always a good bet. Save the more dramatic transitions to add extra impact to your title slides and section dividers.

❌ CLEAN UP **Save the presentation if you want, and then close it.**

Playing sound across slides

Inserting an audio file is basically like inserting anything else. Click the Insert tab, click Audio, and then choose whether you want to add a sound file from your computer or insert a sound file that will download from Office.com.

After the audio file has been inserted into your presentation, you can trim it and fade it just as you can with video. In addition, you can insert a sound file on the first slide and then click the Play In Background button on the Audio Tools Playback tab to have PowerPoint treat your sound as a background track. (The buttons to Start Automatically, Play Across Slides, Loop Until Stopped, and Hide During Show are all activated when you click Play In Background.)

Inserting and playing online video

It's not unusual to want to put a short video clip from an online source (such as YouTube) into your presentation. PowerPoint 2013 makes it easy to do that by using the video's embed code. Be aware that even though you're using an embed code to control the video, it's still online, and it's still linked to your presentation. That means you'll need a good solid Internet connection in order to play the online video during your presentation.

In this exercise, you'll insert an online video into your presentation.

→ **SET UP** **You need the SampleContentC_start presentation located in the Chapter15 practice file folder to complete this exercise. You will also need an Internet connection in order to insert an online video. Open the SampleContentC_start presentation, and save it as SampleContentC. Then follow the steps.**

1   Select slide **5**, choose **Insert**, then **Video**, and then **Online Video**.

2   If necessary, click the **Also Insert From YouTube** icon to enable adding video from YouTube.

3   Enter **Fabrikam Employee Excursion** in the YouTube search box and press **Enter**.

Insert Video

4   There will be only one search result. Select the video, and then click **Insert**.

5   Press **Shift+F5** to play the presentation and test the video. Click the **Play** button on the YouTube video to start it.

TIP Your video must be public in order to search for it. If the video is not public, paste the embed code into the From A Video Embed Code field.

TROUBLESHOOTING If you need to get an embed code from YouTube, on the You-Tube video page, click Share, then Embed, and then Use Old Embed Code. Copy and paste that embed code into the From A Video Embed Code field.

✖ CLEAN UP Save the presentation if you want, and then close it.

Saving your presentation as a video

PowerPoint 2013 gives you the option to save your presentation as either a .wmv or an .mp4-formatted video. It does a very good job of keeping animations and transitions intact, but they are all converted to automatic animations. After all, you can't click to animate an object in a video. PowerPoint also includes most audio and video you've added to the presentation, so you can create a video of a video! However, some files, such as online videos, will not be included when you save your presentation as a video.

If you've added automatic transition timings (Advance After __ Seconds), then PowerPoint will use those as it creates the video. Otherwise, you will have the option of specifying how long PowerPoint will remain on each slide. You also have options to choose different sizes of video, which comes in handy when you're creating videos for various purposes.

In this exercise, you'll save your presentation as a video.

 SET UP **You need the SampleContentD_start presentation located in the Chapter15 practice file folder to complete this exercise. Open the SampleContentD_start presentation, and save it as SampleContentD. Because the Fabrikam Employee Excursion video from YouTube has been inserted into this file, you may receive a security warning, "References to external media objects have been blocked." Click the Enable Content button to allow PowerPoint to reference the YouTube video, and then follow the steps.**

1   Click **File**, **Export**, and then **Create a Video**.

2   In the **Create a Video** settings on the right, change **Seconds Spent on Each Slide** from **5.00** to **7.00**.

SampleContentD_start - PowerPoint

Export

Info
New
Open
Save
Save As
Print
Share
Export
Close

Account
Options

Create PDF/XPS Document

Create a Video

Package Presentation for CD

Create Handouts

Change File Type

Create a Video
Save your presentation as a video that you can burn to a disc, upload to the web, or email
- Incorporates all recorded timings, narrations, and laser pointer gestures
- Preserves animations, transitions, and media

Get help burning your slide show video to DVD or uploading it to the web

Computer & HD Displays
For viewing on a computer monitor, projector, or high definition display (Large — 1280 x 720)

Don't Use Recorded Timings and Narrations
No timings or narrations have been recorded

Seconds spent on each slide: 07.00

Create Video

3   Leave the **Computer & HD Displays** option set at **Computer & HD Displays** (Large size).

4   Click the **Create Video** button, enter a name for the video, and click **Save**.

TIP To save the video in a .wmv format instead of the default .mp4 video format, click the Create Video button. Then in the Save As dialog box, change the Save as Type from MPEG-4 Video to Windows Media Video.

5   A message box appears to explain that some of the media in the presentation can't be included in the video. Click **Continue without media**.

TIP While PowerPoint is saving your video, a progress bar appears on the status bar at the bottom of the PowerPoint window. If you need to cancel the video creation for any reason, click the X to the right of the progress bar.

6   Play the video in your favorite video application. You'll find that the animations and transitions have all become automatic, the YouTube video is missing from the last slide, and just a static picture of the first frame is displayed.

❌ CLEAN UP **Save the presentation if you want, and then close it.**

Key points

- Animations add movement to objects on a slide, whereas transitions move the presentation from one slide to the next.

- When it comes to animations and transitions, "less is more" is a good rule of thumb.

- Audio and video files are embedded into PowerPoint 2013 by default.

- Even if you use an embed code to insert an online video into your presentation, that video is *not* embedded in your presentation.

- You can save your presentation as a video, and PowerPoint will leave animations, transitions, and most multimedia intact.

- Online video is not included when you save your presentation as a video.

Chapter at a glance

Organize

Organize slides by using sections,
page 380

Comment

Insert comments,
page 384

Finalize

Finalize your presentation,
page 391

Present

Practice with Presenter view,
page 401

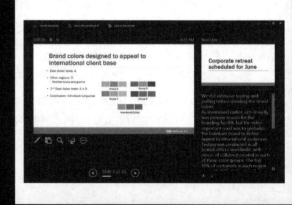

Finalizing and presenting

16

IN THIS CHAPTER, YOU WILL LEARN HOW TO

- Add and rename sections.

- Insert comments.

- Print a presentation.

- Finalize a presentation.

- Deliver a presentation.

- Practice with Presenter view.

You may need to collaborate with others as you develop your presentation. Microsoft PowerPoint 2013 makes this process easy, with features that support commenting, sharing, and broadcasting online. You may also need to use these tools and others as you finalize and deliver your presentation.

In this chapter, you'll work with sections, comments, and tools such as the Document Inspector and the Accessibility Checker.

PRACTICE FILES To complete the exercises in this chapter, you need the practice files contained in the Chapter16 practice file folder. For more information, see "Download the practice files" in this book's Introduction.

Adding and renaming sections

Sections are a useful administrative tool for grouping slides. For example, you might divide a presentation by subject to make it easier to navigate when you're giving the presentation. Or you might divide it among a number of colleagues, each of whom takes responsibility for developing the slides in one section of the presentation. Whatever the reason, sections can be tremendously helpful for managing content within a PowerPoint file.

In this exercise, you'll add and manipulate sections.

➜ SET UP **You need the SampleContentA_start presentation located in the Chapter16 practice file folder to complete this exercise. Open the SampleContentA_start presentation and click Enable Content if you're prompted to do so. Save the presentation as SampleContentA. Then follow the steps.**

1 With slide **6** selected, on the **Home** tab, in the **Slides** group, click **Section**, then **Add Section**. A section called **Untitled Section** will be added, and the slides in it (slides **6** through **10**) will be selected. (Another existing section begins with slide **11**.)

2   With the **Untitled Section** still selected, click the **Section** button on the **Home** tab again and choose **Rename Section**.

> **TROUBLESHOOTING** Click the name of a section to select it. When a section is selected, its name will be bold and orange, and all slides in the section will be selected.

> **TIP** You can add, edit, and manipulate sections by right-clicking a slide thumbnail or section name in the Slides pane.

3   In the **Rename Section** dialog box, enter **Future Growth (Taneyhill)** and click **Rename**. **Untitled Section** changes to **Future Growth (Taneyhill)** in the **Slides** pane.

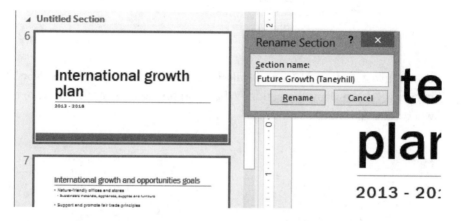

4   On the **View** tab, click **Slide Sorter** to switch to **Slide Sorter** view.

> **TIP** You can access Slide Sorter view from either the View tab or the status bar.

5   On the **Home** tab, click **Section**, then **Collapse All** to collapse all sections.

6   Click the last section, **HR info (Wakefield)**, to select it. Drag the section ahead of the previous **Future Growth** section. When you release the mouse button, the section will be repositioned.

7   Click the arrows next to the **Introduction** and the **New Branding** sections to expand them.

8   Click slide **1** to select it. Drag it into the **New Branding** section just before slide **2**, the Fabrikam rebrand campaign slide. Release the mouse button to place the slide in the **New Branding** section.

9   Click the **Introduction** section, and on the **Home** tab, click **Section**, then **Remove Section** to delete the empty **Introduction** section.

TIP Remove Section removes a section designation, but it doesn't remove any slides. If you want to delete all the slides in a section, right-click the section name in the Slides pane or in Slide Sorter view and choose Remove Section & Slides.

TIP You can double-click a slide thumbnail in Slide Sorter view to return to Normal view.

✖ CLEAN UP **Save the presentation if you want, and then close it.**

Inserting comments

Like sections, comments are also very helpful when developing a presentation. When you add a comment to a slide or an object, anyone reviewing the file in Normal view will be able to view and respond to it, but the comments will not be displayed in Slide Show view. This makes comments a handy way to communicate with colleagues as you're developing a presentation. The introduction of the new threaded Comments pane improves this feature in PowerPoint 2013, especially to enhance collaboration via the cloud.

In this exercise, you'll add comments to your PowerPoint file.

➡ SET UP **You need the SampleContentB_Start presentation located in the Chapter16 practice file folder to complete this exercise. Open the SampleContentB_Start presentation, and save it as SampleContentB. Then follow the steps.**

1   Click the **Comments** button on the status bar to open the **Comments** pane.

TIP You can also access Comments tools on the Review tab of the ribbon.

2   With slide **1** selected, in the **Comments** pane, click the **Next** button to move to the next comment in the file.

You'll be taken to slide **3**.

3   Click **Next** again, and you'll be taken to slide **8**. In the **Comments** pane, click inside the **Reply** box and enter **No, it's an embedded video.** Then press **Enter** to create the comment.

Comments

New

Kate T 53 minutes ago

Is this an online video? I don't think we'll have a good Internet connection in the ballroom.

Robin Wakefield A few seconds ago

No, it's an embedded video.

Reply...

4   Select slide **5** and in the **Comments** pane, click **New** to add a new comment. Enter **Kate, be sure to review notes**, and then press **Enter** to create the comment.

Comments icon

Comments

New

◢ **Robin Wakefield** A few seconds ago ✕
Kate, be sure to review notes

Reply...

Brand colors designed to appeal to international client base

- East Asian tests: A
- Other regions: D

TIP You can click a Comments icon on the slide to open the Comments pane to that comment.

TIP You can move Comments icons on a slide. Just drag them.

5   Click the **Next** button four times, until Kate's comment on slide **13** is selected.

6   Click the **X** in the upper-right corner of Kate's comment to delete it.

TIP To quickly delete all comments in a file, click the bottom of the Delete button on the Review tab and choose Delete All Comments And Ink In This Presentation.

❌ CLEAN UP **Save the presentation if you want, and then close it.**

Printing slides and notes

Although we're moving to a more digital world and printing less and less, sometimes you still need to print your slides or your notes. PowerPoint gives you a number of options for this. You can print full page slides if you need to display one slide per page. Or you can print handouts, which lets you choose how many smaller slide thumbnails should appear on each page. You can also print the note pages, which include a slide thumbnail plus any speaker notes you added in the Notes pane. There are also options to print comments or print only a specific section.

In this exercise, you'll print your PowerPoint file.

SET UP **You need the SampleContentC_Start presentation located in the Chapter16 practice file folder to complete this exercise. Open the SampleContentC_Start presentation, and save it as SampleContentC. Then follow the steps.**

1   Choose **File**, then **Print**.

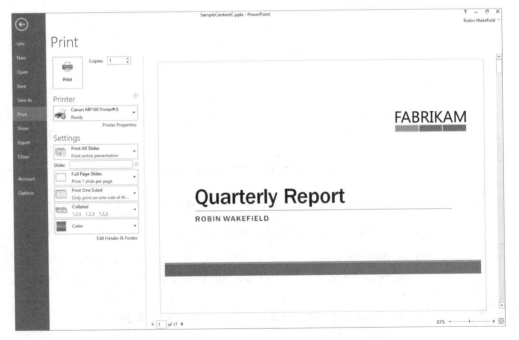

TIP If there are comments in the file, PowerPoint will print them by default. If you do not want to print comments, deselect them by going to File, Print. In the Print Layout options (where you can choose to print full page slides or multiple slides per page), clear the option to Print Comments And Ink.

2   In the **Print** dialog box, click **Print All Slides** to access options for which slides to print. Choose **HR info (Wakefield)** in the **Sections** options to print only slides included in that section.

3   Click **Full Page Slides** to access the **Print Layout** settings.

4   Select **Notes Pages** to print your slides with their speaker notes. Also make sure that **Print Comments and Ink Markup** remains checked so the comments included in the file will print.

Print Layout

| Full Page Slides | Notes Pages | Outline |

Handouts

1 Slide	2 Slides	3 Slides
4 Slides Horizontal	6 Slides Horizontal	9 Slides Horizontal
4 Slides Vertical	6 Slides Vertical	9 Slides Vertical

Frame Slides
✓ Scale to Fit Paper
High Quality
✓ Print Comments and Ink Markup

Notes Pages
Print slides with notes

Print One Sided
Only print on one side of th...

Collated
1,2,3   1,2,3   1,2,3

Portrait Orientation

Color

Edit Header & Footer

5   Below the preview of the slides, use the next and previous arrows to move through the pages to see how your notes pages will look when printed.

6   When you get to page **4**, Use the **Zoom** slider at the lower-right of the **Print** page to help you view the comments more clearly, then click the **Zoom to Page** button to view the entire page again.

Slide 8

KT3   Is this an online video? I don't think we'll have a good Internet connection in the ballroom.
        Kate T. 1/12/2013

RW8   No, it's an embedded video.
        Robin Wakefield, 1/12/2013

◄ 4 of 6 ►   100% —————|————+ ⊡

Print Preview navigation   Zoom to Page button

TIP To create a PDF of your presentation, choose File, Export, Create PDF/XPS Document, then click the Create PDF/XPS Document button to open the Publish As PDF Or XPS dialog box. Click Options in that dialog box if you want to print notes pages or multiple slides per page.

7　Click the **Print Preview** nagivation arrow to show the print preview of page **5**. Click it again to view a preview of page **6**, which displays the leftover notes from slide **5**.

❌ CLEAN UP **If you have a printer connected to your computer, click Print to print the six notes pages. Otherwise, save the presentation if you want, and then close it.**

Finalizing your presentation

PowerPoint has a number of tools you might want to use as you finalize your presentation. Although you can check spelling from the Review tab, most of the other finalization tools are located in the Backstage view. To access them, click the File tab, then Info.

If there are any multimedia files in your presentation, you may find options to Optimize Compatibility and Compress Media. Clicking Optimize Compatibility converts older .wmv files as well as video file types such as QuickTime .mov files to newer Windows Media Video format so they're more likely to play on other PCs. It also prompts you to embed any linked multimedia files so they're not lost if you transfer your presentation to another computer. Use Compress Media to make the media files smaller, which in turn makes your PowerPoint file size smaller. Be sure to run the presentation in Slide Show view after you compress it to ensure that the media quality hasn't suffered.

Protect Presentation includes an option to Mark As Final, which prevents users from making changes to the file. Note that this is only an administrative tool. Its sole purpose is to prevent users from making inadvertent changes to the presentation. Anyone can simply click Mark As Final again to unmark the presentation and allow changes again, or someone can click the Edit Anyway button that appears when a presentation that's been marked as final is opened.

Inspect Presentation includes tools to Inspect Document, Check Accessibility, and Check Compatibility.

The Document Inspector is a great way to remove unwanted or personal content from your presentation all at once. For example, if you want to remove your speaker notes before sending your presentation to a client, click Inspect Document and choose the Presentation Notes option. Be sure to do this on a copy of your presentation, so you don't lose the only copy of your notes! You can also remove all comments and ink annotations in the file by using the Document Inspector.

Check Accessibility helps you make your presentation easier for people with disabilities to read. Select an object in the Accessibility Checker pane and then scroll through the Additional Information to get tips for fixing the associated accessibility problems.

16

Accessibility Checker ▾ ✕

Inspection Results

ERRORS

▷ Missing Alt Text (29)

TIPS

◢ Ensure Caption Usage
Fabrikam Employee Excursion (Slid...
◢ Check Reading Order
Slide 4
Slide 7
Slide 8
Slide 12

Additional Information   ⌄

How To Fix:

To add alternate text to a picture or object:
1) Right-click on the object, and click Format.
2) Click Layout & Properties.

Select and fix each issue listed above to make this document accessible for people with disabilities.

Read more about making documents accessible

The Compatibility Checker tells you what issues you may experience when you save your file in a format for a previous version of PowerPoint (with a .ppt file extension). It runs by default when you save in that earlier file format, but you can access it at any time. For example, running the Compatibility Checker is helpful if you're wondering what types of issues people using previous versions of PowerPoint might encounter when trying to edit or view your .pptx file.

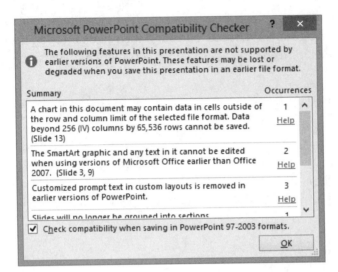

Delivering a presentation

To deliver a presentation to an audience, you must first put the presentation into Slide Show view. There are a number of ways to do this. You can click the shortcut icon on the status bar, click one of the options in the Start Slide Show group on the Slide Show tab, or press F5 on your keyboard.

KEYBOARD SHORTCUT Press F5 to start a presentation from the beginning. Press Shift+F5 to begin the presentation from the slide that's currently selected.

If your computer doesn't have another monitor (or a projector) attached to it, any of those actions will open the Slide Show view of your presentation. This is the full-screen presentation that your audience sees.

Fabrikam rebrand campaign

Pop-up Toolbar

If you have a second monitor or a projector attached to your computer, PowerPoint will also open Presenter view by default when you begin a slide show. Presenter view displays thumbnails of your current slide and the next slide, your speaker notes, a timer, and various navigation and inking tools. Your audience will see everything that happens in Slide Show view, but only you will see Presenter view.

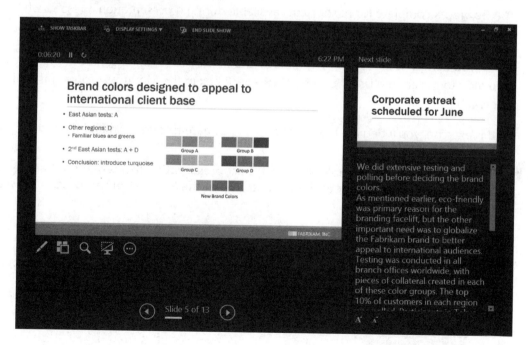

TROUBLESHOOTING If you start a slide show and don't see the full-screen Slide Show view on the correct monitor, choose a different monitor in the Monitors group on the Slide Show tab.

When you're in Slide Show view, there are a number of ways to navigate. Press the mouse button to move forward. On a touch device, you can swipe backward and forward. If you have a keyboard available, you can also press the spacebar, the Right Arrow key, the Down Arrow key, or the N key to move to the next slide. The Left Arrow key, the Up Arrow Key, or the P key will take you to the previous slide. Pressing the B key will black out the screen, which is a great way to bring focus back to you during a question and answer session, for example. If you know your content well, you can also enter the slide number and press the Enter key to jump to that slide. If you don't want to remember all those slide numbers (and who does?), PowerPoint 2013 also has a new See All Slides feature that shows thumbnails of all your slides, which allows you to quickly jump to any slide in the presentation.

TIP To view a complete list of shortcuts available during a presentation, press F1 while you're in Slide Show view.

TIP If you don't want Presenter view to activate when you're running Slide Show view with two monitors, clear the Use Presenter View check box in the Monitors group of the Slide Show tab.

In this exercise, you'll begin a presentation and navigate through some of the slides.

➡ SET UP **You need the SampleContentD_Start presentation located in the Chapter16 practice file folder to complete this exercise. Open the SampleContentD_Start presentation, and follow the steps.**

1   Select slide **2** in the **Slides** pane.

2   With slide **2** selected, click the **Slide Show** button on the status bar to begin your slide show from the selected slide.

TIP You can also begin your presentation by using the From Beginning or From Current Slide buttons in the Start Slide Show group on the Slide Show tab.

3   While in **Slide Show** view, press the **Down Arrow** key to advance one slide.

4   Press the **Up Arrow** key to move back to slide **2**.

5   Press the **Spacebar** to advance to slide **3**.

6   Press the **9** key and then press **Enter** to jump to slide **9**, which is titled **Fabrikam employee community contributions make a difference**.

7   Move your mouse pointer to the lower-left corner of the screen to activate the **Pop-up Toolbar**.

8   Click the **See All Slides** button to open the **Navigation Grid** that displays thumbnails of all the slides in the presentation.

TIP While you're in the Navigation Grid, click a section to go to the first slide of that section.

IMPORTANT If you activate the Navigation Grid in Slide Show view, your audience will see it. If you don't want the audience to see the Navigation Grid, activate it in Presenter view (see the section, "Practicing with Presenter view," later in this chapter).

9   Click the slide **12** thumbnail to see slide **12** in full-screen **Slide Show** view.

10   In **Slide Show** view, right-click anywhere on the screen and choose **Pointer Options**, then **Highlighter**.

TIP All of the tools on the right-click shortcut menu can also be accessed from the Pop-up Toolbar.

11   Drag the yellow highlighter cursor over the words **Conference Area** to highlight them on the slide.

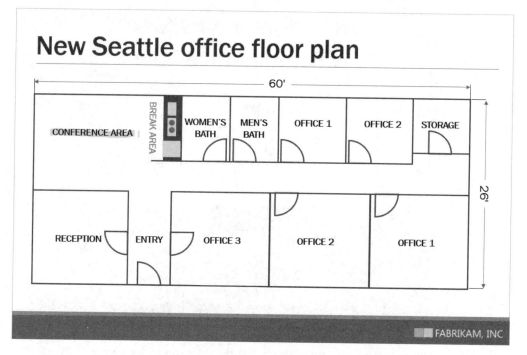

12   Press **Esc** to turn off the highlighter and return to the arrow pointer.

13   Click the **Zoom** tool on the **Pop-up Toolbar**.

14 When the pointer becomes a magnifying glass icon, click near the highlight you just added to zoom in on the conference area of the slide.

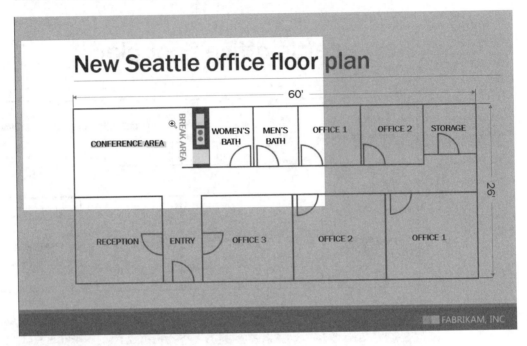

15 When the pointer turns into a hand icon, drag to pan around the slide.

16 Press **Esc** to exit pan and zoom mode.

TIP When you're using a touch-enabled device, you can stretch your fingers apart to zoom in on a slide. Pinch them together to zoom out. When you're not zoomed in on a slide, pinching will take you to See All Slides view.

17   Press **Esc** again to end your slide show and return to **Normal** view.

18   Click **Keep** if prompted to keep or discard your ink annotations.

✖ CLEAN UP **Save the presentation if you want, and then close it.**

TIP If you want your presentation to open in Slide Show view when you double-click it in a window, save the presentation as a PowerPoint Show (*.ppsx).

TIP To edit a presentation that's been saved as a slide show (with a .ppsx extension), open PowerPoint and choose File, then Open, and navigate to the file. When you open it from PowerPoint this way, it opens in Normal view so you can edit as you wish.

16

Practicing with Presenter view

Presenter view has been included in PowerPoint for many versions. It's an option that lets you see your slide thumbnails and speaker notes on your computer, while your audience sees only your full-screen slides on the projected screen.

PowerPoint 2013 takes Presenter view to a whole new level. Not only is it easier to find on the Slide Show tab of the ribbon, but it's also already turned on by default. Probably the most important enhancement is that you can now use Alt+F5 to open Presenter view without having a projector attached to the computer! This makes it simple and convenient to practice your delivery with Presenter view so you're fully prepared once you do get in front of an audience.

In this exercise, you'll open a presentation in Presenter view and navigate through it.

SET UP You need the SampleContentE_Start document located in your Chapter16 practice file folder to complete this exercise. Open the SampleContentE_Start document, and then follow the steps.

1   Press **Alt+F5** to open the presentation on slide **1** and access **Presenter** view.

> **IMPORTANT** If you have a projector or second monitor attached to your computer, Slide Show view will open in addition to Presenter view when you press Alt+F5. Remember, your audience sees Slide Show view, but they won't see Presenter view.

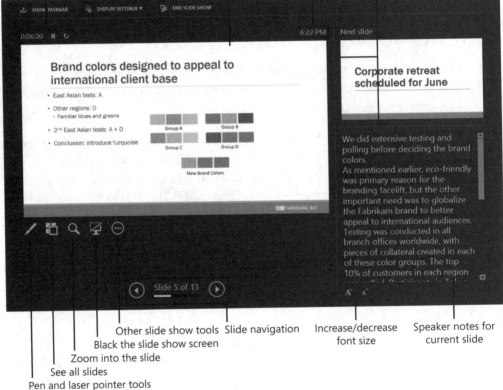

TROUBLESHOOTING If you do not see Presenter view on the correct monitor, try selecting a different monitor in the Monitor options on the Slide Show tab.

2   Click the right arrow at the bottom of the **Presenter** view screen until you get to slide **5**.

3   Move your mouse pointer over the vertical line separating the current slide from the notes and the next slide. When the mouse pointer turns into a double-headed arrow, drag to the left to increase the width of the **Next Slide** and **Notes** panes.

4   Move your mouse pointer over the horizontal line separating the next slide from the notes. When the mouse pointer turns into a double-headed arrow, drag up to increase the height of the **Notes** pane and decrease the height of the **Next Slide** pane.

5   Click the **Increase Font Size** button at the bottom of the screen to increase the size of your notes.

6   Click the **See All Slides** button to open the **Navigation Grid**.

You will see thumbnails of all your slides, but your audience won't.

7   Click slide **8** in the **Presenter** view **Navigation Grid** to advance the presentation to that slide.

8   In the current slide thumbnail in **Presenter** view, click the video to start it.

Your audience won't see this happen. They will only see the video begin to play in **Slide Show** view.

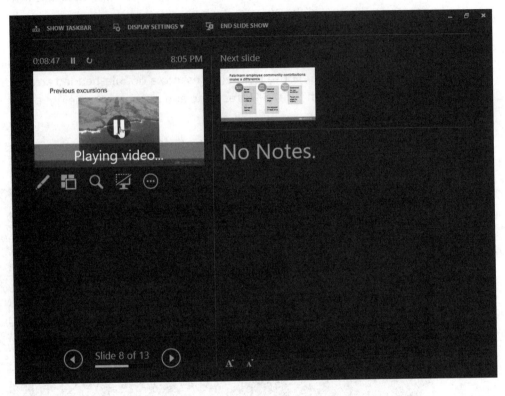

9   Navigate to slide **9** by using the arrows at the bottom of **Presenter** view.

10   Click the **Pen and Laser Pointer Tools** icon and select **Highlighter**.

Your mouse pointer changes to a yellow rectangle.

11   On the slide thumbnail in **Presenter** view, drag over the words **Raked Leaves** to high-light them. When you let go of the left mouse button, the highlight will appear in **Slide Show** view also.

12   Press **Esc** to return to the arrow pointer.

> **TIP** To point to an object on the slide while in Presenter view, select the Laser Pointer in the Pen And Laser Pointer Tools options, and then click the slide thumbnail. If you click the slide thumbnail with the typical arrow pointer, the audience won't see it in Slide Show view.

13   Click the **End Slide Show** button at the top of the **Presenter** view window to end the presentation and leave **Presenter** view.

14   Click **Keep** if prompted to keep or discard your ink annotations.

❌ CLEAN UP **Save the presentation if you want, and then close it.**

Key points

- Sections are very helpful for managing content and for presentation development.

- Mark As Final doesn't keep people from making edits to your presentation.

- PowerPoint 2013 uses a friendly threaded Comments pane.

- The redesigned Pop-up Toolbar makes slide show tools easier to access using touch-enabled devices.

- You can click the Zoom tool in Slide Show view or Presenter view to pan and zoom on your slide.

- You don't have to have a second monitor to practice with Presenter view.

Part 4
Excel 2013

17 Getting comfortable in Excel 2013   431

18 Creating and editing worksheets   443

19 Manipulating numbers and text   473

20 Analyzing data   517

21 Formatting worksheets   559

22 Manipulating workbooks and worksheets   605

23 Creating charts and graphics   645

Chapter at a glance

Flash Fill

Quickly extract text from adjacent data to fill a column, page 413

	First Name		Email		Contact Type	
	Hazem		hazem@fabrikam.com		Business	
	Ahmed		ahmed@fabrikam.com		Personal	
	Pilar		pilar@fabrikam.com		Business	
	Terry		terry@fabrikam.com		Business	
	Nupur		nupur@fabrikam.com		Business	
	Sean		sean@fabrikam.com		Business	
	Dave		dave@fabrikam.com		Business	

Analyze

Use Quick Analysis tools to apply formats, add totals, and more, page 414

Expenses	Jan	Feb	Mar	Apr	May	Jun	Ju
Expense 1	33.00	375.00	33.00	45.00	375.00	201.00	
Expense 2	238.00	238.00	238.00	123.00	111.00	98.00	
Expense 3	110.00	110.00	110.00	125.00	333.00	122.00	
Expense 4	426.00	84.00	84.00	426.00	125.00	187.00	
Expense 5	54.00	54.00	109.00	98.00	33.00	441.00	
Total	861.00	861.00	574.00	117.00	977.00	1,049.00	

FORMATTING | CHARTS | TOTALS | TABLES | SPARKLINES

Data Bars | Color Scale | Icon Set | Greater Than | Top 10% | Clear Format

Conditional Formatting uses rules to highlight interesting data.

Chart

Let Excel provide recommendations based on selected data, page 415

Filter

Use the Timeline feature to display data from a specific timeframe, page 416

Row Labels	Total Sales
⊟Sandals	$11,253.00
02/01/2012	$1,758.00
02/29/2012	$2,464.00
03/31/2012	$1,777.00
04/30/2012	$2,715.00
05/14/2012	$2,539.00
⊟Shirts	$11,277.00
02/01/2012	$2,193.00
02/29/2012	$2,469.00
03/31/2012	$2,388.00
04/30/2012	$1,829.00

Price Date

Feb - May 2012   MONTHS

2012

FEB   MAR   APR   MAY   JUN   JUL   AUG

Getting comfortable in Excel 2013

17

IN THIS CHAPTER, YOU WILL LEARN HOW TO

- Start Excel 2013.

- Identify what's new in Excel.

- Use the new features in Excel 2013.

  Microsoft Excel 2013 is a spreadsheet application that allows you to organize, sort, calculate, and otherwise manipulate data by using formulas. Excel spreadsheets are organized into columns and rows but can also include other features, such as graphs and charts.

  It doesn't matter if your spreadsheet is simple or complex, because this part of the book provides you with the foundation for all of your needs. In this chapter, you'll get familiar with the Excel 2013 user interface and using the ribbon. You will also get a glance at features that are new to this latest version of Excel.

Starting Excel 2013

You typically start Excel 2013 from the Windows Start screen in Windows 8 or the Start menu in Windows 7. You can also start Excel 2013 and open a file at the same time by opening a workbook from an email attachment, or by double-clicking a file on the desktop or in the File Explorer.

When you start Excel without opening an existing file, the new Start screen is displayed.

From the Start screen, you can open a recently used workbook, open an existing workbook, create a new workbook from a template, or just start with a fresh, blank workbook.

File tab Quick Access Toolbar Ribbon Dialog box launcher Group Window controls Ribbon display options Help

Formula bar Status bar

The following list describes some of the most important interface elements; places you'll visit almost every time you employ Excel.

- **Ribbon** The main component of the Excel interface is where you'll find the primary commands for working with the content of your workbooks. The ribbon contains task-oriented tabs; each tab contains groups of related commands. For example, on the Home tab, the Clipboard group contains commands for copying and pasting information in your workbooks. Command groups with additional commands not shown on the ribbon include a dialog box launcher button. Clicking the dialog box launcher displays a dialog box or a pane that contains related options. For example, if you click the dialog box launcher for the Font group, the Font dialog box appears, providing more formatting choices such as Strikethrough, Superscript, and Subscript.

IMPORTANT Your display settings may be different than those used for the graphics shown in this book. The ribbon may appear different on your screen due to its dynamic capabilities. For example, some buttons may appear stacked vertically without labels, or horizontally with labels.

SEE ALSO For instructions on how to modify your display settings and adapt exercise instructions, see Chapter 1, "Getting comfortable in Office Home and Student 2013."

- **File tab** The first tab on the ribbon is unlike other ribbon tabs. Clicking the File tab does not display a ribbon tab; it instead displays the Backstage view, a place where you can find commands that apply to the entire workbook, such as Save As, Print, Share, and Export. The Backstage view is also where application options are located and where you can find information about your user account and your version of Office.

- **Quick Access Toolbar** Holds your most frequently used commands. By default, Save, Undo, and Redo have already been added.

  TIP To add commands that you use the most to your Quick Access Toolbar, right-click the command you want and then click Add To Quick Access Toolbar. To remove a command from the Quick Access Toolbar, right-click it and then click Remove From Quick Access Toolbar.

- **Title bar** Appears at the top of the window and displays the name of the active workbook along with the application name. If your workbook hasn't yet been saved, the title bar displays a name such as *Book1 – Excel*. After the workbook has been saved, the title bar will reflect the name of the saved workbook.

- **Window controls** Along with the standard Minimize, Restore Down/Maximize, and Close buttons available on the right side of the title bar, there are two additional buttons, the Help button and the Ribbon Display Options button, which is new in Excel 2013.

- **Status bar** Appears at the bottom of the window and displays information about the current workbook, such as the total and average of the values in the currently selected cells. On the right side of the status bar are view options for switching your workbook to a different view, along with a zoom slider to change the magnification of your active workbook.

SEE ALSO For a more comprehensive list of ribbon and user-interface elements, along with detailed instructions on how to customize your user interface, including the ribbon and Quick Access Toolbar, see Chapter 1.

Identifying what's new in Excel 2013

A lot of work went into the Windows 8 and Office underpinnings for this release of Excel. Microsoft also invested effort in producing some excellent, helpful new features, plus extensions and improvements of existing features.

- **Flash Fill** When you are entering data, Flash Fill uses predictive fills and offers to autocomplete the remaining pattern for you. Use Flash Fill to split a full name into first and last names, change the case of text, extract a name from an email address, and more.

First Name	Email	Contact Type
Hazem	hazem@fabrikam.com	Business
Ahmed	ahmed@fabrikam.com	Personal
Pilar	pilar@fabrikam.com	Business
Terry	terry@fabrikam.com	Business
Nupur	nupur@fabrikam.com	Business
Sean	sean@fabrikam.com	Business
Dave	dave@fabrikam.com	Business

- **Separate workbook windows** Workbook windows no longer share the same user interface. Now you can display workbook windows on separate monitors and compare formulas between workbooks. Each workbook has its own ribbon that can be used independently of other open Excel windows.

- **Quick Analysis** Get applicable conditional formatting, charts, totals, tables, Pivot-Tables, and in-cell charts, called *sparklines*, for a selected region of data. If you're not sure about what to use, a live preview will help you visualize a suggestion prior to applying it.

- **Table Slicers** These filter lists of information to your selected Slicer items. And, when your list is filtered, Table Slicers show you what you've selected along with other list data that's relevant to your current filter.

Bid Details

BID #	CUSTOMER	DATE RECEIVED	AMOUNT
1	Contoso, LTD	09/21/2012	$2,000.00
9	Contoso, LTD	09/21/2012	$6,949.00
13	Contoso, LTD	09/21/2012	$3,427.00
14	Contoso, LTD	09/21/2012	$6,607.00
21	Proseware, Inc.	09/21/2012	$4,423.00

DATE RECEIVED
09/03/2012
09/11/2012
09/16/2012
09/21/2012
10/14/2012
10/21/2012

CUSTOMER
Contoso, LTD
Fourth Coffee
Litware, Inc.
Proseware, Inc.

- **Recommended Charts** If you know you need a chart, but aren't sure about where to begin, the Recommend Charts feature will display the most relevant chart suggestions by using your selected data to help you determine which chart to use.

- **Recommended PivotTables** Get help summarizing and creating reports for your information. Instead of trying to determine a PivotTable layout prior to adding one, you can use the Recommended PivotTables feature, which will suggest various layouts based on your data that will assist you with creating a PivotTable.

Recommended PivotTables

Sum of Bulk Price Per U...

Row Labels	Sum of Bulk Price Per Unit*
Sandals	257
Shirts	240
Shorts	260
Umbrellas	265
Water bottles	215
Grand Total	1237

Sum of Total Sales ($) ...

Row Labels	Sum of Total Sales ($)
Sandals	670654
Shirts	582884
Shorts	605996
Umbrellas	578939
Water bottles	552232
Grand Total	2990705

Sum of Retail Price Per...

Sum of Bulk Price Per Unit* by Product Name

Row Labels	Sum of Bulk Price Per Unit*
Sandals	257
Shirts	240
Shorts	260
Umbrellas	265
Water bottles	215
Grand Total	**1237**

- **Timeline** When working with information that includes dates, you can add a timeline to filter your content to specific months or years.

Row Labels	Total Sales
Sandals	$11,253.00
02/01/2012	$1,758.00
02/29/2012	$2,464.00
03/31/2012	$1,777.00
04/30/2012	$2,715.00
05/14/2012	$2,539.00
Shirts	$11,277.00
02/01/2012	$2,193.00
02/29/2012	$2,469.00
03/31/2012	$2,388.00
04/30/2012	$1,829.00

Price Date

Feb - May 2012   MONTHS ▾

2012

FEB   MAR   APR   MAY   JUN   JUL   AUG

- **Multiple data sources in PivotTables** Instead of being limited to a single data table, you can relate tables with common information and add fields from those tables to your **PivotTable** report.

PivotTable Fields   ▾ ✕

ACTIVE   ALL

Choose fields to add to report: ☼ ▾

▲ ⊞ Contacts
   ☐ Customer ID
   ☐ Name
   ☐ Title
   ☐ Email

▷ ⊞ Customers

▷ ⊞ Orders

Using the new features in Excel

The following is a list of discussions in this book that explain how to use some of the new features in Excel 2013, with handy cross-references.

- **Flash Fill** See "Introducing Flash Fill" in Chapter 18.
- **Quick Analysis** See "Using the Quick Analysis tools" in Chapter 20.
- **Recommended PivotTables** See "Creating a PivotTable" in Chapter 20.
- **New Templates** See "Exploring a built-in template" in Chapter 20.
- **Recommended Charts and PivotCharts** See "Creating and modifying a chart" in Chapter 23.
- **Timeline** See "Adding a timeline to a chart" in Chapter 23.

Other enhancements, improvements, and feature upgrades

The following are some other changes that you'll notice in Excel 2013:

- **One sheet in a new workbook** There is now only one sheet in a new workbook, not three, as in previous versions of Excel. You add sheets by clicking the **New Sheet** plus-sign button (+).

New sheet

TIP Specifying the number of sheets in a new workbook is one of the many settings that you can change. For example, to construct a number of annual-summary-type workbooks, you might find it helpful to begin with 13 sheets; one for each month plus a summary sheet. To increase or decrease the default number of sheets that appear in new workbooks, change the Include This Many Sheets option on the General page of the Excel Options dialog box. You can specify up to 255 sheets.

SEE ALSO For more information about working with multiple worksheets, see "Creating a multisheet workbook" in Chapter 22, "Manipulating workbooks and worksheets."

- **New functions** There are about 50 new functions in Excel 2013, most of which were added for increased compatibility with Open Document Format (ODF) 1.2, a universal royalty-free document format used by spreadsheet, chart, word-processing, and presentation applications, including StarOffice and OpenOffice.

- **New chart controls** Charts now have new dynamic floating controls—Chart Elements, Chart Styles, and Chart Filters—to make reworking an existing chart quicker and easier.

- **Rich chart data labels** You can now apply more formatting and graphic treatments to data labels in charts. You can even change the chart type, while preserving the label formatting.

- **Chart animation** When you change the underlying data for a chart, rather than changing immediately, the resulting change animates the chart as it changes to show the new values, which serves to emphasize the effects on the bigger picture.

- **Slicers** Slicers have a new interface in Excel 2013, which makes it easier to understand relationships. You can now use Slicers in data tables, not just in PivotTables.

- **PivotTable Field List** The new Field List includes fields from one table or multiple tables.

- **Standalone Pivot Charts** You can now detach a chart created by using PivotTable data, so that it can be repurposed elsewhere without its parent PivotTable.

- **Excel Data Model** Some of the functionality of the PowerPivot add-in is now built in as the Excel Data Model, allowing you to access multiple large data sources quickly and efficiently.

- **PowerView** Create presentation-quality reports by using graphics and data from multiple tables with the PowerView add-in, which uses data from the Excel Data Model exclusively.

- **Strict Open XML file format** For anyone who has experienced problems calculating data by using dates from 1900 or earlier, the Strict Open XML file format is compliant with the ISO8601 specification, solving leap-year and 2-digit-year problems.

Key points

- The major interface elements of Excel 2013 are unchanged from 2010.

- Most of the tools you need to do your work are located on the ribbon; if you need more tools, click a dialog-box launcher button to display a relevant dialog box with more options.

- There are many new features in Excel 2013, which you will learn more about in the upcoming chapters.

17

Chapter at a glance

Adjust

Adjust the width of columns to fit your data, page 423

	A	B	C	D	E	F	G	H
1	LastName	FirstName	Department	Title	Email			
2								
3								

AutoFill

Quickly create a series of numbers or numbered text, page 429

Name

Name cells and ranges for easy reference, page 434

Copy

Copy a cell or range in an operation, page 447

	A	B	C	D	E
1	One to Many		One to Many		
2			One to Many		
3			One to Many		
4			One to Many		
5			One to Many		
6			One to Many		
7				(Ctrl) ▾	
8					
9					

Creating and editing worksheets

18

IN THIS CHAPTER, YOU WILL LEARN HOW TO

- Modify Excel options.

- Format as you enter text.

- Extend a numeric series.

- Extend a series based on adjacent data.

- Assign names to cells and ranges.

- Select and navigate by using the keyboard.

- Customize and move column widths and row heights.

This chapter will cover some of the basics of spreadsheet construction and maintenance, including techniques for entering and organizing data and ways to manipulate cells and move among them.

If you are familiar with Microsoft Excel 2010, you will notice very little functional difference at first glance on the Home tab, beyond the new simplified Microsoft Office look. However, if you are logged into a Windows Live, Microsoft SkyDrive, Outlook, or Hotmail account, your name and image may appear among the window controls in the upper-right corner of the Login menu, This allows you to access your account settings, switch accounts, and even change your profile photo. One more small difference is that the Full Screen button (formerly on the View tab) now lives in the upper-right corner along with the window controls. These changes were designed to facilitate performance on a range of devices and displays, from phones to desktops, tablets, and TVs.

SEE ALSO For more information, see Chapter 4, "Using touch in Office."

So, it may look like not much has changed—Excel is a "mature" application, after all—but there are some great new features, hidden in buttons and commands, some of which may just happen before you know they're there. Exploring the other tabs on the ribbon will reveal more, especially on the Insert and Data tabs.

In this chapter, you'll learn some of the most useful basic techniques for creating and organizing worksheets and workbooks, entering data, making calculations, analyzing data, and preparing for presentation. In such a short discussion, we won't be able to tell you everything there is to know about Excel, but we encourage you to explore at every juncture. When a dialog box is open for a procedure, examine its contents; click other tabs; try a procedure in a different way; use your own data after trying the practice files, and so on. Remember, you can undo up to 100 actions, with a few exceptions like saving workbooks and deleting worksheets.

PRACTICE FILES To complete the exercises in this chapter, you need the practice files contained in the Chapter18 practice file folder. For more information, see "Download the practice files" in this book's Introduction.

Entering and organizing data

The general rule of thumb is to put whatever you have the most of into rows, and try to fit all of your columns across a sheet of paper, even if it will print in landscape mode. That way, if you have more than one page of data, the bottom of a page leads naturally to the top of the next page, not the top of the next column. Your audience is more accustomed to "paging down" than "paging right."

A	1990	1991	1992	1993	1994	1995	1996	1997	1998	1999	2000	2001	2002	2003	2004	2005	2006	2007	2008
Product 1	$ 205.00	$ 157.00	$ 180.00	$ 175.00	$ 182.00	$ 152.00	$ 116.00	$ 200.00	$ 215.00	$ 112.00	$ 160.00	$ 175.00	$ 190.00	$ 208.00	$ 189.00	$ 153.00	$ 192.00	$ 163.00	$ 125.00
Product 2	63.00	74.00	20.00	71.00	21.00	21.00	62.00	61.00	15.00	13.00	12.00	13.00	27.00	44.00	36.00	42.00	50.00	44.00	24.00
Product 3	222.00	140.00	174.00	220.00	194.00	146.00	113.00	114.00	133.00	137.00	178.00	189.00	198.00	158.00	185.00	172.00	150.00	120.00	156.00
Product 4	44.00	60.00	88.00	51.00	58.00	40.00	37.00	80.00	49.00	46.00	64.00	76.00	43.00	38.00	35.00	58.00	80.00	59.00	34.00
Product 5	91.00	95.00	96.00	95.00	99.00	91.00	91.00	93.00	91.00	91.00	96.00	93.00	95.00	98.00	95.00	95.00	89.00	92.00	97.00
Product 6	146.00	175.00	152.00	138.00	128.00	157.00	128.00	183.00	175.00	168.00	169.00	144.00	144.00	131.00	149.00	147.00	127.00	144.00	163.00
Product 7	52.00	72.00	17.00	44.00	42.00	43.00	56.00	37.00	97.00	72.00	74.00	33.00	90.00	18.00	47.00	94.00	59.00	34.00	91.00
Product 8	144.00	137.00	129.00	149.00	138.00	154.00	139.00	143.00	143.00	134.00	130.00	152.00	136.00	139.00	136.00	131.00	124.00	140.00	130.00
Product 9	50.00	103.00	72.00	99.00	111.00	47.00	49.00	104.00	63.00	114.00	155.00	132.00	79.00	80.00	100.00	152.00	147.00	66.00	64.00

	Product 1	Product 2	Product 3	Product 4	Product 5	Product 6	Product 7	Product 8	Product 9
1990	$ 203.00	$ 63.00	$ 222.00	$ 44.00	$ 91.00	$ 146.00	$ 52.00	$ 144.00	$ 50.00
1991	157.00	74.00	140.00	60.00	95.00	175.00	72.00	137.00	103.00
1992	180.00	20.00	174.00	88.00	96.00	152.00	17.00	129.00	72.00
1993	175.00	71.00	220.00	51.00	95.00	138.00	44.00	149.00	99.00
1994	182.00	21.00	194.00	58.00	99.00	128.00	42.00	138.00	111.00
1995	152.00	21.00	146.00	40.00	91.00	157.00	43.00	154.00	47.00
1996	116.00	62.00	113.00	37.00	91.00	128.00	56.00	139.00	49.00
1997	200.00	61.00	114.00	80.00	93.00	133.00	37.00	143.00	104.00
1998	215.00	15.00	133.00	49.00	91.00	175.00	97.00	143.00	63.00
1999	112.00	13.00	137.00	46.00	91.00	168.00	72.00	134.00	114.00
2000	160.00	12.00	178.00	64.00	96.00	169.00	74.00	130.00	155.00
2001	175.00	13.00	189.00	76.00	93.00	144.00	33.00	152.00	132.00
2002	190.00	27.00	198.00	43.00	95.00	144.00	90.00	136.00	79.00
2003	208.00	44.00	158.00	38.00	98.00	131.00	18.00	139.00	80.00
2004	189.00	36.00	183.00	35.00	95.00	149.00	47.00	136.00	100.00
2005	153.00	42.00	172.00	58.00	95.00	147.00	94.00	131.00	152.00
2006	192.00	50.00	150.00	80.00	89.00	127.00	59.00	124.00	147.00
2007	163.00	44.00	120.00	59.00	92.00	144.00	34.00	140.00	66.00
2008	125.00	24.00	156.00	34.00	97.00	163.00	91.00	130.00	64.00
2009	147.00	72.00	151.00	54.00	91.00	143.00	85.00	137.00	139.00
2010	218.00	45.00	190.00	76.00	98.00	153.00	18.00	147.00	42.00
2011	142.00	64.00	216.00	37.00	94.00	153.00	19.00	133.00	79.00
2012	219.00	67.00	172.00	70.00	94.00	168.00	79.00	135.00	81.00
2013	177.00	62.00	143.00	64.00	94.00	159.00	84.00	128.00	131.00
2014	175.00	71.00	220.00	51.00	95.00	138.00	44.00	149.00	99.00
2015	182.00	21.00	194.00	58.00	99.00	128.00	42.00	138.00	111.00
2016	152.00	21.00	146.00	40.00	91.00	157.00	43.00	154.00	47.00
2017	116.00	62.00	113.00	37.00	91.00	128.00	56.00	139.00	49.00
2018	200.00	61.00	114.00	80.00	93.00	133.00	37.00	143.00	104.00

Think about the audience and the output you plan to produce. Size matters: are you printing, emailing, or web-publishing your work? Content matters: will you share your work, or is it just for your own use? Details matter: do you need an executive summary? Appearance matters: how about presentation graphics? Documentation matters: do you need to make sure others know how to use your workbooks in the future without your personal intervention? Sometimes, it's all (or most) of the above.

Generally, the more people you plan to share with, the less data you should share. Find ways to summarize—this is what analysis is all about. It's almost impossible to comprehend the big picture when you're looking at details. Sending the VP a raw worksheet with thousands of rows of data probably won't get your point across as well as a summary table with a few rows and columns and an accompanying chart.

Luckily, you can start small and then create whatever you need later. Virtually everything else in the Excel portion of this book will help you to craft your data to address the questions posed earlier.

Changing column widths

One fundamental requirement of any Excel user is to make sure all your data is visible and readable. If it is not, column widths are probably part, if not all, of the problem. The default 64-pixel column width was chosen to accommodate a typical formatted numeric entry such as $1,234.56 without adjustment. When you enter numbers, Excel usually adjusts the width of the column to accommodate the entry. Not so with text, however. The following graphic shows a simple example of what is possibly the most common spreadsheet task of all time—a list.

	A	B	C	D	E
1	LastName	FirstName	Title	Department	Email
2	Agarwal	Manoj	Accounts Receivable Clerk	Finance	manoj@fabrikaminc.onmicrosoft.com
3	Andersen	Henriette	Benefits Analyst	Human Resources	henriette@fabrikaminc.onmicrosoft.com
4	Axford	Kai	Sales Associate	Sales & Marketing	kai@fabrikaminc.onmicrosoft.com
5	Banti	Ed	Web Services Analyst	Sales & Marketing	ed@fabrikaminc.onmicrosoft.com
6	Bentley	Sean	Training Specialist	Human Resources	sean@fabrikaminc.onmicrosoft.com
7	Brewer	Alan	Advertising Coordinator	Sales & Marketing	alan@fabrikaminc.onmicrosoft.com
8	Burke	Brian	Production Analyst	Manufacturing	brian@fabrikaminc.onmicrosoft.com
9	Carbonati	Cyril	Employee Relations Specialist	Human Resources	cyril@fabrikaminc.onmicrosoft.com
10	Chavda	Ankur	Accounts Receivable Clerk	Finance	ankur@fabrikaminc.onmicrosoft.com
11	Corets	Eva	Systems Analyst	Information Technology	eva@fabrikaminc.onmicrosoft.com
12	David	Willson Raj	Marketing Coordinator	Sales & Marketing	willsonraj@fabrikaminc.onmicrosoft.com
13	DeSeranno	Shane	Communications Analyst	Operations	shane@fabrikaminc.onmicrosoft.com
14	Ersan	Ebru	Product Support Specialist	Sales & Marketing	ebru@fabrikaminc.onmicrosoft.com
15	Fong	Raymond	Research Associate	Research & Development	raymond@fabrikaminc.onmicrosoft.com

A simple list can be used for various purposes; for example, for generating mailing lists, organization charts, and departmental rosters. Most times, it is best to keep your detail data simple and easy to edit and manipulate. Then you can create additional sheets to summarize or otherwise interpret the data.

In this exercise, you begin creating a sheet like this to illustrate a few techniques.

➡ SET UP **You don't need any practice files to complete this exercise. Start Excel and follow the steps.**

1   Click the **File** tab and click **New** to display the opening screen, if it is not already visible.

2   Click **Blank Workbook** to create a new file with a clean, new worksheet.

3   Enter **LastName** in cell **A1** (don't press **Enter**), then press the **Tab** key to activate the next cell to the right.

   TIP The simple act of moving to another cell finalizes your cell entry. Pressing Enter does it, but so does pressing Tab, any arrow key, or clicking another cell. Pressing Esc before leaving a cell discards your entry.

4   Enter **FirstName** in cell **B1**, then press the **Tab** key.

5   Enter **Department** in cell **C1**, then press the **Tab** key.

6   Enter **Title** in cell **D1**, then press the **Tab** key.

7 Enter **Email** in cell **E1**, and then press the **Tab** key.

8 Press the **Home** key to select cell **A1**.

9 Press and hold the **Shift** and **Ctrl** keys and then press the **Right Arrow** key to select all the headings you just entered. Notice that all the columns are the same default width.

	A	B	C	D	E	F	G	H	I	J
1	LastName	FirstName	Departme	Title	Email					
2										

10 In the **Font** group on the ribbon, click both the **Bold** button and the **Bottom Border** button. If the **Bottom Border** button is not currently visible, click the arrow next to the **Border** button and select **Bottom Border** from the list.

11 Click the column heading letter **A** to select the entire column, then, still holding the mouse button down, drag through the column letters from **A** to **E**. Notice as you drag that Excel displays a ScreenTip showing the dimensions of the selected range, which in this case is 1,048,576 rows deep (all the rows in the worksheet, because you selected the entire column) by 5 columns wide. Excel designates rows by appending an *R* to the row number, and it does the same for columns, with a *C* to the column number, as shown in the ScreenTip.

	A	B	C	D	E	1048576R x 5C	G	H	I	J
1	LastName	FirstName	Departme	Title	Email					
2										
3										

12 Point to the border line to the right of any selected column letter until it becomes a double-headed arrow pointer, and then double-click to auto-fit all selected columns to their widest entries. Notice that the columns are now different widths.

	A	B	C	D	E	F	G	H	I	J
1	LastName	FirstName	Department	Title	Email					
2										
3										

13 With the columns still selected, click the right border line of any selected column heading (don't double-click) and drag it to the right to make it wider. Notice that not only are all of the selected columns wider now, they are also all the same width.

	A	B	C	D	E	F
1	LastName	FirstName	Department	Title	Email	
2						
3						

❌ CLEAN UP **Close the workbook without saving.**

The great thing about this feature is that you don't have to scroll down a long worksheet to determine if a column is wide enough for everything it contains; simply double-clicking the column-letter border essentially does that for you. If a column seems too wide after auto-fitting, it may point out a problem somewhere else, such as data entered or imported incorrectly into a cell, or a label out of place.

TIP It works for rows, too. Excel increases row height automatically if you increase the font size or apply the Wrap Text format, but does not decrease it automatically if the cell contents no longer warrant it. Just like columns, you can drag to resize rows, or you can auto-fit them by double-clicking the border below the row number to fit its tallest entry.

Using formatting to alter the appearance of data

A worksheet can be a façade; what is displayed isn't necessarily all there is to it. The displayed values on the screen may not be exactly the same as the underlying values that appear if you select a cell and look in the formula bar. How numeric entries are formatted makes a huge difference in how they appear.

To Excel, everything is a value, including text. What you enter and how you enter it changes the way that Excel responds to the entry. Fractions, dates, times, currency, scientific values, and percentages are all just raw numeric values that are formatted so that they are displayed in familiar ways. This allows Excel to perform calculations on the raw numbers, while allowing you to view the more easily readable formatted values.

For example, Excel uses numeric values to calculate dates. The serial (sequential) value representing Christmas Day 2013 is 41633, which is the actual number of days that have elapsed since (and including) January 1, 1900. If a cell containing this number has the Short Date format applied, it appears in the more understandable form *12/25/2013*.

TIP Enter any date into a cell, then click the Number Format drop-down menu (located in the Number group on the Home tab), and click General to format the date so that it displays its serial value. Then you can click one of the Date formats to display the number as a date again.

> **IMPORTANT** Applying a Date or Time format to a number appears to actually change the underlying value in the formula bar, but you can always change it back by simply applying a numeric format.

In this exercise, you'll find that although you can always apply formatting by using buttons on the ribbon, when entering numeric values, you can specify many kinds of formats "by example" as you enter data, including currency, percentages, and dates.

➡ SET UP **You don't need any practice files to complete this exercise. Start Excel, open a blank workbook, and follow the steps.**

1   In cell **A1**, enter **$1000** and press **Enter**.

2   Press the **Up Arrow** key to reselect the cell, and notice the difference between the entry in the cell itself and the entry as shown in the formula bar above.

3   Now, in cell **A1**, enter **25** (no dollar sign) and notice that even though you replaced the number you first entered in dollars, the cell still displays a dollar sign, because the cell is formatted as currency. After you format a cell "by example," it stays in that format until you explicitly change it by using formatting commands.

4   In cell **A2**, enter **1234.567** and press **Enter**, then enter **$1234.567** and press **Enter**, then enter **1,234.567** and press **Enter** (making sure to add the comma). If you select each cell that contains the numbers you just entered, you'll notice that the numbers all look exactly the same in the formula bar.

This example illustrates the difference between the formatted values displayed on the worksheet and the underlying values displayed in the formula bar. It also shows that Excel interprets numeric entries based on the way you enter them and applies formatting accordingly. Entering a dollar sign in front of a number tells Excel to format the entry as currency, which Excel dutifully applies for you. This particular currency format (there are several) includes a dollar sign and comma separators, and rounds the decimal portion to two places. Because you entered a comma separator along with the value in cell A4, Excel applied a different currency format without dollar signs. However, as shown in the formula bar, the formatting only appears on the worksheet. The actual values you enter are not altered. The underlying values in cells A2, A3, and A4 are identical; only the formatting is different.

TIP Understand that applying formats does not alter underlying values. Even though cell A4 displays 1,234.57, calculations that refer to that cell will always use the underlying value 1234.567.

❌ CLEAN UP **Close the workbook without saving.**

Extending a series with AutoFill

Excel provides a few tools you can use to quickly fill a cell range with a series of numbers, dates, formulas, or even text ending with serial numeric values such as Q1, Q2, and so on. For example, you could enter three numbers or dates into adjacent cells, select them, and then drag to extend a series based on the selected cells. They need not be consecutive. Excel extrapolates the numeric or date series by using the example increments.

In this exercise, you'll create simple series by dragging or by using commands on the ribbon.

➡ SET UP **You don't need any practice files to complete this exercise. Start Excel, open a blank workbook, and follow the steps.**

1   In cell **B1**, enter **Widget 5**.

2   In cell **B2**, enter **Widget 6**.

3   Click cell **B1** and drag to cell **B2** to select both cells.

4   Click the tiny black dot at the lower-right corner of the selection, called the *selection handle*, and drag down to cell **B5**.

    Excel displays a ScreenTip (Widget **9**) showing you what the value in that cell will be.

5   Release the mouse button to apply the fill and reveal a numbered series of widgets.

6   Click the **AutoFill Options** menu—the little box that appears near the lower-right corner of the selection after dragging—to display a few additional options you can apply even after you're done. The default option selected is **Fill Series**, which is what you want, so you can press **Esc** to dismiss the menu.

AutoFill makes it easy to extend a series of numbers, dates, or text/numeric entries, as in the Widgets example. You can also click and drag the fill handle by using the right mouse button. Then, instead of immediately extending the series, Excel presents you with a menu of options first, including trends and dates. (Commands appear gray if they are not applicable to the selected values.) You can also use the Fill menu, located in the Editing group on the Home tab, to apply different types of fills.

CLEAN UP Close the workbook without saving.

SEE ALSO For more about using AutoFill with formulas, see Chapter 19, "Manipulating numbers and text." For more about filling across worksheets, see "Creating a multi-sheet workbook" in Chapter 22, "Manipulating workbooks and worksheets."

Another helpful feature of AutoFill is that it recognizes certain text/number combinations as special cases. For example, if you enter Q1 into a cell, and then drag the fill handle, you'll notice that Excel extends it, stops at Q4, and keeps repeating Q1, Q2, Q3, and Q4, over and over, rather than copying the cell or extending the numeric series. Excel recognizes that these are common designations used to specify annual quarters, and will perform the same trick if you start with "Quarter 1" or "1st Quarter."

TIP If you really just want to make copies, you can temporarily suppress AutoFIll by holding down Ctrl while dragging the fill handle.

Introducing Flash Fill

The new Flash Fill command in the Data Tools group on the Data tab is a clever cousin of AutoFill. It evaluates example data, compares it to existing data in adjacent cells, tries to determine a pattern, and suggests entries for you. (The Flash Fill command is also available on the Fill menu that appears when you click the Fill button in the Editing group on the Home tab.)

For example, suppose your company switches to a brand new email domain, and you need to create a new set of unique email addresses for all of your employees.

In this exercise, you'll quickly create a list of email addresses and combine first and last names from separate cells into a single cell.

➡ SET UP **You need the Fabrikam-Management_start.xlsx workbook located in the Chapter18 practice file folder to complete this exercise. Open the Fabrikam-Management_start.xlsx workbook, and save it as Fabrikam-Management.xlsx.**

1 Open the **Fabrikam-Management.xlsx** sample workbook and make sure cell **E5** is selected.

2   Click the **Fill** menu in the **Editing** group on the **Home** tab, and click **Flash Fill**.

	A	B	C	D	E	F
1	LastName	FirstName	Title	Department	Email	
2	Abercrombie	Kim	Accounting Manager	Finance	kim@fabrikaminc.onmicrosoft.com	
3	Affronti	Michael	Director of Operations	Operations	michael@fabrikaminc.onmicrosoft.com	
4	Agarwal	Nupur	Director of Manufacturing	Manufacturing	nupur@fabrikaminc.onmicrosoft.com	
5	Bebbington	Mark	VP Research	Executive	mark@fabrikaminc.onmicrosoft.com	
6	Bellew	Allie	Recruiting Manager	Human Resources	allie@fabrikaminc.onmicrosoft.com	
7	Bento	Nuno	Director of Human Resources	Human Resources	nuno@fabrikaminc.onmicrosoft.com	
8	Bermejo	Antonio	President	Executive	antonio@fabrikaminc.onmicrosoft.com	
9	Byrne	Randy	Security Manager	Operations	randy@fabrikaminc.onmicrosoft.com	
10	Carvallo	Carlos	IT Operations Manager	Information Technology	carlos@fabrikaminc.onmicrosoft.com	
11	Chai	Sean	VP Marketing	Executive	sean@fabrikaminc.onmicrosoft.com	
12	Chan	Gareth	Social Media Manager	Sales & Marketing	gareth@fabrikaminc.onmicrosoft.com	
13	Chudzik	Terri	CFO	Executive	terri@fabrikaminc.onmicrosoft.com	
14	Circeo	Ken	Sales Manager	Sales & Marketing	ken@fabrikaminc.onmicrosoft.com	
15	Clarkson	John	Product Support Manager	Sales & Marketing	john@fabrikaminc.onmicrosoft.com	
16	Danner	Ryan	IT Services Manager	Information Technology	ryan@fabrikaminc.onmicrosoft.com	
17	Huff	Arlene	Warehouse Manager	Operations	arlene@fabrikaminc.onmicrosoft.com	
18	Käch	Reto	VP Information Systems	Executive	reto@fabrikaminc.onmicrosoft.com	
19	Karásek	Petr	Advertising Manager	Sales & Marketing	petr@fabrikaminc.onmicrosoft.com	
20	Taneyhill	Kate	CEO	Executive	kate@fabrikaminc.onmicrosoft.com	
21	Weber	Gregory	VP Finance	Executive	gregory@fabrikaminc.onmicrosoft.com	
22	Zighetti	Barbara	Web Services Manager	Information Technology	barbara@fabrikaminc.onmicrosoft.com	
23						

These email addresses simply use employees' first names with a common email domain. Excel correctly determined the desired outcome, even though those first names were several columns away. (Both columns need to be part of the same table, though.) Excel analyzed the examples entered into cells E2 through E4, and then with the next cell in the table selected, Flash Fill finished the entries and stopped at the end of the table, saving a lot of time entering text. Flash Fill doesn't always get it right, but if not, add more examples.

TIP When you enter a complete email or web address into a cell, Excel formats it as a hyperlink (blue underlined text). When you click a hyperlink, it opens the target; for example, an email program, web browser, or file. Excel actually applies the hyperlink format as a second action after you press Enter. If you would rather not have active hyperlinks in your worksheet (as in this example), press Ctrl+Z immediately after you enter to undo the last action. Because there were actually two actions that took place after you pressed Enter, (you entering the value in the cell, and Excel applying the hyperlink), only the hyperlink is undone, and the unlinked text remains.

One of the most common list-management tasks is managing contact or address lists. For example, first and last names are often kept together in the same cell (or the same record in an imported database). But sometimes first and last names are kept separate; at times you need just the first or last name. Flash Fill offers options for combining (concatenating) or splitting (parsing) cell entries.

3   Select cell **F2** and enter **Kim Abercrombie**.

4   In cell **F3**, begin entering **Michael Affronti**. Even before you finish entering the word *Michael*, Excel fills in the rest of the name in cell **F3**, and simultaneously shows what **Flash Fill** thinks you're trying to do in the cells following.

▲	A	B	C	D	E	F	G
1	LastName	FirstName	Title	Department	Email		
2	Abercrombie	Kim	Accounting Manager	Finance	kim@fabrikaminc.onmicrosoft.com	Kim Abercrombie	
3	Affronti	Michael	Director of Operations	Operations	michael@fabrikaminc.onmicrosoft.com	Michael Affronti	
4	Agarwal	Nupur	Director of Manufacturing	Manufacturing	nupur@fabrikaminc.onmicrosoft.com	Nupur Aga	
5	Bebbington	Mark	VP Research	Executive	mark@fabrikaminc.onmicrosoft.com	Mark Bebi	
6	Bellew	Allie	Recruiting Manager	Human Resources	allie@fabrikaminc.onmicrosoft.com	Allie Belle	
7	Bento	Nuno	Director of Human Resources	Human Resources	nuno@fabrikaminc.onmicrosoft.com	Nuno Ben	
8	Bermejo	Antonio	President	Executive	antonio@fabrikaminc.onmicrosoft.com	Antonio B	
9	Byrne	Randy	Security Manager	Operations	randy@fabrikaminc.onmicrosoft.com	Randy Byr	
10	Carvallo	Carlos	IT Operations Manager	Information Technology	carlos@fabrikaminc.onmicrosoft.com	Carlos Car	
11	Chai	Sean	VP Marketing	Executive	sean@fabrikaminc.onmicrosoft.com	Sean Chai	
12	Chan	Gareth	Social Media Manager	Sales & Marketing	gareth@fabrikaminc.onmicrosoft.com	Gareth Ch	
13	Chudzik	Terri	CFO	Executive	terri@fabrikaminc.onmicrosoft.com	Terri Chud	
14	Circeo	Ken	Sales Manager	Sales & Marketing	ken@fabrikaminc.onmicrosoft.com	Ken Circe	
15	Clarkson	John	Product Support Manager	Sales & Marketing	john@fabrikaminc.onmicrosoft.com	John Clark	
16	Danner	Ryan	IT Services Manager	Information Technology	ryan@fabrikaminc.onmicrosoft.com	Ryan Dann	
17	Huff	Arlene	Warehouse Manager	Operations	arlene@fabrikaminc.onmicrosoft.com	Arlene Hu	
18	Käch	Reto	VP Information Systems	Executive	reto@fabrikaminc.onmicrosoft.com	Reto Käch	
19	Karásek	Petr	Advertising Manager	Sales & Marketing	petr@fabrikaminc.onmicrosoft.com	Petr Karás	
20	Taneyhill	Kate	CEO	Executive	kate@fabrikaminc.onmicrosoft.com	Kate Tane	
21	Weber	Gregory	VP Finance	Executive	gregory@fabrikaminc.onmicrosoft.com	Gregory W	
22	Zighetti	Barbara	Web Services Manager	Information Technology	barbara@fabrikaminc.onmicrosoft.com	Barbara Zi	
23							

5   Press **Enter** to accept the **Flash Fill** suggestions.

6   Double-click the right border of column heading **F** to auto-fit its contents.

7   Select cell **G2** and enter **Kim in Finance**.

8   Select cell **G3** and enter **Michael in Operations**.

9   Select cell **G4** and begin entering **Nupur in Manufacturing**.

▲	A	B	C	D	E	F	G	H
1	LastName	FirstName	Title	Department	Email			
2	Abercrombie	Kim	Accounting Manager	Finance	kim@fabrikaminc.onmicrosoft.com	Kim Abercrombie	Kim in Finance	
3	Affronti	Michael	Director of Operations	Operations	michael@fabrikaminc.onmicrosoft.com	Michael Affronti	Michael in Operations	
4	Agarwal	Nupur	Director of Manufacturing	Manufacturing	nupur@fabrikaminc.onmicrosoft.com	Nupur Agarwal	Nupur in Manufacturing	
5	Bebbington	Mark	VP Research	Executive	mark@fabrikaminc.onmicrosoft.com	Mark Bebbington	Mark in Ex	
6	Bellew	Allie	Recruiting Manager	Human Resources	allie@fabrikaminc.onmicrosoft.com	Allie Bellew	Allie in Hu	
7	Bento	Nuno	Director of Human Resources	Human Resources	nuno@fabrikaminc.onmicrosoft.com	Nuno Bento	Nuno in H	

10   Press **Enter** to accept the suggested entries.

❌ CLEAN UP **Save the Fabrikam-Management.xlsx workbook.**

This time, it took three examples before Flash Fill figured out the pattern, including an incorrect guess on the second entry. Just keep entering text if the suggestions don't work.

Similarly, you could use Flash Fill to split, or parse, the full names you entered in column F back into individual cells by simply entering *Abercrombie* into cell H2, and *Affronti* into cell H3. Flash Fill springs to life, offering correct suggestions by around the third letter of the second name. This is one very powerful feature that you'll want to experiment with.

Selecting and naming cell ranges

You know how to select a cell—just click it. You know how to select multiple cells—just click and drag to select a range. In Excel, you can also select multiple nonadjacent (also known as *noncontiguous*) ranges, a technique that comes in handy if you need to apply formatting, styles, or certain editing techniques to noncontiguous cells. You can apply most kinds of formatting to noncontiguous ranges, but many editing techniques are prohibited, including copying and pasting.

Sometimes, especially in large worksheets, it is helpful to assign names to cells and ranges. A name is simply an easy way to identify specific cells. Names can be used to quickly select ranges, or they can be used in formulas as proxies for cryptic cell addresses or to identify the results of other formulas; for example, *net_profit*. Names can also be used to identify cells containing often-used static values such as *sales_tax_rate*. Names can be easier to remember and work with than cell or range addresses.

In this exercise, you'll select nonadajacent cells and assign names to cells.

→ SET UP **You need the Fabrikam-Management2_start.xlsx workbook located in the Chapter18 practice file folder to complete this exercise. Open the Fabrikam-Management2_start.xlsx workbook and save it as Fabrikam-Management2.xlsx.**

1   Open the **Fabrikam-Management2.xlsx** workbook.

2   Click cell **A5** and drag to the right, selecting cells **A5:C5**.

    Note that this is how Excel identifies a cell range; the ID of the cell in the upper-left corner and the ID of the cell in the lower-right corner, separated by a colon.

3   Hold the **Ctrl** key while selecting the corresponding cells in columns **A** through **C** for each of the other members of the Executive department (the 1x3 cell ranges **A8:C8**, **A11:C11**, **A13:C13**, **A18:C18**, and a 2x3 range, **A20:C21**).

4   While still holding the **Ctrl** key, press the **B** key to apply **Bold** formatting to all the selected cells. Alternatively, you could click the **Bold** button on the **Home** tab of the ribbon.

	A	B	C	D
1	**LastName**	**FirstName**	**Title**	**Department**
2	Abercrombie	Kim	Accounting Manager	Finance
3	Affronti	Michael	Director of Operations	Operations
4	Agarwal	Nupur	Director of Manufacturing	Manufacturing
5	**Bebbington**	**Mark**	**VP Research**	Executive
6	Bellew	Allie	Recruiting Manager	Human Resources
7	Bento	Nuno	Director of Human Resources	Human Resources
8	**Bermejo**	**Antonio**	**President**	Executive
9	Byrne	Randy	Security Manager	Operations
10	Carvallo	Carlos	IT Operations Manager	Information Technology
11	**Chai**	**Sean**	**VP Marketing**	Executive
12	Chan	Gareth	Social Media Manager	Sales & Marketing
13	**Chudzik**	**Terri**	**CFO**	Executive
14	Circeo	Ken	Sales Manager	Sales & Marketing
15	Clarkson	John	Product Support Manager	Sales & Marketing
16	Danner	Ryan	IT Services Manager	Information Technology
17	Huff	Arlene	Warehouse Manager	Operations
18	**Käch**	**Reto**	**VP Information Systems**	Executive
19	Karásek	Petr	Advertising Manager	Sales & Marketing
20	**Taneyhill**	**Kate**	**CEO**	Executive
21	**Weber**	**Gregory**	**VP Finance**	Executive
22	Zighetti	Barbara	Web Services Manager	Information Technology
23				

18

IMPORTANT Names cannot contain spaces and must begin with either a letter or an underscore.

5   Select all the email addresses.

> **TIP** Be careful if your addresses are hyperlinked. If you click a link directly, it will activate to your email program. Instead, click in an empty part of the cell to avoid activating the link, then drag to select the range.

6   Click the **Formulas** tab on the ribbon.

7   Click the **Define Name** command in the **Defined Names** section to display the **Define Name** dialog box.

The first email address is displayed and highlighted in the **Name** field of the dialog box.

8   Enter **Email**. This replaces the highlighted email address.

9   Press **Enter** and then look at the box on the left side of the formula bar; this is called the **Name** box, and it normally displays the address of the active cell, unless a named cell or complete named range is selected. After you click **Enter**, the **Name** box should display the name **Email**.

Name box

10   Click to select any cell outside the **Email** range.

11   Click the arrow next to the **Name** box and click **Email**, which reselects the named range. You can also click the **Name** box and enter **email** (case-insensitive) to select the associated cell or cells.

SEE ALSO For more information, see Chapter 19.

❌ CLEAN UP Save the Fabrikam-Management2.xlsx workbook and then close it.

TIP When you first create a defined name, you can use the Scope options in the New Name dialog box to limit the usage of the name to a specific sheet in the workbook (which, of course, doesn't matter if there is only one sheet). Normally, Workbook is the selected Scope, meaning that you can use the name on any sheet. If you specify a sheet in the Scope drop-down list, you will only be able to use the name on that sheet.

Using column headers to define names

You can define multiple names at once by using the Create From Selection command on the Formulas tab of the ribbon. Remember that when you defined the name Email in the previous example, you selected the data but not the column heading. When you use the Create From Selection command, you need to select the headers along with the data.

In this exercise, you'll create names by using column headings, and you'll begin by using a keyboard-selection trick to select the table.

➜ SET UP **You need the Fabrikam-Management3_start.xlsx workbook located in the Chapter18 practice file folder to complete this exercise. Open the Fabrikam-Management3_start.xlsx workbook and save it as Fabrikam-Management3.xlsx.**

1   Open the **Fabrikam-Management3.xlsx** workbook.

2   Click cell **A1** to select it.

3   Hold down the **Shift** and **Ctrl** keys and then press the **Right Arrow** key to select the top row of the table.

4   While still holding **Shift** and **Ctrl**, click the **Down Arrow** key to select the entire table.

5   Click the **Formulas** tab if it is not already active, and click the **Create From Selection** command in the **Defined Names** group.

6   Click the **Left Column** option in the **Create Names From Selection** dialog box to deselect it, because you want to create names just from the column headers at this time.

7   Click **OK** to create a set of names based on the column headers you selected.

8   Click the **Name** box in the formula bar to display the list of names you just created.

9   Click the **Name Manager** command on the **Formulas** tab of the ribbon for another way to view the names you just created, including the ranges (shown in the **Refers To** column) and values associated with the names.

Name Manager ? ✕

	New...	Edit...	Delete			Filter ▾

Name	Value	Refers To	Scope	Comment
Department	{"Finance";"Operati...	=Sheet1!$D$2:$D$22	Workbo...	
Email	{"kim@fabrikaminc....	=Sheet1!$E$2:$E$22	Workbo...	
FirstName	{"Kim";"Michael";"N...	=Sheet1!$B$2:$B$22	Workbo...	
LastName	{"Abercrombie";"Aff...	=Sheet1!$A$2:$A$22	Workbo...	
Title	{"Accounting Mana...	=Sheet1!$C$2:$C$22	Workbo...	

Refers to:

✕ ✓ =Sheet1!$D$2:$D$22

Close

18

10   Click the **Close** button.

✖ CLEAN UP **Save the Fabrikam-Management3.xlsx workbook, and then close it.**

SEE ALSO For more information, see Chapter 19.

Moving around in the worksheet

In the previous exercise, you used a keyboard-navigation technique to select a table. Although using the pointer for selecting and navigating is okay, using keyboard short-cuts can save time, frustration, and repetitive movements, especially when working with larger worksheets.

In this exercise, you'll navigate between and among regions, which are defined as blocks of contiguous cells.

SET UP You need the Fabrikam-Employees_start.xlsx workbook located in the Chapter18 practice file folder to complete this exercise. Open the Fabrikam-Employees_start.xlsx workbook, and save it as Fabrikam-Employees.xlsx.

1   Open the **Fabrikam-Employees.xlsx** workbook. Make sure that cell **A1** is selected.

2   Hold down **Ctrl** and press the **Down Arrow** key to jump to the last entry in column **A**.

	A	B	C	D	E
1	LastName	FirstName	Title	Department	Email
2	Agarwal	Manoj	Accounts Receivable Clerk	Finance	manoj@fabrikaminc.onmicrosoft.com
3	Andersen	Henriette	Benefits Analyst	Human Resources	henriette@fabrikaminc.onmicrosoft.com
4	Axford	Kai	Sales Associate	Sales & Marketing	kai@fabrikaminc.onmicrosoft.com
5	Banti	Ed	Web Services Analyst	Sales & Marketing	ed@fabrikaminc.onmicrosoft.com
6	Bentley	Sean	Training Specialist	Human Resources	sean@fabrikaminc.onmicrosoft.com
7	Brewer	Alan	Advertising Coordinator	Sales & Marketing	alan@fabrikaminc.onmicrosoft.com
8	Burke	Brian	Production Analyst	Manufacturing	brian@fabrikaminc.onmicrosoft.com
9	Carbonati	Cyril	Employee Relations Specialist	Human Resources	cyril@fabrikaminc.onmicrosoft.com
10	Chavda	Ankur	Accounts Receivable Clerk	Finance	ankur@fabrikaminc.onmicrosoft.com

	A	B	C	D	E
60	Tupy	Richard	Recruiting Analyst	Human Resources	richard@fabrikaminc.onmicrosoft.com
61	Veronesi	Giorgio	Developer	Information Technology	giorgio@fabrikaminc.onmicrosoft.com
62	Volodin	Viktor	Payroll Analyst	Finance	viktor@fabrikaminc.onmicrosoft.com
63	Weadock	Kelly J.	Client Services Representative	Information Technology	kellyj@fabrikaminc.onmicrosoft.com
64	Wheeler	Wendy	Customer Service Representative	Sales & Marketing	wendy@fabrikaminc.onmicrosoft.com
65	Xylaras	Ioannis	Production Contracts Analyst	Manufacturing	ioannis@fabrikaminc.onmicrosoft.com
66	Yair	Shmuel	Controller	Finance	shmuel@fabrikaminc.onmicrosoft.com
67	Yuan	Joanna	Regional Manager	Sales & Marketing	joanna@fabrikaminc.onmicrosoft.com
68	Zhang	Frank	Social Media Analyst	Sales & Marketing	frank@fabrikaminc.onmicrosoft.com
69					

3   While pressing **Ctrl**, press the **Down Arrow** key again and notice that cell **A1048576** is selected—the last row in the worksheet.

4   While pressing **Ctrl**, press the **Up Arrow** key to return to the previous location (cell **A68**).

5   While pressing **Ctrl**, press the **Right Arrow** key to jump to the last active cell in the table (cell **E68**).

6   While pressing **Ctrl**, press the **Up Arrow** key to jump to the top of the table (cell **E1**).

7   While pressing **Ctrl**, press the **Left Arrow** key to jump back to cell **A1**.

8   Click the **Sheet 2** tab at the bottom of the workbook.

9   Make sure that cell **A3** is selected, then hold down **Ctrl** and press the **Right Arrow** key, pause, then repeat this three more times, pausing to notice what happens each time. Cell **H3** should be selected.

	A	B	C	D	E	F	G	H
1								
2								
3			Agarwal	Manoj		Accounts Receivable Clerk	Finance	manoj@fabrikaminc.onmicrosoft.com
4			Andersen	Henriette		Benefits Analyst	Human Resources	henriette@fabrikaminc.onmicrosoft.com
5			Axford	Kai		Sales Associate	Sales & Marketing	kai@fabrikaminc.onmicrosoft.com
6			Banti	Ed		Web Services Analyst	Sales & Marketing	ed@fabrikaminc.onmicrosoft.com
7			Bentley	Sean		Training Specialist	Human Resources	sean@fabrikaminc.onmicrosoft.com
8			Brewer	Alan		Advertising Coordinator	Sales & Marketing	alan@fabrikaminc.onmicrosoft.com
9			Burke	Brian		Production Analyst	Manufacturing	brian@fabrikaminc.onmicrosoft.com
10			Carbonati	Cyril		Employee Relations Specialist	Human Resources	cyril@fabrikaminc.onmicrosoft.com
11			Chavda	Ankur		Accounts Receivable Clerk	Finance	ankur@fabrikaminc.onmicrosoft.com
12			Corets	Eva		Systems Analyst	Information Technology	eva@fabrikaminc.onmicrosoft.com
13			David	Willson Raj		Marketing Coordinator	Sales & Marketing	willsonraj@fabrikaminc.onmicrosoft.com
14			DeSeranno	Shane		Communications Analyst	Operations	shane@fabrikaminc.onmicrosoft.com
15			Ersan	Ebru		Product Support Specialist	Sales & Marketing	ebru@fabrikaminc.onmicrosoft.com
16			Fong	Raymond		Research Associate	Research & Development	raymond@fabrikaminc.onmicrosoft.com
17			Furse	Kari		Advertising Analyst	Sales & Marketing	kari@fabrikaminc.onmicrosoft.com
18			Garcia	Hugo		Client Services Representative	Information Technology	hugo@fabrikaminc.onmicrosoft.com
19			Gonzalez	Nuria		Sales Associate	Sales & Marketing	nuria@fabrikaminc.onmicrosoft.com
20			Gruber	Eric		Systems Analyst	Information Technology	eric@fabrikaminc.onmicrosoft.com
21			Harteveld	Arno		Product Support Specialist	Sales & Marketing	arno@fabrikaminc.onmicrosoft.com

10   Now hold down **Ctrl** and **Shift** together, and press the **Down Arrow** key to select the data in column **H**.

11   Holding **Ctrl** and **Shift**, press the **Left Arrow** key to select the region **F3:H21**.

	A	B	C	D	E	F	G	H
1								
2								
3			Agarwal	Manoj		Accounts Receivable Clerk	Finance	manoj@fabrikaminc.onmicrosoft.com
4			Andersen	Henriette		Benefits Analyst	Human Resources	henriette@fabrikaminc.onmicrosoft.com
5			Axford	Kai		Sales Associate	Sales & Marketing	kai@fabrikaminc.onmicrosoft.com
6			Banti	Ed		Web Services Analyst	Sales & Marketing	ed@fabrikaminc.onmicrosoft.com
7			Bentley	Sean		Training Specialist	Human Resources	sean@fabrikaminc.onmicrosoft.com
8			Brewer	Alan		Advertising Coordinator	Sales & Marketing	alan@fabrikaminc.onmicrosoft.com
9			Burke	Brian		Production Analyst	Manufacturing	brian@fabrikaminc.onmicrosoft.com
10			Carbonati	Cyril		Employee Relations Specialist	Human Resources	cyril@fabrikaminc.onmicrosoft.com
11			Chavda	Ankur		Accounts Receivable Clerk	Finance	ankur@fabrikaminc.onmicrosoft.com
12			Corets	Eva		Systems Analyst	Information Technology	eva@fabrikaminc.onmicrosoft.com
13			David	Willson Raj		Marketing Coordinator	Sales & Marketing	willsonraj@fabrikaminc.onmicrosoft.com
14			DeSeranno	Shane		Communications Analyst	Operations	shane@fabrikaminc.onmicrosoft.com
15			Ersan	Ebru		Product Support Specialist	Sales & Marketing	ebru@fabrikaminc.onmicrosoft.com
16			Fong	Raymond		Research Associate	Research & Development	raymond@fabrikaminc.onmicrosoft.com
17			Furse	Kari		Advertising Analyst	Sales & Marketing	kari@fabrikaminc.onmicrosoft.com
18			Garcia	Hugo		Client Services Representative	Information Technology	hugo@fabrikaminc.onmicrosoft.com
19			Gonzalez	Nuria		Sales Associate	Sales & Marketing	nuria@fabrikaminc.onmicrosoft.com
20			Gruber	Eric		Systems Analyst	Information Technology	eric@fabrikaminc.onmicrosoft.com
21			Harteveld	Arno		Product Support Specialist	Sales & Marketing	arno@fabrikaminc.onmicrosoft.com
22								

 CLEAN UP   **Close the Fabrikam-Employees.xlsx workbook without saving.**

When you press any Ctrl+Arrow combination when an empty cell is selected, the selection moves to the first active cell in the next region. If you do this when an active cell is selected, the selection moves to the last active cell in the same region. If there are no active cells in the direction you move, Excel selects the last available cell on the worksheet.

Moving and adjusting cells

You probably, already know plenty about clicking and dragging; these are core competencies of anyone who uses a computer. Things work differently in Excel than in writing apps, considering the grid or "graph paper" model. Word-processing programs are linear; most text-based documents are essentially one long string of characters. Excel is modular; you can put strings of characters into each cell, like tiny books on a million-shelf bookcase (1,048,576, to be exact). Of course, the tiny books have skills. For now, let's drag stuff around.

SEE ALSO For more information about formulas and functions, see Chapter 19.

In this exercise, you'll select and drag cell regions to new locations on a worksheet, and you'll quickly adjust column widths and row heights afterward.

➜ SET UP **You need the Fabrikam-Employees.xlsx workbook created in the previous exercise to complete this exercise. Or open the Fabrikam-Employees.xlsx workbook located in the Chapter18 practice file folder and save it as Fabrikam-Employees.xlsx.**

1   Open the **Fabrikam-Employees.xlsx** workbook.

2   Click the **Sheet2** tab at the bottom of the workbook window.

3   Select the region **C3:D21**.

4   Point to one of the borders of the selection, until a 4-headed arrow pointer appears.

5   Click and drag the region one cell up and one cell to the left (cell **B2** becomes the upper-left corner).

6   Select the region **F3:H21**, then drag it one cell up and two cells to the left (adjacent to the first region).

Notice that in some of the cells, single letters are wrapping within the cells, other entries are cut off, and others extend beyond the cell borders.

7 Drag through the column headers **B** through **F** to select them.

8 Click the border to the right of column **F** and drag the column header to the right to make all selected columns wider.

9 All the entries fit in the cells now, but some columns are too wide and some rows are too deep, so click the **Select All** button located at the intersection of the row and column headers to select all the rows and columns in the worksheet.

10　Double-click any border between column headers to auto-fit all columns to their widest entries.

11　Double-click any border between row headers to auto-fit all rows to their tallest entries (notice that the double-headed arrow pointer points up and down when manipulating row heights).

In this example, there was an intentionally introduced "issue" to illustrate one of the problems that may crop up when moving cells around. The cells containing first names were needlessly formatted with text wrapping turned on (it happens), which is why even individual letters wrapped within cells (for example, see cell B3 in the "before" graphic). Excel makes the row taller when text wraps in a cell, but it does not readjust the row height if you widen the column enough to avoid wrapping. To fix this, we first made the cells too wide, then we auto-fit both the rows and the columns.

If you want, you can turn off text wrapping.

12　Select the column containing the first names (column **B** in the "after" graphic earlier).

13　Click the **Wrap Text** button twice (the button is located in the **Alignment** group on the **Home** tab): once to turn wrapping on in all the selected cells, and once to turn it off.

The **Wrap Text** button should turn gray when text wrapping is on, and it turns white again when turned off.

✖ CLEAN UP **Close the Fabrikam-Employees.xlsx workbook without saving.**

Moving and copying rows and columns

Often you just need to move things around in your workbooks, and in a grid like Excel, simple copying and pasting is a needlessly awkward way of doing it. If your worksheet is set up properly, you should be able to drag entire rows and columns around without too much trouble. You simply select and drag to move and replace, or hold down Ctrl and drag to move and insert.

In this exercise, you'll move rows and columns and copy them, too.

➡ SET UP **You need the Fabrikam-Employees.xlsx workbook created in the previous exercise to complete this exercise. Or open the Fabrikam-Employees.xlsx workbook located in the Chapter18 practice file folder and save it as Fabrikam-Employees.xlsx.**

18

1   Open the **Fabrikam-Employees.xlsx** workbook, and make sure **Sheet1** is selected.

2   Scroll down to row **43** and click the row header to select the entire row.

Notice that **Giuseppe Russo** is out of alphabetical order in this table. We'll fix that.

3   Point to any part of the selection border around row **43** until the pointer becomes a 4-headed arrow.

4   Press the **Shift** key, then click and drag row **43** down.

Notice that while you are dragging, an "I-beam" type insertion cursor appears between rows, indicating the new location.

5   Release the mouse button when the insertion cursor is between rows **47** and **48**.

	A	B	C	D	E
41	Phillips	Jeff	Developer	Information Technology	jeff@fabrikaminc.onmicrosoft.com
42	Pogulsky	Grigory	Production Facilities Specialist	Manufacturing	grigory@fabrikaminc.onmicrosoft.com
43	Russo	Giuseppe	Research Associate	Research & Development	giuseppe@fabrikaminc.onmicrosoft.com
44	Railson	Stuart	Web Services Analyst	Sales & Marketing	stuart@fabrikaminc.onmicrosoft.com
45	Rao	Arvind B.	Regional Manager	Sales & Marketing	arvind@fabrikaminc.onmicrosoft.com
46	Richardson	Don	Production Logistics Analyst	Manufacturing	don@fabrikaminc.onmicrosoft.com
47	Roth	Tali	Cost Accountant	Finance	tali@fabrikaminc.onmicrosoft.com
48	Salas-Szlejter	Karolina	Maintenance Technician	Operations	karolina@fabrikaminc.onmicrosoft.com
49	Scholl	Boris	Accounts Payable Clerk	Finance	boris@fabrikaminc.onmicrosoft.com

	A	B	C	D	E
41	Phillips	Jeff	Developer	Information Technology	jeff@fabrikaminc.onmicrosoft.com
42	Pogulsky	Grigory	Production Facilities Specialist	Manufacturing	grigory@fabrikaminc.onmicrosoft.com
43	Russo	Giuseppe	Research Associate	Research & Development	giuseppe@fabrikaminc.onmicrosoft.com
44	Railson	Stuart	Web Services Analyst	Sales & Marketing	stuart@fabrikaminc.onmicrosoft.com
45	Rao	Arvind B.	Regional Manager	Sales & Marketing	arvind@fabrikaminc.onmicrosoft.com
46	Richardson	Don	Production Logistics Analyst	Manufacturing	don@fabrikaminc.onmicrosoft.com
47	Roth	Tali	Cost Accountant	Finance	tali@fabrikaminc.onmicrosoft.com
48	Salas-Szlejter	Karolina	Maintenance Technician	Operations	karolina@fabrikaminc.onmicrosoft.com
18:48 Scholl		Boris	Accounts Payable Clerk	Finance	boris@fabrikaminc.onmicrosoft.com

	A	B	C	D	E
41	Phillips	Jeff	Developer	Information Technology	jeff@fabrikaminc.onmicrosoft.com
42	Pogulsky	Grigory	Production Facilities Specialist	Manufacturing	grigory@fabrikaminc.onmicrosoft.com
43	Railson	Stuart	Web Services Analyst	Sales & Marketing	stuart@fabrikaminc.onmicrosoft.com
44	Rao	Arvind B.	Regional Manager	Sales & Marketing	arvind@fabrikaminc.onmicrosoft.com
45	Richardson	Don	Production Logistics Analyst	Manufacturing	don@fabrikaminc.onmicrosoft.com
46	Roth	Tali	Cost Accountant	Finance	tali@fabrikaminc.onmicrosoft.com
47	Russo	Giuseppe	Research Associate	Research & Development	giuseppe@fabrikaminc.onmicrosoft.com
48	Salas-Szlejter	Karolina	Maintenance Technician	Operations	karolina@fabrikaminc.onmicrosoft.com
49	Scholl	Boris	Accounts Payable Clerk	Finance	boris@fabrikaminc.onmicrosoft.com

 CLEAN UP **Save the Fabrikam-Employees.xlsx workbook and then close it.**

TIP If you press Ctrl while dragging a selection, Excel makes a copy of the selected cells and pastes them in the new location rather than inserting them (and replaces the contents of the destination cells). Pressing Ctrl+Shift while dragging both makes a copy of the selected cells and inserts them at the new location.

You use the same techniques when moving and copying columns, too.

Copying one or more cells to many

In this exercise, you'll use a handy trick for making a lot of duplicate entries, rather than extending a series of entries.

➡️ SET UP **You don't need any practice files to complete this exercise. Open a blank workbook and follow the steps.**

1   In cell **A1**, enter **One to Many**.

2   Select cell **A1** and press **Ctrl+C** to copy it.

3   Click cell **C1** and drag to select cells **C1:C6**.

4   Press **Ctrl+V** to paste, and notice that Excel fills in the entire range of selected cells with the same entry.

5   Select cells **E3:J5** by dragging through the range, and click **Ctrl+V** again to paste the entry into a 2-dimensional range.

	A	B	C	D	E	F	G	H	I	J	K	L
1	One to Many		One to Many									
2			One to Many									
3			One to Many		One to Ma	One to Ma	One to Ma	One to Ma	One to Ma	One to Many		
4			One to Many		One to Ma	One to Ma	One to Ma	One to Ma	One to Ma	One to Many		
5			One to Many		One to Ma	One to Ma	One to Ma	One to Ma	One to Ma	One to Many		
6			One to Many								(Ctrl) ▾	
7												

6   Select cell **A2** and enter **Two to Many**.

7   Select cell **A3** and enter **Three to Many**.

8   Select cells **A1:A3** and press **Ctrl+C** to copy.

9   Select cells **C1:C6** again and press **Ctrl+V** to paste.

10   Select cells **E3:J5** again and press **Ctrl+V** to paste.

	A	B	C	D	E	F	G	H	I	J	K	L
1	One to Many		One to Many									
2	Two to Many		Two to Many									
3	Three to Many		Three to Many		One to Ma	One to Ma	One to Ma	One to Ma	One to Ma	One to Many		
4			One to Many		Two to Ma	Two to Ma	Two to Ma	Two to Ma	Two to Ma	Two to Many		
5			Two to Many		Three to N	Three to N	Three to N	Three to N	Three to N	Three to Many		
6			Three to Many								(Ctrl) ▾	
7												
8												

Excel repeats the sequence to fill your selections. You can select as many cells as you like before you paste, and Excel will keep repeating the sequence you copied until the range is filled.

✖ CLEAN UP Close the workbook without saving.

Key points

- Number formatting changes the appearance of numbers, but not the underlying values.

- You can apply number formatting as you enter data by using currency symbols, percentage symbols, or commas, or by entering dates "in format."

- You can extend a series of numbers, dates, and even text entries with numeric values by dragging.

- Flash Fill learns by example to fill a range of cells based on entries in an adjacent column.

- You can assign names to cells to make it easier to remember values, to quickly select ranges, or to create more understandable formulas.

- Manipulate borders between column letters to change column widths: double-click to auto-fit all selected columns; drag to make all selected columns the same width.

- You can use the Select All button to select the entire worksheet, which is useful for formatting and adjusting row heights and column widths.

- Use the Ctrl key with an arrow key to navigate around in a worksheet.

- You can drag cells, ranges, or entire rows and columns to move them around. Pressing Shift while dragging allows you to insert the item into the new location. Pressing Ctrl makes a copy in the new location.

- In calculations, Excel always uses the underlying values displayed in the formula bar, even though the formatted values displayed on the worksheet may be different.

- If you paste a copied cell or range into a larger selected range, Excel repeats the copied cells as many times as necessary to fill the destination range.

18

Chapter at a glance

Summarize

Use the AutoSum button to create quick totals and more, page 457

Deduce

Create simple formulas by typing operators and clicking cells, page 456

Calculate

Use built-in functions to create complex formulas, page 457

Simplify

Use defined names to make formulas easier to read, page 482

Manipulating numbers and text

19

IN THIS CHAPTER, YOU WILL LEARN HOW TO

- Create, edit, and copy formulas.

- Use functions.

- Work with text in Excel.

- Restrict cell entries.

There are some pretty flashy features in Microsoft Excel, more with every new release. This chapter has possibly the lowest flash quotient of any in this section, because we're covering the basics of Excel—manipulating numbers. In other words, we're talking more about adding, subtracting, multiplying, dividing, rounding, truncating, converting, extrapolating, square-rooting, and otherwise manipulating raw data to create information. It's why Excel exists; it's what Excel does best, and it's all about what you need to know.

As a bonus, we'll look at how to manipulate text. If you routinely process a lot of text-based data like inventory or address lists, and you combine first and last names into full names, Excel may become your favorite tool.

In this chapter, you'll learn to use cell references and functions in formulas, give names to cells and ranges for easier referencing, and use formulas to edit text.

PRACTICE FILES To complete the exercises in this chapter, you need the practice files contained in the Chapter19 practice file folder. For more information, see "Download the practice files" in this book's Introduction.

Creating, editing, and copying formulas

Formulas are "backward" in Excel. In other words, we all learned in elementary school that 1+1=2 is how you write a formula. But in Excel, you flip the equal sign to the other side, so typing =1+1 into a cell returns the desired result. Putting the equal sign in front of the expression is the signal that tells Excel that you are entering a formula for which you want a calculated result. Anything else is just text, as far as calculations are concerned.

1+1=   This is a text entry in Excel.
=1+1   This is a formula in Excel.

TIP Though Excel also allows you to begin a formula with a plus or minus sign instead of an equal sign; after you press Enter, Excel adds a preceding equal sign anyway, and keeps the sign if it's a minus.

So, you begin entering your formula with an equal sign, and then by using the correct language, including numbers (or constants), math operators, cell references, and functions, you can calculate just about anything from a shopping list to an Excel music video.

In this exercise, you will use the most common formula-editing features in Excel to create a simple formula and copy it to other cells.

→ SET UP **You need the Fabrikam-Seven-Year-Summary_start.xlsx workbook located in the Chapter19 practice file folder to complete this exercise. Open the Fabrikam-Seven-Year-Summary_start.xlsx workbook, and save it as Fabrikam-Seven-Year-Summary.xlsx.**

1   Open the **Fabrikam-Seven-Year-Summary.xlsx** workbook, and make sure that cell **B10** is selected.

2   Enter = (an equal sign), then click cell **B8** (containing the 2007 Net Profit figure), and you'll notice several things: cell **B10** remains selected, there is a dotted marquee around cell **B8**, and the cell reference =B8 appears in both cell **B10** and the formula bar.

B8	▼	⋮	✕ ✓ ƒx	=B8				
	A	B	C	D	E	F	G	H
1			Fabrikam, Inc. Seven-Year Summary					
2	$1 = $1,000	2007	2008	2009	2010	2011	2012	2013
3	Income	$134,137.45	$142,728.38	$138,632.47	$151,841.00	$165,049.52	$169,605.83	$179,930.28
4	Expenses	70,962.31	75,924.87	74,167.20	76,773.91	79,380.61	79,805.13	81,684.44
5	Gross Profit	63,175.14	66,803.51	64,465.27	75,067.09	85,668.91	89,800.69	98,245.84
6	Depreciation	4,517.77	4,656.92	4,576.27	4,622.18	4,668.09	4,650.72	4,675.54
7	Interest Expense	2,745.82	2,893.11	2,885.24	2,896.65	2,908.06	2,909.82	2,918.02
8	Net Profit	55,911.55	59,253.48	57,003.76	67,548.26	71,804.47	82,240.15	90,652.28
9	Taxes	19,569.04	20,738.72	19,951.31	23,641.89	25,131.56	28,784.05	31,728.30
10	Aftertax Profit	=B8						
11								

3   Enter − (a minus sign), and then click cell **B9**.

4   Press the **Enter** key, then press the **Up Arrow** key to reselect cell **B10**.

B10	▾	⋮	✕	✓	*fx*	=B8-B9			

⊿	A	B	C	D	E	F	G	H
1				Fabrikam, Inc. Seven-Year Summary				
2	$1 = $1,000	2007	2008	2009	2010	2011	2012	2013
3	Income	$ 134,137.45	$ 142,728.38	$ 138,632.47	$ 151,841.00	$ 165,049.52	$ 169,605.83	$ 179,930.28
4	Expenses	70,962.31	75,924.87	74,167.20	76,773.91	79,380.61	79,805.13	81,684.44
5	Gross Profit	63,175.14	66,803.51	64,465.27	75,067.09	85,668.91	89,800.69	98,245.84
6	Depreciation	4,517.77	4,656.92	4,576.27	4,622.18	4,668.09	4,650.72	4,675.54
7	Interest Expense	2,745.82	2,893.11	2,885.24	2,896.65	2,908.06	2,909.82	2,918.02
8	Net Profit	55,911.55	59,253.48	57,003.76	67,548.26	71,804.47	82,240.15	90,652.28
9	Taxes	19,569.04	20,738.72	19,951.31	23,641.89	25,131.56	28,784.05	31,728.30
10	Aftertax Profit	$ 36,342.51						
11								

Fill handle

Although you could arrive at the same result by typing =55911.55-19569.04 into cell B10, a better way to leverage Excel's talents is to use references to cells containing values that appear on the worksheet. This example formula should always produce a correct result, even if the numbers in cells B8 and B9 change. And sometimes the referenced cells contain other formulas, which is the case in this example (cell B8).

5   Click cell **B8** and notice the formula =**B5-B6-B7**, which calculates net profit by subtracting depreciation and interest expense from gross profit.

6   Click cell **B3** (2007 Income), enter **123456**, and notice that cells **B5**, **B8**, **B9**, and **B10** all change accordingly, because they are all dependent upon the value in cell **B3**, called a precedent cell.

7   Press **Ctrl+Z** to undo your last entry, and the dependent cells return to their previous values.

8   Select cell **B10** and drag the fill handle across to **column H** to fill in the rest of the formulas.

9   Press **Tab** to inspect the formula in cell **C10**; repeat until you reach cell **H10** and notice that the new formulas all reflect their relative locations. The cell references were adjusted by **AutoFill**. This is the easiest way to complete a row or column of identical formulas.

H10	▼	:	×	✓	fx	=H8-H9		

◢	A	B	C	D	E	F	G	H
1				Fabrikam, Inc. Seven-Year Summary				
2	$1 = $1,000	2007	2008	2009	2010	2011	2012	2013
3	Income	$134,137.45	$142,728.38	$138,632.47	$151,841.00	$165,049.52	$169,605.83	$179,930.28
4	Expenses	70,962.31	75,924.87	74,167.20	76,773.91	79,380.61	79,805.13	81,684.44
5	Gross Profit	63,175.14	66,803.51	64,465.27	75,067.09	85,668.91	89,800.69	98,245.84
6	Depreciation	4,517.77	4,656.92	4,576.27	4,622.18	4,668.09	4,650.72	4,675.54
7	Interest Expense	2,745.82	2,893.11	2,885.24	2,896.65	2,908.06	2,909.82	2,918.02
8	Net Profit	55,911.55	59,253.48	57,003.76	67,548.26	71,804.47	82,240.15	90,652.28
9	Taxes	19,569.04	20,738.72	19,951.31	23,641.89	25,131.56	28,784.05	31,728.30
10	Aftertax Profit	$ 36,342.51	$ 38,514.76	$ 37,052.44	$ 43,906.37	$ 46,672.90	$ 53,456.10	$ 58,923.98
11								

Error indicator

You'll notice that there is a small triangle in the corner of cell F8. This is an indication that there is something different about this cell; that it somehow does not match the adjacent cells. It alerts you that there might be a problem with your formula.

10   Click cell **F8** and an **alert symbol** will appear adjacent to the cell; click it to display the menu shown below.

F8	▼	:	×	✓	fx	=F4-F6-F7		

◢	A	B	C	D	E	F	G	H
1				Fabrikam, Inc. Seven-Year Summary				
2	$1 = $1,000	2007	2008	2009	2010	2011	2012	2013
3	Income	$134,137.45	$142,728.38	$138,632.47	$151,841.00	$165,049.52	$169,605.83	$179,930.28
4	Expenses	70,962.31	75,924.87	74,167.20	76,773.91	79,380.61	79,805.13	81,684.44
5	Gross Profit	63,175.14	66,803.51	64,465.27	75,067.09	85,668.91	89,800.69	98,245.84
6	Depreciation	4,517.77	4,656.92	4,576.27	4,622.18	4,668.09	4,650.72	4,675.54
7	Interest Expense	2,745.82	2,893.11	2,885.24	2,896.65	2,908.06	2,909.82	2,918.02
8	Net Profit	55,911.55	59,253.48	57,003.76	67,54◇ ▾	71,804.47	82,240.15	90,652.28
9	Taxes	19,569.04	20,738.72	19,951.31	23,64	Inconsistent Formula	05	31,728.30
10	Aftertax Profit	$ 36,342.51	$ 38,514.76	$ 37,052.44	$ 43,90	Copy Formula from Left	10	$ 58,923.98
11						Help on this error		
12								
13						Ignore Error		
14						Edit in Formula Bar		
15						Error Checking Options...		
16								
17								

11 This menu offers possible solutions for the erring formula, and in this case, you could choose **Copy Formula from Left**, which would solve the problem. Instead, double-click cell **F8** to enter **Editing** mode.

Notice that the word Edit appears in the lower-left corner of the Excel window, and that each cell referenced in the formula is highlighted.

	A	B	C	D	E	F	G	H
SUM ▾ : ✕ ✓ ƒₓ	=F4-F6-F7							
1				Fabrikam, Inc. Seven-Year Summary				
2	*$1 = $1,000*	2007	2008	2009	2010	2011	2012	2013
3	Income	$ 134,137.45	$ 142,728.38	$ 138,632.47	$ 151,841.00	$ 165,049.52	$ 169,605.83	$ 179,930.28
4	Expenses	70,962.31	75,924.87	74,167.20	76,773.91	79,380.61	79,805.13	81,684.44
5	Gross Profit	63,175.14	66,803.51	64,465.27	75,067.09	85,668.91	89,800.69	98,245.84
6	Depreciation	4,517.77	4,656.92	4,576.27	4,622.18	4,668.09	4,650.72	4,675.54
7	Interest Expense	2,745.82	2,893.11	2,885.24	2,896.65	2,908.06	2,909.82	2,918.02
8	Net Profit	55,911.55	59,253.48	57,003.76	67,548.26	=F4-F6-F7	82,240.15	90,652.28
9	Taxes	19,569.04	20,738.72	19,951.31	23,641.89	25,131.56	28,784.05	31,728.30
10	Aftertax Profit	$ 36,342.51	$ 38,514.76	$ 37,052.44	$ 43,906.37	$ 46,672.90	$ 53,456.10	$ 58,923.98
11								
12								
13								
14								
15								
16								
17								
18								
19								
20								
21								
22								
23								

◀ ▶ **Seven-Year Financial Summary** Unit Sales Unit Prices 2015 Projectic ... ⊕ ⋮ ◀

EDIT

This formula was entered incorrectly; subtracting depreciation and interest from cell F4, expenses, instead of cell F5, gross profit. You could simply highlight the reference in the formula and enter the correct reference, or you can manipulate the references directly. Whenever possible, it is always advisable to use direct manipulation with cell references in formulas, in order to minimize errors. Plus, it's just easier to see the relationships among cells.

12   Point to the thick border of the box highlighting cell **F4** and notice that it thickens just a bit when you pass over it.

13   Click the border and drag the box from cell **F4** down to cell **F5**; the formula changes to reflect the newly highlighted cell.

LOOKUP	▼	⋮	✕	✓	*fx*	=F5-F6-F7		

	A	B	C	D	E	F	G	H
1				Fabrikam, Inc. Seven-Year Summary				
2	$1 = $1,000	2007	2008	2009	2010	2011	2012	2013
3	Income	$ 134,137.45	$ 142,728.38	$ 138,632.47	$ 151,841.00	$ 165,049.52	$ 169,605.83	$ 179,930.28
4	Expenses	70,962.31	75,924.87	74,167.20	76,773.91	79,380.61	79,805.13	81,684.44
5	Gross Profit	63,175.14	66,803.51	64,465.27	75,067.09	85,668.9⫦	89,800.69	98,245.84
6	Depreciation	4,517.77	4,656.92	4,576.27	4,622.18	4,668.09	4,650.72	4,675.54
7	Interest Expense	2,745.82	2,893.11	2,885.24	2,896.65	2,908.06	2,909.82	2,918.02
8	Net Profit	55,911.55	59,253.48	57,003.76	67,548.26	=F5-F6-F7	82,240.15	90,652.28
9	Taxes	19,569.04	20,738.72	19,951.31	23,641.89	25,131.56	28,784.05	31,728.30
10	Aftertax Profit	$ 36,342.51	$ 38,514.76	$ 37,052.44	$ 43,906.37	$ 46,672.90	$ 53,456.10	$ 58,923.98
11								

14   Press **Enter**; the triangle indicator disappears, and the newly edited formula returns the correct net profit amount.

You can drag the formula-editing boxes anywhere on the sheet, or if you click one of the square dots in the corners, you can drag to expand the cell reference to include more rows and columns of cells.

✖ CLEAN UP **Save the Fabrikam-Seven-Year-Summary.xlsx workbook, and then close it.**

Using functions

You can create a lot of formulas by using math operators: addition, subtraction, multiplication (asterisk), division (forward slash), square root (caret), parentheses, and percentage symbols. But far more computational power is at your disposal with functions, which are essentially prepackaged formulas that perform specific calculations. All functions are followed by a set of parentheses, and most require specific arguments to be entered between them.

Although you can use cell references with math operators in simple formulas, you cannot use range references. But when you use functions, range references are perfectly acceptable to use as arguments, when appropriate.

The simplest and most-often-used function is SUM, which accommodates any number of arguments up to 255. For example, the following formulas all return totals:

```
=12+334
=C6+C7+C8
=SUM(C6:C8)
=SUM(12,334)
=SUM(12,334,C6:C8)
```

With most functions, you can combine different types of arguments, including single cell references, cell ranges (C6:C8), static values (12), and even other formulas. (Formulas within formulas are said to be *nested*.)

TIP It is usually better to enter cell references in formulas, rather than entering static values, because you can see and change values entered into cells, but they are "hidden" in formulas; only the result of the formula is displayed. Keeping your numbers visible makes it easier to troubleshoot and audit worksheets.

19

Using the AutoSum button and built-in function

You might expect that Excel would offer a quick and easy way to apply the most-often-used function in the galaxy, and you would be correct.

In this exercise, you will use the "epsilon" button, also known as the Sum button or AutoSum, for more than just totals.

 SET UP **You need the Fabrikam-Seven-Year-Summary.xlsx workbook from the previous exercise to complete this exercise. Or, you can open the Fabrikam-Seven-Year-Summary_start.xlsx workbook located in the Chapter19 practice file folder and save it as Fabrikam-Seven-Year-Summary.xlsx.**

1 Open the **Fabrikam-Seven-Year-Summary.xlsx** workbook, and click the **Unit Sales** worksheet tab.

2 Click cell **A3**, then hold down the **Ctrl** key and press the **Right Arrow** key to jump to the rightmost end of the table. Cell **CG3** should be selected.

> **IMPORTANT** Rows in Excel are numbered 1 through 1,048,576 down the left side of the worksheet, but because there are only 26 letters in the alphabet, column letters are repeated. Column Z is followed by columns AA, AB, AC, and so on. After AZ comes BA; after ZZ comes AAA, and so on until you reach XFD, the 16,384th column.

3   Press the **Right Arrow** key once to select cell **CH3**.

4   Click the **AutoSum** button, located in the **Editing** group on the **Home** tab. (You can also hold down the **Alt** key and press = to enter a **SUM** function.)

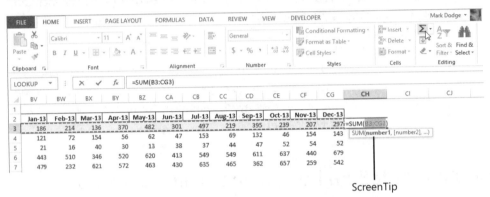

ScreenTip

Notice what just happened. After you clicked the AutoSum button, Excel inserted an equal sign, the function name, a set of parentheses, and the suggested argument, eliminating the need to type them. In this case, Excel correctly identified the range you want to sum. You can scroll back to the left to check this before you press Enter to lock in the formula. The AutoSum button sometimes gets it wrong, especially if the row or column label (for example, "FABK-0001" in cell A3) is a calculable numeric value such as a date, so you always need to check. You can also get help on the function before you press Enter.

5   Click the **SUM** function name that is displayed in the ScreenTip floating just below cell **CH3**, and the **Excel Help** window appears, displaying information about the function.

Excel Help ·

SUM function

This article describes the formula syntax and usage of the **SUM** function in Microsoft Excel.

Description

The **SUM** function adds all the numbers that you specify as arguments. Each argument can be a range, a cell reference, an array, a constant, a formula, or the result from another function. For example, **SUM(A1:A5)** adds all the numbers that are contained in cells A1 through A5. For another example, **SUM(A1, A3, A5)** adds the numbers that are contained in cells A1, A3, and A5.

Syntax

```
SUM(number1, [number2], ...)
```

The SUM function syntax has the following arguments:

- **number1**   Required. The first number argument that you want to add.

- **number2,....**   Optional. Number arguments 2 to 255 that you want to add.

6 Close the **Help** window by clicking the **X** in the upper-right corner.

7 Press **Enter** to finish the formula in cell **CH3**.

8 Click the tiny downward-pointing arrow to the right of the **AutoSum** button to display a menu of additional functions you can apply by using this button, in addition to SUM.

9   Click **Average** to enter the function on the worksheet; you'll see that cell **CH3** is the suggested argument to the **AVERAGE** function, which is definitely not what you want.

CF	CG	CH	CI	CJ	CK

Nov-13	Dec-13				
207	297	26283			
154	143	=AVERAGE(CH3)			
54	52	AVERAGE(**number1**, [number2], ...)			
440	679				
259	542				
28	60				
224	242				

10   With the **AVERAGE** function still visible and the cell still in **Edit** mode, click cell **CG4**, just to the left of the new formula.

11   Hold down **Ctrl** and press the **Left Arrow** key to jump all the way to the left end of the table (cell **A4**), then release the **Ctrl** key and press the **Right Arrow** key to select cell **B4** instead.

12   Hold down both the **Shift** and **Ctrl** keys, and then press the **Right Arrow** key to select cells **B4:CG4**.

CF	CG	CH	CI	CJ	CK

Nov-13	Dec-13		
207	297	26283	
154	143	=AVERAGE(B4:CG4)	
54	52	AVERAGE(**number1**, [number2], ...)	
440	679		
259	542		
28	60		
224	242		

13 Press **Enter**, then press the **Up Arrow** key to reselect cell **CH4** so you can see the formula, which now displays the average unit sales for this product, 100.8928571.

14 Decimal values in your averages are distracting, so to fix this, make sure that cell **CH4** is still selected and click the **Decrease Decimal** button, located in the **Number** group on the **Home** tab, and keep clicking until the decimal portion of the number is hidden from view and until the rounded integer value **101** appears. (Remember that the actual value has not changed, only the displayed value.)

TIP An integer value is, quite simply, a number without decimals.

CF	CG	CH	CI	CJ	

lov-13	Dec-13		
207	297	26283	
154	143	101	
54	52		
440	679		
259	542		
28	60		
224	242		

❌ CLEAN UP Close the Fabrikam-Seven-Year-Summary.xlsx workbook without saving it.

As you can see, when you click the menu arrow next to the AutoSum button, it offers other functions, including:

- **Count Numbers** Returns only the number of cells in the referenced area that contain numbers; cells containing text are ignored.

- **Max** Returns the maximum value in the referenced area.

- **Min** Returns the minimum value in the referenced area.

- **More Functions** Opens the **Insert Function** dialog box, where you can select any function. Contrary to what you might expect, this does not add the selected function to the **AutoSum** menu.

Using the status bar to check totals and more

The status bar is another handy feature you can use to quickly check the sum or average of any selected cells. Select some cells containing, well, anything, and then look at the bottom of the Excel window at the status bar. There you'll see the Average, Count, and Sum. (Note that the default status bar readout for Count is a tally of cells with contents of any kind, not just cells containing numbers.) If you don't need to create a formula, this is a real timesaver. You can modify the items displayed in the status bar by right-clicking the status bar to display the Customize Status Bar menu.

Customize Status Bar

✓ Cell Mode	Ready
✓ Flash Fill Blank Cells	
✓ Flash Fill Changed Cells	
✓ Signatures	Off
✓ Information Management Policy	Off
✓ Permissions	Off
Caps Lock	Off
Num Lock	On
✓ Scroll Lock	Off
✓ Fixed Decimal	Off
Overtype Mode	
✓ End Mode	
✓ Macro Recording	Not Recording
✓ Selection Mode	
✓ Page Number	
✓ Average	165.9761905
✓ Count	42
✓ Numerical Count	42
Minimum	
Maximum	
✓ Sum	6971
✓ Upload Status	
✓ View Shortcuts	
✓ Zoom Slider	
✓ Zoom	100%

(E)	May-07	Jun-07	Jul-07	Aug-07	Sep-07	Oct-07	Nov-07	Dec-07
81	231	362	130	360	451	456	250	318
36	65	83	80	80	149	121	51	56
28	14	23	28	56	18	27	24	53
30	651	604	442	477	420	330	414	570
81	515	362	287	589	535	291	539	430
43	95	97	76	110	30	96	79	70
30	320	240	388	305	252	321	326	282
93	91	96	81	86	83	106	79	84
10	186	63	155	72	137	116	110	193
79	86	96	95	91	69	97	79	68
53	57	27	37	53	39	29	56	33
52	471	638	523	424	640	587	493	373
65	101	176	187	179	181	129	198	191
29	73	78	46	25	66	22	51	52
96	260	234	247	237	229	306	325	231
23	60	66	117	105	71	111	102	120
35	37	20	18	29	19	17	18	37
26	18	17	17	14	24	29	28	19
60	140	128	114	143	124	163	165	179
37	348	534	418	452	530	483	481	479
88	352	483	368	964	617	811	973	232
	61	76	86	91	53	93	52	56

it Sales | Unit Prices | 2015 Projectic ...

AVERAGE: 165.9761905   COUNT: 42   NUMERICAL COUNT: 42   SUM: 6971

Status bar readout area

All items with check marks on the Customize Status Bar menu are currently active, even if there is no current corresponding item visible in the status bar. When, for example, you use Flash Fill, one of the two Flash Fill "mode" messages appears on the left side of the bar. Most of the menu items are mode indicators that appear only when appropriate. The last three—View Shortcuts, View Slider, and Zoom—turn the controls on the right end of the status bar on and off. You can add status bar readouts for Numerical Count, Minimum, and Maximum; to do so, click the corresponding menu item.

Inserting functions

The SUM function is pretty easy to figure out, but there are hundreds of functions available, and most of them are not nearly as intuitive. Click the Insert Function button—the little fx button on the formula bar—to display the Insert Function dialog box, which comes in handy when you need to use functions with multiple arguments. Offering assistance in context, it explains the function and its possible variations, and makes it easy to enter even the most complex nested-formula arguments correctly. If you want more information and "live examples," you can still access the Help system from the Insert Function dialog box by clicking the question mark in the title bar.

In this exercise, you'll create a formula and work with the formula bar.

→ SET UP **You need the Loan_start.xlsx workbook located in the Chapter19 practice file folder to complete this exercise. Open the Loan_start.xlsx workbook, and save it as Loan. xlsx.**

1   In the **Loan.xlsx** workbook, make sure that cell **C6** is selected.

2   Click the **Insert Function** button in the formula bar, and notice that Excel inserts an equal sign (=) in the selected cell, in preparation for the formula that you are about to enter.

3   In the **Or Select a Category** list in the **Insert Function** dialog box, click the downward-pointing arrow and select **Financial**.

4   In the **Select a Function** box, scroll down the list and select **PMT**, which calculates the monthly payment on a simple loan; the syntax and description of the selected function appears below the function list.

5 Click **OK** to insert the function into the cell, which dismisses the **Insert Function** dialog box and displays the **Function Arguments** dialog box.

6 The first box in the **Function Arguments** dialog box—the **Rate** box—is active; click cell **B6** (containing the percentage **5.00%**) to insert that cell's reference as the **Rate** argument. Notice that a short description of the selected argument appears in the bottom half of the dialog box. If you need more information, click the **Help on This Function** link at the bottom of the dialog box.

7 After the cell reference has been inserted, the cursor is still flashing in the **Rate** box; enter **/12** to convert the rate from annual to monthly to create a nested formula within the PMT function; you can create up to 64 levels of nesting by using parentheses.

8   Click in the **Nper** box and then click cell **C3** to insert the cell reference for the **Years** entry.

9   While the cursor is still in the **Nper** box, enter ***12** to convert the time periods from years into months.

10   Click in the **Pv** box (present value), and then click cell **C5**; the loan amount is the present value.

As you add arguments in the Function Arguments dialog box, you'll notice that Excel displays the actual calculated value of each argument to the right of each edit box, and shows the overall result that will be returned by the function, just below the argument values. If you watch cell C6 or the formula bar, you can keep an eye on the formula as it takes shape. Only the arguments that are displayed in bold in the dialog box are required; the Fv (future value) and Type arguments are optional.

11   Press **OK** to enter the formula.

This simple formula shows that your payments would be $189, but the result is displayed in parentheses as a negative number, because payments represent money spent rather than received. You might need to express cash outflows as negative values in a double-entry accounting worksheet, for example. However, if you don't, it is common practice to reverse the sign for display purposes.

12   Select cell **C6**.

13   In the formula bar, click between the equal sign and the PMT function and enter – (a minus sign).

14   Press **Enter**.

| C6 | ▼ | : | ✕ | ✓ | ƒx | =-PMT(B6/12,C3*12,C5) |

◢	A	B	C	D	E	F
1						
2		Loan Payment Formula				
3		Years:	5			
4			Amount			
5		Rate	$ 10,000			
6		5.00%	189			
7						

✖ CLEAN UP Save the Loan.xlsx workbook, and then close it.

You can explore the Insert Function dialog box to give yourself some perspective on the array of functions available and how they are organized.

Using relative, fixed, and mixed cell references

There are three kinds of references in Excel: fixed, relative, and mixed. All of the cell references we have used thus far have been relative references, such as C4. Using relative references in formulas allows you to copy or fill the formula, and the relative references will adjust automatically. This is fine for many one-dimensional purposes like totals, as long as the data cells and the formula cells are always in the same relative positions.

For example, suppose in cell A1, you enter the formula =B1+C1. What this formula says, essentially, is "take the value in the next cell to the right, and add it to the value two cells to the right." You can copy this formula anywhere, and the relative references will adjust automatically; the formula will always add the two cells to the right of the formula, wherever it is located.

But frequently, you might want to use a single value in multiple formulas, such as a percentage rate. You could use a relative cell reference, but only if you didn't need to copy it elsewhere. Otherwise, you could use a fixed reference, such as $C$4. A dollar sign preceding the row number and column letter tells Excel to hold that position so it will not adjust when you copy it. You can use $C$4 in a formula, copying it as needed, and the cell reference will not change, because both the row and column are fixed.

You can also specify mixed references, in which one row or column is fixed and the other is relative; for example, $C4. When you copy this reference, the row adjusts automatically, but the column does not. You'll use this ability to fix and mix your references in the next exercise.

19

In this exercise, you'll change the reference style by using the F4 function key, which is a special unnamed reference-switching key that only works when you are editing formulas. This makes it easier and more reliable to edit formulas and requires a lot less squinting and typing the dollar signs yourself.

➡ SET UP **You need the Loan_start.xlsx workbook from the previous exercise to complete this exercise. Or, you can open the Loan_start.xlsx workbook located in the Chapter19 practice file folder. Save the workbook as Loan.xlsx.**

1   In the **Loan.xlsx** workbook, click the **Loan Table** worksheet tab.

2   Make sure cell **C6** is selected, and enter **=-PMT(** to begin the formula. (Make sure to include the minus sign after the equal sign.)

3   Click cell **B6**, which contains the **3.00%** rate, to add the cell reference into the formula.

4   Press the **F4** key and notice that the reference changes to the fixed form, **$B$6**.

5   Press **F4** again, and it changes to **B$6**.

6   Press **F4** a third time to change the reference to **$B6**, which is what you want; if you press **F4** again, the reference returns to normal; you can keep pressing **F4** to cycle through the sequence.

7   Following the reference **$B6**, enter **/12** to convert the annual interest rate into a monthly amount.

C6	▼	:	✕	✓	ƒx	=-PMT($B6/12	

⊿	A	B	C	D	E	F	G
1							
2		**Loan Payments Table**					
3		Years:	5				
4				Loan Amount			
5		Rate	$ 10,000	$ 20,000	$ 30,000	$ 40,000	
6		3.00%	=-PMT($B6/12				
7		3.50%	PMT(rate, nper, pv, [fv], [type])				
8		4.00%					
9		4.50%					
10		5.00%					
11							

8   Enter a comma to separate the first argument from the next, then click cell **C3**, which contains the number of years.

9   Press the **F4** key just once this time, settling on the locked-row-and-column version of the mixed reference, **$C$3**.

10   Following the reference **$C$3**, enter ***12** to convert years into months.

11   Enter a comma (,) and then click cell **C5**, which contains the **$10,000** loan amount.

12   Press the **F4** key twice this time to enter the locked-row version of the mixed reference, **C$5**.

13   Enter a closed parenthesis sign ()) to finish the function arguments.

14   Press **Enter**. Now you're ready to copy the formula.

> **TIP** When you are in Edit mode and are working on a formula with multiple cell references, click the one you want to fix or mix; pressing F4 adjusts that reference only. And yes, you could just type the dollar signs yourself, but F4 actually does make it easier if you're working with more than one reference.

19

C6			×	✓	f_x	=-PMT($B6/12,$C$3*12,C$5)	

	A	B	C	D	E	F	G
1							
2		**Loan Payments Table**					
3		Years:	5				
4				**Loan Amount**			
5		Rate	$ 10,000	$ 20,000	$ 30,000	$ 40,000	
6		3.00%	180				
7		3.50%					
8		4.00%					
9		4.50%					
10		5.00%					
11							

15   Select cell **C6** and drag the fill handle to the right to cell **F6**.

16   Drag the fill handle from cell **F6** down to cell **F10**.

17   Press **Shift+Tab** to highlight cell **F10**. (You can press **Tab** to move the selected cell to the right or down in a selected block of cells without losing the selection; pressing **Shift+Tab** moves the selection in reverse.)

fx =-PMT($B10/12,$C$3*12,F$5)

	A	B	C	D	E	F	G
1							
2		**Loan Payments Table**					
3		Years: 5					
4				Loan Amount			
5		Rate	$ 10,000	$ 20,000	$ 30,000	$ 40,000	
6		3.00%	180	359	539	719	
7		3.50%	182	364	546	728	
8		4.00%	184	368	552	737	
9		4.50%	186	373	559	746	
10		5.00%	189	377	566	755	
11							
12							

In all of the copied formulas, the fixed reference $C$3 stayed locked on the Years cell, and the mixed references performed as expected, adjusting to use the correct rate in column B, and the proper loan amount in row 5. Filling in formulas even in a table this small would have been an unduly tedious and error-prone endeavor, had we entered each formula manually. Spending a little time crafting the formula made the table easier to create and rendered the results more reliable.

✖ CLEAN UP **Save the Loan.xlsx workbook, and then close it.**

Using names in formulas and validating cell entries

Another way to construct formulas is to use named ranges instead of cell references. Applying familiar names to cells and ranges makes them easier to remember.

In this exercise, you'll create names to apply to cell references and ranges.

➡ SET UP **You need the Fabrikam-Seven-Year-Summary2_start.xlsx workbook located in the Chapter19 practice file folder to complete this exercise. Open the Fabrikam-Seven-Year-Summary2_start.xlsx workbook, and save it as Fabrikam-Seven-Year-Summary2.xlsx.**

1 Open the **Fabrikam-Seven-Year-Summary2.xlsx** workbook.

2 Click the tiny arrow in the **Name** box on the left end of the formula bar, and select **NamesRange** from the list to select the range **A3:H10**.

3 On the **Formulas** tab, click **Create From Selection** in the **Defined Names** group.

Name box

4   Select the **Left Column** check box, if it is not already selected, and then click **OK**.

5   Select cell **B10**.

6   Enter **=Net_Profit-Taxes** and press **Enter**.

7   Select cell **B10** again and drag the fill handle to cell **H10** to copy the formula.

D10			fx	=Net_Profit-Taxes			
	A	B	C	D	E	F	G	H
1				Fabrikam, Inc. Seven-Year Summary				
2	$1 = $1,000	2007	2008	2009	2010	2011	2012	2013
3	Income	$ 134,137.45	$ 142,728.38	$ 138,632.47	$ 151,841.00	$ 165,049.52	$ 169,605.83	$ 179,930.28
4	Expenses	70,962.31	75,924.87	74,167.20	76,773.91	79,380.61	79,805.13	81,684.44
5	Gross Profit	63,175.14	66,803.51	64,465.27	75,067.09	85,668.91	89,800.69	98,245.84
6	Depreciation	4,517.77	4,656.92	4,576.27	4,622.18	4,668.09	4,650.72	4,675.54
7	Interest Expense	2,745.82	2,893.11	2,885.24	2,896.65	2,908.06	2,909.82	2,918.02
8	Net Profit	55,911.55	59,253.48	57,003.76	67,548.26	78,092.76	82,240.15	90,652.28
9	Taxes	19,569.04	20,738.72	19,951.31	23,641.89	27,332.47	28,784.05	31,728.30
10	Aftertax Profit	$ 36,342.51	$ 38,514.76	$ 37,052.44	$ 43,906.37	$ 50,760.29	$ 53,456.10	$ 58,923.98
11								

These formulas all create the same totals as the ones that you created in the first exercise in this chapter, except that now all the formulas in row 10 are exactly the same. This illustrates one of Excel's hidden features, implicit intersection. The names Net_Profit and Taxes each represent a range of cells, not a single cell, but Excel correctly assumed that you wanted to use only the cell in each range that appears in the same column as the formula.

8 Select the **Net Profit** formulas in cells **B8:H8**.

9 Enter = (an equal sign), then click the **Use in Formula** menu in the **Defined Names** group.

10 Select **Gross_Profit** from the list of names, and then enter – (a minus sign).

11 Select **Depreciation** from the **Use in Formula** menu, and then enter – (a minus sign).

12 Select **Interest_Expense** from the list.

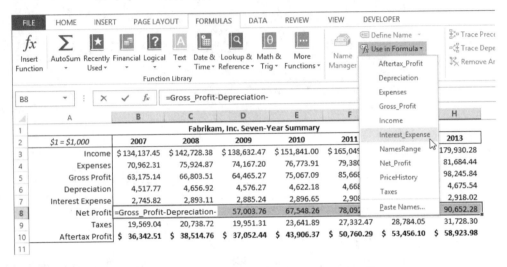

13 Press **Ctrl+Enter** to insert the formula into all the selected cells at once.

There is one more row of formulas you can edit yourself. Just perform the last four steps of this procedure on row 5 instead of row 8, and create the formula =Income-Expenses.

✖ CLEAN UP **Save the Fabrikam-Seven-Year-Summary2.xlsx workbook, and then close it.**

Looking at useful functions

The categories listed in the Insert Function dialog box represent all functions, including very specialized functions that are used for such things as programming, engineering, and querying databases. There are frequently used functions in every category, of course, but for most of us, some categories will never have representatives in our favorites list. Viewing the Formulas tab on the ribbon reveals the types of functions available.

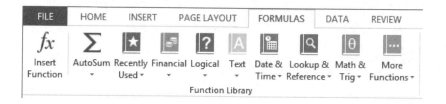

Next to giant versions of the Insert Function and AutoSum buttons (everyone's favorites), the Function Library reveals the categories that we all use most; less frequently used functions are relegated to the More Functions menu. The Recently Used menu collects your own personal favorites.

TIP When you have an idea of what you're looking for, the Formulas tab may be more beneficial to you than the available choices in the Insert Function dialog box. When you select a function from the Function Library group, you skip the Insert Function dialog box and go directly to the Function Arguments dialog box.

In this section, we'll focus on some helpful functions from the six categories represented on the Formulas tab, and you'll be provided with brief explanations of each category. We encourage you to use the Excel Help system to enhance your understanding. You can access the Help system at any time by pressing F1 on your keyboard or clicking the Help button on the ribbon. You can also directly access a specific Help topic by clicking the More Help On This Function link at the bottom of the Insert Function dialog box.

In the Help topics, you'll find descriptions and definitions, and most function topics will include live examples that you can download and test for yourself.

Handy math and trig functions

The following eight math and trig functions can be accessed through the AutoSum button:

- **SUMIF(range, criteria, sum_range)** This command combines the IF and SUM functions to add specific values in a range according to the criterion you supply. For example, the formula =SUMIF(G5:G12, "X", J5:J12) returns the total of all numbers in J5:J12, in which the cell in the same row in column G contains an X.

- **COUNTIF(range, criteria)** This command is similar to SUMIF, but counts cells in the specified range that match your specified criterion.

- **SUMPRODUCT(array1, [array2], [array3], ...)** This function multiplies each value in array1 by the corresponding value in array2, array3, and so on, then adds the totals. All the arrays (up to 255) must consist of an identical shape and size.

- **PRODUCT(number1, [number2], ...)** This function multiplies all of its arguments (up to 255). If you need to multiply a lot of numbers, using this function is easier than creating a formula such as =A1+A2+A3+A4.

- **RANDBETWEEN(bottom, top)** This function generates a random integer that falls between two provided integer values, inclusive. It is also volatile, meaning that it recalculates every time you open or edit a worksheet or press F9 (recalculate).

- **ROUND(number, num_digits)** You can round a number by using this function for a specified number of digits. When num_digits is zero, number is rounded to an integer value; if num_digits is greater than zero, number is rounded to the specified number of decimal places; if num_digits is less than zero, the number is rounded to the indicated number of places to the left of the decimal point.

- **ROUNDDOWN(number, num_digits)** Similar to ROUND, this function always rounds a number down, toward zero.

- **ROUNDUP(number, num_digits)** Also similar to ROUND, this function rounds a number up, away from zero.

> **IMPORTANT** The rounding result produced by applying a number format does not change the underlying value entered into a cell. Using one of the rounding functions will effectively truncate the value for any dependent calculations.

Handy logical functions

You can use logical functions to create complex conditional formulas, such as those mentioned in the following list:

- **IF(logical_test, [value_if_true], [value_if_false])** This function applies a logical test (for example, C5>200) that results in a true or false and optionally allows you to specify different values for both True and False results.

- **Nested IF** This function creates a hierarchy of tests. For example, the formula: =IF(A1=1, "Yes", IF(AND(A1>=1, A1<10), "Maybe", IF(AND(A1>=10, A1<20), "No", "N/A"))) returns Yes if the value is 1, Maybe for values of 2 through 9, No for values between 10 and 20, and N/A if none of these conditions is true.

- **AND(logical1, logical2, ...)** This function returns FALSE if any of its arguments are false, and returns TRUE only if all of its arguments are true. Generally, this function is used as an argument to another function, such as IF, which allows you to apply multiple logical tests instead of just one. Conversely, the OR function returns FALSE only if all of its arguments are false, and returns TRUE if any of its arguments are true. Either function can accept up to 255 arguments.

- **IFERROR(value, value_if_error)** This function returns a specified value (or a message enclosed in quotation marks, such as "We have a problem!") if the value argument evaluates to FALSE. You can use this function to test the results of other formulas by nesting them within the IFERROR function as the value argument.

Handy text functions

Many functions can manipulate text. Some of them are pretty esoteric; for example, the BAHTTEXT function coverts any number into text in the Thai language.

Following are a few of the more useful text functions, shown with their arguments.

- **CLEAN(text)** Removes all nonprintable characters. This is useful when you are importing data from other sources, which sometimes includes errant code symbols, returns, or line-break characters.

- **CONCATENATE(text1, text2, ...)** See "Combining text from multiple cells into one string" later in this chapter.

- **EXACT(text1, text2)** This function compares two text strings to see if they are the same. The function returns TRUE if they are exactly the same; otherwise, it returns FALSE. It is case-sensitive, but not formatting-sensitive.

- **LEFT(text, num_characters)** This function returns the first num_characters in a text string. For example, the formula =LEFT("Step by Step",4) returns Step. Note that text entered directly into a formula must be enclosed in quotation marks. This tells Excel that you have entered a text string; the quotation marks don't count as characters. If you use references to text in other cells; no quotation marks are needed. If cell C3 contained the text Step by Step, the formula =LEFT(C3,4) would also return Step.

- **LEN(text)** Returns the number of characters in a text string. For example, the formula =LEN("Step by Step") returns a value of 12.

- **LOWER(text)** Converts text into all-lowercase characters.

- **PROPER(text)** See "Changing the case of text" later in this chapter.

- **RIGHT(text, num_characters)** Returns the last num_characters in a text string. For example, the formula =RIGHT("Step by Step",7) returns the text by Step. Yes, spaces count as characters.

- **TRIM(text)** See "Removing extra spaces," later in this chapter.

- **UPPER(text)** Converts text into all-uppercase characters.

Handy date and time functions

You can use dates in formulas and functions as you would any other value. If cell A1 contains the date 7/4/2013, the formula =A1+300 returns the date that falls exactly 300 days later: 4/30/2014 (or the serial date value 41759).

To find the elapsed number of weeks between two dates, you can enter a formula such as =(("12/13/14")-("11/12/13"))/7, which returns 56.6 weeks. If you enter dates "in format," then enclose them in quotation marks. Or you can use serial date values. But it's always better to use cell references instead of entering any values into formulas directly, simplifying the previous formula to something like =(C4-D4)/7.

Following are several functions that do things that formulas cannot accomplish:

- **TODAY()** Inserts the current date. This function takes no arguments, but you must include the empty parentheses anyway. You may also need to apply a date format, if the date appears as an integer. This function is said to be volatile, meaning that it recalculates every time you open or edit the worksheet.

- **NOW()** Similar to the TODAY function, but it inserts both the current date and time. This function is also volatile and takes no arguments. The result includes an integer (the date) and a decimal value (the time).

- **WEEKDAY(serial_number, return_type)** Returns the day of the week for a specific date. The serial_number can be a date value, a cell reference, or text such as "1/27/11" or "January 27, 2011" (you need to include the quotation marks). The function returns a number that represents the day of the week on which the specified date falls, where day 1 is Sunday if the optional return_type argument is 1 or omitted. If return_type is 2, then day 1 is Monday, if return_type is 3, then Monday is day 0, and Sunday is day 6.

- **WORKDAY(start_date, days, holidays)** Returns a date for a specified number of working days before or after a given date. If the days argument is negative, the function returns the number of workdays before the start date; if days is positive, then it returns the number of working days after the start date. Optionally, you can include an array or range of other dates you wish to exclude as the holidays argument.

- **NETWORKDAYS(start_date, end_date, holidays)** This function is similar to the WORKDAY function but calculates the number of working days between two given dates. This function does not count weekends.

Handy lookup and reference functions

These two lookup functions are designed to search for the largest value (either numerically or alphabetically) in a specified row or column of a table that is less than or equal to the lookup value, not for an exact match. The functions return errors if all the values in the first row or column of the table are greater than the lookup value, but if all the values are less than the lookup value, the function returns the largest value available.

- **VLOOKUP(lookup_value, table_array, col_index_num, [range_lookup])** Searches the first column of table_array and returns a value from the same row, in the column indicated by col_index_num. The values can be numbers or text, but it is essential that table_array is sorted in ascending order, top to bottom. No lookup_value should appear more than once in a table. This function returns the largest value that does not exceed lookup_value, not necessarily an exact match, unless you set the optional range_lookup argument to FALSE.

- **HLOOKUP(lookup_value, table_array, row_index_num, [range_lookup])** Searches the first row of table_array and returns a value from the same column, in the row indicated by row_index_num. Otherwise, this function performs identically to the VLOOKUP function, except that table_array must be sorted in ascending order from left to right rather than top to bottom.

- **ROW([reference])** Returns the row number of the reference; if the reference argument is omitted, returns the current row.

- **ROWS(array)** Returns the number of rows in the specified range.

- **COLUMN([reference])** Returns the column number (not the letter) of the reference; if the reference argument is omitted, returns the current column.

- **COLUMNS(array)** Returns the number of columns in the specified range.

Handy financial functions

Most of the financial functions involve various aspects of amortizing or annuitizing. There are clusters of functions that address such specifics as T-bills, mortgages, loans, and depreciation.

The following lists some of the most commonly used financial functions:

- **PMT(rate, number of periods, present value, future value, type)** Computes the payment required to amortize a loan over a specified number of periods. For an example, see "Using relative, fixed, and mixed references," earlier in this chapter.

- **IPMT(rate, period, number of periods, present value, future value, type)** Computes the interest portion of an individual loan payment, assuming a constant payment and interest rate. PPMT takes the same arguments as IPMT but returns the principal portion of the payment.

- **NPER(rate, payment, present value, future value, type)** Computes the number of periods required to amortize a loan, given a specified payment.

- **SLN(cost, salvage, life)** Calculates straight-line depreciation for an asset.

Working with text in Excel

People always think numbers when they think about Excel, but in reality, Excel is frequently used as a layout grid for text. Most of the time, this sort of thing would be better accomplished with Microsoft Word, but people use what they know and are comfortable with. However, there are some things you can do with text in Excel that you can't do in Word. After learning a few more tricks, you may think about massaging text in Excel first, before copying it into a Word document.

Combining text from multiple cells into one string

In this exercise, you'll put strings of text together any way you want by using the CONCATENATE function. Whenever you use a cell reference in the function, you use the ampersand (&) as a connector to the next item, which can be another cell reference, or text enclosed in quotation marks. Anything you enter between the quotation marks is treated as text.

SET UP **You need the Fabrikam-Management2_start.xlsx workbook located in the Chapter19 practice file folder to complete this exercise. Open the Fabrikam-Management2_start.xlsx workbook, and save it as Fabrikam-Management2.xlsx.**

1   In the **Fabrikam-Management2.xlsx** workbook, make sure that cell I2 is selected.

2   Begin entering **=CON**.

A suggested list of functions appears below the cell.

	G	H	I	J	K	L
	State	Zip	FullName	FullAddress	CityStZip	
	PA	98006	=Con			
	PA	98272	*fx* CONCATENATE	Joins several text strings into one text string		
	PA	98008	*fx* CONFIDENCE.NORM			
	PA	98004	*fx* CONFIDENCE.T			
	PA	98201	*fx* CONVERT			
	PA	98006	*fx* CONFIDENCE			
	OH	83720				

3   Double-click **CONCATENATE**.

4   Click cell **B2** and then enter **&" "&** (a space enclosed with quotation marks and ampersands).

5   Click cell **A2** and press **Enter**.

6   Press the **Up Arrow** key, reselecting cell **I2** to view the formula.

I2	▼ : × ✓ *fx*	=CONCATENATE(B2&" "&A2)								
▲	A	B	C	D	E	F	G	H	I	J
1	LastName	FirstName	Title	Department	Address	City	State	Zip	FullName	FullAddress
2	Abercrombie	Kim	Accounting Manager	Finance	1234 S 34th	Erie	PA	98006	Kim Abercrombie	
3	Affronti	Michael	Director of Operations	Operations	123 Broadway	Meadville	PA	98272		

7   Select cell **J2**.

8   Enter **=CON** and double-click **CONCATENATE**.

9   Click cell **E2** and enter **&", "&** (a comma and a space enclosed with ampersands and quotation marks).

10   Click cell **F2** and enter **&", "&**

11   Click cell **G2** and enter **&" "&**

12   Click cell **H2** and press **Enter**.

J2	▼ : × ✓ *fx*	=CONCATENATE(E2&", "&F2&", "&G2&" "&H2)				
▲	E	F	G	H	I	J	K	L
1	Address	City	State	Zip	FullName	FullAddress	CityStZip	
2	1234 S 34th	Erie	PA	98006	Kim Abercrombie	1234 S 34th, Erie, PA 98006		
3	123 Broadway	Meadville	PA	98272				

13   Double-click the **border** next to the Column letter **J** to auto-fit the contents.

14   Double-click cell **J2** to activate **Edit** mode.

15   In the formula bar, drag through the entire formula you just created and press **Ctrl+C** to copy it.

16   Press **Esc** to leave **Edit** mode.

17   Click cell **K2** and press **Ctrl+V** to paste the formula. Notice that the cell references did not adjust. When you copy a formula using **Edit** mode, you can paste it into a new cell and the references are preserved.

18   Double-click cell **K2** to activate **Edit** mode.

19   Drag to select the first part of the formula in parentheses **E2&", "&** and press the **Delete** key. Notice that the formula argument selection box disappears from cell **E2**.

20   Press **Enter**.

21   Select cells **I2** to **K2**, then drag the fill handle down to row **23** to copy the relative-reference formulas.

	E	F	G	H	I	J	K	L
I2		f_x	=CONCATENATE(B2&" "&A2)					

	Address	City	State	Zip	FullName	FullAddress	CityStZip	
1	Address	City	State	Zip	FullName	FullAddress	CityStZip	
2	1234 S 34th	Erie	PA	98006	Kim Abercrombie	1234 S 34th, Erie, PA 98006	Erie, PA 98006	
3	123 Broadway	Meadville	PA	98272	Michael Affronti	123 Broadway, Meadville, P	Meadville, PA 98272	
4	456 Center St	Erie	PA	98008	Nupur Agarwal	456 Center St, Erie, PA 9800	Erie, PA 98008	
5	2345 N 56th	Erie	PA	98004	Mark Bebbington	2345 N 56th, Erie, PA 98004	Erie, PA 98004	
6	123 First St	Edinboro	PA	98201	Allie Bellew	123 First St, Edinboro, PA 98	Edinboro, PA 98201	
7	456 12th Ave	Erie	PA	98006	Nuno Bento	456 12th Ave, Erie, PA 98000	Erie, PA 98006	
8	3456 Main St	Ashtabula	OH	83720	Antonio Bermejo	3456 Main St, Ashtabula, OH	Ashtabula, OH 83720	
9	345 Cherry St	Erie	PA	98020	Randy Byrne	345 Cherry St, Erie, PA 9802	Erie, PA 98020	
10	890 1st Ave	Girard	PA	98012	Carlos Carvallo	890 1st Ave, Girard, PA 9801	Girard, PA 98012	
11	12 State St	Erie	PA	98003	Sean Chai	12 State St, Erie, PA 98003	Erie, PA 98003	
12	456 Second St	Conneaut	OH	83702	Gareth Chan	456 Second St, Conneaut, O	Conneaut, OH 83702	
13	4567 Maple	North East	PA	98007	Lee Theng Chia	4567 Maple, North East, PA	North East, PA 98007	
14	678 W 23rd	Edinboro	PA	98201	Terri Chudzik	678 W 23rd, Edinboro, PA 98	Edinboro, PA 98201	
15	345 Third St	Erie	PA	98003	Ken Circeo	345 Third St, Erie, PA 98003	Erie, PA 98003	
16	5678 Central Ave	Ripley	NY	97303	John Clarkson	5678 Central Ave, Ripley, N	Ripley, NY 97303	
17	3456 Fourth St	Erie	PA	98011	Ryan Danner	3456 Fourth St, Erie, PA 980	Erie, PA 98011	
18	23 S 34th	Meadville	PA	98272	Arlene Huff	23 S 34th, Meadville, PA 98	Meadville, PA 98272	
19	6789 Meridian	Erie	PA	98012	Reto Käch	6789 Meridian, Erie, PA 980	Erie, PA 98012	
20	367 Center St	Erie	PA	98007	Petr Karásek	367 Center St, Erie, PA 9800	Erie, PA 98007	
21	2345 10th Ave	Erie	PA	98005	Kate Taneyhill	2345 10th Ave, Erie, PA 9800	Erie, PA 98005	
22	34 N 56th	Sherman	NY	97322	Gregory Weber	34 N 56th, Sherman, NY 973	Sherman, NY 97322	
23	345 12th Ave	Erie	PA	98002	Barbara Zighetti	345 12th Ave, Erie, PA 9800:	Erie, PA 98002	
24								

✖ **CLEAN UP** **Save the Fabrikam-Management2.xlsx workbook, and then close it.**

If you were to concatenate cell references with only ampersands, the concatenated contents of the cells may not be separated by spaces, which is why we added them. You can also concatenate cells containing formulas; only the displayed results are included, not the formulas themselves. Thus, you could use a formula like the following to create a sentence that changes depending on the formula's result:

```
=CONCATENATE("Sales for the month came in at "&E5&"!!")
```

Assuming that cell E5 contains a monthly sales formula; this would result in a displayed value such as:

```
Sales for the month came in at $67,890!!
```

Removing extra spaces

It's inevitable that extra spaces will appear, especially in a document containing a lot of text that was entered by hand at some point in its history. In the previous exercise, for example, you might create or propagate double spaces when combining the contents of other cells. Fortunately, there's a function in Excel to remove extra spaces.

In this exercise, you'll remove extra spaces using formulas, and then you'll copy and paste the results—only the displayed values from those formulas—to replace the spaced-out text.

➡ SET UP **You need the Fabrikam-Management2.xlsx workbook from the previous exercise to complete this exercise. Or, you can open the Fabrikam-Management2_start.xlsx workbook, located in the Chapter19 practice file folder, and save it as Fabrikam-Management2.xlsx.**

1   In the **Fabrikam-Management2.xlsx** file, make sure that **Sheet2** is selected and that the cell range **I2:I23** is selected.

Some entries in column **C** have extra spaces in them; for example, **C7**.

2   Click the **Insert Function** button in the formula bar.

3   Click the **Or Select a Category** list and click **Text**.

4   Scroll down through the list of **Text** functions and double-click **Trim**.

5   Click cell **C2** to enter the cell reference into the **Text** box.

6   Press the **Ctrl** key and click the **OK** button; if you press **Ctrl** when entering any formula, Excel not only inserts the formula into the active cell, it also inserts it into all the selected cells.

Now, the cells that previously contained extra spaces have the spaces removed due to the use of the TRIM function (specifically, rows 7, 13, 16, 19, and 23).

	C	D	E	F	G	H	I
1	Title	Department	Address	City	State	Zip	
2	Accounting Manager	Finance	1234 S 34th	Erie	PA	98006	Accounting Manager
3	Director of Operations	Operations	123 Broadway	Meadville	PA	98272	Director of Operations
4	Director of Manufacturing	Manufacturing	456 Center St	Erie	PA	98008	Director of Manufacturing
5	VP Research	Executive	2345 N 56th	Erie	PA	98004	VP Research
6	Recruiting Manager	Human Resources	123 First St	Edinboro	PA	98201	Recruiting Manager
7	Director of Human Resources	Human Resources	456 12th Ave	Erie	PA	98006	Director of Human Resources
8	President	Executive	3456 Main St	Ashtabula	OH	83720	President
9	Security Manager	Operations	345 Cherry St	Erie	PA	98020	Security Manager
10	IT Operations Manager	Information Technology	890 1st Ave	Girard	PA	98012	IT Operations Manager
11	VP Marketing	Executive	12 State St	Erie	PA	98003	VP Marketing
12	Social media manager	Sales & Marketing	456 Second St	Conneaut	OH	83702	Social media manager
13	Director of Public Relations	Sales & Marketing	4567 Maple	North East	PA	98007	Director of Public Relations
14	CFO	Executive	678 W 23rd	Edinboro	PA	98201	CFO
15	SALES MANAGER	Sales & Marketing	345 Third St	Erie	PA	98003	SALES MANAGER
16	Product Support Manager	Sales & Marketing	5678 Central Ave	Ripley	NY	97303	Product Support Manager
17	IT Services Manager	Information Technology	3456 Fourth St	Erie	PA	98011	IT Services Manager
18	Warehouse Manager	Operations	23 S 34th	Meadville	PA	98272	Warehouse Manager
19	VP Information Systems	Executive	6789 Meridian	Erie	PA	98012	VP Information Systems
20	Advertising Manager	Sales & Marketing	367 Center St	Erie	PA	98007	Advertising Manager
21	CEO	Executive	2345 10th Ave	Erie	PA	98005	CEO
22	VP Finance	Executive	34 N 56th	Sherman	NY	97322	VP Finance
23	Web Services Manager	Information Technology	345 12th Ave	Erie	PA	98002	Web Services Manager

 CLEAN UP Save the Fabrikam-Management2.xlsx workbook, but keep it open for the next exercise.

Copying cells containing formulas and pasting only their resulting values

The previous exercise used formulas to create a clean set of titles in column I, but now how do you get them back into column C? If you copy cells I2:I23 and simply paste them into column C, you get errors, because what you actually copied were formulas.

In this exercise, you'll copy only the formulas' results into column C.

 SET UP You need the Fabrikam-Management2.xlsx workbook from the previous exercise to complete this exercise.

1   Make sure that **Sheet2** is selected and that the range **I2:I23** is selected, and then press **Ctrl+C** to copy it.

2   Click cell **C2**.

3   Click the menu arrow below the **Paste** button on the **Home** tab of the ribbon to display the **Paste Options** palette.

4   Click the **Values** button in the **Paste Values** group to replace the **Titles** in column **C** with the newly trimmed titles from your formulas.

TIP When you copy a range of cells, you don't need to select an equivalent range of cells before copying. You can just click the cell where you want the copy function to begin, and then paste. Just make sure you don't paste over existing data.

5   Click the heading in column **I** to select the entire column.

6   Click the **Clear** button in the **Editing** group on the **Home** tab of the ribbon, and then click **Clear Contents**.

✖ CLEAN UP **Save the Fabrikam-Management2.xlsx workbook, but keep it open for the next exercise.**

Changing the case of text

Case is another issue that comes up frequently when working with large amounts of text. You might have some text in caps and some in all lowercase, for example. Excel provides the tools you need to make the text formatting consistent.

In this exercise, you'll change the case of text entries.

SET UP You need the Fabrikam-Management2.xlsx workbook from the previous exercise to complete this exercise. Or, you can open the Fabrikam-Management2_start.xlsx workbook, located in the Chapter19 practice file folder, and save it as Fabrikam-Management2.xlsx.

1. In the **Fabrikam-Management2.xlsx** workbook, make sure **Sheet2** is selected.

2. Click cell **I12** and then click the **Insert Function** button in the formula bar.

3. Select the **Text** category, then scroll down through the function list, click **PROPER**, and then click **OK**.

4. Click cell **C12** to enter its reference in the **Text** box, and then press **Enter**.

5. Select cell **C12** and drag the fill handle down to cell **C15** to copy the formula.

The Proper function did its job, but at the same time, it created other issues. The four text values in column I are now in proper case, meaning that the first letter of every word is capitalized. This is what you wanted in cells I12 and I15. However, the text in cells I13 ("Of") and I14 ("Cfo") contain some incorrect capitalization, but they serve to illustrate the function's effect. We'll copy only the ones we want and paste them, but this time we'll use the right mouse button to display a shortcut menu.

6. Click cell **I12** and press **Ctrl+C** to copy.

7. Click cell **C12**, then click the right mouse button. Select **Paste Special**, and then click the **Values** button.

8. Click cell **I15** and press **Ctrl+C** to copy.

9. Click cell **C15**, then click the right mouse button, select **Paste Special**, and then click the **Values** button.

10   Select cells **I12** to **I15** and press the **Delete** key to delete the formulas.

❌ CLEAN UP **Save the Fabrikam-Management2.xlsx workbook, and then close it.**

Restricting cell entries

Wouldn't it be nice if there were ways to prevent people (ourselves included) from entering the wrong type of data in critical cells? For example, let's say you have a workbook that several people use to enter collected sales data every month—sales totals, inventory, and contact information—in dollars, integers, and text. A stray text character entered into a cell used in calculations could result in error values popping up all over the workbook. Worse yet, sometimes entry errors produce no visible errors, just bogus results. Excel addresses these concerns and offers Data Validation features to enhance the integrity of your data.

In this exercise, you'll restrict cell entries to protect your data.

SET UP You need the Real-Estate-Transition_start.xlsx workbook located in the Chapter19 practice file folder to complete this exercise. Open the Real-Estate-Transition_start.xlsx workbook, and save it as Real-Estate-Transition.xlsx.

1   In the **Real-Estate-Transition.xlsx** workbook, make sure that cell **B2** is selected.

2   Enter any letter into cell **B2** and press **Enter**.

Notice that many #VALUE! errors suddenly appear.

3   Press **Ctrl+Z** to undo the last entry.

4   With cell **B2** selected, click the **Data** tab on the ribbon and click the **Data Validation** button in the **Data Tools** group.

5   In the **Data Validation** dialog box, select **Whole number** in the **Allow** list.

6   In the **Data** box, select **greater than**.

7   Enter **0** (zero) into the **Minimum** box.

8   Click **OK**.

9   Enter any letter into cell **B3** and press **Enter**.

Notice that Excel will not allow text to be entered into this cell, and an error message is displayed when you try to enter text into the cell.

10   Click **Cancel**.

11   Click the **Data Validation** button again.

12   Click the **Input Message** tab.

13   In the **Title** box, enter **Values Only**.

14   In the **Input Message** box, enter this text: **Enter the asking price for your existing home**.

15   Click the **Error Alert** tab.

16   In the **Title** box, enter **Oops!**

17   In the **Error Message** box, enter **Make sure you enter only numbers in this cell.**

19

18   Click **OK**.

19   Enter any letter into cell **B3**, and press **Enter**.

Now, any time you try to make an invalid entry into cell B3, a customized error message appears.

20   In the **Oops!** dialog box, press **Cancel**.

21   Click the **Home** tab.

22   Click the **Format** button in the **Cells** group, and then click **Protect Sheet** to display the **Protect Sheet** dialog box.

23   Click **OK** in the **Protect Sheet** dialog box.

24   Press **Tab**, and continue pressing **Tab**; you'll notice that only the white cells with borders are selected.

The last two steps show what happens when you protect a sheet with specific cells unlocked. In the original practice file for this exercise, the bordered cells were unlocked, but the sheet wasn't protected. By definition, all cells are "locked" in a new workbook, which actually means that the "locked format" has been applied. You can see this by clicking the Format button on the Home tab and looking at the Lock Cell command near the bottom of the menu. If the icon next to the Lock Cell command has a box around it, then the cell is locked; if not, it is unlocked. But this has no effect on anything until you click the Protect Sheet command (located above the Lock Cell command). When you click the Protect Sheet command, the Protect Sheet dialog box is displayed, offering editing options that allow changes to be made in unlocked cells when the sheet is protected. And, as shown in Step 24, when a sheet is locked, pressing the Tab key will always move the selection to the next unlocked cell; locked cells are ignored.

25 Click the **Home** tab on the ribbon, then click the **Format** button in the **Cells** group, and click **Unprotect Sheet**.

26 Select cell **B21** (Estimated Rate of Return).

27 Click the **Data** tab, click **Data Validation**, and in the **Allow** list on the **Settings** tab, select **List**.

28 Click in the **Source** box and enter **=rates**.

29 Click **OK**.

30 Click the **Home** tab, then click the **Format** button in the **Cells** group, and click **Protect Sheet**.

Now, when you reselect cell B21, a small menu arrow appears alongside it, offering a number of different interest rates. Cells A35:A39 contain this list of options (the range is named rates). We could have entered the formula =$A$35:$A$39 into the Data Validation dialog box, but the name is not only easier to enter, it also makes it easier to edit. If you move or add more items to the list, just select the new list and redefine the name.

B21	▾	:	✕	✓	*fx*	3%

◢	A	B	C
			Net Proceeds:
18			
19	New Home Cost	$ 295,000	*Net after New Home Purchase*
20	Current Investments	$ 65,000	*Total Available to Invest*
21	Estimated Rate of Return	3.00% ▾	*Potential Monthly Return*
22		1.00%	
23		2.00%	
24		3.00%	
		4.00%	
25		5.00%	
26			
27			
28			
29			
30			
31			
32			
33			
34			
35	1.00%		
36	2.00%		
37	3.00%		
38	4.00%		
39	5.00%		
40			

The Data Validation and Lock Cells features allow you to build bulletproof worksheets and maintain control of available options for specific data points. These features are beneficial when creating workbooks that will be used by new Excel users.

❌ CLEAN UP **Save the Real-Estate-Transition.xlsx workbook, and then close it.**

Key points

- All formulas in Excel begin with an equal sign.

- Double-click an existing formula to change cell references directly by dragging.

- Excel automatically adjusts relative references in formulas when you copy or fill the cells containing them.

- Adding a dollar sign before either the row number or column letter in a cell reference makes it a mixed reference, fixing that position and allowing the other to change automatically when copied.

- Adding dollar signs before both the row number and column letter in a cell reference makes it a fixed reference, allowing you to copy the formula anywhere; it will always refer to the same cell.

- If you double-click a cell containing a formula (putting it into Edit mode), you can copy the formula in the cell and paste it into another cell while preserving the references, whether they are mixed, fixed, or relative.

- Using the AutoSum button is the easiest way to enter formulas to compute totals and averages, find the maximum or minimum value, and more.

- The Insert Function dialog box provides a helpful user interface when you are using functions in formulas, and it provides information about the function, along with descriptive text and assistance for entering arguments.

- You can use the CONCATENATE function to combine separate strings of text into one.

- You can use the PROPER function to capitalize the first letter of every word in a text string.

- When you copy cells containing formulas, you can use the Paste Special Values button to paste only their displayed values.

- You can restrict cell entries to accept only numbers, dates, times, text, and more.

- All cells are locked by default; when you protect a worksheet, only the unlocked cells are available for editing.

19

Chapter at a glance

Use

Use Goal Seek to determine the optimum value needed to solve a problem, page 498

Track

Track changing values with the Scenario Manager, page 500

Apply

Apply an appropriate function to selected data using the Quick Analysis tools, page 503

Examine

Examine your data in new ways with PivotTables, page 526

Analyzing data

20

IN THIS CHAPTER, YOU WILL LEARN HOW TO

- Perform goal-seeking operations and manage multiple scenarios.
- Use the Quick Analysis tools.
- Apply conditional formatting.
- Import data from outside sources.
- Create, edit, and manipulate Excel tables.
- Perform customized sorting procedures.
- Create a PivotTable.

After the data is entered into a workbook, your most tedious work is done. In this chapter, you'll learn to work with many of Excel's analysis features to help reveal the truths that are hidden beneath the numbers.

PRACTICE FILES To complete the exercises in this chapter, you need the practice files contained in the Chapter20 practice file folder. For more information, see "Download the practice files" in this book's Introduction.

Exploring a built-in template

Microsoft Excel 2013, like all the Microsoft Office Home and Student 2013 applications, comes with numerous ready-made templates you can use right out of the cloud (the old aphorism *right out of the box* no longer seems appropriate). Many of the built-in templates are sophisticated applications all by themselves; the astute spreadsheet student would do well to study them.

Many of these templates represent hundreds of hours of work and deep understanding of features, some of which will be introduced in this book. They are aspirational and provide examples of many of the features that you'll use, as building blocks to create your own mini-applications. Use these excellent template applications if you can, or modify them to fit your needs, but learn from them as well.

In this exercise, you'll create a new document based on a template.

SET UP **You don't need any practice files to complete this exercise. Start Excel, open a clean, blank workbook, and follow the steps.**

1   Click the **File** tab, and then click **New**.

2   Click any of the template sample images once to view a visual preview.

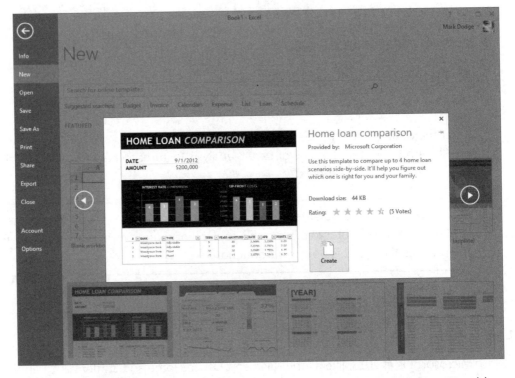

3   Click the **Create** button to open a new worksheet based on the template. (Double-clicking a template sample image is the same as clicking the **Create** button in the preview window.)

4   Click the menu arrow next to the **Name** box in the formula bar, and then click **Loans**. A selected table will be displayed below the charts.

5   Click the **View** tab.

6   Click the **Zoom** button.

7   Click the **Fit Selection** option to adjust the size of the worksheet so that it fits on the screen. (Note that depending on your screen size, this zoom option may either increase or decrease the size of the worksheet.)

Zoom	?	X

Magnification

- ○ 200%
- ○ 100%
- ○ 75%
- ○ 50%
- ○ 25%
- ● Fit selection
- ○ Custom: [69] %

[OK] [Cancel]

20

8   Click **OK**. The entire width of the worksheet should be visible on your screen.

9   Click any cell to deselect the table.

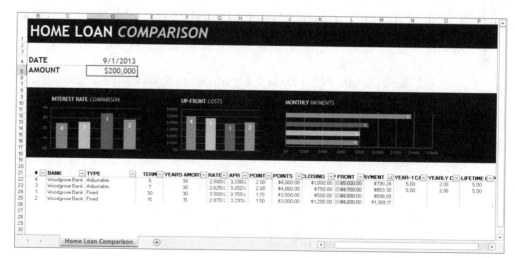

This is one of the simpler templates, but it's useful and instructive, just like all the templates that are available in Excel 2013. Before you start building a workbook for a specific task, you should take the time to look for an existing template that may perfectly suit your needs. If you enter a keyword or two into the Search Online Templates box on the New page, a vast and ever-growing catalog of cloud-based templates will be displayed. New ones are added constantly; all are updated if bugs, typos, or other issues arise, making this a preferred source for safe and useful tools.

✖ CLEAN UP **Close the workbook without saving the file.**

Performing what-if analyses

You do it every day. You probably have thoughts such as, "What if I get stuck in traffic with no gas in the tank?" or "What if I get a raise?" or "What if we downsize the house?" Excel can help you answer at least two of those questions, but for the next exercise, let's use the latter question.

In this exercise, you'll work with the workbook created in the previous chapter. It explores the costs within a range of acceptable prices when selling a home and purchasing a less expensive and less expansive home (values only, ignoring loan and equity issues).

➜ SET UP **You need the RealEstateTransition_start.xlsx workbook located in the Chapter20 practice file folder to complete this exercise. Open the RealEstate-Transition_start.xlsx workbook, and save it as RealEstateTransition.xlsx.**

1 On the **Data** tab, in the **Data Tools** group, click **What-If Analysis**, and then click **Goal Seek**.

2 With the cursor in the **Set Cell** box, click cell **H21**.

3 In the **To Value** box, enter **0** (zero).

4 Click the **By Changing Cell** box, and then click cell **B19**.

Real Estate Transition Worksheet

			Full price	- $9000	- $18000	- $27000	- $36000
Home Asking Price	$399,000	Home Sale Price $	399,000 $	390,000 $	381,000 $	372,000 $	363,000
Decreasing Increment	$ 9,000						
Real Estate Fees	3.00%		11,970	11,700	11,430	11,160	10,890
	3.00%		11,970	11,700	11,430	11,160	10,890
	0.10%		399	390	381	372	363
Settlement Costs	0.21%		846	827	808	789	769
	$ 1,788		1,788	1,788	1,788	1,788	1,788
	1.78%		7,102	6,942	6,782	6,622	6,461
Mortgage Costs	$ 125	Document Prep Fee	125	125	125	125	125
	$ 75	Recording Fee	75	75	75	75	75
Estimated Selling Costs		Total	34,275	33,547	32,818	32,090	31,362
		As a percentage	8.59%	8.60%	8.61%	8.63%	8.64%
		Net Proceeds:	364,725	356,453	348,182	339,910	331,638
New Home Cost	$255,000	Net after New Home Purchase	109,725	101,453	93,182	84,910	76,638
Current Investments	$ 65,000	Total Available to Invest	174,725	166,453	158,182	149,910	141,638
Rate of Return	2.50%	Potential Monthly Return $	364 $	347 $	330 $	312 $	295

Goal Seek dialog:
Set cell: $H$21
To value: 0
By changing cell: $B$19

5 Click **OK** in the **Goal Seek** dialog box, and then click **OK** again to dismiss the **Goal Seek Status** dialog box.

Now when you examine the worksheet, the Goal Seek command has increased the cost of a new home until all of the money (both net proceeds from the existing home sale and current investments) is used up at the lowest acceptable sale price in column H (thus yielding a zero potential monthly return). This tells you that you can spend up to about $396,000 on a new home, if you don't mind spending some or all of your savings.

You could have used the good old trial-and-error method to do this, but by using the Goal Seek command, Excel allows you to reach a faster and more precise conclusion.

✖ CLEAN UP Save the RealEstateTransition.xlsx workbook, but keep it open for the next exercise.

Managing multiple what-if models

When you use the Goal Seek command, you can instantly view the results of one possible scenario, and then you can use the Undo command to revert to the original values on the worksheet. Usually, however, there is more than one possible scenario, and it would be helpful if you could keep track of them. Excel provides the Scenario Manager for just this purpose.

IMPORTANT If you want to access a workbook online by using Excel Web App, don't add scenarios. The presence of a scenario will prevent you from opening the workbook with the Web App.

In this exercise, you'll save sets of variables in scenarios, naming them so you can display them again later.

➡ SET UP **You need the RealEstateTransition.xlsx workbook you created in the previous exercise to complete this exercise.**

1   On the **Data** tab, click the **What-If Analysis** button in the **Data Tools** group and choose **Scenario Manager**.

2   Click the **Add** button to display the **Add Scenario** dialog box.

3   In the **Scenario name** box, enter **Maximum New Home Cost**.

4   In the **Changing Cells** box, enter **B19**, if it is not already entered (the active cell appears here).

5   Click **OK**, and the **Scenario Values** dialog box appears, showing the current value in cell B19. Make sure it says **396,638** (and if not, change it).

6   Click **OK**, and the **Scenario Manager** dialog box reappears with your new scenario in the **Scenarios** list.

TIP There are normally no scenarios listed in the Scenario Manager, but a scenario called Normal was created with the original value of $255,000 that appeared in cell B19. When creating multiple scenarios, you might want to first create one using the starting values.

7   Close the **Scenario Manager** dialog box.

8   Click the **What-If Analysis** button and then click **Goal Seek**.

9   With the cursor in the **Set Cell** box, click cell **D21**.

10 In the **To Value** box, enter **500**.

11 Click the **By Changing Cell** box, and then click cell **B19**.

12 Click **OK** in the **Goal Seek** dialog box, and then click **OK** to dismiss the **Goal Seek Status** dialog box.

13 Click the **What-If Analysis** button, and then click **Scenario Manager**.

14 In the **Scenario Manager** dialog box, click **Add**.

15 In the **Scenario Name** box, enter **Maximum monthly income**.

16   Make sure that **B19** is specified as the **Changing Cell**.

17   Click **OK** in the **Add Scenario** dialog box, and then click **OK** to dismiss the **Scenario Values** dialog box.

18   With the **Scenario Manager** dialog box open, you can select each scenario on the list, click the **Show** button, and view the results on the worksheet. Otherwise, you can double-click the name of the scenario you want, which will dismiss the dialog box.

You can also build multivariable scenarios, perform goal seeking, or just enter values you want to use in cells. You can also add a different set of scenarios for each new changing cell. Then you can test one set of scenarios with other sets of scenarios and save the most compelling combined results as yet another scenario with all the changing cells specified.

TIP Although you can only solve for one changing cell at a time with the Goal Seek command, you can specify up to 32 changing cells in a scenario. To seek goals using more than one variable, use the Solver—a sophisticated analysis tool that is beyond the scope of this book. Excellent Solver help and examples are available in the online Help system.

❌ CLEAN UP **Save the RealEstateTransition.xlsx workbook.**

Using the Quick Analysis tools

You may have noticed that every time you select more than one cell in the worksheet (as long as the cells are not empty), an icon appears near the lower-right corner of the selection. This is called the *Quick Analysis* button, and it offers a menu containing many of the commands and features available on the ribbon that can be applied to cell ranges. The Quick Analysis menu is like a mini-ribbon, with categories (tabs) across the top. Click a category to change the available command buttons, as illustrated in the following exercise.

In this exercise, you'll use the Quick Analysis tools to apply formatting and add totals to a selected range.

 SET UP **You need the 2015Projections_start.xlsx workbook located in the Chapter20 practice file folder to complete this exercise. Open the 2015Projections_start.xlsx workbook, and save it as 2015Projections.xlsx.**

1   Make sure that the **2015 Projections** worksheet tab is selected.

2   Click the small downward-pointing arrow in the **Name** box to the left of the formula bar, and select the name **projections** to select all the values in the table.

B3			f_x	186					
Prices		B	C	D	E	F	G	H	I
profit	ns		Jan		Feb		Mar		Total
projections	ber	Units	Sales	Units	Sales	Units	Sales	Units	Sales
SummaryTotal		186	8,515	214	9,797	136	6,226	536	24,538
total2015sales		121	36,114	72	21,489	154	45,963	347	103,566
5 FABK-0003		21	16,416	16	12,508	40	31,269	77	60,193
6 FABK-0004		443	2,786	510	3,208	346	2,176	1,299	8,171

3   Scroll to the bottom of the selection and click the **Quick Analysis** button. (Point to each command icon on the menu to display an instant preview.)

	A	B	C	D	E	F	G	H	I	J	K	L	M
projecti...					f_x	186							
126	FABK-0124	88	2,222	90	2,273	93	2,348	271	6,843				
127	FABK-0125	2,863	764,106	1,813	483,872	2,297	613,046	6,973	1,861,024				
128	FABK-0126	15	11,821	18	14,185	15	11,821	48	37,826				
129	FABK-0127	217	68,190	195	61,277	197	61,905	609	191,372				

FORMATTING   CHARTS   TOTALS   TABLES   SPARKLINES

Data Bars   Color Scale   Icon Set   Greater Than   Top 10%   Clear Format

Conditional Formatting uses rules to highlight interesting data.

4   Click the **Totals** category, and then click the first **Sum** button to add a row of totals below the selected table. (The second **Sum** button adds totals on the right instead of at the bottom.)

	A	B	C	D	E	F	G	H	I	J	K	L	M
120	FABK-0118	275	34,304	303	37,796	225	28,067	803	100,166				
121	FABK-0119	131	20,477	208	32,512	147	22,978	486	75,967				
122	FABK-0120	63	5,868	80	7,451	70	6,520	213	19,839				
123	FABK-0121	379	113,116	901	268,912	411	122,667	1,691	504,696				
124	FABK-0122	73	34,470	68	32,109	35	16,527	176	83,105				
125	FABK-0123	21	729	34	1,181	27	938	82	2,848				
126	FABK-0124	88	2,222	90	2,273	93	2,348	271	6,843				
127	FABK-0125	2,863	764,106	1,813	483,872	2,297	613,046	6,973	1,861,024				
128	FABK-0126	15	11,821	18	14,185	15	11,821	48	37,826				
129	FABK-0127	217	68,190	195	61,277	197	61,905	609	191,372				
130		20,437	2,896,214	19,546	2,663,088	19,950	2,748,040	59,933	8,307,341				

FORMATTING   CHARTS   TOTALS   TABLES   SPARKLINES

Sum   Average   Count   % Total   Running Total   Sum

Formulas automatically calculate totals for you.

5   Click the **Quick Analysis** button and then click the **Totals** category.

6   Click the **Running Total** button.

⊿	A	B	C	D	E	F	G	H	I	J	K
1				Fabrikam, Inc. Seven-Year Summary							
2	$1 = $1,000	2007	2008	2009	2010	2011	2012	2013			
3	Income	$ 134,137.45	$ 142,728.38	$ 138,632.47	$ 151,841.00	$ 165,049.52	$ 169,605.83	$ 179,930.28			
4	Expenses	70,962.31	75,924.87	74,167.20	76,773.91	79,380.61	79,805.13	81,684.44			
5	Gross Profit	63,175.14	66,803.51	64,465.27	75,067.09	85,668.91	89,800.69	98,245.84			
6	Depreciation	4,517.77	4,656.92	4,576.27	4,622.18	4,668.09	4,650.72	4,675.54			
7	Interest Expense	2,745.82	2,893.11	2,885.24	2,896.65	2,908.06	2,909.82	2,918.02			
8	Net Profit	55,911.55	59,253.48	57,003.76	67,548.26	78,092.76	82,240.15	90,652.28			
9	Taxes	19,569.04	20,738.72	19,951.31	23,641.89	27,332.47	28,784.05	31,728.30			
10	Aftertax Profit	$ 36,342.51	$ 38,514.76	$ 37,052.44	$ 43,906.37	$ 50,760.29	$ 53,456.10	$ 58,923.98			
11	Running Total	$ 36,342.51	$ 74,857.27	$ 111,909.71	$ 155,816.08	$ 206,576.37	$ 260,032.47	$ 318,956.45			

FORMATTING   CHARTS   **TOTALS**   TABLES   SPARKLINES

Sum   Average   Count   % Total   Running Total   Sum

Formulas automatically calculate totals for you.

This time, because you selected the label in column A in the selection, Excel added the Running Total label in row 11. When you select an appropriate label, along with the data, Excel adds a new label for you.

An example of inappropriate labels would be the year numbers at the top of the table on the Seven-Year Summary tab in the 2015Projections.xlsx workbook; dates are numeric, so any formulas you apply using AutoSum or Quick Analysis will attempt to include them in calculations.

A running total simply combines the values in the selected cell(s) one by one, creating an incremental tally, from either left to right or top to bottom.

Take a few minutes to explore all the options on the Quick Analysis menus. More features will be explained later.

❌ CLEAN UP Save the 2015Projections.xlsx workbook.

Formatting conditionally

Sometimes astute analysis may consist of simply being aware when something in your worksheet reaches a limit or crosses a threshold. The conditional formatting features in Excel do that and a lot more, such as highlighting cells that contain specific text or proximate dates, and using icons or shading to give visual cues about cell contents. On the Quick Analysis menu, all of its formatting commands are actually conditional formats.

In this exercise, you'll use Conditional Formatting to highlight the important details on a worksheet.

SET UP **You need the 2015Projections.xlsx workbook from the previous exercise to complete this exercise.**

1   Make sure the **2015 Projections** worksheet tab is active.

2   Click the downward-pointing arrow in the **Name** box, to the left of the formula bar, and select the name **total2015sales** to select the values in column I.

3   Click the **Conditional Formatting** button on the **Home** tab, click **Top/Bottom Rules**, and click **Top 10%**.

A dialog box appears that allows you to change the format and the percentage. (This does not happen when you use the equivalent command on the Quick Analysis menu. Instead, it uses the default settings.) With the dialog box open, you can choose options and view the results displayed on the worksheet before clicking OK.

	A	B	C	D	E	F	G	H	I
112	FABK-0110	85	15,973	86	16,161	92	17,289	263	49,423
113	FABK-0111	117	1,659	100	1,418	121	1,716	338	4,793
114	FABK-0112	80	11,242	52	7,308	113	15,880	245	34,430
115	FABK-0113	113	1,066	142	1,339	186	1,754	441	4,159
116	FABK-0114	26	245	61	575	46	434	133	1,254
117	FABK-0115	81	381	39	183	47	221	167	785
118	FABK-0116	84	11,673	111	15,425	135	18,760	330	45,857
119	FABK-0117	43	8,081	37	6,953	27	5,074	107	20,107
120	FABK-0118	275	34,304	303	37,796	225	28,067	803	100,166
121	FABK-0119	131	20,477	208	32,512	147	22,978	486	75,967
122	FABK-0120	63	5,868	80	7,451	70	6,520	213	19,839
123	FABK-0121	379	113,116	901	268,912	411	122,667	1,691	504,696
124	FABK-0122	73	34,470	68	32,109	35	16,527	176	83,105
125	FABK-0123	21	729	34	1,181	27	938	82	2,848
126	FABK-0124	88	2,222	90	2,273	93	2,348	271	6,843
127	FABK-0125	2,863	764,106	1,813	483,872	2,297	613,046	6,973	1,861,024
128	FABK-0126	15	11,821	18	14,185	15	11,821	48	37,826
129	FABK-0127	217	68,190	195	61,277	197	61,905	609	191,372

Top 10%

Format cells that rank in the TOP:

`10` % with `Light Red Fill with Dark Red Text`

OK   Cancel

4   In the **Top 10%** dialog box, enter or select the percentage that you want to change to **20%**.

Click **OK**, and all the products projected to be in the top 20 percent of sales in 2015 are highlighted.

5   Click the **Unit Sales** worksheet tab.

6   Click the downward-pointing arrow in the **Name** box to the left of the formula bar and select the name **unitsales** to select all the values in the table.

7   Click the **Conditional Formatting** button, click **Highlight Cells Rules**, and then click **Less Than**.

8   In the **Format Cells that are Less Than** box, enter **0** (zero); there should be no unit sales less than zero, so a negative entry must be a typo.

9   Click **OK**, and notice that cell **BY87** is highlighted.

	BT	BU	BV	BW	BX	BY	BZ	CA	CB	CC
85	99	95	91	101	79	96	108	82	105	102
86	93	84	62	96	83	94	73	62	63	85
87	86	76	92	72	75	-90	81	68	71	93
88	180	175	193	196	172	150	111	102	157	163
89	56	32	36	23	27	23	48	56	28	52
90	114	110	115	120	114	110	110	114	101	100

10   Select cell **BY87** and enter **90**, and notice that the highlight disappears.

Because you have applied the *less than zero* formatting parameter to this table, any time another negative value appears, the errant cell will be highlighted unless you remove the formatting. You can do so by using the Conditional Formatting button, Clear Rules command, and clicking either the Clear Rules From Selected Cells command, or the Clear Rules From Entire Sheet command.

Experiment with the other commands in the Conditional Formatting menu, but use these formats carefully; they may provide too much clutter to be helpful. The Data Bars command inserts a small one-bar chart into each cell that indicates the cell's value in relation to other selected cells. The Icon Sets offer graphic alternatives to bars, but you will probably need to widen some cells; for these; icons are actually inserted into cells, though all other conditional formats are more or less transparent. The Color Scales command tints each cell in a solid color according to its rank, and the Data Bars command puts varying sizes of bars of the same color into cells like individual columns in a horizontal column chart.

11   Click the **Seven-Year Financial Summary** tab.

12   Click the downward-pointing arrow in the **Name** box to the left of the formula bar and select the name **SummaryTotal** to select all the values in the table.

13   Click the **Conditional Formatting** button, click **Data Bars**, and position your mouse pointer to point to the **Orange Data Bar** command to preview the results on the worksheet. (Click the command if you want to apply the previewed formatting.)

❌ CLEAN UP   **Save the 2015Projections.xlsx workbook.**

Analyzing data from another source

Sometimes data you work with does not reside in a workbook, but in a corporate database, a document created by another program, on the web, or elsewhere. Click the Data tab and take a look at the commands in the Get External Data group. Including the commands on the From Other Sources menu, Excel provides ten different connection options, but in this next exercise, you'll focus on importing data from a text file. Even if your data is stored in a Microsoft Access database or another program, you can save it as a text-based document; this is called a *universal sharing format*.

In this exercise, you'll import data from a text file created by another program.

SET UP You need the FabrikamJan2013Sales.txt file located in the Chapter20 practice file folder to complete this exercise. Start by opening a new, blank workbook.

1   Click the **Data** tab on the ribbon.

2   In the **Get External Data** group, click the **From Text** button to display the **Import Text File** dialog box.

3   Select the **FabrikamJanSales2013.txt** file and click the **Import** button to display the **Text Import Wizard**.

4   Select the **My Data Has Headers** check box.

5   Make sure that the **Delimited** option is selected, and then click the **Next** button.

6   Make sure that **Tab** is the selected delimiter (a sample is available in the **Data Preview** area), and then click the **Next** button.

7   In the **Data Preview** area, click the **Date** column.

8   Click the **Column Data Format** option button labeled **Date** and make sure that **MDY** is selected.

9   Click the **Finish** button to display the **Import Data** dialog box.

10   Select the **Add This Data to the Data Model** check box.

The options at the top of the dialog box become active.

11   Click **OK** to import the data formatted as a table, which is the default selection in the **Import Data** dialog box.

▲	A	B	C	D	E	F	G
1	Product Number ▼	Date ▼	Group ▼	Channel ▼	Qty ▼		
2	FABK-0012	1/10/2013	Epsilon	B	100		
3	FABK-0074	1/8/2013	Alpha	E	42		
4	FABK-0115	1/22/2013	Beta	A	10		
5	FABK-0009	1/4/2013	Alpha	A	50		
6	FABK-0125	1/11/2013	Omega	A	130		
7	FABK-0115	1/1/2013	Beta	A	10		
8	FABK-0003	1/3/2013	Alpha	C	6		
9	FABK-0046	1/7/2013	Omega	E	110		
10	FABK-0088	1/3/2013	Omega	C	30		
11	FABK-0054	1/10/2013	Gamma	B	50		
12	FABK-0001	1/1/2013	Alpha	A	37		
13	FABK-0112	1/10/2013	Beta	E	20		
14	FABK-0027	1/8/2013	Kappa	E	48		
15	FABK-0012	1/24/2013	Epsilon	B	100		
16	FABK-0125	1/28/2013	Kappa	B	130		

12   Click the header for column **B** to select the entire column.

13   Click the **Number Format** drop-down menu on the **Home** tab of the ribbon, and click **Short Date**.

14   Click the **Save** button (located on the **Quick Access Toolbar**); because the data was imported into a new workbook, the **Save As** dialog box appears.

15   Name the file **Fabrikam-Jan-2013-Sales.xlsx** and click the **Save** button.

✖ CLEAN UP **Keep the new workbook open for the next exercise.**

20

The Excel Data Model

The Data Model is a new concept in Excel 2013. It allows you to analyze disparate data sources in the same workbook and allows Excel to perform relational database–style analysis using multiple tables. Although you use only one table in the Fabrikam January Sales example, activating the Data Model allows this data to be analyzed by using PivotTables and PivotCharts. You can add other tables to the Data Model, from different sources such as websites, SQL tables, Microsoft Access databases, other workbooks, and text files. Excel collects information about all the tables within a workbook that have been added to the Data Model, which allows you to build relationships among them, similar to relational database programs. You can search for more information about the Excel Data Model in the online Help system.

Filtering data with tables

Tables have evolved a lot over the years. In previous versions of Excel, tables were called lists. In the 1990s, Microsoft did a lot of usability research, and they were surprised to find that *list management* was the number one reason that people used Excel. In Excel 2013, tables not only offer prepackaged formats (like them or not), but they also contain sophisticated mechanisms you can use to sort, filter, and summarize data.

In this exercise, you'll turn a cell range into a table, and use Excel's table features to manipulate it.

SET UP You need the Fabrikam-Jan-2013-Sales.xlsx workbook you created in the previous exercise to complete this exercise. When you open the workbook, if the Enable Content button appears, click it to allow editing; if the Trusted Document dialog box appears, then make the data source a trusted document.

1 Click anywhere in the table on **Sheet1**, then click the **Table Tools Design** tool tab that appears whenever a table is selected.

2 Click the **More** button on the **Table Styles** drop-down palette to display the full complement of available styles.

3 Select **Table Style Light 19** from the palette.

4 In the **Table Style Options** group, select the **Banded Columns** check box, and clear the **Banded Rows** check box.

5 Click the **Date** column's **Filter Button** (the arrow adjacent to the **Date** header) to display the **Filter** menu.

	A	B	C	D	E	F
1	**Product Number** ▼	Date ▼	Group ▼	Channel ▼	Qty ▼	

A↓ Sort Oldest to Newest	B 100
Z↓ Sort Newest to Oldest	E 42
Sort by Color ▶	A 10
	A 50
✗ Clear Filter From "Date"	A 130
Filter by Color ▶	A 10
Date Filters ▶	C 6
	E 110
Search (All) 🔍 ▼	C 30
⊟ ☑ 2013	B 50
⊟ ☑ January	A 37
☑ 01	E 20
☑ 02	E 48
☑ 03	B 100
☑ 04	B 130
☑ 05	C 22
☑ 07	E 110
☑ 08	C 13
☑ 09	B 130
	B 93
OK Cancel	

22	FABK-0079	1/29/2013	Alpha	D	46
23	FABK-0084	1/31/2013	Beta	B	24
24	FABK-0062	1/23/2013	Omega	B	40
25	FABK-0106	1/15/2013	Kappa	A	10

Sheet1 ⊕

6 Click the **Sort Oldest to Newest** option in the **Date** column's **Filter** menu to put the dates in ascending order.

7 Click the **Channel** column's **Filter** button, and then select the **Select All** check box, which actually clears all the check boxes, because all of the channels were already selected.

8   Select the **A** check box, and then click **OK**.

9   Click the **Group** column's **Filter** button, and then select the **Select All** check box to deselect all the groups.

10 Select the **Alpha** check box, and then click **OK**.

	A	B	C	D	E
1	**Product Number** ▾	Date ▾⌐	Group ▾⌐	Channel ▾⌐	Qty ▾
3	FABK-0001	1/1/2013	Alpha	A	37
22	FABK-0008	1/1/2013	Alpha	A	34
42	FABK-0009	1/3/2013	Alpha	A	50
58	FABK-0009	1/4/2013	Alpha	A	50
97	FABK-0001	1/8/2013	Alpha	A	37
147	FABK-0001	1/11/2013	Alpha	A	93
160	FABK-0007	1/14/2013	Alpha	A	44
180	FABK-0008	1/15/2013	Alpha	A	34
182	FABK-0009	1/15/2013	Alpha	A	57
226	FABK-0007	1/18/2013	Alpha	A	44
249	FABK-0006	1/22/2013	Alpha	A	45
259	FABK-0007	1/22/2013	Alpha	A	44
306	FABK-0009	1/25/2013	Alpha	A	100
346	FABK-0009	1/29/2013	Alpha	A	50
374	FABK-0007	1/31/2013	Alpha	A	44
380	FABK-0006	1/31/2013	Alpha	A	46

The Excel table features make it easy to create quick reports like this one that shows all January 2013 sales of Fabrikam's Alpha product line through marketing channel A. The filters allowed you to instantly collapse nearly 400 rows of data into just 16 (look at the row numbers on the left). The table hides any rows eliminated by your filters. When you apply a column filter, a tiny funnel icon appears in the Filter button, so it's more evident to you which filters have been applied to the table.

TIP You may sometimes find the filter buttons annoying, especially when you want to print a table, but it's easy to hide them by clearing the check box adjacent to the Filter button in the Table Tools Design tool tab, in the Table Style Options group.

Because this table was created by importing data from a text file, Excel has established a connection to the text file that can be easily updated.

11   Click the arrow below the **Refresh** button on the **Table Tools Design** tool tab to display the **Refresh** menu.

12   Click the **Connection Properties** command to display a dialog box of the same name.

13   Select the **Refresh Data when Opening the File** check box.

Connection Properties ? x

Connection name: FabrikamJan2013Sales

Description:

Usage | Definition

Refresh control

Last Refreshed: 9/9/2012 11:36:31 AM

☑ Prompt for file name on refresh

☐ Refresh every 60 ⌃⌄ minutes

☑ Refresh data when opening the file

☐ Remove data from the external data range before saving the workbook

☑ Refresh this connection on Refresh All

OLAP Server Formatting

Retrieve the following formats from the server when using this connection:

☐ Number Format   ☐ Fill Color

☐ Font Style   ☐ Text Color

OLAP Drill Through

Maximum number of records to retrieve: [   ] ⌃⌄

Language

☐ Retrieve data and errors in the Office display language when available

OK   Cancel

14   Click **OK**.

15   On the **Table Tools Design** tool tab, click the **Properties** button in the **External Table Data** group.

Note that there are two different Properties dialog boxes available for this table.

16   Click **Insert entire rows for new data, clear unused cells**.

17   Click **OK**.

When the data in the text file changes, Excel automatically updates the workbook each time you open it. Because this is a database-style, row-oriented file, you will be inserting entire rows of new data to eliminate errors caused by the possible insertion of individual cells.

❌ CLEAN UP **Save the Fabrikam-Jan-2013-Sales.xlsx workbook and keep it open for the next exercise.**

Filter menu commands

You've already used the Filter buttons to sort a column and focus on a particular data set. The Filter menu offers the following additional features you should know about:

- **Sort** There are two Sort commands that may perform different functions, depending on the contents of the column. For example, for a column of text, the commands are Sort A To Z and Sort Z To A. If the column contains numbers, the commands are Sort Smallest To Largest, and Sort Largest To Smallest. If the column contains dates, the commands are Sort Oldest To Newest and Sort Newest To Oldest.

- **Clear Filter** This command removes the filter from the selected column.

- **Sort by Color/Filter by Color** This means exactly what it says, and is used when your data uses a hierarchical color scheme.

- **Date Filters** This command appears only when the column contains dates, and offers a list of options, such as Today, Next Week, and Last Month, as well as customizable options like Before and Between that display a dialog box that allows you to add date criteria.

- **Text Filters** This command appears only when the column contains text; it offers a list of options, such as Begins With, Ends With, Contains, and Does Not Contain.

- **Number Filters** This command appears only when the column contains numeric data, and offers a list of options such as Greater Than, Between, Top 10, and Below Average.

Adding data to tables

Adding data is actually easier with a range converted to an Excel table than it is with a regular cell table on a worksheet. One thing you can do in a table is use the Tab key to jump to the next cell in the table. When you press Tab to move to the last cell in a row, pressing Tab again jumps the selection to the first cell in the next row. But when you reach the last row of data in a table, the Tab key adds a row instead.

In this exercise, you'll insert a new row and a new column into an existing table.

SET UP **You need the Fabrikam-Jan-2013-Sales.xlsx file saved in the previous exercise to complete this exercise. In the Import Text File dialog box, click the Import button to update the data connection. (This happens because the Refresh Data When Opening File option was set in the Connection Properties dialog box.)**

1 If your table still has filters applied from the previous exercise, clear them. To do so, click the **Filter** button in a filtered row (the button displays a funnel image when there is an active filter), and click the **Clear Filter** command.

2 Click the **Total Row** button in the **Table Tools Design** tool tab, in the **Table Style Options** group. This adds a row of totals to the bottom of the table and activates the new row so that it is visible on the screen. In this case, it adds only one total, to the **Qty** column, because this is the only column that contains numeric data. (The active cell must be somewhere within the table for the **Table Tools Design** tab to appear.)

3   Select cell **E387**, just above the new total.

4   Press the **Tab** key.

	Product Number	Date	Group	Channel	Qty	F
E387 ✗ ✓ *fx* 120						
383	FABK-0051	1/31/2013	Lambda	B	29	
384	FABK-0004	1/31/2013	Beta	D	152	
385	FABK-0016	1/31/2013	Alpha	D	33	
386	FABK-0030	1/31/2013	Kappa	A	64	
387	FABK-0021	1/31/2013	Beta	B	120	
388	Total				20349	
389						
390						
391						

	Product Number	Date	Group	Channel	Qty	F
A388 ✗ ✓ *fx*						
383	FABK-0051	1/31/2013	Lambda	B	29	
384	FABK-0004	1/31/2013	Beta	D	152	
385	FABK-0016	1/31/2013	Alpha	D	33	
386	FABK-0030	1/31/2013	Kappa	A	64	
387	FABK-0021	1/31/2013	Beta	B	120	
388						
389	Total				20349	
390						
391						

All you need to do is press the Tab key with the last cell in the table selected. Even when there is a totals row, Excel adds the new row above the total and adds any new values to the totals in the summarized columns. Also, adding a table row this way automatically propagates the table formatting and formulas (if any) to the new row.

5   Press the **Undo** button to remove the unneeded row.

6   Press **Ctrl+Home** to jump to the first cell in the worksheet.

7   Select cell **F1**, located to the right of the **Qty** column header.

8   Enter **Note** and press **Enter**, and notice that Excel automatically expands the table with a new formatted column, and a **Filter** button is added to the new heading.

9   Click the **AutoCorrect Options** button and notice that the menu that appears offers a command to undo the previous auto-expansion, or you can keep it from happening again by clicking the **Stop Automatically Expanding Tables** command. In addition, you can click the **Control AutoCorrect Options** command to open a dialog box that lets you choose whether you want to enable or disable these and other **AutoCorrect** options.

10   Press the **Esc** key to dismiss the **AutoCorrect** options menu.

	A	B	C	D	E	F	G	H	I	J
O2 ✗ ✓ *fx*										
1	Product Number	Date	Group	Channel	Qty	Note				
2	FABK-0115	1/1/2013	Beta	A	10		⌸ ▾			
3	FABK-0001	1/1/2013	Alpha	A	37		↶ Undo Table AutoExpansion			
4	FABK-0020	1/1/2013	Delta	B	93		Stop Automatically Expanding Tables			
5	FABK-0102	1/1/2013	Omega	C	30		⌸ Control AutoCorrect Options...			
6	FABK-0112	1/1/2013	Beta	E	20					
7	FABK-0071	1/1/2013	Beta	A	47					

✕ CLEAN UP **Save the Fabrikam-Jan-2013-Sales.xlsx workbook.**

TIP Tables are great tools, but there are times when you may want to lose the strict table structure. Click the Convert To Range button in the Tools group on the Table Tools Design tool tab to remove the table architecture and return the table to plain cells, which still contain the formatting.

Sorting data

You explored one way to sort data in "Filtering data with tables" earlier in this chapter, but not all data will be in tables, and the sorting commands on the Filter menus only go so far. The Excel Sort and Filter commands offer a few more tricks you can use to get your data in order.

In this exercise, you'll use Excel's sorting tools to rearrange data on a worksheet.

➡ SET UP **You need the JanSales2_start.xlsx workbook located in the Chapter20 practice file folder to complete this exercise. Open the JanSales2_start.xlsx workbook, and save it as JanSales2.xlsx.**

1   In the **JanSales2.xlsx** workbook, select cell **B2** (the first date in the **Date** column).

2   Click the **Sort Z to A** button in the **Sort & Filter** group to sort the table by date (newest first).

3   Click the **Sort** button in the **Sort & Filter** group to display the **Sort** dialog box.

4   Clear the **My data has headers** check box, and notice what happens to the selected cells in the table (the headers are included in the sort range, which in this case would not be a good thing).

5   Select the **My data has headers** check box again.

6   In the **Sort by Area** (called a *level*), make sure that **Date** is selected in the **Column** drop-down list.

7   Make sure that the **Values** option is selected in the **Sort On** drop-down list.

8   In the **Order** drop-down list, select **Oldest to Newest**.

9   Click the **Add Level** button to add a **Then by** level after the **Sort by** level. (The **Sort** dialog box allows you to specify up to 64 levels of sorting criteria.)

	A	B	C	D	E	F	G	H	I	J	K	L	M	N	O
A2	▼ : ✕ ✓ fx		FABK-0115												

	A	B	C	D	E
1	Product Number	Date	Group	Channel	Qty
2	FABK-0115	1/1/2013	Beta	A	10
3	FABK-0001	1/1/2013	Alpha	A	37
4	FABK-0020	1/1/2013	Delta	B	93
5	FABK-0102	1/1/2013	Omega	C	30
6	FABK-0112	1/1/2013	Beta	E	20
7	FABK-0071	1/1/2013	Beta	A	47
8	FABK-0125	1/1/2013	Alpha	B	130
9	FABK-0096	1/1/2013	Theta	E	34
10	FABK-0008	1/1/2013	Alpha	E	35
11	FABK-0108	1/1/2013	Delta	B	25
12	FABK-0059	1/1/2013	Omega	D	25
13	FABK-0075	1/1/2013	Alpha	B	33
14	FABK-0107	1/1/2013	Kappa	B	60
15	FABK-0038	1/1/2013	Lambda	E	44
16	FABK-0049	1/1/2013	Lambda	A	80

Sort dialog box:

Add Level | Delete Level | Copy Level | ▲ ▼ | Options... | ☑ My data has headers

Column		Sort On		Order	
Sort by	Date ⌄	Values	⌄	Oldest to Newest	⌄
Then by	⌄	Values	⌄	A to Z	⌄

OK | Cancel

10   In the **Then by** level, click the **Column** drop-down list and select **Channel**.

11   Make sure that the default **Sort On** option is selected (**Values**).

12   In the **Order** drop-down list, make sure that **A to Z** is selected.

13   Click the **Options** button and note the possibilities here (just so you know).

14   Click **Cancel** to dismiss the **Sort Options** dialog box.

15   Click **OK**.

	A	B	C	D	E	F
1	**Product Number**	Date	Group	Channel	Qty	
2	FABK-0115	1/1/2013	Beta	A	10	
3	FABK-0001	1/1/2013	Alpha	A	37	
4	FABK-0071	1/1/2013	Beta	A	47	
5	FABK-0049	1/1/2013	Lambda	A	80	
6	FABK-0036	1/1/2013	Lambda	A	71	
7	FABK-0008	1/1/2013	Alpha	A	34	
8	FABK-0020	1/1/2013	Delta	B	93	
9	FABK-0125	1/1/2013	Alpha	B	130	
10	FABK-0108	1/1/2013	Delta	B	25	
11	FABK-0075	1/1/2013	Alpha	B	33	
12	FABK-0107	1/1/2013	Kappa	B	60	
13	FABK-0102	1/1/2013	Omega	C	30	
14	FABK-0055	1/1/2013	Gamma	C	25	
15	FABK-0059	1/1/2013	Omega	D	25	
16	FABK-0112	1/1/2013	Beta	E	20	

The result of this exercise gives you a list of sales made each day during January 2013, sorted by sales channel. If you click the Sort button again and change the Then by column option to Group, you get a similar result, sorted by product group.

✖ CLEAN UP Save the JanSales2.xlsx workbook.

TIP If you get unexpected results, check the data in the cells adjacent to the apparent sorting error to check if there are any numbers formatted as text, or leading spaces in cells. If so, delete the leading spaces, or select the entire column and format it as text, because Excel will sort numbers first, followed by numbers formatted as text. If all the numbers are in the same format, Excel will sort them correctly.

Creating a custom sort list

Sometimes neither numerical sequences nor the alphabet provide the criteria you would like to use to sort data. Let's say, for example, that you want to sort your list by Product Group, but not in order of sales or names or dates, but by some other arbitrary criteria for which there are no standard ways to sort, such as strategic value.

In this exercise, you'll create your own sorting criteria.

➜ SET UP You need the JanSales2.xlsx workbook created in the previous exercise to complete this exercise.

1   In the **JanSales2.xlsx** workbook, click the **Data** tab.

2   Click the **Sort** button in the **Sort & Filter** group on the **Data** tab, and notice that the sort criteria you used in the previous exercise is still there.

3   Click the **Delete Level** button twice to remove both criteria levels.

4   Click the **Add Level** button.

5   In the **Column** drop-down list, select **Group**.

6   In the **Sort On** drop-down list, make sure that **Values** is selected.

7   In the **Order** drop-down list, select **Custom List**.

8   Make sure that **New List** is selected in the **Custom lists** box, and then click the **Add** button. (Clicking the **Add** button simply activates the **List Entries** box; a flashing cursor will appear.)

9   Enter **Lambda** and press **Enter**.

10 Enter **Beta** and press **Enter**.

11 Enter **Alpha** and press **Enter**.

12 Enter **Gamma** and press **Enter**.

13 Enter **Omega** and press **Enter**.

14 Enter **Theta** and press **Enter**.

15 Enter **Epsilon** and press **Enter**.

16   Enter **Kappa**, and then press the **Add** button to add your new list to the **Custom Lists** box.

17   Click **OK** to dismiss the **Custom Lists** dialog box.

18   Click **OK** to dismiss the **Sort** dialog box and apply the sorting criteria to the sales table.

	A	B	C	D	E	F
1	**Product Number**	Date	Group	Channel	Qty	
2	FABK-0049	1/1/2013	Lambda	A	80	
3	FABK-0036	1/1/2013	Lambda	A	71	
4	FABK-0038	1/3/2013	Lambda	A	44	
5	FABK-0049	1/4/2013	Lambda	A	80	
6	FABK-0038	1/8/2013	Lambda	A	44	
7	FABK-0087	1/15/2013	Lambda	A	23	
8	FABK-0038	1/16/2013	Lambda	A	42	
9	FABK-0049	1/31/2013	Lambda	A	80	
10	FABK-0037	1/4/2013	Lambda	B	39	
11	FABK-0051	1/10/2013	Lambda	B	27	
12	FABK-0051	1/15/2013	Lambda	B	27	
13	FABK-0050	1/15/2013	Lambda	B	43	
14	FABK-0042	1/15/2013	Lambda	B	43	
15	FABK-0050	1/25/2013	Lambda	B	43	
16	FABK-0051	1/28/2013	Lambda	B	27	

You can create as many custom sorting lists as you like. Your custom lists are pre-served with the workbook and will be available the next time you open it. In fact, for every custom sort list that you create, Excel automatically creates a second one for you, in reverse order.

19   On the **Data** tab, click the **Sort** button.

20   Click the arrow adjacent to the **Order** drop-down list, and notice that there are two custom lists there now; the second one is the reverse of the one you entered.

21   Click the **Cancel** button.

❌ CLEAN UP **Save the JanSales2.xlsx workbook.**

Creating a PivotTable

PivotTables are powerful tools for summarizing and analyzing data that is stored in work-books, or data collected from external sources. PivotTables do not contain data; they link to it. That disconnection from the source data allows you the freedom to rearrange PivotTable information without fear of corrupting the underlying values.

PivotTables work best on data with common relationships. For example, the Fabrikam sales data you worked with in the previous exercises comprises a lot of individual rows (records), but every record includes one of eight product groups, one of six sales channels, one of 31 dates, and one of 127 product numbers. So, by using a PivotTable, you can display the unit sales from each product group by sales channel, by date, or by product number. And, with a few clicks of the mouse, you can *pivot* your results using any other combination of these criterion.

New in Excel 2013 is the Recommended PivotTables feature, which starts with the PivotTable command and jumps ahead a step, saving you some time by making educated guesses about the kind of PivotTables you can build, based on the data you select. It offers several options in visual form, showing an example of the results before you commit.

In this exercise, you'll create a new PivotTable and manipulate it.

➡ SET UP **You need the FabrikamQ1SalesDetail_start.xlsx workbook located in the Chapter20 practice file folder to complete this exercise. Open the FabrikamQ1Sales-Detail_start.xlsx workbook, and save it as FabrikamQ1SalesDetail.xlsx.**

1   In the **FabrikamQ1SalesDetail.xlsx** workbook, click the **Insert** tab.

2   Making sure that the active cell is within the table of data, click the **Recommended PivotTable** button in the **Tables** group on the **Insert** tab, which automatically selects your data and displays a dialog box of the same name. (If you were to click the **Blank PivotTable** button at the bottom of the dialog box, it would be the equivalent of clicking the **PivotTable** button on the **Insert** tab, which bypasses the recommendations.)

> **IMPORTANT** Worksheet tables need to be set up properly for PivotTables to work. The columns need headers, each row must represent a unique data item (also known as a *record*), and the table cannot contain empty rows or columns.

3   Scroll down the list of recommendations, click the **Sum of Qty by Group** option, and click **OK**, which inserts a PivotTable on a new worksheet and displays the **PivotTable Fields** pane.

4   Move the mouse pointer toward the top of the **PivotTable Fields** pane until the pointer turns into a four-headed arrow.

5   Drag the **PivotTable Fields** pane to the left, so that it "undocks" from the side of the window and becomes a floating pane.

6   Drag the floating pane all the way to the left side of the screen, until it docks on the left, just for fun. (Feel free to move about the window. Note that this works only when the Excel window is maximized.)

7   Select the **Channel** check box. Now **Channel** appears under **Rows** on the right side of the **PivotTable Fields** pane. This adds the data to the PivotTable, but it is buried in detail rows, as indicated by the tiny plus-sign icons adjacent to each **Product Group** name.

8   Under **Rows**, drag the **Channel** box up, and place it under **Columns**. The result is that each channel gets its own column, and the total quantities appear below it for each product group.

IMPORTANT If suddenly the PivotTable Fields pane disappears, don't panic. You probably just clicked a cell outside the PivotTable. The pane is context-sensitive; just click any cell in the table (or click a PivotChart) to redisplay the pane, and the PivotTable Tools tabs on the ribbon, as well.

	A	B	C	D	E	F	G
3	Sum of Qty	Column Labels					
4	Row Labels	A	B	C	D	E	Grand Total
5	⊞ Lambda	1139	943	1076	361	617	4136
6	⊞ Beta	1303	2744	1430	1384	1164	8025
7	⊞ Alpha	1679	1947	811	320	984	5741
8	⊞ Gamma	719	1049	413	314	526	3021
9	⊞ Omega	2410	3847	2352	1880	2696	13185
10	⊞ Theta	2470	3430	1418	597	2108	10023
11	⊞ Epsilon	1286	1981	1123	640	1223	6253
12	⊞ Kappa	1316	1800	699	571	897	5283
13	⊞ Delta	368	1828	710	285	967	4158
14	Grand Total	12690	19569	10032	6352	11182	59825

PivotTable Fields

Choose fields to add to report:

☑ Product Number
☐ Date
☑ Group
☑ Channel
☑ Qty
☐ Unit Price

MORE TABLES...

Drag fields between areas below:

▼ FILTERS

▦ COLUMNS
Channel ▼

▦ ROWS
Group ▼
Product Nu... ▼

Σ VALUES
Sum of Qty ▼

A3 — Sum of Qty

Sheet3 | Q1-2013

9 Click the plus-sign icon adjacent to the **Lambda** product group label to display the detail data.

	A	B	C	D	E	Grand Total
Sum of Qty	Column Labels					
Row Labels	A	B	C	D	E	Grand Total
⊟ Lambda	1139	943	1076	361	617	4136
FABK-0035				156	84	240
FABK-0036	152		73			225
FABK-0037		76			47	123
FABK-0038	217	105	47	51	128	548
FABK-0039	31	37	29			97
FABK-0040	50	167	391		102	710
FABK-0041	231	51	357	50	58	747
FABK-0042		89		51		140
FABK-0049	324	172	90			586
FABK-0050	47	86		53	97	283
FABK-0051	64	137	56		101	358
FABK-0087	23	23	33			79
⊞ Beta	1303	2744	1430	1384	1164	8025
⊞ Alpha	1679	1947	811	320	984	5741
⊞ Gamma	719	1049	413	314	526	3021
⊞ Omega	2410	3847	2352	1880	2696	13185
⊞ Theta	2470	3430	1418	597	2108	10023
⊞ Epsilon	1286	1981	1123	640	1223	6253
⊞ Kappa	1316	1800	699	571	897	5283
⊞ Delta	368	1828	710	285	967	4158

This PivotTable now shows the total unit sales for each product, by product group and by sales channel. PivotTables allow you to try different arrangements of rows and columns in the easiest way imaginable. It would be prohibitively difficult to do this manually, working with the actual raw data in cells. Plus, using the PivotTable insulates the original data for inadvertent harm.

10 Click the **Lambda** plus-sign icon again to collapse the detail rows.

11   In the **PivotTable Fields** pane, clear the **Product Number** check box.

The plus-sign icons disappear, and the icons and detail rows are hidden for a cleaner presentation. The totals remain unchanged, except that they are no longer displayed with a bold font.

12   On the right side of the **PivotTable Fields** pane, drag the **Channel** box down and put it under **Rows**, then drag the **Group** box up and put it under **Columns**; the result is that the table *pivots*.

13   On the left side of the **PivotTable Fields** pane, select the **Date** check box, and the table immediately expands to include every date in the quarter.

14   Select cell **A5**.

15   Click the **PivotTable Tools Analyze** tab.

16   Click the **Collapse Field** button in the **Active Field** group.

Sum of Qty	Column Labels										
Row Labels	Lambda	Beta	Alpha	Gamma	Omega	Theta	Epsilon	Kappa	Delta	Grand Total
A		1139	1303	1679	719	2410	2470	1286	1316	368	12690
B		943	2744	1947	1049	3847	3430	1981	1800	1828	19569
C		1076	1430	811	413	2352	1418	1123	699	710	10032
D		361	1384	320	314	1880	597	640	571	285	6352
E		617	1164	984	526	2696	2108	1223	897	967	11182
Grand Total		4136	8025	5741	3021	13185	10023	6253	5283	4158	59825

❌ CLEAN UP **Save the FabrikamQ1SalesDetail.xlsx workbook.**

Clicking the Collapse Field button was a shortcut; you could have clicked each plus-sign icon individually. But consider this your formal introduction to the two PivotTable Tools tabs, Analyze and Design, brimming with buttons. The Design tab has controls similar to the table controls you learned about earlier in this chapter. Tools on the Analyze tab will be discussed in later chapters.

SEE ALSO For information about creating a PivotChart, a Slicer, or a Timeline, see Chapter 23, "Creating charts and graphics."

Pivot and Power features

PivotTables debuted as a feature in Microsoft Excel back in 1993. Since then, pivot functionality has matured and expanded into a suite of features, at the core of which is the Excel Data Model. (See the sidebar "The Excel Data Model," earlier in this chapter.) The essence of *pivot* functionality is that the PivotTable is separate from, but linked to the underlying data, which enhances the ability to instantly, and non-destructively, change the entire analysis.

The Data Model transparently adds the ability to address more than one table of data at a time (think of a cube consisting of stacked layers of tables). The combination of these concepts provides a foundation for expanded relational PivotTable functionality, and unleashes the PowerPivot and PowerView features, each of which leverages the Data Model to explore relationships among tables. Each of these features would take several chapters to explore; indeed, there is an entire book just on PowerPivot, which takes PivotTable functionality way beyond the scope of this book. You are encouraged to explore the excellent Excel Help topics available on PowerPivot and PowerView, which range from philosophical overviews to detailed tutorials.

As of this writing, the PowerPivot and PowerView features are included only with specific configurations of Office Home and Student 2013. The PowerPivot feature, which was available in all versions of Excel 2010, is available only in Office Professional Plus 2013, Microsoft SharePoint 2013 Enterprise Edition, SharePoint Online 2013 Plan 2, and the E3 or E4 editions of Microsoft Office 365. The PowerView feature, new in Excel 2013, is included with the same versions as PowerPivot. Happily, the Excel Data Model is supported in all configurations of Excel 2013. The variety of available configurations may change, however, so stay tuned.

Key points

- You can use the Goal Seek command to arrive at individual scenario values, and you can manage multiple goals and values by using the Scenario Manager.

- Use the Quick Analysis menu to perform many relevant operations on a selected cell range without using the ribbon.

- You can use conditional formatting to highlight important values in a worksheet when they meet or exceed predetermined thresholds.

- You can easily import data from remote sources by using the Get External Data commands on the Data tab.

- The Excel table format is a sophisticated mechanism you can use to sort, filter, and summarize data.

- You can sort data by using up to 64 criteria, including custom sort lists that you can create yourself.

- PivotTables allow you to quickly change your perspective and directly manipulate relationships among data sets by dragging.

20

Chapter at a glance

Format

Format with styles,
page 542

Create

Create custom themes,
page 546

Work

Work with custom number formats,
page 551

Set

Set view options,
page 574

Formatting worksheets 21

IN THIS CHAPTER, YOU WILL LEARN HOW TO

- Apply number formatting.

- Format with styles.

- Create custom themes.

- Create custom number and date formats.

- Protect worksheets.

- Open extra windows in the same workbook.

Most of you have used formatting controls, buttons, and commands, so you're most likely familiar with fonts and styles. In this chapter, you'll learn how to format numbers and dates in Microsoft Excel, how to use styles, and how to create custom themes. In addition, you'll open extra windows in your workbook and use worksheet protection.

It's been mentioned before, but it bears repeating: formatting does not change the underlying values in cells, even though it may appear to do so. So feel free to experiment. Ctrl+Z (Undo) is your friend.

PRACTICE FILES To complete the exercises in this chapter, you need the practice files contained in the Chapter21 practice file folder. For more information, see "Download the practice files" in this book's Introduction.

Applying number formatting

Formatting is the easiest way to turn a group of numbers into something resembling information, and it really doesn't take much work to get results.

In this exercise, you'll work with a worksheet that is devoid of formatting, which means that everything is in the *General* format. Though you may have viewed similar worksheets before, this one is much harder to decipher without formatting.

	A	B	C	D	E	F	G	H
1	Fabrikam, Inc. Seven-Year Summary							$1 = $1,000
2								
3		2007	2008	2009	2010	2011	2012	2013
4	Income	134137.45	142728.38	138632.4724	151840.9952	165049.518	169605.8256	179930.2767
5	Expenses	70962.31	75924.87	74167.2032	76773.9078	79380.6124	79805.1313	81684.44067
6	Gross Profit	63175.14	66803.51	64465.2692	75067.0874	85668.9056	89800.6943	98245.836
7	Depreciation	4517.77	4656.92	4576.2732	4622.1812	4668.0892	4650.7198	4675.535333
8	Interest Expense	2745.82	2893.11	2885.2396	2896.6476	2908.0556	2909.8244	2918.019333
9	Net Profit	55911.55	59253.48	57003.7564	67548.2586	78092.7608	82240.1501	90652.28133
10	Taxes	19569.0425	20738.718	19951.31474	23641.89051	27332.46628	28784.05254	31728.29847
11	Aftertax Profit	36342.5075	38514.762	37052.44166	43906.36809	50760.29452	53456.09757	58923.98287
12								
13								

 SET UP You need the FabrikamSummary_start.xlsx workbook located in the Chapter21 practice file folder to complete this exercise. Open the FabrikamSummary_start.xlsx workbook, and save it as FabrikamSummary.xlsx. Then follow the steps.

1　In the **FabrikamSummary.xlsx** workbook, select all the cells containing numbers (except the dates)—cells **B4** to **H11**.

2　Click the **Comma Style** button, located in the **Number** group, on the **Home** tab.

　All the decimals in the selected cells are rounded to the nearest hundredth.

3　Click the **Accounting Number Format** button, also in the **Number** group, on the **Home** tab, which adds dollar signs to the format.

4　Click the tiny downward-pointing arrow adjacent to the **Accounting Number Format** button to display a menu of the same name.

Comma style
Percent style Increase decimal
Dialog box launcher Accounting number format Decrease decimal

FILE HOME INSERT PAGE LAYOUT FORMULAS DATA REVIEW VIEW DEVELOPER

Calibri 11 A A Wrap Text Accounting

Paste
Cut
Copy
Format Painter
B I U Merge & Center $ % $\overset{+.0}{\ }$ $\overset{.00}{\ }$ Conditional Form:
Formatting Tabl

Clipboard Font Alignment Styles

$ English (United States)
£ English (United Kingdom)
€ Euro (€ 123)
¥ Chinese (PRC)
fr. French (Switzerland)
More Accounting Formats...

B4 : f_x 134137.45

	A	B	C	D	E	F	
1	Fabrikam, Inc. Seven-Year Summary						
2							
3		2007	2008	2009	2010	2011	
4	Income	$ 134,137.45	$ 142,728.38	$ 138,632.47	$ 151,841.00	$ 165,049.52	$ 169,605.83	$ 179,930.28
5	Expenses	$ 70,962.31	$ 75,924.87	$ 74,167.20	$ 76,773.91	$ 79,380.61	$ 79,805.13	$ 81,684.44
6	Gross Profit	$ 63,175.14	$ 66,803.51	$ 64,465.27	$ 75,067.09	$ 85,668.91	$ 89,800.69	$ 98,245.84
7	Depreciation	$ 4,517.77	$ 4,656.92	$ 4,576.27	$ 4,622.18	$ 4,668.09	$ 4,650.72	$ 4,675.54
8	Interest Expense	$ 2,745.82	$ 2,893.11	$ 2,885.24	$ 2,896.65	$ 2,908.06	$ 2,909.82	$ 2,918.02
9	Net Profit	$ 55,911.55	$ 59,253.48	$ 57,003.76	$ 67,548.26	$ 78,092.76	$ 82,240.15	$ 90,652.28
10	Taxes	$ 19,569.04	$ 20,738.72	$ 19,951.31	$ 23,641.89	$ 27,332.47	$ 28,784.05	$ 31,728.30
11	Aftertax Profit	$ 36,342.51	$ 38,514.76	$ 37,052.44	$ 43,906.37	$ 50,760.29	$ 53,456.10	$ 58,923.98
12							

5   Click **fr. French (Switzerland)**.

Note that changing the currency symbol does not change the values of the numbers (as with all formatting), but notice that the values in row 4 now display a series of pound signs (########), indicating that the contents of those cells are too wide to display. This is because the format adds a space and *fr.* to the right of each number, which takes up more space in a cell than any of the other currency symbols.

6   Click the **Accounting Number Format** button and then click **$ English (United States)**.

7   Select cells **B5:H10** (all the numbers except those for **Income** and **Aftertax Profit**). Standard accounting style dictates that dollar signs should only appear in the first and last rows of a table. You don't necessarily need to follow that rule, but it does make the table a lot easier to read.

8   Click the **Comma Style** button (which removes dollar signs from the selected cells).

9   Select all the cells containing numbers (not dates): **B4:H11**.

10   In the **Number** group, on the **Home** tab, click the **Decrease Decimal** button *twice*.

      In a summary worksheet like this, where large sums of money are being reported, pennies are a distraction and don't need to be displayed.

11   Click the **Center** button, in the **Alignment** group, on the **Home** tab, and notice that nothing happens; the numbers remain right-aligned. The alignment properties of number formatting override text alignment formatting.

12   Select the year headings: cells **B3:H3**.

13   Click the tiny dialog box launcher in the lower-right corner of the **Number** group, on the **Home** tab, to display the **Format Cells** dialog box.

      TIP You can also press Ctrl+1 to open the frequently used Format Cells dialog box.

14   In the **Category** list, on the **Number** page, click **Number**.

15   In the **Decimal places** box, enter or select **0**.

16   In the **Negative numbers** box, click the third option, **(1234)**.

17   Click **OK**.

18 Press **Ctrl+Z** to undo your changes.

19 Press **Ctrl+Y** to redo your changes. Now the date headers line up with the columns.

TIP If you press Ctrl+Z (Undo) repeatedly, Excel steps back through the last 100 actions.

	A	B	C	D	E	F	G	H
1	Fabrikam, Inc. Seven-Year Summary							$1 = $1,000
2								
3		2007	2008	2009	2010	2011	2012	2013
4	Income	$ 134,137	$ 142,728	$ 138,632	$ 151,841	$ 165,050	$ 169,606	$ 179,930
5	Expenses	70,962	75,925	74,167	76,774	79,381	79,805	81,684
6	Gross Profit	63,175	66,804	64,465	75,067	85,669	89,801	98,246
7	Depreciation	4,518	4,657	4,576	4,622	4,668	4,651	4,676
8	Interest Expense	2,746	2,893	2,885	2,897	2,908	2,910	2,918
9	Net Profit	55,912	59,253	57,004	67,548	78,093	82,240	90,652
10	Taxes	19,569	20,739	19,951	23,642	27,332	28,784	31,728
11	Aftertax Profit	$ 36,343	$ 38,515	$ 37,052	$ 43,906	$ 50,760	$ 53,456	$ 58,924
12								

 CLEAN UP Save the FabrikamSummary.xlsx workbook, but keep it open for the next exercise.

Accounting formats and the phantom parentheses

After step 10 in the previous exercise, the date headers no longer lined up with the columns. So what happened? The rows with dollar signs were formatted by using the Accounting Format button. The Comma Style button was used on the middle rows, but it actually applied an accounting format without currency symbols. Accounting formats conform to standard accounting practices, which include the addition of parentheses around negative numbers.

To make positive and negative numbers line up in a column, Excel adds a blank space after positive numbers that is exactly as wide as one parenthesis. The accounting formats force comma separators for thousands, millions, and so on, which are not welcome in dates (such as the year headers in row 3 from the previous exercise). Instead, a number format was selected, because it uses parentheses for negatives, but allows the option of eliminating the comma separators.

Yes, it would have been much easier to use text headings, but less instructive. You can create your own custom formats by using special codes, and you can create different display options for positives, negatives, zero values, and text. We'll describe this in more detail later in this chapter, in the section titled "Working with custom number formats."

Formatting with styles

Styles are not always useful in sheets full of numbers, but they can come in handy for more presentation-oriented uses, and of course, if you like the design. Styles can be created by using the regular formatting tools, so if you don't like something about a style, you can modify it and save it for future reference. Because the numbers were formatted in the previous exercise, let's continue formatting the sheet.

In this exercise, you'll apply formatting to the FabrikamSummary worksheet and save it as a style that can be used elsewhere.

SET UP **You need the FabrikamSummary.xlsx workbook you saved at the end of the previous exercise to complete this exercise. Open the FabrikamSummary.xlsx workbook (if it is not already open), and follow the steps.**

1   Select cells **A1:I12** (one row deeper and one column wider than the table).

2   On the **Home** tab, click the **Cell Styles** button to display the **Styles** gallery.

3   Click **20% - Accent 1**.

4   Select all the numbers below the year headings (cells **B4:H11**).

5   Click the **Cell Styles** button and then click **20% - Accent 6**.

6   Select cell **A1**.

7   Click the **Cell Styles** button and then click **Title**.

8   Select all the numbers in the **Gross Profit** row (cells **B6:H6**).

9   Hold down the **Ctrl** key and select all the numbers in the **Net Profit** row (cells **B9:H9**), adding them to the selection.

	A	B	C	D	E	F	G	H
1	Fabrikam, Inc. Seven-Year Summary							$1 = $1,000
2								
3		2007	2008	2009	2010	2011	2012	2013
4	Income	$ 134,137	$ 142,728	$ 138,632	$ 151,841	$ 165,050	$ 169,606	$ 179,930
5	Expenses	70,962	75,925	74,167	76,774	79,381	79,805	81,684
6	Gross Profit	63,175	66,804	64,465	75,067	85,669	89,801	98,246
7	Depreciation	4,518	4,657	4,576	4,622	4,668	4,651	4,676
8	Interest Expense	2,746	2,893	2,885	2,897	2,908	2,910	2,918
9	Net Profit	55,912	59,253	57,004	67,548	78,093	82,240	90,652
10	Taxes	19,569	20,739	19,951	23,642	27,332	28,784	31,728
11	Aftertax Profit	$ 36,343	$ 38,515	$ 37,052	$ 43,906	$ 50,760	$ 53,456	$ 58,924
12								

21

10   Click the **Cell Styles** button and then click **Heading 3**.

11   Select all the numbers in the **Aftertax Profit** row (cells **B11:H11**).

12   Click the **Cell Styles** button and then click **Total**.

13   Select the year headers (cells **B3:H3**).

14   Click the **Cell Styles** button and then click **Heading 3**.

15   Select all the labels (cells **A4:A11**).

16   Click the **Cell Styles** button and then click **Heading 4**.

17   Select the blank cells between the table and the headings (cells **A2:H2**).

18   On the **Home** tab, in the **Font** group, click the arrow adjacent to the **Fill Color** button and click a slightly darker shade of blue.

19   Click cell **I2**.

20   On the **Home** tab, in the **Cells** group, click the **Format** button, and then click **Row Height**.

21   Enter **5** and press **Enter**.

22   Click the **Format** button, and then click **Column Width**.

23   Enter **3** and press **Enter**.

24   Click anywhere outside the table and look at the results.

	A	B	C	D	E	F	G	H	I
1	Fabrikam, Inc. Seven-Year Summary							$1 = $1,000	
3		2007	2008	2009	2010	2011	2012	2013	
4	Income	$ 134,137	$ 142,728	$ 138,632	$ 151,841	$ 165,050	$ 169,606	$ 179,930	
5	Expenses	70,962	75,925	74,167	76,774	79,381	79,805	81,684	
6	Gross Profit	63,175	66,804	64,465	75,067	85,669	89,801	98,246	
7	Depreciation	4,518	4,657	4,576	4,622	4,668	4,651	4,676	
8	Interest Expense	2,746	2,893	2,885	2,897	2,908	2,910	2,918	
9	Net Profit	55,912	59,253	57,004	67,548	78,093	82,240	90,652	
10	Taxes	19,569	20,739	19,951	23,642	27,332	28,784	31,728	
11	Aftertax Profit	$ 36,343	$ 38,515	$ 37,052	$ 43,906	$ 50,760	$ 53,456	$ 58,924	
12									

Perhaps it's not the most beautiful worksheet you've ever seen, but it's certainly easy to read. You can enhance the appearance of the table by modifying fonts, colors, borders, fills, and number formats any way you like. Then you can save the new formats for easy retrieval directly from the Cell Styles menu. Try it.

25 Click cell **A2**.

26 Click the **Cell Styles** button, and then click the **New Cell Style** command at the bottom of the gallery.

27 In the **Style name** box, enter **AccentColor** and press **Enter**.

Now when you click the Cell Styles button, AccentColor appears at the top of the gallery.

Unfortunately, custom formats travel with the workbook and are not even available to other workbooks that might be open at the same time. However, you can use the Merge Styles command located in the lower-left corner of the Cell Styles gallery to propagate custom styles from one open workbook to another. You can also save collections of colors, fonts, and effects as a theme, which we'll explore next.

❌ CLEAN UP **Save the FabrikamSummary.xlsx workbook.**

Keyboard access to menus and commands

Pressing the Alt key activates keyboard access to the menus and commands in Microsoft Office applications, and this functionality remains active until you either complete a command or press the Alt key again. The feature turns on and off or toggles an action with each press of the Alt key; keep pressing and watch the ribbon. Letter labels appear adjacent to each available command whenever the feature is activated. The first letter you press activates a tab (menu). For example, when you press Alt, and then press H, it activates the Home tab and displays the letters you need to press in order to activate the next menu or command. If you like using keyboard shortcuts, you can memorize a few of the key sequences. Don't worry if you forget a letter—just press Alt and look at the ribbon.

TIP It's easy to fix a bad formatting experiment. Click the Clear button in the Editing group on the Home tab, and then click Clear Formats. Here's the keyboard equivalent: press Ctrl+A (select all), then press Alt, H, E, F (in succession).

Creating custom themes

When you apply a theme, you change the appearance of everything in the workbook, regardless of what is currently selected. Themes are made up of colors, fonts, and effects. They do not apply number, alignment, or protection formats. Themes are not workbook dependent. When you save a custom theme, it is available to use with other workbooks, and it's also available for use in other Office applications.

In this exercise, you'll apply a theme, then modify it, and then save it as a new theme.

SET UP **You need the FabrikamSummaryTheme_start.xlsx workbook located in the Chapter21 practice file folder to complete this exercise. Open the FabrikamSummaryTheme_start.xlsx workbook, and save it as FabrikamSummaryTheme.xlsx.**

Fabrikam, Inc. Seven-Year Summary							$1 = $1,000
	2007	2008	2009	2010	2011	2012	2013
Income	$ 134,137	$ 142,728	$ 138,632	$ 151,841	$ 165,050	$ 169,606	$ 179,930
Expenses	70,962	75,925	74,167	76,774	79,381	79,805	81,684
Gross Profit	63,175	66,804	64,465	75,067	85,669	89,801	98,246
Depreciation	4,518	4,657	4,576	4,622	4,668	4,651	4,676
Interest Expense	2,746	2,893	2,885	2,897	2,908	2,910	2,918
Net Profit	55,912	59,253	57,004	67,548	78,093	82,240	90,652
Taxes	19,569	20,739	19,951	23,642	27,332	28,784	31,728
Aftertax Profit	$ 36,343	$ 38,515	$ 37,052	$ 43,906	$ 50,760	$ 53,456	$ 58,924

1   In the **FabrikamSummaryTheme.xlsx** workbook, click the **Page Layout** tab and then click the **Themes** button.

2   Point to a theme in the gallery to display a preview on the worksheet. Because this table was formatted by using cell styles, all the fonts and colors used in the table change according to the selected theme (along with effects, if any graphic objects were present).

3   Click the **Integral** theme.

Fabrikam, Inc. Seven-Year Summary							$1 = $1,000
	2007	2008	2009	2010	2011	2012	2013
Income	$ 134,137	$ 142,728	$ 138,632	$ 151,841	$ 165,050	$ 169,606	$ 179,930
Expenses	70,962	75,925	74,167	76,774	79,381	79,805	81,684
Gross Profit	63,175	66,804	64,465	75,067	85,669	89,801	98,246
Depreciation	4,518	4,657	4,576	4,622	4,668	4,651	4,676
Interest Expense	2,746	2,893	2,885	2,897	2,908	2,910	2,918
Net Profit	55,912	59,253	57,004	67,548	78,093	82,240	90,652
Taxes	19,569	20,739	19,951	23,642	27,332	28,784	31,728
Aftertax Profit	$ 36,343	$ 38,515	$ 37,052	$ 43,906	$ 50,760	$ 53,456	$ 58,924

IMPORTANT Software continues to be updated long after books are published, and newer versions of Excel may offer a somewhat different selection of themes, color sets, font sets, and effects. Installed fonts vary from system to system, and any themes that you or members of your workgroup created with Excel or any other Office application may also be visible. Use whatever is available (or whatever you prefer).

4   On the **Page Layout** tab, in the **Themes** group, click the **Colors** button. (Point to various color sets to preview their effects.)

5   Click the **Blue Green** color set.

6   In the **Themes** group, click the **Fonts** button. (Point to various font sets to preview their effects.)

7   Scroll down the list and click the **Arial Black** font set (or your favorite, if **Arial Black** is not available on your system).

8   In the **Themes** group, on the **Page Layout** tab, click the **Themes** button and then click **Save Current Theme** at the bottom of the gallery. You'll notice that the default folder is the **Microsoft\Templates\Document Themes** folder, a global settings folder that is available to other Office applications.

9   Enter **Fabrikam1** in the **File name** box.

10   Click **Save**.

11   Click the **Themes** button again, and the **Fabrikam1** theme appears at the top of the gallery, beneath the **Custom** heading.

You can create as many themes as you want, and you can add themes from other disk or network locations by using the Browse For Themes command located in the lower-left corner of the Themes gallery. If you later decide you don't want to keep it, it's easy to delete a custom theme.

12   Click the **Themes** button.

13   In the **Themes** gallery, right-click the **Fabrikam1** theme to display a shortcut menu.

14   If you want to remove a custom theme, click **Delete** to remove it from both the **Themes** gallery and the **Document Themes** folder. But make sure this theme isn't in use in other workbooks or other Office documents.

15   Press the **Esc** key.

✖ CLEAN UP **Save the FabrikamSummaryTheme.xlsx workbook, but keep it open for the next exercise.**

Formatting in cells

This is a little-used feature that went largely unnoticed when it appeared in a previous version of Excel. Prior to that version, it was possible to apply formatting only to the entire contents of a cell, but today, you can format individual characters within a cell. This is a useful feature when you are organizing workbooks and trying to fit into the cell structure with linear content like headings and paragraphs of text.

In this exercise, you'll apply formatting to individual characters in a cell.

➡ SET UP **You need the FabrikamSummaryTheme.xlsx workbook you saved at the end of the previous exercise to complete this exercise. Open the FabrikamSummaryTheme.xlsx workbook (if it is not already open), and follow the steps.**

1   Double-click cell **G1**.

A flashing text cursor appears in the cell.

2   Drag through the words **Seven Year Summary** to select them.

A small floating toolbar called the mini toolbar appears. You can use this toolbar to edit the selected text (or you can use the tools in the **Font** group, on the **Home** tab).

3   Select **Arial** from the **Font** list.

4   Reduce the font size to **11**.

5   Click the **Italic** button.

6   Change the font color to your favorite theme color (we chose **Aqua**).

7   Click anywhere outside the table to view the changes.

Fabrikam, Inc.	Seven-Year Summary	
	2007	**2008**
Income	$ 134,137	$ 142,728
Expenses	70,962	75,925
Gross Profit	63,175	66,804

CLEAN UP **Save the FabrikamSummaryTheme.xlsx workbook.**

Individuals who have used Excel for a long time (before in-cell formatting was possible) might attempt to put *Fabrikam, Inc.* and *Seven-Year Summary* into two separate cells and then apply formats to each cell individually. That process works, too, but the cells won't line up correctly. The result will look something like the text in the following graphic.

Fabrikam, Inc.		Seven-Year Summary	
	2007	**2008**	**2009**
Income	$ 134,137	$ 142,728	$ 138,632
Expenses	70,962	75,925	74,167
Gross Profit	63,175	66,804	64,465

Working with custom number formats

Custom number formats are like programming code; very easy programming code. Excel has its own number-formatting language. Every built-in number format can be expressed by using code, and thus can be easily modified for your own purposes.

In this exercise, you'll work with some of these formatting codes.

➡ SET UP **You don't need any practice files to complete this exercise. Open a blank workbook and follow the steps.**

1 Select cells **A1:A4**.

2 Click the **Accounting Number Format** button ($) on the **Home** tab.

3 Press **Ctrl+1** to display the **Format Cells** dialog box (or click the dialog box launcher in the **Number** group on the **Home** tab).

4 Click the **Number** tab, if it is not already active.

5   Click the **Custom** category.

The following table further describes the code behind the format applied by using the Accounting Number Format button. You can view the code behind any format in the Format Cells dialog box, in the Category list, by first clicking the category and then selecting the format you want to use. Then click the Custom category. The code for the currently selected format is displayed in the Type box, and it is editable. You cannot overwrite a built-in code, so if you edit a code and click OK, a new code is added to the Type list and is available the next time you open the Format Cells dialog box.

We created a modified version of the Accounting Number Format code, as shown in the following table. Format codes have four components separated by semicolons:

($* #,##0.00_);_($* (#,##0.00);_($* "-"??_);_(@_)			
Values	Positive	Negative	Zero	Text
Code	_($* #,##0.00_)	_($* (#,##0.00)	_($* "-"??_)	_(@_)
Entered	1234	–1234	0	Hello!
Displayed	$ 1,234.00	$ (1,234.00)	$ –	Hello!

6   Click **OK** to exit the dialog box.

7   Click cell **A1**. Enter **1234** and press **Enter**.

8   In cell **A2**, enter **-1234** and press **Enter**.

9   In Cell **A3**, enter **0** and press **Enter**.

10   In cell **A4**, enter **Hello!** and press **Enter**.

	A	B
1	$ 1,234.00	
2	$(1,234.00)	
3	$ -	
4	Hello!	
5		

11   Select cells **A1:A4**.

12   Press **Ctrl+1** to display the **Format Cells** dialog box (or click the dialog box launcher on the **Home** tab, in the **Number** group).

13   Click the **Custom** category.

14   In the **Type** box, replace the dash (–) in the third section of the format code with the word **Zero**. Be careful not to delete the quotation marks.

15   Click **OK**.

If you were wondering why they went to the trouble of specifying codes for the text section of the Accounting Number format, because text would display anyway, you'll notice that *Hello!* lines up perfectly with the dollar signs, which would not be the case without the special code. Details matter.

TIP You can create a formatting code that explicitly excludes one or more of the four value types from being displayed. For example, simply delete everything after the third semicolon (but not the semicolon itself) in the Accounting Number Format code to hide all text entries. The code 0.00;;; displays only positive numbers and hides everything else. And the handy ;;;; (four semicolons) code hides everything. You might use this trick to hide a formula on the worksheet; the result of which you need to use elsewhere, but don't need to display.

Following are the descriptions of the formatting codes that were used in the table shown previously:

- **Underscore (_)** Adds an invisible space that is exactly the same width as the character immediately following it. Each section in the previous code begins with an underscore and an opening parenthesis. (This adds a parenthesis-sized space before anything else in the cell, for visual balance. In all but the negative values section, there is a matching underscore at the end of the code section. This adds a balancing blank space on the right side of the cell. Negative values are, of course, surrounded by fully visible parentheses. Adding these spaces allows positive and negative numbers to be correctly aligned in a column.

- **Asterisk (*)** The character immediately following is to be repeated sufficiently to fill the column width. So, in this case, the dollar sign always stays on the left side of the cell, with as many spaces added between it and the number as necessary.

- **Zero (0)** This is a required digit placeholder. If there are no other digits to display in that position, Excel will always display zeros.

- **Pound sign (#)** This is an optional digit placeholder; if there is no digit in that position, it remains blank.

- **Question mark (?)** This is a required spaceholder. Even if there are no other digits to display in that position, Excel will always add a space. It is employed in the previous code to add two spaces after the dash, corresponding to two decimal places. This ensures that dashes (indicating zero values) will always line up with decimal points in a column of otherwise-nonzero numbers.

- **Quotation marks (" ")** These indicate a text component. In the code created previously, a dash is enclosed in quotation marks in the zero values position. In the accounting formats, only a dash is displayed if an entry equals zero.

- **At symbol (@)** This is a text placeholder, similar to the # that is a number placeholder. If there is text in the cell, it is displayed at this position.

- **Comma (,)** Otherwise known as a comma separator, this tells Excel to add commas to separate numbers, such as thousands, millions, and so on. It can also be used to apply gross rounding and scaling. For example, the format code #,###,### would display 4567890 as 4,567,890, but if you apply the code #,###, to the same number, the cell displays the number as 4,568. This kind of rounding/scaling can be used to make reports easier to read when they're displaying numbers in the millions and billions.

TIP For the complete inventory of custom formatting codes, click the question-mark Help button in the upper-right corner of the Excel window, and enter **custom number format** into the search box. The topic Create Or Delete A Custom Number Format contains all the options available.

21

16   Select cell **D1**.

17   Press **Ctrl+1** to display the **Format Cells** dialog box (or click the dialog box launcher on the **Home** tab, in the **Number** group).

18   Click the **Special** category and click **Social Security Number**.

19   Click the **Custom** category to view the custom formatting code **000-00-0000**, which is used to format social security numbers.

If you go back to the **Special** category and click either of the **Zip code** options, similar codes appear that are made up of zeros (and dashes). This indicates that each of these format codes will correctly display the exact number of digits indicated, and if no digit exists, a zero is displayed.

20 Click the **Special** category, select **Phone Number**, and click **OK** to apply the format to cell **D1**.

21 Press **Ctrl+1** and click the **Custom** category.

TIP When you create a custom format, it is saved with the workbook and remains available in the Format Cells dialog box's Custom category. If you want to use it elsewhere, you can copy a formatted cell from one workbook to another; the custom format travels with it.

Let's take a closer look at this formatting code in the following table. Notice that it has only two sections separated by a semicolon. This would seem to indicate that only positive and negative numbers are specified in this code, but actually, because there is a *comparison operator* (<=) involved, the semicolon is used to specify an either/or alternative. If the condition specified in the first section does not apply, then the second section is used.

SEE ALSO For information about Excel's Conditional Formatting command that allows you to easily apply selective formatting depending on the contents of the cells, see Chapter 20, "Analyzing data."

		[<=9999999]###-####;(###) ###-####	
Values	Condition 1	Condition 2
Code	[<=9999999]###-####	(###) ###-####
Entered	5551212	2065551212
Displayed	555-1212	(206) 555-1212

This is a clever code. The bracketed comparison value eliminates anything larger than 7 digits, displaying only phone numbers that do not include area codes. If the number entered is larger than 7 digits, the second section of the formatting code takes over and adds parentheses around the first three numbers. Let's modify it.

22 Edit the second section of the code in the **Type** box as follows (delete the first parenthesis and replace the second one with a dash):

[<=9999999]###-####;###-###-####

23 Click **OK**.

24 Enter **2065551212** and press **Enter**.

Custom formats remain available for use in the workbook in which they were created during the current session. However, if you save the workbook without actually applying a custom format to any values, it will not be available the next time you open the workbook. These are all good reasons to keep track of the custom formats you want to keep.

✖ CLEAN UP **Save the workbook as Custom Formats.xlsx, and keep it open for the next exercise.**

21

TIP For more information about using operators in formatting codes, click the Help button in the upper-right corner of the Excel window and enter **custom number format** into the search box. In the topic Create Or Delete A Custom Number Format, scroll down to Guidelines For Using Decimal Places, Spaces, Colors, And Conditions.

Note that the special Phone Number code will display as many numbers as you enter the digits for (unlike the social security number and ZIP code formats, which always display the same number of digits, adding leading zeros if necessary). For example, if you were to enter an incorrect numbers of digits into cells formatted with the Phone Number code, the numbers will be displayed as entered, such as in *23-4567* or *(12) 345-6789 or (1234) 567-8909*. Leading zeros are ignored in the Phone Number code, but not in the other Special codes.

TIP You can add bracketed conditions such as [<=9999999] to any formatting code, but be aware that when you use conditions, the usual four-part *positive-negative-zero-text* code structure changes to *condition1-condition2-condition3*, where the optional condition3 is essentially the *else* condition to be applied if the first two conditions are not met. If you still want to control negative values, then you can manually add the [<0] operator to the second condition.

Working with percentage formats

When you apply a percentage format to a number, Excel essentially moves the decimal point two places to the right, adds a percent sign, and rounds to a specified number of decimal places (depending on the format selected). For example, if a cell contains the number .3456 and you format it by clicking the Percent Style button (which applies a percentage format with no decimal places), Excel displays 35% in the cell.

Note this fact about percentage formats: after you apply one, Excel assumes there should be a decimal point even if you don't enter one. So, if you want to change the percentage in that same cell to 38%, you can just enter 38 (which is really 3800%) rather than .38. Microsoft learned that when changing a number displayed as a percentage, most people just enter an integer, not a decimal, so they made the format smart enough to deal with it. But, of course, if you really meant to enter 3800% when you entered 38, you'll have to go back and enter 3800.

There's not much you need to modify with percentages. You just need to decide whether or not you want to display decimals. You can display up to 30 decimal places. You can also add custom formatting. In this exercise, you'll do both.

SET UP You need either the Custom Formats.xlsx workbook you saved at the end of the previous exercise or the Custom Formats_start.xlsx workbook located in the Chapter21 practice file folder to complete this exercise. If you are using the Custom Formats_start.xlsx workbook, open it and save it as Custom Formats.xlsx.

1 In the **Custom Formats.xlsx** workbook, click the **New Sheet** button next to the **Sheet1** tab at the bottom of the workbook window to create a new worksheet. You will save the custom formats from each exercise on a separate sheet in this workbook.

2 In cell **A1**, enter **45.67** and press **Enter**.

3 Select cells **A1:A2**.

4 On the **Home** tab, in the **Number** group, click the **Percent Style** button.

5 Select cell **A2**.

6 Enter **45.67** and press **Enter**.

Notice the difference between applying the format before or after entering values. Most of the time, you'll apply percentage formats to cells containing formulas that generate actual percentages, but if not, check the values after applying a percentage format to a large range of cells containing existing values.

7 Select cell **A1**, enter **45.67**, and then press **Enter**.

8 Select cells **A1:A2**.

9 Press **Ctrl+1** to display the **Format Number** dialog box, and notice that **Decimal Places** is the only option you can change in the **Percentage** category.

10 Click the **Custom** category.

11   In the **Type** box, replace the existing code (**0%**) with the following:

"**Profits are up** "0%;[Red][<0]"**Profits are down** "0%

12   Press **Enter.**

13   Enter **-45.67** into cell **A2**

14   Press **Enter.**

 CLEAN UP **Save the Custom Formats.xlsx workbook, and keep it open for the next** **exercise.**

Working with fraction formats

If you want the look of fractions and do not require the precision of decimals, Excel offers formatting options that allow plenty of control over their display. However, you may need to adjust fraction formats to suit your needs. Though fraction formats often apply a round-ing factor to the actual value in the cell (unless there is no remainder, or MOD value), doing so changes the display, but as always, does not alter the underlying value.

In this exercise, you'll apply fraction formatting and work around some of its idiosyncrasies.

SET UP **You need either the Custom Formats.xlsx workbook you saved at the end of** **the previous exercise or the Custom Formats 2_start.xlsx workbook located in the Chap-** **ter21 practice file folder to complete this exercise. If you are using the Custom Formats** **2_start.xlsx workbook, open it and save it as Custom Formats.xlsx.**

1   In the **Custom Formats.xlsx** workbook, click the **New Sheet** button next to the sheet tabs at the bottom of the workbook window to create a new worksheet. You will save the custom formats from each exercise on a separate sheet in this workbook.

2   In cell **A1**, enter **67.89** and press **Enter**.

3   Select cell **A1**.

4   On the **Home** tab, in the **Number** group, click the **Number** list and select **Fraction**.

The fraction displayed in the cell uses a denominator (9) not commonly used in fractions. This may be the closest actual fractional value (67.8888...), but we need to adjust our fraction so that it uses a more conventional denominator.

5   Press **Ctrl+1** to display the **Format Cells** dialog box.

6   In the **Type** list, scroll down to the bottom.

7   Select **As tenths (3/10)**.

Format Cells

Number	Alignment	Font	Border	Fill	Protection

Category:

- General
- Number
- Currency
- Accounting
- Date
- Time
- Percentage
- **Fraction**
- Scientific
- Text
- Special
- Custom

Sample

67 9/10

Type:

- Up to three digits (312/943)
- As halves (1/2)
- As quarters (2/4)
- As eighths (4/8)
- As sixteenths (8/16)
- As tenths (3/10)
- As hundredths (30/100)

OK   Cancel

8   Click **OK**.

	A	B
1	67 9/10	
2		
3		
4		
5		

There are a number of fraction formats available, some of which seem barely usable. Consider the Up To Three Digits (312/943) format, which would actually raise precision considerably, while equally reducing intelligibility and making the use of decimals seem more prudent. But the essential options are all here: Halves, Quarters, Eighths, Sixteenths, and Hundredths. But what if you need a few more?

9   Select cell **A1**, and then press **Ctrl+1** to display the **Format Cells** dialog box.

10   Click the **Custom** category.

11   In the **Type** box, replace the existing code (**# ?/10**) with the following:
        # ?/32.

12   Click **OK**.

	A	B
1	67 28/32	
2		
3		
4		
5		

13   Press **Ctrl+1** to open the **Format Cells** dialog box again.

14   Click the **Custom** category.

15   In the **Type** box, replace the existing code with the following:
        # ?/64.

16   Click **OK**.

21

	A	B
1	67 57/64	
2		
3		
4		
5		

When you open the Format Cells dialog box, the two formats you just created appear somewhere in the list of Custom formats. These two happen to show up at the bottom.

Format Cells dialog box showing the Number tab.

CLEAN UP Save the Custom Formats.xlsx workbook, and keep it open for the next exercise.

Working with date formats

Excel stores dates as serial numeric values starting from January 1, 1900; each day counts as 1. For example, this sentence was written at around 41182.66937 (decimal values, as you might guess, indicate exact time of day), otherwise known as 4:03 P.M. on September 30, 2012. This numeric date system allows you to manipulate dates and times in Excel as easily as other numbers. The time and date formatting options and their associated codes are appropriately different from any of the others.

In this exercise, you'll apply date formatting and create custom date formats.

SET UP You need either the Custom Formats.xlsx workbook you saved at the end of the previous exercise or the Custom Formats 3_start.xlsx workbook located in the Chapter21 practice file folder to complete this exercise. If you are using the Custom Formats 3_start.xlsx workbook, open it and save it as Custom Formats.xlsx.

1   In the **Custom Formats.xlsx** workbook, click the **New Sheet** button next to the sheet tabs at the bottom of the workbook window to create a new worksheet. You will save the custom formats from each exercise on a separate sheet in this workbook.

2   In cell **A1**, enter **41182.66937**, and then press **Enter**.

3   Select cell **A1**, click the **Number** drop-down list on the **Home** tab, and then click **Short Date**.

4   Press **Ctrl+1** to display the **Format Cells** dialog box.

5   Click the **Custom** category.

6   In the **Type** box, replace the selected formatting code **m/d/yyyy** as follows:

dddd mmmm dd, yyyy hh:mm:ss am/pm

7   Click **OK**.

The format now spells out months and days, and includes hours, minutes, and seconds. But if you were timing races or scientific experiments, you might need even more precision.

8   Press **Ctrl+1** again to display the **Format Cells** dialog box.

9   Make sure the **Custom** category is still active, and edit your custom formatting code, adding **.00** after the seconds, as follows:

dddd mmmm dd, yyyy hh:mm:ss.00 am/pm

10   Click **OK**.

Because the time component now includes fractional seconds, this moment in time actually occurred a few hundredths of a second earlier.

A1	▼	⋮	✕	✓	*fx*	9/30/2012 4:03:54 PM			
		A				B	C	D
1	Sunday September 30, 2012 04:03:53.57 PM							
2								
3								
4								
5								

11   In cell **A2**, enter **41198.7**, and then press **Enter**.

12   Reselect cell **A2**, click the **Number** list on the **Home** tab, and then click **Time**.

Cell **A2** displays only the time of day represented by the number you entered.

21

A2	▼	⋮	✕	✓	*fx*	10/16/2012 4:48:00 PM		
		A			B	C	
1	Sunday September 30, 2012 04:03:53.57 PM						
2	4:48:00 PM						
3							
4							
5							

With cell A2 selected, look in the formula bar. The full date and time is displayed there, rather than the number that you entered. The underlying value is still there. This is an aspect of Excel formatting that's quite helpful. If you really need to view that serial value again, apply the General format from the Number Format list. (If you did this, press Ctrl+Z to undo before proceeding.)

13   Select cell **A3**, enter **=A2-A1** and press **Enter**.

This simple formula returns a result that is formatted as a time value, similar to cell **A2**. (Excel adds formatting to an unformatted cell containing a formula that refers to formatted values.)

14   Reselect cell **A3**, click the **Number Format** list on the **Home** tab, and select **Long Date**.

Excel reveals the date Monday, January 16, 1900. This rather cryptically reveals the number of days that have elapsed between the two dates in the formula (16 days, given that 1/1/1900 is day 1). However, in this case, the desired outcome is to display elapsed *time*.

15   Press **Ctrl+1** to open the **Format Cells** dialog box.

16   Click the **Custom** category.

17   Replace the formatting code in the **Type** box with the following:

[hh]:mm:ss.000

18   Click **OK**. Now the elapsed time is 384 hours (16 days), 44 hours, and 6.432 seconds.

SEE ALSO For more information about using functions in Excel to calculate dates, see Chapter 19, "Manipulating numbers and text."

	A	B
1	Sunday September 30, 2012 04:03:53.57 PM	
2	4:48:00 PM	
3	384:44:06.432	
4		
5		

When you add brackets around the first component of a time format, Excel returns elapsed time. The brackets must be around the first component only; they will not work in any other position. However, you can change the code to show only elapsed minutes by deleting [hh]: and adding brackets around *mm* instead. Or, you can use the code [ss] to show only elapsed seconds. The code .000 appended to the seconds component of the format adds precision down to *milliseconds* (thousandths of a second), which is as precise as Excel will go. You can't add more than three zeros to the code.

❌ CLEAN UP **Save the Custom Formats.xlsx workbook and close it.**

What do the asterisks mean?

You may have noticed that some of the format codes that are listed in the Custom category begin with an asterisk (*). This indicates that the code will adjust according to the regional date and time settings of the computer on which Excel is running. To view how this might change from location to location, select a cell containing any date and click Short Date in the Number Format list. Press Ctrl+1 and then click the Locale list and select Estonian. Or, if you are in Estonia, select English (United States). Then try Yoruba.

You'll need to click OK each time to view the results, because the Locale options do not display in the Preview area of the dialog box. (Note that Locale options appear in the Date and Time categories of the Format Cells dialog box, but not in the Custom category.) This may not be an issue for you at all, unless you share workbooks with colleagues in different locales (and even then, you may prefer Excel's automatic localizing). But if you don't want your dates and times to adjust for locales, select a non-asterisk format in the Format Cells dialog box or choose the Custom category and delete the asterisk from the format code.

Following is a list with descriptions for several date formatting codes:

- **d (Day)** This code displays either numbers or text, depending on how many of them you include in the format. A single **d** displays the date as a number without leading zeros (1 or 16). A double **dd** displays the date as a number *with* leading zeros (01 or 16). Instead of displaying a date, using a triple **ddd** code displays the name of the day of the week, abbreviated (Sat). Similarly, using a quadruple **dddd** code displays the full name of the day of the week (Saturday). You can use both numeric dates and day names in formats. For example, a cell containing the date 12/6/2013 that is subsequently formatted using the code **dddd mmmm d** displays *Friday December 6*.

- **m (Month)** Like the day code, the month code displays either numbers or text, depending on how many you include in the format. A single **m** displays the month as a number without leading zeros (1 or 12). A double **mm** displays the month as a number *with* leading zeros (01 or 12). The triple **mmm** code displays an abbreviated month name (Dec). A quadruple **mmmm** code displays the full name of the month (December). (See also **mm (Minutes)**, later in this list.)

- **y (Year)** You can use the code **yy** to display just the last two digits of the year (13), or use **yyyy** to display the full year (2013).

- **h (Hour)** There are two ways to use the hour code: **h** displays the hour without leading zeros (2, 22), while the code **hh** displays the hour with leading zeros (02, 22). Note that Excel always uses a 24-hour clock unless you add the **am/pm** code.

- **mm (Minutes)** Obviously, minutes and months use the same code letter (**m**), so it's all about where you put them. In a date code, the **m** stands for months, in a time code (separated by colons), it's minutes. A single **m** displays minutes without leading zeros (5, 55), while the double **mm** displays minutes with leading zeros (05, 55).

- **s (Seconds)** A single **s** displays seconds without leading zeros (3, 33), and a double **ss** displays seconds with leading zeros (03, 33). Adding a period and one or two zeros to the end of a seconds code (**s.0, ss.0, s.00, or ss.00**) adds tenths or hundredths of a second to the display, respectively.

- **am/pm or a/p** Adding **am/pm** to the end of a date or time format code instructs Excel to display the time component based on a 12-hour clock. Case doesn't matter.

- **[ ] (Brackets)** Brackets around a time code tell Excel to return elapsed time rather than actual time. It is necessary to apply this format to formulas that calculate elapsed time, otherwise the results may not be what you expect. You can only use brackets with time codes, and only in the first section of the code, for example **[hh]:mm:ss** or **[mm]:ss**.

There are some code combinations that won't work. For example, you cannot use the am/pm format code with a bracketed elapsed-time code, which makes sense if you think about it. Mixing date codes and numeric format codes doesn't work, either. Feel free to experiment; Excel will let you know what doesn't work by displaying an error message if you try to create an unusable code.

TIP For more about date and time formatting codes, click the Help button in the upper-right corner of the Excel window, and enter **custom number format** into the search box. The topic Create Or Delete A Custom Number Format contains all the options available.

Protecting worksheets

You and I might not think of protection as a format, but Excel does. You can use it like a format in the sense that you can apply it to some cells and not others. This allows you to lock all the cells in a worksheet to protect them from modification, or you can leave specific cells unlocked, allowing users of the workbook to enter data, and allowing you to specify exactly which areas in the worksheet you want to protect.

Excel assumes that you want to lock all the cells in a workbook if and when you activate protection, so all cells are formatted as *locked* by default.

In this exercise, you'll work with protection formatting by unlocking cells on a worksheet that you want to be able to edit after protection is turned on.

SET UP **You need the Real-Estate-Transition_start.xlsx workbook located in the Chapter21 practice file folder to complete this exercise. Open the Real-Estate-Transition_start. xlsx workbook, and save it as Real-Estate-Transition.xlsx.**

1   In the **Real-Estate-Transition.xlsx** workbook, click the arrow next to the **Name** box in the **Formula** bar, and select the name **Entries** to select all the user-input cells in column **B**.

	B19		f_x	295000						
	Entries	A	B	C	D	E	F	G	H
	Rates								
1		...e Transition Worksheet							
2	Home Asking Price	$425,000		Full price	- $9000	- $18000	- $27000	- $36000
3	Decreasing Increment	$ 9,000	Home Sale Price $	425,000 $	416,000 $	407,000 $	398,000 $	389,000
4								
5	Real Estate Fees	3.00%	Listing	12,750	12,480	12,210	11,940	11,670
6		3.00%	Selling	12,750	12,480	12,210	11,940	11,670
7								
8		0.10%	Escrow/Closing (incl. tax)	425	416	407	398	389
9	Settlement Costs	0.21%	Title Policy (incl tax)	901	882	863	844	825
10		$ 1,788	Property Tax	1,788	1,788	1,788	1,788	1,788
11		1.78%	Excise Tax	7,565	7,405	7,245	7,084	6,924
12								
13	Mortgage Costs	$ 125	Document Prep Fee	125	125	125	125	125
14		$ 75	Recording Fee	75	75	75	75	75
15								
16	Total Selling Costs		Total Estimated Seller Costs	36,379	35,651	34,922	34,194	33,466
17			As a percentage	9.36%	9.37%	9.39%	9.40%	9.41%
18			Net Proceeds:	388,621	380,349	372,078	363,806	355,534
19	New Home Cost	$ 295,000	Net after New Home Purchase	93,621	85,349	77,078	68,806	60,534
20	Current Investments	$ 65,000	Total Available to Invest	158,621	150,349	142,078	133,806	125,534
21	Estimated Rate of Return	3.00%	Potential Monthly Return $	397 $	376 $	355 $	335 $	314
22								

2   Click the **Format** button, on the **Home** tab, and take a look at the **Lock Cell** command.

Protection
  Protect Sheet...
  Lock Cell

The icon adjacent to the Lock Cell command is enclosed in a gray box, which indicates that it is currently active, or locked, as is the case with all cells in a worksheet unless you specify otherwise.

3   Click the **Lock Cell** command to unlock the selected cells.

4   Click the **Format** button again, and this time, click the **Protect Sheet** command to display a dialog box of the same name.

You'll notice that the only allowed default settings involve selecting cells, unless you click additional options.

5   Click **OK** to turn on sheet protection without adding a password or selecting additional options.

6   Select cell **B3**.

7   Enter **8000** and then press **Enter**; Excel accepts the entry and **B4** becomes the active cell.

8   When you try to enter anything into a cell other than those you unlocked in column **B**, Excel prevents any entry and displays a warning message.

✖ CLEAN UP **Save the Real-Estate-Transition.xlsx workbook, and then close it.**

You can protect formulas and data on worksheets that you need to share with others by using protection formatting. Or you can lock all cells on a sheet and optionally apply a password to prevent any changes from happening at all. Protection is applied per worksheet, so a workbook may contain both protected and unprotected sheets.

Protecting workbooks

Protection in Excel has many levels. You protected cells and sheets, so to display the various options for workbook protection, click the File tab to display the Backstage view, click Info, and then click the Protect Workbook button.

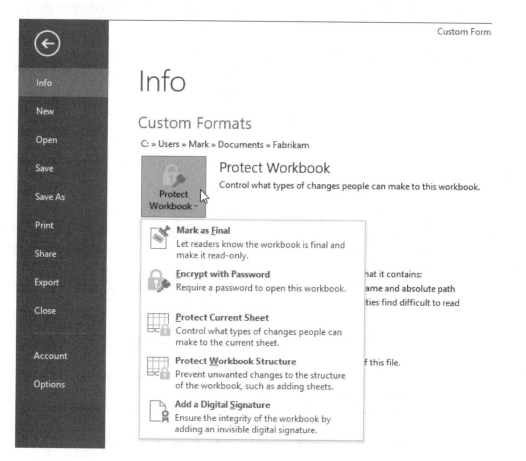

- **Mark as Final** Makes the workbook read-only

- **Encrypt with Password** Displays a dialog box allowing you to specify a password necessary to open the workbook

- **Protect Current Sheet** Prevents the editing of any locked cells on the current sheet and displays the same Protect Sheet dialog box shown earlier in this chapter, with which you specify allowable editing actions for the current sheet

- **Protect Workbook Structure** Allows you to open workbooks and edit worksheets, but not to rename tabs or move, hide, or unhide worksheets and windows

- **Add a Digital Signature** Allows you to apply authentication to a workbook by using a digital stamp, which you must purchase from an authorized digital certificate–issuing authority such as Verisign

Setting view options

When creating workbooks designed for presentation, you can control a variety of display settings by using commands on the View tab. The ribbon and controls of the Excel program and the workbook structure can be a distraction in themselves. Some of these settings are saved with the workbook, and thus can for all intents and purposes be considered among your formatting options. We'll start with the simplest worksheet imaginable to illustrate the remarkable amount of visual clutter you can eliminate if you want to.

In this exercise, you'll change the way your worksheet is displayed on screen.

➡ SET UP **You need the FabrikamSummary2_start.xlsx workbook located in the Chapter21 practice file folder to complete this exercise. Open the Fabrikam-Summary2_start.xlsx workbook, and save it as FabrikamSummary2.xlsx.**

1   With the **FabrikamSummary2.xlsx** workbook open, click the **View** tab.

2   On the **View** tab, in the **Show** group, clear the **Gridlines**, **Headings**, and **Formula Bar** check boxes to deselect those options.

3   Double-click the **View** tab to collapse the ribbon and transform the tabs into a menu bar.

4   Click the **Ribbon Display Options** button, located in the upper-right corner of the screen, and click the **Auto-Hide Ribbon** command, which hides the ribbon and the status bar, maximizes the window and hides the **Quick Access Toolbar** and the tabs. (The formula bar and headings would be visible in this display mode if you hadn't already turned them off on the **View** tab.)

	2010		2011		2012		2013
						$1 = $1,000	
$	151,841	$	165,050	$	169,606	$	179,930
	76,774		79,381		79,805		81,684
	75,067		85,669		89,801		98,246
	4,622		4,668		4,651		4,676
	2,897		2,908		2,910		2,918
	67,548		78,093		82,240		90,652
	23,642		27,332		28,784		31,728
$	43,906	$	50,760	$	53,456	$	58,924

5   Click the **…** (three dots) in the upper-right corner of the screen to temporarily display the ribbon.

6   Click the **Ribbon Display Options** button again and click **Show Tabs** to redisplay the tab names, the status bar, and the **Quick Access Toolbar**. The ribbon is still hidden.

7   Click the **View** tab to temporarily redisplay the ribbon.

When you click a collapsed tab, it appears and stays visible until you click a command or click in the worksheet area.

8   Click anywhere in the worksheet area. The ribbon collapses again.

9   Double-click the **View** tab to redisplay the ribbon (or you can click **Ribbon Display Options**, and then click **Show Tabs and Commands**).

TIP You can double-click any ribbon tab to toggle the ribbon display on or off. If the ribbon is visible, double-clicking any tab hides it; if the ribbon is not visible, double-clicking any tab redisplays it.

You can create another view of a worksheet by using the New Window command on the View tab. This creates not another worksheet, but another window on the same worksheet, within which you can have an entirely different set of view options, regardless of whether the ribbon is collapsed.

10 Click the **New Window** command on the **View** tab; a new window appears entitled **FabrikamSummary2.xlsx:2**, displayed with the default **View** settings.

11 Click the **Zoom** button on the **View** tab, select **200%** and click **OK**.

12 Click the **Switch Windows** button and select the unchecked window (**FabrikamSummary2.xlsx:1**).

13 Click the **Zoom** button, select **75%** and click **OK**.

14 Click the **Arrange All** button, and accept the default **Tiled** option.

15 Click **OK**.

TIP You can click the View Side By Side button to do a row-by-row comparison of two workbooks or windows together onscreen. (If you have more than two workbooks or windows open, a dialog box appears allowing you to select one.) When you click the View Side By Side button, the Synchronous Scrolling button is engaged as well. If you want, click the Synchronous Scrolling button to turn it off, and scroll freely in either window.

Many of the settings you select on the View tab are saved with the workbook, including the display of gridlines, headings, and Zoom settings. When you save the workbook with any of these options changed, they persist the next time you open the workbook, including any additional windows created using the New Window command. However, you cannot save the layout of windows, such as the Tiled layout just discussed. But the windows are there, saved with the workbook; you'll just have to use the Arrange All command again to reset the layout. This is something you can't do in Excel 2013 that you used to be able to do. As a byproduct of the Single-Document Interface, the Save Workspace command had to be removed, because new windows are no longer contained within a workbook-specific workspace, but now are created in an entirely separate instance of Excel.

TIP You lose a lot of screen real estate with multiple windows open and a ribbon and Formula bar in each one. Click the Formula bar option on the View tab to hide it. Double-click any tab to collapse the ribbon (double-click the tab again to restore it).

Collapsing the ribbon and hiding the Formula bar are application settings that are not saved with workbooks. The configuration in place when you exit is displayed the next time you start Excel.

❌ CLEAN UP **Close both windows of the FabrikamSummary2.xlxs workbook without saving.**

Storing formats in templates

If you go to the trouble of creating beautiful and useful worksheets, chances are you would like to use them again, or at least repurpose parts of them. Custom formats you create only apply to the workbook in which you created them. But you can transfer them by copying custom-formatted cells and pasting them into other workbooks. So, you could create a boilerplate workbook to store your number formats created by using custom codes, as well as cell formats, tables, and so on. Or you can create a template. In addition, you can also store workbooks and formats in a location where you can easily retrieve a copy.

TIP You can save specific formatting options (fonts, colors, and effects) as themes, which can be easily used in other Excel workbooks as well as in other Office documents. See "Creating custom themes," earlier in this chapter.

If you have created and used templates in Office applications before, the procedure for saving and accessing templates works a bit differently in Office Home and Student 2013. Before you save your own templates, you need to first specify a Default Personal Templates Location. In order to do this properly, you need to create it first. So before you do anything else, open File Explorer and create a folder to store templates on your computer in a location of your choice. You can place a copy of a random Excel workbook in there too, if you want.

In this exercise, you'll save a workbook as a template.

➡ SET UP **You don't need any practice files to complete this exercise. Start Excel, open a blank workbook, and follow the steps.**

1 Click the **File** tab and then click **Options** to display the **Excel Options** dialog box.

2 Click the **Save** category.

3 In the **Default Personal Templates Location** box, enter the path to the folder you will use to store your templates (or for now, you can copy whatever is in the **Default Local File Location** box and edit it later).

4 Click **OK**.

5 Click the **File** tab, and then click **New**.

New

Search online templates

Suggested searches: Budget   Invoice   Calendars   Expense   List   Loan   Schedule

FEATURED   PERSONAL

Custom Formats

On the New page, next to Featured, which previously stood alone, there is now a Personal category. When you click this category, any templates stored in your designated personal templates folder are displayed on the screen for you to open with a single click. (We added one for the purposes of this discussion; otherwise, the Personal category would not appear at all unless there was a subfolder in your Default Personal Templates folder.) As a matter of fact, any Excel workbooks stored in this folder will be presented as options in the Personal template category and will open as templates, whether or not you save them as such.

You can create as many templates as you choose, from workbooks containing only custom number formats to fully developed applications, and you can store them in your Default Personal Templates Location. When you open any workbook from the New page of the Backstage view, a copy is opened in Excel, using the original filename with an appended number. For example, a workbook or template named Custom Formats would open as Custom Formats1, which makes it harder to inadvertently overwrite the original file.

When you save a workbook created from a template, the Default Local File Location (specified in the Excel Options dialog box) is offered as the default folder, rather that the Default Personal Templates Location, which further protects the original file from being overwritten.

✖ CLEAN UP Press Esc to close the Backstage view, and exit Excel without saving.

Key points

- Formatting helps transform raw numeric data into more accessible information.

- You can format cells, and you can format individual characters in cells.

- You can modify and create your own variations of Excel's built-in number formats.

- You can modify and create your own date formats, including special elapsed-time formats.

- Styles and themes are collections of formatting options that help you maintain consistency among documents.

- You can selectively apply protection formatting to lock and unlock individual cells, allowing you to ensure the integrity of formatting and critical formulas on the worksheet.

- You can open more than one window on the same workbook, and you can arrange all the open workbooks and windows onscreen for simultaneous viewing.

- You can store your formatting choices as templates, making them available for easy duplication.

21

Chapter at a glance

Freeze

Freeze worksheet panes so that you always know where you are, page 592

Print

Print specific rows and columns on every page of output, page 599

Break

Break your printed pages by dragging borders in Page Break Preview, page 602

Drag

Drag worksheets between workbooks, page 610

Manipulating workbooks and worksheets

IN THIS CHAPTER, YOU WILL LEARN HOW TO

- Use Excel's table features to insert and delete rows and columns.

- Keep row and column labels in view, in print and on screen.

- Adjust page breaks.

- Create and work with multisheet workbooks.

- Create multisheet formulas.

- Arrange workbooks and windows on screen.

Regardless of what you plan to put in them, it's important to know the basics of workbooks and worksheets. How do they actually work? Being able to to manipulate the structure of your workbooks may change your thinking about how to organize your data.

In this chapter, you'll learn how to insert and delete cells, rows, and columns; how to change display and print options; and how to use multiple sheets in a workbook.

PRACTICE FILES To complete the exercises in this chapter, you need the practice files contained in the Chapter22 practice file folder. For more information, see "Download the practice files" in this book's Introduction.

Inserting rows and columns

There are certain actions that accrue more usage in applications. Like copying and pasting in Microsoft Word, inserting and deleting rows and columns in Microsoft Excel is near the top of that list.

In this exercise, you'll insert some rows and add a column of totals with the help of Excel's table features. But first, you'll sort the existing worksheet.

 SET UP **You need the FabrikamQ1_start.xlsx workbook located in the Chapter22 practice file folder to complete this exercise. Open the FabrikamQ1_start.xlsx workbook, save it as FabrikamQ1.xlsx, and then follow the steps.**

1 With the **FabrikamQ1_start.xlsx** workbook open, make sure that cell **A2** is selected, and then click the **Data** tab.

2 Click the **Sort** button in the **Sort & Filter** group.

Because the active cell is in a table, Excel automatically selects the entire table when the **Sort** dialog box appears.

3 In the **Sort by** list, select **Group**.

4 Click the **Add Level** button.

5 In the **Then by** list, select **Channel**.

	A	B	C	D	E	F
1	Product Number	Date	Group	Channel	Qty	Unit Price
2	FABK-0008	1/1/2013	Alpha	A	34	29.98
3	FABK-0001	1/1/2013	Alpha	A	37	45.78
4	FABK-0075	1/1/2013	Alpha	B	33	14.18
5	FABK-0125	1/1/2013	Alpha	B	130	266.89
6	FABK-0008	1/1/2013	Alpha	E	35	29.98
7	FABK-0115	1/1/2013	Beta	A	10	4.70
8	FABK-0071	1/1/2013	Beta	A	47	314.24
9	FABK-0112	1/1/2013	Beta	E	20	140.53
10	FABK-0108	1/1/2013	Delta	B	25	29.98
11	FABK-0020	1/1/2013	Delta	B	93	45.78
12	FABK-0111	1/1/2013	Delta	E	117	14.18
13	FABK-0052	1/1/2013	Epsilon	E	25	140.53
14	FABK-0055	1/1/2013	Gamma	C	25	4.70
15	FABK-0034	1/1/2013	Gamma	E	91	29.98
16	FABK-0107	1/1/2013	Kappa	B	60	124.74
17	FABK-0036	1/1/2013	Lambda	A	71	29.98

Sort dialog box:

Add Level | Delete Level | Copy Level | Options... | ☑ My data has headers

Column	Sort On	Order
Sort by **Group**	Values	A to Z
Then by **Channel**	Values	A to Z

OK | Cancel

6 Click **OK** to sort the table.

7 Scroll down to row **648**, the first row of the **Omega** group listings. Notice the tiny ScreenTip near the scroll bar, for a live readout of the current row number as you drag the scroll box.

Row: 648

TIP Another way of navigating to a remote cell is to enter the cell address into the Name box on the left end of the formula bar. For this example, entering **A648** would get you to row 648.

8   Select the entire row by clicking the **648** row heading number.

9   Click the **Omega A** worksheet tab at the bottom of the window.

10   Select row **2** by clicking the row heading number.

11   Hold the **Shift+Ctrl** keys and then press the **Down Arrow** key, which selects all the rows in the table.

12   Click the **Copy** button on the **Home** tab (or press **Ctrl+C**).

13   Click the **Q1-2013** worksheet tab at the bottom of the window.

14   Click the arrow below the **Insert** button, located in the **Cells** group on the **Home** tab of the ribbon.

15   On the **Insert** menu, click **Insert Copied Cells**.

The new rows are inserted above the selected row. (Note that if you click the **Insert** button itself, rather than clicking the arrow button to display the **Insert** menu, **Insert Copied Cells** is still the default action.)

22

16   Click the **Find & Select** button in the **Editing** group on the **Home** tab, and then click **Go To**.

17   In the **Reference** box, enter **E:E**, and then press **Enter**.

You'll notice that the entire column E is selected, just as if you had clicked the header. (You can use this same trick with rows; for example, entering **648:648** selects the entire row **648**.)

18   With column E selected, click the **Insert** button arrow, and then click **Insert Sheet Columns**. (Again, pressing the button arrow and pressing the button itself both yield the same result.)

19   Select cell **E1**, enter **Sale**, and press **Enter**.

The next step is to add formulas to calculate totals. However, entering a formula into cell **E2** and then dragging the fill handle to copy the formula down the column, with 1043 rows of data, is a lot of dragging. There's an easier way.

20   With cell **E2** still selected, click the **Insert** tab, and then click the **Table** button in the **Tables** group.

21   In the **Create Table** dialog box, click **OK**.

22   Select cell **E2**.

23   Enter = (an equal sign), and then press the **Right Arrow** key once.

24   Enter * (an asterisk), and then press the **Right Arrow** key twice.

25   Press **Enter**, and watch as Excel automatically fills the rest of the column with equivalent formulas.

The Excel table features made inserting these formulas very easy.

E2		fx	=[@Qty]*[@[Unit Price]]				
	A	B	C	D	E	F	G	H
1	Product Number	Date	Group	Channel	Sale	Qty	Unit Price	
2	FABK-0008	1/1/2013	Alpha	A	1019.32	34	29.98	
3	FABK-0001	1/1/2013	Alpha	A	1693.86	37	45.78	
4	FABK-0009	1/3/2013	Alpha	A	2289	50	45.78	
5	FABK-0009	1/4/2013	Alpha	A	2289	50	45.78	
6	FABK-0001	1/8/2013	Alpha	A	1693.86	37	45.78	
7	FABK-0001	1/11/2013	Alpha	A	4257.54	93	45.78	
8	FABK-0007	1/14/2013	Alpha	A	2709.08	44	61.57	
9	FABK-0008	1/15/2013	Alpha	A	1019.32	34	29.98	
10	FABK-0009	1/15/2013	Alpha	A	2609.46	57	45.78	
11	FABK-0007	1/18/2013	Alpha	A	2709.08	44	61.57	
12	FABK-0007	1/22/2013	Alpha	A	2709.08	44	61.57	
13	FABK-0006	1/22/2013	Alpha	A	9166.5	45	203.70	

TIP If youdon't like the default table formatting, you can always choose another style. For example, you can switch back to the plain worksheet style used at the beginning of the exercise, by clicking the Table Tools Design tab (only available when the active cell is inside a table) and clicking the very first style in the Table Styles palette. You could also convert the table back to a regular cell range by clicking the Convert To Range button on the Table Tools Design tab. When you do so, the formulas are preserved, but they are converted from table reference formulas to regular Excel formulas.

✖ CLEAN UP **Save the FabrikamQ1.xlsx workbook, and then close it.**

Inserting and deleting cells

Believe it or not, inserted cells are among the most common worksheet problems. When you insert text in Word, for example, existing text shifts to accommodate it, because text processing is essentially linear.

Spreadsheets (and tables in Word) are modular. When you insert cells, you force existing cells, rows, or columns to move out of the way. Unlike with text insertion, you have options when inserting cells: you can push existing cells either to the right or down. Inserting rows and columns is fairly safe, because this usually keeps related data aligned properly. But inserting cells can easily misalign data.

In this exercise, you'll use the right approach to inserting and deleting cells, and you'll discover what happens when you do it the wrong way.

➜ SET UP **You need the FabrikamQ1-B_start.xlsx workbook located in the Chapter22 practice file folder to complete this exercise. Open the FabrikamQ1-B_start.xlsx workbook, save it as FabrikamQ1-B.xlsx, and then follow the steps.**

1   With the **FabrikamQ1-B.xlsx** workbook open, the **Omega A** tab active, and cell **B2** selected, click the arrow below the **Insert** button in the **Cells** group on the **Home** tab, and then click the **Insert Cells** command to display the **Insert** dialog box.

2   Make sure the **Shift cells down** option is selected. (Even though the **Entire row** option would be the appropriate choice in this case, leave the default option selected.)

22

3   Click **OK**. Notice that all the other cells in the same column have been pushed down, and in the process, all the data in column **B** is now misaligned with all the other data in the table.

4   Scroll down to row **41**, and notice that all the data in the column is now one cell lower, and all the sales records are now adjacent to incorrect dates.

⬓	A	B	C	D	E	F	G
34	FABK-0062	3/4/2013	Omega	A	36	77.35	
35	FABK-0102	3/7/2013	Omega	A	-2	156.31	
36	FABK-0056	3/13/2013	Omega	A	24	138.96	
37	FABK-0125	3/13/2013	Omega	A	128	266.89	
38	FABK-0091	3/14/2013	Omega	A	55	140.53	
39	FABK-0059	3/19/2013	Omega	A	3	156.31	
40	FABK-0058	3/21/2013	Omega	A	33	124.74	
41	FABK-0044	3/21/2013	Omega	A	68	18.91	
42		3/22/2013					
43							

5   Press **Ctrl+Z** to undo.

6   Click the **Q1-2013** worksheet tab at the bottom of the screen; the worksheet contains an Excel table, and cell **E2** is selected.

7   Click the arrow below the **Insert** button in the **Cells** group on the **Home** tab, click **Insert Cells**, and then click **OK**; this time Excel inserted an entire row in the table instead of a single cell (and duplicated the **Sale** formula automatically), demonstrating how Excel's table features help ensure the integrity of your data.

	A	B	C	D	E	F	G
1	Product Number ▼	Date ▼	Group ▼	Channel ▼	Sale ▼	Qty ▼	Unit Price ▼
2					0		
3	FABK-0008	1/1/2013	Alpha	A	1019.32	34	29.98
4	FABK-0001	1/1/2013	Alpha	A	1693.86	37	45.78
5	FABK-0009	1/3/2013	Alpha	A	2289	50	45.78
6	FABK-0009	1/4/2013	Alpha	A	2289	50	45.78
7	FABK-0001	1/8/2013	Alpha	A	1693.86	37	45.78
8	FABK-0001	1/11/2013	Alpha	A	4257.54	93	45.78
9	FABK-0007	1/14/2013	Alpha	A	2709.08	44	61.57
10	FABK-0008	1/15/2013	Alpha	A	1019.32	34	29.98

8   Click the arrow below the **Delete** button in the **Cells** group on the **Home** tab, and notice that, when a table is selected, two additional commands appear for table rows and table columns. (The equivalent commands also appear on the **Insert** menu.)

9   Click **Delete Table Rows**, which allows you to easily make modifications while leaving adjacent data on the worksheet undisturbed. Doing so removes only the selected rows in the table (in contrast, the **Delete Sheet Rows** command would remove selected rows all the way across the worksheet). Keep in mind, however, that inserting or deleting table rows or columns will still shift, and possibly misalign, adjacent cells.

TIP Consider the possibility of future modifications when building worksheets. If you'd like to put more than one table of data on a single worksheet, inserting and deleting rows in one table could affect tables to the right, and inserting and deleting columns could affect tables following it. Instead, consider putting additional tables on separate sheets in the same workbook. For more information, see "Creating a multisheet workbook" later in this chapter.

22

10   Click the **Seven-Year Financial Summary** worksheet tab at the bottom of the screen.

11   Select row **8** by clicking its heading number.

12   Click the **Delete** button on the **Home** tab, and notice the small triangles that now appear in the upper-left corner of each cell in rows **8** through **10**, indicating that there is a problem with the formulas in those cells.

13   Click cell **B8**, and then click the action menu that appears adjacent to the cell.

      There is not much the menu can offer that will help this time, other than **Edit in Formula Bar**, but there are a lot of cells to edit.

B8	▼	:	✕	✓	*fx*	=B6-B7-#REF!				

◢	A	B	C	D	E	F	G	H
1	Fabrikam, Inc. Seven-Year Summary							$1 = $1,000
3		2007	2008	2009	2010	2011	2012	2013
4	Income	$ 134,137	$ 142,728	$ 138,632	$ 151,841	$ 165,050	$ 169,606	$ 179,930
5	Expenses	70,962	75,925	74,167	76,774	79,381	79,805	81,684
6	Gross Profit	63,175	66,804	64,465	75,067	85,669	89,801	98,246
7	Depreciation	4,518	4,657	4,576	4,622	4,668	4,651	4,676
8	Net Profit	⬦ ▾ #REF!	#REF!	#REF!	#REF!	#REF!	#REF!	#REF!
9	Taxes	Invalid Cell Reference Error		#REF!	#REF!	#REF!	#REF!	#REF!
10	Aftertax Profit			#REF!	#REF!	#REF!	#REF!	#REF!
11		Help on this error						
12								
13		Show Calculation Steps...						
14		Ignore Error						
15		Edit in Formula Bar						
16		Error Checking Options...						
17								

14   Press the **Esc** key to dismiss the menu.

15   Press **Ctrl+Z** to undo the last action and restore the deleted cells.

      This is just a reminder that deleting cells can have consequences. In a large spreadsheet, you might not even be able to tell that something is wrong.

❌ CLEAN UP **Save the FabrikamQ1-B.xlsx workbook, and then close it.**

Removing stuff

You say *delete*, I say *erase*, she says *clear*. But let's be "clear" about what this means in Excel. What you remove, and how you do it, can make a huge difference to the integrity of your worksheet. Previously, you learned that removing cells, rows, or columns can adversely affect your worksheet structure. And of course, inadvertently removing formulas can have serious effects as well.

In Excel, removing cells completely is called *deleting*. The Delete commands on the Home tab (Delete Cells, Delete Sheet Rows, Delete Sheet Columns, and, if a table is selected, Delete Table Rows and Delete Table Columns) all change the worksheet structure by shifting remaining cells, rows, or columns up or to the left to fill the gap. Note that the Delete key on your keyboard does not "delete," in Excel terminology.

In Excel, deleting data in cells, but not the cells themselves, is called *clearing*. You can clear data by using one of the Clear commands on the Home tab (Clear All, Clear Formats, Clear Contents, Clear Comments, and Clear Hyperlinks). All of these commands remove specific cell contents, but do not alter the worksheet structure. Note that pressing the Delete key on your keyboard is equivalent to issuing the Clear command. The Backspace key also clears data in selected cells, unless you are editing text or a formula within a cell, in which case it just erases the character to the left.

SEE ALSO For more information, see "Moving and copying rows and columns" in Chapter 18, "Creating and editing worksheets."

22

Working with panes and page layout options

When you hear the words *page layout*, you probably think of printing, which used to be one of the top five issues reported by y product support. For Excel in 2013, printing has slipped down the list of issues considerably, perhaps because printing is easier than it used to be, or maybe because more people share data electronically or embedded in other documents like Microsoft PowerPoint presentations.

Of course, page layout is not just about printing, and especially in Excel, layout settings can actually affect not just printability, but the usability of a large worksheet.

In this exercise, you'll work with panes, hidden columns, margins, and the print area.

➡ SET UP **You need the UnitSales_start.xlsx workbook located in the Chapter22 practice file folder to complete this exercise. Open the UnitSales_start.xlsx workbook, save it as UnitSales.xlsx, and then follow the steps.**

1   In the **UnitSales.xlsx** workbook, select cell **B3**.

2   Click the **View** tab.

3   Click the **Split** button in the **Window** group, and observe that Excel divides the worksheet into four segments, or *panes*, divided by gray bars. Each pane is more or less independent; the panes at the top will remain in place as you scroll down, and the panes at the left will stay in place as you scroll to the right. The **Split** button is a toggle; click it again to remove the split. If you needed only a single horizontal or vertical split, you could click and drag either gray bar off of the worksheet to remove it.

	A	B	C	D
1	Unit Sales			
2	Product Number	Group	Jan-07	Feb-07
3	FABK-0001	1	397	235
4	FABK-0002	1	144	125
5	FABK-0003	1	19	56
6	FABK-0004	2	413	654
7	FABK-0005	2	373	447
8	FABK-0006	1	88	34

4   Making sure that cell **B3** is still selected (and that the panes are still split), click the **Freeze Panes** button, and then click the **Freeze Panes** command in the menu that appears; the gray bars turn into thinner gray lines. Now the panes are locked; you can only scroll the lower-right pane. Rows **1** and **2** and column **A** all remain in place, which enables you to locate where you are in the worksheet at all times.

5   Scroll to the right and down.

You can now navigate anywhere you want on the worksheet, and you'll always be able to view the row and column headers. The following graphic illustrates this. Both cells **A1** and **CH129** are visible together onscreen.

	A	CC	CD	CE	CF	CG	CH
1	Unit Sales						
2	Product Number	Jul-13	Aug-13	Sep-13	Oct-13	Nov-13	Dec-13
118	FABK-0116	124	138	140	122	80	128
119	FABK-0117	13	39	28	28	39	19
120	FABK-0118	289	233	327	226	233	440
121	FABK-0119	148	204	167	196	177	199
122	FABK-0120	47	63	59	56	36	94
123	FABK-0121	246	360	286	786	982	655
124	FABK-0122	38	81	57	42	79	83
125	FABK-0123	38	21	37	29	40	22
126	FABK-0124	93	96	96	99	91	93
127	FABK-0125	3126	1766	1569	1643	3055	594
128	FABK-0126	18	17	12	18	17	15
129	FABK-0127	176	188	171	190	191	168
130							

6   Press **Ctrl+Home** to return to the upper-left corner of the worksheet. Notice that, with **Freeze Panes** active, the upper-left cell in the active pane (**B3**) is selected rather than **A1**, which is normally the case.

7   Click the column letter **C** to select the entire column.

8   Scroll to the right until column **BV** (labeled **Dec-12**) is visible.

9   Hold down the **Shift** key and click the column letter **BV** to select all the columns except the 2013 totals.

10   Click the right mouse button anywhere in the selected column headers.

22

⊿	A	BL	BM	BN	BO	BP	BQ	BR	BS
1	**Unit Sales**								
2	**Product Number**	**Feb-12**	**Mar-12**	Apr-1			Jul-12	**Aug-12**	**Sep-12**
3	FABK-0001	459	289	15			372	366	334
4	FABK-0002	134	74	11			74	114	62
5	FABK-0003	36	53	1			21	37	14
6	FABK-0004	310	505	68			540	646	481
7	FABK-0005	589	629	32			297	477	402
8	FABK-0006	76	110	7			46	89	29
9	FABK-0007	306	345	24			387	345	411
10	FABK-0008	106	94	10			85	103	103
11	FABK-0009	198	233	17			218	120	95
12	FABK-0010	82	95	8			86	91	90
13	FABK-0011	23	50	3			38	43	25
14	FABK-0012	542	414	23			545	629	475
15	FABK-0013	156	143	12			197	136	141
16	FABK-0014	42	39	58	26	27	68	24	72
17	FABK-0015	269	240	244	261	277	285	249	277

11 Click the **Hide** command to remove the selected columns from view, leaving only the 2013 columns visible.

(The **Hide** command can also be found on the **Format** menu's **Hide and Unhide** submenu.) The relevant data on the worksheet is now easier to use, and the sheet is much easier to navigate. But you might want to print it, too.

12 Click the **File** menu, and then click **Print** to display the **Print Preview** window. Look at the preview image; not all the columns are visible; look at the bottom of the screen and notice that it will take six pages to print this sheet.

Print

Copies: 1

Print

Printer ⓘ

HP3DC86D (HP Officejet 450...
Ready

Printer Properties

Settings

Print Active Sheets
Only print the active sheets

Pages: ___ to ___

Print One Sided
Only print on one side of th...

Collated
1,2,3   1,2,3   1,2,3

Portrait Orientation

Letter
8.5" x 11"

Normal Margins
Left: 0.7" Right: 0.7"

No Scaling
Print sheets at their actual size

Page Setup

1 of 6

13 Click the **Margins** button (which currently displays **Normal Margins**), and then click **Custom Margins** to display the **Page Setup** dialog box.

14 Double-click each number in the **Top**, **Bottom**, **Left**, and **Right** boxes, and change them all to **.25**. Then select **Vertically** for the **Center on page** option. (Headers and footers are not used in this exercise, so don't worry about changing those numbers. Headers and footers wouldn't fit with such narrow margins, anyway.)

22

Page Setup

Page | Margins | Header/Footer | Sheet

Top: .25
Header: 0.5

Left: .25
Right: .25

Bottom: .25
Footer: 0.5

Center on page
☐ Horizontally
☑ Vertically

Print... Print Preview Options...

OK Cancel

15   Click **OK**.

16   Click the **Scaling** button (which is currently set to **No Scaling**) and click **Fit All Columns on One Page**; notice that now, January through December are visible in the preview, and that this sheet will now require only three pages to print.

17 Press the **Esc** key to close the **Print Preview** window. These and any other print and
    page layout settings you make are preserved the next time you save, so that the
    sheet will print the same way the next time you open it.

18 Press **Ctrl+Home** to return to cell **B3**.

19 Drag through the **B** and **BW** column headers to select them.

20 On a selected column header, click the right mouse button, and then select the **Unhide** command.

	A	B	BW	BX	BY	BZ	CA	CB	CC
1	Unit Sales								
2	Product Number	Group	Jan-13	Feb-13	Mar-13	Apr-13	May-13	Jun-13	Jul-13
3	FABK-0001	1	186	214	136	370	482	301	497
4	FABK-0002	1	121	72	154	56	62	47	153
5	FABK-0003	1	21	16	40	30	13	38	37
6	FABK-0004	2	443	510	346	520	620	413	549

	A	B	C	D	E	F	G	H	I
1	Unit Sales								
2	Product Number	Group	Jan-07	Feb-07	Mar-07	Apr-07	May-07	Jun-07	Jul-07
3	FABK-0001	1	397	235	285	481	231	362	130
4	FABK-0002	1	144	125	139	136	65	83	80
5	FABK-0003	1	19	56	10	28	14	23	28
6	FABK-0004	2	413	654	502	330	651	604	442

21 Click the **View** tab, and then click the **Split** button to turn off the split/frozen panes.

22 Press **Ctrl+Home** and notice that this time, with panes unfrozen, cell **A1** is selected.

23 Press **Ctrl+G** to display the **Go To** dialog box.

24 Enter **Z119** in the **Reference** box.

25 Hold down the **Shift** key and click **OK** to select the range **A1:Z119**.

26 Click the **Page Layout** tab, click the **Print Area** button, and then click **Set Print Area**.

27   Click the **File** tab and click **Print** to display the **Print Preview** screen; notice that the sheet is still set up to include all the columns on one page.

28   Click the **Orientation** button (which currently shows **Portrait**), and then click **Landscape**.

TIP The print area, along with other page setup settings, is saved with the worksheet. This is invaluable when you need to repeatedly print only a certain area of a worksheet.

✕ CLEAN UP Close the UnitSales.xlsx workbook without saving.

Printing row and column labels on every page

The Print Titles command, located on the Page Layout tab, allows you to specify rows and columns—typically containing labels identifying your detail data—to print on every page. This is similar to freezing panes, except that it only applies to printing, and you can specify any cell range on the worksheet, whether or not it happens to be adjacent to the labels.

In the previous exercise, you used the Hide command to conceal data that you didn't need to either display or print. In this exercise, you'll define the print area and print titles to customize your printed work.

➔ SET UP You need either the UnitSales.xlsx workbook from the previous exercise or the UnitSales_start.xlsx workbook located in the Chapter22 practice file folder to complete this exercise. If you are using the UnitSales_start.xlsx workbook, open it and save it as UnitSales.xlsx. Then follow the steps.

1   Open the **UnitSales.xlsx** workbook, if it is not already open.

2   Click the **Name** box at the left end of the formula bar, and select the named range **thirteen**.

	Group	Jan-07	Feb-07	Mar-07	Apr-07	May-07	Jun-07
	1	397	235	285	481	231	362
	1	144	125	139	136	65	83
	1	19	56	10	28	14	23
	2	413	654	502	330	651	604
	2	373	447	330	381	515	362
8 FABK-0006	1	88	34	79	43	95	97
9 FABK-0007	1	388	377	266	230	320	240

Name box: A1 — dropdown list: eight, eleven, nine, Print_Area, seven, ten, thirteen, twelve

Formula bar: Unit Sales

3   Click the **Page Layout** tab.

4   Click the **Print Area** button, and then click **Set Print Area**.

5   Click the **Print Titles** button in the **Page Setup** group on the **Page Layout** tab to display the **Page Setup** dialog box with the **Sheet** tab active.

Notice that the **Print Area** box already displays the reference **BW3:CH129**, the definition of the named range **thirteen**.

6   Click in the **Rows to repeat at top** box and then, on the worksheet, drag through row headings **1** and **2** to select the entire rows.

Notice that when you click the worksheet, the dialog box collapses, revealing any cells that were hidden beneath. (You may need to scroll up a bit to view rows **1** and **2**.) This type of box enables you to navigate around the worksheet, and then select cells, rows, or columns, which serves to enter their references into the box.

7   Click in the **Columns to repeat at left** box, and then click the column **A** heading to select it. (Again, scroll to the left if necessary to make column **A** visible.)

Page Setup

| Page | Margins | Header/Footer | **Sheet** |

Print area: BW3:CH129

Print titles

Rows to repeat at top: $1:$2

Columns to repeat at left: $A:$A

Print

☐ Gridlines

☐ Black and white

☐ Draft quality

☐ Row and column headings

Comments: (None)

Cell errors as: displayed

Page order

◉ Down, then over

○ Over, then down

Print...   Print Preview   Options...

OK   Cancel

8   Click the **Print Preview** button in the **Page Setup** dialog box.

9   Click the **Orientation** button (which usually displays **Portrait Orientation**), and select **Landscape Orientation**.

22

CLEAN UP **Save the UnitSales.xlsx workbook and close it.**

Using the Print Titles command enables you to specify any range on the worksheet that you want to print, and includes the appropriate titles for you. This setting is saved with the worksheet. If you want to print another range, all you need to do is specify a different print area; you won't need to change the print titles again unless you add more rows or columns of information that you want to include.

Adjusting page breaks

When you're printing large Excel worksheets, the location of page breaks can be a real problem. If your table is a little bit too wide to fit on a sheet, for example, you may need to print a second page containing a single column, doubling the necessary size of the printout (for example, 10 pages become 20). Excel provides some help with this.

In this exercise, you'll control page breaks and page size by using Page Break Preview.

SET UP You need either the UnitSales.xlsx workbook from the previous exercise or the UnitSales2_start.xlsx workbook located in the Chapter22 practice file folder to complete this exercise. If you are using the UnitSales2_start.xlsx workbook, open it and save it as UnitSales.xlsx. Then follow the steps.

1   In the **UnitSales.xlsx** workbook, click the **Name** box at the left end of the formula bar and enter the cell address **BW3**.

2   Click the **View** tab, and then click the **Page Break Preview** button.

This workbook already has a defined print area (as shown in the previous exercise): the white area visible in **Page Break Preview** mode. Each printed page has a watermark number superimposed on it in this view. Don't worry, the numbers won't print.

BT	BU	BV	BW	BX	BY	BZ	CA	CB	CC	CD	CE	CF	CG	CH	CI
282	331	476	186	214	136	370	482	301	497	219	395	239	207	297	
118	109	113	121	72	154	56	62	47	153	69	132	46	154	143	
34	44	27	21	16	40	30	13	38	37	44	47	52	54	52	
379	358	319	443	510	346	520	620	413	549	549	611	637	440	679	
585	293	416	479	232	621	572	463	430	635	465	362	657	259	542	
100	74	51	91	76	68	101	54	101	92	110	52	34	28	60	
234	296	314	222	362	411	442	432	341	371	295	387	309	224	242	
81	91	110	103	77	104	94	101	79	87	79	80	88	110	85	
81	93	63	257	200	149	172	111	99	244	149	291	282	235	203	
81	81	67	70	81	94	78	87	75	68	83	70	88	91	74	
64	47	61	24	64	49	61	67	64	26	46	35	42	41	42	
433	371	529	600	259	544	278	392	678	296	358	276	295	498	518	
166	154	177	123	114	184	195	178	151	175	136	103	136	179	181	
73	59	23	63	24	48	74	70	20	67	39	80	30	50	45	
256	243	259	286	301	250	299	259	282	246	242	282	248	281	310	
100	81	99	101	100	56	95	98	34	84	57	65	101	107	117	
43	27	12	26	45	20	42	37	23	21	41	13	31	20	34	
10	33	10	14	13	27	26	17	17	21	34	30	33	34	11	
114	162	156	206	196	146	164	197	132	221	121	202	122	121	194	
463	497	474	465	418	417	468	491	527	515	482	467	488	432	500	
994	225	795	726	565	258	318	804	333	244	638	506	318	327	763	
35	74	84	89	70	89	36	35	61	54	44	52	62	78	51	
379	392	458	460	536	616	570	513	598	363	451	560	381	533	535	
310	385	126	419	162	398	398	454	237	152	305	259	368	435	339	
50	64	72	55	27	83	73	84	50	31	58	55	22	34	88	
150	475	394	315	454	306	137	162	497	260	227	483	318	171	331	
118	145	56	145	141	112	71	49	90	59	74	93	116	70	98	
29	51	35	36	43	41	54	10	34	28	32	18	28	23	17	
38	80	63	51	63	41	65	70	46	34	32	86	83	79	62	
315	326	333	239	275	329	292	296	240	300	268	254	227	310	223	
110	56	109	33	65	66	50	88	44	81	92	42	111	36	60	
242	253	255	272	289	261	251	264	283	277	312	313	271	292	239	
94	81	111	101	85	104	102	108	102	105	95	94	93	98	105	
288	94	181	182	220	102	108	257	142	85	174	194	157	287	107	
90	97	82	77	70	66	76	76	93	73	98	91	98	94	95	
31	84	67	71	87	56	37	49	55	54	48	51	50	43	70	
115	37	111	39	92	72	34	79	106	91	142	120	60	83	127	
148	108	144	175	151	161	192	142	199	113	129	109	190	105	128	

60%

3   Click the **Zoom** button, in the **Zoom** group, on the **View** tab.

4   In the **Custom** box, enter **20**, and press **Enter**. (Your screen size may differ, so feel free to scroll and adjust your zoom so that all of the white areas of the worksheet are visible in **Page Break Preview**.)

5   Click the **Page Layout** tab.

6   Click the **Orientation** button, and then click **Portrait**; the display adjusts and shows that you will now print six pages; the dotted blue lines indicate page breaks. You can drag the blue lines around in **Page Break Preview** mode. Page breaks will adjust accordingly, and the worksheet will be scaled to accommodate, if necessary.

7   Point to the vertical dotted line until the pointer turns into a double-headed arrow.

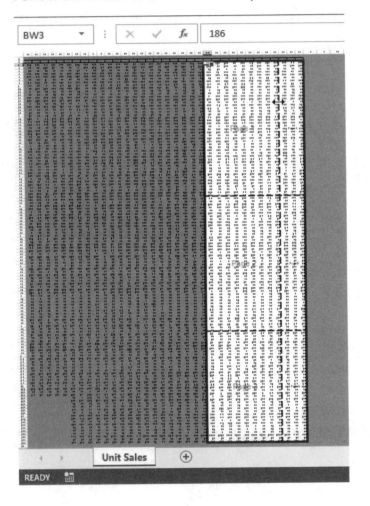

8   Click the vertical dotted blue line and drag it to the right, past the solid blue line. Take a look at the **Scale** percentage in the **Scale to Fit** area of the **Page Layout** tab; after you dragged the line, it changed to the percentage necessary to squeeze all the columns across one page for printing.

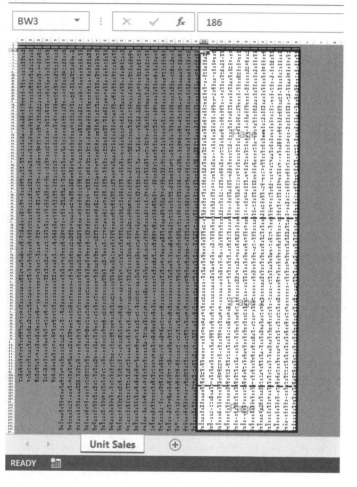

9   Click the **View** tab, and then click the **Normal** button to cancel **Page Break Preview** mode.

10   Press **Ctrl+Home** to display cell **A1**.

TIP Many View tab settings are saved with the workbook, including Page Break Preview. When you open a workbook, these settings as well as the active cell (or cell range) that was selected when you last saved are visible onscreen. You might want to change the view and select cell A1 or another cell in the main area of the worksheet before saving, especially if you share the workbook with others. In a multisheet workbook, the active sheet is also saved.

✕ CLEAN UP Save the UnitSales.xlsx workbook and close it.

Creating a multisheet workbook

Workbooks can contain as many worksheets as you can create, limited only by your good sense and your computer's memory. Putting multiple tables, data sets, presentation graphics, and similar items on a single sheet is not only unnecessary, it's probably unwise, as tempting as it may be to leverage a million rows and 16 thousand columns of sheet real estate. You can help maintain the integrity of your data and make it easier to work with by breaking free of the single-worksheet mindset. (For some good reasons not to put more than one table on a sheet, see "Inserting and deleting cells," earlier in this chapter.)

In this exercise, you'll create a multisheet workbook, format the sheets together, and then use selection and copying techniques to move data into them.

➜ SET UP You need the Q1-Transactions_start.xlsx workbook located in the Chapter22 practice file folder to complete this exercise. Open the Q1-Transactions_start.xlsx workbook, save it as Q1-Transactions.xlsx, and the follow the steps.

1   In the **Q1-Transactions.xlsx** workbook, click the **New Sheet** button *twice* (the plus-sign button next to the sheet tab at the bottom of the worksheet window) to add two new sheets to the workbook.

2   Double-click the **Q1-2013** tab, so that the name of the tab is highlighted.

3   Enter **Jan 2013** and press **Enter**.

4   Double-click the **Sheet1** tab, enter **Feb 2013,** and press **Enter**.

5   Double-click the **Sheet2** tab, enter **Mar 2013,** and press **Enter**.

22					
23					
24					
25					

◄ ► | Jan 2013 | Feb 2013 | **Mar 2013** | ⊕

READY

6   Click the **Jan 2013** sheet tab.

7   Select cells **A1:F1** (the column labels).

8   Press **Shift**, and then click the **Mar 2013** sheet tab to select all three sheets. Notice that **[Group]** now appears after the file name at the top of the Excel window.

9   Click the **Home** tab on the ribbon.

10   Click the **Fill** button in the **Editing** group, and then click **Across Worksheets**, a command that only appears when you have multiple worksheets selected.

11   Make sure that **All** is selected in the **Fill Across Worksheets** dialog box, and then click **OK**. After this, you need to make sure that only one worksheet is selected, otherwise all the edits you make to the active sheet will be performed on the other selected sheets as well.

12   Click the **Feb 2013** sheet tab (which serves to deselect the group of sheets), then click the **Jan 2013** tab again.

22

13   Select cell **B2** (the first date in the **Date** column).

14   Click the **Data** tab on the ribbon.

15   Click the **Sort A to Z** button in the **Sort & Filter** group; the button is now labeled **Sort Oldest to Newest** because the currently selected cell contains a date value.

16   Press **Ctrl+F** to display the **Find and Replace** dialog box.

17   Enter **3/1/2013** into the **Find What** box and press **Enter**.

18   Click the **Close** button or press **Esc** to close the dialog box.

19   Press the **Left Arrow** key to select the cell in column **A** adjacent to the date.

20   Hold down the **Shift** and **Ctrl** keys, and then press the **Right Arrow** Key to select all the data in the row.

	A	B	C	D	E	F	G
738	FABK-0116	2/28/2013	Theta	B	31	138.96	
739	FABK-0119	2/28/2013	Theta	B	73	156.31	
740	FABK-0122	2/28/2013	Theta	B	42	472.19	
741	FABK-0124	2/28/2013	Theta	B	31	25.25	
742	FABK-0119	2/28/2013	Theta	C	72	156.31	
743	FABK-0098	2/28/2013	Theta	D	43	29.98	
744	FABK-0125	2/28/2013	Theta	E	138	266.89	
745	FABK-0075	3/1/2013	Alpha	A	36	14.18	
746	FABK-0001	3/1/2013	Alpha	B	40	45.78	
747	FABK-0008	3/1/2013	Alpha	B	33	29.98	

21   Press the **Shift** and **Ctrl** keys, and then press the **Down Arrow** key to select all the rows of the table below, containing March transactions.

22   Press **Ctrl+X** to cut the selected cells.

23   Click the **Mar 2013** sheet tab.

24   Select cell **A2**, and then press **Ctrl+V** to paste the cut cells.

25   Click the **Jan 2013** sheet tab, and then click any cell to deselect the empty range where you just removed cells. (If you don't do this, the next step won't work, because **Find** searches only the selected cells if more than one is selected.)

26   Press **Ctrl+F**, enter **2/1/2013**, and press **Enter**.

27   Close the dialog box, and then press the **Left Arrow** key to select the adjacent cell in column **A**.

28   Hold down the **Shift** and **Ctrl** keys, and then press the **Right Arrow** key to select the row of data.

29   Press the **Shift** and **Ctrl** keys, and then press the **Down Arrow** key to select all the February transactions.

30   Press **Ctrl+X** to cut the selected cells.

31   Click the **Feb 2013** sheet tab.

32   Select cell **A2**, and then press **Ctrl+V** to paste the cut cells.

	A	B	C	D	E	F	G
1	Product N	Date	Group	Channel	Qty	Unit Price	
2	FABK-007!	2/1/2013	Alpha	A	43	14.18	
3	FABK-012!	2/1/2013	Alpha	A	139	266.89	
4	FABK-000:	2/1/2013	Alpha	C	45	45.78	
5	FABK-0008	2/1/2013	Alpha	E	43	29.98	
6	FABK-011!	2/1/2013	Beta	B	15	4.70	
7	FABK-011:	2/1/2013	Beta	C	25	140.53	
8	FABK-007:	2/1/2013	Beta	E	57	314.24	
9	FABK-002(	2/1/2013	Delta	A	102	45.78	
10	FABK-0108	2/1/2013	Delta	C	30	29.98	
11	FABK-005:	2/1/2013	Epsilon	A	30	140.53	
12	FABK-010:	2/1/2013	Kappa	E	67	124.74	
13	FABK-003(	2/1/2013	Lambda	A	81	29.98	
14	FABK-004!	2/1/2013	Lambda	B	89	14.18	
15	FABK-0038	2/1/2013	Lambda	D	51	156.31	
16	FABK-005!	2/1/2013	Omega	A	35	156.31	
17	FABK-010:	2/1/2013	Omega	B	38	156.31	
18	FABK-009(	2/1/2013	Theta	B	39	29.98	
19	FABK-001(	2/4/2013	Alpha	B	33	77.35	
20	FABK-000:	2/4/2013	Alpha	D	16	781.73	
21	FABK-0008	2/4/2013	Alpha	E	44	29.98	
22	FABK-007<	2/4/2013	Alpha	E	50	108.96	
23	FABK-008<	2/4/2013	Beta	A	29	123.15	
24	FABK-007:	2/4/2013	Beta	B	53	314.24	
25	FABK-011:	2/4/2013	Beta	D	65	9.43	

Jan 2013   **Feb 2013**   Mar 2013   ⊕

READY

22

❌ CLEAN UP   **Save the Q1-Transactions.xlsx workbook and keep it open for the next exercise.**

Working with grouped sheets

When you select multiple sheets, [Group] appears next to the name of the workbook displayed at the top of the screen. If all the sheets in a workbook are selected (as in the previous exercise), just click any tab (other than the active sheet) to ungroup them.

However, if not all sheets in the workbook are selected, clicking another grouped tab activates the sheet, but does not release the group. Instead, click any non-grouped sheet to release the group. If you save a workbook with grouped sheets, the group will be there the next time you open it. Don't do it.

When sheets are grouped, anything you enter or edit in any one of them is duplicated in the others, including entering and formatting data, inserting graphics, changing column widths, and so on. This is a great feature when you need to create an assort-ment of similar worksheets. But be careful. Check that [Group] indicator and make sure it's gone before you start editing individual sheets.

Manipulating sheets

After you add sheets to a workbook, you can change their order; insert, delete, move, or copy sheets to other workbooks; or even create new workbooks from sheets.

In this exercise, you'll move, rename, and copy sheets in a workbook, and drag sheets between workbooks.

➡ SET UP **You need either the Q1-Transactions.xlsx workbook from the previous exercise or the Q1-Transactions2_start.xlsx workbook located in the Chapter22 practice file folder to complete this exercise. If you are using the Q1-Transactions2_start.xlsx workbook, open it and save it as Q1-Transactions.xlsx. Then follow the steps.**

1   In the **Q1-Transactions.xlsx** workbook, click the **Add Sheet** button (the plus sign) next to the sheet tabs at the bottom of the workbook window. **Sheet1** appears be-tween the **Jan 2013** and **Feb 2013** tabs.

2   Click the **Sheet1** tab and drag it until the black arrow indicator is to the left of the **Jan 2013** tab.

3   Release the mouse button.

22			
23			
24			
25			

◄ ► | Jan 2013 | **Sheet1** | Feb 2013 | Mar 2013 | ⊕

READY

22			
23			
24			
25			

◄ ► | **Sheet1** | Jan 2013 | Feb 2013 | Mar 2013 | ⊕

READY

4   Double-click the **Sheet1** tab, enter **Summary**, and press **Enter**.

5   Right-click the **Jan 2013** tab to display the shortcut menu.

14	FABK-0055	1/1/2013	Gamm			4.70
15	FABK-0034	1/1/2013	Gamm			9.98
16	FABK-0107	1/1/2013	Kappa			4.74
17	FABK-0036	1/1/2013	Lambc			9.98
18	FABK-0049	1/1/2013	Lambc			4.18
19	FABK-0038	1/1/2013	Lambc			6.31
20	FABK-0102	1/1/2013	Omeg			6.31
21	FABK-0059	1/1/2013	Omeg			6.31
22	FABK-0096	1/1/2013	Theta			9.98
23	FABK-0010	1/2/2013	Alpha			7.35
24	FABK-0074	1/2/2013	Alpha			8.96
25	FABK-0071	1/2/2013	Beta			4.24

Shortcut menu:
Insert...
Delete
Rename
Move or Copy...
View Code
Protect Sheet...
Tab Color   ►
Hide
Unhide...
Select All Sheets

◄ ► | Summary | **Jan 2013** | Feb 2013 | Mar 2013 | ⊕

READY

22

TIP Hiding a worksheet may be desirable if it contains information that others don't need to view but that may be vulnerable or unnecessarily confusing (such as formulas used to calculate values used elsewhere, or critical reference data that never changes). Hide the current worksheet by clicking the Format button on the Home tab and selecting Hide Sheet on the Hide & Unhide menu, or by right-clicking the tab of the sheet you want to hide and then clicking Hide. Once a sheet is hidden, you can unhide it with the Unhide command, which appears in the same locations as the Hide command, but only if a hidden sheet is present.

6   Click the **Move or Copy** command on the shortcut menu.

7   Click the **To Book** list and select **(new book)**.

8   Select the **Create a copy** check box.

9   Click **OK**, and Excel creates a new, unnamed workbook containing a copy of the **Jan 2013** worksheet.

10   Click the **View** tab.

11   Click the **Arrange All** button, select **Horizontal**, and then click **OK**.

12   Click the **Feb 2013** tab in the **Q1-Transactions.xlsx** workbook.

13   Hold down the **Ctrl** key and drag the **Feb 2013** tab to the other workbook; you'll notice that a small page icon with a plus sign in it appears next to the pointer, indicating a copy operation (if you didn't hold down **Ctrl**, you would move the sheet rather than copy it, and no plus sign would appear in the icon).

14   Release the mouse button and the **Ctrl** key.

15   Close the unnamed workbook without saving.

✖ CLEAN UP Save the Q1-Transactions.xlsx workbook and close it.

Summarizing a multisheet workbook

Now that you've created a multisheet workbook, you need to be able to work with the data on those sheets. The sample workbook used in the following exercise is similar to the Q1-Transactions workbook used in the previous exercise, but formatting was added on the Summary sheet, and a column of totals was added to each detail sheet by using the technique described in "Inserting rows and columns," earlier in this chapter.

In this exercise, you'll use a basic summary sheet to summarize important data by using formulas that calculate data located on the detail sheets.

 SET UP You need the **Q1-Summary_start.xlsx** workbook located in the Chapter22 practice file folder to complete this exercise. Open the **Q1-Summary_start.xlsx** workbook, save it as **Q1-Summary.xlsx**, and then follow the steps.

1 On the **Summary** sheet of the **Q1-Summary.xlsx** workbook, select cell **C5**.

2 Enter **=SUMIFS(**.

3 Click the **Jan 2013** sheet tab, and then click the **E** column header to select the entire column.

4 Press **F4** to change the reference to fixed (**$E:$E**).

5 Enter a comma.

6 Click the **C** column header to select the entire column.

7 Press **F4** to change the reference to fixed (**$C:$C**).

8 Enter a comma.

9 Click the **Summary** sheet tab, click cell **B5**, and then press **F4** three times to change the reference to mixed (**$B5**).

10 Press **Enter**.

11 Select cell **C5**, right-click the fill handle in the lower-right corner of the cell, and drag to the right to cell **E5**; a menu appears.

12 Click **Fill Without Formatting** to copy the formula without disturbing the border formats.

Top spreadsheet screenshot

Cell reference	Formula
C5	=SUMIFS('Jan 2013'!$E:$E,'Jan 2013'!$C:$C,Summary!$B5)

2013 First Quarter Sales

Product Group	Jan	Feb	Mar
Alpha	284,115.32		
Beta			
Delta			
Epsilon			
Gamma			
Kappa			
Lambda			
Omega			
Theta			
TOTAL			

Context menu:
- Copy Cells
- Fill Series
- Fill Formatting Only
- Fill Without Formatting
- Fill Days
- Fill Weekdays
- Fill Months
- Fill Years
- Linear Trend
- Growth Trend
- Flash Fill
- Series...

Bottom spreadsheet screenshot

Cell reference	Formula
C5	=SUMIFS('Jan 2013'!$E:$E,'Jan 2013'!$C:$C,Summary!$B5)

2013 First Quarter Sales

Product Group	Jan	Feb	Mar
Alpha	284,115.32	284,115.32	284,115.32
Beta			
Delta			
Epsilon			
Gamma			
Kappa			
Lambda			
Omega			
Theta			
TOTAL			

22

13   Select cell **D5**, double-click the formula bar to enable **Edit** mode (indicated in the status bar at the lower-left corner of the window), and change **Jan** to **Feb** in both references (being careful not to disturb adjacent spaces and apostrophes when deleting and typing.)

14   Press **Enter**.

15   Select cell **E5**, double-click the formula bar, and change **Jan** to **Mar** in both references.

16   Press **Enter**.

17   Select cells **C5:E5**.

18   To copy the formulas to the rest of the table, right-click the fill handle in the lower-right corner of cell **E5** and drag down to cell **E13**; a menu appears.

19   Click the **Fill Without Formatting** command to copy the formulas down the table without disturbing the border formats.

20   With all the formulas still selected, click the **Decrease Decimal** button in the **Number** group on the **Home** tab *twice*.

21   Select cells **C14:E14**.

22   Click the **AutoSum** button in the **Editing** group on the **Home** tab.

| C14 | ▼ | ⋮ | ✕ | ✓ | *fx* | =SUM(C5:C13) |

◢	A	B	C	D	E
1					
2		2013 First Quarter Sales			
3					
4		Product Group	Jan	Feb	Mar
5		Alpha	284,115	318,173	263,228
6		Beta	228,515	245,948	206,211
7		Delta	82,885	98,216	62,884
8		Epsilon	171,536	191,136	173,057
9		Gamma	172,824	167,607	143,306
10		Kappa	379,359	371,717	331,894
11		Lambda	189,831	220,828	175,183
12		Omega	711,961	750,069	630,351
13		Theta	674,544	647,147	554,125
14		TOTAL	$ 2,895,571	$ 3,010,841	$ 2,540,240
15					

✖ CLEAN UP Save the Q1-Summary.xlsx workbook, but keep it open for the next discussion.

Working with sheet references

Let's take a closer look at one of the monthly Product Group formulas created in the previous exercise. The SUMIF function simply allows you to use criteria to select specific values to add, all of which reside on other worksheets in the example. Each of the three sections of this formula contains a *sheet reference*, characterized by the presence of an exclamation point separating the sheet name from the cell address.

Formula	=SUMIFS('Jan 2013'!$E:$E,'Jan 2013'!$C:$C,Summary!$B5)		
Function and arguments	SUMIFS(Sum_Range, Criteria_Range1, Criteria1, ...)		
	Sum_Range	Criteria_Range	Criteria
Sheet references	'Jan 2013'!$E:$E	'Jan 2013'!$C:$C	Summary!$B5
Description	Refers to the totals in the Sale column on the Jan 2013 sheet	Refers to the totals in the Group column on the Jan 2013 sheet	Refers to the names in the Product Group column on the Summary sheet

A cell reference such as *$B5* used in a formula always refers to a cell on the same sheet. But if you precede a cell reference with a sheet reference, such as *Summary!*, you can access values on the Summary sheet from any sheet in the workbook.

Just one criterion was used in these formulas (the Product Group name), but you can add up to 127 criteria, each with its own criteria range. Notice the difference between the references for Criteria Range and Criteria. The Criteria Range sheet name is enclosed in single quotation marks (apostrophes, if you prefer), but the Criteria reference is not. If a reference includes a space character, as in the sheet name Jan 2013, you must enclose it in single quotation marks.

If you have a set of identical sheets in a workbook (unlike the Q1-Summary workbook), you can use a *multisheet reference* to summarize values located in the same cell on each sheet. These are sometimes called "3-D references," since they escape the two-dimensional spreadsheet grid, drilling down into a stack of worksheets. For example, if a workbook contains a set of sales totals sheets for each month (named Jan, Feb, Mar, and so on) and cell B5 contains the equivalent value on each sheet, the following formula on the Summary sheet adds up the values in cell B5 on all the monthly sheets.

```
=SUM(Jan:Dec!B5)
```

The multi-sheet reference is similar to the sheet reference in the SUMIFS formula. Just take the names of the first and last sheets in the stack you want to summarize, and separate them with a colon to create a multisheet reference. And, of course, you need to surround the multisheet reference with single quotation marks if the sheet names include spaces.

```
=SUM('Jan 2013:Dec 2013'!B5)
```

Managing multiple workbooks

You can open as many workbooks at once as your computer's memory allows, and you can move among them by pressing Alt+Tab, the system shortcut for switching windows. This is relatively new behavior in Excel. Earlier versions embraced all open workbooks under one umbrella, so to speak; a single "instance" of Excel. Now, each workbook you open generates a new window—another instance of Excel—each with its own ribbon, sheet tabs, status bar, and so on. You may appreciate this behavior if you use multiple monitors.

In the previous chapter, we explored opening additional windows to view other areas of the same workbook, or to simultaneously view the same area in different ways. (For more information about view options, see "Setting view options" in Chapter 21, "Formatting worksheets.") Windows that you create this way look nearly identical to windows of other open workbooks, because they both create separate instances of Excel. One way to tell the difference is by looking at the workbook name displayed at the top of the screen. It is a window on a workbook if the name includes a colon followed by a number (indicating which window you're looking at, such as *Book1.xlsx:5*). Otherwise, the instance in question is a different workbook.

In this exercise, you'll create another workbook window and arrange workbooks and windows together on the screen.

➡ SET UP **You need both the UnitSales_start.xlsx and FabrikamQ1_start.xlsx workbooks located in the Chapter22 practice file folder to complete this exercise. Open the Unit-Sales_start.xlsx workbook, and save it as UnitSales.xlsx. Open the FabrikamQ1_start.xlsx workbook, and save it as FabrikamQ1.xlsx. Then follow the steps.**

1   Activate the **UnitSales.xlsx** workbook.

2   Click the **View** tab, and then click **New Window**.

UnitSales.xlsx - Excel

DATA	REVIEW	VIEW	DEVELOPER

Zoom   100%   Zoom to Selection   New Window   Arrange All   Freeze Panes ▾   Split   Hide   Unhide   View Side by Side   Synchronous Scrolling   Reset Window Position

Zoom   Window

New Window

Open a second window for your document so you can work in different places at the same time.

F	G	H						M	N	O
pr-07	May-07	Jun-07	Jul-07	Aug-07	Sep-07	Oct-07	Nov-07	Dec-07	Jan-	
481	231	362	130	360	451	456	250	318	3	
136	65	83	80	80	149	121	51	56	1	

Notice that the workbook name displayed in the title bar becomes UnitSales.xlsx:2.

3   Click the **Arrange All** button in the **Window** group on the **View** tab, and then select the **Windows of active workbook** check box.

Arrange Windows   ?   X

Arrange
- ● Tiled
- ○ Horizontal
- ○ Vertical
- ○ Cascade

☑ Windows of active workbook

OK   Cancel

4   Click **OK**, and you'll notice that both active workbook windows are displayed side by side, ignoring the other open workbook. The title bars of the windows display the names **UnitSales.xlsx:1** and **UnitSales.xlsx:2**.

5   On the **View** menu of the **UnitSales.xlsx:2** window, click the **View Side by Side** button.

6   In the **Compare Side by Side** dialog box, select **UnitSales.xlsx:1** and click **OK**; the windows rearrange to horizontal tiling orientation. Notice that in the **Windows** group on the **View** tab, the **Synchronous Scrolling** button is highlighted automatically when you click the **View Side by Side** button.

7   Scroll up and down in the active window; the inactive window scrolls along with it.

22

8   Click the **View Side by Side** button again to turn it off; the windows rearrange to vertical tiling.

9   Click the **Arrange All** button again, select **Tiled**, and make sure that the **Windows of active workbook** check box is cleared.

10   Click **OK**, and another window appears, displaying the **FabrikamQ1.xlsx** workbook (as well any other workbooks that you may have open).

11   Click the **UnitSales.xlsx:1** window to activate it.

12   On the **View** tab, click the **Hide Window** button in the **Window** group, and the window disappears from the screen. Notice, however, that the remaining window still displays **UnitSales.xlsx:2** in its title bar.

13   Click the **Save** button at the top of the **Unit Sales** window.

14   Click the close window button (the **X**) in the upper-right corner of the **Unit Sales** window.

15   Click the **File** tab, click the **Open** command, and select the **Unit Sales** workbook you just closed (which should be near the top of the **Recent Workbooks** list). Notice that nothing seems to happen. Because the main window was hidden when you saved the **Unit Sales** workbook, it is open, but not visible.

16   On the **View** tab, click **Unhide**, which is only available if a hidden window is present. The **UnitSales.xlsx** filename is highlighted in the dialog box.

17   Click **OK** to unhide the workbook.

18   Click the **Save** button to save the workbook without the hidden window.

❌ CLEAN UP **Save the UnitSales.xlsx workbook and close it.**

Key points

- Excel's table features make it easier and safer to insert and delete rows and columns, as well as add rows or columns of formulas.

- You can convert tables back to regular cells by using the Convert To Range command.

- Use the Print Titles command to specify row and column labels to be printed on each page.

- Use the Freeze Panes command to keep row and column labels in view on screen.

- Page Break Preview allows you to adjust page breaks by dragging.

- To keep track of related data in the same workbook, click the New Sheet button to create additional sheets.

- You can summarize data in a multisheet workbook with formulas, by using sheet references.

- You can arrange all open workbooks and windows together on your screen by using the Arrange All button.

22

Chapter at a glance

Modify

Modify and change the style and color scheme of a selected chart, page 623

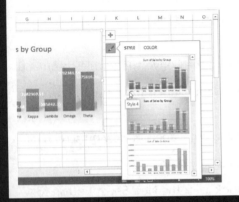

Filter

Filter data by using a slicer to focus on a specific category of data, page 629

Specify

Specify periods of time by using a timeline, page 637

Arrange

Arrange and position objects by using the drawing alignment tools, page 645

Creating charts and graphics

23

IN THIS CHAPTER, YOU WILL LEARN HOW TO

- Create and modify a chart.

- Add a slicer to a PivotChart.

- Add a timeline to a chart.

- Manipulate objects.

- Create and share graphics.

  You may not think of Microsoft Excel as the program you go to when you need to create graphics (other than charts), but most of the graphical tools available in Microsoft PowerPoint and Word are also available in Excel. In this chapter, we'll show you how to create charts, slicers, and timelines, and we'll show you some tricks that have graphical consequences.

PRACTICE FILES To complete the exercises in this chapter, you need the practice files contained in the Chapter23 practice file folder. For more information, see "Download the practice files" in this book's Introduction.

Creating and modifying a chart

Not surprisingly, charts are the most often used graphics available in Excel, complementing Excel's number-crunching prowess. Charts can "wake up" dry numeric data, revealing underlying trends and unanticipated fluctuations that might otherwise be difficult to discern.

In this exercise, you'll explore a new feature in Excel 2013 called Recommended Charts that makes the process of adding a relevant graphic just a little bit easier. After you create it, you'll use some new chart-formatting controls to modify it.

SET UP You need the FabrikamSalesTable_start.xlsx workbook located in the Chapter23 practice file folder to complete this exercise. Open the FabrikamSalesTable_start.xlsx workbook, and save it as FabrikamSalesTable.xlsx.

1   In the **FabrikamSalesTable.xlsx** workbook, make sure that cell **A2** is selected (or any cell within the table).

2   Click the **Insert** tab, and then in the **Charts** group, click **Recommended Charts** to display the **Insert Chart** dialog box with the **Recommended Charts** tab selected.

3   Select the fourth thumbnail, **Clustered Column**, in which the chart title reads **Sum of Sales by Channel**. Excel automatically determined that a PivotTable can be used to analyze this data; six of the seven charts offered are PivotCharts, as indicated by the "pivot" icons displayed in the upper-right corner of each thumbnail.

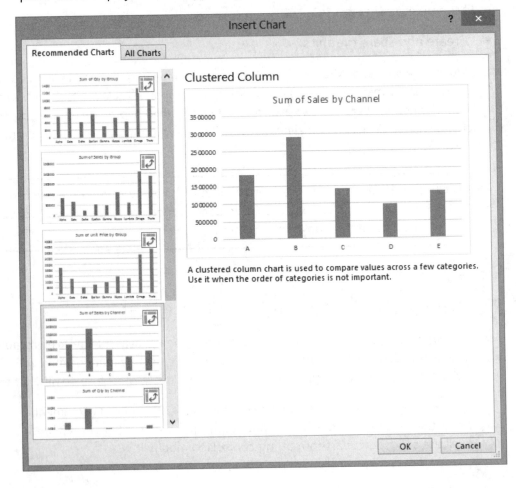

4   Click **OK**, and you'll notice that Excel creates a new worksheet, inserts a PivotChart and a PivotTable, displays the **PivotChart Fields** pane, and displays three **PivotChart Tools** tabs on the ribbon.

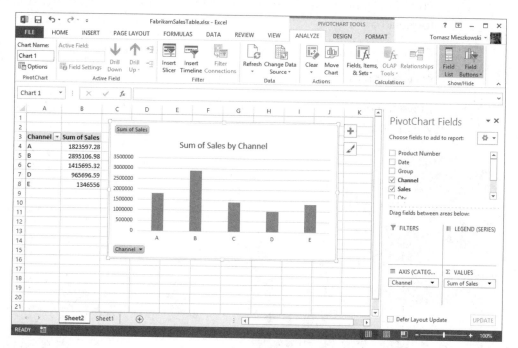

TIP If you click in the worksheet while a PivotChart is selected, the PivotChart Fields list and the PivotChart Tools tabs disappear. Click the chart to redisplay them.

5   In the **PivotChart Fields** pane, select the **Group** check box.

6   Clear the **Channel** check box. You'll notice that both the PivotTable and the PivotChart change accordingly, although the chart title is now incorrect.

7   Close the **PivotChart Fields** pane by clicking the close button (the **X** in the upper-right corner).

8   Click the chart title to select it.

TIP Don't double-click the chart title, or you'll display the Format Chart Title pane instead of selecting the title. This is a nice feature that you don't need right now, so if this happens, click the pane's close button (the X in the upper-right corner) to dismiss it.

23

9   Enter **Sales by Group**; the title does not appear to change, but the text appears in the formula bar as you enter it.

10   Press the **Enter** key, and the text in the title changes to match the text in the formula bar.

11   Click in the white area next to the chart title to deselect it.

12   Click the **Chart Styles** button to display the **Style** menu.

13   Move the pointer over any thumbnail to view a live preview of that style displayed on your PivotChart.

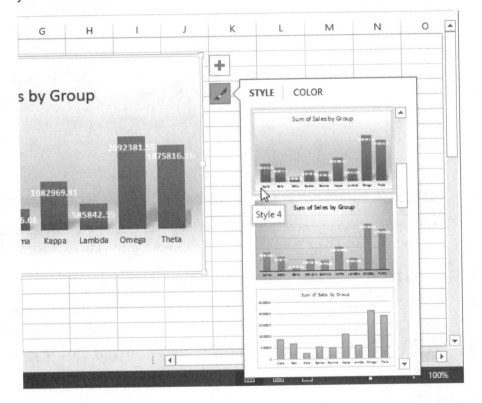

14   Click **Style 4**, a chart with 3-D shading, and then click the **Chart Styles** button again to dismiss the pane.

15   With the chart selected, click the **Chart Elements** button (the plus sign button above the **Chart Styles** button) to display its menu.

16   Clear the **Data Labels** check box; the sales totals disappear.

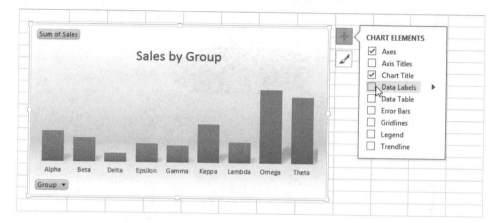

17   Click the chart to select it.

18   Click the **PivotChart Tools Analyze** tab.

19   Click the **Field Buttons** button in the **Show/Hide** group to hide the two grey buttons labeled **Sum of Sales** and **Group** that are displayed on the chart.

20   Click the **PivotChart Tools Design** tab.

21   Click the **Change Chart Type** button in the **Type** group.

22   Click **Pie** and then click the second pie type (**3-D Pie**) from the sketches displayed across the top of the **Change Chart Type** dialog box.

23   Click **OK**.

24   Click the **Chart Styles** button and select **Style 8**, a solid 3-D chart with rounded edges.

25   Click the **Chart Styles** button again to dismiss the menu.

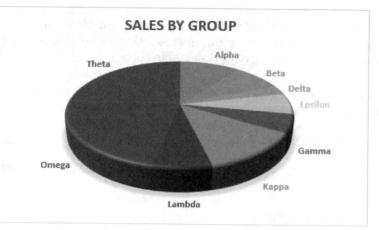

SALES BY GROUP

❌ CLEAN UP **Save the FabrikamSalesTable.xlsx workbook, and then close it.**

TIP 3-D charts are great for presentations and publications, but when accurate representation of relative values is more important than cosmetics, use 2-D charts. The foreshortening that is applied to achieve the 3-D effect distorts the shape of the chart. Areas that appear "closer" seem proportionally larger.

Adding a slicer to a PivotChart

The cryptically named slicers feature was introduced in Excel 2010 for exclusive use with PivotTables, but new in Excel 2013, you can also use them with any kind of data table as well. Slicers are interactive filters that make it easy to determine both the cause and the result of changes in your worksheet, PivotTable, or PivotChart.

In this exercise, you'll add a simple slicer to a PivotChart.

23

SET UP You need the FabrikamSalesTable2_start.xlsx workbook located in the Chapter23 practice file folder to complete this exercise. Open the FabrikamSalesTable2_start.xlsx workbook, and save it as FabrikamSalesTable2.xlsx.

1   In the **FabrikamSalesTable2.xlsx** workbook, click the chart to activate all the context-sensitive tools and tabs.

2   Click the **PivotChart Tools Analyze** tab.

3   Click the **Insert Slicer** button in the **Filter** group; a dialog box of the same name appears.

4   Select the **Channel** check box.

Insert Slicers	?	×

- ☐ Product Number
- ☐ Date
- ☐ Group
- ☑ Channel
- ☐ Sales
- ☐ Qty
- ☐ Unit Price

OK   Cancel

5   Click **OK** to dismiss the **Insert Slicers** dialog box.

6   Drag the **Slicer** box to the side, away from the chart. (We also resized the box a bit by dragging the square handles.)

7   Click the **Slicer Tools Options** tab that appeared on the ribbon after you created the slicer.

8   Click the **More** button (the downward-pointing fast-forward button) in the lower-right corner of the **Slicer Styles** palette to open it.

9   In the **Slicer Styles** palette, click the thumbnail called **Slicer Style Other 2**.

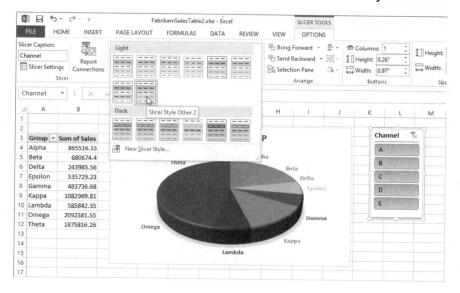

10   Click the **C** button in the slicer box to display the result in the chart. After you click, only the sales made through **Channel C** are represented, the **C** button is highlighted, and the **Clear Filter** button in the upper-right corner of the slicer box becomes active.

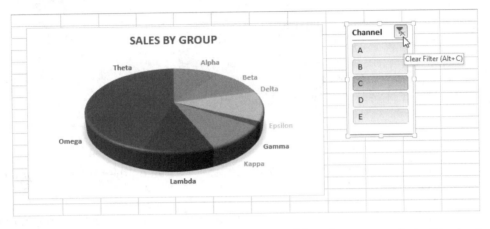

11   Click the other slicer buttons and notice the resulting changes made to the chart.

12   Click the **Clear Filter** button.

✖ CLEAN UP **Save the FabrikamSalesTable2.xlsx workbook, and then close it.**

Manipulating chart elements

After you create a chart, there is a lot you can do to change it. Sometimes it takes experimentation to arrive at the perfect chart that highlights salient information in a way that gets your point across. When a chart is selected, Excel provides many tools you can use to modify it, including context-sensitive tabs that appear on the ribbon, and the Chart Elements and Chart Styles buttons that appear adjacent to a selected chart.

In this exercise, you'll try using additional chart elements to look at your data in a different way.

SET UP You need the FabrikamSalesTable3_start.xlsx workbook located in the Chapter23 practice file folder to complete this exercise. Open the Fabrikam-SalesTable3_start.xlsx workbook, and save it as FabrikamSalesTable3.xlsx.

1   In the **FabrikamSalesTable3.xlsx** workbook, click the chart to activate the context-sensitive chart tools and tabs.

2   Click the **PivotChart Tools Design** tab.

3   Click the **Change Chart Type** button in the **Type** group.

4   Click **Column**, and then click **OK**.

5   Click the **Chart Elements** button, point to **Data Labels**, and then click the small arrow that appears to the right of the option to display the submenu.

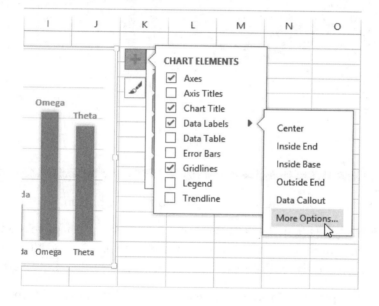

6   Click **More Options** to display the **Format Data Labels** pane.

7   In the **Label Options** section of the pane, select the **Value** check box, and clear the **Category Name** check box.

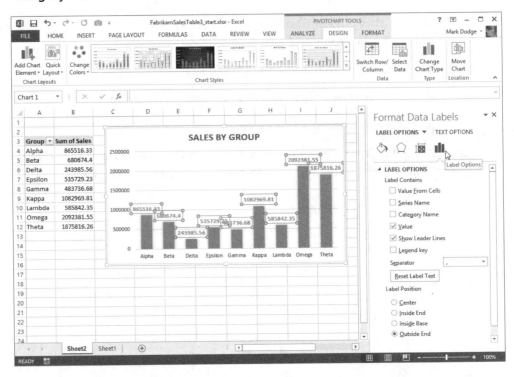

8   Dismiss the **Format Data Labels** pane by clicking its close button.

9   On the worksheet, select all the cells in column **B** containing values, cells **B4:B12**; you'll apply a format that scales them appropriately, so that they won't take up quite as much space on the screen—for example, using *$1.00 M* instead of *$1,000,000.00*.

10 Press **Ctrl+1** to display the **Format Cells** dialog box, and click the **Custom** category.

11 In the **Type** box, drag through the existing code to select it, and replace it by entering **$0.00,," M"**

Format Cells

Number	Alignment	Font	Border	Fill	Protection

Category:

General
Number
Currency
Accounting
Date
Time
Percentage
Fraction
Scientific
Text
Special
Custom

Sample

$0.87 M

Type:

$0.00,," M"

General
0
0.00
#,##0
#,##0.00
#,##0_);(#,##0)
#,##0_);[Red](#,##0)
#,##0.00_);(#,##0.00)
#,##0.00_);[Red](#,##0.00)
$#,##0_);($#,##0)
$#,##0_);[Red]($#,##0)

[Delete]

Type the number format code, using one of the existing codes as a starting point.

[OK]   [Cancel]

12   Click the **OK** button.

> **TIP** In a custom number format code, putting a comma between digit placeholders tells Excel to include thousands separators. But if you put a comma following digit placeholders, Excel scales the number by a multiple of one thousand. Adding one comma scales the number to thousands, adding two commas scales the number to millions, and so on. For example, the format code 0.0,K would display the entry 12345 in thousands as 12.3K.

> **SEE ALSO** For more information about number formatting codes, see Chapter 21, "Formatting worksheets."

13   Click in a blank area of the chart to activate it.

14   Click the **Chart Elements** button, point to **Chart Title**, and then click the small arrow that appears to the right of the option to display the submenu.

15   Click the **Centered Overlay** option, which allows the columns to sit a little taller in the chart.

CHART ELEMENTS
- ☑ Axes
- ☐ Axis Titles
- ☑ Chart Title   ▶   Above Chart
- ☑ Data Labels   Centered Overlay
- ☐ Data Table   More Options...
- ☐ Error Bars
- ☑ Gridlines
- ☐ Legend
- ☐ Trendline

TIP Double-click any chart element to open a corresponding pane docked on the right side of the screen. For example, double-click the chart title to display the Format Chart Title pane.

16   With the **Chart Elements** menu still visible, point to **Axes**, and then click the small arrow that appears to the right of the option to display the submenu.

17   Clear the **Primary Vertical** check box.

18   Click the **Chart Elements** button to dismiss the menu.

19   Click cell **A1** on the worksheet to dismiss the chart controls and **PivotChart Tools** tabs.

20   Click the **View** tab on the ribbon and clear the **Gridlines** check box in the **Show** group.

21   Click the **C** button in the slicer box.

22   Click the other slicer buttons and notice the resulting changes made to the chart.

23   Click the **Clear Filter** button.

Especially when using slicers, this column chart works better than the original pie chart to visualize the sales of each product group and display the differences among channels.

❌ CLEAN UP **Save the FabrikamSalesTable3.xlsx workbook, and then close it.**

Adding a timeline to a chart

If your data includes dates, you can use Excel's new timeline feature to zero in on specific time periods, much like the slicer feature allows you to zero in on specific categories of data.

In this exercise, you'll add a timeline to your evolving chart.

➡ SET UP **You need the FabrikamSalesTable4_start.xlsx workbook located in the Chapter23 practice file folder to complete this exercise. Open the Fabrikam-SalesTable4_start.xlsx workbook, and save it as FabrikamSalesTable4.xlsx.**

1   Click the chart to activate the context-sensitive chart tools and tabs. (You may notice that the PivotTable is no longer visible on the worksheet. It was moved out of the way, to cells **X67:Y76**.)

2   Click the **A** button in the slicer box to display only sales through **Channel A**.

3   Click one of the borders of the chart to select it; three **PivotChart Tools** tabs—
     Analyze, **Design**, and **Format**—appear on the ribbon.

4   Click the **PivotChart Tools Analyze** tab.

5   Click the **Insert Timeline** button in the **Filter** group, and then click the **Date** option
     (the only option available in the dialog box) to select it.

     TIP You can also access the timeline feature by clicking the Timeline button on the
     Insert tab.

6   Click the **OK** button to create a timeline box; it will most likely appear on top of the
     chart.

7   Drag the timeline box to the side, out of the way.

8   Click in the worksheet to deselect the chart and timeline box.

9   Click the scroll bar at the bottom of the timeline box and drag it to the left so that
     JAN is visible.

10   Click the segment of the timeline bar below **FEB** to select it, and watch while the
     chart adjusts to display only February sales.

11   Drag the handle on the right side of the **FEB** timeline bar segment to expand the
     timeframe to include **MAR**.

     At this point, you have isolated the data displayed on the chart to include only those
     sales from **Channel A** that occurred in February and March.

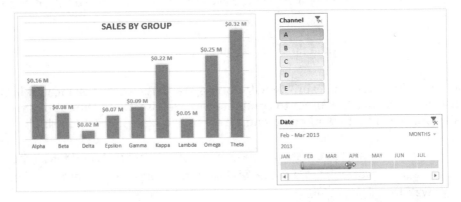

12   Click the **APR** timeline bar segment and notice that the chart goes blank, remind-
     ing you that data only exists for the first three months of the year in this particular
     workbook.

13   In the timeline box, click the small arrow adjacent to the word **Months** to display its menu, and click **Days**. Notice that the timeline bar now displays a separate bar segment for each day.

14   Scroll back to January and click the **Jan 7** segment on the timeline bar.

15   Click the handle on the right side of the selected timeline bar, and drag it to the right until January 7th through January 11th is selected.

     The chart changes to display only the selected data.

16   Make sure that the **Timeline Tools Options** tab on the ribbon is selected.

17   In the **Show** group, clear all four check boxes (**Header**, **Scrollbar**, **Selection Label**, and **Time Level**).

     These options are useful for cleaning up the layout and helping to limit user modifications.

18   In the **Show** group, select the **Header** check box (displaying the **Clear Filter** button).

19   Click the **Clear Filter** buttons in both the slicer box and the timeline box.

❌ CLEAN UP   **Save the FabrikamSalesTable4.xlsx workbook, and then close it.**

Manipulating objects

So far in this chapter, you have created three objects: a PivotChart, a slicer box, and a time-line box. Essentially, anything that does not go into a cell is an object that "floats" above the worksheet. Most of the tools on the Insert tab create objects, including shapes, SmartArt, WordArt, text boxes, and pictures.

When you click an object to select it, the appropriate tabs appear on the ribbon containing tools you can use to format and manipulate the object. An additional Drawing Tools Format tab appears whenever you select more than one object (by holding down the Shift key and selecting multiple objects); this tab contains tools for grouping, stacking, and aligning objects.

In this exercise, you'll rearrange objects and do a little resizing and formatting, as well.

➡ SET UP **You need the FabrikamSalesTable5_start.xlsx workbook located in the Chapter23 practice file folder to complete this exercise. Open the Fabrikam-SalesTable5_start.xlsx workbook, and save it as FabrikamSalesTable5.xlsx.**

1   In the **FabrikamSalesTable5.xlsx** workbook, click one of the borders of the chart to select it.

2   Hold down the **Shift** key and click the slicer box to add it to the selection; thick bor-ders appear around both selected objects.

3   Click the **Drawing Tools Format** tab that appears on the ribbon.

4   Click the **Align Objects** button in the **Arrange** group and click the **Align Top** com-mand. The tops of the two objects are now aligned. (The **Align Objects** button is la-beled **Align** if your screen is wide enough to display it. But when you point to it, the ScreenTip says **Align Objects**.)

5   Click the timeline box, and then drag it below the chart.

6   Click the **Timeline Tools Options** tab on the ribbon.

7   Clear the **Header** check box in the **Show** group (which makes the timeline box narrower).

8   Press the **Shift** key and click the chart to add it to the selection; thick borders appear around both selected objects.

9   Click the **Drawing Tools Format** tab that appears on the ribbon.

10   Click the **Align Objects** button in the **Arrange** group, and then click the **Align Left** command. The left sides of the two objects are now aligned.

11   Click anywhere in the worksheet to deselect the two objects.

12   Click the timeline box.

13   Click the center square handle on the right side of the timeline box and drag it to the right to make it wider, until it is a little too wide; past the edge of the slicer box above it.

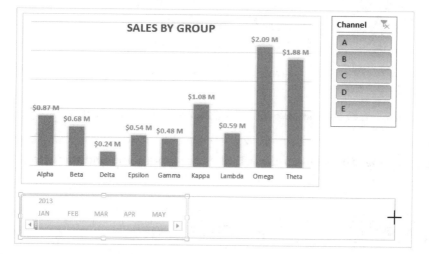

14   With the timeline box still selected, press **Shift** and click the slicer box to add it to the selection; thick borders appear around both selected objects.

15   Click the **Drawing Tools Format** tab that appears on the ribbon.

16   Click the **Align Objects** button in the **Arrange** group and then click the **Align Right** command; all the outside edges of the three objects should now be aligned.

17   Click anywhere in the worksheet to deselect the objects.

18 Click the slicer box to select it.

19 Click the lower-left square handle and drag it down and adjust until the bottom edge is lined up with the bottom edge of the chart.

20 Click the border of the chart to select it.

21 Click the **PivotChart Tools Format** tab that appears on the ribbon.

22 Click the **Shape Effects** button in the **Shape Styles** group, click **Shadow**, and then click the first option in the **Outer** section (**Offset Diagonal Bottom Right**).

23 Click in the worksheet to deselect the objects.

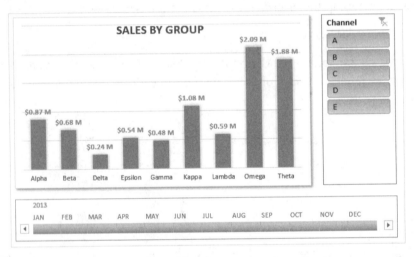

✖ CLEAN UP **Save the FabrikamSalesTable5.xlsx workbook, and then close it.**

Creating and sharing graphics

Excel probably doesn't immediately come to mind when you need to do some graphic design work, but why not? Excel has the same drawing tools that are available in other Microsoft Office applications, including Microsoft Word and Publisher. Excel workbooks can contain multiple sheets, which can be handy for filing graphic elements or sketches into categories. And of course, Excel doesn't only offer a drawing-grid feature; Excel is a grid that you can adjust.

Although no Office application will replace a dedicated graphics program, there's still a lot you can do with Excel, and you won't have to trek a steep learning curve to do it.

In this exercise, you'll take advantage of a few essential object-manipulation tricks as you create a simple logo.

→ SET UP **You need the FabrikamLogo_start.xlsx workbook located in the Chapter23 practice file folder to complete this exercise. Open the FabrikamLogo_start.xlsx workbook, and save it as FabrikamLogo.xlsx.**

1 In the **FabrikamLogo.xlsx** workbook, click the **Insert** tab on the ribbon.

2 In the **Illustrations** group, click the **Shapes** button, and then click **Oval** in the **Basic Shapes** group, and the pointer turns into a crosshair.

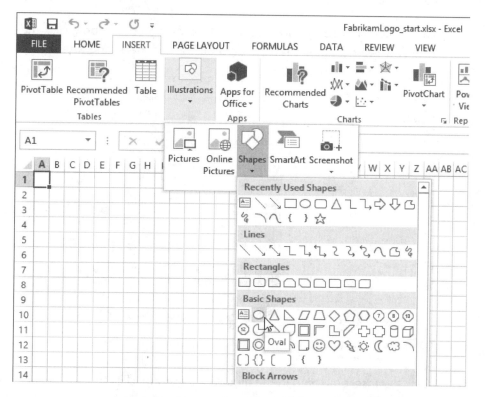

3 Position the crosshair pointer near the upper-left corner of cell **E7**.

4 Drag a shape while holding both the **Shift** and **Alt** keys, and draw a circle that is three cells wide (and of course, being a circle, is also three cells deep); **Shift** constrains the oval tool to create a perfect circle; **Alt** aligns ("snaps") the object to the cell gridlines.

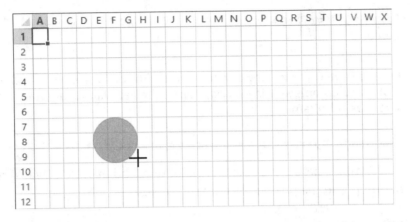

5   On the **Drawing Tools Format** tab that appears on the ribbon, click the **More** button
     (the downward-pointing fast-forward button) on the **Shape Styles** palette, and click
     Intense Effect – Blue, Accent 1.

6   Click the **Insert** tab, and in the **Illustrations** group, click the **Shapes** button, and then
     click **Oval** in the **Basic Shapes** group.

7   Position the crosshair pointer near the upper-left corner of cell **D6**.

8   While holding both the **Shift** and **Alt** keys, click and drag to draw a concentric circle that is one cell wider (and one cell taller) than the first circle.

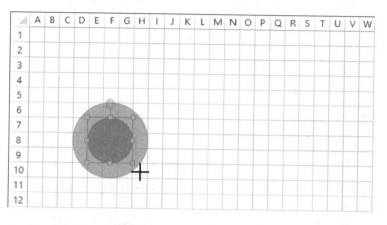

9   On the **Drawing Tools Format** tab, in the **Shape Styles** palette, click **Intense Effect – Blue, Accent 1**.

10   On the **Drawing Tools Format** tab, click the **Send Backward** button.

11   Click the **Insert** tab, and in the **Illustrations** group, click the **Shapes** button, and then click **Oval** in the **Basic Shapes** group.

12   Position the crosshair pointer near the upper-left corner of cell **C5**.

13   While holding both the **Shift** and **Alt** keys, draw a third concentric circle that is one cell wider than the second circle.

14   Click the **Drawing Tools Format** tab, and in the **Shape Styles** palette, click **Intense Effect – Blue, Accent 1**.

15   On the **Drawing Tools Format** tab, click the **Send Backward** button twice.

16   Press **Ctrl+A** to select all three objects.

17   Click the **Drawing Tools Format** tab, and in the **Arrange** group, click the **Align** button and then click **Align Bottom**.

18   Click any cell to deselect the objects.

23

19   Click the **Insert** tab, and in the **Text** group, click **Text Box** and then click anywhere on the worksheet.

20   Enter **fabrikam, inc.**

21   Press **Ctrl+A** to select the text.

22   Make sure the **Home** tab is active, and then click the **Font** drop-down list and select your favorite display font (we used **Haettenschweiler**).

23   Click the **Font Size** drop-down list and select a large size (we chose **60** points).

24   Click the **Drawing Tools Format** tab, and in the **WordArt Styles** group, click the **Text Effects** button, click **Shadow**, and then click **Shadow Options** at the bottom of the menu.

25   In the **Format Shape** pane, set the color to white, set **Blur** to **0 pt**, set **Angle** to **50°**, and set **Distance** to **3 pt**; this will allow the black text to stand out against the blue circles.

Format Shape

SHAPE OPTIONS | **TEXT OPTIONS**

◢ **SHADOW**

Presets	▢ ▾
Color	◌ ▾
Transparency	0%
Size	100%
Blur	0 pt
Angle	50°
Distance	3 pt

▷ **REFLECTION**

▷ **GLOW**

▷ **SOFT EDGES**

▷ **3-D FORMAT**

▷ **3-D ROTATION**

26 Click the dotted edge of the text box, and drag it so that the *f* is near the center of the circles.

23

27   Click anywhere in the worksheet to deselect the objects.

✖ CLEAN UP **Save the FabrikamLogo.xlsx workbook, and then close it.**

Using graphics elsewhere

Over the years, Office applications have become increasingly interoperable, making it easy to leverage the output of an application like Excel for use in other applications like Word and PowerPoint. Today, Office programs share many of the same underlying technologies, such as graphics and charting features, AutoCorrect, fonts, styles, and more. But in terms of graphics, you can usually copy something you want to share, such as a chart, and then paste it where you need it. Doing so will usually work, but not always, especially if you want to scale it—that is, make it smaller (larger often doesn't work well), as with pictures and clip art.

In this exercise, you'll use techniques that will allow you to make a static, scalable graphic image from almost anything you can display on your computer. You'll create it in one workbook and copy it to another, but you can copy the image and use it anywhere.

SET UP You need the Logo_start.xlsx and the Report_start.xlsx workbooks located in the Chapter23 practice file folder to complete this exercise. Open the Logo_start.xlsx workbook, and save it as Logo.xlsx. Open the Report_start.xlsx workbook, and save it as Report.xlsx.

1   Activate the **Logo.xlsx** workbook; if it is not visible, press **Alt+Tab** to switch windows (hold down **Alt** and press **Tab** repeatedly to cycle through all the open windows).

2   Click any of the blue circles in the logo to select it.

3   Press **Ctrl+A** to select all the objects.

4   Click the **Drawing Tools Format** tab.

5   In the **Arrange** group, click the **Group Objects** button and then click **Group**.

6   Press **Ctrl+C** to copy the selected, grouped logo.

7   Press **Alt+Tab** (repeatedly, if necessary) and activate the **Report.xlsx** workbook.

23

8   Make sure cell **A1** is selected.

9   Press **Ctrl+V** to paste the copied logo at the location of the active cell, and you'll notice that it's just a bit too large.

10 Click the selection handle on the lower-right corner of the logo and, while pressing the **Shift** key, drag to the left to make it smaller.

Although the circles seem to scale properly, the text does not. You can select the text in the pasted logo and change the font size directly, but that might not work in other situations, so we'll try a different approach.

11 With the logo selected, press the **Delete** key to remove the logo from the report.

12 Press **Alt+Tab** to return to the **Logo.xlsx** workbook.

13 Click the **View** tab on the ribbon.

14 In the **Show** group, clear the **Gridlines** check box.

15 Press **Alt+Tab** to return to the **Report.xlsx** workbook.

16 Click the **Insert** tab on the ribbon.

17 In the **Illustrations** group, click **Screenshot**.

Notice that thumbnail images of open windows are represented in the Available Windows area of the menu that appears, including Excel workbooks and other open applications.

TIP The only window from which you cannot take a screenshot is the current window—the window in which you clicked the Screenshot button. So, if you need to shoot the screen you're in, open another workbook and shoot from there. Then copy the resulting image anywhere you like.

18   Click the **Logo.xlsx** thumbnail.

19   Click the **View** tab, click the **Zoom** button in the **Zoom** group, choose **50%**, and click **OK**, allowing you to view the entire pasted image on your screen.

20   Click the **Picture Tools Format** tab and click the **Crop** button in the **Size** group.

21   Drag the center black handles on each side of the image and adjust them to crop out the rest of the image around the logo.

22   When you're done cropping the image, click the **Crop** button in the **Size** group again to finalize your edits.

23   Click the **View** tab, click the **Zoom** button in the **Zoom** group, choose **100%**, and click **OK**.

24   Drag the cropped logo image to the upper-left corner of the worksheet.

25   Drag the selection handle in the lower-right corner of the logo image and make the logo smaller, so that it fits above the chart.

26   Click anywhere in the worksheet to deselect the object.

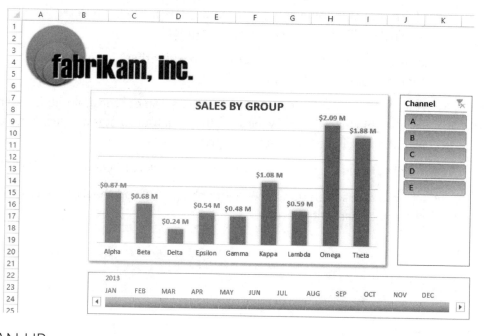

✖ CLEAN UP   **Save the Report.xlsx and Logo.xlsx workbooks, and then close them.**

Key points

- The Recommended Chart feature makes intelligent assumptions about your data and suggests the most useful chart options.

- Slicers make it easy to filter underlying chart data with just one click.

- Timelines allow you to filter chart data by specifying specific date ranges to display.

- Charts and other objects in Excel can be scaled, sized, formatted, and otherwise manipulated just like any other type of graphic.

- Excel charts and graphics are compatible with other Office programs and can be copied and pasted directly.

- Holding down the Shift key while drawing an object constrains it; for example, pressing the Shift key while drawing with the Oval tool creates a circle; doing the same with the Rectangle tool creates a square.

- Holding down the Alt key while drawing an object forces it to align with the cell grid.

- You can take screen shots of Excel graphics (and worksheets) that you can easily crop, scale, and share with anyone.

Part 5
OneNote 2013

24 Getting comfortable in OneNote 2013   679

25 Working with notebooks, sections, and pages   691

26 Using organizational tools   709

27 Sharing notes with others   735

28 Using OneNote everywhere   757

29 Saving time with OneNote   773

Chapter at a glance

View

View the normal view of OneNote, page 659

Dock

Use OneNote in Docked To Desktop view, page 660

Capture

Capture ideas with a OneNote Quick Note, page 663

Getting comfortable in OneNote 2013

24

IN THIS CHAPTER, YOU WILL LEARN HOW TO

- Get started with OneNote 2013.

- Explore the OneNote 2013 user interface.

- Modify the way OneNote looks.

- Identify new and improved features in OneNote 2013.

Microsoft OneNote 2013 is a free-form note-taking, collaboration, and research tool. It's a powerful place to capture all of your notes in the classroom or in business meetings, or even just random ideas that come into your head. You can share your notes with co-workers, family members, or anybody else you'd like to. You can also synchronize your notes across a wide variety of devices from desktops to laptops, tablets, and even your smartphone.

In this chapter, you'll explore the OneNote 2013 interface and learn about new and improved features.

Getting started with OneNote 2013

You typically start OneNote 2013 from the Start screen in Windows 8 or the Start menu in Windows 7.

The very first time you start OneNote, it will walk you through a quick process to create your first notebook. Every time you start OneNote after that, the new OneNote main screen will appear.

From the main screen, you can access your opened notebooks, create new notes, or open other notebooks.

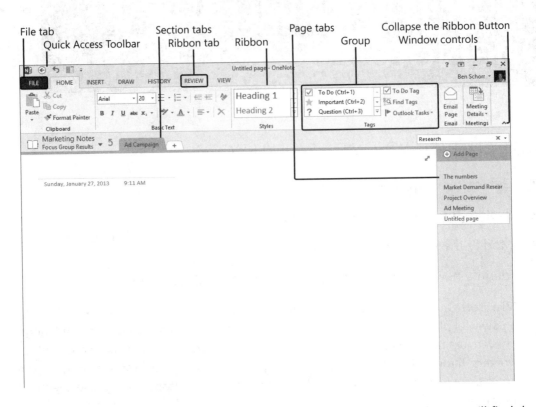

Quick Access Toolbar   Section tabs   Ribbon tab   Ribbon   Page tabs   Group   Collapse the Ribbon Button   Window controls

File tab

- **Ribbon** The main component of the OneNote interface and where you'll find the primary commands for working with the content of your notes. The ribbon is made up of task-oriented tabs, and each tab has groups of related commands. For example, on the **Home** tab, the **Clipboard** group contains commands for copying and pasting information in your OneNote notebooks.

> **IMPORTANT** The screen shots of the ribbon were captured with a screen resolution of 1024 x 768, at the default 100% magnification. If your display settings are different, then the ribbon will appear differently on your screen due to its dynamic capabilities. For example, buttons may appear stacked vertically instead of horizontally. If you notice these differences, you can either adapt the exercise instructions to your screen or modify your display settings to match ours.

> **SEE ALSO** For instructions on how to modify your display settings and adapt exercise instructions, see Chapter 1, "Getting comfortable in Office Home and Student 2013."

- **File tab** The first tab on the ribbon. Unlike other ribbon tabs, the **File** tab displays the **Backstage** view, where commands for working with the entire contents of a notebook, such as **New**, **Print**, **Share**, and **Export**, are located. The **Backstage** view is also where application options are located, and where you can find information about your user account and your version of Microsoft Office.

- **Quick Access Toolbar** Holds your most frequently used commands. By default, **Back**, **Undo**, and **Dock to Desktop** have already been added.

  TIP To add other commands you use the most to your Quick Access Toolbar, right-click the command you want on the ribbon, and then click Add To Quick Access Toolbar. To remove a command from the Quick Access Toolbar, similar to adding a command, you right-click the command you wish to remove and then click Remove From Quick Access Toolbar.

- **Title bar** Appears at the top of the window and displays the name of the active page along with the application name.

- **Notebook pane** Appears at the left side of the screen and provides access to your open notebooks and sections.

- **Section tabs** Appear across the top of the page and provide another means of access to your sections and section groups.

- **Page tabs** Appear at the right side of the screen and give you access to your individual pages.

SEE ALSO For a more comprehensive list of ribbon and user interface elements, along with detailed instructions on how to customize your user interface, including the ribbon and Quick Access Toolbar, see Chapter 1.

Exploring the OneNote interface

24

OneNote 2013 has a few options that let you control how it looks, which can significantly change your experience with the product. Most of these options can be found on the View tab of the ribbon in OneNote.

- **Normal view** A bit self-explanatory; this is the view you'll normally use in OneNote with the ribbon, **Notebook** pane, section, and page tabs all accessible.

- **Full Page view** Pushes all of the tools off the screen so that you have the maximum amount of room for notes. This is most often used on small screens or tablets, or if you just really want to minimize distractions and like to work on a "clean canvas." To exit **Full Page** view, click the **Normal View** button that appears as a double-headed arrow in the upper-right corner of the screen.

- **Dock to Desktop** A handy view when you want to work on other things but keep your notes visible to the side of the screen. **Dock to Desktop** will appear as a column on the right side of your screen (by default) where you can read, edit, and create your notes while leaving the rest of the screen free for other applications. To return to **Normal** view, click the **Normal View** button, which appears as a double-headed arrow at the upper-right of the window.

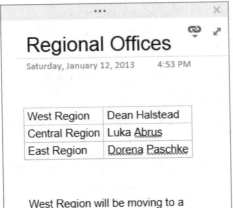

> **TIP** A common approach is to have a OneNote page docked to the desktop, as a "scratch pad" of sorts to take notes on random phone calls, articles you want to remember for later, and so on. You can use it as something of a daily work journal, creating a new page each day.

> **TIP** The docked window is on the right side of the screen by default, but you can move it to the top, bottom, or left side of the screen by simply grabbing the title bar at the top of the window and dragging it to where you want it.

- **Page Color** Enables you to choose different background colors for your pages. The colors you can choose from are very subtle but can be handy for differentiating different types of pages in your section. These colors apply only to the "paper" of your page, not to the page tab.

- **Rule Lines** This button lets you turn on or off line guides on the background of your page; this is essentially turning your clean sheet of blank paper into a college-ruled page or graph paper. They are mostly helpful if you're using ink to take notes and want the guides to align your writing or sketching. For typed notes, they're often a hindrance, because it's difficult to align your typing with the lines.

TIP The rule lines are light blue by default; you can change the color of them by selecting the Rule Line Color option in the Rule Lines gallery.

- **Hide Page Title** A surprisingly dangerous option. In fact, it should more properly be called "Remove Page Title," because it doesn't just hide the title. It actually removes the title, not only from the top of the note page, but from the page tab as well. If you use this option, your page will take on the name of whatever the first thing you've written on the page is. If you attempt to rename the page from the page tab, the page title area that you previously hid will reappear with that new name.

- **Paper Size** Lets you specify the size of your note page. Unless you're planning to print your notes, there is rarely any need to change the paper size.

- **Zoom group** The options in this group let you display your notes larger or smaller so that you can read them more easily or display more of them on the screen at a time.

- **New Window** Opens an additional OneNote window. By default, the new window will have the same note page that you're currently looking at, and you would typically then navigate in that new window to a different page so that you could have multiple OneNote pages open at the same time. You can use **New Window** to open as many windows as your computer has resources to display.

- **New Docked Window** Opens an additional OneNote window as a docked window that sits along the side of your screen, so you can have another application visible on the rest of the screen. Unlike the **Dock to Desktop** button we talked about earlier, this one opens an additional OneNote window instead of changing the view of your existing OneNote window.

- **Send to OneNote Tool** Perhaps this seems a little out of place on the **View** tab, since the dialog box it launches doesn't immediately appear to have much to do with viewing OneNote. Look all the way to the right side of the dialog box, however, and you'll find the **New Quick Note** command. That opens a small window similar to a sticky note on the screen, where you can quickly capture notes or ideas much as you might scribble on a scrap of paper.

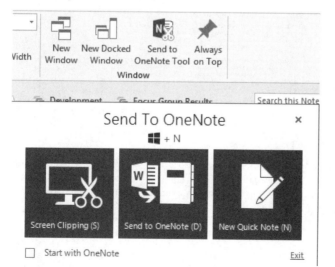

TIP Any Quick Notes you take will be found in the Quick Notes section at the bottom of the Notebook pane. You can easily move them to other notebooks and sections so you can more easily find and reference them later.

- **Always on Top** Pins the current note page so that it always appears on top of any other applications you have running. Obviously, this works best when OneNote is running in a window, rather than full screen, so that you can still view and work with other applications while OneNote is in the foreground on part of the screen.

Identifying new and improved features in OneNote 2013

This section introduces you to key application features for OneNote 2013 and includes screen shots where applicable. The majority of the features included are discussed in detail along with step-by-step instructions throughout this part of the book.

Identifying new and improved features in OneNote 2013

This section introduces you to key application features for OneNote 2013 and includes screen shots where applicable. The majority of the features included are discussed in detail along with step-by-step instructions throughout this part of the book.

- **Full Screen Mode** In **Full Screen Mode**, OneNote tucks almost all of the user interface out of the way.

- **Tighter Microsoft SkyDrive Integration** When you create a new notebook, OneNote now defaults to offering to store it on your SkyDrive, where it can be easily shared with your other devices, colleagues, or family.

24

New Notebook

- Roland Schorr Tower
- **Ben Schorr's SkyDrive**
- Other Web Locations
- Computer
- Add a Place

Ben Schorr's SkyDrive

Notebook Name:

Create
Notebook

Create in a different folder

- **Enhanced Export** OneNote can export your notes into a variety of formats, including PDF and .docx (Microsoft Word).

What's OneNote? - OneNote

Export

1. Export Current:

- Page
- **Section**
- Notebook

2. Select Format:

File Types

- OneNote 2010-2013 Section (*.one)
- OneNote 2007 Section (*.one)
- Word Document (*.docx)
- Word 97-2003 Document (*.doc)
- PDF (*.pdf)
- XPS (*.xps)
- Single File Web Page (*.mht)

Export

- **Embedded Content** OneNote 2013 has the ability to embed Microsoft Excel or Visio content. That content is dynamic, meaning that as it changes in the original file, the changes will be reflected in OneNote. The files can't be directly edited in OneNote, but a handy **Edit** button will open the file in Excel or Visio where it can be easily updated.

The numbers
Wednesday, October 17, 2012   9:18 PM

The numbers - Spreadsheet

January	10
February	20
March	15
April	25
May	27
June	30
July	32
August	35
September	31
October	36
November	40
December	44

Key points

- OneNote 2013 is a free-form note-taking and research software product. You can use it to capture notes, ideas, or web content; record audio or video; annotate images; and draw with ink or shapes—everything you can do with a paper note pad and more.

- There are a number of new features in OneNote 2013, including increased integration with SkyDrive for improved sharing and synchronizing; new views like Full Screen Mode; and improved integration with Excel and Visio for integrating dynamic content.

Chapter at a glance

Organize

Organize notebooks and sections,
page 671

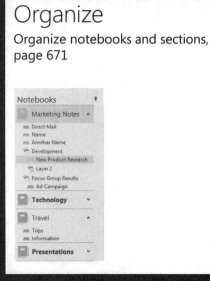

Images

Insert images and ink,
page 676

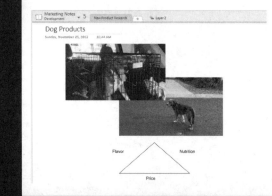

Recover

Recover deleted sections or pages,
page 684

Working with notebooks, sections, and pages

25

IN THIS CHAPTER, YOU WILL LEARN HOW TO

- Create and organize notebooks.

- Create, organize, and manage sections and section groups.

- Create and organize pages and subpages.

- Add and organize notes.

- Insert images and work with ink and shapes.

- Recover deleted sections or pages.

Microsoft OneNote is built around the metaphor of a spiral-bound notebook—though of course you can have multiple notebooks in OneNote if you like. Each notebook is divided into sections, and each section contains the pages where your notes are located.

Before you can get started capturing ideas and research with OneNote, you need to get your notebooks, sections, and pages set up. Adding notebooks is easy. You need to decide where you want to store them and what you want to call them, but after that, you're ready to go. You can have as many notebooks as you have storage space for. Notebooks must have at least one section, but they don't have to have more than one. Likewise, each section has to have at least one page, but can have only one. It's not likely you'll want to have a notebook that has only a single section and single page in it, but you can.

PRACTICE FILES You don't need any practice files to complete the exercise in this chapter.

Creating a notebook

Creating a notebook is quite simple to do. Simply click the File tab to go to the Backstage view and then choose New. The New Notebook page appears, and it's time to make your first important choice—where to put your new notebook.

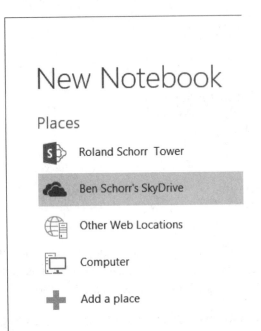

OneNote shows you the list of places it recognizes and gives you the option to add a place that it doesn't. It's worth noting that the Add A Place option only offers choices of places in the cloud. You won't get local or network locations there. The default location in OneNote 2013, as in many programs of the Microsoft Office Home and Student 2013 suite, is on your Microsoft SkyDrive. On the list shown just previously, you may notice from the icon that the first place listed is a Microsoft SharePoint site.

When you are choosing a location to store your new notebook, there are a few things you should know:

- If you plan to share this notebook with mobile devices, only the Windows Phone version of OneNote mobile can access notebooks stored on SharePoint. If you're an iPhone, iPad, or Android user, you'll need to store the notebook on SkyDrive.

- If you plan to share this notebook with other PCs, you can select any network location those PCs also have access to. A network file share, network storage device, Share-Point, or SkyDrive will all work fine as long as all of the PCs involved can access that location.

- After you've selected your location, give your notebook a name. Choose a name that makes sense to you, but try not to make it too long. *Marketing* and *Clients* are great names. *Collection of notes about my trips throughout North Carolina, California, Canada, and much of Southern Mississippi* is a poor name.

- With your location chosen and notebook named, click **Create Notebook**. Your new notebook is created and opened in OneNote with a single section and a single page within that section.

Creating and organizing sections

OneNote helpfully creates the first section for you, and it's a safe bet that you don't really want that section to be named *New Section 1*. To rename the section, right-click the section tab and select Rename from the menu that appears (or just double-click the name on the section tab).

The same naming guidelines you followed for the notebooks apply to sections, as well. The names should be descriptive but not ridiculously long or detailed.

TIP Try to avoid using too much punctuation in notebook or section names. Notebooks are stored as folders and sections as files; too much punctuation can cause problems with synchronization and file storage.

Creating a new section is as simple as clicking the + tab. When you do so, OneNote creates a new section and names it *New Section x*. Rename it to whatever you'd like, as described previously.

If you'd like to rearrange the order of your sections, just click a tab and drag it left or right along the tab row above your page or drag a section up or down on the Navigation pane at the left.

SEE ALSO If you need a refresher on section tabs or the Navigation pane, see Chapter 24, "Getting comfortable in OneNote 2013."

Section groups

Now that we've looked at notebooks and sections, you're probably wondering what section groups are. Section groups are merely an organizational construct that let you group your sections together in a logical fashion (hence the name).

- To create a section group, right-click any of the section tabs or the empty space to the right of the section tabs and select **New Section Group**.

- A group called **New Section Group** will be created, which you can right-click and rename.

- Click the section group to go into it, and click the green swirly arrow at the left side of the section tabs to go back up to the previous level.

TIP You can create just about as many layers of section groups as you want, but don't get too crazy about it. Nine layers of section groups could be rather difficult to easily navigate.

To add a section to a section group, click in that section group and create a new section. To move existing sections into a section group, drag them onto the section group.

25

Creating and organizing pages

The real york in OneNote gets done on pages. All the rest (notebooks, sections, section groups) are just a framework to help organize those pages. Everything we talk about when it comes to typing notes or inserting images or ink happens on pages.

Creating a page is quite simple:

- At the top of the page list on the right side of the screen, click **Add Page**. A new page is created.

As with sections and section groups, your page will have a default name; for example, *Untitled Page*, which you are encouraged to change. There are several ways to rename your page:

- Right-click the page tab and select **Rename**
- Click in the page title area of the page (above the horizontal line) and enter a name for your page.
- Enter some text on the page. In the absence of a formal name, OneNote will use whatever the first line of text is for the title of the page.

TIP You can create as many pages as you like in a particular section.

After you've created your page, you can change the order by dragging it up or down in the page list on the right side of the window.

TIP A popular feature request is the ability to sort pages alphabetically. OneNote 2013 doesn't include that feature, but there have been Microsoft PowerToys available for download in the past that could do it.

After the page is created, click anywhere on the page to begin adding notes and content.

Creating subpages

A subpage is a regular page that is indented a bit in the page list in order to show that it is a subpage of the page above it. Do you have to use subpages? No, but you might want to, because an organizational construct will separate related data onto multiple pages.

To create a subpage, follow these steps:

1   Create a new page, as described previously, below the page where you want the subpage to appear.

2   Right-click the tab of that new page and select Make Subpage, or drag the subpage tab to the right.

Adding and organizing notes

Adding notes to a page in OneNote is as simple as clicking where you'd like the note to appear and adding your content. Most often, that content tends to be typed notes, but it can also be ink, images, web content, and more.

To add typed text, click where you want the text to appear and begin entering text. Don't be too concerned if you decide to change the layout later. You can move your notes around on the page whenever you want.

To format your text, select the text you want to format and use the formatting tools on the Home tab of the ribbon or on the Mini Toolbar that appears just above the selected text. You can apply various font colors, font sizes or types, effects like Bold or Underline, and also highlights to your text.

OneNote makes a basic set of Styles that you can use to format your notes. To apply a style, select the text you want to apply the style to, and then select the style you want to apply from the Styles gallery on the ribbon.

TIP The styles in OneNote 2013 can't be customized, and you can't create your own style. You're limited to the predefined styles that are included with the product.

Inserting images

There are a number of ways you can insert images into your notes in OneNote 2013. First, select the note page where you want the image to appear. Then use one of the following techniques to insert your image:

- On the **Insert** tab, click **Pictures** to select an image from your hard drive or **Online Pictures** to search online sources for an image or piece of clip art to insert.

- On the **Insert** tab, click **Screen Clipping** to use the **Screen Clipping** tool to select and insert a portion of your screen. This is great for inserting images of error messages or other on-screen content.

- If you have a scanner connected to your computer or device, you can click **Scanned Image** on the **Insert** tab to insert an image from your scanner.

- In some cases, you can drag images from other applications right into your notes.

- You can press the **Windows logo key+N** to open the **Send to OneNote** tool, then press **N** again to start a screen clipping action. Select a section of the screen you want to clip, and then paste it into your notes.

SEE ALSO We'll talk more about screen clipping in Chapter 35, "Getting better results with less work."

- After you've inserted an image into OneNote, you can move it to wherever you would like it to appear on the page. Just drag the image to place it. You can also resize the image by dragging one of the image's handles that appear at the sides and corners of the image when you select it.

Working with ink and shapes

OneNote was originally created to be the "killer app" on the original tablet PCs. Back in the early 2000s, Microsoft got on board to promote a variant of the laptop computer that had a touch screen. Some were laptops where the screen could lie flat; these were called *convertibles*. Others had screens that detached entirely from the keyboard, much like early, primitive, iPads. These were called *slates*. The devices ran a version of Windows that was designed specifically for tablets, and OneNote (then OneNote 2003) was a powerful tool for those early efforts at tablet computing. Though those tablets never really took off, OneNote has endured and thrived, and the ink capability of those early devices has continued in OneNote.

In this exercise, you'll explore the inking capabilities of OneNote.

➡ SET UP **You don't need any practice files to complete this exercise. Just open One-Note and open a blank page that you can practice drawing on.**

1   Click the **Draw** tab.

2   On the **Draw** tab, in the **Tools** group, you'll find a selection of pen colors and thicknesses. Click one of the pens from the pen gallery to select it, or click the **More** button on the right edge of the gallery to expand it and show more pen choices.

25

3   After you've selected a pen, click in the page area. Then draw, write, or annotate with that pen, using your mouse or a stylus.

4   To change back to entering text, click the **Type** button at the left end of the **Draw** tab.

❌ CLEAN UP **Delete the practice drawing page if you want to.**

Custom pens

If you can't find the pen you want, you can create a custom pen by clicking the Color & Thickness button in the middle of the Draw tab.

Shapes

Next to the Color & Thickness button you'll find the Shapes gallery. These shapes may look like the kind of shapes you're used to in other applications, but actually, they're just pre-defined ink strokes. That's important to understand, because you use the pens gallery to select the color and thickness of the lines in your shape.

To create a shape, select the pen you want to use from the pens gallery, and then select the shape you want to draw from the shapes gallery. Use your mouse or stylus to drag the shape onto the page where you want it to appear.

Didn't get it exactly the right size or precisely where you want it? Just drag and drop the shape where you want it or grab one of the resizing handles and make the shape larger or smaller.

25

If you want multiple copies of the same shape, select your shape, click Copy (or press Ctrl+C), then move to another part of the page and click Paste (or press Ctrl+V). You can make as many copies of the same shape as you like, then drag those shapes to various places on the page.

If you want to select multiple shapes and move them as a group, you should use the Lasso Select option. Click Lasso Select button on the Draw tab and draw a line around the shapes you want to select. When you've completed the loop, OneNote will select all of the items within that Lasso. Then you can drag the shapes or delete the group as you choose.

If the shape isn't aligned the way you'd like, you can rotate it to the right or left. Select your item and click Rotate on the Draw tab (or right-click the shape and select Rotate from the shortcut menu) to display more choices for how you can rotate the shape.

Erasing ink or shapes

If you don't like what you've drawn, you can use a couple of methods provided by OneNote to erase it. The first way, if it's something you just drew, is to simply use Undo (press Ctrl+Z). You can undo several steps in case you wish to go back further than one step. Just continue pressing the key combination until you've removed the steps you don't want.

If you accidentally undo one too many steps, you can use Redo (press Ctrl+Y) to advance one step.

If you want to do a somewhat more determined sculpting of your ink, you can use the Eraser tool on the Draw tab. When you click the Eraser tool, the pointer turns into an eraser that you can use to erase ink or shapes (or parts of them) from your page.

TIP The eraser can be used to erase parts of drawings but not of inserted images.

You have four different types of erasers to choose from. To select one, click the arrow below the Eraser button to view the menu.

The types of erasers are described in the following list.

- **Small Eraser** An eraser with a small head for very fine work.

- **Medium Eraser** An eraser that is a bit bigger than the small eraser; used for faster erasing.

- **Large Eraser** A rather large eraser head; used for wiping large swathes of the page in quick strokes.

- **Stroke Eraser** A special eraser that removes entire ink strokes with a single click. This eraser is useful for quickly removing a specific ink stroke without disturbing other ink around it.

25

Inserting space

Sometimes you'll want to move items down the page so that you can insert other items above them. The Insert Space tool helps you do that. Just point above the items you want to move down, click the Insert Space button on the Draw tab, and drag down to move all of the items below that point down.

Insert space

You can also insert space horizontally with the Insert Space tool. Simply point to the side of the page; the Insert Space line will change from a horizontal line to a vertical line. Then you can drag left or right to move everything over.

TIP The Insert Space button can also be used to remove space. If you have some blank space in your page and you want to move everything below that space up, point above the items you want to move up, click Insert Space, and drag up to remove the excess space.

To illustrate how this works, enter some text on the page. Then enter some text in a different note container that appears somewhat lower on the page. Next, click Insert Space on the Draw tab, and point to the space between those two note containers. Then drag down to insert more space between them.

Arranging shapes

Shapes don't only exist in two dimensions in OneNote. You can also layer them front to back, and for that you use the Arrange tool.

To place a shape in front of another shape, select that shape, click the Arrange tool on the Draw tab, and select Bring To Front.

After you've brought the shape to the front, drag it on top of the shape you want it to be in front of. In the following graphic, you can see that the Arrange tool has been used to bring the photo of the dog in the crate to the front of the image, and send the other dog photo to the back. Then the front photo was moved so that it overlaps the back photo.

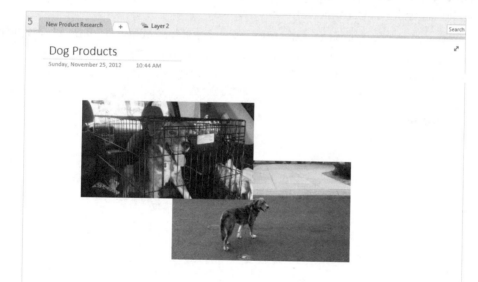

If you play around with the Arrange features, you'll find that you can create some complex layers of shapes.

Recovering deleted sections or pages

If you've deleted a page or section and want to get it back, then the Notebook Recycle Bin is your friend.

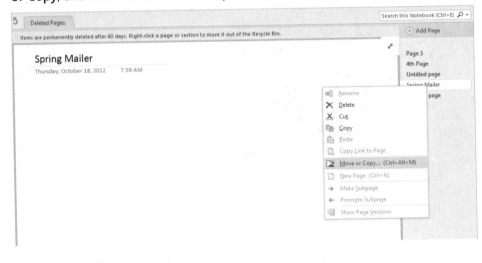

Following are the steps for restoring deleted sections or pages.

1. On the **History** tab, click the **Notebook Recycle Bin** button , and then select **Notebook Recycle Bin** from the menu that appears. OneNote displays deleted pages or sections it still has from the current notebook.

2. To restore a section or page, right-click the tab for the section or page, choose **Move or Copy**, and move it back to where you'd like it in the notebook.

TIP You can also drag to move deleted pages from the Notebook Recycle Bin back to the regular notebooks.

3   If you're sure that you don't need anything in the **Recycle Bin**, you can empty it to save a little bit of space. Just click **Notebook Recycle Bin** on the **History** tab. Then select **Empty Recycle Bin** from the menu.

Key points

- OneNote 2013 uses notebooks, sections, and pages to help you organize your notes. You can have as many notebooks as you like, each containing one or many sections. Each section can contain one or many pages.

- You can move pages and sections between notebooks.

- On a page, you can take notes with text, images, ink, shapes, or other kinds of content.

- Ink and shapes are drawn with pens, which can have many different colors or thicknesses.

- Ink and shapes can be moved, resized, or rotated as needed.

- OneNote's eraser provides several options for cleaning up any mistakes.

- If you accidentally delete a section or page, it can be recovered from OneNote's Notebook Recycle Bin.

25

Chapter at a glance

Apply

Apply tags to notes in OneNote,
page 688

New Marketing Plan

Sunday, October 28, 2012   7:12 PM

- Social Media
  - o   Twitter
  - o   Facebook
  - o   LinkedIn
? • Television Ads
  - o   Evening Drama
  - o   Weekend Comedy
  - • Radio

Connect

Connect an Outlook meeting to a
OneNote page, page 693

Flagstaff Professionals Mixer

Saturday, January 12, 2013   4:39 PM

Meeting Date: 1/10/2013 5:30 PM
Location: Marriott
Link to Outlook Item: *click here*
Invitation Message (Expand)
Participants (Collapse)
    Ben M. Schorr (Meeting Organizer)

Notes

Remember:
- Business Cards
- Lapel pin
- Name tag

Points:
- Managed Services
- New products

Organize

Organize data in tables,
page 704

West Region	Dean Halstead
Central Region	Luka Abrus
East Region	Dorena Paschke

Using organizational tools

26

IN THIS CHAPTER, YOU WILL LEARN HOW TO

- Tag your notes to make them easier to find and understand.

- Use styles to do basic formatting of your notes.

- Connect OneNote to Outlook for a power-integrated experience.

- Use hyperlinks to tie your notes together.

- Create and organize tables.

- Search your notes to find information fast.

In Chapter 25, "Working with notebooks, sections, and pages," you learned how to create notes. In this chapter, you'll examine some of the tools Microsoft OneNote 2013 gives you to organize your notes more effectively. Data capture is only half of the note-taking process. If you can't find those notes later, they aren't really very effective. Fortunately, OneNote provides a number of tools to make it easy to organize and locate those notes once you've taken them.

PRACTICE FILES You don't need any practice files to complete the exercises in this chapter.

Using tags

One of the powerful organizational features of OneNote is the ability to flag your notes with tags. Tags let you categorize and even prioritize your notes in certain ways. OneNote 2013 comes with a couple of dozen predefined tags, plus the ability to create as many of your own custom tags as you'd like. You can apply a tag that indicates that a particular note is a question, or a to-do item, or perhaps an action item that has been delegated to some-body else. You can tag items as contact information or a book to read. You can use tags to indicate that a particular item is important, or even critical.

You'll find the tags for OneNote on the Home tab of the ribbon, in the Tags gallery.

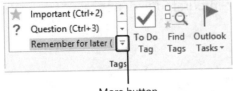

More button

In this exercise, you'll use tags to categorize some notes.

➡ SET UP **You don't need any practice files to complete this exercise. Start OneNote and use existing notes or enter some practice notes on your own. Then follow the steps.**

1   Navigate to the page where you want to tag some notes.

2   Click a note you'd like to tag.

3   Make sure you're on the **Home** tab of the ribbon, and click the **More** button to expand the **Tags** gallery.

Tags

- ☑ To Do (Ctrl+1)
- ★ Important (Ctrl+2)
- ? Question (Ctrl+3)
- Remember for later (
- 💡 Idea (Ctrl+5)
- ☺ Good! (Ctrl+6)
- ! Critical (Ctrl+7)
- ☹ Bad! (Ctrl+8)
- Definition (Ctrl+9)
- Highlight
- Contact
- Address
- Phone number
- Web site to visit
- Password
- Project A
- Project B
- Book to read
- Source for article
- Remember for blog
- Discuss with Matti
- Discuss with Jon
- Discuss with Jeff
- Send in email
- Schedule meeting
- Call back
- To Do priority 1
- Customize Tags...
- Remove Tag

4   Click the tag you would like to apply to the selected note.

You can apply several tags to the same note if you'd like. To remove a tag, right-click it and select Remove Tag.

✖ CLEAN UP There's no cleanup required unless you wish to undo the changes you made to your tags. You'll have to do it manually though, because there's no option to reset a tag.

26

Creating and customizing tags

You can customize any of the built-in tags, or you can create entirely new tags of your own.

In this exercise, you'll customize one of the built-in OneNote tags.

 SET UP **You don't need any practice files to complete this exercise. Start OneNote and follow the steps.**

1   Make sure you're on the **Home** tab of the ribbon. Click the **More** button to expand the **Tags** gallery.

2   Click **Customize Tags**.

3   Select the **Remember for Later** tag to modify, and click it.

4   Click **Modify Tag**.

5   Click the **Symbol** button.

6   Select an alternate symbol for that tag and click it.

7   Click **OK** twice to get back to your notes page.

❌ CLEAN UP **No cleanup is necessary after this exercise.**

26

It's just that easy to modify any existing tags that you like. Note that any modifications you make will not affect any notes that have already been tagged with that tag.

Creating your own custom tags is essentially the same procedure as the previous one. The only difference is that in Step 4 you would click New Tag instead of Modify Tag, and you would need to type a name in the Display Name field in the dialog box.

Using styles to format your notes

Though styles have been an important feature in Microsoft Word for years, OneNote 2010 introduced the concept of styles to OneNote. The feature has not changed much in OneNote 2013, but it remains a useful way to apply consistent formatting to your notes.

Heading 1	Phon
Heading 2	Web
Heading 3	Passw
Heading 4	ion Group
Heading 5	
Heading 6	
Page Titl	
Citation	
Quote	
Code	
Normal	
A Clear Formatting	

To use a style, select a piece of text that you would like to format with that style, then select the style you want to apply from the Styles gallery on the Home tab of the ribbon.

Styles in OneNote are especially useful for headings, quotes, and code samples. They help them stand out from the rest of your notes.

TIP The styles in OneNote can't really be customized natively, and there's no facility for adding custom styles to the list. The exception to this is the Normal style, which can be customized, in a manner of speaking, by accessing the menu bar and clicking File, Options, General and then changing the default font. There are third-party utilities, such as OneTastic, that offer some facility for customizing styles.

TIP If you really need to create a custom style, you can get part of the way there by creating a custom tag instead. The elements of a tag include font color and font highlighting. So although you can't set the font typeface or size, you could at least create a style, of sorts, that changes the color and highlighting of your selected text. Revisit the previous section for instructions about how to use and create custom tags.

Connecting OneNote to Outlook

One of the things that makes OneNote a powerful tool for task and project management is its ability to tie into another member of the Microsoft Office Home and Student 2013 suite—Microsoft Outlook.

There are really two kinds of integration that are important for you to know: integrating Outlook to OneNote, and integrating OneNote to Outlook.

There are a number of items in Outlook that you can connect to OneNote. The first and surprisingly least useful of these types of items is the email message.

Sending email messages to OneNote

You can easily send email messages to OneNote, which leads some people to try to use OneNote as some sort of massive archive system for email messages. Unfortunately, that's a task for which OneNote is not really well suited. It's better if you use Outlook itself to archive your messages. Its search capabilities are better, and the messages are more useful in their native format.

That said, it can be useful to send an email message to OneNote in order to add it to an archive of research or a project plan.

26

To send an email message to OneNote, you can select the message in the message list (or open the email message) and click the Send To OneNote button on the Home tab of the ribbon.

OneNote will display a dialog box that asks where you'd like to put that email message. If you select an existing page, OneNote will append the contents of that email message to that existing page. If you select a section, then OneNote will create a new page in that section, populated with the contents of the email message.

OneNote will insert your email message content into the selected location and even preface it with a header that indicates the subject, whom the message was from, to whom it was sent, and when it was sent.

Connecting appointments to OneNote

Far more useful than email messages are appointments or meeting items from the Outlook calendar. By sending these to OneNote, you create a workspace where you can take (and share) detailed notes about the meeting while retaining a two-way link between the OneNote page and the Outlook appointment item.

Sending an appointment or meeting item to OneNote is done almost exactly the same way as sending an email message (see the previous section). You select or open the item in Outlook and click the Meeting Notes button on the ribbon.

When you click Meeting Notes, a dialog box is displayed that asks if you'd like to share your notes with the meeting, or if you're going to take notes on your own.

26

If you select Share Notes With This Meeting Occurrence, OneNote will prompt you for a notebook and section to locate these shared notes. You may notice that not all of your notebooks are listed as possible choices. The reason is that shared notes can only be located in notebooks that are stored in shared locations, such as SkyDrive or Microsoft SharePoint. Notebooks you have on your local hard drive won't be listed as options here.

If you choose Take Notes On Your Own, OneNote will offer you any notebook you have, because sharing is not a consideration.

With either choice, subject to the aforementioned limits, as with the email messages, OneNote will ask where you'd like to send the appointment item and append it to an existing page or create a new page for you, whichever you choose.

| Direct Mail | Name | Another Name | + | New Section Group | Test Group | Search |

Weekly Review - 1/14/2013

Saturday, January 12, 2013   11:17 PM

Meeting Date: 1/14/2013 10:00 AM
Link to Outlook Item: *click here*
Participants (Collapse)
Ben M. Schorr (Meeting Organizer)

Notes

The appointment page in OneNote will include a header that tells when the meeting was scheduled for, a link back to the original Outlook item, and a list of participants (hyperlinked so that clicking on a name will initiate an email message to an individual), followed by a large area for taking extensive notes.

TIP In Chapter 29, "Saving time with OneNote," recording audio in your notes is mentioned. You can use that to capture an even richer version of the meeting, but first you should make sure you have permission from the other participants before you start the recording.

Annotating contacts

Perhaps what you'd like to take notes on is not a what or a when but rather a who. You can send an Outlook contact item to OneNote in order to create a rich set of notes on that contact.

To send the contact item to OneNote, simply select or open the contact item in Outlook and click the Linked Contact Notes button on the ribbon.

As with the other types of items, OneNote will ask you where in OneNote you'd like to place this contact item. If you select an existing page, OneNote will append the contact to that page. If you select a section, OneNote will create a new page for you, in that section, with the contact information.

Humongous Insurance
Penor, Lori

Saturday, January 12, 2013   11:39 PM

Contact	Humongous Insurance Penor, Lori
Business Phone	(310) 555-1212
Business Address	1234 Main Street Los Angeles, CA 90068
E-mail	lorip@humongousinsurance.com

Link to Outlook item

Notes

26

The page title will include the company name (if any) and the person's name (if any). Below that, a table repeats the name information, displays the phone and address information, and then displays the hyperlinked email address.

TIP Obviously, the information that can be displayed is limited by the information that's available. If you don't have the contact's email address, it won't magically appear here.

Finally, below the contact information you'll have an extensive area to take notes.

TIP This can be a good place to insert photos or images of the person, satellite photos, maps of their office location, or captured content from the contact's website.

Connecting OneNote tasks to Outlook

In past versions of OneNote, there were several different kinds of content that it would attempt to connect to Outlook, especially addresses and contact information. None of that worked especially well, so in OneNote 2013, there is just one piece that integrates to Outlook.

If you have an action item in OneNote, you can flag it with an Outlook task flag and the item will automatically appear on the Outlook Tasks list. Better still is that the connection is a two-way sync, which means that if you mark the task as complete in either OneNote or Outlook, it will be marked as complete in the other program, too.

Let's try flagging a task for follow-up. In this exercise, you'll flag a task for follow-up.

 SET UP **You don't need any practice files to complete this exercise. Start Outlook 2013 and start OneNote. Then follow the steps.**

1   In OneNote, navigate to or create a page you can use for practice.

2   Enter a note that is a sample action item, such as **Call Bob**.

3   Click the **Outlook Tasks** button on the **Home** tab of the ribbon.

4 Click **Today** to flag the item for follow-up today.

Outlook will place a red follow-up flag in front of your item. Even more important is that a corresponding item will be automatically added to your Tasks list in Outlook.

Task list

Saturday, January 12, 2013   11:57 PM

▶ Call Bob

Arrange by: Flag: Due Date | Today

Type a new task

▲ ▶ Today

Call Bob

▲ ▶ Tomorrow

Palma: Follow-up

✖ CLEAN UP You probably will want to delete that test item from your Outlook tasks list.

You can take notes on the task in OneNote, and when you've completed the task, simply left-click the flag in either OneNote or in the Outlook Tasks list. The item will be marked as complete in both products.

TIP The text that appears in the Outlook Task list is the exact text you flagged in OneNote. There isn't any context to it. That means that if you have multiple identical tasks on multiple pages (for example, "Follow Up"), you will find it difficult to differentiate those items in the Outlook tasks list. Try being a little more verbose in those cases. For example, use "Follow up: Tailspin Toys Project;" "Follow up: Contoso Marketing;" or "Follow up: Wingtip Toys proposal," and so on.

Using hyperlinks to tie your notes together

The concept of hyperlinks in information access goes back nearly 50 years, and almost nobody who uses the Internet today can remember a time when the Internet didn't use hyperlinks to navigate from place to place. OneNote 2003 supported hyperlinks to outside content and websites, but it was OneNote 2007 that introduced the concept of internal hyperlinks—links between notes in OneNote.

Internal hyperlinks let you create a link on any page that will take you to any note, page, section, or notebook you have. There are a couple of different ways to create internal hyperlinks. Let's take a look at the traditional way to do it first.

In this exercise, you'll create hyperlinks that take you from one location in your notes to a different location in your notes.

➡ SET UP **You don't need any practice files to complete this exercise. Start OneNote, and open one page where you can create your link and another page that you want to link to. Refer to the page you're creating the link on as Source and the page you're linking to as Destination.**

1   Locate the page you want to link to (**Destination**, in this example) in your page tabs.

2   Right-click the page tab of the **Destination** page and click **Copy Link to Page**.

3   Navigate to or create a page referred to as **Source**.

4   Click the **Source** page and click **Paste** on the **Home** tab of the ribbon.

OneNote will paste the link you just copied.

Source

Sunday, January 13, 2013   9:16 PM

Destination

5   Click the link you just created (**Destination**) to make sure the hyperlink takes you
directly to the **Destination** page.

In this manner, you can easily create links from any page to any page. Some people use these techniques to build a Table of Contents page that simply contains
links to the pages they use most often, even if those pages are located in totally
different notebooks. It's a quick and simple way to navigate if you have an extensive set of notebooks.

26

If you right-click any section or notebook in the Notebook pane at the left, you'll find a Copy Link To item on the shortcut menu. That lets you use the same technique you just learned to create links to notebooks or sections.

TIP Right-click the note handle to the immediate left of any note paragraph in OneNote. You'll find Copy Link To Paragraph listed there. Click it, then paste that link into your Source page. Yes, you've just created a hyperlink directly to a specific paragraph of notes.

✄	Cu̲t
📋	C̲opy
📋	**Paste Options:**
	📋
✕	D̲elete
🗐	Copy Link to P̲aragraph
	S̲elect ▸
👤	Ben M. Schorr at 12/17/2012 10:54 AM

✕ CLEAN UP No cleanup is required.

Creating custom hyperlinks to other pages

One thing you'll notice in what you've done with hyperlinking so far is that the link you're creating has the same text as the name of what you're linking to. But what if you want to have a completely different piece of text that is a link to the page?

In this exercise, you'll create hyperlinks with custom text that take you from one place in your notes to another page in your notes.

→ SET UP You don't need any practice files to complete this exercise. Start OneNote and use the same Source and Destination pages that were created in the previous exercise.

1   Right-click the **Destination** page and click **Copy Link to Page**.

2   Navigate to the **Source** page.

3   Enter **Where we want to go** anywhere on the page.

4   Select the text you just entered.

5   Click the **Insert** tab on the ribbon, and then click **Link** or press **Ctrl+K** to open the **Link** dialog box.

6   Click in the **Address** field and paste in the link you copied to the **Destination** page by right-clicking and selecting **Paste** or pressing **Ctrl+V**.

7   Click **OK**.

	Link	✕

Where we want to go

Text to display:

Where we want to go

Address:

onenote:///\\BEN-PC8\Users\Ben\Documents\Marketing%2C

Or pick a location in OneNote:

Search by text in title

All Notebooks

⊞ Flagstaff Clients

⊞ RST Clients

⊞ RST Prospects

⊞ Technology

⊞ Personal (Web)

⊞ Presentations

OK   Cancel

8   Click the **Where we want to go** link to confirm that it takes you to the **Destination** page.

The power of this technique may not be immediately obvious, but what it means is that by using the Link dialog box (via clicking Insert and then clicking Link, or pressing Ctrl+K), you can attach hyperlinks to any item in OneNote. That can be a word within a sentence or an item in a table—even a picture or piece of clip art on a page can have a hyperlink attached to it; it will take you to another notebook, section, page, or paragraph whenever you click it.

26

OneNote 2010 introduced a new way to create hyperlinks between pages. Capitalizing on the popular concept of a *wiki*, OneNote now supports what are called *wiki-style links*. A wiki link is traditionally created by enclosing the text you want to be the source of the link in double square brackets ([[text]]).

TIP Try this: On your Source page, enter **Let's go to the [[Destination]]**. When you press the spacebar after that last square bracket, OneNote should automatically convert the word *Destination* to a link to your Destination page.

When you enclose a word or phrase in double square brackets, OneNote looks in the current section to determine if a page already exists with that name. If a page by that name doesn't exist, then OneNote will check all of the other sections in the current notebook for a page with that name. If it can't find one, OneNote will automatically create a new, blank page in the current section with the enclosed text as its name.

❌ CLEAN UP **No cleanup is required.**

Creating and organizing tables

Tables are a useful organizational construct in OneNote. They allow you to arrange and organize data within a familiar structure.

Creating a basic table is quite easy. In this exercise, you'll create a basic table.

➡ SET UP **You don't need any practice files to complete this exercise. Start OneNote and open a blank page to create some practice tables.**

1   Navigate to or create your practice page for tables.

2   Click anywhere on the page and enter a piece of text.

3   Press the **Tab** key and enter some more text.

4   Press **Tab** again and enter some more text.

5   Press **Enter**.

Tables

Sunday, January 13, 2013   10:20 PM

A piece of text	Some more text	Even more text

Each time you press Tab on that first line, you'll add another column onto your table. When you press Enter, you'll create a new row. From then on, your table will have just that many columns (three in this exercise), and pressing Tab will simply move you across those three columns and then on to the next row.

 CLEAN UP **You may want to keep the practice tables page you just created for the next exercise. If you don't plan to do the next exercise, you can delete the practice tables page.**

Using the Insert Table feature

Another way to create a table, if you already know the size of the table you want, is to use the Insert Table feature.

In this exercise, you'll use the Insert Table feature to create a new table.

SET UP **You don't need any practice files to complete this exercise. Start OneNote. If you deleted the page you created in the previous exercise, create a blank new page to use in this exercise.**

1   Locate your practice tables page.

2   Click at the location on the page where you'd like to insert the table.

3   Click the **Insert** tab on the ribbon.

26

4   Click the **Table** button.

5   On the table tool that drops down, select a table up to a maximum of 10 columns wide by 8 columns long. Using your mouse pointer, select a table that fits your needs, and click it.

In the following example graphic, a table has been selected that is 7 columns wide by 6 columns long. A blank table is inserted into your notes that's the size you specified.

TIP If you want to create a table larger than the 10 x 8 maximum that the Insert Table tool allows, click Insert Table at the bottom of the Insert Table gallery instead. In the dialog box that appears, you can create a table with up to 99 columns and 99 rows.

If you need to add (or delete) columns or rows from your table after it's been created, just click in your table, click Table Tools, and then click the Layout tab that appears on the ribbon.

Here you'll find tools for selecting particular cells, rows, or columns; deleting rows or columns (or the entire table); or inserting rows or columns. You can also hide the borders of your table, add shading, or change the alignment of your text within the cells.

Another useful setting lets you sort your data in the table according to the currently selected column, either ascending or descending.

Finally, if your table has a lot of data in it, and you'd like to do some analysis or calculations on that data, you can convert it to an Excel spreadsheet.

✕ CLEAN UP You can delete the table practice page if you want.

Searching your notes to find information quickly

Having great notes is only half the battle. Being able to find those notes later is every bit as important. The search function in OneNote makes it easy for you to quickly find notes across pages, sections, or notebooks.

Above the page list on the right side of your notebook, you'll find the Search box. You can click there to enter a query or you can press Ctrl+E on your keyboard.

When you're in the Search box, enter your search term, and OneNote will search the selected scope (by default it's All Notebooks) for the term.

26

| Business | ✕ ▾ |

Finished: This Notebook (change)　　　Find on page (Ctrl+F)

In title: Business (1)

　　📄　The Morning Download: Clo...　(Marketing Notes>Direct M...

On page: Business (5)

　　📄　Humongous Insurance　　　　(Marketing Notes>Direct M...
　　📄　Ben M. Schorr　　　　　　　(Marketing Notes>Direct M...
　　📄　Flagstaff Professionals Mixer　(Marketing Notes>Direct M...
　　📄　subcontractor survey - com...　(Marketing Notes>New Sect...
　　📄　Inserting Space　　　　　　(Marketing Notes>New Sect...

　　📌　Pin Note and Audio Search results pane (Alt+O)

If you click any of the results, OneNote will display the page on the left side with the search term highlighted. Click any other search result and that page will be displayed in a similar manner. Note that once you click away from the Search Results pane, it will disappear, and you'll have to click the Search box again and re-enter your search phrase before the results will be displayed again.

TIP It's not just text that OneNote is going to search. You can search for audio recordings, the audio portion of video recordings, text recognized in pictures you've inserted, and any handwritten notes in OneNote.

Changing your search scope

Perhaps you want to narrow (or broaden) the search scope. When you click in the Search box, the Search Results pane opens, and at the upper left OneNote indicates what your current search scope is. If you'd like to search more (or less) of your content, you can change that scope. Click that link, and OneNote will allow you to change the scope to one of the following:

- This Section
- This Section Group
- This Notebook
- All Notebooks

In this exercise, you'll change the scope of your search to search across a larger (or smaller) selection of your notes.

 SET UP **You don't need any practice files to complete this exercise. Start OneNote, and then follow the steps.**

1   Click in the search box at the upper right of the screen.

2   Click **This Notebook (change)**.

3   Select the scope you want to search.

OneNote will perform your search across that scope.

TIP If you want that scope to be the default from now on, click the scope link at the upper-left corner of the Search Results pane again, and click Set This Scope As Default at the bottom of the list.

TIP Instead of clicking the Search box and changing the scope each time you only want to search the current page, press Ctrl+F on your keyboard and enter your search term.

⊗ CLEAN UP **No cleanup is necessary for this exercise.**

TIP To find an exact phrase in OneNote, enclose your phrase in quotation marks like this: "Key products in the eastern region." To limit your search results to a page that contains multiple words (not necessarily together), use AND in your query like this: *Sales AND Bicycles.*

OneNote will find variations of words if you don't use the quotation marks. For example, a search for *serving* will also find *serves*.

If you want to do a more leisurely examination of your search results without the Search Results pane constantly closing, click the Pin Note And Audio Search Results Pane link at the bottom of the Search Results pane. That will cause the pane to open as a task pane along the right side of the screen and stay open until you close it.

Key points

- Tags let you categorize, highlight, and even prioritize notes.
- Styles help you apply consistent formatting to your notes.
- Integration between OneNote and Outlook makes both products better at supporting your productivity.
- Hyperlinks let you connect notes with each other as well as the outside world.
- Tables give you a structure for organizing certain kinds of information.
- A powerful search capability makes it easy to find your notes.

26

Chapter at a glance

Share

Share your OneNote notes via SkyDrive, page 716

Collaborate

Connect to teammates by storing notebooks on a common network drive, page 718

Communicate

Use OneNote and Outlook together to send your notes to anybody, page 728

Sharing notes with others

27

IN THIS CHAPTER, YOU WILL LEARN HOW TO

- Share notes by using SkyDrive.

- Make notes available to your team on a network drive.

- Use SharePoint to share notes with your entire department.

- Send notes via email.

- Export your notes to other formats.

  In Chapter 25, "Working with notebooks, sections, and pages," you learned how to create notes. In this chapter, you'll examine some of the tools OneNote gives you to share those notes with others. Data capture is made even more powerful by collaborating on those notes with others.

  PRACTICE FILES You don't need any practice files to complete the exercises in this chapter.

Creating a new notebook on SkyDrive

In Chapter 25, you learned that the preferred storage location for OneNote files is Microsoft SkyDrive. When you store notebooks on SkyDrive, you can synchronize them with other computers and devices you own (described in Chapter 28, "Using OneNote everywhere"), and you can also share them with other people.

In this exercise, you'll create a new notebook located on SkyDrive.

SET UP You don't need any practice files to complete this exercise. Log into your Microsoft Account, and then start OneNote. If you don't already have a Microsoft Account, go to *http://www.live.com* and sign up for one (it's free).

1   In OneNote, click the **File** tab, and then click **New**.

2   Make sure your SkyDrive is selected as the storage location.

3   Give the notebook a name, and click **Create Notebook**.

4   OneNote will ask if you want to invite other people to share the notebook. Click **Invite people**.

5   OneNote will open the **Share Notebook** page and give you some options for inviting people.

6   In the **Type names or e-mail addresses** field, enter the names or email addresses of people you'd like to share this notebook with. If there are multiple names, you can separate them with semicolons (;).

7   Enter a personal message in the box provided, with a quick explanation of what the notebook is that you're sharing.

8   Click **Share** to send the invitations.

❌ CLEAN UP **You may want to delete the practice notebook you just created; otherwise, no cleanup is required.**

You do have some control over the permissions these users will have.

To the right of the field where you list he people to share with, you'll find a control that lets you specify if those people can edit the notebook or if they are to have Read-Only access. If you need to give some people Edit permissions and others Read-Only, then invite them in two separate steps. Invite the editors first, then click the File tab on the ribbon, click Share, and repeat steps 6-8 with the permissions field set to Can View.

TIP If you're paranoid about security, you can check the Require User To Sign In Before Accessing Document check box to make it more difficult for a passerby to open your notebook from the intended user's computer by using cached credentials.

After the other users start using your notebook, if they have Can Edit permissions, any changes they might make will be seamlessly synchronized to your notebook, and your changes will be seamlessly synchronized to theirs. Under ideal circumstances, these changes may appear in nearly real time. Under most circumstances, due to Internet performance and other factors, the appearance of changes may be delayed by a matter of minutes.

If you've got an existing notebook that is already on SkyDrive that you would like to share, you can simply click the File tab on the ribbon, then click Share and go through steps 6-8 as described previously.

Moving a notebook to SkyDrive

If you have an existing notebook that is not on SkyDrive that you would like to share via SkyDrive, clicking the File tab and then Share will cause OneNote to prompt you to move the notebook to SkyDrive.

In this exercise, you'll move an existing notebook to SkyDrive.

➡ SET UP **You don't need any practice files to complete this exercise. Start OneNote, open a local notebook, and then follow the steps.**

1   Select the notebook you want to share.

2   Click the **File** tab, and then click **Share.**

3   Make sure your SkyDrive account is selected as the destination location. Click it once if you need to select it.

4   You may change the notebook's name if you want to.

5   Click **Move Notebook**.

6   OneNote will notify you that the notebook is now syncing to the new location. Click **OK**.

7   OneNote will return you to the **Share Notebook** page and ask if you want to invite other people to share the notebook. If so, click **Invite people**.

OneNote will open the Share Notebook page and give you some options for inviting people.

8   In the **Type names or e-mail addresses** field, enter the names or email addresses of people you'd like to share this notebook with. If there are multiple names, you can separate them with semicolons (;).

9   Enter a personal message in the box provided with a quick explanation of what the notebook is that you're sharing.

27

10   Click **Share** to send the invitations.

OneNote will give you the same options to control what kind of sharing you'd like to offer: Can Edit or Can View.

 CLEAN UP **No cleanup is required unless you want to remove the notebook you just created.**

Stopping sharing in SkyDrive

If you'd later like to remove permissions for one or more users who share the notebook, click File, then click Share. A list of users that the notebook is shared with is displayed near the bottom of the screen. Right-click the name of the person whose permissions you'd like to change, and you'll have the option to change their permissions to Can View (or Can Edit if they were already Can View people), or you can remove their access entirely.

IMPORTANT Removing a user's sharing permissions only removes that person's access to the version of the notebook that is on your SkyDrive. If that person has already made a copy of the notebook elsewhere, there's nothing you can do to revoke her access to that notebook.

Using a file server to share notes

Many companies have a network file server (or many file servers) where it's common for users to store and share documents, spreadsheets, and other files with others in the company. This can be an excellent place to store OneNote notes for several reasons:

- It's central and presumably accessible to all members of your team.
- It's always on, which means there's no need to worry if turning your computer off at the end of the day will disrupt others' access to the notebooks.
- It's presumably secure, within the corporate firewall and thus not easily accessible to the outside world. If the information in your notes is sensitive, you may be reluctant to store those notes on a server outside the company walls (like SkyDrive).

- Your information technology (IT) department should be making sure it's regularly backed up to protect against data loss.

There are also a few disadvantages to storing your notes on the company file server:

- It's more difficult to share the notes with people outside the company.
- Unless you have a facility in place for remote access, your user may not be able to synchronize changes when they're outside of the office.
- You can't synchronize the notebooks to any mobile devices like iPads or Android phones, because those (currently) require SkyDrive for sharing.
- Sharing your notebooks via the company server is more or less like sharing any other kind of file via the company server. You'll need a folder on the company server that everybody you want to share with has the proper permissions to (read, or read/write).

  TIP This will be easier if you map a drive letter on your local computer to the share where the destination folder exists. You can do that in File Explorer by clicking Map Network Drive, entering the destination share, and selecting an available drive letter.

In this exercise, you'll create a notebook on a network file share.

➡ SET UP **You don't need any practice files to complete this exercise. Start OneNote.**

1 Click the **File** tab, then click **New.**

2 Select **Computer** as the destination location.

3   Click **Create in a different folder**.

OneNote will open the browser dialog box to let you select a different location.

4   In the **Places** pane on the left, expand **Computer** and find the drive letter that you mapped to the destination share. If you didn't map a drive letter to it, expand the **Network** group instead, find the server where the notebook is to be hosted, expand that device, and select the share where the folder is located.

5   In the **Folders** pane on the right, navigate to and select the folder where you want the notebook to be hosted. Remember, because you intend to share this notebook, you'll have to choose a folder that the people you intend to share with can access.

6   Enter a notebook name into the field at the bottom of the dialog box.

7   Click **Create**. OneNote will create the notebook with the initial section and page.

8   Click **File**, then click **Share**.

9   Click **Email Others About the Notebook**. OneNote will create an Outlook email message with a link to the new notebook already in the body of the message.

10   Address the message to the people you want to share with, enter any explanatory text you want, and then click **Send**.

Any changes you make to the notebook will be automatically and immediately synchronized to any of the other users who have that notebook open in their OneNote at the time. Synchronizing changes to a corporate server over a local network can be extremely fast, sometimes approaching real-time speeds.

✖ CLEAN UP If you didn't intend to keep the notebook you just created, you can close it from OneNote and delete it from the folder where it was created. If you actually invited others to share it in step 10, you may want to let them know it was just practice.

Stopping sharing on a file server

There are a couple of ways to stop sharing via a file server. First, you can revoke the access permissions to the file or folder where the notebook exists.

Second, you can relocate the notebook from the server to a different location that others don't have permission to, like your local hard drive.

In this exercise, you'll move a notebook from its location on the network file share to a different location.

➡ SET UP You don't need any practice files to complete this exercise. Start OneNote, and open a notebook that is being shared on your network server that you want to stop sharing.

1   Right-click the notebook that you want to relocate in the **Notebook** pane at the left.

2   Select **Properties**.

27

3 Click **Change Location**.

4 OneNote will prompt you to navigate to the new location for the notebook. Select a folder to move the notebook to.

5 OneNote will acknowledge your success. Click **OK**.

ay name: Sharing Test

Does not affect the actual notebook folder name.

r: Sharing Test

tion:

Microsoft OneNote

ⓘ Your notebook is now syncing to the new location.

OK

ult Format:

e Location...

t to 2010-2013

vert to 2007

OK   Cancel

❌ CLEAN UP   **No cleanup is required.**

Sharing notes via SharePoint

Sharing your notebooks via Microsoft SharePoint gives you some of the advantages of sharing via SkyDrive, along with some of the advantages of sharing via your local network. SharePoint is more likely to be remotely accessible than your local network drive is, and companies may feel that they have more control over SharePoint from a security standpoint (especially if your SharePoint server is hosted on premises). If you're using a Windows Phone and Windows tablets, you'll be able to sync your SharePoint-hosted notebooks to your mobile devices, but (currently) if you're using Android or iOS, you can't.

The first step in sharing a notebook via SharePoint is to select or create a document library on the SharePoint site where your OneNote notebooks will be hosted. For this example, a dedicated document library just for OneNote notebook was created, named *OneNote*.

If your SharePoint site is an Office 365 or SharePoint Online site, then you've got an easy path ahead of you. When you click File and then New your Office 365 or SharePoint account is listed as one of the options. Select that option, and OneNote will display a list of recent folders that you can choose from. If the folder you want to use is not visible, click Browse, select the OneNote document library you created (or any other document library you want), name your notebook, and click Create. Job done.

27

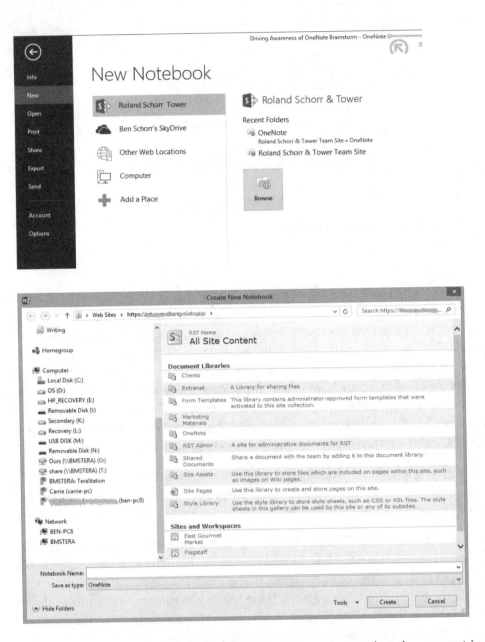

TIP If you have an Office 365 or SharePoint Online account, but the account isn't listed, you may have to add it. Click File, then Account, and add the service.

If you don't have an Office 365 or SharePoint Online account, then your route to hosted SharePoint notebooks may be slightly more primitive, but it's still not difficult to do.

In this exercise, you'll create a new notebook and move it to a corporate SharePoint server.

SET UP You don't need any practice files to complete this exercise. Start OneNote. Log into your SharePoint account if you aren't already logged in. Remember, this exercise is for people who are using corporate SharePoint. If you have SharePoint Online or Office 365 SharePoint, you can create new notebooks in essentially the same way SkyDrive users do.

1. Click the **File** tab, then click **New**.

2. Select **Computer** for your location.

3. Enter a name in the **Notebook Name** field, and then click **Create Notebook**.

4. In the OneNote **Notebook** pane, right-click your notebook and select **Properties**. Be sure to remember the notebook's location.

5. Click **Cancel**.

6. Right-click your new notebook again and choose **Close this notebook**.

7   Open your SharePoint site in Windows Internet Explorer.

8   Navigate to the document library where you want your OneNote notebook to be. You'll probably find your list of libraries along the left side of the window.

9   Upload your notebook to the document library.

> **TIP** If you don't want that notebook to stay in your SharePoint library, you can delete it from SharePoint.

> **TIP** It is often easiest to upload your notebook to the document library by clicking the Library tab in SharePoint and selecting Open With Explorer. Then you can just drag the OneNote folder to the document library.

10 Confirm that your OneNote notebook now appears in the document library, and then click the down arrow to the right of the OneNote notebook's name.

☐	Type	Name		M
	(N)	Flagstaff Clients	▾	8/
	(N)	RST Clients		8/
	(N)	RST Competitors		7/
	(N)	RST Prospects		8/
	(N)	Technology		8/
✚ Add document				

Menu:
- View Properties
- Edit Properties
- View in Browser
- Edit in Browser
- Edit in Microsoft OneNote
- Connect to Client
- Compliance Details
- Alert Me
- Manage Permissions
- Delete

11 Select **Edit in Microsoft OneNote**.

At this point, your new notebook will re-open in OneNote, and you're all set for sharing. Make sure anybody else you want to share it with has the proper permissions in SharePoint to access the notebook. They'll only need to do steps 10 and 11 in order to open it for themselves.

Now that your notebook is shared via SharePoint, OneNote will automatically sync any time you have a connection to that SharePoint server.

❌ CLEAN UP **You can delete that notebook from your SharePoint server if you want to.**

Sharing notes with others during a meeting

One of the new features of OneNote 2013 is the ability to easily share notes with others in a meeting. When you create, or accept, a meeting item in Outlook 2013, you can click the Meeting Notes button to create a OneNote page that will serve as a place to take notes during the meeting. That's not new; OneNote has done that for years. What's new is that now when you do that, OneNote will ask you if you want to take notes on your own or share notes with others in the meeting.

Select Share Notes With The Meeting and OneNote will prompt you to select a section (and page, if desired) from among your shared notebooks. If you select an existing page, that page will be attached to the meeting invitation in Outlook and shared with the other attendees. If you merely select a section, a new page will be created (and shared with those attending the meeting).

27

TIP In order to share meeting notes, the notebook containing the shared page has to be in a location that the other attendees can access. If the other attendees are all within your own company, then you can probably use a notebook shared on the company SharePoint server or a Windows file server. If some of the attendees don't have access to that resource, then you're better off using a notebook stored on SkyDrive.

During the meeting, you and the other attendees can take notes in the shared page, and you'll all be able to view each other's notes, almost like a shared whiteboard.

Sending notes via email

If you don't want to share a live notebook, another option is to send your notes via email. OneNote makes that very easy to do. Simply go to the page you want to share and click the Email Page button on the Home tab of the ribbon. OneNote will launch Outlook and create a new email message with the note page in the body of the message. All you need to do is address the message and click send. The recipient does not need to have OneNote in order to read the notes.

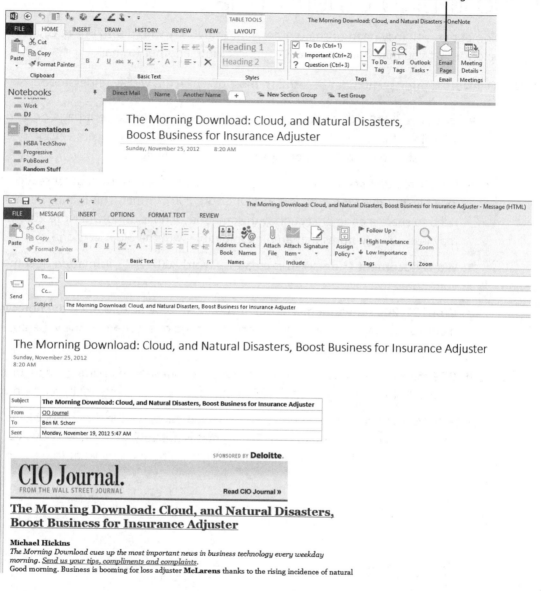

Email Page

TIP OneNote can optionally include a .one file containing the page you're emailing as an attachment to the email item. If that attachment doesn't appear when you create a new email message, then you need to enable that option. In OneNote, click the File tab, click Options, and then click Advanced, and in the Email Sent From OneNote section, make sure that the Attach A Copy Of The Original Notes As A OneNote File check box is selected.

Exporting to other formats

Sometimes you may need to share notes with somebody who doesn't have OneNote at all, and for that you may want to export your notes into another format.

OneNote supports a number of formats, most of which are widely understood.

- **OneNote 2010-2013 section (*.one)** This exports the current page or section as a .one file in the OneNote 2010-2013 format. Anybody with a recent version of OneNote will be able to open it, except those who have OneNote 2007.

- **OneNote 2007 section (*.one)** This also exports the current page or section as a .one file, but this time it does it in a OneNote 2007 format. This is convenient if you need to share a page or section with somebody who is using OneNote 2007, but you may lose a few features that aren't compatible with the older version.

- **Word document (*.docx)** This creates a Word 2007-2013 formatted document from your notes.

- **Word 97-2003 document (*.doc)** If you need to be able to open the notes in an older version of Word, you can export your page or section into the venerable .doc format.

- **PDF (*.pdf)** With this option, you can export your selected page, section, or notebook into the widely accepted PDF format. This format is essentially read-only.

- **XPS (*.xps)** You can also export your selected page, section, or notebook into XML Paper Specification (XPS) format. This format is not very widely used, however, so don't be surprised if the person you send it to isn't quite sure what to do with it.

- **Single file webpage (*.mht)** This option exports your selected page or section as an HTML document that can be viewed in most common web browsers.

- **OneNote package (*.onepkg)** Exports your selected notebook into a special *package* file that can be unpacked by OneNote 2007, OneNote 2010, or OneNote 2013. This is a great option for archiving a OneNote notebook, or if you need to ship an entire notebook to a user who has OneNote but doesn't want to use SkyDrive or SharePoint to share the file.

Exporting your notes into one of these formats is easy.

In this exercise, you'll export notes into another format.

SET UP **You don't need any practice files to complete this exercise. Start OneNote and open a notebook, section, or page that you can practice exporting.**

1   Select the page, section, or notebook you want to export.

2   Click **File**.

3   Click **Export**.

4   Select the scope of your export (page, section, or notebook).

5   Select the format you want to export to (see the bulleted list before this exercise).

6   Click **Export**.

7   Select a destination to save to (such as your local hard drive).

8   Give your exported file a name.

9   Click **Save**.

After that is done, you can send the exported file to the person you want via email, flash drive, or any other file sharing mechanism you choose.

CLEAN UP **You can delete the exported file you created.**

TIP Though you can export to a variety of formats, you can really only import from the .one or .onepkg formats. You can insert content from the other formats, but it's not the same as re-creating native OneNote content.

Key points

- OneNote 2013 makes it easy to share your notes with other people.

- You can store notebooks on a commonly accessible location such as SkyDrive, SharePoint, or a Windows file share and invite others to open those notebooks in their copy of OneNote.

- When you share notebooks from a common storage location, everyone's edits and changes will be synchronized to all of the other participants for a truly collaborative experience.

- You can email notes to people who don't have OneNote, and they'll be able to read your notes in their email client.

- You can export your notes into a wide variety of compatible formats, such as .docx or PDF, and send those files to others.

27

Chapter at a glance

Synchronize

Synchronize notebooks to multiple computers, page 735

Edit

Edit your notes in any web browser with OneNote Web App, page 738

Access

Access OneNote with OneNote Mobile on Windows Phone 8, page 741

Using OneNote everywhere

28

IN THIS CHAPTER, YOU WILL LEARN HOW TO

- Sync your notes among multiple computers.

- Access your notes in a web browser.

- Use OneNote on your phone or tablet.

In Chapter 27, "Sharing notes with others," you learned to use your notes to collaborate with others. In this chapter, you'll share notes with yourself. These days it's common for people to have multiple devices that they use on a regular basis, and your notes are more powerful and useful if you can have them with you no matter what device you're using.

The most important thing to sort out, when you're going to sync your notes among multiple computers, is the platform you're going to use to host the notes. Will you use Microsoft SkyDrive, SharePoint, a USB flash drive, or some sort of network-attached storage?

After you've figured that part out, then keeping your notes synchronized is fairly easy. With Microsoft OneNote 2013, the most common platform to use for syncing notes is going to be SkyDrive, because Microsoft Office Home and Student 2013 makes it so easy to locate your notebooks there.

PRACTICE FILES You don't need any practice files to complete the exercises in this chapter.

Syncing your notes by using SkyDrive

So let's try creating a notebook that we'll use on multiple computers. One of the natural ways to want to do that is by using the Microsoft SkyDrive cloud storage service.

In this exercise, you'll create a notebook in SkyDrive and then synchronize it to a second computer.

1   Open OneNote and click the **File** tab, then click **New**.

2   Make sure that your SkyDrive account is selected in the first column of the **New Notebook** page.

3   Give your notebook a name, and click **Create Notebook**.

4   OneNote will ask if you want to share the notebook with other people. If you want to invite other people, click **Invite People** and invite them to the notebook. As you may recall, this process was discussed in Chapter 27. If you're only going to share the notebook with yourself on other devices, then click **Not Now**.

5　Go to the other computer you want to synchronize this notebook with.

6　Open OneNote.

7　Click **File**, then click **Open**.

8　A list of notebooks that you can open on SkyDrive is displayed. Find the notebook you just created, and click that notebook. It will open in OneNote.

Just like that, you've now got a notebook open on both devices.

TIP Click the default first page created in the new notebook and enter some text. Then look at the same notebook on the other device. Assuming that both devices are connected to the Internet, the text should be displayed within a matter of seconds or a couple of minutes.

28

TIP Go to SkyDrive in Internet Explorer and find a SkyDrive-hosted notebook that isn't open in your OneNote desktop yet. Right-click the notebook and click Open In OneNote to add it to your OneNote desktop.

SEE ALSO To review the procedures for creating notebooks, read the material in Chapter 25, "Working with notebooks, sections, and pages."

This same process works for other locations as well. You can store your notebooks on a network drive, as long as all of your PCs can access that network drive. Then they'll be able to sync. You can also store your notebooks on Microsoft SharePoint and sync them that way. Just remember that as of this writing, only PCs can sync notebooks located on a network drive, and only PCs or a Windows Phone can sync notebooks located on SharePoint.

 CLEAN UP **No particular cleanup is necessary.**

Accessing your notes in a web browser

There's another good reason to store your notebooks on SkyDrive (or SharePoint). It's known as OneNote Web App.

Any notebooks you store on SkyDrive can be opened and edited in the web browser, even on computers and devices that don't have OneNote installed.

In this exercise, you'll open a notebook in OneNote Web App on SkyDrive.

➡ SET UP **You don't need any practice files to complete this exercise. You'll need to have created at least one notebook in SkyDrive to complete this exercise. Refer to the previous exercise for a refresher.**

1   Open your web browser and navigate to **https://skydrive.live.com**.

2   Log in, if prompted.

3   Find your notebooks. They should be easy to locate, because they'll be displayed in a purple color and they'll have the OneNote icon. By default, they should be located in the **Documents** folder, though you could have chosen a different folder when you created them.

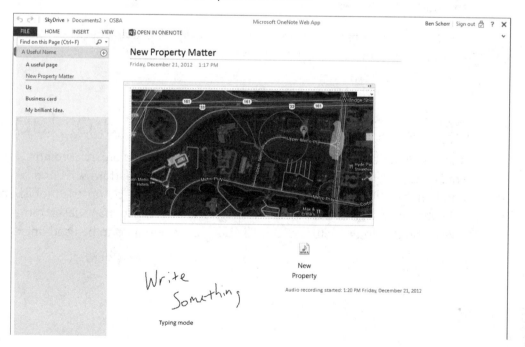

4   Select the notebook you'd like to open, and click it.

28

At this point, the notebook you select will open in the browser. OneNote Web App is considerably more limited than the desktop program, but it's perfectly sufficient to let you read or edit notes.

 CLEAN UP **No cleanup is necessary. Simply close your web browser when you're finished.**

> **IMPORTANT** OneNote Web App does not currently support opening password-protected sections. If you've got any of those, you'll need the desktop client in order to open them.

There are a couple of other limitations of OneNote Web App:

- It will display inked notes but can't create any.
- There is support for tags but no customized tags.
- It doesn't support audio or video recording.

You can easily add pages in OneNote Web App by clicking the plus sign next to the section title in the upper-left of the browser window. After you've created the new page, enter a title in the title area at the top of the page, and you can then click anywhere on the page and start typing notes.

Any pages and notes you create will automatically sync to any devices you have that are connected to your SkyDrive with OneNote.

Using OneNote on your phone or tablet

The best notes are the ones that go with you wherever you are. Accordingly, Microsoft has created OneNote Mobile apps for a number of different platforms: iPhone, iPad, Android, and Windows Phone, just to name a few. Like OneNote Web App, the mobile apps are considerably more limited than the desktop OneNote is and, in many cases, more limited than a web app due to the nature of the devices they're designed to be used on.

Any notes you create in the mobile apps can be synchronized to your desktop version of OneNote or even shared with other users. Previously, you learned how to synchronize your notes among multiple computers. In Chapter 27, you learned how to use your notes with others.

These apps are slightly different from each other and evolve so quickly that it's likely that most of them will have changed by the time you read this book. With that recognition, this section offers information on how to use each application without being so specific that this content will be outdated before the ink dries.

Using OneNote on an iPhone or iPad

OneNote Mobile for the iPhone or iPad (they are two separate apps) can be found in the iTunes App store. Currently, it's free for up to 500 pages of notes, which is actually quite a few. If you need to exceed that number of pages, then the upgrade is just a one-time charge of $4.99 currently.

Both versions of OneNote Mobile for iOS have the following key features:

- Support for multiple notebooks
- Support for viewing tables
- The ability to create bulleted lists or checklists
- The ability to insert photos in notes
- Support for OneNote tags
- The ability to search for notes

28

Both versions of OneNote Mobile for iOS have the following key limitations:

- Synchronization requires a (free) Windows account with SkyDrive.
- They do not currently support inked notes.
- Creating new notebooks or renaming sections has to be done in the desktop or Web App; they will then sync to the Mobile app.
- They do not support password-protected sections.
- They are not available in all countries.
- They require iOS 4.3 or later.

To be honest, the only real difference between the two versions is that the iPad version is optimized for the larger screen of the iPad.

In this exercise, you'll install OneNote Mobile for iOS on your iPhone or iPad.

SET UP You don't need any practice files to complete this exercise. You need an iPhone or iPad with at least iOS 4.3 and an active Internet connection to complete this exercise.

1   To get OneNote for iOS, turn on your iPhone or iPad.

2   Navigate to the App Store.

3   Search for OneNote.

4   Locate the official OneNote Mobile for iOS app.

5   Click the app to download and install it.

   TIP Be sure to select the correct app. The OneNote Mobile for iPhone app won't look right on the larger screen of the iPad, and the OneNote Mobile for iPad app won't run on the iPhone.

CLEAN UP No cleanup is required.

When you've installed OneNote Mobile for iOS and you run it for the first time, it will ask you to sign into your Microsoft Account (SkyDrive). If you don't have one, you can sign up for the account, for free, by going to *www.live.com* or clicking the link the OneNote Mobile app will offer you.

After you've signed into your Live account, you'll find that the OneNote Mobile app already has one notebook created. It's called *Personal (Web)*, and it's required for OneNote Mobile to store unfiled notes. You can't create additional notebooks in the Mobile app; however, you can create additional notebooks in the SkyDrive OneNote Web App or on your desktop OneNote (make sure they're stored on SkyDrive), and those notebooks will synchronize to the OneNote Mobile app.

TIP Do you own an iPhone and an iPad? You can install OneNote Mobile on both devices, and the notes you take on one will automatically sync to the other!

Creating new notes is easy. Navigate to the notebook and section where you want to locate the page, and click the New Page button at the bottom of the app. You can enter in any notes you like, and when you're finished, just go back to the page list in the section.

To create bulleted lists or checklists in your notes, tap the appropriate button (just above the keyboard) and then start typing your list. Each time you tap the return button, a new list item will be created.

If you want to insert a photo into your notes, just tap the location in your notes where you want the picture to appear. Then tap the camera button that appears just above the keyboard.

To find notes on your iPhone or iPad, click the Search button in the lower-left corner of the screen, and then enter your search term or phrase into the search box that appears at the top of the screen.

TIP You can save a lot of time by using the Recents feature. Click the Recents button at the bottom of the screen to view a list of recently used pages. If you have one (or more) that you plan to refer to often, you can even pin them to the top of the Recents list by clicking the pushpin icon to the right of the page name on the Recents list.

Using OneNote Mobile for Android

OneNote Mobile for Android can be found in the Google Play store. Unlike the iOS version, there is just one version of the Android app, which works on both Android phones and Android tablets. Currently, it's free for up to 500 pages of notes, which is actually quite a few. If you need to exceed that number of pages, the upgrade is just a one-time charge of $4.99 currently.

28

OneNote Mobile for Android has the following key features:

- Support for multiple notebooks
- Support for tables
- Support for hyperlinks to external sites (but not internal hyperlinks, yet)
- Spell check
- The ability to insert photos into notes

OneNote Mobile for Android has the following key limitations:

- Synchronization requires a (free) Windows account with SkyDrive.
- It does not currently support inked notes.
- Creating new notebooks has to be done in the desktop or Web App; they will then sync to the Mobile app.
- It is not available in all countries.
- It requires Android 2.3 or later.

In this exercise, you'll install OneNote Mobile for Android on your Android device.

➡ SET UP **You don't need any practice files to complete this exercise. You need an Android phone or tablet with at least Android version 2.3 installed and an active Internet connection to complete this exercise.**

1   To get OneNote for Android, turn on your Android device.

2   Navigate to the **Google Play Store**.

3   Search for **OneNote**.

4   Locate the official OneNote Mobile for Android app and click the app to install.

✖ CLEAN UP **No cleanup is required.**

When you've installed OneNote Mobile for Android and you run it for the first time, it will ask you to sign into your Microsoft account (SkyDrive). If you don't have one, you can sign up for the account, for free, by going to *http://live.com.*

After you've signed into your Live account, you'll find that the OneNote Mobile app already created a notebook for you called *Personal (Web).* It's required for OneNote Mobile to store unfiled notes. You can't create additional notebooks in the Mobile app; however, you can create additional notebooks in the SkyDrive OneNote Web App or on your desktop OneNote (make sure they're stored on SkyDrive), and those notebooks will synchronize to the OneNote Mobile app.

There are two ways to create new pages in OneNote Mobile for Android, and the difference tends to confuse new users a bit. The New Page button at the top of the screen is actually a New Quick Note button. Any notes you create with that button will be stored in the Unfiled Notes section just like Quick Notes you create with OneNote 2013. If you want to create a new page in the current section, however, click the menu button and select New Page from the menu that appears.

To create a bulleted or numbered list or a checklist, tap the appropriate button from the menu at the top of the screen when you're editing a note. Then start typing your list items. Each time you tap the return key, a new line appears for your next list item.

To insert a photo into your notes, tap where you'd like the image to appear, then tap the camera button on the left end of the menu at the top of the screen.

TIP You can save a lot of time navigating around by using the Recents feature. Click the Recents button (it looks like a clock) at the top of the screen. and a list of your recently used pages will appear.

28

Using OneNote Mobile on a Windows Phone

OneNote Mobile comes preinstalled on Windows Phone 7.x and 8.x. Currently, it's free for as many notes as your device can store. Not surprisingly, OneNote Mobile for Windows Phone is the most capable of the Windows Mobile versions.

OneNote Mobile for Windows Phone has the following key features:

- Support for multiple notebooks
- Support for tables
- Support for SkyDrive and SharePoint synchronization
- Support for inserting photos and audio recordings in your notes
- The ability to create bulleted or numbered lists or checklists
- The ability to display inked notes
- Support for searching within the app

OneNote Mobile for Windows Phone has the following key limitation:

- Creating new notebooks has to be done in the desktop or Web App. In turn, they will sync to the Mobile app.

The first time you run OneNote for Windows Phone, it will give you the option to open any notebooks you have stored in your OneNote folder. If you're a SharePoint user, especially via Microsoft Office 365, you'll also have the option to sign into that service and open any notebooks you have stored there.

As with the other OneNote Mobile apps, the Windows Phone version always has one notebook created called *Personal (Web)*, and it's required for OneNote Mobile to store unfiled notes. You can't create additional notebooks in the Mobile app. However, you can create additional notebooks in the SkyDrive OneNote Web App or on your desktop OneNote (make sure they're stored on SkyDrive), and those notebooks will synchronize to the OneNote Mobile app.

To create pages on OneNote Mobile for Windows Phone, click the New Page button that looks like a plus sign (+) at the bottom of the screen. Then you can enter your notes on the page that appears.

To insert a photo into your notes, tap where you'd like the photo to appear, and then tap the camera button at the bottom of the screen.

To insert an audio recording, tap where you'd like the recording to be placed in your notes, tap the microphone button at the bottom of the screen, and then start speaking.

TIP You can add a new note in Windows Phone 8 at any time. Just long-press and release the Windows button at the bottom of the phone. When the phone displays *Listening* say "Note," then speak the text of the note you'd like to take.

Using OneNote with a Windows 8 tablet

Windows 8 tablets are a bit of an anomaly. They are capable of running the full version of Office Home and Student 2013, but they also come with a special version of OneNote that is optimized for the touch interface.

28

The touch-enabled version of OneNote is in the Windows 8 store on any Windows 8 device (not just tablets). Though it does have some innovative features (like the radial user interface, as shown following this text), it also has significant limitations in the current version. For example:

- Only SkyDrive-shared notebooks are easily accessed.
- Audio or video recording is not supported.
- There is a limited set of note tags and no customization.

Like most of the Windows Store (formerly called *Metro*) apps in Windows 8, the special Windows 8 OneNote app is fairly limited compared to the full-fledged desktop version.

You can find the OneNote Windows Store app in the Windows Store on any Windows 8 computer.

TIP Windows RT is different from Windows 8. The version of OneNote that comes bundled with Windows RT is substantially the same as OneNote 2013.

Key points

- OneNote gives you a lot of opportunities to use your notes wherever you are.

- Using SkyDrive, SharePoint, a network drive, or even a simple USB flash drive, you can share notes between multiple devices.

- If your notes are stored in SkyDrive or SharePoint, you can access them from any computer with a web browser via OneNote Web App.

- OneNote Mobile lets you access your notes on the go on your iPhone, iPad, Android, Windows tablet, or Windows Phone devices.

28

Chapter at a glance

Find

Find tags in your notes with the Tags Summary pane, page 752

![Tags Summary pane showing Search completed, Group tags by Tag name, Show only unchecked items, Important section with Sales-PC and Web sites, Question section with How many users in North America?]

Record

Record audio in your notebook, page 755

Capture

Capture ideas quickly and easily with Quick Notes, page 756

![Quick Note showing Carter Project with bulleted items: Meet with designers, Call EricB!, Set deadline for design ideas, Focus group to evaluate and recommend proposed design.]

Saving time with OneNote

IN THIS CHAPTER, YOU WILL LEARN HOW TO

- Find tags.

- Record audio.

- Capture ideas and information with Quick Notes.

- Insert screen clippings into your notes.

- Create linked notes that connect to documents, presentations, webpages, or other notes.

- Create templates on which to build your notes.

Microsoft OneNote 2013 is a surprisingly powerful tool for collecting and organizing ideas and research, and getting your projects moving in the right direction. In this chapter, you will learn about tools that you may not have even realized OneNote 2013 has.

OneNote is for unstructured data, so it's appropriate for this chapter to introduce you to these tools in no particular order.

PRACTICE FILES To complete the exercises in this chapter, you need the practice files contained in the Chapter29 practice file folder. For more information, see "Download the practice files" in this book's Introduction.

Finding tags

In Chapter 27, "Sharing notes with others," you learned about adding tags to notes. You can tag a note as a phone number, as *Important*, as a to-do item, or even as a question. There's a tags gallery right there on the Home tab of the ribbon that offers you many tags, as well as the ability to create your own custom tags.

Did you know there's a powerful tool in OneNote for finding those tags after you've used them? Immediately to the right of the Tags gallery, you'll find Find Tags, and if you click it, the Tags Summary pane on the right side of the screen shows you all the tags you've used. You have a few options for what you can do with that tool.

At the bottom of the pane, you can use the Search option to set the scope that the Tags Summary is going to apply to. Click the arrow on the right end of the field to display a drop-down list of choices.

Following are several useful options:

- All notebooks
- This notebook
- This section
- This page group (which is as close to *this page* as you can get)
- Today's notes

The Tags Summary pane is a static pane. That means that if you add, change, or remove a tag from the notes, the Tags Summary results don't automatically change. To update the pane, click the Refresh Results button located below the Search field.

In this exercise, you'll use the Find Tags feature to quickly locate tags that you've assigned to your notes.

➡ SET UP **Start OneNote and open a OneNote page with a few sample notes.**

1   Click a paragraph in your notes.

2   Assign a tag to that paragraph from the **Tags** gallery on the **Home** tab of the ribbon.

3   Repeat steps 1 and 2 as desired.

4　Click **Find Tags** on the **Home** tab of the ribbon.

5　The **Tags Summary** pane appears on the right side of the screen, showing all tagged items within the selected scope (**Page**, **Section**, **Notebook**, **This Week**, and so on).

6   Select a tag and click it. OneNote will immediately take you to the page and paragraph where that tag is located.

✖ CLEAN UP You'll probably want to reuse your page of sample notes for other exercises, so you don't need to do anything with them at this point.

Tags are great organizational tools when you're browsing your notes, because they help you quickly identify what you've written. They're even more powerful when you can find them later.

TIP The next time you're in a meeting, take notes with OneNote. When you have questions, flag them with the Question tag. When you get to the part of the meeting where it's time to ask questions, use the Find Tags feature to gather all of your questions into one pane so you can quickly refer to them.

Recording audio

While you're attending those meetings, there's another powerful feature available that gives you the ability to record audio. The audio recording appears right on your note page, so it's readily available when you want to play it back later.

TIP Be sure you have permission to record the audio in your meeting. In some cases, it's required by law, but in all cases, it's just good manners to let folks know they're being recorded.

To start recording audio, click the Insert tab on the ribbon, and then click Record Audio. Be warned that the recording will start as soon as you click the button. Therefore, don't click Record Audio until you're ready to start recording.

While the audio is recording, continue taking notes normally. When you're ready to stop recording, click the Stop button on the ribbon (it looks like a square). It's as easy as that. OneNote will insert your audio recording into your notes as an icon along with a portion of text that details when the audio was recorded.

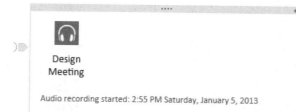

To play your audio back later, just double-click the icon that OneNote inserts into the notes.

Later, when you're playing the audio, OneNote highlights the notes you were taking while the audio was being recorded. As a bonus, you can take notes while listening to the audio playback, and OneNote will synchronize those notes to the recording as well.

TIP If you plan to do a lot of audio recording, you should invest in a decent microphone. The ones built into most laptops are good enough to record your voice, but they aren't likely to produce excellent quality audio in a large meeting.

TIP The next time you're on a technical support phone call, put the support person on speakerphone and use the OneNote recording feature to record the call as he or she helps you. Any notes you take during the call will be synchronized to the audio. This enables you to save the instructions for future use. Just make sure it's legal to record phone calls where you are.

Using Quick Notes

Have you ever been sitting at your desk when some brilliant idea that's unrelated to what you're working on hits you? When that happens, just press the Windows key+N and then another N; OneNote will open a Quick Note window for you that looks like a small sticky note on the screen. This enables you to write down the thoughts you had for future reference.

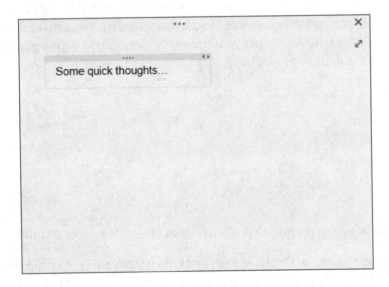

You can have as many Quick Notes open at a time as you want, and you can easily file them, print them, share them, or delete them if they turn out to not be so brilliant.

To access the ribbon commands in a Quick Note, click the three dots on the bar at the top of the Quick Note window.

If you close a Quick Note without filing it, OneNote will automatically put it in the Quick Notes section at the bottom of the OneNote Notebook pane on the left.

To access Quick Notes, press Windows key+N and then press N again when the Send To OneNote window appears.

Quick Notes are a great way to take notes during phone calls or when you just want to capture random ideas that occur during the day, rather than scribbling them on the back of pieces of paper.

Using screen clipping

OneNote has always had a very good integrated screen clipping capability. What's screen clipping? It's the ability to take a picture of an area of your screen, which is great for capturing error messages, images, or other content.

To use the screen clipping capability, press the Windows key+S (OneNote doesn't even have to be open at the time). Your screen will dim somewhat, and your mouse pointer will turn into a crosshair pointer, and you can use the left mouse button to drag the mouse pointer across an area of the screen that you want to capture. When you release the mouse button, OneNote will ask you what page of your notebook you'd like to put that screen clipping on. It's as simple as that.

In this exercise, you'll use OneNote's screen clipping feature to capture part of your screen and insert it into your notes.

➡ SET UP **You need a page in OneNote where you can place an image clipped from your screens to complete this exercise.**

1   Check to make sure that the **Send to OneNote tool** is on your system tray (where the clock is; usually in the lower-right corner of your screen). It should be there by default, but if it isn't, start OneNote, click the **File** tab, click **Options**, and then click **Display**. Then ensure that the **Place OneNote icon in the notification area of the taskbar** check box is selected.

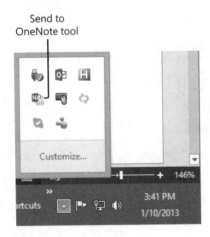

2   Press **Windows key+S**.

3   When the screen dims, move your mouse pointer to the upper-left corner of the area of the screen you would like to clip.

4   Press and hold the left mouse button while dragging down and right across the area of the screen you want to capture.

5   When you've selected the area you want, release the left mouse button.

6   OneNote will ask you what page you would like to place the clipping on. Select a page, and click **OK**.

❌ CLEAN UP **You can delete the page where you sent your practice screen clippings, if you want.**

Screen clippings are a powerful way to capture things happening on your screen (like a portion of a webpage or an error message) in your notes.

Using linked notes

OneNote 2010 introduced the ability to take linked notes. What that means is that while you're working on a Microsoft Word document, a Microsoft PowerPoint presentation, or even when you're browsing websites in Windows Internet Explorer, you can have OneNote docked to the side of the screen where you can take notes. As you take notes, OneNote stores a link with the notes to the document or websites you were working with when you took those notes, so that you can easily return to them.

To use linked notes, open the document, presentation, or website you want to take notes on, open or create the OneNote page where you want to take the linked notes, and then click the Dock To Desktop button on the View tab in OneNote.

When you're done taking notes, you can click the Normal View button on the View tab of the OneNote ribbon or just close the docked page.

In this exercise, you'll use OneNote to take notes that are linked to a Word document.

➡ SET UP **Start OneNote.**

1   Start Word.

2   Open a document in Word that you want to take notes about.

3   In OneNote, navigate to the page where you want to take those notes.

4   Click the **View** tab on the ribbon.

5   Click the **Dock to Desktop** button. OneNote will dock itself to the right side of the screen, by default. The Word document should now occupy the rest of the screen.

6   Take notes in the OneNote page while navigating up or down in the Word document. Your notes will be linked to the Word document.

7   To exit docked view, click the **Normal View** button, which looks like a two-headed arrow at the upper-right corner of the docked window.

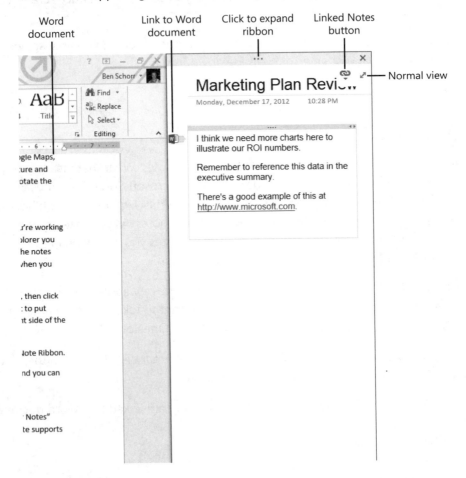

760   Chapter 29   Saving time with OneNote

TIP Your Word document must be saved and named at least once for the linking to work. If you want to create linked notes on a brand new document, you'll need to save it first.

✖ CLEAN UP **No cleanup is required.**

To use those linked notes later, navigate to the page where you took those notes, and you can click the provided links to jump back to the document or website you were working with.

Searching your images

In Chapter 25, "Working with notebooks, sections, and pages," you learned how to insert a photo image or document into OneNote. You can use the screen clipping feature, print from the original application to OneNote, or go to the Insert tab in OneNote and select Pictures, Online Pictures, Screen Clipping, or even Scanned Image.

Did you know that OneNote can automatically try to recognize any text that appears in those images? That process is called *OCR* or *Optical Character Recognition*.

Naturally, the results will vary by the quality of the picture and the legibility of the text. However, a photo of handwritten text on a whiteboard could be successfully recognized, if the photo is clear and the handwriting is fairly easy to read. A photo of a printed stop sign will very likely be recognized.

In this exercise, you'll insert an image into a page of notes.

 SET UP **You need the 29 Practice image 1.jpg image located in the Chapter29 practice file folder to complete this exercise. Create a practice OneNote page that you can insert an image into.**

1   Navigate to the OneNote page you want to insert the image on.

2   Click the location on the page where you want to place the image.

3   Click the **Insert** tab on the ribbon.

4   Click the **Pictures** button.

5   Navigate to and insert the **29 Practice image 1.jpg** file

6   Next, confirm that the page will be indexed. Right-click the image you just inserted and select **Make Text in Image Searchable**.

7   Set the language you want to use.

Right-click
the image

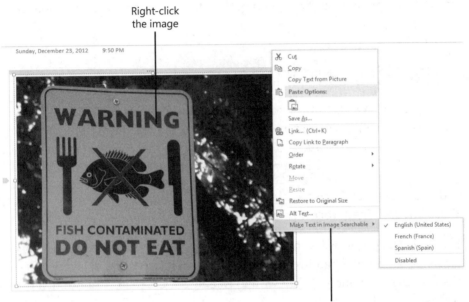

Select Make Text in
Image Searchable

OneNote will attempt to index the text in the image in the background, and that text will subsequently appear in your search results if you look for that string (or part of it).

❌ CLEAN UP **You can delete the practice images page you created in this exercise.**

TIP The next time you get a long PDF report, print it to OneNote instead of to paper. As long as Make Text In Image Searchable is enabled, OneNote will index the text of the PDF, which will make it easy to find specific items even in long PDF files.

Inserting a spreadsheet

One of the features folks have been asking for in OneNote since the very beginning has been the ability to embed content from other file types in a OneNote document other than just being able to print it there. OneNote 2013 has some of that capability with the Insert Spreadsheet feature.

In this exercise, you'll embed a Microsoft Excel spreadsheet on a OneNote page.

➡ SET UP **You need the 29 PracticeSpreadsheet.xlsx workbook located in the Chapter29 practice file folder to complete this exercise.**

1   Open OneNote.

2   Navigate to a page where you want to insert the sample spreadsheet.

3   On the **Insert** tab, click **Insert Spreadsheet**.

4   OneNote will ask if you want to insert a new spreadsheet or an existing spreadsheet.

5   Select **Existing Excel Spreadsheet**.

6   Navigate to the folder containing the **29 Practice Spreadsheet** and select it.

7   Click **Insert**.

8   OneNote will ask if you want to **Attach File**, **Insert Spreadsheet**, or **Insert a Chart or Table**.

Insert File

▣ **Attach File**

▦ **Insert Spreadsheet**

▥ **Insert a Chart or Table**

9   Choose **Insert Spreadsheet**. OneNote will insert the spreadsheet you selected onto the note page.

TIP If your workbook has multiple sheets and you only want to insert one sheet of the workbook, right-click the spreadsheet in OneNote and click Select What To Display from the shortcut menu. OneNote will display a list of the sheets in the workbook, and you can select the one you want.

❌ CLEAN UP **There are no specific clean-up tasks.**

Any changes that were made to the sheet will automatically be updated in OneNote. However, you can't edit the sheet in OneNote. To do that, you would have to click the Edit button in the upper-left corner of the window, which will open Excel. Then you can make and save your changes, which will appear in OneNote.

Annual Sales Numbers
Saturday, January 12, 2013   3:39 PM

▣ 35 Practice Spreadsheet 1

	January	February	March	April	May	June	July	August	September	October	November	December
2009	$2,134.00	$2,045.00	$2,232.00	$2,235.00	$2,188.00	$2,210.00	$2,254.00	$2,216.00	$2,263.00	$2,207.00	$ 2,445.00	$2,872.00
2010	$2,345.00	$2,132.00	$2,443.00	$2,332.00	$2,192.00	$2,256.00	$2,314.00	$2,273.00	$2,308.00	$2,254.00	$ 2,567.00	$2,999.00
2011	$2,534.00	$2,234.00	$2,654.00	$2,429.00	$2,196.00	$2,302.00	$2,374.00	$2,330.00	$2,353.00	$2,301.00	$ 2,689.00	$3,126.00
2012	$2,754.00	$2,456.00	$2,865.00	$2,526.00	$2,200.00	$2,348.00	$2,434.00	$2,387.00	$2,398.00	$2,348.00	$ 2,811.00	$3,253.00

New Marketing Plan
Dog Products
Inserting Space
Marketing Plan Review
Outlining
subcontractor survey ~
Math
Annual Sales Numbers

Using the Napkin Math feature

If you asked 100 OneNote users what Napkin Math was. about 98 respondents wouldn't know the answer. Napkin Math is the name given to the feature in OneNote where you can enter a mathematical equation and OneNote will solve it for you.

For example: enter 2+2= then press Enter, and OneNote will insert the 4 for you. Napkin Math understands a surprising number of mathematical operators. In addition to addition, subtraction, multiplication, and division, it can also do exponents (squared, cubed, x5, and so forth), square roots, percentages, and more. You can use the currency symbol ($) to have it treat the result as currency, and you can even enter some fairly long formulas.

$5*4=$20.00

Napkin Math cannot calculate with variables or references like Excel does. It won't let you create a calculated cell in a table, for example. In that instance, you would do better to use the inserted spreadsheet tool discussed in the previous section.

Formatting with templates

If the plain white sheets of electronic paper are just a little too plain for you, then you can dip into the OneNote collection of templates. Templates are precreated pages that already contain specific elements such as formatting, tables, graphics, or instructions.

In this exercise, you'll use a template to create a new page in OneNote.

 SET UP **Start OneNote.**

1   Click the **Insert** tab on the ribbon.

2   Click the **Page Templates** button.

3   From the **Recently Used** list, select a template you use often (if any), or click the **Page Templates** item at the bottom of the menu to open the **Templates** pane on the right side of the screen.

4   Select a template from the **Templates** pane by expanding the category (such as **Academic** or **Business**) and clicking the template you like. If you don't like the template you selected, simply repeat step 3 and select a different template. After you enter notes onto the page, you won't be able to change the underlying template and keep your notes. You'll have to create a new page with the new template and move your notes to it.

On the Templates task pane, you can select from among a couple dozen pre-created templates, including special types of notes pages, planners, and more. Or, you can create your own.

TIP To create your own template, create a page that is exactly the way you want it— page title, paper color, any tables or content you want inside—and then click the Templates pane. Click the Save Current Page As A Template link at the bottom of the Templates pane. OneNote will ask you to give your template a name. Then you can save it in the My Templates section at the top of the Templates pane.

CLEAN UP You can delete any practice pages you created during this exercise.

Page templates are a unique way to create pages that have pre-existing formatting so they are ready for you to enter notes without having to create new formatting parameters each time.

Key points

- OneNote 2013 has some powerful features that aren't obvious to the casual observer.

- Tags help you organize and categorize your notes, and the Find Tags feature makes it easy to find your tagged items later.

- OneNote has the ability to record audio and video that can help you more accurately capture notes in a meeting or conference.

- Quick Notes make it possible to quickly capture ideas or events (like phone calls) as they occur and make them searchable and shareable later.

- Screen clippings let you save anything visible on your screen in your notes.

- If you're taking notes on a document, presentation, webpage or other OneNote page, you can link your notes to that item to quickly return to it when you review the notes later.

- If there is text in your picture, OneNote can recognize that text and make it searchable.

- OneNote 2013 lets you insert spreadsheets (and Microsoft Visio files) into your notes and keeps the inserted spreadsheet updated so if the source data changes, the table in your notes changes too.

- Napkin Math lets you make quick and simple calculations within your notes.

- Templates let you create pre-formatted pages that you can use and reuse in your notes.

Index

Index

Index

Symbols

0 (zero), as Excel formatting code, 554
1 Page per Sheet print option, 246
2-D vs. 3-D charts in presentations, 318
3-D charts, 629
3-D effects, applying to shapes, 346–349
3-D Format tools, in Format Shape pane, 346
3-D vs. 2-D charts in presentations, 318
$ (dollar) sign, in Excel formulas, 467–470, 493
* (asterisk), in Excel formatting, 554, 569
@ (at symbol), as Excel formatting code, 555
[ ] (brackets)
   adding to formatting code in Excel, 558
   as Excel date formatting code, 570
^ (caret), entering from keyboard, 168
: (colon), entering from keyboard, 168
, (comma)
   as Excel formatting code, 555
   using in custom number format code, 635
= (equal) sign, in Excel formulas, 452
(pound sign), as Excel formatting code, 554
" " (quotation marks)
   as Excel formatting code, 555
   using in searches, 710
=Rand(), 85
~ (tilde), entering from keyboard, 168
_ (underscore), as Excel formatting code, 554

A

accent colors, 274–275

Accessibility Checker pane
   in PowerPoint, 393
   in Word, 237
Account page
   connecting to cloud service, 79–81
   switching to another Office account, 76–77
Account page, Backstage, 12–13
Add a Digital Signature option, 574
adding
   commands to Quick Access Toolbar, 28–29
   frames to images, 359
   sections, 380–383
   shapes in PowerPoint, 336–341
   text boxes to slides, 308–313
   text to slides, 304
   timelines to charts, 637–639
Add To Quick Access Toolbar command, 28–29
adjustment handles, using, 349–351
After spacing option, in Paragraph dialog box, 288
aligning
   objects button, 640, 645
   objects in PowerPoint, 289, 340
   text using tabs, 214
   using alignment guides, 127
   using Smart Guides in PowerPoint, 289, 311, 352
Align Objects button, 640–641, 645
All Caps font format option, 201
Also Insert From YouTube icon, 374
Always on Top option, OneNote, 664
am/pm (a/p), Excel date formatting code, 570
AND() functions, 476
Android, sharing notes via SharePoint on, 723
Android, using OneNote on, 743–745
Animation gallery, 366
Animation Painter, in PowerPoint, 369
Animation pane, PowerPoint, 368–370
animations
   number next to, 369
   playing one at a time, 370

reordering, 370

Animations tab, PowerPoint
Effect Options on, 367
Fade command on, 366

application Start screen
about, 4–5
templates in, 58

application window, elements in, 6–13
Account commands, 12–13
dialog box launcher, 8
galleries, 8–9
KeyTips, 11
Live Preview, 9
Mini Toolbar, 10
Quick Access Toolbar, 8
ribbon, 6
Screen Tips, 10–11
status bar, 8
title bar, 7
tool tabs, 8

appointments, connecting to OneNote, 695–697
Apps for Office, inserting in Office documents, 47
Arrange All button, 612, 621
Arrange button, 360
Arrange group, Align Objects button in, 640–641
Arrange tool, OneNote, 683
Artistic Effects button, 357
asterisk (*), in Excel formatting, 569
in Excel formatting, 554
at symbol (@), as Excel formatting code, 555
audio. *See also* video
linking files to PowerPoint, 371
playing across slides, 373
recording with OneNote, 755–756
searching notes in OneNote for recordings, 708
Audio Tools Playback tab, 373
AutoComplete ScreenTip, 179–180
AutoCorrect
deleting entries that were added in error, 175
entering symbols using, 167–168
using, 172–175
AutoCorrect dialog box, 173–174, 211
AutoCorrect Options button, 520
autofill
extending series with, 429–431

suppressing, 431
AutoFill Options menu, in Excel, 429
AutoFit to contents option, in Insert Table dialog box, 219
AutoFit to window option, in Insert Table dialog box, 219
AutoFormat As You Type feature
for numbering and bulleting lists, 210
turning off, 210
Auto-hide Ribbon option, 7–8
auto-hide state, setting ribbon to, 27
AutoRecover information, turning on, 23
autosave files, setting feature to, 23–24
AutoSum button, 457–460
Available Windows area of menus, 651
AVERAGE() function, 460–461
Axes option, in Chart Elements list, 636

B

Background Removal tab, 361
backgrounds
applying styles to presentations, 281–283
playing audio file in presentations, 373
preferred setting for, 12
removing from pictures in PowerPoint, 361–363
Background Styles menu choice, in PowerPoint, 282
Backstage pages
Account, 12–13, 76–77, 79–81
Export, 22
Info, 16–17, 23–25
New, 17–19
Open, 20, 91
Print, 21–22
Save As, 21, 86–87
Share, 22, 88–89
Sign in to Office, 74
Backstage view
closing, 13
displaying, 11
Before spacing, in Paragraph dialog box, 288
Bezier Curves, 351
Bing, searching from Research pane using, 152

Blank layout, in PowerPoint, 343

Blank Workbook, creating, 424

Blur field, in Format Shape pane, 345

body fonts, in PowerPoint, 272

bolding selected text, 310

Border button, in Excel, 425

borderless tables, 226

Border Painter command, in Word, 125

Border Painter, in Word, 125

Border Sampler command, 224

Border Sampler, in Word, 125

borders, removing from shapes, 345

Border Styles gallery

    for tables in Word, 125

    on Table Tools Design tool tab, 224

bottom page margins, toggling in Print Layout
    view, 120

brackets ([ ])

    adding to formatting code in Excel, 558

    as Excel date formatting code, 570

Bring to Front menu option

    in OneNote, 683

    in PowerPoint, 360

browser, accessing notes in, 738–740

building blocks

    composing documents using, 176–180

    in Word, 128

Building Blocks Organizer dialog box, 180

built-in functions

    AVERAGE, 460–461

    SUM, 460–461

    using, 460–462

bulleted lists

    about, 209

    formatting, 210–213

bullet points

    changing list text into SmartArt graphic, 321–325

    changing size and color of, 285

    changing spacing before and after paragraph
        levels of bulleted text, 288

    creating second level bulleted text in slides, 308

    troubleshooting slide, 306

Bullets gallery, in PowerPoint, 286

buttons

    Align Objects, 640–641, 645

Animation pane, 368

Arrange, 360

Arrange All, 612, 621

Artistic Effects, 357

AutoCorrect Options, 520

AutoSum, 457–460

Border, in Excel, 425

buttons, 356

Cell Styles, 542–545

Change Chart Type, 627–628, 633

Chart Elements, 627, 632, 633, 636

Chart Styles, 626–627, 632

Collapse Field, 533

Color, 344, 362

Comma Style, 539

Conditional Formatting, 505, 506

Convert To Range, 521, 587

Convert to Shapes, 110

Create PDF/XPS, 239

Crop, 356

Data Validation, 488

Decrease Decimal, 461

Decrease Font Size, 285

Decrease List Level, 306

Dock to Desktop, 663

"epsilon", 457–460

Field Buttons, 627

Fit Slide to Current Window, 289

Freeze Panes, 592

From Beginning or From Current Slide, 397

Group Objects, 649

Help, 7

hiding filter, 516

Increase Font Size, 285

Increase List Level, 306, 307

Ink Comment, 109

Insert Function, 464–467

Insert Slicer, 630

Insert Space, 682

Insert Timeline, 638

Layout, in PowerPoint, 336

Layout Options, in Word, 127

Linked Contact Notes, 697

More Options, 319

New Slide, 305, 313–316

Next, 137
Notebook Recycle Bin, 684–685
Orientation, 604
Outlook Tasks, 698
Page Templates, 765
Pictures, 51
Previous, 137
Print, 22
Protect Workbook, 573
Publish, 242
Recents, OneNote Mobile apps, 743
Remove Background, 361–362
Remove Gradient Stop, 345
Reset Picture, 359
Ribbon Display Options
    in Excel, 413, 575
    in Office, 7–8
    in PowerPoint, 256
    in Word, 118
Rule Lines, 661–662
Running Total, 504
Save, green arrows on Quick Access Toolbar, 91
Screenshot, 355, 651
See All Slides, 397
Select All, in Excel, 443
Send Backward, 645
Set As Default, in Find Options dialog box, 140
Shape Effects, 642
Shape Fill, 343
Shape Options Effects, 345
Shapes, 643, 645
Show/Hide ¶, 163, 201, 215
Slicer, 637
Slide Master, 272
SmartArt, 52
Start Inking, 108
Symbol, 165–166
Symbol, OneNote, 691
Synchronous Scrolling, 578
Text Effects, 348, 646
Text Highlight Color, 187
Themes, 49, 549
Timeline, 638–639
Touch Mode, 103
Trim Video, 372

Undo, 156
using, 502
Values
    in Paste Special, 486
    in Paste Values group, 485
View Side By Side, 578
What-If Analysis, 501
Window control
    in Excel, 413
    in Office, 7–8
    in PowerPoint, 256
    in Word, 118
Wrap Text, 444
Zoom, 652
Zoom to Page, 389

C

Capitalize each word option, 202
caret (^), entering from keyboard, 168
case of text, changing in Excel, 485–487
Category Name option, of Format Data Labels task
        pane, 634
cell ranges, selecting and naming
        spreadsheet, 434–437
cell references vs. static values in formulas, 457
cells, spreadsheet
    copying and pasting range of, 485
    copying one or more cells to many, 447–448
    creating bottom border in, 425
    extending series with autofill, 429–431
    finalizing entry in, 424
    format for email and web addresses, 432
    formatting, 426–427, 550–551
    maximum number of characters in, 442
    maximum number of rows, 458
    moving and adjusting, 442–444
    pasting formulas as resulting values, 484–485
    restricting entries in, 487–492
    using references, 467–470
    validating entries, 470–472
    working with text in
        changing case of text, 485–487
        combining into one string, 479–482

pasting formulas as resulting values, 484–485
removing extra spaces, 482–484
Cell Styles button, 542–545
Centered Overlay option, in Chart Title option list, 636
centering text, 316
Change Case command, 202–203
Change Chart Type button, 627–628, 633
Change Chart Type dialog box, 627–628
Change File Type option, 243
changing
bulleted list text into SmartArt graphics, 321–325
bullet size or color, 285
case of text in Excel, 485–487
font size, 285
Office Theme, 12
permissions on shared files, 90
presentation to widescreen format, 297–300
search scope in, 709–710
spacing before and after paragraph levels of bulleted text, 288
widths of columns, 423–426
widths of spreadsheet rows, 426
character formats
exploring, 200–201
resetting, 196
using styles for, 192–196
characters, international, 167–168
Chart Elements button, 627, 632, 633, 636
chart elements, double-clicking, 636
Chart Elements list
Axes option in, 636
Chart Title option in, 636
Chart Elements list, seeing icons next to, 318
Chart Filters tool (funnel icon), 320
charts
adding slicers to PivotCharts, 629–632
adding timelines, 416, 637–639
creating and modifying, 623–629
formatting, 43–44
inserting in Office documents, 54
inserting in PowerPoint, 316–320
manipulating elements in, 632–637
manipulating objects in, 640–642
Recommended Chart feature, 415

viewing in Read Mode, 147
Chart Styles button, 626–627, 632
Chart Title option, in Chart Elements, 636
Chart Tools Design tool tab, 57
circular text, making, 348
CLEAN() function, 476
Clear Filter command, 518
Clear Formats option, 546
cloud services. See also Office cloud accounts; See also SkyDrive
about, 71–73, 78–79
changing permissions, 90
computer requirements to access, 72
connecting to, 79–81
Office 365, 83
opening files from, 42, 90–91
personal, 80–81
saving files on, 42, 85–87
sharing files from, 88–90
signing into Office cloud account, 74–76
syncing files for offline use with, 92–96
Clustered Column thumbnail, 624–625
co-authoring Office documents, 97–98
Collapse All Headings option, 143
Collapse Field button, 533
collapsing ribbon, 27
Collated print option, 246
colon (:), entering from keyboard, 168
Color button
in Format Shape pane, 344
under Picture Tools Format tab, 362
colors
changing bullet color, 285
Create New Theme Colors dialog box, 282
customizing PowerPoint, 273–275
Sort by Color/Filter by Color commands, 518
theme vs. direct, 341–342
using absolute, 276
Colors dialog box, in PowerPoint, 279
column headers, in Excel, using in defining names, 437–439
COLUMN([reference]) functions, 478
columns
changing widths of spreadsheet, 423–426
deleting OneNote table, 707

deleting Word table, 222–223

inserting in Excel, 583–587

moving and copying spreadsheet, 445–446

printing column labels in Excel, 599–602

COLUMNS(array) functions, 478

Column Width, as Read Mode option, 145

comma (,)

as Excel formatting code, 555

using in custom number format code, 635

commands

Account, 12–13

adding commands from Quick Access Toolbar

in Excel, 412

in Office, 28–29

in OneNote, 659

in Word, 118

Border Painter command in Word, 125

Border Sampler, 224

Change Case, 202–203

Clear Filter, 518

Control AutoCorrect Options, 520

Create From Selection

in Defined Names group, 470–471

in Excel, 437–439

Date Filters, 519

Define and Translate, 152

Draw Table, 219

Excel worksheets Hide, 611

file tab, Excel, 412

Filter by Color command, 518

Filter menu, 518–519

Flash Fill, in Excel, 431–433

Freeze Panes, 592

keyboard access to, 546

Lock Cell, 491

Number Filters, 519

Page Width, 120

Print Titles, 599, 602

Remove Split, 123

removing commands from Quick Access Toolbar, 28–29, 118

ribbon vs. Quick Access Toolbar, 32

screen tips for, 10–11

Scroll Here, 135

Sort, 518

Sort by Color, 518

split control on ribbon of, 6–7

Stop Automatically Expanding Tables, 520

Text Filters, 519

Comma Style button, 539

comment indicator, in Word, 126

Compare Side by Side dialog box, 619

Compatibility Checker, PowerPoint, 394

Compatibility Mode, in Word, 129

composing documents

inserting special characters, 169–171

inserting symbols, 165–166, 168

using AutoCorrect, 167–168, 172–175

using building blocks, 176–180

using formatting marks in, 161–164

using international characters, 167–168

Compress Pictures dialog box, 358

Computer & HD Displays option, 376

CONCATENATE() function, 476, 479–482

Conditional Formatting button, 505

conditional formatting features, 504–507

contacts, annotating contacts in OneNote, 697–698

Continuous section breaks, 191

Control AutoCorrect Options, 173

Control AutoCorrect Options command, 520

Convert Text to Table dialog box, 219–220

Convert To Range button, 521, 587

Convert to Shapes button, 110

copying

columns and rows on spreadsheets, 445–446

formulas, 452–456

formulas and pasting as resulting values, 484–485

one or more spreadsheet cells to many, 447–448

range of cells, 485

copying selected text or object, 311

Copy Link to Page option, OneNote, 700

Copy Link To Paragraph option, OneNote, 702

COUNTIF() functions, 474

Count Numbers function, 462

Create a Video setting, 376

Create From Selection command

in Defined Names group, 470–471

in Excel, 437–439

Create Graphic group, 323

Create New Building Block dialog box, 178
Create New Theme Colors dialog box, 282
Create PDF/XPS button, 239
Create PDF/XPS Document option, 241
creating
    blank document, 179
    bottom border in spreadsheet cells, 425
    charts, 623–629
    coordinating documents across applications, 128
    creating notebooks on SkyDrive, 713–716
    creating notes in OneNote Mobile apps, 743
    custom shapes, 349–354
    custom slide layouts, 291–297
    custom sort list, 523–526
    custom themes in Excel, 546–549
    formulas, 452–456
    graphics in Excel, 642–648
    hyperlinks to pages in OneNote, 702–704
    new files, 17–19
    notebooks, 670–671
    OneNote tables, 704–707
    pages in OneNote, 675
    PDFs
        in OneNote, 666
        in PowerPoint, 389
        in Word, 239–244
    perfect shapes, 336
    PivotTables, 526–533
    presentations using theme variants, 268
    sections in OneNote, 671–673
    tables in Word, 217–223
    tags, OneNote, 690–692
    theme font set, 277
Crop button, from Picture Tools Format tab, 652
cropping pictures, in presentations, 356
cursor
    keyboard shortcuts for moving, 155–156
    moving to beginning of sentence, 171
Custom category, of Format Cells dialog box, 634–635
Customize Quick Access Toolbar list, 27
Customize Status Bar list, 30–31
Customize Status Bar menu, 462
Customize Status Bar options, 191
customizing
    PowerPoint fills, 342–349
    PowerPoint themes, 271–276
    Quick Access Toolbar, 28–29
    ribbon, 32–35
    shapes, 349–354
    slide layouts, 291–297
    status bar, 30–31
    user interface, 25–31
custom keyboard shortcut, assigning to character or symbol, 168
custom number format code, using comma (,) in, 635
Custom Print option, 247

D
data, Excel
    adding to tables, 519–521
    analyzing from outside source, 508–511
    entering and organizing data, 422–423
    formatting, 426–429
    sorting, 521–523
data labels, 44
Data Labels option, in Chart Elements, 627, 633
data model, Excel, 512, 534
Data Tools group, in Excel, Flash Fill command in, 431–433
Data Validation dialog box, 488, 492
Date Filters command, 519
date formats, Excel, 564–570
date() function, 477–478
d (Day), Excel date formatting code, 569
decimal tabs, 214, 220, 226
Decrease Decimal button, 461
Decrease Font Size button, 285
Decrease List Level button, 306
default formatting, setting for documents, 128
Define and Translate commands, 152
Defined Names group, Create From Selection in, 470–471
Define Name command, in Excel, 435
Define option, as research tool, 149
deleting
    AutoCorrect entries that were added in error, 175
    cells in Excel, 587–591

custom color theme in PowerPoint, 280
decimal tabs, 220
Word tables, 222–223
demoting text in slides, 306
Design tab
in PowerPoint, 270, 272, 277, 282, 299
in Word, 128
diagrams. *See* charts
dialog box launcher, 8
dictionary
adding words to, 232
definitions and synonyms, 152
direct colors vs. theme colors, 341–342
Dock to Desktop button, 663
Dock to Desktop view, OneNote, 660
Document Inspector
in PowerPoint, 392–393
in Word, 234–237
documents
alignment guides in, 127
collapsible headings, 126
collapsing and expanding headings in, 141–144
composing
inserting special characters, 169–171
inserting symbols, 165–166, 168
using AutoCorrect, 167–168, 172–175
using building blocks, 176–180
using formatting marks in, 161–164
using international characters, 167–168
correcting proofing errors, 230–232
created in earlier versions of Word, 129
creating across applications coordinating, 128
editing
PDFs, 124
selecting text, 156–160
formatting
about, 183–188
changing case of text, 200–201
exploring character, 200–201
exploring paragraph, 196–198
managing pagination through, 203
setting default documents, 188
setting section formatting, 190–192
using styles for, 192–196
heading styles in, 141–144

inspecting before publishing, 233–237
making final, 238
navigating, 135–141
opening from Internet, 148
PDFs
creating, 239–244
editing, 239, 243–244
presenting information in
enhancing tables, 223–227
inserting tables, 217–223
using bulleted lists, 209, 210–213
using numbered lists, 209, 210–213
using tabbed lists, 210, 213–217
using tables, 210
printing, 245–249
printing documents, 245
Read Mode
exploring research tools in, 148–152
viewing documents in, 144–148
scrolling, 134–135
searching, 135–141
setting default formatting for, 128
tables in, 125
threaded comments in, 126
tracking changes in, 126
using tables for page layouts, 226
views in, 119–122
.docx file extension, 116
dollar ($) sign, in Excel formulas, 467–470, 493
double-clicking, chart elements, 636
double quotes ("), as Excel formatting code, 555
Double Strikethrough font format option, 201
Draft view
in Word, 120
opening documents in, 122
dragging
animations into Animation pane, 370
Drawing Tools Format tab
Align button from, 645
Align Objects button from, 640–641
formatting illustrations using, 52
Group Objects button from, 649
Merge Shapes tool from, 353
Send Backward button from, 645
Shape Fill button from, 343

Shape Styles from, 337
Shape Styles palette from, 644
WordArt Styles group in, 646
Draw Table command, 219
duplicating objects, 311

E

Edit Document, as Read Mode option, 145
editing
custom color theme in PowerPoint, 280
documents, 155–156
formulas, 452–456
PDFs, 124, 239, 243–244
saved slide show presentations, 401
video, 371–373
Edit mode, activating formula, 469, 481, 493
Edit Points, in PowerPoint, 351
Effect Options in PowerPoint
Animations tab in, 367
effects
applying enhanced fills and, 342–349
customizing PowerPoint theme, 277–281
email addresses
Excel format for, 432
selecting in Excel, 435
email messages
sending notes via, 728–729
sending to OneNote, 693–695
em and en spaces, formatting marks for, 170
embed codes, in videos, 374–375
Emphasis animations, 368
empty paragraphs, 162
Encrypt with Password option, 573
enhanced fills, applying in PowerPoint, 342–349
Entrance animations, 368
"epsilon" button, using, 457–460
equal (=) sign, in Excel formulas, 452
eraser, OneNote, 681
error messages, chart, 318
Even Page or Odd Page section breaks, 191
EXACT() function, 476
Excel
about, 421–422

about new features in, 417–418
about starting, 409–413
adding data to tables, 519–521
analyzing data from outside source, 508–511
cells in
changing case of text, 485–487
copying and pasting range of, 485
copying one or more cells to many, 447–448
deleting, 587–591
extending series with autofill, 429–431
format for email and web addresses, 432
formatting, 426–427, 550–551
inserting, 587–591
maximum number of characters in, 442
moving and adjusting, 442–444
pasting formulas as resulting values, 484–485
restricting entries, 487–492
using references, 467–470
validating entries, 470–472
working with text, 479–487
changing widths of spreadsheet columns, 423–426
charts
adding slicers to PivotCharts, 629–632
adding timelines to, 416, 637–639
creating and modifying, 623–629
manipulating objects in, 640–642
conditional formatting features, 504–507
creating and sharing graphics in, 642–648
creating custom sort list, 523–526
custom formatting codes, 554–555
data model, 512, 534
entering and organizing data, 422–423
filtering data with tables, 512–518
Filter menu commands, 518–519
Flash Fill command in, 413, 431–433
formatting cells, 550–551
formatting data, 426–429
formatting worksheets
applying number formatting, 538–541
applying percentage format to numbers, 558–560
Clear Formats option, 546
creating custom themes, 546–549
custom number formats, 551–558

lining up positive and negative numbers in columns, 541

protection in, 570–572

setting view options, 574–578

with styles, 542–545

working with dates, 564–570

working with fractions, 560–564

formulas

   about, 452

   activating Edit mode, 469, 481, 493

   dollar ($) sign in, 467–470, 493

   entering, 452–456

   equal (=) sign in, 452

   static values vs. cell references, 457

   using cell references, 467–470

   using Formulas tab, 473–479

   using names in, 470–472

functions

   CONCATENATE(), 476, 479–482

   date, 477–478

   financial, 478–479

   inserting, 464–467

   logical, 475–476

   math and trig, 474–475

   PROPER(), 476, 486

   reference, 478

   text, 476–477

   time, 477–478

   TRIM(), 477, 483

   using, 456–457

   using AutoSum button, 457–460

   using AVERAGE() function, 460–461

   using status bar for checking totals, 462

graphics in

   creating and sharing, 642–648

   using in other Office Applications, 648–653

inserting columns and rows, 583–587

inserting spreadsheets in OneNote, 763–764

jumping to first cell in worksheet, 520

manipulating elements in charts, 632–637

moving and copying columns and rows, 445–446

moving around worksheets, 439–441

online pictures feature in, 45

page layout options, 591–599

pages in

adjusting page breaks, 602–606

   printing row and column labels, 599–602

panes, 591–599

performing What-If Analysis, 498–502

PivotTable Fields pane, 528

PivotTables. *See also* PivotTables

   creating, 526–533

Recommended PivotTables feature, 415, 527

recovering unsaved files in, 24

Scenario Manager, 499

selecting and naming cell ranges, 434–437

sheet references in, 617–618

Simple to-do list workbook in, 49

sorting data, 521–523

table slicers, 415

templates

   built-in, 495–498

   storing formats in, 579–580

using column headers in defining names, 437–439

using Quick Analysis, 502–504

using touch mode in, 105

values in, 426, 429

workbooks

   changing number of sheets setting in, 417

   creating multisheet, 606–610

   displaying separate windows, 414

   managing multiple, 618–621

   manipulating sheets in, 610–613

   summarizing multisheet, 613–616

Zoom group, 603

exercise steps in book, adapting to, 26

Exit animations, 368

Expand/Collapse heading option, 143

expanding ribbon, 27

Export command, in Excel, 412

exporting

   OneNote to other formats, 730–732

Export page

   about, 22

   OneNote, 666

Eyedropper menu choice, 339–340

Eyedropper Text Fill tool, 263, 340

F

Facebook, connecting to personal cloud service in, 80–81
Fade, PowerPoint, 366
Field Buttons button, 627
Field List, PivotTable, 418
files. *See also* Office documents
    changing permissions, 90
    creating new, 17–19, 60
    customizing PowerPoint, 271–276
    opening, 20
    opening from cloud, 42, 90–91
    pinning and unpinning, 20
    recovering unsaved changes to, 23–25
    saving as PDF, 22
    saving in XPS format, 22
    saving on cloud service, 42
    selecting multiple, 107
    setting feature to autosave, 23–24
    sharing files from cloud service, 88–90
    syncing for offline use with SkyDrive, 92–96
    viewing information about active, 16–17
    viewing recent files, 20
file server
    sharing notes on, 718–723
    stop sharing on, 721–723
File tab
    Excel, 412
    OneNote, 658
    PowerPoint, 255
    Word, 118
Filled Round Bullets menu choice, 286
Fill menu, in Excel, Flash Fill command from, 431
filter buttons, hiding, 516
Filter by Color command, 518
Filter group; a dialog box, 630
Filter menu commands, 518–519
financial functions, 478–479
Find Options dialog box, 140
Fit Slide to Current Window button, 289
Fixed Column Width option, in Insert Table dialog box, 218
Flash Fill command, in Excel, 413, 431–433
folders, pinning and unpinning, 20
Followed Hyperlink color, in PowerPoint, 280

Font dialog box, 200
fonts
    creating theme font set, 277
    customizing PowerPoint, 271–276
    decreasing font size, 285
    glyph, 166
    increasing font size, 285
    serif and sans serif, 188
Font Size box, PowerPoint, 285
Format Background pane, in PowerPoint, 290
Format Cells dialog box, 561–563, 565–567
    Custom category in, 634–635
    using comma (,) in custom number format code, 635
Format Chart Title task pane, 625
Format Data Labels task pane, 634
Format Shape pane, 258
    3-D Format tools, 346
    accessing, 344
    Blur field, 346
    in Excel, 646–648
    Shape Options Effects button in, 345
formatting
    accessing PowerPoint picture formatting tools, 358
    cells in Excel, 426–427
    changing presentation to widescreen format, 297–300
    charts
        controlling, 43–44
        in PowerPoint, 316–320
    conditional, 504–507
    data in Excel, 426–429
    documents
        about, 183–188
        changing case of text, 200–201
        exploring character formatting, 200–201
        exploring paragraph formatting, 196–198
        managing pagination through, 203–207
        setting default documents, 188–190
        setting section formatting, 190–192
    illustrations using Drawing Tools Format tool tab, 52
    in OneNote using styles, 692–693
    lists using bullets, 210–213
    lists using numbering, 210–213

manual text boxes in slides, 308–313

OneNote with templates, 765–767

options in all galleries, 273–275

pictures in presentations, 354–360

placeholders on slide master, 283–288

reusing slides and keeping source, 326–333

setting for documents default, 128

shapes in PowerPoint, 336–341

table borders in, 125

tables in PowerPoint, 313

Total Row, 223

worksheets

  applying number formatting, 538–541

  applying percentage format to numbers, 558–560

  cells, 550–551

  Clear Formats option, 546

  creating custom themes, 546–549

  custom number formats, 551–558

  formatting with styles, 542–545

  lining up positive and negative numbers in columns, 541

  protecting, 570–572

  setting view options, 574–578

  working with dates, 564–570

  working with fractions, 560–564

formatting marks

  using during document composition, 161–164

formulas. *See also* functions

  about, 452

  activating Edit mode, 469, 481, 493

  creating, 464–467

  dollar ($) sign in, 467–470, 493

  entering, 452–456

  equal (=) sign in, 452

  inserting, 464–467

  pasting as resulting values, 484–485

  static values vs. cell references in, 457

  using cell references, 467–470

  using Formulas tab, 473–479

  using names in, 470–472

  using status bar for checking totals, 462

Formulas tab, in Excel

  about, 473

  Create From Selection command on, 437–439

Defined Names section on, 435

Fragment tool, PowerPoint, 264

Freeform icon, 351

Freeze Panes command, 592

From a Video Embed Code field, 375

From Beginning or From Current Slide buttons, 397

Full Page view, Notebook, 660

Full Screen mode

  OneNote, 665

  vs. Read mode, 119

Function Arguments dialog box, 465–466, 473

Function dialog box, 473

functions. *See also* formulas

  about, 456–457

  AVERAGE, 460–461

  CONCATENATE(), 476, 479–482

  Count Numbers(), 462

  date, 477–478

  financial, 478–479

  inserting, 464–467

  logical, 475–476

  math and trig, 474–476

  Max(), 462

  Min(), 462

  PROPER(), 476, 486

  reference, 478

  text, 476–477

  time, 477–478

  TRIM(), 477, 483

  using, 456–457

  using AutoSum button, 457–460

  using AVERAGE() function, 460–461

  using Formulas tab, 473–479

  using status bar for checking totals, 462

funnel icon (Chart Filters tool), 320

G

galleries

  about, 8–9

  Animation, 366

  Border Styles, 224

  Bullets, 286

  Bullets and Numbering, 211–212

Reuse Slides, 326–333
Rule Lines, 662
Shapes, 679–680
SmartArt Styles, 324
Styles
    Excel, 542
    Word, 184
Table Styles, 223
Tags, 688–689, 752
Theme, 270
Theme Colors, 278, 280
Theme Font, 272
Theme Fonts, 277
Themes, 49, 549
Variants, 270, 277
gestures
    in touch mode, 105–106
    zoom on slide in touch-enabled device, 400
Get a Sharing Link option, 46
Get External Data group, 508
glyph fonts, 166
Goal Seek command, 499, 502
Goal Seek dialog box, 499, 501
gradient fills, applying and editing, 342–349
grammar errors
    correcting, 230–231
    correcting in touch mode, 105
graphics. *See also* illustrations; *See also* pictures
    (photos)
    adding to presentations, 288
    copying to slides, 290, 341–342
    creating and sharing in Excel, 642–648
    distortion changing to presentation wide-screen
        format, 300
    using between Office applications, 648–653
Gridlines option, in Excel, 636
grouped worksheets, Excel, 610
Group Objects button, 649
guides
    document alignment, 127
    in PowerPoint, 311

H

handwriting recognition vs. ink, 108
hanging indent markers, 198, 214
HD Displays option, Computer &, 376
heading fonts, in PowerPoint, 272
headings in documents
    collapsible, 126
    collapsing and expanding, 141–144
    styles of, 141–144
Headings section, in Navigation pane, 137
heading text, 185
Help button, 7
h (Hour), Excel date formatting code, 570
hidden text
    font format option, 201
    printing, 201
Hide Background Graphics
    in Format Background pane, 290
    on layout in PowerPoint, 290
Hide command, Excel worksheets, 611
Hide Page Title, OneNote, 662
HLOOKUP() function, 478
Home tab
    Excel
        Flash Fill command from, 431
        Wrap Text button on, 444
    PowerPoint
        about, 256–257
        Layout button from, 336
        Order Objects tools from, 360
        Paragraph dialog launcher from, 287
        Word, Bullets and Numbering galleries from, 211–
            212
Horizontal Bullet List Smart Art, 321
Hotmail, 73
HTML, saving Word documents as, 243
Hyperlink color, in PowerPoint, 279, 280
hyperlink format
    for email and web addresses in Excel, 432
    selecting cells in Excel in, 435
hyperlinks
    creating to pages in OneNote custom, 702–704
    tying OneNote notes together using, 700–702

I

IFERROR() functions, 476
IF() function, 475
illustrations. *See also* graphics
    formatting using Drawing Tools Format tool
        tab, 52
    inserting in Office documents, 51
Illustrations group, in Excel
    Screenshot button, 651
    Shapes button, 645
    Shapes button in, 643
images. *See also* graphics
    adding frames to, 356
    cropping in presentations, 356
    displaying layout options for, 127
    embed from online locations directly into Office
        documents, 44
    inserting in Office documents, 51
    inserting in OneNote pages, 676–677
    inserting in presentations, 355–357
    online pictures feature for, 44–45
    placement in documents of, 127
    removing backgrounds from, 361–363
    resizing, 289
    searching, 761–762
Import Text dialog box, 511
Increase Font Size button, 285
Increase List Level button, 306, 307
Indentation option, 197
indent markers, controlling on ruler, 287
Info page
    about, 16–17
    tools for recovering unsaved files, 23–25
ink
    tools in OneNote, 108
    vs. handwriting recognition, 108
    working in OneNote with, 677–683
    working in touch mode with, 107
    working with, 108–112
Ink Comment button, 109
Ink Tools Pens tool tab, 108
Insert Chart dialog box, 56, 624
Insert Function dialog box, 462, 464–465, 473
inserting pictures, in presentations, 355–357
Insert Slicer button, 630

Insert Slicers dialog box, 630
Insert Space tool, 682
Insert tab
    inserting illustrations using, 51
    in Tables group, 217
Insert Table dialog box, 218
Insert Table feature, OneNote, 705–707
Insert Timeline button, 638
Insert Video page, 374–375
Inspect Document heading, 235
installation, Office, getting information about, 12–
    13
integers, about, 461
international characters, 167–168
Internet, opening documents from Internet, 148
Inverse screen color, in Read Mode, 146
Invite People section
    on Share Notebook page, 715
    Share page, 88–89
iOS, sharing notes via SharePoint on, 723
iPad or iPhone, using OneNote on, 741–743
IPMT() functions, 479
italicizing selected text, 310

K

Keep lines together paragraph options, 205
Keep Source Formatting option
    in Reuse Slides pane, 329
    Paste Option to, 331
Keep with next page option, 205
keyboard access to menus and commands, 546
keyboard shortcuts
    assigning to character or symbol custom, 168
    bolding selected text, 310
    centering text, 316
    centering text in documents, 195
    changing case of text, 203
    clicking Previous button, 139
    collapsing and expanding ribbon, 27
    copying selected text or object, 311
    creating new blank document, 85
    decreasing font size, 285
    demoting text in slides, 306

displaying characters in uppercase, 201
displaying hidden text, 201
displaying small caps, 201
duplicating objects, 311
entering international characters, 167–168
entering SUM function, 458
entering symbols using, 167
formatting marks, 161
increasing font size, 285
italicizing selected text, 310
jumping to first cell in worksheet, 520
left aligning text, 316
manual page breaks, 203
moving around worksheets using Ctrl key, 440–441
moving cursor, 155–156
moving cursor to beginning of sentence, 171
moving cursor to top of document, 195
navigating documents, 134
Nonbreaking space, 171
opening Font dialog box, 200
opening Link dialog box, 703
pasting selected text or object, 311, 331
promoting text in slides, 306
resetting character and paragraph formats, 196
saving files, 86–87
screen clipping capability, 758
Search box, 139
selecting Navigation pane check box, 139
selecting text, 157
starting presentations, 394
translating phrase, 151–152
underlining selected text, 310
undo the previous action, 270
KeyTips, 11

L

Label Options section, of Format Data Labels task pane, 634
Layout, as Read Mode option, 146
Layout button, in PowerPoint, 336
Layout Options button, in Word, 127
layouts

PowerPoint. *See also* slides
    adding graphics to, 288–291
    creating custom slides, 291–297
    Word, using tables for page, 226
Layout tab, PowerPoint, viewing, 315
left aligning text, 316
LEFT() function, 476
LEN() function, 476
line breaks, manual line, 170
Line spacing, in Paragraph dialog box, 288
Line Spacing option, 198
Link dialog box, 703
Linked Contact Notes button, 697
linking
    multimedia files to PowerPoint, 371
    notes, 759–761
lists, formatting bulleted and numbered, 210–213
Live Layout, in Word, 127
Live Preview, 9
Lock Cell command, 491, 492
logical functions, 475–476
lookup functions, 478
Lowercase option, 202
LOWER() function, 476

M

Manage Styles dialog box, 190
manual line break, 170
manual page breaks, 203
manual tabs, 162
    decimal tab as type of, 214, 220, 226
    text alignment using, 214
    using, 214–217
manual tab stops, 213
margin marker, in PowerPoint, 286
margins, toggling in Print Layout view, 120
Mark As Final option
    in Excel, 573
    in PowerPoint, 392
    in Word, 238
math functions, 474–476
Max function, 462

meetings, presentation through Office Presentation Service at, 62

menus, keyboard access to, 546

Merge Shapes tool, 353

messages, email
    sending notes via, 728–729
    sending to OneNote, 693–695

microphones, for recording audio, 756

Microsoft account
    about, 73
    signing into, 74–76
    signing out of, 78
    switching to another account, 76–77

Microsoft Excel
    about, 421–422
    about new features in, 417–418
    about starting, 409–413
    adding data to tables, 519–521
    analyzing data from outside source, 508–511
    cells in
        changing case of text, 485–487
        copying and pasting range of, 485
        copying one or more cells to many, 447–448
        deleting, 587–591
        extending series with autofill, 429–431
        format for email and web addresses, 432
        formatting, 426–427, 550–551
        inserting, 587–591
        maximum number of characters in, 442
        moving and adjusting, 442–444
        pasting formulas as resulting values, 484–485
        restricting entries, 487–492
        using references, 467–470
        validating entries, 470–472
        working with text, 479–487
    changing widths of spreadsheet columns, 423–426
    charts
        adding slicers to PivotCharts, 629–632
        adding timelines to, 416, 637–639
        creating and modifying, 623–629
        manipulating objects in, 640–642
    conditional formatting features, 504–507
    creating custom sort list, 523–526
    custom formatting codes, 554–555
    data model, 512, 534

entering and organizing data, 422–423

filtering data with tables, 512–518

Filter menu commands, 518–519

Flash Fill command in, 413, 431–433

formatting cells, 550–551

formatting data, 426–429

formatting worksheets
    applying number formatting, 538–541
    applying percentage format to numbers, 558–560
    Clear Formats option, 546
    creating custom themes, 546–549
    custom number formats, 551–558
    lining up positive and negative numbers in columns, 541
    protection in, 570–572
    setting view options, 574–578
    with styles, 542–545
    working with dates, 564–570
    working with fractions, 560–564

formulas
    about, 452
    activating Edit mode, 469, 481, 493
    dollar ($) sign in, 467–470, 493
    entering, 452–456
    equal (=) sign in, 452
    static values vs. cell references, 457
    using cell references, 467–470
    using Formulas tab, 473–479
    using names in, 470–472

functions
    CONCATENATE(), 476, 479–482
    date, 477–478
    financial, 478–479
    inserting, 464–467
    logical, 475–476
    math and trig, 474–476
    PROPER(), 476, 486
    reference, 478
    text, 476–477
    time, 477–478
    TRIM(), 477, 483
    using, 456–457
    using AutoSum button, 457–460
    using AVERAGE() function, 460–461

using status bar for checking totals, 462
graphics in
    creating and sharing, 642–648
    using in other Office Applications, 648–653
inserting columns and rows, 583–587
inserting spreadsheets in OneNote, 763–764
jumping to first cell in worksheet, 520
manipulating elements in charts, 632–637
moving and copying columns and rows, 445–446
moving around worksheets, 439–441
online pictures feature in, 45
page layout options, 591–599
pages in
    adjusting page breaks, 602–606
    printing row and column labels, 599–602
panes, 591–599
performing What-If Analysis, 498–502
PivotTable Fields pane, 528
PivotTables. See also PivotTables
    creating, 526–533
Recommended PivotTables feature, 415, 527
recovering unsaved files in, 24
Scenario Manager, 499–502
selecting and naming cell ranges, 434–437
sheet references in, 617–618
Simple to-do list workbook in, 49
sorting data, 521–523
table slicers, 415
templates
    built-in, 495–498
    storing formats in, 579–580
using column headers in defining names, 437–439
using Quick Analysis, 502–504
values in, 426, 429
workbooks
    changing number of sheets setting in, 417
    creating multisheet, 606–610
    displaying separate windows, 414
    managing multiple, 618–621
    manipulating sheets in, 610–613
    summarizing multisheet, 613–616
Zoom group, 603
Microsoft Office 365, 83
Microsoft Office cloud accounts. See also cloud
    services

about, 73
signing into, 74–76
signing out of, 78
switching to another account, 76–77
using cloud services with, 78–79
Microsoft Office Home & Student 2013 RT, 101
Microsoft OneNote. See also OneNote Mobile apps
about, 669
about getting started, 657–660
about navigating interface, 659–664
about new features in, 665–667
accessing notes in web browser, 738–740
changing search scope in, 709–710
connecting to Outlook
    about, 693
    annotating contacts, 697–698
    appointments, 695–697
    sending email messages to OneNote, 693–695
    tasks, 698–700
correcting grammar errors in touch mode, 105
creating and organizing
    pages, 674–677
    sections, 671–673
creating custom hyperlinks to other pages, 702–704
creating notebook, 670–671
custom styles in, 693
exporting to other formats, 730–732
file server
    sharing notes on, 718–723
    stop sharing on, 721–723
finding tags, 751–754
inking tools in, 108
inserting spreadsheets in, 763–764
linking notes, 759–761
printing PDFs to, 762
recording audio, 755–756
Require User To Sign In Before Accessing
    Document check box, 716
searching images, 761–762
searching notes, 707–710
section groups in, 673
sharing notes
    during meetings, 727–728
    on file server, 718–723

via email messages, 728–729

via SharePoint, 723–726

SkyDrive

    accessing notes in, 738

    creating notebooks on, 713–716

    moving notebook to, 716–718

    stop sharing in, 718

    syncing notebooks using, 743

    syncing notes using, 735–738

tables

    creating and organizing, 704–705

    Insert Table feature, 705–707

    maximum size of, 706

tags

    creating and customizing, 690–692

    using, 688–689

templates, 765–767

tying notes together using hyperlinks, 700–702

using Napkin Math feature, 765

using on phone or tablet, 740–741

using Quick Notes, 756–757

using screen clippings, 758–759

using styles to format notes, 692–693

working with ink and shapes, 677–683

Microsoft Outlook, connecting to OneNote

    about, 693

    annotating contacts, 697–698

    appointments, 695–697

    sending email messages to OneNote, 693–695

    tasks, 698–700

Microsoft PowerPoint

    about, 253–256

    about new features in, 259–264

    adding and formatting shapes, 336–341

    alignment tools in, 289, 340. *See also* Smart
        Guides, in PowerPoint

    applying enhanced fills and effects, 342–349

    converting inked drawing to shape in, 110–111

    creating custom shapes, 349–354

    customizing, 271–276

    inserting and formatting charts in, 316–320

    online pictures feature in, 45

    placeholders in

        formatting on slide master, 283–288

        inserting pictures in, 355

selecting, 284

troubleshooting selecting, 366

turning off title and footer, 293

presentations. *See also* presentations

    changing presentation to widescreen
        format, 297–300

    creating PDFs of, 389

    delivering, 394–401

    editing video, 371–373

    finalizing, 391–394

    formatting pictures in, 354–360

    inserting comments in, 384–385

    inserting online video into, 65, 374–375

    practicing, 401–406

    removing backgrounds from pictures, 361

    saving as video, 375–377

    using theme variant, 268

recovering unsaved files in, 24

Shapes gallery in, 309

slide master, 283–291

slides

    adding and formatting tables in, 313–316

    adding and renaming sections, 380–383

    adding manual text boxes, 308–313

    adding text to placeholders, 304–308

    applying transitions to, 371–373

    bullet points in, 306, 321–325

    choosing layout for, 304, 313–316

    copying graphics to, 341–342

    creating and formatting charts, 313–316

    creating and formatting SmartArt
        diagrams, 320–325

    creating custom layout, 291–297

    default size of, 259

    editing video, 371–373

    Fit Slide to Current Window button, 289

    inserting comments in, 384–385

    notating using inking tools, 109

    placeholders, 304

    playing sound across, 373

    printing, 386–390

    reusing and keeping source formatting, 326–
        333

    selecting animations on, 367

    selecting groups of, 331

transitions in, 261

Smart Guides in, 289, 311, 352

starting, 253

starting presentation using theme variant, 268

templates, 297

themes. *See also* themes

    applying background styles to presentations, 281–283

    applying to existing presentations, 269–271

    creating presentations using theme variants, 268

tools in, 256–258

word completion, in touch mode, 105

Microsoft SharePoint, sharing notes via, 723–726

Microsoft SkyDrive

    about, 84

    accessing notes in, 738

    changing permissions, 90

    connecting to, 79–81

    creating notebooks on, 713–716

    moving notebook to, 716–718

    opening files from, 42

    opening files from cloud, 90–91

    saving files on, 42, 85–87

    sharing files from, 88–90

    signing into, 84

    stop sharing in, 718

    syncing files for offline use with, 92–96

    syncing notebooks on, 743

    syncing notes using, 735–738

Microsoft Surface

    automatic phrase translation on, 151

    viewing documents in, 239

Microsoft Surface, using Read Mode on, 146

Microsoft Windows 7

    modifying screen resolution, 14–15

    starting Office application in, 4–5

Microsoft Windows 8

    modifying screen resolution, 14–15

    starting Office application in, 4–5

    tablet edition of, 101

    Window control buttons, 7–8

    Windows Explorer vs. File explorer, 92

Microsoft Windows RT

    about, 101

    on Windows 8 tablet, 748

Microsoft Word

    about new features in, 123–129

    alignment guides in, 127

    composing documents

        inserting special characters, 169–171

        inserting symbols, 165–166, 168

        using AutoCorrect, 167–168, 172–175

        using building blocks, 176–180

        using formatting marks in, 161–164

        using international characters, 167–168

    correcting proofing errors, 230–232

    creating across applications coordinating documents, 128

    documents created in earlier versions of, 129

    editing documents

        moving cursor by keyboard shortcuts, 155–156

        selecting text, 156–160

    file extension for, 116

    formatting documents

        about, 183–188

        changing case of text, 200–201

        exploring character formatting, 200–201

        exploring paragraph formatting, 196–198

        managing pagination through, 203–207

        setting default documents, 188–190

        setting section formatting, 190–192

        using styles for, 192–196

    heading styles in documents, 141–144

    inspecting documents before publishing, 233–237

    Layout Options button in, 127

    Live Layout in, 127

    making documents final, 238

    modifying document view, 119–120

    online pictures feature in, 45

    opening files from cloud, 90–91

    PDFs

        creating, 239–244

        editing, 239, 243–244

        Reflow feature, 124

    presentations, inserting online video into, 65–69

    presenting information in

        inserting tables, 217–223, 223–227

        using bulleted lists, 209, 210–213

        using numbered lists, 209, 210–213

using tabbed lists, 210, 213–217
using tables, 210
printing documents, 245–249
Read Mode
    exploring research tools in, 148–152
    viewing documents in, 144–148
recovering unsaved files in, 24
resume reading feature in, 124
ribbon, 117–119
saving files on cloud, 85–87
scrolling documents, 134–135
selecting document content, 157
setting default formatting for documents, 128
splitting screen in, 122–123
starting, 115–116
tables, 125
threaded comments in, 126
turning on ruler display, 122
using Navigation pane, 135–141
word completion, in touch mode, 105
Zoom group in, 120–121
Min function, 462
Mini Toolbar, 10
mm (Minutes), Excel date formatting code, 570
mobile phones, using OneNote on, 740
More Options button, 319
mouse
    scrolling documents using, 134–135
    selecting text using, 157, 159
Move Notebook option, on Share Notebook
    page, 717
mp4 formatted video, saving presentation as, 375–
    377
multimedia files, linking to PowerPoint, 371

N

names
    using in Excel column headers in defining, 437–439
    using in formulas, 470–472
naming, cell ranges in Excel, 434–437
Napkin Math feature, 765
Navigation Grid, in PowerPoint, 397–398
Navigation pane

about, 136
Headings section, 137
Word
    as mini table of contents, 137
    options, 136–138
    searching and navigating documents, 135–141
    selecting heading with, 159
Navigation Pane option, in Read Mode, 145
Nested IF() function, 475
NETWORKDAYS() function, 478
New Docked Window, OneNote, 663
New Name dialog box, in Excel, 436, 437
New page, 17–19
New Slide button, 305, 313–316
Next and Previous buttons, using in
    documents, 137
Next Page section breaks, 191
Nonbreaking space, 171
Normal view
    in OneNote, 659–660
    in Word, 120
Notebook pane, OneNote, 659
Notebook Recycle Bin button, 684–685
notebooks, OneNote
    about, 669
    creating, 670–671
        in OneNote Mobile apps, 743
        in SkyDrive, 713–716
    creating and organizing
        pages, 674–677
        sections, 671–673
    moving to SkyDrive, 716–718
    working with ink and shapes, 677–683
notes, OneNote
    accessing in SkyDrive, 738
    adding and organizing OneNote, 675–676
    creating in OneNote Mobile apps, 743
    linking, 759–761
    sharing
        during meetings, 727–728
        on file server, 718–723
        via email messages, 728–729
        via SharePoint, 723–726
    stop sharing on file server in, 721–723
    syncing notes in SkyDrive, 735–738

notes pane, in PowerPoint, 256

notes, printing presentation, 386–390

NOW() function, 477

NPER() functions, 479

numbered lists
    about, 209
    formatting, 210–213

Number Filters command, 519

Number Format drop-down menu, in Excel, 426–427

number formatting, Excel
    applying number formatting, 538–541
    applying percentage format to, 558–560
    lining up positive and negative numbers in columns, 541
    working with custom number formats, 551–558
    working with fractions, 560–564

number next to PowerPoint animation, 369

O

objects, manipulating in Excel, 640–642

Odd Page or Even Page section breaks, 191

Office 365
    about, 83

Office applications
    elements in application window, 6–13
        Account commands, 12–13
        dialog box launcher, 8
        galleries, 8–9
        KeyTips, 11
        Live Preview, 9
        Mini Toolbar, 10
        Quick Access Toolbar, 8
        ribbon, 6
        Screen Tips, 10–11
        status bar, 8
        title bar, 7
        tool tabs, 8
    shared features in, 42
    starting, 4–5
    streaming, 83
    supporting touch, 47, 101–112
    using graphics between, 648–653

Office cloud accounts. *See also* cloud services
    about, 12, 73
    signing into, 74–76
    signing out of, 78
    switching to another account, 76–77
    using cloud services with, 78–79

Office documents. *See also* files
    co-authoring, 97–98
    creating new, 60
    inserting
        apps in, 47
        charts in, 54–57
        illustrations in, 51
        pictures in, 51
        shapes into, 52
        SmartArt graphic in, 52
    online pictures embed directly into, 44
    online presentations, 44, 62–65
    online sharing of, 44
    online video in, 45–46, 65–69
    sharing with social networks, 46

Office Home & Student 2013 RT, 101–103

Office installation, getting information about, 12–13

Office on Demand, 83

Office Presentation Service
    PowerPoint presentation through, 62–65
    sharing Office documents through, 44

Office themes
    applying, 47–50
    changing, 12

OneNote. *See also* OneNote Mobile apps
    about, 669
    about getting started, 657–660
    about navigating interface, 659–664
    about new features in, 665–667
    accessing notes in web browser, 738–740
    changing search scope in, 709–710
    connecting to Outlook
        about, 693
        annotating contacts, 697–698
        appointments, 695–697
        sending email messages to OneNote, 693–695
        tasks, 698–700
    correcting grammar errors in touch mode, 105

creating and organizing
    pages, 674–677
    sections, 671–673
creating custom hyperlinks to other pages, 702–704
creating notebook, 670–671
custom styles in, 693
exporting to other formats, 730–732
file server
    sharing notes on, 718–723
    stop sharing on, 721–723
finding tags, 751–754
inking tools in, 108
inserting spreadsheets in, 763–764
linking notes, 759–761
printing PDFs to, 762
recording audio, 755–756
Require User To Sign In Before Accessing Document check box, 716
searching images, 761–762
searching notes, 707–710
section groups in, 673
sharing notes
    during meetings, 727–728
    on file server, 718–723
    via email messages, 728–729
    via SharePoint, 723–726
SkyDrive
    accessing notes in, 738
    creating notebooks on, 713–716
    moving notebook to, 716–718
    stop sharing in, 718
    syncing notebooks using, 743
    syncing notes using, 735–738
tables
    creating and organizing, 704–705
    Insert Table feature, 705–707
    maximum size of, 706
tags
    creating and customizing, 690–692
    using, 688–689
templates, 765–767
tying notes together using hyperlinks, 700–702
using Napkin Math feature, 765
using on phone or tablet, 740–741

using Quick Notes, 756–757
using screen clippings, 758–759
using styles to format notes, 692–693
working with ink and shapes, 677–683
OneNote Mobile apps
    about, 740
    creating notebooks in, 743
    creating notes in, 743
    using on Android, 743–745
    using on iPad or iPhone, 741–743
    using on Windows phone, 746–747
    using on Windows Phone 8 tablet, 747
OneNote Web App, 738–740
online
    pictures feature, 44–45
    presentations, 44, 62–65
    templates, 42, 58–62
    video
        inserting into presentations, 65–69, 374–375
        playing back in Office documents, 45–46
        saving in video presentation, 377
on-screen keyboard, 105
Open Document Format ODF 1.2, 418
OpenDocument, saving Word documents as, 243
Open page, 20, 91
Option commands, 13
Options dialog box, in Word, 242
Order Objects tools, 360
Orientation button, 604
Or Select a Category list, in Insert Function dialog box, 464
Outline level document option, 197
Outline view
    in Word, 120
Outlook.com, signing up for, 73
Outlook, connecting to OneNote
    about, 693
    annotating contacts, 697–698
    appointments, 695–697
    sending email messages to OneNote, 693–695
    tasks, 698–700
Outlook Tasks button, 698

P

Page break before page option, 205
Page Break Preview mode, 604
page breaks, adjusting Excel, 602–606
Page Color, as Read Mode option, 146
page layout options, in Excel, 591–599
pages
    Excel
        adjusting page breaks, 602–606
        printing row and column labels, 599–602
    OneNote
        creating and organizing, 674–677
        recovering deleted, 684–685
Page Setup dialog box, 601
pages feature, in Navigation pane, 137
Page tabs, OneNote, 659
Page Templates button, 765
Page Width command, in Word, 120
pagination, managing through formatting, 203–207
panes, in Excel, 591–599
Paper Size, OneNote, 662
Paragraph dialog box
    After spacing, 288
    Before spacing, 288
    Line spacing in, 288
    Paragraph pagination options in, 204
Paragraph dialog launcher, from Home tab, 287
paragraph formats
    exploring, 196–198
    pagination options for, 203–207
    resetting, 196
    using styles for, 192–196
Paragraph group, Bullets and Numbering galleries in, 211–212
Paragraph group dialog box, 197
Paragraph pagination options, 204
Paste Options
    palette, 485
    to keep source formatting, 331
Paste Special, Values button in, 486
Paste Values group, Values button in, 485
pasting
    formulas as resulting values, 484–485
    range of cells, 485
pasting selected text or object, 311, 331
PDF (Portable Document Format)
    creating from presentations, 389
    editing in Word, 124
    printing to OneNote, 762
    saving files as, 22
PDF Reflow feature, in Word, 124
Pen and Laser Pointer Tools icon, in PowerPoint, 404, 406
pens, OneNote, 679
permissions
    removing on file server user, 721–723
    removing on SkyDrive user, 718
Permissions drop-down box, 90
personal cloud services, connecting to, 80–81
Personal (Web), 743
phones, using OneNote on, 740
Pictures button, 51
pictures (photos). *See also* graphics
    adding frames to, 356
    cropping in presentations, 356
    displaying layout options for, 127
    embed from online locations directly into Office documents, 44
    inserting in Office documents, 51
    inserting in OneNote pages, 676–677
    inserting in presentations, 355–357
    online pictures feature for, 44–45
    placement in documents of, 127
    removing backgrounds from, 361–363
    resizing, 289
    searching, 761–762
Picture Tools Format tab, 52
    accessing PowerPoint picture formatting tools from, 358
    Crop button on, 356, 652
    in slide master, 289
    Remove Background button on, 361–362
    Reset Picture button on, 359
    Transparent Wand tool from, 362
pinch gestures, in touch mode, 106
pinning files, 20
PivotChart Fields task pane, 625
PivotCharts
    adding slicer to, 418, 629–632

creating and modifying, 623–629
PivotChart Tools Analyze tab, 627, 630, 638
PivotChart Tools Design tab, 627, 633
PivotChart Tools Format tab, 642
PivotChart Tools tabs, 625, 638
pivot icons, 624–625
PivotTable Fields pane, 528
PivotTables
    creating, 526–533
    Field List, 418
    in determining to use, 624–625
    Recommended PivotTables feature, 415
pixels, in screen resolution, 15
placeholders
    about, 256
    formatting on slide master, 283–288
    inserting pictures in, 355
    selecting, 284
    slide
        about, 304
        adding text to, 304–308
    troubleshooting selecting, 366
    turning off title and footer, 293
Play in Background button, 373
pm/am, Excel date formatting code, 570
PMT() functions, 479
Pointer Options, in Slide Show view, 398
Popup Toolbar, activating during PowerPoint
    presentations, 397
Post to Social Networks option, 46
pound sign (#), as Excel formatting code, 554
PowerPoint
    about, 253–256
    about new features in, 259–264
    adding and formatting shapes, 336–341
    alignment tools in, 289, 340. See also Smart
        Guides, in PowerPoint
    applying enhanced fills and effects, 342–349
    converting inked drawing to shape in, 110–112
    creating custom shapes, 349–354
    customizing files, 271–276
    inserting and formatting charts in, 316–320
    online pictures feature in, 45
    placeholders in
        formatting on slide master, 283–288

inserting pictures in, 355
selecting, 284
troubleshooting selecting, 366
turning off title and footer, 293
presentations. See also presentations
    changing presentation to widescreen
        format, 297–300
    creating PDFs of, 389
    delivering, 394–401
    editing video, 371–373
    finalizing, 391–394
    formatting pictures in, 354–360
    inserting comments in, 384–385
    inserting online video into, 65, 374–375
    practicing, 401–406
    removing backgrounds from pictures, 361–363
    saving as video, 375–377
    using theme variant, 268
recovering unsaved files in, 24
Shapes gallery in, 309
slide master, 283–291
slides
    adding and formatting tables in, 313–316
    adding and renaming sections, 380–383
    adding manual text boxes, 308
    adding text to placeholders, 304–308
    applying transitions to, 371–373
    bullet points in, 306, 321–325
    choosing layout for, 304, 313–316
    copying graphics, 341–342
    creating and formatting charts, 313–316
    creating and formatting SmartArt
        diagrams, 320–325
    creating custom layout, 291–297
    default size of, 259
    editing video, 371–373
    Fit Slide to Current Window button, 289
    inserting comments in, 384–385
    notating using inking tools, 109
    placeholders, 304
    playing sound across, 373
    printing, 386–390
    reusing and keeping source formatting, 326–
        333
    selecting animations on, 367

selecting groups of, 331

selecting in touch mode, 107

transitions in, 261

Slide Sorter view

selecting slides in touch mode, 107

Smart Guides in, 289, 311, 352

starting, 253

templates, 297

themes. *See also* themes

applying background styles to presentations, 281–283

applying to existing presentations, 269–271

creating presentations using theme variants, 268

tools in, 256–258

word completion, in touch mode, 105

PowerView, 418

presentations

3-D charts in, 629

adding and formatting shapes, 336–341

adding graphics to, 288–291

applying background styles to, 281–283

applying enhanced fills and effects, 342–349

applying text formatting in, 283, 347

changing to widescreen format, 297–300

creating PDFs of, 389

customizing, 271–276

delivering, 394–401

editing saved slide show, 401

editing video, 371–373

finalizing, 391–394

formatting pictures in, 354–360

inserting comments in slides or objects, 384–385

inserting online video into, 65–69, 374–375

playing sound across slides, 373

practicing, 401–406

printing slides and notes, 386–390

removing backgrounds from pictures, 361–363

saving as video, 375–377

sharing Office documents in online, 44

starting using theme variant, 268

theme colors vs. direct colors, 341–342

themes, 269–271

through Office Presentation Service, 62–65

viewing on two monitors, 396

Presenter view, PowerPoint, 260, 401–406

presenting information in Word

using bulleted lists, 209, 210–213

using numbered lists, 209, 210–213

using tabbed lists, 210, 213–217

using tables, 210, 217–223, 223–227

Previous and Next buttons, using in documents, 137

Print All Slides option, 387

Print button, 22

Print command

in Excel, 412

Print Heading and Content option, 249

printing

documents, 245–249

hidden text, 201

presentation slides and notes, 386–390

Print Layout view, in Word, 119–120

Print One-Sided option, 246

Print page, 21

Print Titles command, 599, 602

PRODUCT() function, 475

Product Information, getting information about Office installation, 13

promoting text in slides, 306

PROPER() function, 476, 486

Protect Current Sheet option, 574

Protect Document button, 238

Protect Sheet dialog box., 490

Protect Sheet option, 491

Protect Workbook button, 573

Protect Workbook Structure option, 574

Publish button, 242

Q

Question tag, OneNote, 754

Quick Access Toolbar

about, 8

adding commands to

in Excel, 412

in Office, 28–29

in OneNote, 659

in PowerPoint, 255

in Word, 118
backing up to share with others, 35
customizing, 123
displaying through KeyTips, 11
green arrows on Save button, 91
moving below ribbon, 27
removing commands from, 28–29, 118
vs. ribbon commands, 32
Word, 118
Quick Analysis tools, using, 502–504
Quick Notes, 756–757
Quick Parts option, 178
quotation marks (" ")
as Excel formatting code, 555
using in searches, 710

R

RANDBETWEEN() functions, 475
range of cells, copying and pasting, 485
Read Mode
as document view, 119
closing, 145
exploring research tools in, 148–152
viewing documents in, 144–148
vs. Full Screen mode, 119
recent files, viewing, 20
Recent Folders list
pinning and unpinning folders to, 20
Recents button, OneNote Mobile apps, 743
Recommended Chart feature, 415, 623
Recommended PivotTables feature, 415
Recommended PivotTables feature, Excel, 527
recording audio, OneNote, 755–756
recovering
deleted sections or pages in OneNote, 684–685
unsaved files, 23–25
Rectangle tool, 336
reference functions, 478
Remove Background tool, 361–362
Remove From Quick Access Toolbar, 412
Remove Gradient Stop button, 345
Remove Section option, 383

Remove Section & Slides option, in Slide Sorter
view, 383
Remove Split command, 123
removing. *See* deleting
Rename Master menu choice, from Slide Master
view, 291
Rename Section dialog box, 381
reordering animations, 370
Require User To Sign In Before Accessing Document
check box, in OneNote, 716
Research pane, 152
research tools, exploring in Read Mode, 148–152
resizing
objects in touch mode, 106, 110–112
pictures, 289
presentation, troubleshooting, 300
split screens in Word, 122–123
Results option, in Navigation pane, 138
resume reading feature
in PowerPoint, 261
in Word, 124
Retrospect theme, 268, 270
Reuse Slides gallery, 326–333
Review tab, Define and Translate commands
on, 152
revising documents, using simple markup, 126
ribbon
about, 6
adjusting display of, 14–15
backing up to share with others, 35
collapsing and expanding, 27
customizing, 32–35
Excel, 411
moving Quick Access Toolbar below, 27
OneNote, 658
PowerPoint, 254–255
setting to auto-hide state, 27
vs. Quick Access Toolbar commands, 32
Word, 117–119
Ribbon Display Options button, 575
in Excel, 413
in Office, 7–8
in PowerPoint, 256
in Word, 118
right-clicking objects

to format shapes, 345
troubleshooting, 338
right-clicking pictures, to access PowerPoint picture formatting tools, 358
RIGHT() function, 477
roaming profiles, 72
rotating, text boxes, 312
ROUNDDOWN() functions, 475
ROUND() functions, 475
ROUNDUP() functions, 475
ROW([reference]) functions, 478
rows
    deleting OneNote table, 707
    deleting Word table, 222–223
    spreadsheets in Excel
        changing widths of, 426
        inserting in, 583–587
        moving and copying, 445–446
        printing row labels in, 599–602
ROWS(array) functions, 478
Rule Line Color option, OneNote, 662
Rule Lines button, 661–662
ruler display
    controlling indent markers on, 287
    setting indents in, 198–199
    viewing measurements on, 216
ruler display, turning on, 122
Running Total button, 504

S

sans serif and serif fonts, 188
Save As command, in Excel, 412
Save button, green arrows on Quick Access Toolbar, 91
Save Selection to Quick Part gallery, 178
Scenario Manager, 499
Scenario Manager dialog box., 501
Scope options, in New Name dialog box in Excel, 437
screen clippings, 758–759
Screen Clipping tool, 676
screen colors, in Read Mode, 15, 146
screen resolution, modifying, 14–15

Screenshot button, 355, 651
Screen Tips, 10–11
scroll bars, 134–135
Scroll Here command, 135
scrolling
    documents, 134–135
    in touch mode, 105–107
Search document
    as Navigation pane option, 138
    screen colors in Read Mode, 136
searching
    for online templates, 58–62
    notes in OneNote, 707–710
    notes in OneNote Mobile apps, 743
    using quotation marks in, 710
Search with Bing option, in Research pane, 152
section groups, OneNote, 673
sections
    adding and renaming, 380–383
    printing documents with, 248
sections, OneNote
    creating and organizing, 671–673
    recovering deleted, 684–685
Section tabs, OneNote, 659
security
    protecting worksheets, 570–572
    Require User To Sign In Before Accessing Document check box in OneNote, 716
    restricting entries in worksheets, 487–492
See All Slides button, 397
Select All button, in Excel, 443
selecting
    cell ranges in Excel, 434–437
    content in touch mode, 106–107
    phrase for translation, 151–152
    text in documents, 156–160
    Word tables, 225
selection handle, in Excel, extending series using, 429
selection mode, selecting text in, 158
Send Backward button, 645
Send to OneNote Tool, 663–664
Sentence case option, 202
Sepia screen color, in Read Mode, 146
serif and sans serif fonts, 188

Set As Default button, in Find Options dialog
box, 140
Set Transparent Color tool, 362
shadow options, accessing, 345, 646
Shape Effects button, 642
Shape Fill button, 343
Shape Options Effects button, 345
Shape Options Fill and Line icon, 344
shapes
adding and formatting in PowerPoint, 336–341
adding animation to presentation, 366–370
applying 3-D effects to, 346–349
creating custom, 349–354
creating perfect, 336
displaying layout options for, 127
inserting in Office documents, 52
placement in documents of, 127
removing border from, 345
selecting, 337
using adjustment handles, 349–351
working in OneNote with, 677–683
Shapes button, 643, 645
Shapes gallery, in PowerPoint, 309, 336
Shapes icon, 336
Shape Styles group
Drawing Tools Format tool tab in, 52
Shape Effects button in, 642
Shape Styles palette, from Drawing Tools Format
tab, 337, 644
Share command, in Excel, 412
shared features in Office 2013, identifying new, 42
Share Notebook page
Invite People section on, 715
Move Notebook option on, 717
Share Notes With This Meeting Occurrence,
OneNote, 696
Share page
about, 22
Invite People section on, 88–89
SharePoint Online
accessing locations hosted by school or
company, 92
changing permissions, 90
connecting to, 79–81
opening files from, 42

opening files from cloud, 90–91
saving files from, 42
saving files on, 85–87
sharing files from, 88–90
SharePoint, sharing notes via, 723–726
sharing files
changing permissions, 90
form cloud, 88–90
sheet references, Excel, 617–618
Show Comments, as Read Mode option, 145
Show/Hide ¶ button, 163, 201, 215
Show Tabs and Commands option, 576
Sign in to Office screen, 74
simple markup, for tracking changes in
documents, 126
Simple to-do list workbook, 49
Size group, Crop button from, 652
SkyDrive
about, 84
accessing notes in, 738
changing permissions, 90
connecting to, 79–81
creating notebooks on, 713–716
moving notebook to, 716–718
opening files from, 42
opening files from cloud, 90–91
saving files on, 42, 85–87
sharing files from, 88–90
signing into, 84
stop sharing in, 718
syncing files for offline use with, 92–96
syncing notebooks on, 743
syncing notes using, 735–738
Slicer buttons, 637
slicers feature
about, 418
adding to PivotCharts, 629–632
Slicer Styles palette, 631
Slicer Tools Options tab, 631
Slide Library feature, companies using, 328
slide master
adding graphics to, 288–291
formatting placeholders on, 283–288
Slide Master view, 272, 284, 291
slides

adding and formatting tables in, 313–316
adding and renaming sections, 380–383
adding manual text boxes, 308–313
applying transitions to, 371–373
bullet points in, 306, 308
choosing layout for, 304, 313
copying graphics, 290, 341–342
creating and formatting charts, 313–316
creating and formatting SmartArt diagrams, 320–325
creating custom layouts for, 291–297
default size of, 259
Fit Slide to Current Window button, 289
inserting comments in, 384–385
notating using inking tools, 109
placeholders, 304
playing sound across, 373
printing, 386–390
reusing and keeping source formatting, 326–333
selecting animations on, 367
selecting groups of, 331
selecting in touch mode, 107
transitions in, 261
Slide Show
    pop-up toolbar, 261
    view, 260
    zoom, 261
Slide Show view
    comments and, 384–385
    opening presentation in, 401
    Pointer Options in, 398
    seeing full-screen, 396
    view complete list of shortcuts available during presentations, 396
    ways to navigate in, 396
Slide Size menu choice, 299
Slide Sorter view, 107
    accessing, 381
    Remove Section & Slides option in, 383
slides pane, in PowerPoint, 256
SLN() functions, 479
Small Caps font format option, 201
SmartArt button, 52
SmartArt diagrams
    creating and formatting, 320–325

troubleshooting size of text in SmartArt diagrams, 325
SmartArt graphics
    changing bulleted list text into, 321–325
    inserting in Office documents, 52
SmartArt Styles gallery, 324
SmartArt Tools Design tool tab, 54, 323
Smart Guides, in PowerPoint, 289, 311, 352
smart phones, using OneNote on, 740
social networks, sharing Office documents with, 46
Sort commands, 518
Sort dialog box, Excel, 521, 584
sorting data, 521–523
sort list, creating custom, 523–526
sound
    linking files to PowerPoint, 371
    playing across slides, 373
Space Before and Space After option in document formatting, 198
special characters inserting, 169–171
spell checking, 230–231
Spelling And Grammar Check icon, 230–231
split control
    of commands on ribbon, 6–7
    Text Highlight Color, 187
splitting screen, in Word, 122–123
spreadsheets
    cells in, 424, 425
        changing case of text, 485–487
        copying and pasting range of, 485
        deleting, 587
        formatting, 550–551
        inserting, 587–591
        pasting formulas as resulting values, 484–485
        removing extra spaces, 482–484
        restricting entries, 487–492
        using references, 467–470
        validating entries, 470–472
        working with text, 479–487
    changing widths of columns, 423–426
    changing widths of rows, 426
    charts in, 623–629. *See also* charts
    creating and sharing graphics, 642–643
    creating PivotTables, 526–533
    formatting

applying number formatting, 538–541

applying percentage format to numbers, 558–560

Clear Formats option, 546

creating custom themes, 546–549

custom number formats, 551–558

lining up positive and negative numbers in columns, 541

setting view options, 574–578

with styles, 542–545

working with dates, 564–570

working with fractions, 560–564

inserting columns, 583–587

inserting in OneNote, 763–764

inserting rows, 583–587

jumping to first cell in, 520

moving and copying columns and rows on, 445–446

moving around, 439–441

page layout options, 591–599

pages in

adjusting page breaks, 602–606

printing row and column labels, 599–602

panes, 591–599

performing What-If Analysis, 498–502

protecting, 570–572

selecting entire, 443

sheet references in, 617–618

storing formats in templates, 579–580

using built-in templates, 495–498

square bullet character, formatting mark for paragraph pagination options, 205

s (Seconds), Excel date formatting code, 570

Start Automatically setting, in Video Tools Playback tab, 371

Start Inking button, 108

Start On Click setting, in Video Tools Playback tab, 371

Start screen, application

about, 4–5

templates in, 58

Word, 115–116

static values vs. cell references in formulas, 457

status bar

customizing, 30–31

in Excel, 413, 462

in Office, 8

in PowerPoint, 256

in Word, 119

Stop Automatically Expanding Tables command, 520

Stop option, on AutoCorrect feature, 172–175

streaming, Office applications, 83

Strict Open XML file format, 418

Strikethrough font format option, 201

Stroke Eraser, OneNote, 681

Style menu, Chart Styles button in, 626–627

styles

formatting in Excel with, 542–545

formatting in Word using, 192–196

in OneNote, 676, 692–693

Style Sets gallery, in Word, 128

Styles galleries

Excel, 542

Word, 184

subpages, creating OneNote, 675

SUM function, 457–460

SUMIF() function, 474

SUMPRODUCT() functions, 475

Surface

automatic phrase translation on, 151

viewing documents in, 239

Surface, using Read Mode on, 146

switching to another Office account, 76–77

Symbol button, OneNote, 691

Symbol dialog box, 165–166

symbols, inserting in documents, 165–166, 168

Synchronous Scrolling button, 578

syncing files, for offline use with SkyDrive, 92–96

T

tabbed lists

about, 210

creating, 213–217

Table gallery, in Word, 217

table of contents, Navigation pane as mini, 137

tables

Excel

adding data to tables, 519–521
filtering data with, 512–518
OneNote
creating and organizing, 704–705
maximum size of, 706
using Insert Table feature, 705–707
PowerPoint, adding and formatting in, 313–316
Word, 125
about, 210
borderless, 226
enhancing, 223–227
inserting, 217–223
selecting, 223–227
Tables group, Insert tab in, 217
table slicers, in Excel, 415
Table Style Options group, on Table Tools Design
tool tab, 223
Table Styles gallery, in PowerPoint, 315
Table Styles gallery, on Table Tools Design tool
tab, 223
tablet computers
sharing notes via SharePoint on, 723
touch mode
about, 47, 101–103
disabling, 103
handwriting recognition vs. ink, 107
selecting content in, 106–107
using, 103–106
working with ink in, 107
using Read Mode on, 146
Windows 8 for, 101
Table Tools Design tool tab, 223–224, 315, 513
Table Tools Layout tool tab, 222
tabs
decimal, 214, 220, 226
manual tab stops, 213
text alignment using, 214
using manual, 214–217
tags, OneNote
creating and customizing, 690–692
using, 688
Tags Summary pane, OneNote, 752, 753
Take Notes On Your Own, OneNote, 696
tasks, connecting Outlook to OneNote, 698–700
Tell Me More is display, on Screen Tips, 11

templates
accessing online, 42
Excel
built-in, 495–498
storing formats in, 579–580
OneNote, 765
saving PowerPoint, 297
searching for online, 58–62
Simple to-do list workbook, 49
text
adding animation to presentation, 366–370
adding text to slides, 304
aligning using tabs, 214
applying formatting in presentations to, 283, 347
disappearing when copying slides, 283
formatting. See also keyboard shortcuts
about, 183–188
changing case of text, 200–201
exploring character, 200–201
exploring paragraph, 196–198
setting section formatting, 190–192
using styles for, 192–196
functions, 476–477
making circular, 348
selecting in documents, 156–160
using Eyedropper Text Fill tool, 340
working in Excel with
changing case of text, 485–487
combining into one string, 479–482
copying and pasting range of cells, 485
pasting formulas as resulting values, 484–485
removing extra spaces, 482–484
text boxes
adding to slides manual, 308
rotating, 312
Text Effects button, in WordArt Styles group, 646
Text Filters command, 519
Text Highlight Color button, 187
Text Import Wizard, 509–510
text wrapping, turning off, 444
Theme Colors gallery
in PowerPoint, 278, 280
theme effects, 47
Theme Effects sets, in PowerPoint, 280–281
Theme Font gallery, in PowerPoint, 272, 277

themes
    applying, 47–50
    changing, 12
    creating in Excel custom, 546–549
Themes button, 49, 549
Themes gallery, 49, 270, 549
themes, presentation
    applying background styles to, 281–283
    applying to existing presentations, 269–271
    creating presentations using variants, 268
    customizing, 272–273, 273–275, 277–281
    theme colors vs. direct colors, 341–342
theme variant, starting presentation using, 268
Thesaurus, as research tool, 152
threaded comments, in Word, 126
tilde (~), entering from keyboard, 168
time() function, 477–478
Timeline bar, 639
Timeline button, 638
timelines, adding to charts, 416, 637–639
Timeline Tools Options tab, 639, 641
title bar
    in Excel, 413
    in Office, 7
    in OneNote, 659
    in PowerPoint, 255
    in Word, 118, 129
Title Slide, 304
TODAY() function, 477
Toggle case option, 202
tool tabs, 8
top page margins, toggling in Print Layout
    view, 120
Total Row formatting, 223
total screen count, in Read Mode, 146
touch-enabled devices, gesture to zoom on
    slide, 400
touch mode
    about, 47, 101–103
    disabling, 103
    handwriting recognition vs. ink, 107
    selecting content in, 106–107
    using, 103–106
    working with ink in, 107
touch mode, Office applications, 47

touchpad, scrolling documents on, 134–135
tracking changes in documents, using simple
    markup, 126
transitions, applying to animations in slides, 371–
    373
Translate feature, as research tool, 151–152
translating service, 151–152
Transparent Wand tool, 362
trig functions, 474–476
TRIM() function, 477, 483
Trim Video dialog box, 372
troubleshooting
    bullet points, 306
    chart error messages, 318
    getting embed code from YouTube, 375
    Presenter view, 402
    resizing presentation, 300
    right-clicking objects, 338
    selecting placeholders, 366
    selecting sections, 381
    size of Shapes gallery in PowerPoint, 309
    size of text in SmartArt diagrams, 325
    Slide Show view, 396
    Start On Click setting in Video Tools Playback
      tab, 371
    text disappearing when copying slides, 283
Twitter, connecting to personal cloud service
    in, 80–81
Type group
    Change Chart Type button in, 627–628, 633

U

underscore (_), as Excel formatting code, 554
Undo button, 156
unpinning files, 20
Unprotect Sheet option, 491
Up and Down arrows, using in Animation
    pane, 370
Uppercase option, 202
UPPER() function, 477
USB flash drive, sharing OneNote notes using, 749
user interface, customizing, 25–31

V

Values button
  in Paste Special, 486
  in Paste Values group, 485
values, in Excel, 426, 429
Variants gallery, in PowerPoint, 270, 277, 280
variants, in PowerPoint
  about, 268
  applying to existing presentations, 268
  creating presentations using theme, 268
versions file, opening previous, 24
video. *See also* online: video
  canceling conversion of presentation into, 377
  editing, 371–373
  inserting and playing in presentations online, 374–375
  linking files to PowerPoint, 371
  placement in documents of, 127
  playing back in Office documents online, 45–46
  previewing, 67
  saving presentation as, 375–377
Video Tools Playback tab, Start On Click setting in, 371
View Ruler command, in Word, 123
views
  modifying document, 119–122
  OneNote, 659–660
  setting options in Excel for, 574–578
View Side By Side button, 578
View tab
  changing document view in, 119–122
  Navigation pane from, 136
  Slide Master view, 291
VLOOKUP() function, 478

W

web addresses
  Excel format for, 432
  selecting in Excel, 435
web browser, accessing notes in, 738–740
Web Layout view, in Word, 120
WEEKDAY() function, 477
What-If Analysis, performing, 498–502

widescreen format, changing presentation to, 297–300
Widow/Orphan Control option, 204
wiki links, 704
Window control buttons
  in Excel, 413
  in Office, 7–8
  in PowerPoint, 256
  in Word, 118
Windows 7
  modifying screen resolution, 14–15
  starting Office application in, 4–5
Windows 8
  modifying screen resolution, 14–15
  starting Office application in, 4–5
  tablet edition of, 101
  Window control buttons, 7–8
  Windows Explorer vs. File explorer, 92
Windows 8 tablet, using Onenote on, 747–748
Windows Explorer vs. File explorer, 92
Windows Phone
  sharing notes via SharePoint on, 723
  using OneNote on, 746–747
Windows Phone 8, adding new note in, 747
Windows RT
  about, 101
  on Windows 8 tablet, 748
.wmv formatted video, saving presentation as, 375–377
Word
  about new features in, 123–129
  alignment guides in, 127
  composing documents
    inserting special characters, 169–171
    inserting symbols, 165–166, 168
    using AutoCorrect, 167–168, 172–175
    using building blocks, 176–180
    using formatting marks in, 161–164
    using international characters, 167–168
  correcting proofing errors, 230–232
  creating across applications coordinating documents, 128
  documents, 134–135
  documents created in earlier versions of, 129
  editing documents

moving cursor by keyboard shortcuts, 155–156

selecting text, 156–160

file extension for, 116

formatting documents

about, 183–188

changing case of text, 200–201

exploring character formatting, 200–201

exploring paragraph formatting, 196–198

managing pagination through, 203–207

setting default documents, 188–190

setting section formatting, 190–192

using styles for, 192–196

heading styles in documents, 141–144

inspecting documents before publishing, 233–237

Layout Options button in, 127

Live Layout in, 127

making documents final, 238

modifying document view, 119–122

online pictures feature in, 45

opening files from cloud, 90–91

PDFs

creating, 239–244

editing, 239, 243–244

Reflow feature, 124

presentations, inserting online video into, 65–69

presenting information in

inserting tables, 217–223, 223–227

using bulleted lists, 209, 210–213

using numbered lists, 209, 210–213

using tabbed lists, 210, 213–217

using tables, 210

Read Mode

exploring research tools in, 148–152

viewing documents in, 144–148

recovering unsaved files in, 24

resume reading feature in, 124

ribbon, 117–119

saving files on cloud, 85–87

scrolling documents, 134–135

selecting document content, 157

setting default formatting for documents, 128

splitting screen in, 122–123

starting, 115–116

tables, 125

threaded comments in, 126

tracking changes in documents, 126

turning on ruler display, 122

using Navigation pane, 135–141

word completion, in touch mode, 105

Zoom group in, 120–121

WordArt Styles group

from Drawing Tools Format tab, 646

Text Effects button from, 348

Text Effects button in, 646

word completion, in touch mode, 105

Word Start screen, 116

Word Web App, viewing documents in, 239

workbooks

changing number of sheets setting in, 417

creating multisheet, 606–610

displaying separate windows, 414

managing multiple, 618–621

manipulating sheets in, 610–613

summarizing multisheet, 613–616

WORKDAY() function, 477

worksheets

cells in. See also cells, spreadsheet

creating bottom border in, 425

deleting, 587–591

finalizing entry in, 424

inserting, 587–591

maximum number of rows, 458

changing widths of columns, 423–426

changing widths of rows, 426

charts in, 623–629. See also charts

creating and sharing graphics, 642–648

creating PivotTables, 526–533

formatting

applying number, 538–541

applying percentage format to numbers, 558–560

cells, 550–551

Clear Formats option, 546

creating custom themes, 546–549

custom number formats, 551–558

dates, 564–570

lining up positive and negative numbers in columns, 541

setting view options, 574–578

with styles, 542–545

working with fractions, 560
inserting columns, 583–587
inserting rows, 583–587
jumping to first cell in, 520
moving and copying columns and rows on, 445–446
moving around, 439–441
page layout options, 591–599
pages in
adjusting page breaks, 602–606
printing row and column labels, 599–602
panes, 591–599
performing What-If Analysis, 498–502
protecting, 570–572
sheet references in, 617–618
storing formats in templates, 579–580
using built-in templates, 495–498
Wrap Text button, 444
Wrap Text format, 426

in Word, 120–121
zoom, in touch mode, 106
Zoom slider, 389
Zoom tool, in PowerPoint during presentations, 399–400
Zoom to Page button, in viewing presentation comments, 389

X

XML Paper Specification (XPS) format, saving files in, 22
XPS (XML Paper Specification) format, saving files in, 22

Y

YouTube
getting embed code from, 375
inserting videos into presentations, 374–375
YouTube video page, 375
y (Year), Excel date formatting code, 569

Z

zero (0), as Excel formatting code, 554
Zoom button, 652
Zoom dialog box, 121
Zoom group
in Excel, 603
in OneNote, 663

About the authors

Beth Melton, Microsoft Office MVP since 2000 and Microsoft Office Specialist Master Instructor, has been teaching others how to use Office applications more efficiently and developing custom Microsoft Office solutions for almost 20 years. She co-authored *Microsoft Word 2007 Inside Out* (Microsoft Press) and is a regular contributor to several websites, including Microsoft Office Online.

Beth spends her leisure time with her three children and enjoys finding different ways to give back to her community by integrating her love of technology, newly developed culinary skills, and passion for healthy eating.

Mark Dodge has been working with and writing about Microsoft software since 1989, and is co-author of the Microsoft Press titles *Microsoft Office Excel 2013 Inside Out* and the *MOS 2013 Study Guide for Excel Expert*. As a senior writer in the Office group at Microsoft, he created print, online, and multimedia documentation for all Microsoft Office software, and continues to work as a contract technical writer and editor, most recently in emergency management planning at FEMA. Mark is a lifelong jazz and rock musician, as well as an award-winning fine art photographer.

A Microsoft PowerPoint MVP since 2000, **Echo Swinford** began her PowerPoint career in 1997. She holds a Master's degree in New Media from the Indiana University-Purdue University at Indianapolis School of Informatics. Echo is the owner of Echosvoice, a PowerPoint consulting firm specializing in custom template development; presentation creation, makeovers and cleanup; and PowerPoint training for large and small corporate clients. Echo has written and co-written three PowerPoint books and has a string of tech editing credits to her name. Visit her Web site at *www.echosvoice.com*.

Ben M. Schorr is a technologist and Chief Executive Officer for Roland Schorr & Tower, a professional consulting firm headquartered in Honolulu, Hawaii with offices in Los Angeles and Arizona. He is also the author of several books and articles on technology including "The Lawyer's Guide to Microsoft Outlook", "The Lawyer's Guide to Microsoft Word" and "OneNote in One Hour". He's been a Microsoft MVP for more than 15 years and involved with management and technology for more than 20. In his free time he's an Ironman triathlete and a high school football coach. He currently lives in Flagstaff, Arizona with his wife Carrie.